Ancient Greek Athletics

Ancient Greek Athletics

Primary Sources in Translation

Charles H. Stocking

Susan A. Stephens

OXFORD
UNIVERSITY PRESS

OXFORD
UNIVERSITY PRESS

Great Clarendon Street, Oxford, OX2 6DP,
United Kingdom

Oxford University Press is a department of the University of Oxford.
It furthers the University's objective of excellence in research, scholarship,
and education by publishing worldwide. Oxford is a registered trade mark of
Oxford University Press in the UK and in certain other countries

Published in the United States of America by Oxford University Press
198 Madison Avenue, New York, NY 10016, United States of America

British Library Cataloguing in Publication Data
Data available

Library of Congress Control Number: 2021937943

ISBN 978–0–19–883959–0 (hbk.)
ISBN 978–0–19–883960–6 (pbk.)

Printed and bound by
CPI Group (UK) Ltd, Croydon, CR0 4YY

CONTENTS

I TEXTS

II INSCRIPTIONS

III PAPYRI

APPENDICES

ACKNOWLEDGMENTS

This project would not have been possible without a great number of people. First, we would like to thank the editors at Oxford University Press, who have showed great care and support throughout the lifetime of this project, including Charlotte Loveridge, who originally proposed the idea for a new sourcebook, as well as Karen Raith, Georgina Leighton, Samantha Downes, Celine Louasli, Gwen Colvin, and our copy editor. Three former and current graduate students were absolutely critical in the production of this text, including Jonathan Weiland, for his detailed work on the site plans and charts in this volume, Nolan Epstein for his contributions to the section on Pindar, and above all to Annie Lamar for her care and effort in preparing the charts, timeline, glossary, images, and index. Finally, we must thank the anonymous reviewers whose suggestions have considerably improved the content and structure of the material presented here.

We have been able to present material from this sourcebook on several occasions, and we are grateful to our colleagues and audiences at the University of Virginia, the University of Toronto, the USC Institute of Sports Media and Society, the International Olympic Academy, and the Harvard Center for Hellenic Studies for much helpful advice.

We are especially grateful for the work of our colleagues in the field of ancient Greek athletics, on whom we have relied, and it is with great sadness and regret that we were not able to complete this text before the passing of one of the most important scholars of ancient athletics, Mark Golden. This sourcebook would not have been possible without him.

The endless patience and support of our partners and families during this project deserves more appreciation than can be expressed in words.

And finally, we would like to thank the many students and student athletes we have taught over the years in our courses on ancient athletics. Your curiosity, engagement, and enthusiasm have been and will continue to be a constant source of inspiration.

LIST OF ABBREVIATIONS

AB	C. Austin and G. Bastianini (eds), *Posidippi Pellaei quae supersunt omnia* (Milan, 2002)
BE	*Bulletin épigraphique*
BGU	*Aegyptische Urkunden aus den Königlichen Museen zu Berlin, Griechische Urkunden, Berlin*
CEG	P. A. Hansen, *Carmina epigraphica Graeca* (Berlin and New York, 1983, 1989)
CID	*Corpus des inscriptions de Delphes* (Paris, 1977–)
CIG	A. Boeckh, *Corpus Inscriptionum Graecarum* (Berlin, 1828–77)
CRAI	*Comptes rendus de l'Académie des Inscriptions et Belles-lettres*
Delph.	*Fouilles de Delphes* (Paris, 1909–)
Ebert	J. Ebert, *Griechische Epigramme auf Sieger an gymnischen und hippischen Agonen* (Berlin, 1972), *Abhandlungen der sächsischen Akademie der Wissenschaften zu Leipzig, Philologisch-historische Klasse* 63.2
I Eph.	H. Wankel, R. Merkelbach et al., *Die Inschriften von Ephesos* 1979–81
IG	*Inscriptiones Graecae* (Berlin, 1873–)
ILindos	C. Blinkenburg, *Lindos 2 Inscriptions 1–2* (Berlin and Copenhagen, 1941)
IvO	W. Dittenberger and K. Purgold, *Inschriften von Olympia* (Berlin, 1896)
NIvO	P. Siewert and H. Taeuber (eds), *Neue Inschriften von Olympia* (Vienna, 2013)
OGIS	W. Dittenberger, *Orientis Graeci Inscriptiones Selectae* (Leipzig, 1903–5)
PCairo Zenon	C. C. Edgar, *Zenon Papyri, Catalogue general des antiquités du Musée de Caire*
PHal	*Dikaiomata: Auszüge aus alexandrinischen Gesetzen und Verordnungen in einem Papyrus des philologischen Seminars der Universität, Halle* (Berlin, 1913)
POxy	*The Oxyrhynchus Papyri* (London, 1898–)
PRyl	*Catalogue of the Greek Papyri in the John Rylands Library, Manchester* (Manchester 1911–52)
PSI	*Papiri greci e latini: Pubblicazioni della Società italiana per la ricerca dei papyri greci e latini in Egitto*
REA	*Revue des études grecques*
SEG	*Supplementum Epigraphicum Graecum* (Leiden, 1923–)
SIG³	W. Dittenberger, *Sylloge Inscriptionum Graecarum*, 3rd edn (Leipzig, 1915–24)

LIST OF FIGURES

LIST OF PLANS

LIST OF TABLES

HISTORICAL TIMEFRAME FOR ANCIENT GREEK ATHLETICS

Archaic Period (*c.*800–480 BCE)

776 BCE	Foundation of Olympic Games (traditional date)
753 BCE	Foundation of Rome (traditional date)
720 BCE	Athletic nudity introduced at Olympic Games
632 BCE	Cylon attempts to seize power in Athens
594 BCE	Solon elected archon; writes laws for the Athenians
586 BCE	Foundation of Pythian Games at Delphi
582 BCE	Foundation of Isthmian Games
573 BCE	Foundation of Nemean Games
566 BCE	Greater Panathenaea first held at Athens
mid-sixth century BCE	Earliest evidence for gymnasium
520 BCE	Foundation of Asclepieia at Epidaurus
509 BCE	Foundation of Roman Republic (traditional date)
490 BCE	First Persian invasion of Greece; battle of Marathon
480 BCE	Second Persian invasion of Greece; battle of Salamis

Classical Period (*c.*480–323 BCE)

479 BCE	Foundation of Eleutherian Games at Plataea
470–457 BCE	Construction of Temple of Zeus at Olympia
425 BCE	Nemea destroyed by warfare
416 BCE	Athenian invasion of Sicily
*c.*400 BCE	Hippias of Elis' Olympic victor lists
399 BCE	Trial and death of Socrates
*c.*380 BCE	Prize list from Greater Panathenaea
371 BCE	Festival of Basileia at Lebadeia
364 BCE	Arcadians and Eleans wage war at Olympia
356 BCE	Olympic victory of Philip II of Macedon
	Birth of Alexander the Great
323 BCE	Death of Alexander the Great

Hellenistic Period (323–31 BCE)

c.280 BCE	Foundation of Ptolemeia at Alexandria
279 BCE	Foundation of Soteria at Delphi
264 BCE	First gladiatorial games at Rome
250 BCE	Nemean Games moved to Argos
242 BCE	Foundation of Asclepieia on Cos
c. second century BCE	Beroia inscription
196 BCE	Foundation of Eleutheria at Larisa
186 BCE	Fulvius Nobilior introduces Greek athletes at a Roman festival
c.175–167 BCE	Building of the gymnasium at Jerusalem
146 BCE	Greece becomes the Roman province of Achaea
	Isthmian Games moved to Sicyon
80 BCE	Cornelius Sulla stages Greek games at Rome (*ludi victoriae Sullanae*)
73 BCE	Revolt of Spartacus

Roman Imperial Period (31 BCE–fourth century CE)

31 BCE	Battle of Actium; Octavian defeats Antony and Cleopatra
30 BCE	Death of Cleopatra; Egypt becomes a Roman province
27 BCE	Augustus becomes Roman emperor
	Augustus establishes Actian Games at Nicopolis
4 BCE	Olympic chariot victory of Tiberius
2 CE	Sebastan Games established at Naples
40 CE	Isthmian Games return to Isthmia
mid-first century CE	Athletic guilds begin to be formed
60 CE	Nero establishes Neronia at Rome
66–7 CE	Nero competes in Greek games
80 CE	Colosseum dedicated
86 CE	Domitian establishes Capitoline Games at Rome
117–38 CE	Reign of Hadrian
180 CE	Commodus becomes Roman emperor.
393 CE	Theodosius I bans pagan festivals
395 CE	Last known Olympic victor
520 CE	Last Olympic Games at Antioch

Introduction

Athletic competition was deeply embedded in ancient Greek life from as early as Homer, and it continued to exert its influence well into the Christian period, as we can see from the fact that the fourth-century Christian bishop Eusebius included our only complete list of Olympic victors in his *Ecclesiastical History*. This historical persistence coincides roughly with the establishment and conduct of the Olympic Games, which ancient sources place at 776 BCE, until they ceased around 394 CE. Ancient Greek athletics remains one of the very few connections between that ancient world and our modern world that commands instant recognition, if only for the institution of the modern Olympic Games that were supposedly modeled on ancient practice. College and university courses on ancient athletics draw large numbers of students, many of whom are athletes themselves and can readily identify with their ancient counterparts. In teaching such courses we have found that using as many ancient sources as possible and in as complete a form as is feasible considerably enriches the students' experience, allowing for a much more nuanced understanding of the range of expectations, hardships, benefits, debates about, and praise or condemnation of ancient athletes, which ancient sources can provide.

The material of this Sourcebook comes out of that experience. Written evidence, of course, is only part of the information available on athletic practices. Archaeological work on the wide range of festival and game sites, civic gymnasia, statuary, inscriptions, and ceramic materials must all be used in tandem to give as full a picture as possible. Each of these sources has its own social context and rationale, but they constitute far more material than one book can encompass, thus requiring decisions about how much, what, and in what order the sources should be presented. We have chosen to focus on written sources, which we have arranged in three categories: literary sources, by far the largest section, which range from Homer to Eusebius; inscriptions, which are publicly displayed documents and constitute a small subset of the vast number that have been published; and finally papyri, material written in Hellenistic and Roman Egypt, which de facto form a narrowly focused data set. From the papyri we have mainly personal letters that provide perspectives that differ from the other two categories. Within each unit our selections are organized by time period (Archaic and Early Classical, Classical, Hellenistic, and Roman), then by genre (for the literary material of the Archaic and Classical Periods), and by site for the inscriptions. This has several benefits:

(1) It does not distort the historical development of Greek athletics by importing material from much later periods to explain earlier phenomena. As becomes clear, our central sources of information come from Roman period writers, particularly Lucian's *Anacharsis*, Pausanias' description of Olympia, and Philostratus' *Gymnasicus*, and

Sourcebook of Ancient Greek Athletics. Charles H. Stocking and Susan A. Stephens, Oxford University Press (2021).
© Charles H. Stocking and Susan A. Stephens. DOI: 10.1093/oso/9780198839606.003.0001

each author has a specific agenda though which it is necessary to filter the truth value of the statements. With respect to inscriptions, for example, the site and chronological order again indicates that most of what we know about the actual workings of the gymnasium within a city comes from one source: the Beroia Inscription from Macedon (280 BCE).

(2) It allows readers to see the interaction between writers. For example, what we know about Spartan practices comes mainly from Xenophon (early fourth century BCE), but six centuries later, we find much of this repeated in Plutarch. It thus becomes clear that we do not have two independent sources, but one early and one later source dependent on the earlier.

(3) It allows readers to see the way arguments that first develop in the Classical Period, such as the relationship of medicine and athletic training, evolve over time, as later writers often quote their earlier predecessors as sources.

(4) It allows readers to understand more clearly how various genres condition responses to athletic practices. Victory poems, for example, treat athletic success quite differently than do philosophical writers; dramatic and oratorical texts are more focused (for good or ill) on chariot and horse racing, the events for the super-rich, than the events that the average Greek male citizen might be expected to participate in. In the Roman period, reading Galen's medical texts along with Philostratus' *Gymnasticus* provides us with a glimpse of the agonistic environment in which these writers contended for respect and audience.

But the most significant benefit is that it allows readers to see how deeply the experience of athletics permeated Greek civic and social life and even influenced the ways in which elite writers like Isocrates and Plato borrowed from the realm of athletic practice to model ideas about training the soul. In short, ancient athletics was not just about training the body, but it served as a vehicle for thinking, speaking, and writing about all aspects and issues of the ancient world, from the earliest periods of Greek history to the Roman Imperial era and beyond.

Organization of this Sourcebook

Each section (Archaic and Classical, Classical, Hellenistic, Roman, Inscriptions, Papyri) is prefaced by an introduction that summarizes the most important historical events and the general trends found in the section readings; there is also an introduction to each individual author, inscription, or papyrus.

The individual entries are organized into three sections: Texts, Inscriptions, Papyri. Within the **Text** section the readings are ordered numerically by author, e.g., Pindar = **2** (each entry receives a separate letter, e.g., **2a** = Pindar, *Olympian* 1; **2m** = *Nemean* 5); Plato = **22**; Pausanias = **37**. These entries are of unequal length: some are quite long, as is Philostratus' *Gymnasticus* (**40a**); others are of no more than a few lines, e.g., Theognis, on athletic nudity (**6a**) or Diogenes Laertius on athletic emoluments (**44a**). Section numbers are provided in the longer passages for ease of reference, i.e., Pausanias' discussion of the athlete Theagenes of Thasos is cited as **37q** (6.11.2–9, 6.15.3).

Entries in the **Inscriptions** section are prefaced by **I** (for Inscription) plus a number for the site (**1** = Olympia, **2** = Delphi, **3** = Sparta, **4** = Athens, **5** = Other regions), and a letter for an individual entry; thus, **I1m** = the Zanes base inscription at Olympia, **I4f** = the Panathenaic prize list.

Papyri are listed by number preceded by **P** (for Papyrus); thus, **P6** = a papyrus fragment of a wrestling manual.

In addition to the chronological organization of the texts, we have provided a series of **Appendices**, accompanied by site plans, and charts, that take up many of the standard topics relevant to the teaching and understanding of Greek athletics, including cultural values (heroization, the gymnasium, nudity, status, female athletics, record-keeping, cheating), the organization of games and game sites, and the types of events and their development. These sections can be read independently and are cross-referenced to the readings. In addition, there is a **Glossary of Greek Terms** relevant to athletics. These terms are transliterated Greek and italicized in the texts and the **Glossary**, where they are explained and cross-referenced to the readings.

Our translations are based on standard editions of the relevant Greek text or on the Loeb Classical Library editions, when Loeb provides the most recent or most accessible edition of the text. The selections of Pausanias are revised and modified from the 1918 Jones translation. Throughout, we have used Latinized Greek spellings when they are in common use; otherwise we have transliterated the Greek. Most passages of poetry are set out as prose (e.g., epic, drama); the exceptions are the epinician odes of Pindar and Bacchylides, for which we have tried to keep the intricate order of the poetic lines, some short poems like epigram, and poetry that is quoted by a prose author.

Part I
Texts

Sourcebook of Ancient Greek Athletics. Charles H. Stocking and Susan A. Stephens, Oxford University Press (2021).
© Charles H. Stocking and Susan A. Stephens. DOI: 10.1093/oso/9780198839606.011.0001

1 The Archaic and Early Classical Period

The Greek Archaic period is normally dated from the eighth century through the Persian Wars (c.750–480 BCE). It was characterized by rapid population growth and the beginning of the institutions that came into prominence in the Classical period. The most notable was the rise of city states of varying sizes from the smaller units of a few thousand male citizens to Athens, by far the largest, with a population of around 30,000 male citizens in the fifth century BCE, and of course, women, children, slaves, and non-citizen resident aliens would have considerably increased the populations. The political arrangements of individual city states ranged from the radical democracy of Athens, which was also the greatest economic power, to oligarchies like Sparta, ruled predominantly by two families, to the tyrants, most prominently, of Sicily (see 2a, 2b, and 3a). Economic growth was facilitated by the introduction of coinage for the exchange of goods, expanded trade with the wider Mediterranean world, and colonization, as cities from the mainland dispatched some of their citizens to regions of the Black Sea in the north, along the Turkish coast in the east, to North Africa in the south, and to Sicily and southern Italy in the west, where they established colonies, though these new cities normally maintained their ties with the mainland. For example, Epizephyrian (or Western) Locri in southern Italy was founded around 680 BCE by colonists from Opuntian Locris in mainland Greece, and the cities shared common myths (see 2c and 2d). These individual city states, well over one hundred, never unified and fought numerous local wars against each other. They did, however, form alliances, usually along political lines (democracies united with Athens, for example). What gave Greeks a sense of common identity was not their national unity so much as a common language (though there was considerable dialect variation) and belief in a common set of gods who were ruled over by Zeus and his extended family. These divinities were worshiped in similar ways in festivals sponsored by city states and in Panhellenic shrines that also came to sponsor athletic events. The evolution of city states from the older palace-based societies that we see in Homer's poems was propelled in part by the development of the citizen soldier and a new way of fighting. The heavy infantry of the Bronze Age, armed with spears and protected by oblong shields that covered most of the body, gave way to phalanxes of lighter armed soldiers (called hoplites) who required concentrated training for fighting in close combat. The need to train these new fighting men is closely connected to the rise of the gymnasium (see Appendix AII). Cavalry continued to be important, though the battle chariot so prominent in the Iliad became obsolete (see Appendix BI).

At the beginning of the Archaic period, the Iliad and the Odyssey, epic poems attributed to Homer, came to epitomize Greek values of honor and shame. Although originally oral in their composition and performance, they must have been written down sometime between the eighth and sixth centuries, and later were often recited by dedicated performers (called rhapsodes) at civic festivals throughout Greece. In this way, the characters and stories found in these poems also contributed to a sense of collective Greek identity. Although these poems are set in a world that predates the city state, they are

Sourcebook of Ancient Greek Athletics. Charles H. Stocking and Susan A. Stephens, Oxford University Press (2021).
© Charles H. Stocking and Susan A. Stephens. DOI: 10.1093/oso/9780198839606.003.0002

*our earliest literary sources for athletic practices, including vivid descriptions of many of the contests (boxing, wrestling, running, chariot racing) that came to be staples of later festival games. The Greeks themselves trace the origin of the Olympic Games to this period (776 BCE), at a sanctuary (Olympia) dedicated to Zeus, the king of the gods. Open to all Greeks, it came to be used by city states for displays of civic power and pride (see **16b**, **18a**, **18b**, and **38a**). It housed, for example, treasuries of various Greek colonies in which often quite valuable dedications were deposited (see **37r**; other Panhellenic sites, particularly Delphi, also had treasuries). Prestige also accrued to cities from the athletic victories of their citizens. This is best seen in the victory poetry of Pindar and Bacchylides, also located in this chapter. Although much of their work was produced in the decades immediately after the Persian Wars (480–458 BCE), we include them here because, like the Homeric material, they belonged to a performance culture that gives us detailed information about athletic behaviors, contests, and games sites. Seventh- and sixth-century elegy and epigram also belonged to performance culture, specifically, with the symposium a venue for reinforcing elite male bonds.*

Epic

1. Homer

Athletic competition in Homeric poetry occupies a privileged, yet problematic position in the study of ancient Greek athletics. On the one hand, Homeric poetry offers our earliest and most detailed account of Greek athletic practice. On the other hand, because the Homeric epics are fictional and the product of an oral poetic tradition, they cannot be used to reconstruct the historical practice of athletics. Nevertheless, in order to be intelligible to the audience, contests cannot have strayed too far from reality. The poetic descriptions also provide insights into the role athletic competition plays within the narrative of the poems and how that poetic significance may in turn reflect the ideological importance of athletics in early Greek culture. We have set out these sections in continuous prose, not keeping the line breaks of verse.

1a. *Iliad* bk. 22.157–66: Achilles Pursues the Trojan Prince Hector before the Walls of Troy

There the two were running, the one running away and the other pursuing from behind.

A good man ran out in front, but a far better man pursued eagerly. It was not for a sacrificial oxhide that the two were striving, (22.160) the sort that are prizes (*aethlia*) won by men with their feet. No, they were running for the life (*psychē*) of horse-taming Hector. As when single-hoofed prize-winning horses run around the turning post, and the great prize is placed there, (22.165) either a tripod or the wife of a man who has been killed, so the two rushed around the city of Priam with their eager feet. And all the gods were watching.

1b. *Iliad* bk. 23.257–897: The Funeral Games of Patroclus, Companion of Achilles (with omissions)

The most extensive description of athletic competition in Homer occurs as part of the funeral of Patroclus, who was killed in battle when he fought in the Trojan War on behalf of Achilles, the main hero of the Iliad. *These games are described as an* agōn, *which literally means a "leading together" or "gathering" of people. Used in this way,* agōn *becomes synonymous with competition, starting with Homer. The competition involved eight events, and prizes were given with a value scaled to reflect the results of the contest. The term for prizes,* aethla, *also became a synonym for the contests for such prizes. Historically, the Funeral Games for Patroclus may reflect athletic practice in the Iron Age and early Archaic periods. Many of the prizes correspond to prestige goods found in Iron Age and early Archaic phases of sanctuaries known for their athletic contests, such as Olympia. In addition, we have significant archaeological evidence indicating that funerals for elite individuals were one of the earliest occasions for athletic competition. Other references to funeral games in the epics and in related traditions include* Iliad *23.629–45 (Amarynceus' funeral; see* **1b***) and Odyssey 24.85–97 (Achilles' funeral; see* **1f***).*

Then Achilles gathered the people and sat them down in a wide gathering (*agōn*), and he brought out prizes (*aethla*) from the ships, cauldrons and tripods, horses and mules, strong head of oxen, well-girdled women and gray iron.

First, as shining prizes for swift charioteers, he set forth a woman who knew how to do faultless handiwork and a tripod holding twenty-two measures. And for second place, a six-year-old unbroken mare, who was pregnant with a mule. For third place he set down a beautiful unfired cauldron, still bright, which held four measures. For fourth place, he set down two talents of gold, and for fifth an unfired jar with two handles (23.270). Then he stood up right away and uttered an authoritative command to the Argives:[1]

"Son of Atreus and other well-greaved Achaeans, the prizes for the chariot race lie in the middle of the gathering for the charioteers. If now we Achaeans should contend with each other for the sake of another hero, then I would easily take the first-place prizes to my tent. For you know by how much my horses stand out in excellence (*aretē*), since they are immortal. Poseidon gave them to my father, who in turn handed them to me. But I and my single-hoofed horses will stay behind. For they lost the noble glory (*kleos*) of their chariot driver (23.280), him who often anointed their manes with soft olive oil, after washing them with bright water. Standing there, they grieve for him, and their manes drag along the ground; they stand motionless with troubled heart. But others of you in the camp, get ready, whoever of the Achaeans trusts in his horses and well-constructed chariot."

Thus, Achilles son of Peleus spoke, and the swift charioteers (*hippēes*) gathered. By far the first to rise was the lord of men Eumelus, the dear son of Admetus, who excelled in

---

[1] In Homeric poetry, the name for the Greeks is given variously as Argives, Achaeans, or Danaans.

horsemanship. Then rose the son of Tydeus, dominant Diomedes (23.290), and he yoked his Trojan horses, which he took from Aeneas, although Apollo saved Aeneas.[2] Then up rose the fair-haired son of Atreus, divine-born Menelaus, and he led his swift horses under the yoke. Menelaus had a mare, Aithe, which belonged to Agamemnon…(23.300). Fourth, Antilochus, the glorious son of courageous Nestor fitted out his well-maned horses. The horses that pulled his chariot were from Pylos.

Strategy for the Chariot Race

His father, standing nearby and thinking about what was best for his young son, gave him the following advice: "Antilochus, although you are young, Zeus and Poseidon love you and taught you all manner of horsemanship. And so, I do not need to teach you anything. For you know well how to drive the turn. But your horses are the slowest in speed, and so I think it will be difficult for you (23.310). Their horses are swifter, but they do not know more than you how to use their skill (*mētis*). But you, dear boy, place all manner of skill in your heart in order that the prizes not escape you…Through skill, chariot driver surpasses chariot driver. But he who thoughtlessly places confidence in his horses and chariot, he drives his chariot here and there (23.320), and his horses get off track, and he cannot restrain them. But he who thinks upon profit, although driving inferior horses, with an eye always on the turning post, he takes the turn tightly, and he does not forget to grip the reins tightly as at the beginning of the race, but he holds fast and looks upon the man out in front. And I will point out to you a sign (*sēma*) on the track you cannot miss. A dry stump either of oak or of pine stands out from the ground by about six feet. It is not rotted by the rain, and two white stones are leaned against it at the joining of the road, and the path is smooth around it (23.330). Either it was a grave marker (*sēma*) for a man who died long ago or it was fashioned as a turning post for a previous generation of men. Now swift-footed Achilles has made it the turning post for this race. Drive your horses and chariot close to it, and you, in the well-made chariot, keep to the left with your horses. And calling out, drive your right horse with the goad, and relax its reins. And at the turning post, let the left horse be held tight in order that the edge of your wheel seems to touch it. But take care not to hit the rock (23.340), lest you wound your horses and break your chariot. That would be a source of joy for others and lamentable for you. But above all, dear boy, be thoughtful and safe. For if you are behind and pass them at the turning post, there is no one who can overtake you…" Thus spoke Nestor the son of Neleus, and he sat back down, after explaining each part of the race to his son (23.350). And then fifth, to fit out his well-maned horses was Meriones.

---

[2] Aeneas was a Trojan, second cousin to the sons of Priam; he escaped the burning of Troy to become the founder of Rome.

The Chariot Race

Then they mounted their chariots and cast lots (*klērous*). Achilles shook the lots and that of Antilochus jumped out first. After that was the lot of mighty Eumelus, and then the son of Atreus, spear-famed Menelaus, and then Meriones received his lot to drive his horses. And last Diomedes, who was the best, received his lot to drive his horses. Then they stood in order, and Achilles pointed out the turning post far off on the smooth plain. And as a lookout he placed god-like Phoenix, the follower of his father (23.360), in order that he might bear witness to the race and speak forth the truth.

Then they all raised their whips above their horses, struck them with the reins, and called out with eager words. And quickly they ran over the field far from the swift ships. The dust rose up striking the chests of the horses like a cloud or storm, and their manes flowed from the blast of wind. And then at one point a chariot would run close to the nourishing earth and then it would be lifted off the ground. And drivers stood in the chariots, and the heart of each was beating, desirous of victory (23.370). Each one called to his horses, and the horses flew, digging up dirt of the plain as they went.

But when the swift horses were completing the final part of the race at the gray sea, then the excellence (*aretē*) of each was apparent, and the course stretched forth for the horses. Then quickly the swift-footed horses of the son of Pheres, Eumelus, were out in front. The stallions of Diomedes followed after them, Trojan horses, not far behind, but very near. For they always seemed like they were about to mount the chariot in front of them, and with their breath they were warming the back and broad shoulders of Eumelus (23.380). The horses were closing in on Eumelus with heads lowered and then Diomedes would have passed Eumelus or caused a disputed finish, if Phoebus Apollo was not angry at the son of Tydeus and struck the shining whip from Diomedes' hand. Then tears poured from Diomedes' eyes, since he saw the horses of Eumelus go far ahead, while his horses were hindered without a goad to urge them on. But Apollo's trick did not escape the notice of Athena, and she quickly urged Diomedes on and gave him back his whip and placed force (*menos*) in his horses (23.390). She went behind the son of Admetus, Eumelus, because she was angry at him, and the goddess broke the yoke. Eumelus' horses ran on each side of the course, and the pole dragged on the ground. And then Eumelus himself rolled out beside the wheel, and his elbows were torn and his mouth and his nose, and his face above his eyebrows was smashed. And tears filled his eyes, and his stout voice was checked in him. And Diomedes swerved in order to pass Eumelus, and he held on to his single-hoofed horses. Diomedes drove them far out beyond the others, for Athena placed force (*menos*) in the horses and gave glory (*kudos*) to him (23.400).

After Diomedes, the son of Atreus, fair-haired Menelaus was coming up after him. But then Antilochus called out to the horses of his father: "Go you two! Pull as fast as you can. I am not commanding you to contend with the horses of the brave son of Tydeus, Diomedes, since Athena has given speed to them and glory to him. But catch up quickly to the horses of the son of Atreus, Menelaus, and do not be left behind, lest Menelaus' mare Aithe pour mockery on you. Why are you falling behind, oh mightiest of horses? For I will tell you this, and it will be accomplished (23.410). You will not be cared for by Nestor, but right away he will slaughter you two with the sharp bronze if we take away a lesser prize because of your lack of effort. Go forth and hurry as fast as possible. For I myself will contrive this and plan it, so that we pass at the narrowing in the course, and Menelaus will not get past me."

Thus he spoke, and the horses ran more quickly in a short burst out of fear of their master's voice. And then Antilochus, delighting in his strength, saw the narrowing of the course. There was a break in the ground where winter water collected (23.420) and broke out over the road, and there was a sinkhole all around it. Menelaus steered there, avoiding a collision with the other chariots. Antilochus held his horses and also turned outside the course, following after Menelaus. And Menelaus, the son of Atreus, was afraid and shouted to Antilochus: "Antilochus, you are driving your horses recklessly! But restrain your horses, for the course is narrow; soon it will be wider for passing. Do not hurt us both by hitting me with your chariot!"

Thus he spoke, but Antilochus drove on harder still, urging his horses on with the whip, as though he had not heard him (23.430). And they ran as far as the range of a discus thrown by a vigorous young man when testing his strength. Then the mares of Menelaus drew back, for he himself willingly let up on his driving, fearing that the single-hoofed horses would crash on the course, overturn the well-made chariots, and that they themselves would fall in the dust when pressing for victory. Then fair-haired Menelaus spoke to him with threatening words: "Antilochus, no one of mortal men is more destructive than you. To hell with you. We Achaeans did not tell the truth when we said you were sensible (23.440). But you will not carry away the prize without an oath."

He spoke and called to his horses: "Do not hold back; do not stop though grieved in heart. Their feet and knees will become weary before yours, for those horses have lost their youth." Thus Antilochus spoke, and the horses ran faster out of fear of their master's voice, and quickly they came near.

The Spectators

The Argives sitting in the gathering then saw the horses, which were flying and kicking up dirt from the plain. Idomeneus, leader of the Cretans, was first to see the horses (23.450). For he was sitting outside the gathering, up high on a lookout point. He recognized Diomedes separate from the others and heard him calling out, and Idomeneus saw one of his very recognizable horses out front, which was red with a white mark on its forehead, round like a full moon. And Idomeneus stood up right away and spoke to the Argives:

"Friends, leaders and counselors of the Argives, do I alone see the horses or do you as well? Another chariot driver and different horses seem to be out in front (23.460).

Perhaps the horses of Eumelus, which were out in front on the way out, were injured in the plain. For I saw them first going around the turn, but now I am unable to see them, although my eyes scan all over the entire Trojan plain. Or perhaps Eumelus lost the reins, and he was not able to hold them around the turn and did not manage to make the turn. I think he must have fallen out and his chariot must have broken, and the horses must have swerved from the course, after they were startled. But stand up and look for yourselves. For I do not see him (23.470). The leader seems to me to be Aetolian by birth, and he rules among the Argives—it is the son of horse-taming Tydeus, dominant Diomedes."

Then swift Ajax,[3] the son of Oileus, spoke words of reproach to him: "Why do you brag beyond measure? The swift-footed horses are still far off from the great plain. You are not the youngest of the Argives, nor do the eyes in your head see the most sharply. Always you say empty things with speeches. But there is no need for you to be so empty in your speech, for there are others better than you. The horses out in front are those which were out in front before, those of Eumelus, and he goes with the reins in hand" (23.480). And then the lord of the Cretans, angered, spoke in reply: "Ajax, best in quarreling, bad in counsel, of the Argives you are the worst, since your mind is thoughtless. Here now, let us wager a tripod or a cauldron, and let us make Agamemnon son of Atreus a witness to see which horses are out in front. Only by paying the price will you gain some knowledge." Thus he spoke, and right away in anger swift Ajax, son of Oileus, rose up to respond with harsh words. And now the quarrel between them would have gone farther, if Achilles himself did not stand up and speak (23.490): "Ajax and Idomeneus, no longer react with harsh and evil words, since it is not fitting. You would resent another man if he were doing such things. But sit back down in the gathering and watch the horses. For soon the men drive the horses here, pushing for victory. Soon each of you will recognize the horses of the Argives, whose are first and whose second."

The Race's Finish

Thus he spoke, and quickly Diomedes came near, driving always with the whip (23.500). And his horses lifted their feet high, going on the path. But always the splash of dust fell on the charioteer, and the chariot fitted with gold and tin ran on with the swift-footed horses. Nor was there much of a chariot track from the tires left behind in the light dust. And the two horses flew on in their haste. And Diomedes stopped them in the middle of the gathering, and much sweat from the manes and the chests of the horses poured to the ground. Diomedes himself jumped to the ground from his all-gleaming chariot, and he leaned his whip on the yoke…

---

[3] In the *Iliad*, there are two heroes named Ajax. There is Ajax, son of Telamon, known for his size and strength, and Ajax, son of Oileus, known for his speed.

(23.514) And after Diomedes, Antilochus, the son of Neleus drove his horses, having passed Menelaus by cunning and not by speed. But even so Menelaus held his swift horses near. By as much distance as a horse from the wheel of a chariot, which strains pulling its master on the plain and the end hairs of the tail touch upon the wheel and it runs close on it and there is not much space, while running over the great plain (23.520); by that much distance Menelaus was behind the blameless Antilochus. At first, he was left by the distance of a discus throw, when fair-haired Aithe, the mare of Agamemnon, increased her noble force. If the race had gone on farther for both, Menelaus would have overtaken him and there would not have been a dispute. After them, Meriones, attendant of Idomeneus, was behind Menelaus by a spear's throw. For his beautiful-maned horses were the slowest (23.530), and he himself was worst of them in driving the chariot in the contest. But last of all came the son of Admetus, Eumelus, dragging his beautiful chariot, and leading his horses in front.

Awarding Prizes

Swift-footed divine Achilles took pity on him when he saw him, and he stood up and addressed the Argives with winged words: "The best man (*aristos*) drives his single-footed horses last. But come let us give a prize as is fitting—the second-place prize. And let the son of Tydeus, Diomedes, take the first." Thus he spoke, and everyone shouted in approval of his command (23.540). And Achilles would have handed over the mare to him, for all the Achaeans approved, if Antilochus, the son of great-spirited Nestor, had not stood up and called for justice:

"Achilles, I will be angry with you, if you do what you say. For you are about to rob me of my prize, thinking it best because this man, though he is noble, crashed his chariot and swift horses. But he ought to have prayed to the immortals. Then he would not have come last in the race. But if you feel pity for him and he is dear to you, you have much gold in your tent, and bronze and animals, and you also have slaves and single-hoofed horses (23.550). Taking from these, give him a better prize later or now even, in order that the Achaeans praise you. But the mare I will not give up. He who is willing, let him fight with his own hands against me for her."

Thus he spoke, and swift-footed divine Achilles smiled, taking delight in Antilochus, since he was a dear companion. And in reply Achilles spoke winged words: "Antilochus, if you command me to give to Eumelus something else of my own, I will do so. I will give him the armor which I stripped from Asteropaeus (23.560). It is bronze with a covering of shining tin around it. It will be worth much to him." Thus he ordered his dear companion Automedon to carry it from his tent. And he went away and brought it to him and placed it in Eumelus' hands. And he accepted it with joy. But then Menelaus stood up, grieving in his heart and full of insatiable anger at Antilochus. And the herald placed the scepter in his hand and ordered the Argives to be silent. And then the god-like man spoke:

"Antilochus, formerly wise, what a thing you have done (23.570). You shamed my excellence (*aretē*), and you hindered my horses by urging yours out in front, which are far inferior. But come leaders and councilors of the Argives, make a judgment here in the middle of the gathering, but not strictly for my benefit, lest someone of the bronze-clad Achaeans say 'Menelaus overpowered Antilochus with lies and goes off with the mare, since his horses were inferior, and he himself was superior in excellence (*aretē*) and force (*biē*).' But come, I myself will make the judgment, and I claim that no one of the Danaans will rebuke me. For the judgment will be straight (23.580). Antilochus, divinely reared, come here as is right. Stand before your horses and your chariot and take the narrow whip in your hand with which you drove your horses. Touch the horses and swear by Poseidon, who holds and shakes the earth, that you did not willingly hinder my chariot with deceit."

Then wise Antilochus answered him: "Hold on now. For I am much younger than you Lord Menelaus, and you are older and better. You know the sorts of transgressions a young man commits in his youth. My mind is rushing, and my intelligence (*mētis*) is light (23.590). But let your heart endure. I myself will give the horse to you which I earned. And if you should request something better from me personally, I would wish to give it to you right away, oh divinely reared one, rather than fall from your favor and be condemned by divinities." Then the son of great-spirited Nestor led the horse and placed it in the hands of Menelaus…(23.600). Indeed, Menelaus, your heart was softened. And he spoke winged words to Antilochus: "Now I will give up my anger, since you were never reckless and witless before this. Only now your youthful mind conquered you. Be careful not to cheat your superiors a second time. Nevertheless, you have suffered much and have toiled much, you and your father, for the sake of me and my brother. Thus, I will obey your entreaty, and I will give *you* the horse, although it is mine, in order that these men here may know that my mind is never overbearing and harsh" (23.610).

And Menelaus then gave the horse to Noemon, the companion of Antilochus, to lead away, and Menelaus himself took the shining cauldron. Then Meriones took the two talents of gold, since he drove in fourth.

Funeral Games of Amarynceus Remembered

Only the fifth-place prize remained, the two-handled jar. Achilles, carrying it through the gathering of the Argives, gave it to Nestor, and said: "May this object now be yours as a memento (*mnēma*) of the burial of Patroclus, since you will no longer see him among the Argives. But I give it to you as a prize all the same (23.620). For you will not fight in boxing, nor will you wrestle, nor anoint yourself with dust, nor will you run with your feet, since difficult old age already presses upon you."

Speaking thus, Achilles placed it in his hands. And Nestor accepted the prize with delight and spoke winged words to him: "You have spoken all these things appropriately, child. For my limbs are no longer stable, nor do my feet or the arms from both my shoulders move lightly. Would that I had my youth and that my force (*biē*) were stable (*empedos*), as in a time before, when the Epeians buried the mighty Amarynceus at Bouprasion (23.630), when the children of the king set up prizes. There no man was equal to me, not among the Epeians, the Pylians, nor among the great spirited Aetolians. In boxing, I conquered Clytomedes, son of Enops; in wresting I conquered Ancaeus of Pleuron, who went against me. In the foot race, I outran Iphiclus, good though he was, and in the spear throw I surpassed Phyles and Polydorus. In the chariot race alone, the sons of Actor surpassed me; they passed me in the crowd, intent on victory, since the greatest prize was reserved for that event (23.640). For they ran as a team. The one held the reins and the other urged on the horses with the whip. Such a one was I once. But now let younger men partake in such work. It is necessary that I obey painful old age, though I was preeminent among heroes once. But come, pay honors to your companion Patroclus with contests. And this prize I willingly accept, and it delights my heart, since you remember me and my kindness, nor do I forget you and the honor it is fitting that I receive among the Achaeans. May the gods give to you a pleasing recompense (*charis*)" (23.650). Thus he spoke, and Achilles went back among the great crowd of the Achaeans, after he heard the praise of Nestor, son of Neleus. But he then set up prizes for painful boxing. He led into the gathering a six-year-old mule, hard-working and unbroken, the sort hardest to break. But for the one who was defeated, he set down a two-handled cup.

Boxing

Then he stood and spoke among the Argives: "Son of Atreus and other well-greaved Achaeans, we command two men among you who are the best (*aristos*) to fight in boxing (*pyx*) with your hands up. For the one to whom Apollo gives endurance (23.660) and whom the Achaeans recognize, let him go to his tent, leading away the hard-working mule. But the one who is conquered will take away this two-handled cup." Thus he spoke and a man brave and good, knowledgeable in boxing, Epeius the son of Panopeus, seized upon the hard-working mule and said: "Let him approach who will lead away the two-handled cup. I claim that no one else of the Greeks will take away the mule, victorious in boxing, since I boast to be the best (*aristos*). Is it not enough that I am deficient in battle? Nor was it ever possible for a man to be experienced in all matters (23.670). For I will tell you this, and it will be accomplished. Right away I will rip his skin and break his bones. And let others remain around him as caretakers who will carry him out after being conquered by my hands."

Thus he spoke, and all sat in silence. But then Euryalus alone rose up against him, a man equal to the gods, the son of Lord Mecisteus, the son of Talaon, who once came to the burial of Oedipus. There he conquered all the Cadmeans (23.680). The spear-famed son of Tydeus, Diomedes, was his handler and encouraged him with words, and he wished great victory for him. First, he put his belt around him and then gave him the well-cut straps of leather from a field ox. And the two, belted, went into the middle of the contest. They held their heavy hands up opposite each other and fell upon each other, and they traded blows with heavy hands. There was a terrible crashing of jaws, and sweat poured from their limbs. And divine Epeius rose up and struck Euryalus on the cheek as he was looking up (23.690). Nor did Euryalus stay standing long, for his glorious limbs gave way. As when under the blast of the north wind a fish jumps onto a shore full of seaweed, and the dark wave crashes upon it, thus Euryalus fell after being hit, but great-hearted Epeius took him in his hands and put him upright. And Euryalus' companions stood around him, and they led him from the contest, feet dragging, coughing up thick blood, with his head falling to the side. His mind was confused as they sat him among them, and they went and picked up the two-handled cup.

Wrestling

Then the son of Peleus set up a third set of prizes (23.700), revealing them to the Danaans, these for painful wrestling (*palaismosynē*). To the victor would go a great fired tripod, which the Achaeans valued at twelve oxen. And for the one who was conquered, he placed in the middle a female slave who was very skilled at handiwork, and they valued her at four oxen. And he stood up and spoke among the Argives: "Rise up, you who will test yourselves for this prize." Thus he spoke and up rose great Ajax, son of Telamon, and wily (*polymētis*) Odysseus, who knows tricks. The two put on their belts and entered the middle of the contest (23.710), and they held each other's elbows with their thick hands as when a famous craftsman fits together the rafters of a high house to protect it from the force of the winds. Their backs creaked when struck solidly with their brave hands. And sweat poured from their backs, and bruises red with blood ran thick along their ribs and shoulders. And the two were ever straining for victory for the sake of the well-made tripod. Odysseus was unable to defend himself and move in any way, nor was Ajax able, but the force of Odysseus held strong (23.720). But when they began to cause stress for the well-greaved Achaeans, then great Ajax, son of Telamon, said to him: "Divine born son of Laertes, much-contriving Odysseus, either you lift me, or I you. All will be left to Zeus."

Speaking thus, he lifted him. But Odysseus did not forget a trick. He struck him, taking hold behind his knee, and loosened his limbs, and Ajax fell backwards. And Odysseus fell upon his chest. And the people were watching and shouting. And a second time divine Odysseus lifted him and moved him only a little from the ground, but could not keep lifting him (23.730), and hooked his knee. Both fell to the ground close to each other, and they were sullied in the dirt. And jumping up, they would have wrestled a third time, if Achilles had not stood up and made an announcement: "Do not keep contending, nor wear yourselves out with troubles. Victory goes to you both. Go take away equal prizes, in order that the rest of the Achaeans may compete for prizes." Thus he spoke, and the two listened and obeyed, and they brushed off the dust and put on their tunics.

Running

Then right away the son of Peleus, Achilles, set up prizes for speed (23.740), a silver mixing bowl, finely wrought, which held only six measures but surpassed all in beauty, since the Sidonians, skilled craftsmen, made it, and Phoenicians brought it over the misty sea and placed it in the harbor and gave it to Thoas as a gift. But Euneus, son of Jason, gave it to Patroclus as ransom for Lycaon, son of Priam, and Achilles made it a prize for his companion that would go to whoever would be lightest with their swift feet. And for second place he placed a great ox, thick with fat (23.750), and he placed a half-talent of gold for last place. And he stood and spoke to the Argives: "Rise up you who will test yourselves for this prize." Thus he spoke, and right away swift Ajax, son of Oileus, rose up, as did wily Odysseus, and then Antilochus, son of Nestor, for he already conquered all the young men with his feet. And they stood in the middle, and Achilles pointed out the turning post. The course was measured at a distance from the turn. When the race began, Ajax, son of Oileus, was soon out in front, and divine Odysseus rose up nearby (23.760)…And then divine Odysseus poured his breath on the back of the head of Ajax, running ever swiftly. And the Achaeans cheered for him, since he was desirous of victory. But when they reached the uttermost part of the track, right away Odysseus prayed to gray-eyed Athena in his heart: "Hear me, goddess, come as a good helper to my feet" (23.770). Thus he prayed. And Pallas Athena heard him, and she made his limbs light, his feet below and his hands above. But when they were about to rush for the prize, then Ajax slipped while running, where the detritus had accumulated from the oxen Achilles sacrificed for Patroclus. Athena hindered him. And his mouth and nose were filled with the detritus. And much-enduring divine Odysseus seized the mixing bowl, since he got there first. But glorious Ajax seized the ox and stood holding the horn of the field ox with his hand. He spat out the refuse and spoke among the Argives. "Oh! The goddess hindered my feet who has always stood beside Odysseus and helped him as though she were his mother." Thus he spoke, and all the Achaeans laughed with pleasure at him. But Antilochus, smiling took away the last-place prize…

Fight in Armor

But then Achilles, son of Peleus, placed a long spear in the middle of the gathering, and on it he put a shield and helmet—the arms of Sarpedon, which Patroclus had taken (23.800). He stood up and spoke to the Argives: "I call for two men, who are the best (*aristos*), to put on armor, to take up the skin-tearing bronze spears, and to face each other. Whoever is first in breaking the beautiful skin, and touches the inside and dark blood, to him I will give this beautiful Thracian silver sword, which I stripped from Asteropaeus. But let both take the armor in common. And for both we will prepare a good feast in the tents" (23.810).

Thus he spoke, and then rose up the great Ajax, son of Telamon, and the son of Tydeus, dominant Diomedes. And then after they put on their armor on either side of the crowd, they came into the middle, staring fiercely, desirous to fight, and awe came upon the all the Achaeans. Then when the two went near to each other, three times they charged, and three times they rushed. Then Ajax struck on the shield of Diomedes, which was a perfect circle, but he did not break through. And Diomedes from over his shield was about to strike upon the neck of Ajax with the point of his shining spear (23.820). And then all the Achaeans were afraid for Ajax and called for them to stop and to take up equal prizes. But the hero Achilles gave to the son of Tydeus the great sword along with its scabbard and well-cut strap.

Throwing a Weight

Then Achilles, the son of Peleus, set down a lump of iron, which Eëtion in his strength used to throw, but swift-footed divine Achilles killed him and brought the iron with his other possessions on the ships. He stood and spoke to the Argives (23.830): "Rise, you who will test yourselves for this prize. Although his rich fields are far away, he will have use of this iron there for five years in a row. Neither his shepherd nor his plowman will have to go to the city for iron, but he will have it ready at hand." Thus he spoke, and Polypoetes, steadfast in battle, stood up, as did Leonteus, equal to the gods in his mighty force, as well as Ajax, son of Telamon, and divine Epeius. They stood in order, and Epeius seized the iron, and whirling about, he released it. And all the Achaeans laughed (23.840). And second Leonteus, scion of Ares, threw it, and third Ajax hurled it from his thick hand, and he surpassed the marks of all. But when Polypoetes grabbed the iron, he threw past the entire competition by as far as an oxherd can throw his stick, which whirls in the air and lands among the field oxen. And the crowd shouted. The companions of mighty Polypoetes stood up and carried the prize of the king to the curved ships.

Archery

Then Achilles set forth dark iron again for the archers (23.850). He set down ten double-bladed axes and ten single-bladed axes. And he planted far away a mast of a dark-prowed ship and tied a timorous pigeon to it with a string attached to its foot, and he ordered them to hit it: "Whoever strikes the timorous pigeon, let him collect up all the axes and take them home. But if one misses the bird and hits the string, that man is less skilled and will carry away the single-bladed axes."

Thus he spoke, and up rose Lord Teucer in his force and brave Meriones, the attendant of Idomeneus (23.860). And they shook lots in a bronze helmet, and Teucer received the first spot. And confidently he shot his arrow, but he did not promise to Apollo, the god of archery, a glorious sacrifice of firstborn lambs. He missed the bird, for Apollo hindered him, but he did strike the string which held the bird, and the bird flew to the sky and the string fell to the ground. And the crowd shouted. And quickly, Meriones grabbed the bow from the hands of Teucer (23.870). He already had an arrow in hand, while Teucer was aiming. And immediately he promised to the far shooter Apollo a glorious sacrifice of firstborn lambs. And high up under the clouds he saw the timorous pigeon, and he struck it in the middle under the wing as it flew about, and the arrow went clean through and fell back to the ground beside Meriones' foot. But the bird fell upon the mast of the dark-prowed ship, with its neck hanging down and wings relaxed. And the spirit flew from its limbs and it fell far from the mast (23.880). The people gazed upon it and were amazed. And Meriones collected ten axes, and Teucer took the single-bladed axes to his curved ships.

Spear Throwing

Then Achilles set down in the middle of the gathering a long spear and an unfired cauldron embossed with flowers worth one ox. And the spear throwers stood up—wide-ruling Agamemnon, son of Atreus, and Meriones, brave attendant of Idomeneus. To them swift-footed divine Achilles spoke (23.890): "Son of Atreus, we know by how much you have excelled all others, and by how much you are the best (*aristos*) in power (*dynamis*) and with the spear throw. Take this prize and go to the curved ships. But let us give the spear to the hero Meriones, if you should wish it in your heart, for I at least command it." Thus he spoke, nor did the lord of men Agamemnon disobey. And Achilles gave the bronze spear to Meriones, and Agamemnon gave his very beautiful prize to the herald Talthybius.

1c. *Odyssey* bk. 6.85–100: Nausicaa and Her Attendants Play Ball

When Nausicaa and her handmaidens arrived at the beautiful streams of the river, where the water troughs were full and much beautiful water flowed to clean dirty garments, there they freed the mules from the wagon and drove them to feed on the honey-sweet grass by the eddying river. They took up the clothes from the wagon with their hands and placed them in the dark water, and they trampled them in the trenches, making a contest (*eris*) of the work. After they washed and cleaned all the dirty clothes, they spread them out in a row on the shore of the sea, where the sea washed away the pebbles on the dry land. Then they bathed and anointed themselves with olive oil and they took a meal beside the banks of the river, while they waited for the clothes to be dried by the rays of the sun.

But after Nausicaa and her handmaidens had their fill of food, they cast off their head-dresses and played with a ball (*sphairē*) (6.100), and white-armed Nausicaa led with a song.

1d. *Odyssey* bk. 8.94–198: The Games of the Phaeacians (with omissions)

Odysseus has been washed ashore in Phaeacia after being shipwrecked. His identity is as yet unknown to his hosts, who are entertaining him. The king of Phaeacia is Alcinous. Note in this passage how athletic prowess is a mark of social distinction.

Alcinous alone noticed Odysseus, who was sitting nearby, and he heard him groaning deeply. Right away he spoke among the oar-loving Phaeacians: "Hear me lords and counsel-lors of the Phaeacians, we have satisfied our hearts equally with feasting and with the lyre, which is the companion to the rich feast, but now let us go and test ourselves at all manner of contests (8.100) in order that this stranger may say to his friends at home how much we excel all others in boxing (*pyx*), wrestling (*palaimosynē*), jumping (*halma*), and running."

Speaking thus, he led them out and they followed on the same road upon which the best of the Phaeacians were going in order to marvel at the games. Then they went to the agora, and a great crowd followed, countless people. And many young and noble men stood by…(8.110) First, they tested themselves in the foot race (8.120). The track was measured from the turning post. And quickly all together they rushed, kicking up the dirt of the plain. And of them, blameless Clytoneus was best (*aristos*) in running. As far as a trench in fallow land made by mules, by that distance he ran out in front and the group was left behind. Then they tested painful wrestling. In that event, Euryalus con-quered all the best. In jumping, Amphialus excelled all. And in the discus throw (*diskos*), Elatreus was by far the best of all. And in boxing Laodamas, noble son of Alcinous was best (8.130).

But after they delighted themselves in the contests, Laodamas, the son of Alcinous, spoke to them: "Come friends, let us speak to the stranger to see if he is familiar with contests. His stature is not that of a base man, from the look of his thighs, calves, hands, his thick neck, and great strength. Nor is he lacking in youth, although he has met with many troubles: For I say that nothing is more harmful to come upon a man than the sea, even if he has force." Then Euryalus answered him (8.140): "Well spoken, Laodamas; now you call to him and make the challenge."

When the noble son of Alcinous heard this, he stood in the middle and spoke to Odysseus: "Come, stranger, sir, test yourself in contests, if you have learned any. You seem to know contests. For there is no greater glory (*kleos*) for a man than what he accomplishes with his hands and feet. But come, test yourself and shake off the pains from your heart. The way home will not be long for you (8.150), but already a ship has been launched and the crew is ready."

Then wily Odysseus answered him: "Laodamas, why do you taunt me and command these things? I have cares in my heart more than contests, I who have suffered much and have toiled much, and now I sit here in your gathering entreating the king and his people, desiring a return home." Then Euryalus began to quarrel with him in response: "I do not think you are a man of contests (*athla*), of which there are many types among men (8.160). No, you seem to me to be a captain of merchant seamen, going here and there, mindful of his cargo and looking out for profit and gain. No, you do not appear to be an athlete."

Then, looking out from under his furrowed brow, wily Odysseus spoke: "Stranger, you have not spoken well. You appear to be a reckless man. The gods do not give all that is pleasing to all men, namely physical form, mind, and eloquence. For one man may be weak in appearance, but the god crowns his form with words (8.170), and men take delight when they look at him. And he speaks steadily with sweet modesty, and he is preeminent in the crowd, and they look upon him like a god as he goes through the city. But another man is like the gods in form, but there is no grace (*charis*) upon his words. Your physical form is distinguished, nor could a god add to it, but your mind is empty. Now you have stirred the spirit in my dear breast, since you spoke beyond measure. I am not ignorant of contests, as you claim (8.180). I was among the best as long as I had confidence in my youth and my hands. But now I am seized with hardship and pain. And I endured much after passing through waves and the painful wars of men. Nevertheless, although having suffered many ills, I will try out the contests. For your speech has bitten my spirit and you have roused me with your words." And he leapt up with his cloak on and seized a discus (*diskos*), larger, massive, and much thicker than those which the Phaeacians were throwing against each other. Whirling about, he threw it from his thick hand. It made a booming noise (8.190), and the Phaeacian oarsmen, famed for seafaring, were amazed at the throw and ducked to the ground. And Athena, in the form of a man, placed the mark for the throw and spoke out: "Stranger, even a blind man could make out the mark by feeling for it, since it is not mixed with the crowd, but is by far the first. You can be confident in this contest. No one of the Phaeacians will reach it or overtake it."

1e. *Odyssey* bk. 18.40–107: Odysseus Boxes with Irus

After twenty years, Odysseus, who was presumed dead, has returned to his home, Ithaca, to find his palace occupied by local elites who are eager to marry his wife. He prudently assumes the disguise of a beggar to monitor their actions. In this incident he is challenged by another beggar trying to take his place. The two trade insults and are then goaded into boxing by one of the suitors. The match is closer to a street brawl than a formal boxing match. Note that they do not use thongs.

All jumped up and gathered around the poorly clothed beggars. Antinous, son of Eupeithes, spoke among them: "Listen to me, noble suitors, in order that I may say something: On the fire lie the goat stomachs, which we filled with fat and blood in preparation for dinner. Whichever of the two is victorious and proves to be the stronger, let him come and take however much he wishes of this food. And he will always eat with us, nor will we let any other beggar who comes asking to join."

Thus Antinous spoke, and his speech pleased them (18.50). But crafty, deceptive Odysseus spoke to them: "Friends, it is not possible for an old man, racked with agony to fight a younger man. But the wrong-doing stomach compels me even if I am conquered by its blows. Come now, all of you swear a mighty oath, lest someone, wishing to help Irus, strike me with a heavy hand in his insolence and conquer me by force on that man's behalf." Thus he spoke, and all swore an oath as he commanded. But when they swore and completed the oath (18.60), then Telemachus, in his sacred strength, spoke to them: "Stranger, if your heart and spirit compels you to ward off this man, fear no one of the Achaeans, since whoever strikes you will fight with many. And I am your host, and the kings agree, Antinous and Eurymachus, who are both wise."

Thus he spoke, and all gave approval. But Odysseus belted his rags around his loins, and he revealed his large and beautiful thighs, and his broad shoulders and chest and thick arms. But Athena, standing nearby, strengthened the limbs of the shepherd of the people (18.70). And all the suitors were especially amazed. And one person looking to another would say: "Soon Irus will be Un-Irus'ed and will suffer evil which he brought upon himself, such a thigh does the old man reveal from his rags." Thus they spoke, and Irus' spirit grew cowardly. But the workers girded him by force and led him out, afraid though he was. And the flesh of his limbs was trembling. And Antinous spoke a word and called out to him: "You are better off dead, if you tremble and are terribly afraid of this old man (18.80), racked with the pain which comes upon him. But I say this to you, and it will be accomplished: If that man wins and proves to be better, I will throw you in a black ship and send you off to the mainland, to king Echetus, a scourge for all men. He will cut your nose and ears from your face with the pitiless bronze, and he will rip off your limbs and feed your raw flesh to the dogs."

Thus he spoke, and even more fear seized his limbs. They led them into the middle, and the two held up their hands. Then much-enduring divine Odysseus thought to himself (18.90) whether he should hit him so that Irus' life would leave him right away as he fell, or whether he should strike him lightly and stretch him out on the ground. It seemed to him to be better to strike him lightly, so that the Achaeans might not suspect him. Then Irus struck his right shoulder as he approached, but Odysseus struck his neck under the ear and broke the bones there. Right away, dark blood came up from his mouth, and he fell to the ground groaning, gnashing his teeth and kicking the ground. But the noble suitors held up their hands, dying with laughter (18.100). Then Odysseus took him and dragged him from the doorway by the foot until he came to the courtyard and the portico gates. He sat him up and leaned him on the wall of the courtyard, and placed his walking stick in his hand, and spoke winged words to him: "Sit there and ward off the pigs and the dogs. But do not try to be prince of strangers and beggars, miserable as you are, lest you meet a far greater evil."

1f. *Odyssey* bk. 21.1–4, 67–139, 404–30: The Contest of the Bow

The goddess Athena contrives this contest so that Odysseus, still in disguise as a beggar, may gain access to his favored weapon, a bow, in order to kill the suitors. The contest also serves as an occasion for Odysseus to prove his worthiness to continue as the king of Ithaca. Aside from funeral contests, another early occasion for athletic contests is the wedding contest (see also Pindar Olympian *1,* **2a***).*

21.1–4. And then gray-eyed Athena put an idea into the mind of the daughter of Icarius, very wise Penelope, to set down the bow and gray iron for the suitors in the halls of Odysseus, a contest (*aethlia*) that would be the beginning of the slaughter.

21.67–187. Right away Penelope spoke, addressing the suitors: "Hear me, noble suitors, who have used this house for eating and drinking without end, while my husband has been absent for so long (21.70). You have not been able to make any excuse except that you wish to marry me and make me your wife. But come, suitors, since this prize is here before you. For I will set down the great bow of divine Odysseus. Whoever strings the bow with his hands easily and shoots an arrow through all twelve axes, that man I will follow, leaving the house where I was a bride (21.79). Thus she spoke and ordered Eumaeus the swineherd to place the bow and gray iron before the suitors. And Eumaeus received it with tears and put it down and cried aloud when he saw the bow of his master. But the suitor Antinous spoke out to them:

"Uncivilized fools, thinking only of today, how miserable you are. Why do you now shed tears and rouse the spirit in the chest of this woman? Her spirit is already in pain, since she lost her dear husband. Now sit and eat in silence, or go outside the gates and cry, but leave the bow here (21.90), although it is an impossible contest for the suitors. For I do not think the polished bow will be easily stretched, since no man among all those here is comparable to Odysseus. I myself saw him and I remember him, though I was but an innocent child." Thus he spoke, but his spirit in his chest still hoped to string the bow and shoot an arrow though the iron. Yet Antinous was going to be the first to taste the arrow shot from the hands of blameless Odysseus, since he dishonored Odysseus when he sat in the halls and encouraged all his companions (21.100).

And then Telemachus, inspired by the god, spoke among them: "Ah, Zeus made me mindless. My dear mother tells me, since she is wise, that she will leave this house and follow another man. But I, in my mindless spirit, laugh and am pleased at this. Come suitors, since the prize is there, there is no woman like her throughout the land of the Achaeans, not in sacred Pylos, nor in Argos, nor in Mycenae, not here in Ithaca, nor throughout the dark mainland. And you yourselves know it. What need is there, then, for praise of my mother? (21.110) But come, do not drag this out with pretenses and do not turn from stringing the bow, in order that we may know. And I myself should test the bow. Perhaps if I string it and shoot an arrow through the iron, my queenly mother would not go off with another and leave me sorely grieved in this house, since I would remain here, able to take up the beautiful prizes of my father."

Then he jumped up right away and hurled away his purple cloak and sharp sword from his shoulders. First, he stood up the axes (21.120), digging a single long trench for all of them, and made it straight with a carpenter's measure, and he covered them with earth. And astonishment seized all looking upon him, because he set them up in such an orderly fashion. He went and stood upon the threshold and tried the bow. Three times he shook, desiring to string it, and three times his force failed him, though he had hope in his spirit that he would string the bow and shoot through the iron. And he would have strung it on the fourth attempt, pulling on it with force, but Odysseus shook his head and prevented him, though he was desirous to do it. And then Telemachus, with his divine power, spoke among them (21.130): "Ah, I will be a coward and a weakling, or I am too young and I do not yet have confidence in my hands to ward off a man, when someone older gives me a hard time. But come, those who are more preeminent in force than me, try the bow and let us finish this contest." Speaking thus, he put the bow on the ground, leaning it against the polished and compact doors, and there placed the swift arrow against the polished handle, and he sat back down in his chair from which he had stood up.

After each of the suitors in turn tries to string the bow and fails, Odysseus asks for the chance to string the bow. After considerable discussion and an exchange of insults, he is permitted to do so. When he succeeds, he then proceeds to kill all the suitors.

…crafty Odysseus lifted the bow and looked it all over, as when a man who knows well the lyre and song easily strings a chord of well-twisted sheep's gut over a new peg, so without effort Odysseus strung the great bow. Then with his right hand he tested the bowstring (21.410). It sung beautifully, like the voice of a swallow. And great grief came upon the suitors, and their color changed. And Zeus, showing portents, thundered greatly. And the much-enduring divine Odysseus felt joy that the son of crooked-counseling Cronus sent him a sign. He took up an arrow which lay uncovered on the table. The other arrows lay inside the hollow quiver; with these the Achaeans were soon to be tested. Taking up this one arrow on his arm, he drew back the bowstring, and sitting from his chair (21.420), he released it, nor did he miss any of the axes, but the bronze-weighted arrow went straight through. And he spoke out to Telemachus: "Telemachus, the guest sitting in your halls does not shame you. I did not miss any part of the target nor did I fail in stringing the bow. My life force is still stable. And I am not as the suitors mocked me in disrespect. But now is the time to prepare a feast for the Achaeans in the daylight; then let there be amusement with the song and the lyre, for these are the complements of the feast" (21.430).

1g. bk. *Odyssey* 24. 85–97: The Funeral Games of Achilles

When the dead Agamemnon encounters the spirit of Achilles in the Underworld, he proceeds to describe the funeral games that Achilles' mother Thetis held for him at his death.

Your mother requested beautiful prizes from the gods and placed them in the middle of the gathering for the best of the Achaeans. At that time, I had already visited the graves of many heroes, where youth girded themselves and competed for prizes when a king had perished. But you would have admired these above all others if you had seen them. Such beautiful prizes the goddess silver-footed Thetis set up for you were especially dear to the gods. But in death, you did not lose your name, but always you will have noble glory (*kleos*) among all men, Achilles. But what pleasure was there for me, when I finished the war? Upon my return home (*nostos*), Zeus contrived a terrible destruction at the hands of Aegisthus and my wretched wife.

Victory Odes

2. Pindar

Pindar (517–438 BCE), from Thebes in Boeotia, was considered the greatest of the nine Greek lyric poets who wrote in the Archaic period and was best known for his writing of victory odes (epinicia) for successful athletes. Forty-five of these poems survive and, although written over many years, they were gathered together in antiquity and organized into collections by the games sites: Olympian, Pythian (Delphi), Isthmian, Nemean. These odes may have been performed at the site of the victory or in the victor's hometown or both. They are also likely to have been reperformed well after the occasion of the victory. The primary goal of the ode was to celebrate the extraordinary qualities that led an individual to athletic victory, but Greeks also had a strong cultural inhibition against excessive pride or boastfulness. Many of their myths are about the gods punishing humans for overstepping normative boundaries. For that reason, the poet also needed to present the event in a way that demonstrated the importance of the victory (and the virtue of the victor) for the world of mere mortals. In addition, he reminds the victor of these limits and his audience that the individual being honored in turn honored the gods and his fellow citizens. Pindar's poems usually have the following elements: (1) reference to the event and place of victory; (2) praise of the victor's city; (3) praise of the victor's family; (4) myths that celebrate the games site or the victor's city or legendary heroes in the victor's ancestry; and (5) a warning against excessive pride. Pindar also uses the venue of these public displays of song to elevate the status and importance of his own poetry. He often does this with analogies that liken his song-making to athletic prowess or victory. Pindar's poetry was written in a variety of choral meters that were both sung and danced. His language is elevated in style and full of difficult expressions; in translating we have attempted to keep the structure of his stanzas and to translate his dense thoughts as exactly as possible within the limits of intelligibility. We have chosen a representative sample of his epinicia, translated in whole or in part, to illustrate how he celebrated individuals, places, and events. At the end of this section is the complete list of Pindar's surviving odes, their addressees, and the event (see Table 1).

2a. *Olympian* 1: Hieron of Syracuse, Single-Horse Race, 476 BCE

*Hieron I was the ruler of Syracuse from 478–467 BCE, and during that time the city was distinguished by numerous victories at Panhellenic games. Hieron himself won both a single-horse victory (kelēs) and later added a chariot victory at the Pythian Games that Pindar also commemorated (Pythian 1). His single-horse victory was also celebrated by Bacchylides (see **3a**).*

This poem was placed first in the ancient collection of Pindar's odes for Olympic victors, we are told, because it treats a myth important for the site: Pelops defeating Oenomaus, the king of Elis, in a chariot race in order to win the hand of Hippodamia. The tomb of Pelops is in the Olympic sanctuary (92–3), and the east pediment of Zeus's temple at Olympia commemorates the race between these two men. Pelops was from Lydia, the child of Tantalus, but after his race, in which Oenomaus was killed, he became king of Elis. In some versions of his story, Tantalus cut up and served his own children to the gods in a stew. The goddess Demeter unwittingly ate part of Pelops' shoulder. When the gods revived him, they replaced the missing portion with ivory. Pindar's version of the myth alludes to but avoids telling this gruesome tale; rather, he has Pelops born with an ivory shoulder given him by Clotho, one of the threes Fates who determined the length of human life. The god of the sea, Poseidon, fell in love with the adolescent Pelops and transported him to Olympus. Hence, Pelops' later appeal to Poseidon for aid in his competition with Oenomaus.

> Best is water, and gold like flaming fire
> is to be seen preeminent in the night above great wealth.
> But if to sing of athletic victory
> delights, dear heart,
> look no farther than the sun
> for another star, shining more warmly in daylight,
> > through the empty ether.
> Let us proclaim no contest greater than Olympia,
> from which comes the much-spoken-of hymn that encloses
> the imaginations of wise men,
> coming to celebrate the son of Cronus at the rich
> and blessed hearth of Hieron, (1–11)
>
> who is guardian of the rightful scepter in Sicily,
> rich in flocks. Plucking the blooms of all excellence,
> he is glorified as well
> at the height of songs,
> the kind that we men often perform playfully
> at table among friends. Now

take the Dorian lyre from its peg
if the glory of Pisa[4] and Pherenicus[5]
imbued your mind with the sweetest thoughts,
when he sped along the Alpheus,[6]
giving his body to the race without need of a goad,
and merged his master, Syracuse's chariot-driving king, (12–22)

with great power.
   His fame shines
in the manly colony of Lydian Pelops,
with whom the mighty Earth-shaker Poseidon
fell in love when from the pure cauldron
   Clotho pulled him,
equipped with a bright ivory shoulder.
There are many marvels and sometimes also men's
speech exceeds literal truth,[7]
stories embellished with
   ornate falsehoods deceive. (23–29)

Now Charis,[8] who fashions all things to be delightful for mortals,
in bestowing honor often makes
even the unbelievable believable.
But the days to come
are the wisest witnesses.
It is reasonable for a man to tell fine stories
   about the divine, since the blame is less.
Son of Tantalus, I shall speak of you in a way contrary to those who have gone
   before,
of how when your father summoned the gods
to a most propitious banquet in friendly Sipylus,[9]
providing a feast for the gods in reciprocation,[10]
then the Lord of the Shining Trident [= Poseidon] seized you, (30–40)

---

[4] The site of Olympia.   [5] The name of Hieron's victorious horse.

[6] The Alpheus is a river that runs along the western side of the site of Olympia. The hippodrome, where this race was run is now thought to have been much farther to the east (see Plan 2, p. 374). The ancients thought that there was an underground connection between this Peloponnesian river and a fountain in Hieron's Syracuse (mentioned in *Nemean 1*).

[7] There is an extra line (28b) here in the Greek.

[8] Charis (compare English "*char*-ity") is here personified as a goddess or "Grace" representing the appeal of praise and poetry. Elsewhere in Pindar the word is used as a common noun to mean "charm," "splendor," "favor," or "glory."

[9] A city in Lydia.   [10] That is, in reciprocation for a feast given by the gods previously.

his wits overcome with desire; and with his golden horses
he carried you off to the lofty home of widely honored Zeus.
There at a later time
Ganymede also came
For this same purpose for Zeus.[11]
When you disappeared [i.e., from Tantalus' banquet] and not even,
    after much searching, did men return you to your mother,
someone of the envious neighbors immediately spoke in secret
that into the water boiling on the fire
they had cut up your limbs with a knife,
and for the last course they distributed
your flesh to the tables and ate it. (41–51)

For me it is impossible to call
    any of the blessed gods a glutton—I do not take a side.
Frequently the lot of slanderers is without profit.
If indeed the guardians of Olympus honored
any mortal man, it was this Tantalus.
    But to digest his great good fortune,
he was unable, and from his insolence he reaped
an overwhelming penalty; over him the father [of the gods]
hung a massive rock which,
in his eagerness to cast it away from his head,
    keeps him from happiness. (52–58)

He has this helpless life burdened with weariness.
With three sufferings a fourth,[12] because, having stolen from the immortals,
he gave to his drinking companions
the nectar and ambrosia
by means of which they [i.e., the gods] made him
immortal. Now if a man hopes
    to keep secret some deed from a god, he is making a mistake.
For these reasons, the immortals cast his son back
among the short-lived race of men again.
When coming into the age of blooming youth
and down covered his darkening chin,
he turned his mind to a ready marriage, (59–69)

---

[11] The boys were cupbearers for the gods, but also served a pederastic purpose. Pindar's language is discreetly neutral.

[12] This can be taken to mean that Tantalus joins the three famously punished sinners: Tityus, Sisyphus, and Ixion (for whom, see *Pythian* 2); or that Tantalus' punishments of hunger, thirst, and the hanging stone also include a fourth element of an eternally wretched life, which is described immediately following.

to gaining the famous Pisan girl Hippodamia from her father.
Coming close to the gray sea alone in the dark,
he called to the deep-thundering
Lord of the Fair Trident, who
appeared to him by his feet.
He said to him: "If the loving gifts of Cypris [= Aphrodite]
    have accomplished anything of gratitude, Poseidon,
then hold back Oenomaus' bronze spear,
and bring me in the swiftest chariot
to Elis[13] to be victorious;
for, having killed three and ten men
who were her suitors, he pushes back the marriage (70–80)

of his daughter. Great risk
    does not attract the cowardly man,
for whom to die is a necessity. But who would cling to
an anonymous old age, sitting in darkness in vain,
without a share of all that is noble? For my part,
    this contest will be undertaken.
For yours, grant me the desired outcome."
Thus he spoke, and did not touch upon unfulfilled
words. Honoring him, the god
gave him a golden chariot
    and winged, tireless horses. (81–7)

He defeated Oenomaus' might and took the girl as his wife.
He sired six sons to be leaders, eager for valor.
Now he has a share in
splendid blood sacrifices,
reclining by the course of the Alpheus,
with a well-attended tomb nearby the much-
    visited altar [of Zeus Olympios]. From afar
flashes the fame of the Olympic festivals, on the racecourses
of Pelops, where is contested swiftness of foot,
and the bold-laboring peaks of strength.
The victor, for the remainder of his life,
has a honey-sweet calm (88–98)

because of the games. But having good fortune daily
is supreme for every mortal. It is for me
to crown that man with

---

[13] The area that contains Pisa, Olympia, and the Alpheus.

an equestrian tune in Aeolic song.[14]
I am persuaded that there is no other host
of those who are now alive
    both expert in fair deeds and more commanding in his power
to adorn within the famous layers of hymns.
God as a guardian takes heed of your things,
keeping in mind, Hieron,
your desires. Unless he should quickly abandon you,
I should hope even more sweetly still (99–109)

to celebrate once more your swift chariot,
    having found a helpful road of words
coming to the hill of Cronus[15] open to the sun. For me
the Muse nourishes the mightiest weapon for defense;
in other respects, others are great,
    but the peak is crowned
by kings. Search no further.
May you walk exalted for the time that is yours.
May I be a companion to the victors
as often as they win, being far-famed for wisdom
    among the Greeks everywhere. (110–16)

2b. *Olympian* 3: Theron of Acragas, Chariot Race, 476 BCE

The ode celebrates Theron's victory with the four-horse chariot at Olympia. Olympian 2 treats the same victory, but this poem includes a foundation myth of the games by Heracles (see Pausanias 37a). Theron was the son of the Emmenid Aenesidamus (see lines 8 and 38); he ruled Acragas in Sicily from 488 until his death in 473. He won this victory in the same Olympiad as Hieron (celebrated in Olympian 1).

To please the hospitable sons of Tyndareus [= Castor and Polydeuces]
    and fair-haired Helen [= their sister],
while praising famous Acragas, I pray,
as I raise up for Theron an Olympic victory
    hymn, which is the choicest for the indefatigable feat
of his horses. For this reason, I suppose, the Muse
was at my side as I found a newly shining way
to harmonize my voice of splendid celebration with the Dorian sandal.[16] (1–5)

---

[14] Compare *Pythian* 2.70.   [15] In Olympia.
[16] i.e., the Dorian "rhythm" or "meter." Compare the metrical term "foot" in English.

The crowns of victory that yoke his hair
　　require from me this god-built duty,
to intermingle in a fit way the multi-toned lyre
with the cry of the *aulos* and placement of words
　　for the son of Aenesidamus,
celebratory acts which Pisa too urges of me—from there
god-allotted songs come to those men (6–10)

over whose brow and hair
the stern Aetolian *Hellanodikēs* [= judge] places,
in accordance with Heracles' ancient instructions,
the adornment of gray-skinned olive,
that olive which once
from the Ister's[17] well-shaded
　　springs the son of Amphitryon [= Heracles] brought back
to be the fairest memorial of the contests at Olympia, (11–15)

after he persuaded the Hyperborean folk,
　　Apollo's servants, with his words.
With honorable intent he requested
for the all-welcoming sanctuary of Zeus a tree
　　for the communal purposes of a source of shade for men and of crowns for
　　　　victories.
Now the altars of his father [= Zeus] had already
　　been consecrated, and, in the middle of the month, from her golden chariot
the Moon shone forth her full eye at evening.[18] (16–20)

He established the sacred judging of the great contests
　　with their four-year cycle
by the sacred banks of the Alpheus.
But Pelops' land in the valleys of Cronus' hill [= Olympia]
　　did not bloom with fair trees.
Naked of them, the garden seemed to him
　　to be under the sway of the fierce rays of the sun.
At that point his spirit urged him to go (21–5)

to the Istrian land. There Leto's horse-driving daughter [= Artemis]
received him once as he came from the mountain glens
　　of Arcadia and the winding valleys
where, on the orders of Eurystheus,
　　a necessity from his father [Zeus]

---

[17] The far northern region of the Upper Danube where the mythical Hyperboreans were said to live.
[18] The first full moon after the summer solstice marked the beginning of the Olympic truce.

urged him to bring back the doe
    of golden horns which once
Taygeta had inscribed as a sacred offering dedicated to [Artemis] Orthosia.[19] (26–30)

While tracking the deer, he saw that land
    beyond the blasts of the cold north
wind. He stood there marveling at the trees.
A sweet desire overtook him
    to plant them around the boundaries of the twelve-lapped racecourse
for horses.[20] So now, to this festival
he comes gladly with the twin, godlike
children [= Castor and Polydeuces] of Leda of the wide sash, (31–5)

For when he went to Olympus,[21] he entrusted them
    to take charge of the marvelous competition
involving the valor of men and the swift
driving of chariots. I think that my heart
    urges me to say that to the Emmenidae
and to Theron fame has been given by the
    sons of Tyndareus, who are skilled horsemen, because most of all men
did they host them at their hospitable tables, (36–40)

and with reverent minds they guard the rites of the blessed gods.
If water is best, and of possessions
    gold is the most honored,[22]
then now Theron has come to the furthest point by his valor
    and from his home touches
the pillars of Heracles.[23]
What lies beyond is inaccessible to both the wise
and the unwise. I shall not pursue it. That would be foolish. (41–5)

2c. *Olympian* 10: Hagesidamus of Epizephyrian Locri, Boys' Boxing, 476 BCE

Pindar begins this ode by claiming that he had forgotten about it and will now write something that will praise the victor "with interest." In 476 Pindar was committed to three other victory odes

---

[19] Taygeta was one of the Pleiades; when she was pursued by an amorous Zeus, Artemis changed her into a deer. Upon returning to her normal shape, she dedicated a deer to the goddess.

[20] This line offers evidence that the chariot competition consisted of twelve laps.

[21] That is, became immortal.   [22] See the beginning of *Olympian* 1 above.

[23] The Strait of Gibraltar, where, according to Greek myth, Heracles established the promontory.

(Olympians 1, 2, and 3), which probably accounts for his delay in writing for this event. He devotes much of the ode to the foundation of the games by Heracles, which were paid for in part with the spoils of Heracles' war against Augeas, and his bringing of shade trees to the sanctuary. Pindar also names those who won early victories in gymnic events. Olympian 11 is another ode for the same victor and event. Apart from these odes, Hagesidamus is unknown.

> The Olympic victor, read me his name,
> the son of Archestratus, from the place in my mind
> where it is written, for I had forgotten that I owe him
>   the debt of sweet song. Oh Muse, you and your sister
> Truth, the daughter of Zeus, with an upright hand
> hold off from me a rebuke for false promises
> to the harm of a guest-friend. (1–6)

> For the time that was about to come has now arrived from afar
> and has brought deep shame to my debt.
> Nevertheless, it is possible with interest
>   to redeem bitter reproach. Let him see now how a flowing wave
> washes over the rolling stone
> and how with a public accounting
> we shall repay for his dear pleasure. (7–12)

> For Strictness rules the city of the Western Locrians,
> and they cultivate Calliope
> and brazen Ares [= the god of war]. A battle with Cycnus[24]
>   turned back even Heracles, who was larger than life.
> As one victorious in boxing at the Olympic Games,
> let Hegesidamus express gratitude
> to Ilas [i.e., his trainer] just as
> Patroclus did to Achilles.
> Through sharp training a man may compel
> one born to excellence to unfathomable fame
> with help from a god. (13–21)

> Few have found a joy without effort
> that beyond all deeds is a light for life.
> The ordinances of Zeus have urged me to sing of the greatest contest
>   that beside the ancient tomb of Pelops
> Heracles established, six in number…[25]

---

[24] A son of the war god Ares, who challenged Heracles to a fight.
[25] The text is corrupt: Either six [altars] or six [contests] would be the best choice.

Now having gathered his whole army in Pisa
and all his people, the glorious son of Zeus
measured out a sacred precinct for his almighty father.
     Placing fencing around the Altis, he marked it off in a clear space,
and the encircling plain
he made a respite for dining,
honoring the stream of the Alpheus (43–8)

along with the twelve ruling gods. And he named
the hill of Cronus. Before then
it was without a name and, when Oenomaus ruled, it was wetted
     with many snows. In that first festival moment
the Fates stood nearby
and the single assayer
of what is really true, (49–54)

Time, which as it progressed, revealed clearly
how, dividing the gifts of war,
he sacrificed the best part
     and established a quadrennial festival
with the first Olympiad
and its victory bearers.
Who won the new
crown with hands or
feet or chariot, setting
a triumph in the contest in his mind,
     and in his deed accomplishing it? (55–63)

He was best in the *stadion*, running with his feet
on a straight course, Oeonus the child of Licymnius,
who came from Midea, leading his army.
     In wrestling (*palē*), Echemus brought *kudos* to Tegea,
and Doryclus bore the victory in boxing (*pygmē*),
living in the city of Tiryns.
With four horses from Mantinea (64–9)

Samos, the son of Halirrhothius, won.
With his javelin (*akōn*) Phrastor hit the mark.
Niceus, whirling a stone with his hand, cast it
     a distance beyond all others, and the army
raised a great clamor. In the evening
the fair light of the lovely-
faced moon shone forth. (70–5)

The whole sanctuary was filled with the sounds of pleasant feasts
in the way of the victory celebration.
In the manner of those ancient beginnings
    even now we shall celebrate the song named for
noble victory singing of the thunder
and fire-thrown bolt
of Thunder-wakening Zeus,
the flaming lightning, suitable
in every victory.
The subtle play of songs
    shall answer the reed pipe...(76–84)

And whenever, having accomplished great deeds unaccompanied by song,
Hagesidamus, a man may come into the house of Hades
having breathed to no purpose, he has attained for his toil
    little joy. But upon you the sweet-speaking lyre
and dulcet flute shed grace.
The Pierian daughters of Zeus[26]
tend your widespread fame. (91–6)

I, eagerly taking part, have embraced
the famous race of Locrians, imbuing
their city of noble men with honey.
    The beloved child of Archestratus
I celebrate, whom I saw conquering
with strength of hand near the
Olympian altar at that time
both fair in form
and touched with a youthfulness that once
kept shameful death from Ganymede[27]
    with the help of the Cypris-born one [= Aphrodite]. (97–105)

2d. *Olympian* 9: Epharmostus of Opous, Wrestling, 468 BCE

Olympian 9 was written for a victor who had won in all four of the crown games. Someone who achieved this feat, which is comparable to today's grand slam in professional tennis, was known as a periodonikēs ("one who has completed the victory circuit"). Epharmostus was, as we learn in this poem, also very successful as a young competitor, who easily continued his victory streak after advancing

[26] The Muses, whose home was Pieria in northern Greece.
[27] See n. 11 on line 45 of *Olympian* 1.

from the boys' tournament to the men's. We have omitted Pindar's treatment of the two central myths: Heracles' battles against three Olympian gods (an appropriate myth for a wrestler), and the story (also found in other versions across the Mediterranean) of the destruction of the earth by flood and the subsequent resettling of a race of stone-born men at Opous (the victor's hometown on the shore of the Greek mainland opposite Euboea).

The song of Archilochus
was intoned at Olympia.
    The loud-sounding thrice-repeated victory ode[28]
was enough to lead Epharmostus and his companions
to the hill of Cronus in their celebration.
But now from the bow of the far-shooting Muses,
take aim at Zeus of the scarlet thunderbolt
and at the holy peak of Elis[29]
with arrows such as these[30]—
Elis, which once the hero, Lydian Pelops,
won as Hippodamia's fairest dowry.[31] (1–10)

And cast a sweet winged arrow
toward Pytho.[32] No words
that you touch will fall upon the ground,
when you make the lyre strings vibrate for the wrestling
of a man who comes from famous Opous. Praise her and her son,
whom Themis and her daughter the savior, glorious Eunomia, have
received as their lot. She [= Opous] blooms
with the glories had by your stream,
Castalia, and the Alpheus,[33]
from where the choicest crowns exalt
the Locrians' mother city shining in its trees.[34] (11–20)

I make that dear city alight
with the flames of my songs,

[28] The song of Archilochus (c. 680s–640s BCE), though of questionable origins and content, began, "*tenella kallinike.*" Because the verses were constructed for a victory in a contest of religious song, the first word of this short, repeated refrain, "*tenella*" was meant to imitate the sound of a kithara ("*kallinike*" is likely an address to the, "glorious victor"). In this Pindaric ode, we hear how Archilochus may be invoked as an early example of epinician song.
[29] The hill of Cronus at Olympia.
[30] Referring to the song (i.e., the singer is a sort of warrior or athlete of the Muses).
[31] See *Olympian* 1 above.   [32] i.e., another site of victory for Epharmostus.
[33] Waters near Pytho and Olympia, respectively.
[34] Whereas *Olympian* 10 was written for the Epizephyrian ("Western") Locrians, who inhabited the toe of Italy, *Olympian* 9 was for the Opountian Locrians on the eastern shore of Greece, who may have established the Italian colony around 680 BCE (therefore, Opous is a "mother city").

and, faster than a valiant horse
or a winged ship,
I shall send this news everywhere [21–5]

[26–79 omitted]

May I be one who finds appropriate words
as I mount the chariot of the Muses.
May daring and abundant power
attend me. On account of friendship and glory, I have come
to honor Lampromachus' Isthmian crowns of ribbons,
    since both won victories (77–84)

on the same day.[35]
Two other victorious moments
    were at the gates of Corinth [= the Isthmian Games],
and those for Epharmostus were in the Nemean valley [= Nemean Games];
At Argos he won glory (*kudos*) in the men's contest, and in the boys' contest
at Athens, and what a contest at Marathon did he endure for silver cups
against older men, when taken out of the unbearded class (*ageneioi*).
Without a fall and with swift feints,
conquering men, he moved
through the encircling crowd to such a shout,
being beautiful in his prime while accomplishing the fairest deeds. (85–94)

His astonishing prowess was seen
by the Parrhasian people
    during the festival of Zeus Lycaeus,[36]
and at Pellana[37] he won the warm remedy
for cold winds [= a wool cloak]. The tomb of Iolaus
and Eleusis by the sea were witness to his glories.[38]
That which is natural is everywhere best. Many men
strive to achieve fame
with skills that are taught,
but anything which is without the god
is none the worse for remaining unsaid. (95–104)

---

[35] Lampromachus was related to Epharmostus.   [36] In Arcadia (see Pausanias, **37y**).
[37] In the region of Achaea on the north shore of the Peloponnese.
[38] The Iolaea was a festival and competition held in Thebes. Eleusis, which is on the coast immediately
west of Athens, also held games.

Some roads are longer than others.
No one regimen suits us all.
There is a steep path to skill,
but in presenting this prize
be bold and shout straight out:
This man was born, thanks to divine will,
with quick hands, nimble limbs, a fierce glance.
At your feast, Ajax, son of Ilias,[39]
    this victorious man has placed his garland at your altar. (105–12)

2e. *Olympian* 12: Ergoteles of Himera, *Dolichos*, 466 BCE

Himera is in Sicily; Ergoteles, who was exiled from his homeland of Cnossus (in Crete), competed from Himera. Pausanias states that he was a double periodonikēs *at the* dolichos *and that his statue was erected at Olympia (6.4.11; see* **37q***).*

I entreat you, child of Zeus the Deliverer,
saving Fortune, keep protecting Himera, and make her powerful.
For by your favor swift ships are steered on the sea,
and on dry land rushing battles
and assemblies where counsel is given. But men's expectations
are often tossed up and then back down,
as they cleave the waves of vain falsehood. (1–6a)

Never yet has any man on earth
found a reliable token of what will happen from the gods.
Our understanding of the future is blind.
And, therefore, many things fall out for men contrary to their judgment,
bringing to some reversal of delight, while others, having encountered grievous storms,
in a short time exchange their troubles
for high success. (7–12a)

Son of Philanor, truly,
like a cock that fights at home, at your native hearth
the fame of your swift feet would have shed its leaves ingloriously
if hostile civil strife had not deprived you of your Cretan fatherland.[40]
But as things are, having been crowned with garlands at Olympia,

---

[39] This Ajax led the Locrian contingent of Greeks at Troy. He is not the same as the great fighter at Troy of the same name who hailed from Aegina (see **1b**, n. 3).

[40] i.e., Ergoteles' victory would not have been celebrated, given the hostility of his former homeland, but in exile he has found a more receptive community.

and twice from Delphi, and at the Isthmus, Ergoteles,
you bathe in the hot baths of the Nymphs,[41]
   while keeping company with them beside fields belonging to you. (13–19)

2f. *Olympian* 7: Diagoras of Rhodes, Boxing, 464 BCE

The victor, from the Rhodian city of Ialysus, was one of the most famous boxers in ancient times. He was a periodonikēs *and the first of a successful line of later competitors that included his sons and grandsons. According to Pausanias, Diagoras' daughter, Kallipateira ("girl with a lovely father"), was the only woman outside of those with religious functions to have seen the Olympic Games. She was discovered dressed up as a male trainer to watch her son but was not punished on account of her victorious lineage. After her, the story goes that all trainers were required to appear naked (see Pausanias* **37q**, *6.7.2–5).*

As someone with a rich hand taking up a bowl,
bubbling within with the dew of the wine,
will give it to
his young son-in-law toasting
from one household to another, a bowl all golden, a crowning possession,
as he honors the joy of the symposium
and his connection by marriage, and with his friends
present he makes him an object of envy for the harmonious marriage. (1–6)

So I, by sending nectar poured out, the gift of the Muses,
to men who have won victories, sweet fruit of the mind,
gladden them, the victors
at Olympia and Pytho.
   Happy is he who enjoys a good report.
Grace [= *Charis*] looks at one man now, then another,
   tending life's flower,
often with sweet-sounding lyre and in all modes of the flutes. (7–12)

And now with both
   I have disembarked with Diagoras,
hymning the sea child of Aphrodite
   and bride of the Sun, Rhodes,
so that a straight-fighting, mighty man,
   crowned for his victory by the Alpheus,
and at Castalia [= Delphi]
I may praise as a recompense for his boxing,

---

[41] In reference to the hot springs and sanctuary complex at Himera.

and may praise his father
Damagetus, who delights Justice.
They live on an island with three cities near
the projection of broad Asia among Argive spearmen. (13–19)

[20–79, which tell the myth of the creation of the island of Rhodes and the establishment of its three main cities, have been omitted]

[At Lindos] With blooms Diagoras
was crowned there twice;
    at the famous Isthmus he was four times victor,
time after time at Nemea and in rocky Athens. (80–82)

The bronze at Argos knew him, and the prizes in Arcadia
and Thebes, and the games
ordained by the Boeotians,[42]
and at Pellana and Aegina he was victorious
    six times. In Megara the stone
record tells no different tale. But,
    oh Father Zeus, ruler of Atabyrion's ridge,[43]
honor the Olympic ordinance of victory hymn (83–8)

and the man finding his distinction
    at boxing; give him the favor of regard
both among the citizens and among strangers.
    For he travels straight along an insolence-hating road,
having learned clearly that which the upright minds of his noble forebears
    have revealed to him.
Do not keep hidden the common
seed descended from Callianax.[44]
    With the joys of the Eratidae[45] the city too
holds a feast. In one moment of time
the winds are variable, blowing in different directions. (89–95)

2g. *Olympian* 13: Xenophon of Corinth, *Stadion*/Pentathlon, 464 BCE

Olympian 13 celebrates Xenophon, who had won the stadion *and pentathlon in the same Olympiad, as well as his family. Pindar credits the Corinthian clan with three Olympic victories, six Pythian,*

---

[42] The region of central Greece where Thebes is located.
[43] Rhodes's highest peak, on which was a temple of Zeus.   [44] An ancestor of the victor.
[45] Diagoras' clan.

sixty combined at Nemea and Isthmia, and an unstated number at local games throughout Greece (indeed, the catalogue of local victories is one of the longest and most geographically widespread in the entire corpus). Fittingly for so extraordinary an athletic family, Olympian 13 is loaded with myths that are particular to the city of Corinth, including an account of Bellerophon's taming of the winged horse Pegasus and his invention, through the aid of Athena, of the bridle. This aetiology of horse-taming is not inspired by the victor's event (stadion/pentathlon), but a theme of Corinthian "inventiveness."

Three times victorious at Olympia,
is the house I praise, gentle to her own citizens,
and hospitable to strangers,
and I shall recognize prosperous Corinth,
Poseidon's portal on the Isthmus, land of glorious youth.
In her lives Eunomia[46] and her sisters,
    the secure foundation of cities,
Justice and her sister Peace,
    dispensers of wealth for men,
the golden daughters of Themis [= Divine Law] with her wise counsel. (1–8)

They are eager to repel
Hubris, the bold-speaking mother of Satiety.
I have fair stories to tell, and upright courage
moves my tongue to speak.
It is impossible to hide one's inborn nature.
As for you, sons of Aletes,[47] many times
    the Seasons gave you the splendor of victory
for your consummate excellence
    won in sacred contests, and many times,
with their abundant blooms, they cast into the hearts of your men, (9–16)

ancient wisdom. But every work is due to its inventor.
    Whence did the delights of Dionysus appear
with the ox-driving dithyramb?[48]
Who invented the bridle for horse's equipage[49]
or upon the temples of the gods placed two eagles?
And in Corinth the sweet-breathing Muse,
and Ares blossoms as well,
with young men's deadly spears. (17–23)

---

[46] The personification of the good order of laws.   [47] An old king of Corinth.

[48] A type of choral song and dance produced by Pindar, Bacchylides, and others. It was associated with the ritual worship of Dionysus (which involved sacrifice of oxen) and said to have been first practiced by the hero Arion at Corinth.

[49] The story of the bridle is told in the myth of Bellerophon that has been omitted.

Lofty, wide ruler of Olympia,
father Zeus, may you be ungrudging
of our words for all time,
and governing this people in freedom from harm,
make straight the wind of Xenophon's fortune.
Receive the lawful song of praise in honor of the garlands
that he brings from Pisa's plains [= Olympia],
in both the pentathlon and the foot race,
    having posted victories; he has a share of
what no mortal man has ever attained before. (24–31)

Two wreaths of wild celery crowned
his appearance at the Isthmian festival;
and Nemea does not gainsay this.
The splendor of his father Thessalus' victory in the foot race
is dedicated by the streams of the Alpheus [i.e., at Olympia],
and at Delphi he has honor of the *stadion*
    and the *diaulos* in a single day;
and in the same month, in rocky Athens,
    one swift-footed day placed
the three fairest prizes on his head; (32–9)

seven times he was victor at the Hellotian Games.[50]
    In the festivals of Poseidon between the seas [i.e., the Isthmian Games],
the songs would need to be longer to catch up to the victories
won by Thessalus' father Ptiodorus and by Terpsias and Eritimus.[51]
How many times your family won at Delphi,
and in the pastures of the lion [= Nemea], I dispute with many
over the number of your victories for clearly
I would not know how to number the pebbles in the sea. (40–6)

[47–77 omitted, the story of the capture of Pegasus]

Due measure follows for everything.
To recognize the moment is best.
The power of the gods accomplishes easily what
    is beyond oath and beyond hope.
And indeed, mighty Bellerophon
    strove and captured the winged horse
by stretching the mild drug (78–85)

---

[50] Games held at Corinth in honor of Athena.
[51] Terpsias is said to be an uncle of Thessalus, whose son or grandson was Eritimus.

around its jaw. He mounted him and in his bronze armor
   he immediately performed to the tune of battle.
With the horse he once,
shooting from the chill folds of the empty air,
killed the female army of archers, the Amazons,
and fire-breathing Chimaera and the Solymoi.[52]
I for my part shall remain silent about his own doom.[53]
The horse at least was received into the ancient stalls of Olympian Zeus. (86–92)

But I, having sent forth the straight whirl of my javelins,
must not miss the target[54]
while casting many darts stoutly from my hands,
for I have come to the splendid-throned Muses
and to the Oligaethidae[55] as a willing helper.
All their accomplishments at the Isthmus and Nemea I shall
   clarify in a brief account: The truth for me
will come, under oath, from the sweet-tongued cry
of the noble herald, heard sixty times from the two places. (93–100)

Their Olympic victories,
it seems, have been stated before.
Their future victories I shall make clear in the event.
As of now I hope for this, but the outcome
is with the god. If the good fortune of the line continues
we shall leave it for Zeus and Enyalius [= Ares] to realize.
   Their victories under the brow of Parnassus are six.
How many in Argos, how many
   in Thebes, how many in Arcadia…[56]
will the altar of the Lycaean witness (101–8)

and Pellana and Sicyon
   and Megara, and the well-fortified sanctuary of the Aeacidae [= Aegina],
and Eleusis and rich Marathon

---

[52] A tribe situated near Lycia (today, the coast of southwest Turkey) that threatened to invade this kingdom. They were repelled by Bellerophon acting on the orders of the Lycian king Iobates, the father of the Corinthian hero's wife, Philonoe.

[53] Bellerophon attempted to ride Pegasus to Mt. Olympus only to be thrown to earth when Zeus, checking the hero's hubris, sent a fly to bite the horse, which caused the animal to toss the rider. Bellerophon spends the rest of his life aimlessly traveling in the south of Asia Minor through the "Plain of Wandering."

[54] The Greek can mean that the javelin is thrown out of play, or that it misses or comes short of a target (compare *Nemean* 7.71).

[55] i.e., Xenophon's clan.   [56] There is a problem with this line in the Greek.

and the fair and prosperous
cities under Aetna's high peak and Euboea? If you search
throughout all of Greece, you will find more than it is possible to see.
Come, swim away with nimble feet;
Zeus the Accomplisher, grant them modesty and the sweet fortune of delight.
   (109–15)

2h. *Pythian* 10: Hippocleas of Thessaly, Boys' *Diaulos*, 498 BCE

This Pythian ode is considered by many to be Pindar's earliest surviving epinician (he was perhaps 20 when it was performed). Thessalians were well-known competitors, especially in the early history of athletics. While the victor was from the city state of Pelinna, nevertheless the work was commissioned not by his family or local citizens, but by an influential leader from the nearby city of Larisa.

Happy Sparta,
blessed Thessaly: The race of one man, best in battle, Heracles,
rules over both.[57]
Why do I boast beyond what is fit for the occasion (*kairos*)?
But Pytho and Pelinna call me,
as do the children of Aleuas,[58] who come in order to bring
the glorious voices of men's revelry to Hippocleas. (1–6)

For he has tasted the contests:
The glen of Parnassus [= Delphi] has proclaimed him to the host of neighbors
to be the best of boys in the *diaulos* race.
Apollo, the beginning and end of men's deeds increases in power sweetly,
when a god urges.
In part, he accomplished what he did through your plans.
But through inherited ability, he followed in the footsteps of his father, (7–12)

an Olympic victor twice in
the war-enduring armor of Ares.[59]
The contest under the deep-meadowed rocks of Cirrha [= Pythian Games]
made Phricias[60] a dominant runner.
May it be their family's fate (*moira*) that manly wealth
blooms in days to come. (13–18)

---

[57] Both the Spartans and the Aleuadae clan of Larisa traced their lineage back to the sons of Heracles, as did many other cities in ancient Greece.

[58] The founder of the powerful, aristocratic clan at Larisa to which the commissioner of the ode, Thorax, belonged.

[59] i.e., the *hoplitodromos*.   [60] Father of Hippocleas.

After obtaining no small gift of pleasures in Greece,
may they encounter no envious reversals from the gods.
He who is without pain is a god.
But that man is blessed
and the subject of song among the wise
who conquers through the excellence of his hands and feet,
and seizes upon the greatest of prizes through daring and strength— (19–24)

yes, he is blessed who, while still living,
sees his young son obtain crowns in the Pythian Games.
Although the bronze sky is never mountable for him,
nevertheless, out of all the glories which we obtain as a mortal race,
he makes the farthest voyage.
Neither by ship nor by foot could you discover the path
to the marvelous gathering of the Hyperboreans.[61] (25–30)

[31–54 omitted]

But when the Ephyraeans[62]
pour out my sweet voice by the Peneius river,[63]
I hope, for the sake of his victories, to use my songs to make Hippocleas
still more wondrous among
both his age-mates and the earlier generation,
and a darling thing for young maidens.
Desires of different types excite peoples' minds in different ways, (55–60)

but when each man achieves whatever he has sought after,
let him eagerly keep hold of it, an ever-present care.
But there is no clue to foresee what will happen next year.
I have put my trust in the kind hospitality of Thorax,
who, breathless with desire for my song,
yoked this four-horse chariot of the Pierian Muses,
returning friendship for friendship and gladly leading a leader.[64] (61–6)

---

[61] The conventional statement concerning the extreme distances to which the victorious family's fame extends leads seamlessly into a myth concerning the legendary people at the northernmost edge of the world in the Greek imagination, the Hyperboreans (Greek for, "those beyond the north wind").

[62] Citizens of a city near Pelinna. Their connections with either the victor or with the people from Larisa who commissioned the song are otherwise unclear. Some have suggested that the ode was performed by Ephyraeans at Pelinna, or that there would be a second performance at Ephyra, but there can be no positive confirmation in either case.

[63] A river in Thessaly that ran through the victor's hometown.

[64] i.e., as Thorax is a leader in his *polis*, so Pindar is a leader of songs.

For the man who tests gold on a touchstone,
it shines as does an upright mind.
We shall also praise his noble brothers,[65]
because they lift up and increase the Thessalian regime.
Among good men lies the governance of cities,
a dear thing passed down through families. (67–72)

2i. Pythian 12: Midas of Acragas, Flute Playing, 490 BCE

The last song in the collection of Pythians is unique among Pindaric epinicia for being dedicated to a victor in a musical and not an athletic event. The victor Midas (said to be a teacher of the tragedian Sophocles) won an aulos-*playing contest (the* aulos *is a wind instrument made out of reed and bronze that was believed to have been invented by Athena).*

The myth is of Perseus and the Gorgons and then of the hero's return to the island of Seriphus where he takes revenge on the people who held his mother captive. The image of Medusa with her head of many snakes related to how the Greeks conceived of the aulos, *namely as an instrument of "many heads" (i.e., tonalities or voices) that was thought to make the player of beautiful sounds appear ugly (likely because one had to puff out one's cheeks to play it).*

I ask you,[66] lover of splendor, most beautiful of mortal cities,
abode of Persephone,[67] you who inhabit the well-built hill
on the ridges of sheep-grazing Acragas,
oh Queen, with the favor of men and gods,
graciously accept this crown from Pytho on behalf of well-famed Midas,
and accept Midas himself as one who won over Greece through that craft (*technē*)
which Pallas Athena once discovered
when she wove a song out of the deadly dirge of the savage Gorgons. (1–8)

That song she heard pouring forth amidst grievous toil
from the maidens[68] as they lay low, their unapproachable heads filled with serpents.
Perseus cried out victorious, and then brought one of the three sisters
to Seriphus in the sea, a thing of death for the people there.
Indeed, he blinded the divine race of Phorcus,[69]
and he made Polydectes' feast a painful thing for him as well as

---

[65] Thorax's brothers, Eurypylus and Thrasydaeus, are named in Herodotus, bk. 9.58.
[66] The poet addresses the nymph Acragas, who is also the patron and personification of the Sicilian city.
[67] All of Sicily was given to Persephone by Zeus after she became the bride of Hades.
[68] There are three Gorgon sisters: Medusa, Euryale, and Sthenno.
[69] The Graeae were daughters of Phorcus and they had one eye between them, which Perseus took until they told him how to find the Gorgons, who were also daughters of Phorcus.

the slavery and the bed to which he had subjected Danaë,[70]
after he took the head off beautiful-cheeked Medusa. (9–16)

That was the son of Danaë, who we say was born from flowing gold.[71]
But when the maiden Athena saved the man she favored from these toils,
she fashioned a full-voiced strain for *aulos*,
in order to imitate with instruments the loud-sounding lament
which was forced from the snapping jaws of Euryale.
The god discovered this tune, but she did so in order for mortals to have it.
She named it the many-headed measure,
a famous reminder of the peoples' contests.[72] (17–24)

The song often flows through thin bronze and reeds—
reeds which reside beside the city of the Graces with its beautiful places for
   dancing,[73]
trustworthy witnesses of choruses in the precinct of the daughter of Cephisus,[74]
But if there is any happiness (*olbos*) among men, it does not appear
without struggle. Perhaps today
a divinity will accomplish it—what is fated cannot be escaped—
but that time will come, which will strike a person unexpectedly
and will give one thing beyond belief, but another not at all. (25–32)

2j. *Pythian* 9: Telesicrates of Cyrene, Race in Armor, 474 BCE

Pythian 9 is the only surviving ode dedicated to this particular contest. It contains an extended proph-
ecy of the foundation of Cyrene, a city in North Africa, named for the nymph. Cyrene is celebrated for
her skills at hunting and wrestling. At the end Pindar introduces another mythic athletic event: the
foot race to win the hand of Antaeus' daughter. As the closing image of Pythian 9, *the latter depiction*
recalls the victor, Telesicrates, who had won the hoplitodromos *and the* stadion *at Delphi, as well as*
at multiple local events.

By announcing Telesicrates, that fortunate man,
   as the bronze-shielded Pythian victor,
   with the help of the deep-girded Graces, I wish to proclaim

---

[70] Danaë is Perseus' mother. She was held captive along with her son by Polydectes, the king of the island
of Seriphos when the two washed ashore after being exiled from their native Argos.

[71] Perseus' grandfather, the king of Argos, had received an oracle that he would be killed by his daughter
Danaë's son; to prevent her from having a child, he imprisoned her. Nevertheless, Zeus came to her in a
shower of gold (a common trope of Greek myth), thereby fathering Perseus.

[72] *Auloi* were used to announce the beginning of the games.   [73] Orchomenus in Boeotia.

[74] Cephisus is the god of the Cephisus river in Boeotia, which flowed into (the now drained) Lake Copais
near Orchomenus. The god's daughter was a nymph named Copais.

a crown for horse-driving Cyrene,
whom the long-haired son of Leto [= Apollo] once seized
from the wind-echoing valleys of Pelion.
He carried the wild maiden off in a golden chariot,
and there he established her
as queen of a land with many sheep and fruit,
in order to inhabit the lovely and flourishing
third root of the world.[75] (1–8)

Silver-footed Aphrodite received the Delian guest [= Apollo]
from the divinely built chariot
and placed a gentle hand on him.
Then she cast loving modesty upon their sweet bed.
She joined them together in a common marriage, mixed between god
and the daughter of mighty Hypseus.

[12–16 omitted]

This man raised his fair-armed daughter Cyrene.
But she did not enjoy the back-and-forth
paths of the loom,
nor did she delight in feasts among companions at home,
but with bronze spears and sword,
she fought and cut down wild beasts,
and she provided much peace and quiet for her father's cattle,
and she spent only a little time
with that sweet companion
sleep, which falls upon
eyelids toward dawn.[76] (17–25)

Apollo the far shooter with large quiver
came upon her wrestling with a mighty lion
alone without weapons.
At once he called aloud to Cheiron[77] to come from his halls:
"Son of Philyra, leave your sacred cave and be amazed
at the spirit and great muscle of a woman—
what a fight she makes with a steady bearing—
a young girl with a heart superior to toil.

---

[75] Africa was one of three known continents in the ancient Mediterranean.
[76] The meaning is either that she did not sleep even after working all night or that she did not sleep until just before morning.
[77] Cheiron was a centaur—half-man, half-horse—and noted for his wisdom.

Her mind is not buffeted by fear.
What man fathered her?
From what stock was she plucked (26–33)

so that she now inhabits the hollows of shadowy mountains,
and tests her limitless fighting strength?
Is it lawful to put my famous hand upon her and
to cut the honey-sweet flower of love from the marriage bed?"
The prophetically inspired centaur,
smiling warmly with gentle eyes,
answered him right away with his oracular counsel:
"Wise Persuasion's keys to sacred acts of love lie hidden, Phoebus,
and among the gods and humans this is a source of shame,
to engage the sweet bed for the first time
out in the open. (34–41)

And so a gentle impulse has led you to utter this insincere question,
you for whom it is not right to touch upon a lie.
You ask about the lineage
of this maiden, oh lord?
You who know all paths and the appointed end of all things—
how many leaves the springtime earth sends forth,
and how many grains of sand in the sea and rivers
are driven tumultuously by waves and gusts of wind,
what will happen, and from where
it will come, you see it easily.
But if I must set myself against one who is wise, I shall speak. (42–50)

To be her husband, you came to this place,
and you are going to take her across the sea
to the preeminent garden of Zeus [= the city of Cyrene].
There you will make her ruler of a city,
after you have gathered island people to the hill surrounded by the plain.[78]
But now Mistress Libya with broad meadows
will happily receive your well-famed bride in her golden halls,
where right away she will give her
a portion of land to rightfully possess,
a portion not unblessed with plants of all fruit
nor ignorant of beasts. (51–8)

---

[78] From the island of Thera (Santorini); this foundation is the subject of the mini-epic *Pythian* 4.

[59–96 omitted]

When also they saw you accomplish the most victories
in the seasonal festivals of Pallas Athena,[79]
the maidens each prayed
silently that you were, oh Telesicrates,
their most beloved husband or son, (97–100)

as they did in the Olympic Games
and in the contests of deep-bosomed Earth
and in all the local contests.
While I satisfy my thirst for song, someone compels me
to pay up by awakening again the ancient reputation of his ancestors,
those who came for the sake of the Libyan woman,
to the city of Irasa,[80] the suitors
of the famous, beautiful-haired daughter of Antaeus.[81]
Many natives, the best of men, and many foreigners
sought her hand in marriage,
because her form was marvelous. (101–8)

They wished to pluck the blooming fruit of gold-wreathed Hebe.[82]
But her father was devising a more glorious marriage for his daughter.
He heard how once in Argos
Danaus discovered how to win the swiftest marriage possible for
his forty-eight daughters,
all before the middle of the day.
For he right away placed the entire troop of daughters
at the finish line of a contest.
He ordered that competitions for speed of foot would decide
which hero would have which daughter,
from among those who came in order to be their husbands.[83] (109–16)

Thus, the Libyan offered a similar contest to join a groom to his daughter.
He decorated her and placed her
at the goal as the top prize.
In the middle of the suitors, he said that that man would lead her away
as his own whoever leapt forward first and touched her dress.

---

[79] Held at Cyrene along with the festival dedicated to Earth mentioned below.
[80] A city near Cyrene.
[81] Antaeus was the son of the god Poseidon who ruled over native tribes in Libya.
[82] Goddess of youth.
[83] Wedding contests may have been a traditional and early form of athletic contest in Greece, with a possible Indo-European origin. See discussion of the "Contest of the Bow" (**1f**) and *Olympian* 1 (**2a**).

Then Alexidamus,[84] when he had left the others behind in the swift race,
took the dear maiden hand in hand
and led her through the crowd of nomad horsemen.
Those men threw many
leaves and crowns upon him,
and before that he also received many winged victories. (117–25)

2k. *Isthmian* 2: Xenocrates of Acragas, Chariot Race, *c*.470 BCE

*This ode occurs in the book of Isthmian victories, but in addition to the Isthmian it mentions victories at the Pythian Games, the Panathenaea, and the Olympic Games (17–26). By the time it was written, Xenocrates had died, and the ode is addressed to his son Thrasyboulus, and a man named Nicasippus (= Horse-Victor) is urged to convey it to him (47). Pindar celebrates other victories of this family in Olympian 2 and 3 for Xenocrates' brother Theron (see **2b**). Isthmian 2 is important for its discussion of the payment that victory poets received for their work and for the fact that it includes the charioteer in the praise. Nicomachus was the charioteer commissioned by Xenocrates (and possibly also by Theron). We are told by an ancient commentator that he was an Athenian. Lines 22–6 suggest that he enjoyed special guest status at Elis.*

Thrasyboulus, the men of old,
who mounted the chariot
of the Muses with their golden hairbands
while accompanied with the glorious lyre,
were used to shooting the arrows of their honey-voiced songs of love
freely for any boy who was beautiful and had the sweetest bloom in season,
a bloom that reminds one of well-throned Aphrodite. (1–5)

For the Muse then did not love profit
nor was she a laborer,
nor were sweet, soft-voiced songs
sold like silver
by honey-tongued Terpsichore [= the Muse of dance]
But now she encourages us to preserve the Argive's saying,
which comes…closest to the truth: (6–10)

"Money, money is the man,"
said he who lost his possessions and friends.
Enough of that—for you are wise.
The Isthmian chariot victory of which I sing is not unknown;
Poseidon granted it to Xenocrates,

---

[84] The ancestor of Telesicrates.

sending a wreath of Dorian parsley
to crown his hair. (11–16)

Thus, he honored the well-charioted man,
light of the people of Acragas.
In Crisa [i.e., Delphi], Apollo of broad strength
    saw him and gave him splendor there also.
He also met with the famous gifts of the children of Erechtheus [a mythical king]
in shining Athens. Nor did he blame
the chariot-protecting hand of the horse-driving man, (17–21)

Nicomachus, who at the right time
gave full rein.
Him [= Nicomachus] did the heralds of each festival season also know to recognize,
the Elean truce-bearers of Zeus, son of Cronus,[85]
who (so I venture to guess) experienced some act of his hospitality.
They greeted him with sweet-breathed voice
as he fell upon the knees of golden Nikē [= the goddess of victory] (22–6)

in their land, which they call
the grove of Olympian Zeus.
That is where the children of Aenesidamus[86]
mingled with immortal honors.
So, Thrasyboulus, your home is not ignorant
of revelries, of feasts,
or of sweet-sounding songs. (27–32)

Neither uphill,
nor on a steep road,
goes he who brings to famous men
the honors of the Muses of Helicon.
With a whirling motion may my toss of the javelin equal in length
the extent to which Xenocrates surpassed men in charming behavior.
He kept respectful company with his fellow citizens, (33–7)

He practiced horse-breeding
according to the Panhellenic custom,
and he embraced all the feasts
of the gods. Never did
a windy sky cause him to pull up his sails at his hospitable table.

---

[85] These heralds proclaimed a truce throughout Greece during the season of the Olympic Games at Elis.
[86] Xenocrates' father.

But he went to the Phasis river in the summer,
and in the winter, he sailed to the shore of the Nile.[87] (38–42)

Because envious hopes
hang over the minds of men,
let Xenocrates' son never now keep silent about his paternal excellence,
and may he not keep silent about these songs of praise,
since I did not fashion them to be still.
Nicasippus, deliver these words,
when you come upon my esteemed host. (43–8)

21. *Isthmian* 1: Herodotus of Thebes, Chariot Driver and Victor, *c.*458 BCE

This ode begins with the poet excusing himself from having to finish another work for the people of Ceos to perform in honor of Apollo. But since six Thebans had just won at the Isthmian Games, this extraordinary event caused Pindar, a poet of Thebes, to drop what he was doing and celebrate his home city. Only one of these six victors is celebrated, Herodotus, who is unique for having driven his own chariot. He did not, as was common, commission a charioteer. Fittingly, the ode praises mythological figures, Castor and Iolaus, associated both with horsemanship and with a wider variety of other ancient athletic events.

Mother of mine, Thebe with the golden shield,[88]
I shall put your affairs above my own lack of leisure.
May rocky Delos not resent me,
she upon whom I have poured my voice.
What is dearer to good men than their dear parents?
Give way, island of Apollo.[89]
With the help of the gods, I shall combine the end of both poems, (1–6)

by dancing for Phoebus [= Apollo] with his uncut hair
both on sea-girt Ceos with sea-faring men
and on the ridges of the Isthmus surrounded by water.
For it gave six prizes
to the people of Cadmus,
a triumphant glory to the fatherland,
where Alcmene bore her fearless child,[90] (7–12)

---

[87] The summer and winter being the seasons that produced the best winds for sailing to the Phasis and the Nile, respectively.

[88] The speaker addresses the nymph Thebe. She is the daughter of a river-god and the deity of the city that shares her name. Shields were a typical symbol for Thebes and were found on the city's coins.

[89] Delos was Apollo's birthplace and a major site of his worship.

[90] i.e., Heracles. One of his labors is mentioned directly afterward.

before whom the brave dogs of Geryon once cowered.
But I give honor to Herodotus
for his four-horse chariot victory.
He guided the reins himself, with no one else's hands.
I wish to set him in a hymn for Castor and Iolaus.
For those men were born the most dominant charioteers
in Sparta and Thebes. (13–17)

In athletic contests, they won the most competitions,
and they decorated their houses with tripods
and cauldrons, and golden bowls,
having tasted the crowns of victory.
Their excellence shines clearly
in the naked foot races
and in the races in armor that clatter with shields. (18–23)

Such was their excellence when they threw javelins with their hands,
and when they hurled the stone discus.
For there was no pentathlon,
but there was a prize for each event.[91]
They often crowned their hair with thick wreathes
and they shone forth at the streams
of Dirce and beside the river Eurotas.[92] (24–9)

Iolaus was the son of Iphicles; he belonged to the race of Spartoi.[93]
Castor was a son of Tyndareus, dwelling among the Achaeans
on the high abode of Therapna.
Farewell. But as I adorn song with the trappings of Poseidon,
the sacred Isthmus, and the shores of Onchestus[94]
in honor of this man, I shall sing of the glorious fate
of his father Asopodorus (30–4)

and his paternal land of Orchomenus.
That land received him
from the immeasurable brine in chilling misfortune,

[91] According to Greek myth, the first pentathlon occurred during the expedition of the Argonauts, in which Castor participated (different sources include or exclude Iolaus as one of the heroes who left with Jason). The earliest historical pentathlon documented in the Archaic period was in 708 BCE. The event would undergo several changes before being fixed in the form recognizable to Pindar.

[92] The waters associated with Thebes and Sparta, respectively.

[93] These are the "Sown Men," called such because they were born from the earth after Cadmus had been instructed by the gods to sow a serpent's teeth in the soil.

[94] Both the Isthmus and Onchestus (a city near to Thebes) were sacred places of Poseidon.

when he was hard-pressed by shipwreck.[95]
But now once again his inborn Fate
has placed him in the fair weather of old.
One who has struggled carries foresight in his mind. (35–41)

If one invests every impulse in excellence
through both expenditures and toils,
it is necessary to bring him, in return for the achievements he has found,
a manly boast without begrudging thoughts.
For it is easy to give a gift of noble speech
to a wise man in exchange for all types of toils,
and to set up an object of beauty for all. (42–6)

Different wages for different types of labor
are sweet to men,
whether to a shepherd, a plowman, a bird catcher,
or one whom the sea nourishes.
All are tense to protect the belly from nagging hunger.
He who achieves luxurious renown either in contests or in war,
being spoken well of, he receives the highest profit of
choice praise from the tongues of citizens and strangers alike. (47–51)

It is right for us to celebrate the earth-shaking son of Cronus [= Poseidon],
our neighbor, patron god of horse racing,
in recompense for his aid in the chariot race.
It is right for us also to invoke those sons of yours,
Amphitryon, and the glen of Minyas,[96]
as well as Eleusis, the famous grove of Demeter,
and Euboea, in the races with many turns— (52–7)

Protesilas, I include your precinct
of Achaean men in Phylaka.
The hymn, with its short measure,
prevents me from explaining in full all those events
which Hermes, patron of contests granted to Herodotus and his horses.
Often what is passed over in silence
brings greater joy. (58–63)

---

[95] There was once a large lake in the region of Boeotia where Thebes and Orchomenus are located. This lake was drained in the late nineteenth century.

[96] The Thebans held local games in honor of both Amphitryon's son Heracles and his grandson Iolaus.
 The Minyeia was a festival with games celebrated at neighboring Orchomenus. The list that follows includes several other local games: Eleusis, Euboea, and Thessalian Phylaka.

May it be that he, lifted on the glorious wings of the sweet-voiced
Pierian Muses, hereafter envelop his hand
with the choicest garlands of the Alpheus
from the Pythian and Olympic Games, obtaining honor for Seven-gated Thebes.
But if a man hoards his wealth in secret,
and assails others with laughter, then he does not realize
that he pays his soul to Hades without fame. (64–8)

2m. *Nemean* 5: Pytheas of Aegina, Boys' *Pankration*, *c.*483 BCE

This ode was written for a member of a highly successful family from Aegina. Pindar's Isthmians 5 and 6 praise Pytheas' brother, Bacchylides' Ode 13 also covers this Nemean victory, and Nemean 5 is itself full of praise for other members of Pytheas' family. The myths of Nemean 5 strategically deploy stories of heroic mistakes and mixed blessings to temper the force of the victory boast. The opening image of the first line and its resonance in the conclusion of the ode elegantly demonstrate how song and sports training "create" similar products.

I am not a sculptor who makes statues
that stand motionless on their bases.
So, go, sweet song,
on every ship and boat
from Aegina, announcing that
mighty Pytheas, son of Lampon
won a crown for the *pankration* in the Nemean Games,
not yet showing on his cheeks the ripening season,
tender mother of the grape vine's bloom.[97] (1–6)

He has honored the Aeacidae,
spear-wielding heroes born of Cronus and Zeus
and from the Nereids,[98] and he honored
his mother city, land dear to foreigners.
The well-recognized sons of Endais
and the force of mighty Phocus, the son of the goddess Psamatheia,
who bore him on the shore of the sea, prayed
that the land [= Aegina] would one day
be well-manned and known for sailing,
stretching their hands to the sky together (7–12)

[97] i.e., the victor competed with the other "beardless" young men.
[98] Aeacus, considered the founding mythological figure at Aegina, was the son of Zeus and Aegina, which made him Cronus' grandson. Achilles was born of Peleus, Aeacus' son, and the Nereid Thetis.

beside the altar of their father Zeus Hellanius.[99]
I am ashamed to speak of their grave act,
which was ventured not with justice,[100]
how they left the famous island
and how a certain spirit drove
the mighty men from Oenona [= Aegina].
I shall stop. Not every truth is profitable
which shows its face in detail.
Often to be silent is the wisest thing
for a man to observe. (13–18)

But if it has been decided to praise good fortune or the force of hands
or iron war, someone should dig a jumping pit
for me far from where I stand—
eagles soar across seas—
and I have a light spring in my knees.
With good intent did the most beautiful chorus of the Muses
sing for those men in Pelion.[101]
In the middle of them, Apollo played runs on a seven-tongued lyre
with a golden plectrum. (19–24)

He led with all kinds of melodies.
After a first song to Zeus, they sang of holy Thetis and Peleus,
how once delicate Hippolyta, the daughter of Cretheus,
wished to ensnare him [= Peleus] with a trick,[102]
after she convinced her husband, the overseer of the Magnesians,
to be her accomplice in manifold schemes.
She fabricated a false story,
how that man [= Peleus] made an attempt
at her wifely love in the bed of Acastus. (25–30)

But the opposite was the case.
Many times, with her entire spirit she begged him with gentle words.
But her dizzying words spurred his anger.
Right away he rejected her as wife,

[99] The Aeginetan heroes Telamon and Peleus were sons of Aeacus and Endais. Phocus was the son of Aeacus by Psamatheia.

[100] Telamon and Peleus murdered Phocus and were exiled to Salamis and Iolcus, respectively.

[101] i.e., for the descendants of Aeacus while at Iolcus for the wedding of Peleus and Thetis.

[102] Hippolyta, the queen of Iolcus, was also called Astydameia. She fell in love with Peleus when he was purified of the murder of a neighboring king by her husband, the king Acastus. Through a series of lies Hippolyta effected the suicide of Peleus' first wife and caused Acastus to lead Peleus into an ambush of centaurs. Peleus takes revenge on Hippolyta and the whole of the city.

fearing the anger of the Father of Guests [= Zeus].
Cloud-raising Zeus, king of the immortals, noticed well
and gave his agreement from the sky,
so that in haste he would make
one of the golden-staffed daughters of Nereus
to be his [= Peleus'] queenly wife [i.e., Thetis], (31–6)

after persuading their kinsman Poseidon,[103] who often goes
from Aegae to the Dorian Isthmus,[104]
where happy crowds receive him as a god
with the roar of reed pipes,
and they contend with the bold strength of their limbs.
Inherited fate decides in all affairs.
Euthymenes,[105] you fell into the arms of Victory twice from Aegina,
and came in contact with
colorful songs of praise. (37–42)

Pytheas, your maternal uncle glorifies you,
one who is of the same race and, now indeed, of the same caliber as he.
Nemea suited Euthymenes,
as did the local month, which Apollo holds dear.[106]
He conquered his age-mates at home,
and at the well-hollowed hill of Nisus.[107]
I am delighted that the whole city contends for noble matters.
Know this, that you partook of the sweet reward for your toils
by the fortune of Menander.[108] (43–8)

It is necessary that one who builds *ath*letes comes from *Ath*ens.[109]
But if you have come to sing of Themistius,[110]
no longer shrink from doing so.
Give over your voice; hoist up the sails
to the top of the mast.

---

[103] Poseidon was married to the sea-nymph Amphitrite.

[104] Two cult centers of Poseidon. Aegae is on the northern coast of the Peloponnese.

[105] The victor's uncle.

[106] Euthymenes' two victories were at Nemea and Aegina, the latter being the site of the Aeginetan Delphinia held in the month of Delphinios, which was sacred to Apollo.

[107] A competition at Megara, possibly also celebrated during the April–May period of Delphinios.

[108] Menander is the name of the trainer who was from Athens. This is one of the few direct mentions of trainers in these victory odes.

[109] The pun here is on the sound of the two words which are otherwise unrelated. The word used for "trainer" here is *tektōn*, literally a "builder" or "craftsman" (compare with the opening line).

[110] Pytheas' maternal grandfather.

Proclaim that he as a boxer and in the *pankration* seized upon twofold excellence
in his victories at Epidaurus,
and bring the leafy crowns of flowers
to the front doors of Aeacus
together with the fair-haired Graces.[111] (49–54)

Table 1 List of Pindaric victory odes

Games site	Name of victor	Home city	Event	Year
Isthmian 1	Herodotus	Thebes	chariot race	458?
Isthmian 2	Xenocrates	Acragas	chariot race	470?
Isthmian 3	Melissus	Thebes	chariot race	474/3?
Isthmian 4	Melissus	Thebes	*pankration*	474/3?
Isthmian 5	Phylacidas	Aegina	*pankration*	478?
Isthmian 6	Phylacidas	Aegina	boys' *pankration*	480?
Isthmian 7	Strepsiades	Thebes	*pankration*	454?
Isthmian 8	Cleandrus	Thebes	*pankration*	478?
Isthmian 9	?	Aegina	?	?
Isthmian fr	Casmylus	Rhodes	boxing	?
Nemean 1	Chromius	Aetna	chariot race	476?
Nemean 2	Timodemus	Acharnae	*pankration*	485?
Nemean 3	Aristocleidas	Aegina	*pankration*	475?
Nemean 4	Timasarchus	Aegina	boys' wrestling	473?
Nemean 5	Pytheas	Aegina	youths' *pankration*	483?
Nemean 6	Alcimidas	Aegina	boys' wrestling	465?
Nemean 7	Sogenes	Aegina	boys' pentathlon	485?
Nemean 8	Deinias	Aegina	*diaulos*	459?
Nemean 9	Chromius	Aetna	chariot race	474?
Nemean 10	Theaeus	Argos	wrestling	444?
Nemean 11	Aristogoras	Tenedos	councilor	446?
Olympian 1	Hieron	Syracuse	single-horse race	476
Olympian 2	Theron	Acragas	chariot race	476
Olympian 3	Theron	Acragas	chariot race	476
Olympian 4	Psaumis	Camerina	chariot race?	452
Olympian 5	Psaumis	Camerina	mule race	448
Olympian 6	Hagesias	Syracuse	mule race	472/468
Olympian 7	Diadorus	Rhodes	boxing	464
Olympian 8	Alcimedon	Aegina	boys' wrestling	460

[111] Themistius appears to have been a victor at a local event held in honor of Aeacus.

Games site	Name of victor	Home city	Event	Year
Olympian 9	Epharmostus	Opous	wrestling	468
Olympian 10	Hagesidamus	Western Locri	boys' boxing	476
Olympian 11	Hagesidamus	Western Locri	boys' boxing	476?
Olympian 12	Ergoteles	Himera	*dolichos*	466
Olympian 13	Xenophon	Corinth	Pentathlon and *stadion*	464
Olympian 14	Asopichus	Orchomenus	*stadion*	488?
Pythian 1	Hieron	Aetna	chariot race	470
Pythian 2	Hieron	Syracuse	chariot race	474?
Pythian 3	Hieron	Syracuse	single-horse race	474?
Pythian 4	Arcesilas	Cyrene	chariot race	462
Pythian 5	Arcesilas	Cyrene	chariot race	462
Pythian 6	Xenocrates	Acragas	chariot race	490
Pythian 7	Megacles	Athens	chariot race	456
Pythian 8	Aristomenes	Aegina	wrestling	446
Pythian 9	Telesicrates	Cyrene	race in armor	474
Pythian 10	Hippocleas	Thessaly	boys' *diaulos*	498
Pythian 11	Thrasydaeus	Thebes	boys' *stadion*	474?
Pythian 12	Midas	Acragas	flute playing	490

3. Bacchylides

*Bacchylides, from the island of Ceos, lived from c.518 to c.451 BCE. Little is known about his life. Like Pindar, he wrote poems for choral performance, but the majority of his have been lost. However, a papyrus that was recovered from the sands of Egypt contains about fifteen of his epinicia. It is clear from this find that his style is much simpler than that of Pindar, though he praises men and boys for victories at similar events. Ancient sources state that his father was an athlete and his uncle was the lyric poet Simonides (see **7a–d**).*

3a. 5: Hieron of Syracuse, Single-Horse Race at Olympia, *c.*476 BCE

*Hieron, the ruler of Syracuse in Sicily, commissioned more than one victory ode for this event (see Pindar **2a**). Both poets name Hieron's horse Pherenicus (= "Victory Bearer"). Bacchylides composed another epinician for Hieron's chariot victory at Olympia in 468 BCE.*

Fortunate commander
    of horse-riding Syracusans,
you will rightly recognize the sweet-gifted dedication

of the violet-crowned Muses
all men who are now on the earth.
Cease the cares of
your calm righteous mind,
      and turn your attention here,
where your guest-friend (*xenos*) sends hymns,
      woven with the help of the deep-girdled Graces,
from his sacred island
      to your famous city.
For he is the renowned servant
      of gold-beribboned Urania and wished,
pouring his voice from his chest,
      to praise Hieron. (1–16)

High above, the eagle,
      messenger of wide-ruling,
loud-thundering Zeus, cuts the deep air
      with his swift holy wings;
he takes courage, confident
      in his dominant strength,
while thin-voiced birds
      cower in fear.
The peaks of the great earth do not hold him back,
   nor the rough waves
of the tireless sea.
      He spreads his light wings
in the unplowable void
      on the breeze of the west wind,
      a recognizable sight among men. (17–30)

So there are countless paths for me
      to praise your excellence,
noble sons of Deinomenes,
      by the will of dark-haired Victory
and bronze-chested Ares.
      May the god not tire of doing good.
Golden-armed Dawn saw the chestnut,
      storm-running foal Pherenicus
win beside the wide-flowing Alpheus (31–40)

and also at holy Pytho [= Delphi].
      Touching the earth, I declare:

Never in a contest has the horse been spattered
   by dust from horses ahead of him
when running for the finish.
   Equal in speed to Boreas,
obeying his charioteer,
   he prepares and sends victory
and applause to hospitable Hieron.
Blessed is he to whom the god
has given a share of beautiful things
   and with enviable fortune
a rich life to live out.
   For no one of men on earth
was born happy in all respects. (31–55)

[56–190 omitted. Heracles, who has gone to the Underworld to carry off the three-headed dog of Hades, meets the dead hero Meleager, who tells him about the Calydonian boar hunt.]

A Boeotian man, Hesiod,
   servant of the sweet Muses,
said the following: "The fame of men follows
   whomever the immortals honor."
I am easily persuaded
   to send to Hieron my famous voice on the path
that is not beyond justice.
   In this way the roots of good things flourish.
May Zeus the great father protect
   them safely in peace. (191–200)

3b. 9: Automedes of Phlius, Pentathlon Victor at Nemea

In this epinician Bacchylides includes elements of the foundation myth of the Nemean Games. When the seven heroes set out for Thebes to help Polyneices in his struggle against his brother Eteocles, they stopped at Nemea, where they requested water from a local woman. She was the nurse of Archemorus, the infant son of the local king. She placed the child on the ground before she brought the Seven to a local spring to drink. When they returned, the baby had been bitten by a snake and died. The Seven then instituted the games in his memory. The date of the victory is unknown.

Graces with golden staffs,
   May you grant good reputation (*doxa*),
Which persuades the hearts of men.

Since the divine prophet of the violet-eyed Muses
is ready to sing the praise of Phlius
and the blooming plain of Nemean Zeus,
where white-armed Hera raised
the deep-roaring, flock-slaughtering lion,
the first of the famous labors (*athla*) of Heracles. (1–9)

The red-shielded heroes [= the Seven against Thebes],
   the chosen few of the Argives,
first held games (*athla*) for Archemorus,
whom an insolent, shining-toothed serpent killed while he slept—
a sign (*sēma*) of the slaughter to come.
Overpowering fate (*moira*)!
The son of Oecles [= the seer Amphiaraus] did not persuade them
to go back to the well-manned streets.
Hope robs men of thought. (10–18)

Hope sent Adrastus, son of Talaus,
to Thebes as a guest-friend to Polyneices.
From these well-reputed contests in Nemea,
men become famous
who garland their shining hair with the crown
   in alternate years.
Now a god (*daimōn*) has given a crown
   to Automedon for his victory. (19–26)

For he was preeminent in the pentathlon,
   just as the bright moon shines forth
among the stars on the night of the full moon.
Such was he in the limitless circle of the Greeks.
His amazing body shone forth
when he hurled the circular discus,
and when the shaft of the dark-leaved elder tree
he sent forth into the lofty air,
he inspired an uproar from the people. (27–35)

After he accomplished flashing movement of wrestling,
   and sent strong limbed bodies to the earth
with great high-spirited strength,
then he came to the dark-flowing Asopus,
whose glory (*kleos*) reaches all the earth
and the farthest reaches of the Nile.

And the daughters of horse-driving Ares,
skilled with a spear, who live
beside the fair-flowing stream of Thermodon, (36–44)

they have encountered your descendants,
oh, much-envied lord of rivers, and so has the seat of high-gated Troy.
Everywhere on wide paths
go countless reports
about the generation of your
shining-belted daughters,
whom the gods established
as rulers of unsacked cities. (45–52)

Who does not know of the well-built city
of dark-haired Thebe,
or renowned Aegina, who went to the bed
of great Zeus and bore a hero…who…the land of the Achaeans…
…well-robed…and the maiden Peirane with twisted crown,
and so many other reverent children of the sounding river,
who were conquered long ago in the famous beds of gods.
…the city…victory…the cries of flutes…(53–60)

To speak well of the gold, violet-haired daughter,
the famous mother of unbending desires for mortals…(72–3)

hymn…even for him who has perished…
…would profess your victory at Nemea
for all unwearied time
and always to future generations.
A beautiful deed which has received legitimate hymns of praise
is stored up on high beside the gods.
With that which is not to be forgotten among men,
A thing most beautiful, even if the person has died,
remains behind, a delight of the Muses. (79–87)

[The rest is fragmentary.]

3c. 10: Athenian Victor in a Foot Race at the Isthmian Games

*The ode was commissioned by the brother-in-law of the victor, though neither the victor's
name nor the date of the event is known, because both the beginning and the end of this ode*

are missing. The event seems to have been a long-distance race (vv. 27–8), and the man commemorated seems to have won at multiple venues at the Isthmus; both the Isthmian and Nemean Games are mentioned. He is said to have brought glory to Athens, so he would have been an Athenian citizen.

> Fame (*phēmē*),…you visit the tribes of men with announcements
> …and now for him his sister's husband has
> moved the shrill-tongued island bee [= the poet] (1–10)

> in order that the immortal gift of the Muses
> be a common joy for men,
> revealing your excellence (*aretē*)
>   to those who dwell on earth;
> so often by the will of Victory,
> you crowned your bright head with flowers
> and gave renown (*kudos*) and reputation (*doxa*)
>   to broad Athens and the Oeneidae.
> In the famous contests of Poseidon,
> right away you showed to the Greeks the swift onset of your feet.
> You stood at the boundary of the racecourse,
> expelling your hot breath;
> You wetted the cloaks of the onlookers
> with oil as you fell into the crowd,
> After you turned around the racecourse
> a fourth time.
> Twice the heralds of the games organizers
>   announced you as Isthmian victor. (11–28)

> And twice you won by the holy altar of Zeus, son of Cronus, at Nemea.
> And famous Thebes received him
> appropriately and spacious Argos and Sicyon,
>   as did those who inhabit Pellene,
> and Euboea, rich in grain,
> and the sacred island of Aegina.
> One man seeks one path,
>   another seeks another,
> by which he will obtain a reputation easy to recognize.
> The forms of knowledge are manifold for men.
> A wise man (*sophos*) who has obtained honor from the Graces
> or knows some form of prophecy,
> he blooms with golden hope.
>   Another man stretches

his artful bow toward all.
Others increase their spirit through labor and herds of oxen.
The future gives birth
 to undecided results,
wherever fortune prevails.
But this is the most beautiful good: to be a man much envied
among many men. (29–49)

I know the great power of wealth,
which makes even a useless man useful.
But why with my blessed tongue
do I drive off the path?
Delight is announced for mortals after victory…(50–4)

Elegy

Ancient Greek elegy is a genre of poetry which consists of couplets, (one line of hexameter, one line of pentameter). Most early elegiac poetry seems to have been composed for symposia, small private drinking parties often attended by elite individuals of a given Greek city. The two elegiac poems presented here by Tyrtaeus and Xenophanes offer some of our earliest evidence for anti-athletic sentiment in Greek culture. In particular, both poems criticize the high value placed on athletic achievement, because victory in athletics fails to facilitate any form of civic good or utility. In this respect, these elegiac poems may be contrasted specifically with the genre of epinician poetry, which praises victorious athletes as a benefit to the cities from which they came. We have retained the poetic structure in our translations.

4. Tyrtaeus

4a. 12: Athletic Excellence Contrasted with That of War

Tyrtaeus is a Spartan poet (although some sources say he is of Athenian origin), writing during the seventh century BCE. *Most of his poetry may be classified as a form of "martial exhortation," used to inspire and motivate Spartan soldiers for war. The poem presented here (12) is unique in its focus on the Greek idea of excellence, aretē. Tyrtaeus specifically contrasts athletic aretē, both real and mythical, with excellence in war. As such, the poem may be viewed as part of an ongoing debate throughout Greek literary history as to whether athletic practice was contrastive with or complementary to war. This debate was already introduced in Homeric poetry, when the figure Epeius, who wins the boxing match in the Funeral Games of Patroclus, claimed to be the best (aristos) in boxing but deficient in the practice of war (1b, 660–90) Other later sources, such as Philostratus'* Gymnasticus *(40a) see the origin of athletics in the practice of war. Sparta, in particular, occupies a privileged position in that relationship. Despite the sentiments expressed in this poem, it should be noted that Spartans were historically quite dominant in athletic competitions, especially in the Archaic and early Classical periods. (The text comes originally from* Stobaeus' Anthology *4.10.1+6. This translation is based on the Greek text from Douglas Gerber's* Greek Elegiac Poetry, *Loeb 258 [1999].)*

I would not recall or take account of any man
based on his excellence (*aretē*) in running or wrestling,
not even if he had the size and strength of the Cyclopes,
not if he were victorious in running against Thracian Boreas,
(5)   not if he were more handsome in form than Tithonus,
not if he were richer than Midas and Cinyras,
not if he were more royal than Pelops, son of Tantalus,
not if he had a tongue more honey-sweet than Adrastus,
not if he had a reputation (*doxa*) in all things except courageous fighting strength,
(10)   For no man is good in battle,
unless he can endure the sight of bloody slaughter,
and can lunge at the enemy in close quarters.
This is excellence (*aretē*); this is the best prize (*aethlon*) among men,
and the most beautiful for a young man to take away.
(15)   For this is a common good for the city and all the people:
When a man holds his ground constantly in the front ranks,
and he entirely forgets shameful flight.
Risking his life and enduring spirit,
he stands there urging on the man next to him.
(20)   That man is good in war.
He quickly routs the bristling phalanx of enemy men,
And through his passion, he holds back the tide of battle.
And when he falls in the front ranks and loses his dear life,
he brings glory (*kleos*) to his city, people, and father,
(25)   pierced many times in the chest and bossed shield,
and pierced also through his breastplate.
Young and old alike lament for him,
and the entire city suffers with painful desire.
His tomb and his children are preeminent among the people,
(30)   as are his children's children and the generation after that.
Never do his noble glory (*kleos*) and name perish.
Whomever impetuous Ares destroys, while showing excellence
by standing his ground and fighting for his land and children,
that man becomes immortal, although he is under the earth.

(35)   But if he escapes the fate of long-suffering death,
         and if he makes good the boast of his painful spear through victory,
         all pay honor to him, young and old,
         and he experiences much pleasure before going to Hades.
         When he grows old, he is preeminent among the citizens,
(40)   and no one wishes to harm his sense of shame and justice,
         but all at the benches, young, age-mates, and those older yield their place to him.
         May every man not let up in war and attempt to reach this pinnacle of excellence
            (*aretē*).

5. Xenophanes

5a. Fr. 2.1–11: Critique of Athletes

Xenophanes was a sixth-century poet and philosopher from Colophon in Asia Minor. He is most famous for his criticism of common ancient Greek values. In this fragment, Xenophanes offers our first evidence of a more philosophical criticism of athletic practice in Greek and Roman cultural history. Similar criticism can be found in later works such as Plato's Apology, *in which the figure of Socrates contrasts the public rewards for athletes with the actual, unrewarded good that he himself as a philosopher brings to the city (see* **22a**). *Such criticisms ultimately culminate in the work of the Roman physician and philosopher Galen (see* **39a–c**). *Note that Xenophanes also provides a list of the perks awarded to successful athletes (lines 6–10).*

        But if someone should gain victory by the speed of his feet
        or in the pentathlon, where there is a sanctuary of Zeus
        in Olympia beside the stream of Pisa, or if he were victorious in wrestling
        or painful boxing,
(5)   or in the terrible contest they call the *pankration*,
        the citizens would look upon him with greater admiration,
        he would have front-row seats at the games,
        and he would receive meals from the public stores of the city,
        and a gift, which would be a prized possession for him.
(10)   In horse racing he would also receive all these things too.
        But he is not as worthy as I am. For my wisdom (*sophia*) is better
        than the strength (*rhōmē*) of men and horses.
        This is considered irrational, but it is not right
        to choose strength over noble wisdom.

(15)   Not even if is someone is a preeminent boxer,
           Or good at the pentathlon, wrestling, or even
           in the foot race, which is the most honored
           among the many forms of strength in the contest (*agōn*),
           not because of these things would the city be well ordered (*eunomia*).
(20)   There would be little joy for the city,
           if an athlete were victorious at the banks of Pisa,
           for this does not fatten the storerooms of the city.

6. Theognis

6a. 1335–6: On Athletic Nudity

Theognis is the name of a sixth-century BCE *poet to whom a collection of elegiac poems on varying topics is attributed. He was said to have been an aristocrat from the city of Megara. A number of his poems are addressed to a young man named Cyrnus, while others are clearly meant to be performed at symposia. The fragment here is of an erotic nature, referring to the cultural practice of pederasty, in which an older man would serve as the lover (erastēs, erōn), of a younger boy (erōmenos). This fragment is our earliest attestation for* gymnazein, *the verb typically associated with exercise in the nude. The verbal form is derived from* gymnos, *an adjective that means "naked."*

    Happy is he who goes home and trains naked (*gymnazetai*) in love,
    Sleeping with a beautiful boy, all day long.

Epigram

Epigrams are short poems, usually no more than 4–10 lines, in various meters, the most common of which is the elegiac couplet (see Elegy*).*

7. Simonides

Simonides was a writer of elegy and epigram from the island of Ceos. He was born probably in 556 and lived ninety years. None of his victory poems has survived, apart from very small fragments, but these four epigrams on athletes, modeled on dedicatory inscriptions, are found in the Byzantine collection known as the Greek Anthology *(see* **33**).*

7a. *Greek Anthology* 16.2: Theognetus, Boy Wrestler

When gazing at him, recognize that Theognetus, an Olympian victor,
    as a boy, a dexterous charioteer of wrestling,
the fairest to look upon, at competition no less fair than his form,
    won a crown for the city of his distinguished ancestors.

7b. *Greek Anthology* 16.3: For Diophon, Victorious Pentathlete

At Isthmia and Delphi, Diophon, the son of Philon was victorious,
in jumping (*halma*), swiftness, discus, javelin (*akōn*), and wrestling.

7c. *Greek Anthology* 16.23: Casmylus, Boxer

A.   Say who you are, whose son, what country, what you won.
B.   Casmylus, the son of Euagoras, boxing at Delphi, a Rhodian.

7d *Greek Anthology* 16.24: Milo of Croton, Wrestler

This is a handsome statue of handsome Milo, who at Pisa [= the Olympic Games]
once won seven times without once falling on his knees.

2 The Classical Period

*The Classical period of Greek history witnessed major political and cultural developments. In the latter half of the sixth century BCE Athens was ruled by the Peisistratid family. Called tyrants, these men governed with the support of the poorer classes, whose conditions they ameliorated by measures to promote economic and agricultural growth and to curb the power of the rich. At the end of their reign, the reforms of Cleisthenes (508 BCE) continued the trend toward a more democratic political structure. He organized the citizens into ten groups (called tribes) that included subgroups from different regions—the city proper, the coastal, and the inland areas. Power to select officials for the governing council (boulē) was vested in the tribes. Tribal units were also significant for the training of young citizen soldiers (ephebes) and for the tribal competitions held during the Panathenaea (**14a, 14h**). The Classical period includes most of the fifth and fourth centuries BCE and was bracketed by two wars that involved most of the Greek city states. In response to the threats of invasion from Persia at the opening of the fifth century, many of the city states, including those of the Aegean islands and along the Turkish coastline, formed the Delian League, under the leadership of Athens in 478 BCE. Once the threat was over, Athens continued to use the monies paid into the league for its own purposes, including the rebuilding of the city after the Persian invasion. The roughly sixty years between the battle of Marathon (490) and the onset of the next major conflict, the Peloponnesian War (431–404), saw the rise of Athenian naval power and, with it, economic hegemony over the greater Mediterranean. The threat that Athens posed to other Greek cities, particularly Sparta and its allies led to the Peloponnesian War; it was waged in three phases over a thirty-year period and concluded with Sparta's defeat of Athens, most notably the total route of its fleet at the battle of Aegospotami.*

While Athens grew in power during the fifth century, Sparta, after helping to defeat the Persian invasion, controlled the Peloponnese, but an earthquake in 464 BCE devastated the city, and it was slow to recover, though at the end of the Peloponnesian War it was the leading city state in Greece. Sparta was ruled by two kings chosen from hereditary families (the Agiads and the Eurypontids) during the Classical period. In the fourth century Sparta struggled to maintain its supremacy, sometimes with the aid of Persia. It contended with several other city states during most of this period (particularly Thebes). The rise of Macedon in the north, under the leadership of Philip II (359–336 BCE) posed an ongoing threat to the independence of all of these city states, and they eventually succumbed after the battle of Chaeronea in 338 BCE. Philip II was succeeded by his son Alexander III (the Great), who completed the conquest of Greece proper as well as the rest of the Greek cities of the eastern Mediterranean.

*The majority of the writing that has survived from this period was produced in Athens. In contrast to the material in the Archaic section, these texts introduce new genres that are mainly intended for reading not performance. They include history, the first true example of which was Herodotus' account of the Persian Wars (see **8**), followed by Thucydides' account of the Peloponnesian War (see **9**). The latter was unfinished and continued by Xenophon in his* Hellenica. *Xenophon also produced writings that provide*

Sourcebook of Ancient Greek Athletics. Charles H. Stocking and Susan A. Stephens, Oxford University Press (2021).
© Charles H. Stocking and Susan A. Stephens. DOI: 10.1093/oso/9780198839606.003.0003

*us with our best information on the organization of Spartan society (**10a, 10c–g**). Public speaking took off during this period in Athens, where law courts allowed for both public and private suits, and democratic assemblies were a stage for gifted speakers to offer advice on matters of state. Medical writing in the form of a series of essays now collected together in the Hippocratic corpus (see **14**) explored the nature of disease, health, and the environment as well as the treatment of illness and accidents like fractures. The philosophical writing of Plato and Aristotle also flourished in this period and, as will be apparent from the selections, also took up questions of bodily health, who was best to treat the body—doctors or athletic trainers—and often depended on analogies of bodily training in discussing the care of the soul. The exception to this efflorescence of prose was Attic drama, tragedy and comedy (see **11–12c**) that was written by playwrights selected in competition and staged as part of central Athenian festivals like the Greater Dionysia. Just like oratory, it tended to express the values of the democratic state. In this period, athletics, to the extent that it was considered aristocratic display or useless for the state, was often criticized (**9b, 9g, 12a, 21**). To the extent that athletics could be aligned with the need for citizens who were well trained for war and for the protection of the state, it was praised (**12a, 16b, 18a, 18c, 19e**).*

History

8. Herodotus

Herodotus was a Greek prose author from the ancient city of Halicarnassus on the Aegean coast of Asia Minor (Bodrum in modern Turkey) who lived c. 484–425 BCE. His Histories *presents us with our first complete prose text in the ancient Greek tradition, and he is largely known as the originator of "history" as a genre. The* Histories *had as a primary focus the causes and events of the Greco-Persian Wars, which lasted from roughly 499 to 449 BCE. His* Histories *also offers semi-ethnographic accounts of the customs (nomoi) of many cultures besides those of Greece and Persia, including Egypt, Scythia, Lydia, and Babylon. Hence, it is deeply engaged in questions of cultural practice and identity for both Greeks and non-Greeks alike.*

Herodotus offers a specific account of "Greekness" (to Hellēnikon), which includes "common blood, common language, common temples and sacrifices for the gods, and common habits of practice" (Herodotus 8.144). As Herodotus makes clear throughout his Histories, *one common Greek practice is the naked athletic contest (gymnikos agōn), where the singular refers to the constellation of events in which the participants were naked—wrestling, running, boxing, etc. On the one hand, athletic practice was understood to be a defining feature of elite activity in the Archaic period. At the same time, the practice of athletics is a key attribute of the common Panhellenic religious festivals at Olympia, Delphi, Isthmia, and Nemea in both the Archaic and Classical periods. Indeed, as Herodotus makes clear, participation in games such as those at Olympia might actually qualify a participant as "Greek" (see **8e**), and it is the naked athletic contest (gymikos agōn) which may be seen as a primary means of separating Greek from non-Greek (see **18b, 18c**). Furthermore, we see parallels and contrasts between the agonism involved in athletics and war, and it is this close connection which, according to Herodotus, may help to account for the unlikely success of the Greeks in* *defending themselves against the Persian invasion (see **8g, 8i, 8j**). Lastly, the significance of agonism is relevant not just to the content of the* Histories, *but also for the original performative context of Herodotus' work. For it is said that Herodotus himself first performed his* Histories *at the Olympic Games (see **38b**)*

8a. Bk. 1.31: The Story of Cleobis and Biton

This story of the Argive brothers Cleobis and Biton provides insight into the ethos of ancient Greek athletics through a focus on the extreme physical effort exerted by the brothers, the high value placed on praise for their physical achievement, and, finally, the danger of death that is a constant theme throughout the history of ancient Greek athletics. Herodotus tells us that the physical effort of the brothers was commemorated at the Panhellenic Sanctuary of Delphi, where we find large statues of two young men (kouroi) dedicated by the Argives (see Figure 1).

The story is narrated by the Athenian lawgiver Solon, who, after he had implemented his legal and social reforms for the Athenian people, is reported to have visited Croesus, the king of Lydia, who was known for his extreme wealth. When Croesus asks Solon whom he thinks to be the most fortunate of all men, Solon disappoints him by naming first Tellus, then the two brothers. Solon's point in this vignette is that no one can be called happy until he or she has reached the end of life and that to die young while accomplishing glorious deeds is the best kind of death.

When Solon said the affairs of [the Athenian] Tellus were many and fortunate, he provoked Croesus, and Croesus asked him whom he considered to be the second most fortunate man, expecting that he [Croesus, for his wealth] would take away second-place prize at least. But Solon named Cleobis and Biton. "Their family is Argive, they have sufficient livelihood, and in addition they have this strength (*rhōmē*) of body. For they were both prize-winning athletes, and the following story is said about them. There was a festival of Hera among the Argives, and their mother needed to be conveyed to the festival by their team of oxen. But the oxen did not arrive back from the field in time; constrained by time, the two young men took up the yoke upon themselves and pulled the wagon, and their mother rode on top of the wagon. They traveled forty-five stadia [roughly five miles] to the festival. After they accomplished this task and were seen by everyone, their life came to the best possible end. With these two, the god showed that it is preferable to die rather than to live. For the Argives gathered around the young men and congratulated them for their strength. And the Argive women congratulated their mother for bearing such children. Their mother was very happy with their accomplishment and the praise, and she stood before the statues of the goddess and prayed on behalf of her children Cleobis and Biton that the goddess might give whatever it is best for a man to attain. After this prayer, she sacrificed and held a feast, and the youths went to sleep in the temple. But they never awoke and came to the end of their lives. The Argives made images of them and dedicated them at Delphi because they were the best of men.

Figure 1. Kouroi, c.580 BCE, Parian Marble; Delphi Archaeological Museum no. 497, 1524

8b. Bk. 2.160: The Judges from Elis at Olympia

Book 2 of the Histories *provides an ethnographic description of Egypt as the diametric opposite of Greece in history and cultural practices. In this passage, Herodotus provides a history of the rulers of Egypt, specifically Psammis (also known as Psammeticus), pharaoh of the twenty-sixth, or Saïte dynasty, who ruled from 595 to 589 BCE. For most of their history the ancient Olympic Games were organized and controlled by the city of Elis. In this passage the inherent bias that the Olympics would display in favor of the Eleans is highlighted. Issues of fairness and Elean control plagued the entire history of the Olympic Games. The passage also suggests that the ancient Olympic Games were known outside of Greece in the Archaic period.*

Messengers of Elis came to Psammis, who was ruling over Egypt, and they boasted that the contest they organized at Olympia was the most just and the most beautiful for all humankind, believing that the Egyptians, although the wisest of men, could not devise anything better. But when the Eleans arrived in Egypt and explained why they had come, the king summoned all those Egyptians thought to be wisest. The Egyptians came together and learned all the things that the Eleans said they had to do to put on the contest. After explaining, they said they had come to learn if the Egyptian could discover anything more just. After taking counsel, the Egyptians asked the Eleans if their own citizens took part in the contests. They said that it was possible for anyone of their citizens and the rest of the Greeks to take part in the contests. And the Egyptians responded that in doing this they missed the mark in being entirely just. They said that there was no way not to favor one's own citizen who was competing and to do wrong against the stranger. But if they wish to set up the games justly and this is the reason they came to Egypt, they urged that the contest be set up for foreigners to compete, and that no Elean could compete. This is what the Egyptians suggested to the Eleans.

8c. Bk. 2.91: Greek Customs in Egyptian Chemmis

If Herodotus generally regards the Egyptians as unique among all other people, here he provides an "exception that proves the rule" in his discussion of one particular city in Egypt that practices athletic contests. For Herodotus, the naked athletic contest (gymnikos agōn) is an essentially Greek phenomenon (see Appendix A III). Apart from the naked aspect of these contests, there is ample evidence for the practice of various forms of athletic contests throughout Egyptian history. See especially Decker (1992).

To speak plainly, the Egyptians avoided making use of Greek customs, nor did they use the customs of any other people. Although most Egyptians guard against others' customs, there is a great city called Chemmis, in the area of Thebes, near the New City. In this city is a square temple of Perseus, the son of Danaë, around which palm trees have grown. At the entrance of the temple are great stone columns, and two great stone statues stand before it. In the outer court of the temple there is a standing image of Perseus. The people of Chemmis say that Perseus often appears to them throughout the land and often inside the temple, and that the sandal which he wears, which is four feet long, is often found. When it appears, all of Egypt thrives. They say these things, and they perform Greek customs for Perseus. They organize a naked athletic contest (*gymnikos agōn*) that includes all kinds of events, and they provide prizes of sheep, cloaks, and leather skins. When I asked why Perseus had the habit of appearing only to them and why they put on a naked contest separate from the rest of the Egyptians, they said that Perseus' lineage was from their city. For Danaus and Lynceus were citizens of Chemmis and sailed to Greece, and they traced their pedigree from them to Perseus. And he himself came to Egypt for the same reason as the Greeks say, to carry the head of the Gorgon from Libya and, in addition, to recognize all his relatives. They also said he learned the name of Chemmis before coming to Egypt, having learned it from his mother, and that it was Perseus himself who requested that a naked contest be performed for him.

8d. Bk. 3.137: Democedes of Croton

Herodotus claims that Persia invaded Greece at the suggestion of Democedes of Croton, the enslaved physician who advised the Persian king Darius. But the suggestion was a ploy so that Democedes could find a way to return home. The significance of athletics is conveyed by the final section, in which Democedes marries the daughter of the most famous Greek wrestler, Milo of Croton, as a way for the physician to demonstrate his own significance both to his own people and to Darius as well. For Milo of Croton, see **36a, 37q** *(6.14.5–9),* **39a** *(13),* **40a** *(1),* **42a,** *and* **46.**

And then the Persians set sail in pursuit of Democedes and arrived at Croton, where they discovered him in the marketplace and seized him. Some of the people of Croton who feared Persian power were ready to hand him over, but others struck the Persians with clubs. In response the Persians said the following: "Men of Croton, consider what you are doing. You are taking away a man who has become a runaway from the king. How do you think King Darius will deal with this insult? How will the things done turn out well for you, if he escapes us? Against what city will we wage war first? Which city will we try to enslave first?" But they did not persuade the men of Croton with their words but held on to Democedes and the merchant ship which sailed with him, and the Persians gave him up and sailed back to Asia. Nor did they try to learn by going to further parts of Greece, since they were deprived of their guide. But Democedes gave them a message as they were on their way, ordering that they report to Darius that Democedes was marrying the daughter of Milo. For the name of the wrestler Milo was well known to the king. And it seems to me that Democedes was eager for this marriage and spent a great deal for it in order that he might seem notable both to Darius and in his own country.

8e. Bk. 5.22: Alexander I of Macedon

In this passage, we see how the Olympics might operate as a means of ethnic and cultural legitimation. The issue of ethnic identity between Macedon and Greece would remain a constant question through-out ancient history. Here, one of the early kings of Macedon, Alexander I, validated his own claim to "Greekness" by participating in the Olympic Games. He also set a precedent for establishing Greek identity through involvement with the Olympics that would continue with later Macedonian kings, Phillip II and Alexander III (the Great), although Alexander III never competed directly in the games.

Those men born from Perdiccas say they are Greeks, and I myself happen to have learned this and will show in my later writing that they are Greeks. In addition, the

Hellanodikai,[1] who organize the contests at Olympia recognized them to be Greeks. For Alexander I of Macedon decided to compete and went there for that purpose. But the Greeks who would compete against him prevented him from entering on the grounds that the contest was not for foreign competitors but for Greeks alone. But when Alexander showed that he was Argive by lineage, he was judged to be Greek and he competed in the *stadion*, in which he tied for first place.

8f. Bk. 6.103: Cimon the Elder and the Olympic "Victory" of Peisistratus

Herodotus describes the fate of Cimon the Elder, one of the generals who led the Athenian army against the Persians before the battle of Marathon (490 BCE). Cimon was exiled from Athens by Peisistratus, the first major tyrant of Athens, who ruled c.546–510 BCE. While in exile, Cimon won several four-horse chariot victories at Olympia. For one of these victories, Cimon "gave" his victory to Peisistratus in exchange for being allowed to return from exile. This was possible for two reasons: The victor in the chariot race was the person who owned the horses and chariot, not the chariot driver, and the owner did not need to be present at the event itself. Then, if the owner of the chariot was not present at the event, victory was only solidified by the official declaration of victory after the event. Thus, it would be quite believable to ancient audiences that Peisistratus was victor, even though it was Cimon the Elder who actually owned the team of horses. The burial of Cimon and his Olympic-winning horses described below attests to the high value that the city of Athens placed on Olympic victors (see Appendix C IV).

Ten generals led [the Athenians], of whom the tenth was Miltiades. Miltiades' father, Cimon the son of Stesagoras, had to flee from Athens on account of Peisistratus the son of Hippocrates. While Cimon was in exile, he was victorious at the Olympics in the four-horse chariot race, winning the same prize as his half-brother Miltiades. At the next Olympics, he won with the same horses but allowed Peisistratus to be declared victor. By giving his victory away, he came back to his own property under a truce. But it happened that Cimon died at the hands of the children of Peisistratus when he won another Olympic victory with these same horses, since Peisistratus himself was no longer alive. They murdered him with an ambush of men at night behind the *prytaneion*. Cimon was buried in front of the city, across the road called "Through the Hollow." And the horses that won in three Olympic Games are buried opposite him. The mares of Euagoras the Laconian are the only other horses to have done this [i.e, won three Olympic victories]. The older of Cimon's children, Stesagoras, was raised by his uncle Miltiades in the Chersonese. The younger was with Cimon in Athens but took the name Miltiades from the Miltiades who was the founder of the Chersonese.

---

[1] These "Judges of Greece" were the officials in charge of organizing and running the Olympic Games. For further discussion, see Appendix BI Olympia.

8g. Bk. 6.105–6: Pheidippides Runs from Athens to Marathon

*The marathon race is one of the most popular events in modern history. Although the story of the modern marathon is rooted in ancient history, such a race was not a competitive event in ancient times but was introduced in the first modern Olympics of 1896 as a commemoration of the battle of Marathon during the Persian Wars. There are several sources for the story of the first "marathon" run in antiquity, and Herodotus provides our earliest account. In Herodotus' version there was a herald named Pheidippides who was also a distance runner. The ancient Greek term for distance runner, "hēmerodromos," means "day-runner," and so it was likely that there was some ancient form of what is now called "ultramarathon" running, i.e., running a distance that requires one to run constantly for the length of an entire day. In Herodotus' account, the herald Pheidippides runs from Marathon to Sparta, a distance of roughly 152 miles. There is now a modern race called the Spartathlon meant to retrace the steps of the Athenian herald. The distance of the modern marathon is based on an alternate account of another herald running from the battle of Marathon to Athens, a distance of roughly 26 miles. That story is recounted in Plutarch (**35p**) and Lucian (**38c**).*

(105) While the generals were still in the city, they first sent the Athenian herald Pheidippides, who was also a distance runner (*hēmerodromos*), to Sparta, and this was his primary practice. Pheidippides announced to the Athenians that he encountered the god Pan in the Parthenian mountain above Tegea. He said Pan called Pheidippides by name and bade him ask the Athenians why they paid him no worship, although he was well disposed toward them, often rendered service to them, and would do so in the future. The Athenians believed these things to be true, and when things were going well for them, they set up a sacred precinct of Pan under the Acropolis. And ever since that message, they propitiate him with sacrifices and a torch race (see Appendix C I 5).

(106) This Pheidippides who said that Pan appeared to him was sent by the generals, and he arrived in Sparta from Athens the very next day. When he encountered the Spartan leaders, he said "Oh Spartans, the Athenians need your help. Do not let the most ancient city in Greece fall into slavery at the hands of foreign men. Even now Eretria has been enslaved, and with the loss of that noble city Greece has become weaker." He announced this request to them, and they said they would send help to the Athenians, but they were unable to do so right away because they did not want to break their law. For it was the ninth day of the beginning of the month, and they said they could not march out on the ninth day, if the moon was not full.

8h. Bk. 8.126–9: The Marriage of Agariste

In this passage Herodotus narrates events that preceded the marriage of Agariste, the daughter of Cleisthenes, the tyrant of Sicyon. As different forms of tyranny developed throughout the Greek city states of the Archaic period, elite families often increased their power by way of marriage and also through athletic competition. Thus, Cleisthenes of Sicyon is reported to have won a victory in the chariot race at Olympia, and he used this occasion to announce a marriage contest for his daughter Agariste. This form of contest was not an innovation on the part of Cleisthenes; marriage contests are one of the earliest forms of athletic competition attested for Greece (see the contest of the bow in the Odyssey, 1f). Although marriage contests were traditional, the story of the contest for Agariste stands out because of Hippocleides' behavior.

(126) But later in the next generation [of the Alcmeonidae], Cleisthenes, the tyrant of Sicyon, lifted up the house of Alcmaeon higher still, so that it was more recognizable in Greece than before. Cleisthenes, the son of Aristonymus, the grandson of Myron, and the great-grandson of Andreas, had one daughter named Agariste. He wished to give her as a bride to whomever he found to be the best (*aristos*) in all of Greece. And when Cleisthenes won in the four-horse chariot race at the Olympic Games, he made an announcement that whoever considered himself to be a worthy son-in-law of Cleisthenes should come on the sixtieth day or earlier to Sicyon, and Cleisthenes would make good his promise of marriage in a year from that sixtieth day. Thereupon, all the Greeks there who were proud of themselves and their fatherlands came as suitors. Cleisthenes had a track and *palaistra* made for them for that purpose.

(127) *[Suitors are listed]*

(128) When the suitors arrived on the requested day, Cleisthenes first inquired about the fatherland and the lineage of each, and after he kept them there for a year and tested their manly virtue (*andragathia*), their temperament, their education, and manners. He kept company with each one separately and in a group. Those who were younger he brought to the gymnasium, but most importantly he tested their habits at table. As long as he kept them there, he did all this and entertained them lavishly. Those suitors from Athens pleased him most of all, especially Hippocleides, the son of Tisandrus, who was singled out for his *andragathia* and also because his ancestry came from the Cypselids of Corinth.[2]

(129) When the appointed day came for the marriage banquet and Cleisthenes' announcement of whom he would choose of all the suitors, he sacrificed one hundred oxen and entertained the suitors and all the Sicyonians. When the feast was complete, the suitors held a contest in musical performance and in speaking. As the drinking continued, Hippocleides, who was surpassing the others, ordered that the *aulos* player play a song, and he danced while the *aulos* player played. He danced in a manner that pleased himself, but Cleisthenes, looking on, was suspicious of the whole affair. But after a time, Hippocleides stopped and ordered a table to be brought out, and he jumped on the table and began to dance—first a Spartan dance, then an Attic one, and third, he stood on his head on the table and made gestures with his legs. In the first and second rounds of

---

[2] Cypselus is said to be the first tyrant of Corinth from seventh century BCE. Pausanias describes a richly decorated chest that Cypselus was said to have dedicated at Olympia, see **37i.**

dancing, Cleisthenes was repelled by the idea of Hippocleides as his son in law on account of his dancing and shamelessness, but he restrained himself because he did not want to lash out at him. But when he saw him making hand gestures with his legs, he was no longer able to hold himself back and said, "O son of Tisandrus, you have danced away your marriage prospects." And Hippocleides said in response: "It is no concern to Hippocleides!" And from this comes the saying.

8i. Bk. 8.26: The Olympics during Xerxes' Invasion

After the battle at Thermopylae, a few Greeks deserted to the Persian side, and Xerxes inquired what the Greeks were doing when they left. The deserters explained that those Greeks were competing in the Olympic contests which have no monetary prize. The story is meant to emphasize the truly competitive spirit of the Greeks. The distinction between gymnikoi *(naked) and* hippikoi *(horse) competitions was standard at Greek games.*

Then a few deserters came to him from Arcadia, because they were in need of livelihood and wished to find work. When they came into the presence of the king, the Persians asked what the Greeks were doing, with one person asking questions on behalf of all. They said they were conducting the Olympic festival and watching the naked (*gymnikoi*) and horse (*hippikoi*) competitions. And then he asked what prize it was for which they were contending. They said that the prize was the gift of a crown of olive. Then Tritanaichmes, the son of Artabanes, expressed a most noble opinion, but which seemed cowardly to the king. For when he heard that they were competing not for money but for a crown, he did not restrain himself and keep quiet but said the following to all: "Mardonius! What sort of men are these that you have brought us to fight against! Men who do not compete in contests for money but for the sake of excellence (*aretē*)."

8j. Bk. 9.33, 35: Tisamenus of Elis

Tisamenus was a seer from Elis who gained citizenship status among the Spartans. This passage describes Tisamenus before the battle of Plataea (479 BCE), the last major land battle in the Persian war and a major victory for the Greeks. Tisamenus was important to the Spartans because seers were often employed to predict the outcome of battles on the basis of the sacrifices they made. This passage shows the close connection and confusion between contests in sport and war, an ongoing line of discourse throughout antiquity.

(33) When all were arranged according to tribe and station, then on the second day both sides made sacrifice. Tisamenus, the son of Antiochus, was the sacrificer for the Greeks. For he followed that army as a seer. He was an Elean and a Clytiad from the

lineage of Iamids, and the Spartans made him a fellow citizen. For when Tisamenus consulted the Delphic oracle about children, the Pythia[3] said that he would win five great contests (*agōnes*). But Tisamenus misunderstood the prophecy and turned to athletic training (*gymnasia*) so as to win in athletic contests (*gymnikoi agōnes*). He prepared for the pentathlon (= five contests), and he almost won at Olympia by one wrestling match, when he competed with Hieronymus of Andros.[4]

(35) But the Spartans perceived that the prophecy of Tisamenus applied not to athletic contests but to contests of war (*arēioi agōnes*)...The five contests were as follows: first at Plataea, and then one at Tegea against the Tegeans and the Argives, and after that one at Dipaea against all the Arcadians except for the Mantineans, and then one against the Messenians at Ithome. And finally, there was the battle at Tanagra against the Athenians and Argives. This was the last victory of the five contests.

9. Thucydides

Thucydides (c. 460–400 BCE) was an Athenian by birth and served as a general to Thasos in 424 BCE, and as a result of the battle of Amphipolis was sent into exile. His exiled status enabled him to travel to many states during the Peloponnesian War and to observe the events from more than one political perspective. He wrote about the war in eight books that covered the opening disagreements and the ensuing conflict until 411, when his history breaks off.

9a. Bk. 1.6. 4–6: Sparta and Athletic Nudity

In his discussion of early Greek history Thucydides makes this comment about the origins of the practice of exercising naked. It is one of many attempts to explain the behavior (see Appendix AIII*).*

The Spartans were the first to use modest dress, as is the modern style, and those of greater means adapted their own habits to conform to those of the common people. They were the first to exercise naked, removing their clothing in public and anointing themselves with oil as part of their naked exercise. In ancient times in the Olympic Games, the competing athletes wore a cloth around their genitals, and it has not been many years since they stopped. They still wear loincloths in barbarian countries, especially in the countries of Asia; when boxing and wrestling contests take place, they wear loincloths to

---

[3] The priestess at the sanctuary of Apollo at Delphi, who was thought to have spoken while in a type of trance; Delphic priests would then interpret her words in order to provide answers to the questions posed. In the Herodotean tradition, the responses of the Pythia are often obscure and subject to misinterpretation, as was the case with Tisamenus.

[4] Pausanias echoes this passage when he describes the victor's statue of Hieronymus of Andros at Olympia (see **37q**, 6.14.13).

do this. One might point to many other resemblances between ancient Greek habits of life and the customs of barbarians today.

9b. Bk. 1.126: The Cylon Episode

As part of the ramping up of hostilities between Athens and Sparta, Sparta demanded that the Athenians "drive out the curse of the goddess." This was a not very covert attack on Pericles, whose family was descended on his mother's side from one of the members of the attempted coup. This is Thucydides' version of events; Herodotus, bk. 5.71 also has a brief account.

During this time the Spartans sent ambassadors to the Athenians to make this complaint, so that they would have the greatest reason for war if the Athenians did not comply. In the first place the Spartans sent ambassadors who urged the Athenians to drive out the pollution of the goddess. This was the pollution: Cylon was an Athenian, an Olympic victor of former times, well born and powerful, who had married the daughter of Theagenes, who at that time was the tyrant of Megara. When Cylon inquired at the Delphic oracle, the god told him in the great festival of Zeus [the Olympic Games] to take possession of the Athenian Acropolis. So, when he had received an army from Theagenes and had persuaded his friends, he seized the Acropolis at the time when the Olympic festival began in the Peloponnese in order to become a tyrant, considering that this was the great festival of Zeus and a fitting occasion for him because he had won an Olympic victory. Whether "the great festival of Zeus" was in Attica or elsewhere, he did not consider and the oracle did not make clear (for the Athenian Diasia was called the greatest festival of Zeus Melichios, and celebrated outside of the city, and the whole city makes many sacrifices, not blood offerings, but local produce).Thinking that he judged rightly, he made the attempt. But when the Athenians realized, they all came from the fields in aid and, sitting down, they besieged the Acropolis. But as time passed many of the Athenians became weary of the blockade and went away, entrusting the guarding to the nine archons and with full authority for the arrangement of everything as they judged best. In those days the nine archons performed the bulk of the civic functions. Now those who were besieging with Cylon were in poor condition because of the lack of food and water. Cylon and his brother escaped, but the others, being hard pressed—some even died from starvation—sat down as suppliants by the altar on the Acropolis. The Athenians who were assigned to guard duty, when they saw that they were dying in the sacred space, picked them up, claiming that they would do them no harm, and taking them out, killed them. Those that sat down at the altars of the Furies they killed in the entryway. As a result of this action those men were said to be cursed and to have sinned against the goddesses, and their descendants as well. Now the Athenians drove these polluted men out of the city and later the Spartan Cleomenes with an Athenian faction drove them out again, both the living and the dead, after taking up the bones and casting them out. They came back later, and their descendants are still in the city. This is the pollution that the Spartans ordered them to drive out.

9c. Bk. 3.8.1–2, 3.14.1–2: The Mytileneans Urge Support for Their Revolt at Olympia

This event takes place in the fourth year of the Peloponnesian War (428) during an armistice. The Mytileneans have revolted against Athens. They come to Olympia to claim that their revolt was justified and ask for support. It demonstrates the importance of the Olympic Games as a site where all Greeks gathered and politics as well as athletics were important.

(8.1–2) The Mytilenean ambassadors who had been sent out on the first ship arrived in Olympia, since the Spartans told them to go there, in order that the other allies upon hearing them might make a plan. It was the Olympiad in which Dorieus of Rhodes won for the second time. And after the festival they made their appeal.

[The end of the speech is as follows:]

(14.1–2) "Now in respecting the hopes that the Greeks have placed in you and in Olympian Zeus, in whose temple we are almost suppliants, become allies and aid the Mytileneans and do not forsake us who are risking our own lives since we give a common benefit to all from our success, and we give a yet greater common harm if we fail because you were not persuaded to help. Be the men that the Greeks think you to be and that our necessity requires."

9d. Bk. 3.104: The Reintroduction of Games on Delos

The island of Delos housed an important Greek sanctuary to the god Apollo and served as the meeting place for the Delian League, an association of Greek city states led by Athens.

In that same winter [426/5] the Athenians purified Delos in accordance with an oracle. The tyrant Peisistratus had purified it earlier, not the whole island, but only what could be seen from the temple. At this point they purified the whole island in this manner. The graves of all of those who had died on Delos were taken up and removed, and for the future they decreed that no one should die or give birth on Delos but should be transferred to Rheneia. It is so close to Delos that Polycrates, the tyrant of Samos, when he held power over the sea and ruled the other islands, took Rheneia and dedicated it to Delian Apollo, by binding it to Delos with a chain. After the purification, the Athenians celebrated the quinquennial festival for the first time. There was once long ago a great assembly of the Ionians and the surrounding islanders at Delos. This sacred mission included [choruses of] women and boys, just as now that of the Ionians does at Ephesus, and there was a contest there also of naked athletics (*gymnikos*]) and music, and the cities brought choruses. Homer makes this clear in his poems as follows, from the Hymn to Apollo: "But Apollo, your heart is especially gladdened by Delos, for there the long-robed Ionians gather with their wives and children on your processional way. There in memory of you they take pleasure in boxing and dancing and singing, whenever they have seated themselves for the festival" [*Homeric Hymn to Apollo* 146–50]. That there was a music competition and that they frequented athletic contests is clear from this same hymn. After hymning the Delian chorus of women, he concludes his praise in these words, in which he memorializes himself as well: "But now, may you be favorable, Apollo with Artemis, and farewell, all you maidens. Remember me in the future, whenever some stranger, who has suffered much, should come here and ask, 'Maidens, what man who comes here is most pleasing to you in song? And whom do you most take pleasure in?' You must respond with one voice: 'The blind man; he dwells in rocky Chios'" [*Homeric Hymn to Apollo* 165–73]. To this extent, Homer is a witness that in ancient times there was a great assembly and festival on Delos. Later the islanders and the Athenians sent choruses with the sacred offerings. Most of the contests were dissolved apparently as a result of circumstances, until [in 426/425] the Athenians created the current contest (*agōna*) and the horse races (*hippodromias*), which were not there before.

9e. Bk. 4.121.1: The Scionaeans Receive Brasidas as a Successful Athlete

Scione was a city on the western face of Chalcidice in northern Greece. This brief vignette provides insight into the status of athletic victors in the eyes of the Greeks.

The Scionaeans were uplifted by his speech, and all were likewise encouraged, even those who before had disapproved of what was happening, and they now decided that the war should be vigorously conducted. They received Brasidas with all due honor, publicly gave him a golden crown as the man who freed Greece, and, privately, they tied fillets around him and accorded him honors as if he were an athlete.

9f. Bk. 5.49–50: Spartan Exclusion from the Olympic Games

On this event and its possible aftermath, see **10h, 37k** *and Hornblower (2000).*

(49) The Olympic Games took place during the summer, and the Arcadian Androsthenes took first place in the *pankration* there. The Spartans were interdicted from the temple by

the Eleans and as a result they did not perform the sacrifices or compete in the events, because they did not pay the fine that the Eleans levied against them in accordance with Olympic law, claiming that they [the Spartans] had brought a force against Fort Phorcus and had sent their hoplites into Lepreum during the Olympic truce. The fine was two thousand minas, factored at two minas per hoplite, as the law stipulates. The Spartans sent ambassadors who argued that they had been fined unjustly, saying that the truce had not yet been proclaimed in Sparta when they had sent out their troops. But the Eleans stated that the armistice was already in effect for them (since they first proclaim it in Elis) and the Spartans in their unjust actions took them by surprise since they were keeping the peace and not anticipating anything. The Spartans retorted that it would not have been necessary for them to announce the truce in Sparta if they already thought that the Spartans had acted unjustly, but the Eleans did not think they had done anything wrong, and [after the truce was proclaimed in Sparta] they did not send troops against them anywhere. The Eleans held to their statement and would not be persuaded that they [the Spartans] had not behaved unjustly, but if they wished to return Lepreum to them, they would give up their own portion of the money and the god's portion they would pay for them. (50) When the Spartans did not accede to this, the Eleans proposed instead not to give back Lepreum, if they did not wish to, but ascending the altar of Zeus Olympios, since they desired to use the shrine, to swear an oath that they would pay the fine later. Since they did not at all wish to do these things, the Spartans were interdicted from the temple, the sacrifice, and the competitions, and they sacrificed at home, while the other Greeks apart from the Lepreans attended the festival. Nevertheless, the Eleans, in their fear that the Spartans would sacrifice through the use of force, posted a guard of heavy-armed young men. The Argives and the Mantineans joined them, a thousand of each, and Athenian cavalry, who remained at Harpina during the festival. There was considerable fear at the festival that the Spartans would invade with an army, especially since Lichas, the son of Archesilaus, the Spartan, had been whipped by the umpires (*rhabdouchoi*) in the contest, because he won with his own chariot team, while the Boeotian *dēmos* was proclaimed victor because he [as a Spartan] did not have permission to compete. Lichas came forward at the contest and crowned the chariot driver in his desire to make it clear that the chariot was his. As a result, they were all much more afraid and expected social unrest. But the Spartans made no move, and the festival concluded for them in this way.

9g. Bk. 6.16.1–3: Alcibiades at the Olympics

Alcibiades is speaking in favor of the Sicilian expedition and himself as the best Athenian to lead it. He starts off by mentioning his success in chariot-racing at the Olympic Games. This victory was famous (or infamous). See further **12c, 17a, 17b** *and* **18a.**

(1) It is fitting that I, above all others, Athenians, should lead—I must begin in this way, since Nicias has attacked me, and at the same time I am convinced that I am worthy of the task. The rumors that circulate about me, these things brought fame to my ancestors and to myself, and they are profitable for my country. (2) For the Greeks thought that our city was greater in power than we were, thanks to my distinction at the Olympic festival, although before they expected that it was devastated by the war; this was because I competed with seven chariots, more than any other private citizen before, and won first, second, and fourth place, and I arranged all of the rest [the victory parties] in a way worthy of the victory. Honor is customarily granted for this sort of thing and in the doing there is an attendant sense of power. (3) Then, my splendid undertaking of providing a chorus in the city or other things naturally engenders envy in the citizens but to foreigners it appears as strength.

9h. Bk. 8.9–10.1: The Isthmian Truce

This event takes place in 412 BCE during the Peloponnesian War. It provides information about the conduct of crown games in periods of internal warfare.

(9.1) They [the Athenians] were eager to sail, but the Corinthians did not want to do so before celebrating the Isthmian Games, which were happening at the time. So that they not break the Isthmian truce, Agis [the Spartan king] was prepared to privately undertake the expedition. (9.2) The Corinthians did not agree, and, after a delay, the Athenians began to suspect what was happening in Chios and they sent one of their generals, Aristocrates, who accused them [of planning a revolt], and, when the Chians denied this, they ordered them to send ships as a pledge of their alliance. They sent seven ships. (9.3) The reason for the dispatch of the ships is that the majority of the Chians were unaware of what was happening, while the few who did know did not want to antagonize the majority before they had something secure and they no longer expected the Peloponnesians to arrive because of their delay. (10.1) In this way the Isthmian Games took place and the Athenians (for they had been invited) took part in them.

10. Xenophon

Xenophon (c.430–354) was an Athenian, but closely associated with Sparta. He wrote on a wide number of subjects including the end of the Peloponnesian War (Hellenica), taking up events where Thucydides left off. His political views were antidemocratic, as is evidenced in his admiration for Sparta, with whom he fought against Athens in the battle of Coronea (394 BCE), in his biography of the Spartan king, Agesilaus II, and in the Constitution of the Lacedaemonians. He also admired the Persian king, Cyrus the Great, the putative founder of the Persian Empire. Xenophon wrote a *fictionalized account of him in his* Education of Cyrus (Cyropaedia)*. Xenophon participated in the expedition of ten thousand Greek mercenaries who enlisted to advance the cause of the Persian prince Cyrus the Younger against his brother Artaxerxes II, who was king. When Cyrus was killed at the battle of Cunaxa in 401 BCE, the Greeks were left stranded to make their way back to Greece through central Persia. Xenophon relates their experience in his account of their return (*Anabasis*)*. He also wrote a number of essays on technical subjects (horse-breeding, dog-breeding, how to be a cavalry officer, and household management), and on Socrates, including the* Memorabilia *and the* Symposium*. This last work was on a dinner party that seems modeled on Plato's* Symposium*.*

10a. *Agesilaus* 9.6: Cynisca of Sparta

Agesilaus II was king of Sparta c.398–360 BCE. Xenophon portrays him not just as a successful king, but as a man of simple, manly tastes, including the breeding of dogs and horses. In 396, his sister Cynisca was the first woman to win a victory at the Olympic Games (see also **27o, 35a, 37q** *(5.12.5, 6.1.6),* **37x, I1i***).*

In that respect how noble and dignified it was that he enhanced his own house with the artifacts and possessions worthy of a man, namely, rearing many hunting hounds and war horses. He also persuaded Cynisca, who was his sister, to breed horses for chariot teams, and by her winning [i.e., at Olympia] thus demonstrated that this stable was an example not of manly virtue, but of wealth.

10b. *Anabasis* bk. 4.8.25–8: Spontaneous Games

As they marched north, the ten thousand Greek mercenaries finally reached the Black Sea near ancient Colchis, where this event takes place. These Greeks were from many different city states but sacrifices to the gods and athletic games were used to solidify their collective Greek identity. A little later in the march, the ten thousand celebrate gymnic games in another place, the Greek city of Cotyora (5.5.6).

(25) [When they had acquired] a suitable number of oxen, they made an offering in gratitude for their safe arrival to Zeus the Savior, to Heracles, and to the other gods, as they had vowed. They also celebrated a gymnic contest on the mountain where they were camped. To look out for a racecourse and to oversee the contests they chose Dracontius, a Spartan, who as a boy had been exiled from his home because he had accidentally killed another boy when he struck him with a curved knife.[5] (26) When the sacrifice was

---

[5] The curved knife (*xyēlē*) was used to shape and smooth a javelin. See **15**, in which one boy accidentally kills another while at javelin practice in the gymnasium. Dracontius' accident may have resulted from similar circumstances.

finished, they gave the hides[6] to Dracontius and ordered him take them to where he had laid out the racetrack. Pointing to where they happened to be standing, he said, "This hill is the best for running, wherever you please." "How," they said, "will men be able to wrestle on ground so hard and full of thickets?" He replied, "The one taking the fall will be in rather more pain." (27) Boys, most of them captives, competed in the *stadion*; more than sixty Cretans ran the *dolichos*; and in wrestling, boxing, and the *pankration* there was also a fine showing. For many competed, and seeing as their comrades were spectators, there was considerable rivalry. (28) Horses also raced, and their riders needed to ride them down a slope, turn them at the seashore, and bring them back again to the altar.[7] Many of the horses rolled over as they went down, while, on the way up the extremely steep incline, they were barely able to proceed at a walk. As a result, there was a great deal of shouting, laughter, and advice.

10c–g. Constitution of the Lacedaemonians

*Written between 387–375 BCE, this treatise sets out to illustrate the reasons for the Spartans' success as a result of their unique social practices. The sections below stress the importance of physical health and training for the citizens. In Sparta the children, both boys and girls, were given a rigorous military-athletic training aimed at creating strong men to be citizen soldiers and strong women to bear, rear, and support them. Because the education of Spartan girls paralleled that of boys in many ways, non-Spartan, usually Athenian writers often criticized it (see **12b** and **22g**). Though the historical reality of Lycurgus as a Spartan lawgiver was by no means certain, even in antiquity (see **35f**), Xenophon credits him with creating the constitution and the rules governing civic life as described in these passages.*

10c. *Constitution of the Lacedaemonians* 1.1–4: Spartan Rearing of Girls

(1) When I realized that Sparta was the most powerful and the most recognized of the thinly populated cities in Greece, I wondered how this had come about. But when I came to understand the customs of the Spartans, I was no longer surprised. (2) Indeed, they prosper because they abide by the laws that Lycurgus set out for them. This man I admire and consider him wise in the utmost. For he was not an imitator of other civic entities, but, thinking the opposite of most of them, he brought his fatherland to the height of its prosperity. (3) With respect to the raising of children—for I shall begin at the beginning—the rest of the world nourishes those girls thought to be well brought up and who

---

[6] These hides from the sacrificed animals were used as prizes.
[7] The starting point. Races were normally run to a turning point and then back to the start.

are expected to become mothers with the bare minimum necessary for sustenance, and with almost nothing to supplement. As for wine, they raise them to abstain completely or use it only diluted with water. And because the majority of those who work at handicrafts are sedentary, other Greek cultures think that girls should sit quietly and weave wool. That is all we demand of them. But how are we to expect that women nurtured in this fashion should produce splendid offspring? (4) Lycurgus thought that slave women were suitable for producing clothing, and thinking that for freeborn women it was most important to produce children, he ordered first of all that females exercise their bodies no less than males. Then he organized contests in running and strength for women to compete with one another, just as he did for men, believing that if both parents were robust, their offspring would be even more so.

10d. *Constitution of the Lacedaemonians* 2.1–9: The Education of Boys

(1) Since I have given an account of Spartan practices on issues relevant to childbirth, I now want to explain the educational practices in Sparta and elsewhere. Among the rest of the Greeks those who say that they educate their sons best, as soon as their sons are able to understand spoken language, they immediately appoint attendants, called *paidogōgoi*,[8] to be in charge of them, and send them to teachers in order for them to learn reading, music, and the concerns of the *palaestra*. In addition to this they soften their son's feet with shoes and make their bodies delicate with changes of clothing. And they think that their appetites should govern how much they eat. (2) But Lycurgus, instead of allowing each man individually to appoint a slave *paidogōgos* for his son, appointed a man from among those who had held the highest offices; he was called a *paidonomos*[9] and had authority to gather the boys together,[10] and to watch over them, and, if they misbehaved, to whip them severely. Lycurgus also gave this man whip bearers in the prime of life whose duty it was to chastise whenever necessary, with the result that considerable modesty and obedience went together. (3) Instead of softening their feet with shoes, he ordered them to strengthen their feet by going barefoot, thinking that if they practiced in this manner, they would climb mountains much more easily and would come down from the peaks more safely… (4) Instead of making them delicate with a lot of clothing, he habituated them to a single garment worn throughout the whole year, thinking that they would be better prepared for both heat and cold. (5) Again, as to food, he recommended that they eat so moderately that they would avoid feeling full by over-eating, and accustom themselves to live with scarce rations, thinking that those boys trained in this way would be better able, if they needed, to continue to labor on an empty

---

[8] Literally, "one who guides a boy" (*paidagōgos* is singular, *paidagōgoi* plural).
[9] "Supervisor of boys."   [10] Boys were raised in groups segregated by age, called an *agōgē*.

stomach, and, if they were so commanded, to remain at their posts for a longer time without their rations. They would desire luxuries less and would be the readier to eat any food at hand; thus, they would live in greater health. He thought that a diet that made the body easily increase in height to be preferable to one that encouraged weight gain. (6) But so that they not be too much stressed by hunger, he did not allow them to take without effort whatever they needed but allowed them to steal what there was to alleviate hunger. (7) It was not through lack of what he might give them that he allowed them to devise a manner of getting food—no one, I think, is ignorant of this. But it is clear that the one who is going to steal needs to keep awake during the night and by day be deceptive and lie in ambush, and the one who is ready to take something needs to have spies ready. It is clear that he so educated the boys in all these things because he wished them to be more resourceful at acquiring necessities and more warlike. (8) Now someone might ask, why, then, if he thought it good for them to steal, did he beat with many blows whoever was caught? Because, I say, that even as in other things that men teach, they chastise the one who executes the lesson badly. And the boys who are caught are shamed as bad thieves. [And in this way deeming it good to steal as much cheese as possible from the altar of Artemis Orthia, (9) he ordered them to be beaten by others, wishing to make clear in this respect that it is possible for someone experiencing pain for a short time to gain distinction over the long term.] It is clear from this that where there is need for swiftness, the slacker profits least and gets the most trouble.

10e. *Constitution of the Lacedaemonians* 2.12–14: Homoerotic Relationships

This discussion of erotic relationships between adult males and boys echoes, in many respects, the speech of Pausanias in Plato's Symposium *(180c3–185c4). See also* Appendix A III.

(12) I think that something should be said about erotic relationships with boys, since this is something that is relevant to education. For other Greeks like the Boeotians, a man and boy may be joined together as in marriage or, as with the Eleans, by means of favors they gain intimacy with them in the bloom of youth. Some states completely prevent adult lovers from talking with boys. (13) But Lycurgus, in contrast to all of these, thought that if someone's character was what it should be and in admiration of a boy's soul, he tried to make him a blameless friend and spend time with him. Thus, he approved and thought this would be the fairest form of education. But if it was clear that he was yearning for the boy's body, having decreed that this was most shameful behavior, he made lovers restrain themselves from sexual intercourse with boys no less than parents refrain from their children or siblings with each other. (14) I am not surprised that some do not believe this, since, in many cities, the laws do not prohibit love for boys.

10f. *Constitution of the Lacedaemonians* 5.8–9: The Value of Physical Labor

(8) Lycurgus was well aware that, apart from diet, men who did physical labor had a good complexion, well-toned muscles, and were strong. But men who did not work could be identified by their embarrassingly bloated and weak physiques. He did not ignore this but thinking that when a man makes his own decision to engage in hard work, he will appear to have a sufficiently strong body. He ordered the one who was the oldest at any one time in each gymnasium to see to it that there never be a shortage of food. (9) And it seems to me that he was not tripped up in this matter either.[11] One would not easily find men with healthier or more fitly developed bodies than the Spartans. For in their gymnastic training they exercise equally their legs, their hands, and their necks.

10g. *Constitution of the Lacedaemonians* 10.1–4: Compelling the Practice of Virtue

How, then, is this effort of Lycurgus not worthy of great admiration? When he recognized that those who wanted to practice virtue were not sufficient to grow the fatherland, he compelled them to practice all manner of virtue in Spartan public life. Now just as those practicing virtuous behavior in their private lives differ from those who neglect it, so Sparta reasonably differs from every other city state in virtue, since it alone lives by the public practice of noble conduct (*kalokagathia*).

10h. *Hellenica* bk. 3.2.21–2: Eleans Declare Spartans Breakers of the Olympic Truce

The eruption of violence mentioned here occurred in 399 BCE, but the grievances harbored by the Spartans against the Eleans dated to 420. Elis, as the overseers of the Olympic Games acted as the sole arbiters if rules were thought to have been violated. In 420, the Eleans declared that the Spartans had broken the Olympic truce by sending military support to Lepreum against Elis. The Spartans were fined, but refused to pay, and as a result their citizens were barred from Olympic competitions. (Thucydides also relates the story; see 9f) The incident involving Lichas was part of this ban.

(21) During this time period tensions erupted again between the Spartans and the Eleans, because the Eleans had made an alliance with the Athenians, Argives, and Mantineans, and because in the past the Eleans had claimed that the judgment rendered

---

[11] Xenophon uses a term from wrestling, causing someone to take a fall (*sphalēnai*).

against the Spartans debarred them from both the hippic and the gymnic contests. But this alone was not enough for them; furthermore, after the Spartan Lichas (in 420 BCE) had given his chariot to the Thebans and the team was proclaimed as victor, when Lichas entered to crown his charioteer, they beat him with whips and drove the old man away. [22] At a later time, when Agis[12] was sent to sacrifice to Zeus in accordance with an oracle, the Eleans prevented him from praying for victory in war, saying that from ancient times it was the custom that Greeks could not consult the oracle about a war against other Greeks; so Agis went away without sacrificing.

10i. *Hellenica* bk. 4.5.1–2: Conflict over Isthmian Games

This event occurred in 390 BCE. The Corinthians were the traditional overseers of the Isthmian Games, but during their war with the Argives, the Argives had temporarily taken possession of the sanctuary and were conducting the games. The Spartans were supporting the Corinthians against Argos, so when Agesilaus routed the Argives, the Corinthians with his help celebrated the games. A little later (4.5.4) we learn that the temple to Poseidon was burned down, supposedly by Agesilaus' men, though very likely this was an accident.

(1) [When the Spartans learned that the Argives] were again campaigning against Corinth, at this point Agesilaus was the Spartan general. And first he came to the Isthmus of Corinth. For it was the place where the Isthmian games were taking place and the Argives happened to be making sacrifices to Poseidon as if Argos was Corinth. When they became aware of Agesilaus' approach, in the greatest fear they abandoned both the sacrificial offerings and the preparations for breakfast and ran down the road from Cenchria into the city. (2) When Agesilaus saw this, he did not pursue them but set up camp in the sanctuary, and he himself sacrificed to the god [Poseidon] and remained there while the Corinthian exiles conducted the sacrifice to Poseidon and the games. After Agesilaus left, the Argives celebrated the Isthmia from the beginning, and, in that year, some of the athletes lost twice and some were twice proclaimed victor.

10j. *Hellenica* bk. 7.4.28–32: Military Interruption of Olympic Games

*This event of 364 BCE is the most egregious violation of the Olympic Games recorded in ancient sources. During a war between Elis and Arcadia, and their allies (the Argives, Messenians, and Thebans), the fighting actually broke out within the precinct of Olympia itself and while the games were in progress. Pausanias (**37k,** 5.20.4–5), writing five centuries later, records that many years after the event the body of one of the soldiers was found under the roof of the Heraeum, where he had*

---

[12] Agis II, one of the Spartan kings, who ruled from 427-399 BCE. See **9h.**

apparently fallen during the fighting. For the areas of the Olympic site described in the fighting, see Plan 2 (p. 374).

(28) The Arcadians again turned to the situation with the Eleans, and not only garrisoned Olympia more strongly, but since an Olympic year was approaching, they prepared to celebrate the Olympic Games along with the Pisatans, who claim that they were the first to oversee the sanctuary. But when the month in which the Olympic Games take place had arrived and the days on which the festival gathering was assembled, at this time the Eleans made their preparations openly, requested aid from the Achaeans, and processed along the Olympic route. (29) The Arcadians did not think that the Eleans would attack them, and they were organizing the festival along with the Pisatans. They had just finished the horse races and foot races of the pentathlon. The competitors who had reached the wrestling were no longer on the racetrack but were wrestling in the area between the racetrack and the altar. At this point the Eleans, who were armed, had already reached the sacred precinct. The Arcadians did not advance much farther to meet them but drew up their line along the river Cladeus, which flows by the Altis to empty into the Alpheus. Their allies were together with them (about 2,000 Argive infantry and 400 Athenian cavalry). (30) The Eleans drew up their line on the other side of the Cladeus and as soon as they had slaughtered the sacrificial victims, they advanced . . . (31) But when the Eleans had pursued them into the area between the *bouleutērion* and the shrine of Hestia and the theater next to these buildings, they fought just as fiercely and pushed them toward the altar. But since they were being pelted from the stoas, the *bouleutērion*, and the Temple of Zeus itself, as they were fighting at ground level, some of the Eleans were killed, including Stratolas, the leader of the Three Hundred.[13] When this happened, they retreated to their own camp. (32) But the Arcadians and their allies were afraid of the approaching day and thus did not rest during the night but cut down the tents that had been so carefully erected [i.e., for the various merchants who sold food during the games], and they built a stockade. When the Eleans returned on the next day and found that the wall was stronger and that many men had climbed up onto the roofs of the temples, they departed for their own city.

10k. *Hipparchus* 8.5.3: The Hardship of Athletic Training

This treatise, written in the 360s, focuses on the moral qualities necessary to make a good cavalry commander for the Athenians. Chapter 8 provides some information about the care of horses, but the value of this passage is the claim that it is harder to be an athlete in gymnic events than a rider of horses.

---

[13] Not the Spartan Three Hundred who defended at Thermopylae in 480 BCE, but a later company of Elean soldiers.

(5) If someone considers that it is very burdensome to practice horsemanship in this way, let him consider that those preparing for athletic competitions engage in much more strenuous and difficult labor than those who practice horsemanship, however hard. (6) The majority of gymnic practices are difficult and sweaty labor, but horsemanship is sheer pleasure. It is nothing other than having wings. (7) And, in fact, to win a victory in war is much more glorious than a victory in boxing. For the city has some share in this distinction, but for the most part with the victory in war the gods crown the city with prosperity, not but that I think that anything is more fitting to practice than the military skills.

10l. *Hipparchus* 3.10–13: Description of the *Anthippasia*

This event deployed two units of cavalry in opposing lines. The basis of organization was by tribe, and it is only attested at the Athenian festivals of the Panathenaea and Olympieia. Xenophon provides our only description of it.

(10) Whenever there is a cavalry display in the hippodrome, first it would be good for them to deploy in extended facing lines so that the hippodrome is full of horses, in order to drive out the men in the middle. (11) Then it would be good, when the tribes (*phylai*) in the *anthippasia* flee and swiftly pursue one another in mock battle with the cavalry leader (*hipparchos*) of the contingent of five tribes, to drive each contingent through the other. This is the spectacle: The facing lines ride fiercely toward each other; (12) the solemnity as they stop opposite each other again, having ridden through the hippodrome; the beauty when they charge again more swiftly at the trumpet; the third time they have stopped, when the trumpet sounds, they should ride toward each other as quickly as they can. When they have crossed through each other, they all should wait in their phalanxes until dismissal. (13) Then, as is customary, proceed to the council house (*boulē*). It seems that these maneuvers would be more like warfare and more novel.

10m–o. *Symposium*

This dialogue presents itself as a recollection of a dinner party held in celebration of the victory of a young man who won the pankration in the boys' class at the Greater Panathenaea in 421 BCE. His adult lover Callias hosted the event, and Socrates and a list of other historical figures were said to have been present. At some level this is a parody of Plato's Symposium, an account of a drinking party held on the occasion of Agathon's tragic victory in the Lenaea of 416. The topic of Plato's discussion was Eros—what Eros was, his effects, and how best to praise him. Xenophon's narrative gives us an insight into the erotic aspects of athletics, since the victor, Autolycus, is a beautiful young boy to whom many are openly attracted. The date of its writing is probably around 370.

10m. *Symposium* bk. 1.1–10: Celebration in Honor of a *Pankration* Victor

I think that the serious deeds of distinguished men are not the only things worthy of recording, but also what they do when they relax, and I wish to relate the experience on which I base this conviction. (2) It was the occasion of the horse races at the greater Panathenaea. Callias, the son Hipponicus, happened to be in love with the boy Autolycus, and when the boy had won the *pankration*, Callias brought him to see the spectacle. When the racing was over, Callias went to his house in the Piraeus with Autolycus and the boy's father. Niceratus also accompanied him. (3) But when he saw Socrates, Critobulus, Hermogenes, Antisthenes, and Charmides together, Callias ordered someone to take Autolycus and the others to his home, while he, going over to Socrates and his companions, said: (4) "It's good that I ran into you, for I am about to give a dinner party for Autolycus and his father; and I think that my arrangements would appear much more brilliant if my dining room were adorned by men like you, whose souls have been purified [i.e., by philosophy] than with generals and cavalry commanders and office-seekers." (5) Socrates replied: "You always joke, looking down on us because you have paid a lot of money to Protagoras, Gorgias, Prodicus, and many others for the procurement of wisdom, and see us as philosophical amateurs." (6) And Callias said: "Before, to be sure, I have hidden my great cleverness at speaking from you, but now, if you will come to my house, I shall show you that I am worthy of being taken seriously."

(7) [Socrates and his friends decide to attend the party]; some had exercised in the gymnasium and had a rubdown; others had bathed as well. (8) Autolycus was seated at his father's side; the others, as was customary, reclined. Now, someone observing what happened would have immediately concluded that beauty is naturally something regal, especially when, as with Autolycus, the person possesses it along with modesty and good judgment. (9) For in the first place, just as all eyes are drawn to a light that appears at night, so did Autolycus' beauty draw everyone's gaze. None of the onlookers failed to be moved in his soul by the boy; some grew quieter; others struck poses. (10) Of course, all who are possessed by one of the gods seem well worth gazing at; while those who are possessed by other gods are sterner in their looks, more terrifying in their voice, and more forceful, those inspired by a prudent desire have a more tender look, speak more softly, and adapt a more open bodily posture. Callias, acting like this under the influence of Eros, himself became an object well worth observing for those initiated into the rites of this god.

10n. *Symposium* bk. 2.3–4, 5–8, 11–12, 15–19: Socrates on the Virtues of Dancing

After the meal, entertainers are brought in—first musicians, then dancers. Socrates claims that danc-ing is an excellent exercise for the whole body, especially as men age. The whole exchange is treated as a kind of burlesque. The passage begins with a rejection of perfumes for men in favor of the scent of olive oil used by those who exercise in the gymnasium. Since the civic gymnasia were restricted to citizens, only those who were free, supposedly, would exude this smell.

(3) [Socrates is speaking:] The smell of the olive oil in the gymnasium, when you have anointed yourself, is sweeter than perfume is to women, and when it is absent, it is the more strongly desired. (4) Indeed, when someone, whether free man or slave, has anointed himself with perfume, they all smell the same. But the odors that come from the exercise of free men first of all require the proper habituation for many years if they are to be sweet and a mark of free men." And Lycon said: "For young men this may be true, but what scent do those of us who no longer exercise in the gymnasia need?" "The scent of moral excellence," said Socrates. "And where would someone get this ointment?" "Well, not from the perfume sellers," said Socrates. "Then where?" "Theognis has said: 'You should be taught by the noble deeds of noble men. But if you mingle with bad men, you will destroy the good judgment you had before." (5) Lycon said: "Are you hearing that, my son?" "Yes, indeed he does," said Socrates; "and he follows the advice, because when he wanted to become victorious in the *pankration*,... and again with you looking for the one whom he thinks is most suitable for gaining experience in these matters, and he will associate with him." (6) Then many cried out. One of them asked, "Where will he find an instructor in this subject?" Another said that the subject was not teachable; a third that if anything else could be taught, this could be as well. (7) "Since this is a subject on which we cannot agree," Socrates said, "let's postpone it for another time; for now, let's finish our previous discussion. I see that the dancing girl has taken up her position, and that someone is bringing her some hoops." (8) At this point another girl began to accom-pany her on the *aulos*,[14] and a boy standing near the dancer handed her the hoops until he had given her twelve. She took them as she danced and tossed them to whirl in the air, and simultaneously noting the proper height to throw them in order to catch them without breaking her dance rhythm...

(11) After this a circle was fashioned ringed with upright swords. The dancer turned somersaults into the circle and out again so frequently that as they watched her, they were afraid that she might come to harm. But she finished this performance boldly and safely. (12) Then Socrates, calling to Antisthenes, said: "I doubt that those watching this performance would any longer deny that courage can be taught when she, even though she is a woman, leaps so boldly into the ring of swords!"...

---

[14] A double-reed instrument, most similar to the modern oboe, but often translated as "flute."

(15) Then the boy danced. Socrates said, "Did you see that, although this boy is good-looking, he appears even more so in the positions of the dance than when he is still?" "It's likely that you were praising the dance master," said Charmides. (16) "Well yes," replied Socrates; "and I noticed something else, that no part of his body was idle during the dance, but neck, legs, and hands were all exercised together. And that is the way one who is going to have a well-toned body should dance. And I, for my part," he said, "Syracusan, would like to learn the movements from you." He replied, "What use will you make of them?" "I will dance, by Zeus." (17) At this everybody laughed; but Socrates, looking quite serious, said: "Are you mocking me because I want to exercise to be healthier or because I want to eat and sleep with greater pleasure? Or because I am eager to exercise in this way, and not, like the long-distance runners who develop their legs while their shoulders grow thin, or like the boxers, who develop their shoulders but whose legs are attenuated, but rather with a view to giving my body a symmetrical development by exercising it in every part? (18) Or is the reason for the laugh that I shall not need to look for someone to exercise with, or need as an old man to strip off my clothing in a crowd,[15] but a small room will be sufficient for me (as just now this room was sufficient for the young male dancer to work up a sweat), or because in winter I shall exercise under a roof, and when it is too hot, in the shade? (19) Or is this why you laugh, because I have a paunch that is much greater than it should be and want to reduce it? Don't you know that just yesterday morning Charmides here found me dancing?" "Yes indeed," said Charmides; "and at first I was dumbstruck and thought that you were going crazy; but when I heard you say the same things as you said just now, I myself went home, and did not dance, for I had never learned how, but shadow-boxed (*echeironomoun*), because I knew how to do that."

10o. *Symposium* bk. 8.37–8: Value of an Athletic Victory

This passage sets out the cultural stakes in winning an athletic victory

(37) In your case, Callias, I think it appropriate for you to thank the gods for inspiring you with love for Autolycus. For his desire for glory is transparent, as he has accepted much hard work and many bodily discomforts for the sake of being proclaimed victor in the *pankration*. (38) Now, if he should think that he would not only bring glory upon himself and his father but also by virtue of his display of manly courage become able to help his friends and to exalt his country by setting up trophies of victory over its enemies, and for these reasons be admired by all and be renowned among both Greeks and barbarians, would you not think that he would hold in the highest regard whomever he considered to be the best partner in these circumstances?

---

[15] Socrates refers to attending the gymnasium, where one needed a partner to wrestle, and the rooms for stripping and oiling were open to all.

10p. **Pseudo-Xenophon**, *Constitution of the Athenians* 1.13: Degeneration of the Gymnasium

This essay, also known as the **Old Oligarch**, *was attributed to Xenophon, in part because of its clearly antidemocratic sentiments. In Athens all male citizens, who were referred to collectively as the* dēmos, *were entitled to attend the assembly and make decisions by hand or voice vote, often to the detriment of the wealthy. One-time assessments were imposed on the wealthy to pay for civic services (called liturgies). These services included paying for city-sponsored events like festivals, oversight of the gymnasium, and military needs. The author makes a direct link between Athenian lack of success in athletic endeavors and the desire for wealth.*

(13) The people have destroyed athletic and musical events here, since they consider them not worthwhile, because they are aware that they are incapable of these pursuits. Then they know that with respect to funding athletic contests and overseeing the gymnasium, and providing a warship it is the wealthy who act as the choral leaders, while the people are merely the participants, the wealthy who pay for the warship, while the people row them or compete in the games. At least the people think that they should take money for singing and running[16] and dancing and sailing on ships so that they might have some share in the wealth that the others possess and become less poor. In the courts too they are not interested in justice but rather what is in it for them.

Tragedy and Comedy

*While there are very few sustained passages in Attic drama that describe athletic events, these plays made frequent use of athletic images and metaphors, particularly those of running, wrestling, and boxing and for winning or being crowned for a victory. The most famous passage that survives is the detailed description of a chariot race in Sophocles' Electra (**11a**). A reported description of Hippolytus' fatal chariot crash occurs in Euripides' Hippolytus (1173–242). In his Alcestis, Heracles wrestles Death for the soul of Alcestis (1019–36); in a fragment of Euripides' now lost Alexandros [= Paris], this son of Priam, who was abandoned at birth, returns anonymously to compete in funeral games held in his honor. Fragments of lost plays such as Aeschylus' satyr play on the Isthmian Games (Isthmiastai) and titles of others, such as Alcaeus' Palaestra, Anaxilas' Euandria, or Alexis' Apobates, signal a greater interest in athletics than the surviving plays would lead us to believe.*

For a thorough discussion of athletics in comedy and tragedy, see Larmour (1999).

---

[16] A reference to games like the Panathenaea, where there were money prizes.

11. Sophocles

11a. *Electra* 698–756: Orestes' Chariot Accident at the Pythian Games

This is a false report made to Clytemnestra and Aegisthus that her son Orestes had been killed at Delphi in a chariot contest. According to the old slave making the report, Orestes had already won victories in all of the other contests. He then entered the four-horse chariot event with nine other contenders. The race is described in detail, and in one of the final turns around the post, Orestes' chariot overturns and he is pulled to his death. Orestes is not actually dead, but this deception allows him to enter the palace and later kill his mother and his stepfather as an act of vengeance for their slaying of his father Agamemnon. In his Poetics *(1460a31–2) Aristotle claimed that this long digression was extraneous to the drama. Commentators subsequently objected to the anachronism, because the Pythian Games were established well after the just post-Homeric world of Orestes. Descriptions of chariot crashes seem to have been popular, however (see* **1a**, *23.380–400, 450–500) and* **19e***).*

[Orestes is from Argos.] Now on another day, when at dawn the contests of swift-footed horses took place, (700) he entered with many other charioteers. One was an Achaean, another from Sparta, two were Libyan, skilled at the yoked chariots. And the fifth man among them had Thessalian mares. The sixth was from Aetolia with chestnut foals. The seventh was a man from Magnesia. The eighth with white horses was from Aenus. The ninth was from god-built Athens. A Boeotian filled out the tenth place. (710) Standing where the appointed judges had determined their positions by lot and placed their chariots, at the sound of the bronze trumpet they leapt forward. They shouted out to their horses while they shook the reins in their hands. The whole course resounded with the noise of rattling chariots. Dust was kicked up as, closing with each other, they did not hold back with the goad; each strove to pass the wheels and the neighing horses of the others. Likewise, around their backs and the wheelbases foam and the breaths of the horses fell upon them. (720) Now Orestes, holding his horses close under the turning post, brought the nave of his left wheel close at each turning and, giving his right trace horse his head, he tried to check the man who was coming up behind. Initially everyone stood upright in his chariot, but the hard-mouthed colts of the man from Aenus grabbed the bit and, from the leftward curve as they were finishing the sixth and beginning the seventh lap, smashed their foreheads against the chariot from Barca [i.e., one of the two Libyan contenders]. Then one man crashed into another in one pile-up and (730) the whole field of Crissa was filled with chariot wreckage. When he saw this, the clever Athenian driver checked his horses and pulled up to the side, avoiding the morass in the middle of the course. Orestes was driving in last place, holding his horses back, confident in the result. When he saw that only one was left [the Athenian], he gave a sharp command to his horses' ears and pursued. They brought their chariots level with each other and drove on, with the head of now one, now the other gaining. (740) Now, through all of the previous laps the wretched man [Orestes] had held his chariot on course, but then he relaxed the left rein as the horse was turning and, not paying attention, he struck the edge of the turning post. He broke the axle nave in the middle and slipped over the rail, and he was tangled in the reins. As he fell onto the field, his horses were scattered into the middle of the racecourse. When the people saw him fall from his chariot, (750) they cried piteously for the youth, who was doing such deeds when misfortune befell him. He was carried toward the ground, and then with legs extended toward the sky, until the charioteers with some difficulty checked his horses' course and cut him loose, so bloody that none of his friends on seeing him would have recognized his wretched body.

12. Euripides

12a. *Autolycus* fr. 282: "Tribe of Athletes"

This fragment is from a satyr play on Autolycus, the son of Hermes, an archetypal thief. This long quotation is now found only in Athenaeus (10.413c), who points out that the sentiments expressed are already found in a fragment of Xenophanes (see **5***). A fragmentary philosophical dialogue (POxy 3699) as well as Galen* **39a** *(Protrepticus 10, 13) also quote from this passage. The sentiments expressed about the usefulness of athletics for war may be found again in the* Anacharsis *(***38a***).*

AUTOLYCUS Of the countless evils that exist throughout Greece none is worse than the race of athletes. First, they neither learn to manage a household well, nor would they be able to. How could any man who is a slave to eating and dominated by his belly garner wealth that exceeds his father's? Then, they are unable to cope with poverty or misfortunes; without the acquisition of good habits, a change toward the worse leaves them without resources. In their prime they are brilliant and go about as ornaments to a city. But when bitter old age takes possession of them, they go away, cast out like threadbare cloaks. I blame the customs of the Greeks, who, gathering on account of these men, honor useless pleasures for the sake of a feast. For the man who wrestles well, who is swift of foot, who throws a discus, or boxed well, has he defended his fatherland by winning a crown? Are they going to fight the enemy with a discus in their hands or cast the enemy from their fatherland by penetrating a shield with their fists? No one is this foolish when he is near a sword. Men who are wise and good should be crowned with leaves [a reference to the wreathes at crown games—olive, laurel, celery, pine] and who leads the city in the fairest manner because he is modest (*sōphrōn*) and just, and who transforms base deeds by his words, averting quarrels and factions. Such things as these are good for a city and for all the Greeks.

12b. *Andromache* 590–601: On Spartan Women

Peleus is chastising Menelaus for his cowardice; he brings up the fact that Menelaus let his wife run off with another man, pointing out that she (Helen) was Spartan, and Spartan women were by nature unchaste. He alludes to the Spartan practice of allowing women to exercise in the presence of males (see Xenophon 10c).

Do you belong among men, you who are the basest of the base, whose wife was carried off by a Phrygian, leaving your house unlocked, thinking that your wife in your house was chaste, when in fact she was the worst of all women? Not even if she wished to, could a Spartan girl be chaste; in the company of young men they leave their houses with naked thighs and loose tunics, and they have common running tracks and palaestras—something I cannot bear. Then do you wonder that you do not educate women to be chaste?

12c. **Euripides (?),** *Epinician for Alcibiades*

This fragmentary opening of a victory ode for Alcibiades on the occasion of his placing first, second, and third at Olympia with his chariot teams is recorded in Plutarch's Life of Alcibiades 11 and attributed to the tragic poet. On this event, see 9b, 17a-b, 18a).

I marvel at you, son of Cleinias. Victory is a fine thing, but the finest is to do what no other Greek has done; with your chariot team to have run first, second, and third and to have come without effort, crowned with Zeus's olive, to provide the herald with a victory cry.

13. Aristophanes

Arsitophanes' Clouds gives us a father (Strepsiades) driven into debt because of the cost of sustaining his son Pheidippides' horse and chariot driving habits. Horse racing was particularly associated with the super-rich of Athens, and Strepsiades begins by lamenting that he married into the aristocratic family of Megacles (13a). The solution he proposes to stem his debts is to enroll Pheidippides in Socrates' Think Tank, where he can learn to speak to his advantage, making a worse argument appear to be the better. (This was a frequent complaint against the sophists who trained people for successful public speaking.) In 13b, Better and Worse Argument are setting out the benefits of following their instructions. Better Argument expresses the old-fashioned ideal for training youths. Plato, a student of Socrates, seems to have believed the Clouds was influential in Socrates' trial and execution (see Plato, Apology: 22a). Ironically, the very gymnasium mentioned in this section of the Clouds, the Academy, would later become the home for Plato's school of philosophy.

13a. *Clouds* 1–18, 25–32, 39–48: Complaint about a Horse-Mad Son

STREPSIADES Oh Lord Zeus, how long the nights are! Endless. Will day never happen? A while ago I heard the rooster, (5) but the slaves keep snoring away. But they wouldn't have before. Damn you, war, for many things, when I can't even punish my slaves. But this fine young man here doesn't wake up before daybreak, but farts away, (10) wrapped in five wool coverlets. Okay, then, let me snore away wrapped up in the covers. But I can't sleep, wretch that I am, being bitten by my expenditures and the costs of hay and debts from this son here. With his long hair, (15) he rides horses and races chariots and dreams about horses, while I am ruined, looking at the close of the month because the interest payment is due.

[19–24 omitted]

(25) PHEIDIPPIDES (in his sleep) Philon, you're cheating. Drive in your own lane.
STREPSIADES This is the evil that's destroying me; he dreams of horses when he is sleeping.
PHEIDIPPIDES How many laps for the war chariots?
STREPSIADES It's me, your father, that you are driving many laps. (30) Now what debt overtakes me after Pasias? Three minas to Amynias for a small racing cart and wheels.

[32–8 omitted]

STREPSIADES Now sleep. But know that all these debts (40) will be on your head. Ah, I wish the matchmaker had suffered a nasty death, the one who urged the marriage with your mother. I had a very happy country life, (45) abounding in bees, sheep, and olive cakes. Then I (a rustic) married the niece of Megacles, the son of Megacles from the city, proud, prone to luxury, and given over to the festivals for Aphrodite [the goddess of love].

13b. *Clouds* 1002–23: Gymnasium Education

BETTER ARGUMENT You shall spend your time in the gymnastic schools, sleek and blooming; not chattering in the marketplace like the youths of the present day; nor be dragged into court on some petty, greedy, pettifogging, ruinous charge; (1005) but going down to the Academy and beneath the sacred olives you shall race, crowned with the white reed, against an upstanding young man of your own age, smelling of bindweed, at leisure, taking pleasure in the spring, when the plane tree whispers to the elm. (1010) If you do the things that I tell you and apply your mind to these, you will always have a buff chest, a clear complexion, broad shoulders, a tiny tongue, well-toned glutes, and a small penis. (1015) If you practice what the youths of the present day do, you will have, in the first place, a hollow chest, a pasty complexion, narrow shoulders, a large tongue, flaccid glutes, and a long decree. (1020) [Worse Argument] will persuade you to consider everything that is base to be honorable, and what is honorable to be base; and in addition to this, he will fill you up with the buggery of Antimachus.

Medical Writing

14. Hippocratic Corpus

About sixty treatises of various types, most of which were written between 430 and 330 BCE, were gathered together in antiquity under the name of Hippocrates of Cos, the fifth-century physician widely regarded as the father of western medicine. Of the tracts extracted here, Aphorisms *is a loose collection of observations about health, exercise, and disease that was clearly the product of accretion over time. The seven books of the* Epidemics *consist of a series of a physician's case notes, recording symptoms, treatment, and progress of a disease.* Regimen *consists mainly of a treatise on diet and exercise, with probably more than one author.* On Fractures *is taken to be authentically by Hippocrates; it is a treatise on types of fractures and dislocations and how to treat them.* Places in Man *is an anatomical and physiological treatise. Greek medicine in the period in which these tracts were written was both competitive and intertwined with various ideas developed in philosophical writings. In general, while Greek medicine has the reputation for beginning scientific or rational thinking about the causes and treatments of disease, it did proceed by a series of intellectual models that were easily distorted. Two of the most important were analogy and polarity, which gave scope for medical writers to dispute what the proper analogy or polarity was in promotion of their own practice. In* On Fractures, *for example, the writer criticizes practitioners who set fractures on the basis of a false analogy, considering that the extended left arm of an archer was the arm's "natural" position.* Aphorisms *and* Regimen *depend on the Heraclitan polarities of warm vs. cold and moist vs. dry bodies, in which health depends on the proper balance between these opposites. Hence, much of the discussion of exercise is taken up with what creates various unhealthy states and how to correct them. Another important characteristic of Hippocratic writings is the correlation of place, weather, and the seasons with various states of health. Unlike Galen, the Hippocratic corpus has relatively little to say about athletic training but is more focused on the interrelationship of gymnastic exercise and health, particularly running and wrestling. The final short passage from* On Nourishment *is widely cited as an indication of the general attitude of doctors to athletes; the sentiment is echoed in Galen (see* **39a**, **39b**).

14a. *Aphorisms* 1.3: The Condition of the Athlete

This is later quoted in Galen's Protrepticus *11 (**39a**).*

For those engaged in gymnastic training, peak condition is dangerous if it has reached its limit. For it is unable to be maintained at the same level and remain at this peak. Because it cannot remain as it is, it can no longer improve. Therefore, it is left to decline. For these reasons it is important to end this peak condition quickly so that the body may again initiate growth, but do not bring the body to a complete loss of good condition for it too is dangerous; rather bring the body to whatever condition it can maintain for the future. In the same way extreme fasting is dangerous, and weight gain taken to extremes is dangerous.

14b. *Aphorisms* 1.5: An Athlete's Consumption of Food

The bowels in winter and spring are naturally hotter, and one sleeps for the longest period of time. In these seasons more food should be given, since the innate heat is great. Thus, there is need for more nourishment. Witness the young and athletes.

14c. *Epidemics* bk. 6.3.18: Herodicus the Trainer

*This is a comment on the practice of Herodicus, who appears to be an athletic trainer (see **22f**). He harms those in his care who have fevers by his insistence on exercise.*

Herodicus killed those with fevers by insisting on running, wrestling, and hot baths. That is bad. Inflammation is hostile to wrestling, walking around, running, and massage.

14d. *Regimen* bk. 1.24: Trainers Corrupt Athletes

The point of this comment seems to be that by teaching athletes how to win by strategy and technique they defeat those who are their social superiors.

Trainers teach how to break the law within the confines of the law, to justly act unjustly, to cheat, to steal, to do the most shameful violent acts in a way that seems most noble.

14e. *Regimen* bk. 2.61–5: Health Benefits of Exercise

I shall now go through exercises and what potential they have. Some are natural and some derive from violence...

(62) **Walking** is very much a more natural exercise than the rest, but it does have something of force about it. The properties of each type of walking are as follows. A walk after dinner dries the abdomen and the body and does not allow the belly to become fat for these reasons: As the man moves, the food and the body grow warm, and the flesh draws out the moisture and does not allow it to accumulate around the belly, so the body is full, but the stomach is thinned. It dries out for these reasons: When the body is moving and warmed up, the thinnest part of the nourishment is consumed, on the one hand, by

the innate heat, on the other, expelled by breathing or by urination. The residue is the driest of the food in the body; as a result the belly and the flesh become dry. Walking at daybreak reduces the body, making parts of the head light, pure, with keen hearing, and relaxes the bowels. Walking reduces the body because, as it moves, the body grows warm and moisture is thinned and purified from the breath, from blowing the nose, and from clearing the throat, thus nourishing the heat of the soul. Walking relaxes the bowel because, while it is warm, cold breath rushes in upon it, and heat yields to cold. It lightens the head for these reasons: Whenever the bowel is emptied, since it is warm, it draws moisture into itself from the rest of the body and from the head. When the head is emptied, sight and hearing are clearer, and the individual becomes alert. Walking after gymnastic exercise purges bodies and makes them thin by not permitting the flesh reduced by exercise to regather but purges it away.

(63) With respect to **running**, that which is not on a double track[17] but long-distance, if increased little by little, concocts and dissipates flesh by warming it; this type of running digests the impact of the food in the body; it makes for slower and thicker bodies than running on circular tracks, but is more beneficial to those who consume a lot of food and more in winter rather than in summer. Those who run in a cloak get the same benefit, but, by heating the body more rapidly, it makes it moister but less tanned, because the body is not purified by the circulation of fresh air, but the exercise takes place in stale air [contained within the cloak]. However, running in a cloak is beneficial for dry bodies and those who carry a lot of flesh and wish to reduce it, and for those who are older, because of the coldness of their bodies. **Running the diaulos** in the open air reduces flesh less but thins the body more, because the exercises, since they are for the inner parts of the soul,[18] draw moisture from the flesh in the opposite direction and thin and dry out the body. **Running the circular course** least reduces flesh, but especially thins and contracts the belly; because the runner employs very rapid breathing, this running is the quickest to draw moisture to itself.

(64) **Swinging the arms** [as an exercise] for those of dry disposition, if with abrupt motions, is harmful. For it creates spasms in this way: When the body is warmed, the skin is a lot thinner and swinging the arms compacts the flesh less than running a circular course but drains the flesh of moisture. **Sparring and relaxing**[19] warm the flesh least, but they stimulate the body and soul and leave one breathless.

Wrestling and a **rubdown** provide exercise more for the body's exterior, but they do warm the flesh and harden it and cause it to grow for this reason: The naturally hard parts of the body are compressed by rubbing, while the hollow parts, like the veins, are increased. Flesh that is warmed and dry draws nourishment to itself through these channels and the flesh is increased. **Wrestling in the dust** accomplishes nearly the same

---

[17] A reference to the *diaulos*, which was a course of a fixed distance.

[18] The text seems to be corrupt.

[19] The meaning of the Greek is not entirely clear. The text seems to proceed from arm swinging while running to arm swinging on its own as a form of exercise or as a preliminary to boxing.

thing as **wrestling**,[20] but it dries the flesh more because of the dust and increases the flesh less. **Hand wrestling**[21] thins and draws the flesh up; **punching bag** and **arm exercises** have nearly the same effect. Holding the breath can force open the passages, thin the skin, and expel moisture from the skin.

(65) **Exercises in dust** differ from those in oil in this way: Dust is cold, oil warm; in the winter oil better promotes growth; in summer oil produces an excess of heat and wastes the flesh away, whenever it is heated by the season and by oil and by exercise. Dust, for exercise in summer, better promotes growth; for by cooling the body, it does not allow it to grow excessively warm. But in winter dust is cold and freezing. To linger in the dust after exercise in summer for a short time helps one to cool off, but for a long time it dries the body out too much and makes it hard and like wood. A rubdown with oil and water softens and does not allow the body to become overheated.

14f. *Regimen* bk. 3.67: Relationship between Food and Exercise

It is impossible to write with such accuracy about individual dietary regimens, as I have said above, as to make the expenditure of effort exactly equal to the intake of food. Many circumstances prevent this. First, men differ in their constitutions. And dry constitutions are more or less dry when compared with themselves or with others. Similarly, with wet constitutions, or any other kind. Then, different ages do not need the same things. Further factors include the lay of the land, the variation in the winds, the changes of the seasons, and the general characteristics of the year. Foods themselves differ in many ways: One type of wheat differs from another, wine from wine, as do other elements of diet, and this inhibits the ability to prescribe accurately. But the diagnoses that I have discovered identify the dominant elements in the body [i.e., whether exercise overwhelms food or food exercise], and how it is necessary to remedy each circumstance [i.e., whether excess of food or exercise], and re-establish health in order to ward off disease, unless someone makes very many and serious mistakes. At this stage drugs are necessary, and there are worse conditions that not even drugs can cure.

14g. *On Fractures* 1–2: Injuries and Athletic Movement

(1) It is necessary for the doctor to make the extensions of dislocations and fractures as straight as possible, as this is the most natural conformation. But if [the injured limb]

---

[20] The distinction is probably between wrestling on the ground and upright wrestling; see Poliakoff (1987: 23–33).

[21] This seems to have been a technique used in wrestling that could be practiced in the gymnasium (as opposed to the *palaestra*). See, e.g., Lucian **38c**.

inclines one way or another, it should turn toward the pronation [i.e., with the palm down], for the mistake is less than with the supination [i.e., palm up]. In fact, those who have no preconceived notions, do not usually make this mistake, for [the injured party] extends his arm for binding this way, as its natural disposition compels.

(2) With respect to our subject, a patient presented his arm to be bandaged with the palm down, but the practitioner compelled him to hold it as archers do when they bring their shoulder forward [i.e., with their elbow extended], and he bandaged it in this position, thinking to himself that this was the arm's natural position. He took as his example that fact that all the bones in the forearm lie parallel to one another and the surface, and thus both interior and exterior are in a straight line. In the same way, he said, this is the natural position for the flesh and the tendons and cited the practice of archery as his witness. In what he said and what he did he seemed to be knowledgeable. But he had ignored all the other arts and the all the things done by strength or artistry, not realizing that the natural disposition differs from one to another and in the same task there may be one natural position for the right arm and another for the left. For there is one natural position for throwing the javelin, another for whirling the sling, again another in throwing stones, another in boxing, and yet another when resting. How many arts could one find in which the natural position of the arms is not the same, but the arms are positioned in accordance with the implement used and the work one wishes to accomplish. For the man practicing archery this position is likely to be the best for one arm: The hinge-like part of the humerus pressed in this position into the socket of the ulna makes a straight line for the bones of the humerus and ulna [upper arm and forearm], as if it were one whole unit. The flexure of the elbow is lost in this position. Therefore, it is reasonable that the elbow, when straight and extended, does not weaken or give way when the bowstring is drawn back by the right hand. In this way he will draw the bowstring back as far as possible and release with the strongest force and frequency. Arrows released from such a position are swift and strong, and they fly far. But reducing fractures and archery have nothing in common. For this reason, if having bound up the arm, he intended to hold it in this position [i.e., extended], he would cause much additional pain, greater than the injury. But if he instructed him to bend the elbow, neither the bones nor the tendons nor the flesh would remain in the same place, but would rearrange themselves in another position, despite the binding. What advantage is there, then, for the archer position? Perhaps our wise practitioner would not have made this mistake if he had let the injured man himself present his arm.

14h. *Places in Man* 35: Contrast of the Athletic Trainer and the Doctor

Gymnastic training and medicine are wholly opposite; for gymnastic training does not need to bring about changes, but medicine does. It does no good for the healthy man to change from his present condition, but only those who are suffering.

14i. *On Nourishment* 34: The Unnatural Physical State of the Athlete

This is later quoted in Galen Protrepticus *10 and 36 (**39a**).*

Nourishment is important for growth and for existence; for existence only, as with the old. In addition, it is for strength. The condition of the athlete is not natural; a healthy condition is better in all men.

Attic Oratory

*References to athletics are found only occasionally in the Attic orators, but they do reveal attitudes toward athletic training and competition in so far as they are relevant to Athenian legal and social practices. Antiphon's paired templates for forensic argument provide valuable insights into the ubiquity of gymnastic activities and their supposed value for the citizen, as well as details of how exercise was conducted (**15a**); Lysias (**16a**) provides incidental information about the cost to citizens of sponsoring certain events and (**16b**) the role of the Olympic Games for collective Greek identity; Pseudo-Andocides (**17a**) and Isocrates (**18a**) take opposite positions on Alcibiades' chariot victory at Olympia in 416;[22] Isocrates (**18b**) likens intellectual, specifically philosophical training to athletic training. This is a common viewpoint found also in Plato (**22b–e**) and Aristotle (**23c**). From Demosthenes (**19a**) and Aeschines (**20a**) we learn about the conduct of the Sacred Month and that those convicted of capital crimes were excluded from attendance at the games. This is significant because exile was the normal punishment for citizens so convicted, but this did not preclude them from living in other city states. They were, however, excluded from communal activities. Pseudo-Demosthenes (**19c**) provides one of the few pieces of information we have about the Athenian contest of the* apobatēs; *in addition, he offers the candid observation that people watched chariot races in the expectation of a crash. Lycurgus (**21a**) may account for the paucity of references to athletes in the Attic orators: He records that they were deemed less worthy of memorials in Athens than in other states.*

15. Antiphon

15a. *Second Tetralogy*: An Accidental Death in the Gymnasium

These models of forensic argument suitable for Athenian courts were written around 450 BCE. They do not come from real trials but provide illustrations of typical types of argument. This set of four includes a speech by a father asking for a verdict against a defendant who is charged with causing the accidental death of his son; a reply by the defendant's father (the defendant is too young to speak for himself); a rebuttal by the accuser; and a rebuttal by the defendant. The imagined circumstances are that a boy exercising in the gymnasium accidently struck another boy with his javelin and killed him. Who is responsible? Arguments are (a) the boy throwing the javelin, (b) the boy who ran in front of it and was struck, or (c) the javelin. What

---

[22] As an activity of the super-rich, chariot racing held an ambiguous position in democratic Athens; see Lysias, 19.63; Lycurgus, *Against Leocrates* 139.

lies behind these models is the fact that in Greek law and in the minds of citizens someone who sheds another's blood (whether by accident or intentionally) brings a stain upon the whole citizen group that must be cleansed, either by exiling the person who has shed blood or by a religious cleansing of the pollution. At stake, then, is who must pay for the pollution. Below are sections from the speeches of the fathers of the two boys that provide insight into practice with the javelin in Athenian gymnasia. The terms used for the victim (pais) *and the defendant* (meirakion) *indicate that the victim was younger than the defendant. Note that javelin practice takes place at the same time as other gymnastic activities, though within a restricted place, and it is not clear if the boy who was struck was part of javelin practice or simply ordered by the trainer to help in collecting the weapons. Plutarch* **35a** *refers to a similar event.*

First speech for the Prosecution (spoken by the father of the dead boy)

(α1–2) If there is agreement about the facts, cases are settled either by laws or by decisions of the Assembly, and these cover every aspect of civic behavior. But whenever a matter is disputed, it is your responsibility, gentlemen of the jury, to give a decision. Now I do not think that the defendant will dispute the facts with me. For in the gymnasium my son was struck on his side by a javelin that this young man had thrown, and my son died instantly. (2) I do not accuse him of deliberately killing my son, but of killing him accidentally—though accidentally he caused me harm no less serious than if it were deliberate. For the boy who is dead he has caused no distress, but for those who are alive; and I ask you to pity the parents in their loss of a child, to grieve for the untimely end of this dead boy, to prohibit his slayer from what the law prohibits him from, and not to overlook the fact that whole city is polluted by him.

Reply to a Charge of Accidental Homicide (spoken by the father of the boy who threw the javelin)

(β1–8) It is now clear to me that misfortunes and necessity compel those who are unused to appearing in court to do so and those who are retiring to speak and act in ways contrary to their nature; if I am not mistaken, I am very far from being or wanting to be the sort [i.e., who rushes to litigation], and I am now compelled by sheer misfortune and against my character to appear as defendant in a case in which I found it hard enough to grasp the exact truth, and it leaves me still more confused when I consider how I should explain it to you. (2) I am compelled by harsh necessity and have thrown myself upon your mercy, gentlemen of the jury. I ask you, if my arguments appear more subtle than those generally presented to you, do not allow the aforementioned circumstances to so prejudice you against my defense that you base your verdict upon what appears to be instead of what is the truth. Now it is in the power of the clever speaker to explain what seems to be true, but truth resides with the man whose behavior is just and upright.

(3) I thought that in educating my son in those pursuits that most benefit the common good both of us would be rewarded; but it turned out to be quite contrary to my expectation.

For the young man, not from insolence or maliciousness, but while at javelin practice in the gymnasium with his age-mates, threw his javelin; but he did not kill anyone, if one considers the truth of the matter. Because the other party made a mistake to his own detriment, my son has accidentally incurred the blame. (4) If the javelin had traveled outside the area appointed for its path and had wounded him, no argument would be left to us to maintain that my son was not a murderer. But the boy ran into the path of the javelin and put his body in its way. My son was prevented from hitting the target, while the boy, who moved into the javelin's path, was struck, casting undeserved blame upon us. (5) The boy was struck by running into the javelin's path, and this young man has been accused unjustly, since he struck no one standing clear of the target. But the boy, seeing as it is clear that he was not struck while standing still, but while of his own volition running into the path of the javelin, it is even clearer that he died through his own fault. For he would not have been struck if he had kept still and not run across.

(6) Since both parties agree that the boy's death was accidental, which of the two was at fault would still more clearly identify the murderer. For those who make a mistake when they decide to do something are the makers of accidental mistakes. And those who voluntarily do something or allow it to be done are responsible for the effects suffered. (7) Now the young man, on his part, was not guilty of error in respect of anyone; in practicing he was not doing what was forbidden but what had been ordered, and he was not among those engaged in gymnastics when he threw the javelin, but in his place among the other throwers; nor did he hit the boy because he missed the target and sent his javelin into the bystanders. But in doing everything correctly, as he intended, he was not the cause of any accident, but the victim of one, in that he was prevented from hitting the target. (8) The boy, on the other hand, who wished to run forward, misjudged the moment when he could have crossed without being hit, with results that he did not expect. He was accidentally guilty of an error that affected his own person and has paid the price for his mistake. We do not rejoice or approve; far from it, we feel both sympathy and sorrow.

Rebuttal by the Father of the Dead Boy

[γ6] At that moment the trainer (*paidotribēs*) who was collecting the javelins of the javelin throwers ordered my son to pick them up, and because of the carelessness of the one who threw it he was felled by this one's warlike weapon; without making any mistake at all, he died miserably. But the young man, failing to note the moment for the taking up of the javelins, was not prevented from missing his mark, but found a target (miserable and bitter for me). He did not kill deliberately, but it is more reasonable to claim that he did kill deliberately than that he did not strike my son or did not kill him.

16. Lysias

16a. *On the Charge of Taking Bribes* (the relevant information in this section is given as a summary)

In order to counter the charge that the defendant (whose name is not recorded) was an upright citizen who would not take bribes, we are told of the numerous public expenses (liturgies) that he had undertaken. One of these in 409–408 BCE was to fund the pyrrhic dancers at the Greater Panathenaea at a cost of 800 drachmas (§1). In 405–404 he spent twelve minas to win a victory in the torch race at the Promethea (§4), and in the following year (404–403) he spent seven minas to fund pyrrhic dancers in the category of "beardless youths" (pyrrichistais ageneiois) at the Lesser Panathenaea (§5).

16b. *Olympic Oration* 1–2: Purpose and Value of Olympic Games

This is a fragment from a speech of Lysias quoted by Dionysius of Halicarnassus (On Lysias 29–30). It was not for a trial, but a display speech (panegyric) apparently delivered at Olympia during the festival of 388 or 384 BCE. Lysias uses the assembly of Greeks from all the city states for a political message; he argues that Dionysius I, the tyrant of Syracuse, should be dethroned and Sicily freed from his tyranny. Dionysius' brother was apparently present at Olympia to compete in the four-horse chariot race (Diod. Sic. Bk. 14.105) and to display the wealth and power of the tyrant. Other speeches at Olympia are attributed to Gorgias in 408 and Isocrates in 380. This speech provides evidence that Olympia and similar athletic events might be used for political expression and that in the minds of Greeks the games facilitated a unified sense of Greek cultural identity. Note that "display of wealth" seems to have been an accepted part of the event.

(1) Gentlemen, in addition to the many other excellent deeds for which it is appropriate to remember Heracles, there is the fact that he was the first to gather people together for this contest, because he was well disposed to Greece. For before this time Greek cities treated one another as strangers. (2) But when he had put an end to tyrants and stopped those engaged in insolent behaviors,[23] he established a contest of bodily strength, rivalry of wealth, and a display of intelligence in the fairest part of Greece, so that we might assemble for the sake of all these things, seeing some [i.e., the athletic contests and displays of wealth], hearing others [i.e., musical performances and speeches]. For he considered that the gathering there would become the beginning of mutual friendship among the Greeks.

---

[23] Myths of Heracles stress that he purged the lands he traveled through of monsters, violent criminals, and arrogant kings, thus paving the way for civilized community. For Heracles and the Olympic Games, see Pindar **2b–c**.

17. Pseudo-Andocides

17a. *Against Alcibiades* 26: Alcibiades' Extravagance

*The speaker is giving an alternative account of Alcibiades' acquisition of a chariot team to race at Olympia (cf. **18a**), in which he posits two kinds of owners of teams: an Athenian citizen (Diomedes) of moderate means, who wants only to glorify the city, and the extravagant and lawless behavior of Alcibiades.*

[Let me explain what happened.] Diomedes came to Olympia with a team of horses, a man of moderate wealth, but he desired out of the wealth he had to win a crown for the city and for his house, thinking that chariot races were decided mostly by chance. Now this man, who was no random entrant but an Athenian citizen, Alcibiades, because of his influence with the overseers of the games at Elis, was able to deprive him of his team and compete with them himself.

17b. *Against Alcibiades* 42: Value of Extravagance

In the conclusion of this speech, Alcibiades, who is speaking, notes his Panathenaic victories. This is one of the few mentions we have of the Euandria *or male beauty contest. (see also **42c**).*

I do not deem it necessary to recall my public services, except that I paid for the required expenses not from public funds, but from my own. And, in fact, I happened to be victorious in the *Euandria*, the Torch Race, and in tragic competition, without striking the rival choral dancers, and without being ashamed if I was less powerful than the laws. Citizens of this sort are much more advantageous if they remain in the city than if they go into exile.

18. Isocrates

18a. *On the Chariot Team* 32–4: Alcibiades at Olympia

*Isocrates is said to have written this speech in defense of the son of Alcibiades, who after his famous father's death was sued by a fellow Athenian (Teisias) on the grounds that the elder Alcibiades had stolen his chariot team. The bulk of the speech is a defense of the lifestyle of the elder Alcibiades, who was, during his lifetime, both a successful general and attacked for his scandalous behavior by his fellow Athenians. His extravagance was epitomized by the fact that he entered no fewer than seven four-horse chariot teams in the Olympiad of 416 BCE, taking first, second, and either third or fourth place. The whole of the speech has not survived, and it is quite possible that it was written for display rather than a proper trial. Thucydides (6.16.2) recounts this episode (see **9g**), as does Plutarch, who in* *his* Life of Alcibiades *11 tells us that Euripides wrote a victory ode for the event (see* **12c**). Demosthenes' Against Meidias *145 praises Alcibiades for his skills as a general, his services to democracy, and his Olympic victories in chariot racing but concludes the section by saying, "but nevertheless your ancestors despite all of his accomplishments did not condone his insulting behavior, but cast him out, making him an exile." The speech, entitled* Against Alcibiades, *is attributed to the orator Andocides, but more likely it was written by one of Alcibiades' political rivals. Alcibiades is accused not only of taking another man's team, but of suborning the Olympic judges.*

(32) Around the same time when he saw that the festival at Olympia was loved and admired by all men, and that the Greeks made a demonstration there of their wealth and strength and training (*paideusis*), and that they envied the athletes and the cities that had become well known because of their victorious athletes, and in addition considering that the public services are undertaken here [i.e., at Athens] by private individuals for the benefit of the citizens, but that in that festival venue they happened on behalf of the city for all of Greece, (33) when he considered these things, and although he was inferior to none in natural talent or strength, he dismissed gymnastic competitions, because he knew that some of the athletes were undistinguished in birth and residents of unimportant city states and poorly educated, (34) he put his hand to breeding horses, which is the work of men of the greatest means and no poor man would undertake it, and he surpassed not only those competing against him but even those who had won previous victories. For the number of teams that he entered in competition exceeded those of the greatest cities, and such was their excellence that they came in first, second, and third. In addition to this, in the sacrifices and in the other expenses pertaining to the festival he behaved so lavishly and generously that the expenses paid out of public funds by all the others were less than the private outlay of that man. And when he had ended his mission, he made the successes of his predecessors seem small in comparison to his own and put an end to those who had won victories in his own time being objects of emulation and left those who would train horse teams in the future no space to surpass him.

18b. *Antidosis* 180–5: Physical and Mental Training

*Isocrates likens physical training to the mental training provided by philosophy. Throughout this passage he uses the word for soul (*psychē*), though it is obvious that he is describing the activities and training of the mind. For similar arguments, see Plato (*22d*).*

(180) People agree that our nature is composed of body and soul, and there is no one who would deny that of these two the soul comes first and is more valuable, for it is the function of the soul to make decisions on both private and public matters, and of the body to be servant to the soul's judgments. (181) Since this is so, some of those men long before our times, seeing that many arts had been devised for other things, while no such thing

had been ordained for the body and the soul, invented and left to us two disciplines, physical training for the body, of which gymnastics is a part, and, for the soul, philosophy, which I am going to explain. (182) These are opposed and yoked and complementary to each other. By means of these arts, those mastering them make their minds more intelligent and their bodies more functional, not by separating sharply these educational modes, but by using similar methods of instruction, exercise, and other forms of discipline. (183) Whenever they take on pupils, the physical trainers teach them the techniques that have been developed for competition, while the teachers of philosophy take their pupils through all the concepts that rational discourse makes use of. (184) Then, having made them familiar and thoroughly skilled at these lessons, they give them practice in these matters, accustom them to work hard, and compel them to combine the individual elements that they have learned in order that they may have a firmer grasp of these insights and come into closer touch with the occasions for their application. But in our knowledge of these things complete comprehension is impossible, since the ability to know all cases eludes us. Yet those who most apply themselves and are capable of grasping what happens will most often meet these occasions in the right way. (185) By caring for and educating their pupils in this way, they are able to bring them to the point where they become better and are stronger, both in their minds and in the condition of their bodies. But neither of these teachers [i.e., of rhetoric and of athletics] happens to have the knowledge by which they can make capable athletes or capable orators out of whomever they please. They can bring about partial results but with respect to the entire package, the powers themselves come to maturity in those who excel by virtue both of nature and of training.

18c. *Panegyricus* 1–2: Model of Athletic Competitions for Greek Unity

This speech was written about 380 BCE and is intended to recall Athens to her former glory when the city's political fortune was at a low point after having lost the Peloponnesian War to Sparta and her allies. Isocrates' advice to Athens is to make common cause with former enemies in the face of an increased threat from the Persian Empire. The importance of athletic competition for Isocrates is the way in which it can serve as a model to unite Greeks. In this first passage he comments on the public attention given to athletes in contrast to the neglect of individuals who might benefit the state through their wisdom.

(1) I have often wondered at those who convened festival assemblies and established athletic contests on the grounds that they deemed the excellence of bodies worthy of great rewards, but to those who labor privately for the common good and prepare their own souls so that they can be of help to others, they grant no honor at all. (2) It is reasonable to have a provision for the latter rather than athletes, for if athletes were to acquire as much as twice their strength there would be no greater benefit to others,

but if one man should become wise, all men would enjoy the benefit of his wisdom, if they care to.

18d. *Panegyricus* 43–4: Truces for Festival Games

(43) The founders of our festivals are justly praised because they gave us such an important custom, namely, that when a truce is proclaimed with one another and having set aside existing hostilities we come together into the same place and after making common prayers and sacrifices recall the common kinship that exists between us, and are better disposed toward each other for the future, renewing old guest friendships and forging new ones. (44) Neither for the average man nor for those nobler souls is the time spent idle, but this gathering of Greeks enables some to demonstrate the excellence of their bodies and others to watch them contend against each other, and no one is apathetic. But each has something in which to take pride: When the spectators see the athletes laboring for their sake and the athletes consider that all men have come to watch them. Seeing as the good that accrues to us from this gathering is so great, our city [i.e., Athens] has not been left behind [in the establishment of festivals and spectacles].

18e. *Letter to Antipater* 10–11: Desire for Victory

This excerpt is from a letter written by Isocrates to introduce Diodotus and his son to Antipater, the regent of Macedon, around 340–339 BCE. It reveals the distance between those who compete successfully for athletic crowns and the average citizen. For similar sentiments, see Isocrates, Panegyricus *1–21 and Letter 8.5 to the Rulers of Mytilene.*

I have persuaded Diodotus' son also to take an interest in your affairs and to give himself over to you as a pupil to try to advance himself. When I urged him to this, he said that he was eager for your friendship but that he had nearly the same experience in this as in athletic crowns. He would like to win them but did not dare to enter contests because he did not possess the strength capable of attaining crowns.

19. Demosthenes

19a. *On the Crown* 319.9: The Athlete Philammon

Demosthenes argues that he should be compared not to past but only to contemporary orators. As an analogy, he provides the parallel of a contemporary athlete (Philammon).

Philammon did not leave Olympia without a crown because he was weaker than Glaucus of Carystus or other famous athletes of the past, but because he competed best against those entered against him, he was crowned and proclaimed victor.

19b. *On the False Embassy,* Hypothesis 335: On Thieves at Games

This account provides information about the observation of the Sacred Month during which access to the games was allowed even through territories of states at war. Philip II of Macedon was at war with the Athenians when this event occurred. The details are slightly different in Aeschines' speech on the same topic (see **20a***).*

An Athenian named Phrynon, upon setting out for Olympia, either as a contestant or a spectator, was overpowered by some soldiers of Philip during the Sacred Month (*hieromēnia*) and stripped of his possessions. When he came to Athens, he urged the Athenians to vote for him to be an ambassador, so that by going to Philip he might recover what was taken from him. He persuaded the Athenians to make him an ambassador with Ctesiphon. And when they went to Macedon, Philip received them in a friendly fashion, and returned to him everything that was taken by the soldiers and gave him many things from his own wealth. He claimed in defense that his soldiers were unaware that it was the Sacred Month.

19c. *Against Aristocrates* 40–1: Exclusion of Murderers from Games

This is from a law cited during the trial speech that lists the places from which murderers are excluded.

[They are excluded] also from athletic contests. Why is this? Because the athletic contests in Greece are common to all men. Because all men have a stake in them, the victim also had a stake. And, therefore, the murderer must be excluded from them.

19d. *Against Neaira* 33: Victory Celebration in a Temple

This brief comment provides information about acquiring teams and about celebrating victories when returning to one's city.

When, in the archonship of Socratidas (373 BCE), he won a victory at the Pythian Games with the four-horse chariot that he bought from the sons of Mityus, the Argive, he came to celebrate his victory feast at the temple of Athena Colias.

19e. **Demosthenes (?)**, *Erotic Essay* 22–9: On the *Apobatēs* Race

This essay was attributed to, though almost certainly not written by Demosthenes. It is an encomiastic display piece that praises the virtues of a young man, who is the beloved (erōmenos) of the writer. It is later than a similar erotic speech embedded in Plato's Phaedrus *that was supposedly by Lysias, as well as the erotic speech attributed to Xenophon. The argument that precedes this passage praises the young man's physical attractiveness and moral excellence, before turning to his success in the* apobatēs, *as an example of his courage and good judgment. The* apobatēs *required two contestants: one to drive the chariot, the other to dismount from the moving chariot while holding his shield and then run a race the length of a* stadion. *It was a competition known from the Athenian Panathenaea, images of which occur on the Parthenon frieze. Competition was apparently by tribe, which automatically restricted the agonists to citizen status. This young man was apparently the charioteer. Note the negative comments about other events (see* Appendix C IV*).*

(22) A person might come [to praise] your courage on many other grounds, but especially for your training, of which there have been many witnesses. It is necessary, perhaps, to say at first, that you chose this competition well. For when young, to make the correct choice of what should be done is a common sign of a good nature and sound judgment. (23) For each of these reasons it is not good to omit praise of your choice. Since you were conscious of the fact that slaves and non-citizens took part in other athletic events, but that the option for the dismounting event was only extended to citizens, and that the best men were eager for it, you put your energy into this contest. (24) And further reckoning that those who trained for foot races added nothing to their courage or their well-being, and those training for boxing destroy their minds in addition to their bodies, you have chosen the noblest and best of competitive events and one especially suited to your own nature. From the habit of its weapons [presumably the shield] and the effort of the running it is similar to what happens in warfare, and in the majesty and importance of the equipage [i.e., the chariot] resembles the power of the gods. (25) In addition to this it holds the most pleasurable spectacle, encompassing the greatest number and variety [i.e., of spectators], and is worthy of the greatest prizes. Apart from providing these advantages, the training and practicing of such an event will appear as no small achievement for those who strived even modestly for excellence. One might make the poetry of Homer best witness for this, in which he has made both the Greeks and barbarians war against each other with such equipment. And even now it is customary not in the meanest, but the greatest of the Greek cities to use it in their contests. (26) Your choice [of event] is in this way excellent and admired by all men. Thinking that it is not good to desire the things most worthy of attention, nor for one's body to be naturally good at everything if one's soul is not prepared for ambition, you immediately displayed industry in the gymnasium; and you did not fail in the actual contests, but you especially demonstrated every distinction of your natural ability and the courage of your soul in the games. (27) I hesitate to begin to speak about these things, in case words fail me in giving an account of what took place, but I shall not omit it, for it is shameful to refuse to report what is

enthralling for us, the spectators. If I were to give an account of all of your competitions, the length of my essay would perhaps be excessive, but one, in which you especially excelled, I shall explain as a typical example and thus shall engage the capacity of my listeners more reasonably. (28) When the teams had been released, some rushed ahead, others were being reined in, but you surpassed both, one after the other, as is fitting, and grasped the victory, winning such a fine crown in a manner that, although the victory was fine, that you were safe seemed to be a better and more surprising thing. For when the opponents' chariot was coming straight at you, and everyone thought that the impetus of your horses was unstoppable, seeing that some opponents—although there was no present danger—became very anxious for themselves, you did not become confused or lose your nerve, but by your courage you got control of your rushing team and by your speed passed those contenders who had not suffered such ill luck. (29) Even more you so changed men's minds that, although the many say that nothing in equestrian contests furnishes a more pleasurable spectacle than a crash, and they appear to speak the truth, in your case all the spectators feared the opposite, that some accident should happen to you. Such was the goodwill and the eagerness that your spirit instilled in them.

20. Aeschines

20a. *Against Timarchus* 9–11: Laws Regulating the Gymnasium

The charge against Timarchus, an Athenian citizen, is that he prostituted himself. If it were proven, he would have been disenfranchised and banned from political life, which was Aeschines' goal in bringing the suit. Earlier Timarchus along with Demosthenes had indicted Aeschines for treason. The passages describe the rules that govern teachers and gymnastic trainers with respect to boys. These two passages provide insight into Athenian governance of gymnasia. See also I15g.

[The law] prescribes, first, the hour at which it is fitting for a freeborn boy (*pais*) to go to the schoolroom, then how many boys may enter with him, and when he should leave. It forbids the teachers to open the schoolrooms and the *paidotribai* to open the palaestra before sunrise and orders that they close before sunset, because it has serious concerns about them being alone with a boy or being with him after dark. With respect to the young men (*neaniskoi*) who are admitted, it prescribes who they should be and what their ages are and the official who will be overseeing them and for the oversight of their slave attendants (*paidagōgoi*). It regulates the festivals of the Muses in the schoolrooms and the festivals of Hermes in the palaestras, and finally the companionship that the boys may have and their cyclic dances. It orders that the man who is going to serve as a choral director, spending his own money on your behalf, be above forty years of age when he undertakes the directorship (*chorēgia*), so that he has come to the soberest age of his life when he encounters your sons.

20b. *Against Timarchus* 138: Prohibition against Slaves Exercising in Gymnasia

When our forefathers were setting up the laws to regulate our conduct and those things that necessarily result from our being human, actions that were allowed to freeborn men slaves were prohibited from doing. "A slave," the law says, "may not exercise in the gymnasium or anoint himself in the palaestra." *(See also **10n**. 3–4.)*

20c. *On the Embassy* 12–13: On the Olympic Truce

Not much later Phrynon the Rhamnousian was captured by pirates during the Olympic truce, as he himself alleged. But when he had been ransomed and returned here, he asked you to appoint him as an ambassador to Philip, so that, if possible, he might get back his ransom. *(see **19b**)*

21. Lycurgus

21a. *Against Leocrates* 51: No Victor Statues in Athens

This passage confirms the widespread habit of erecting statues to victorious athletes within the public spaces of Greek cities.

You, Athenians, alone of the Greeks know how to honor brave men. You will find statues erected of athletes in the marketplaces of other cities, but in yours you will find statues of brave generals and those who killed tyrants. It is not easy to find even a few men like these in the whole of Greece, but [statues of] those who have been victorious at crown games are from everywhere and easy to see.

Philosophy

*As a mode of discourse and genre of literature, philosophy in ancient Greece displays an interesting relationship to athletics. Although philosophy is generally assumed to be in opposition to athletics, that assumption is often a function of a broader historical discourse on mind–body (psychē–sōma) dualism. And philosophy itself in Greece is largely understood as one of the main sources for mind–body dualism. However, the philosophic criticism of athletics can be seen already in the Archaic period with the work of Xenophanes (see **5**). As the passages in this section make clear, however, Classical philosophy and athletics are often discussed not just in contrastive ways but also as* *complements. In large part this overlap between philosophy and athletics in the Classical era may be a function of a common background in the history and practices of ancient education* (paideia).

22. Plato

Plato was a citizen of Athens of high status who lived from the 420s BCE *until 347/346* BCE. *He was a student of Socrates, and his works focus on the life and teachings of Socrates represented through dialogues, although it is debated how many of the views expressed in those dialogues are truly those of Socrates and not Plato's own. We see reference to athletics in substantial ways throughout the Platonic corpus. In large part, philosophical practice is often presented in Plato in analogy with athletics. At the same time, Plato himself might have had a background in athletic practice and competition. According to Diogenes Laertius* (Lives of the Eminent Philosophers, *bk. 3.4) Plato is a nickname meaning "wide," referring to his physical frame, and he received this name from his wrestling coach. Plato was also said to have competed in wrestling at the Isthmian Games. Although a wrestler turned philosopher seems unlikely in the modern era, we should recall that athletics was a core aspect of the education of all Athenian citizens, and so some athletic background is to be expected. Plato would eventually establish his own school of philosophy in the Academy, one of the oldest and best-known gymnasia in Athens.*

22a. *Apology* 36b–37e: Socrates' Proposed Punishment

Plato's Apology *narrates the defense of Socrates in a trial in which he was accused of corrupting the youth of Athens and not believing in the gods of the city. The punishment proposed for Socrates was death, but he was allowed to offer a counterproposal. Normally, the convicted individual proposed the alternative of exile or some other less severe punishment. Instead, Socrates proposes that he should receive free meals for life or* sitēsis *in the* prytaneion *in Athens as his "punishment"—a reward that was often reserved for Olympic victors. Needless to say, Socrates' counterproposal was not accepted, and he was put to death c.399* BCE.

(36b) And so, the man proposes for me the punishment of death. Well then, Athenian men, what shall I offer as a worthy counterproposal to you? What is it that I ought to suffer or pay, since, because I did not keep quiet in my life, I neglected what the many care for—money, household management, military positions, public speaking, other offices— nor did I care for conspiracies and factions in the city? In fact, I believed myself to be (36c) more reasonable than to try and save myself through such activities. And I avoided going into those affairs which were going to be of no use to me or to you. Instead, I went to each citizen individually to perform the greatest good, as I said before. I tried to persuade each of you citizens not to care for his own possessions but to care for himself alone and to consider how he might be best and most thoughtful. I also tried to persuade you to not care for the affairs of the city, but to care for the city itself, and to care for other matters in a similar fashion. (36d) Being such a sort of man, what, then, do I deserve to suffer? Men of Athens, if it is necessary to propose a worthy punishment, it would have to be something good. One that is most fitting for me especially. What then is fitting for a poor man who confers gifts and requires leisure in order to offer you advice? Men of Athens, there is nothing more fitting than this, that such a man be given free meals (*sitēsis*) in the *prytaneion*. This reward is much more fitting for me than for any of you who won with a pair of horses or the four-horse chariot at the Olympics. For that man makes it so that you think you are happy (*eudaimōn*), but I make it so that you are actually happy. The Olympic victor has no need of nourishment, but I need it. (36e) So if it is necessary that I propose a just and worthy punishment, I propose this: (37a) free meals in the *prytaneion*.

22b. *Crito* 47a–47d: Expert Knowledge

*This dialogue takes place between Socrates and Crito in Socrates' prison cell after his trial. Crito has made arrangements for Socrates to escape into exile, but Socrates refuses and a conversation about justice (*dikaiosynē*) ensues. In this section, Socrates compares the knowledge of the many (*hoi polloi*) with the knowledge of single individuals or experts. Comparison between knowledge of the body and knowledge of the mind and ethics is frequent in the Platonic corpus. Socrates specifically invokes two types of professionals who have knowledge of the body, the doctor and the trainer.*

(47a) SOCRATES Come then, how did we reason about these things? The one who partakes in physical training (*gymnazein*) and (47b) makes this his business, does he pay attention to the praise, blame, and opinion of every man or only to the one who happens to be a doctor or trainer (*paidotribēs*)?

CRITO To the one only.

SOCRATES And so it is necessary to fear the blame and welcome the praise of the one man but not of the many?

CRITO Clearly.

SOCRATES And so he must act, exercise, eat and drink in the manner that seems best to the one who has knowledge and perception rather than to all the others.

CRITO That is the case.

SOCRATES (47c) Well then, if he disobeys and dishonors the opinion and praises of the one, and he honors those of the many who know nothing, will he suffer evil?

CRITO How would he not?

SOCRATES What is this evil? In what direction does it tend and upon what parts of the one who disobeys?

CRITO Clearly upon the body. For that is what is ruined.

SOCRATES Well said. And so with other matters, not to go over all of them, but especially concerning that which is just and unjust, shameful and beautiful, good and bad, concerning those things which we are considering, does it seem best to follow and fear the opinion of the many or of the one, if there is someone in the know, (47d) whom we ought to fear and respect more than the rest? And if we do not follow him, we will destroy and mistreat that which was made better by justice and destroyed by injustice. Or is this not the case?

CRITO I think it is, Socrates.

22c. *Theaetetus* 169a–169c: Training and Socrates' Agonistic Method

Plato's Theaetetus *is a dialogue in which Socrates converses with the boy Theaetetus and his mathematics teacher Theodorus. The dialogue deals primarily with the nature of knowledge and how it is acquired. In this episode, Theodorus compares Socrates' method of dialogue and argument to wrestling. Theodorus contrasts Socrates relentlessness with the saying of the Spartans that apparently was inscribed above their gymnasia: "Strip or Go Away." Reference is also made to Sciron and Antaeus. Sciron was a mythical bandit who forced passersby to wash his feet and then kicked them into the sea. For Antaeus, see* **22g** *(n. 24). The point of comparison is Socrates' habit of accosting people and relentlessly dragging them into an argument.*

(169a) THEODORUS Socrates, it is not easy to sit beside you and not make an argument, and I was just now speaking foolishly when I said that you would not turn to me and not compel me to strip down, (169b) like the Spartans. You are more like Sciron. For the Spartans command that one strip down or leave, but you seem to play the role of Antaeus. For you do not allow anyone to pass by until you force them to strip down and wrestle with your arguments.

SOCRATES Theodorus, you have made an excellent comparison for my disease, although I am more stubborn than they are. For already a thousand Heracles and Theseus types, strong in argument have labored well, but I do not let up at all, (169c) so terrible is my desire for exercise (*gymnasia*) concerning these matters. So do not hold back from testing yourself and giving me pleasure at the same time.

22d. *Gorgias* 464b–465d: *Technē* of Body and Soul

In Plato's Gorgias, Socrates engages in a dialogue with several figures, including another famous intellectual or "sophist," Gorgias from Leontini in Sicily, a figure who was well known for his rhetorical performances. The dialogue is primarily an attempt to define that particular form of knowledge or expertise (technē) known as rhetoric. In this section, Socrates compares the expertise of rhetoric and its relationship to the mind or soul (psychē) with two forms of expertise related to the body, both medicine and physical training (gymnastikē).

SOCRATES Come then. If I am able, I will show more clearly what I mean. I say there are two forms of expertise (*technai*) with two forms of practice (*pragmata*). I call the one pertinent to the soul politics, but the one pertinent to the body I am not able to name so easily, since there is not one treatment (*therapeia*) of the body, but I say there are two parts—one is called physical training (*gymnastikē*) and the other is medicine (*iatrikē*). With regard to politics, I place legislation in place of physical training and justice in place of medicine.

(464c) In each of these pairs—medicine and physical training, justice and legislation—there is some commonality between them, since each pair is concerned with the same topic. Nevertheless, there are also differences between them. Flattery itself does not partake in these four, which take the best care possible for the body and soul, because it acts not through genuine knowledge but through supposition, and it divides itself into four parts, and then enters into each of the four proper parts, pretending to be what it has entered into and thinking nothing of what is best. (464d) But for the sake of what is most pleasing, it seeks out folly and deceives so that it seems worthy of what is best. Cooking makes its way into medicine and pretends to know the best foods for the body. Thus, if a doctor and a cook had to contend before boys, or before men as mindless as boys, contending as to which knows about useful and harmful foods, I suppose the doctor would starve to death. (465a) But I call it flattery, and I say that sort of thing is shameful, Polus—and I say this to you—that it aims at pleasure without considering what is best. And I assert that it is not expertise (*technē*) but a form of experience (*empeiria*), because it cannot provide an account of that to which it applies and what sort of thing it is in nature, so that it is unable to give an account of each cause. And I do not call an expertise that which is an irrational practice. And if you disagree about these matters, I would like to provide my reasons. (465b) And as I was saying, cooking is a form of flattery for medicine, and cosmetics is the same for physical training; it works evil and is deceptive and ignoble and unfree; with its forms and colors, polish and dress it deceives so as to make a strange type of beauty for those who pursue it to the neglect of proper physical training. In order that I not speak too much about it, I wish to explain it to you like a geometer—perhaps you could follow that. (465c) Cosmetics is to physical training as sophistry is to legislation, and cooking is to medicine just as rhetoric is to justice. Although, as I say, there is a distinction between them by nature, sophists and rhetoricians are mixed and grouped under the same category, and neither can they say what they proclaim to each other nor can other men tell them what they mean. (465d) For if the soul were not in control of the body, but the body was in control of itself, and cookery and medicine were not observed and distinguished by the soul, but the body itself made distinctions based on the pleasures provided to it, this is much what Anaxagoras described—for you have experience of these things—all things would be mixed together, without a distinction between medicine, health, and cooking.

22e. *Hippias Minor* 363c–364a: The Intellectual as Athlete in Olympia

*This dialogue takes place between the figure of Socrates and the intellectual Hippias, who is from the city of Elis. The dialogue's central question concerns the nature and ethics of lying. In this passage, Hippias describes how he would attend the festival at Olympia in order to display his intelligence through public performance. Socrates in turn compares him to the athletes who competed officially in the Olympic Games. Although public debates were not a part of the official program in the ancient Olympic Games, this passage shows how the Olympics operated nevertheless as a place for display of both physical and intellectual prowess. Hippias is credited with constructing the Olympic victor lists (see **35h** and Appendix B II).*

(363c) EUDICUS It is clear that Hippias will not begrudge you, if you ask him something. Hippias, if Socrates asks you something, will you answer? What do you think?

HIPPIAS Eudicus, for me, who always go from my home in Elis to Olympia for the meeting of the Greeks, and (363d) present myself in the sacred precinct to speak on whatever one wishes, on whatever has been prepared by me for demonstration, and to answer anyone who wishes to ask a question, it would be strange if now I were to avoid Socrates' questioning.

(364a) SOCRATES Hippias, you have experienced blessedness, if you arrive in the sacred precinct with so much hope about your soul (*psychē*) and your wisdom (*sophia*) at each Olympiad. And I would be amazed if any of the athletes were so confident and had so much trust in their bodies when they contend for prizes, as you say you do about your intellect.

HIPPIAS I have indeed experienced this. From the time when I began competing at Olympia, I have come across no one stronger than me.

22f. *Republic*, bk. 3, 406a–407b: Care of the Body

*The care of the self and its relationship to care of the body is a theme that runs throughout Plato's works. In this passage, Plato takes up the topic of the relationship between athletics and medicine with regard to excessive attention paid to the body. This same topic will be taken up by Aristotle (**23a**) and Galen (**39a**, **39b**). Socrates is the main speaker; his companion is Glaucon, Plato's older brother, who functions as a sounding board for Socrates' ideas.*

(406a) "[Keep in mind that] before the time of Asclepiades, they did not employ the current medical practice which is 'an education" (*paidagōgikē*) of diseases, until the time of Herodicus. For Herodicus was a trainer (*paidotribēs*) and when he became sick, combined physical training (*gymnastikē*) with medicine. First, he thoroughly exhausted himself, [406b] and then afterward he did the same to others."

"How so?" he said.

"By making death a long process for himself. For he followed the course of his fatal disease closely, and he was not able to cure himself, but he lived his life treating all his maladies without any spare time, and he went about wearing himself out with a strict regimen, and because of his wisdom he arrived at old age and died a difficult death."

"He achieved a beautiful prize for his expertise."

[406c] "It is an appropriate one," I said, "for a man who did not know that Asclepius did not reveal it to his lineage because of inexperience or a lack of knowledge, but he knew that for all well-governed people in a city a certain work is assigned, and that it was necessary to work, and that one could not wear out one's life in leisure treating oneself with medicine. And we observe this quite humorously in the case of craftsmen, but we do not see this with the wealthy and fortunate."

"How so?" he said.

[406d] "A carpenter," I said, "when he is ill, would expect to get rid of the disease by taking a drug from a doctor or he would get rid of it through purging or cautery or by the knife. But if someone prescribed a lengthy regimen, by covering his head in bandages and things that follow from this, the carpenter would quickly say, 'I do not have the leisure to be sick nor to live with such expense, totally preoccupied with the disease,' and he would not care for the existing treatment. And after this [406e] he would say good-bye to such a doctor, and he would embark upon a strict regimen and would become healthy in his lifestyle while attending to his affairs. Or if his body is not sufficient to endure, in dying he is released from his activities."

"For such a man," he said, "this seems to be a fitting use of medicine."

[407a] And I said, "Is that the case because there was work for him, and if he did not do it, there would be no benefit in living?"

"That is clear," he said.

"But the rich man does not have such a task before him, which would make life unlivable if he was forced to abstain from it."

"None comes to mind."

I said, "Have you not heard of the saying of Phocylides, 'When a man has livelihood, then he is to practice excellence (*aretēn askein*).'"

"He should do so beforehand as well I think."

"Let us not fight about this but let us instruct ourselves on what a rich man should care about and what makes life unlivable if he does not care about it. [407b] Or perhaps we should consider that while the nursing of disease is a hindrance to carpentry and the other arts, which require attention, it is not a hindrance to the saying of Phocylides."

"Yes, by Zeus," he said. "The excessive care of the body which goes beyond basic physical training is the greatest hindrance of all. For it is a problem in household affairs, the military, and in civic positions in the city."

"And most of all, it is a hindrance to learning of any sort, and thoughtfulness and makes care of oneself difficult, causing one to always anticipate headaches and blaming philosophy for their cause. So that whenever this 'excellence' is pondered and practiced, in every way it is a hindrance. For it makes you think you are suffering and never stop from suffering with respect to your body."

22g. *Republic* bk. 5, 451d–457b (with omissions): Athletic Training for Women

Socrates has just outlined the kind of education and training he thinks necessary for those who are to be guardians of his ideal city, arguing that women as well as men should fulfill this function. He then turns to the question of the education and the role of women, using analogies to make his points. Socrates is speaking to Glaucon as in **22f**. *For similar ideas, see* **10c–d**.

"Do we think that female guard dogs should guard with the males and hunt with them and do everything in common with them or do we think the females should stay indoors on the grounds that they are incapacitated by the bearing and the rearing of puppies, while the males work to take care of the flock?"

[451e] "They have all things in common," he replied, "except that we treat the females as weaker and the males as stronger."

"Is it possible, then," I said, "to employ different animals for the same purpose if you do not give them the same nurture and education?"

"It is not possible."

"If, then, we are to put the women to the same tasks as the men, they must be taught the same things."

"Yes."

"Now musical and gymnastic training was given to the men."

"Yes."

"Then these two forms of expertise (*technai*) and what pertains to warfare must be taught to women and practiced in the same way."

"What you say is reasonable."

"Perhaps," I said, "much of what we have now said is contrary to custom and would seem laughable if it is carried out as suggested."

"Yes, indeed," he said.

"What then," said I, "is the most laughable thing you see in them? Is it not clearly women exercising naked in the *palaestra* (452b) together with the men, not only the young, but even the older, like old men in gymnasia, when, wrinkled and unattractive to look at, they cling to exercising naked?"

"By god," he replied, "it would seem ridiculous in the present circumstances."

"Then," said I, "since we have determined to speak, we must not fear the mockery of the clever, namely, the sort of things they would say, if such a change happened, about gymnastics (452c) and music, and not least about the wearing of armor and the riding of horses."

"You are right," he said.

"But since we have begun to speak, we must pass to the rough part of our law, after asking these not to mind their own business but to be serious, and reminding them that it is not long since Greeks thought it shameful and laughable, as do most of the barbarians now, for men to be seen naked. And when first the Cretans (452d) and then the Spartans began athletic training, it gave license to the sophisticated of that time to mock these practices, don't you think?"

"I do."

"But when, I suppose, it seemed better to those engaged in athletics to strip than to cover everything up, then what seemed ridiculous to the eye disappeared before the revelation of what was best through reason, and this showed that he who deems anything other than wrongdoing to be laughable and who tries to raise a laugh when looking to any other spectacle than (452e) that of folly and wrongdoing or who takes seriously any other mark of the beautiful than the good is speaking in vain."

[In the omitted section Socrates argues that in order to make the case that women are capable of sharing with males some, if not all types of work, he and Glaucon need to consider the objections others would make to this proposition. After dispensing with these objections by logical argument, he concludes as follows.]

(454d) "Now" I said, "with respect to the male and the female sex, if it seems that they have distinct qualifications for one or another art (*technē*), we shall say that they ought to be assigned respectively to each. But if it seems that they differ only in this, that the female bears (454e) and the male begets children, we shall say that there is no proof that the woman differs from the man for what we are arguing, but we shall continue to think that our guardians and their wives ought to follow the same pursuits."

"And rightly," he said.

"Then, next should we require our opponent tell us (455a) for what practice relevant to the conduct of a state the nature of a woman differs from that of a man?"

"That is fair, surely."

[455b omitted]

(455c) "Do you know, then, of any pursuit of mankind in which the male sex does not surpass the female in every respect? Or shall we string this out by mentioning weaving and the management of sacrificial cakes (455d) and boiled vegetables, at which the female sex seems best and in which their being bested would be most absurd?"

"You are right," he said, "that the one sex far surpasses the other in everything, so to speak. Many women, it is true, are better than many men in many things, but broadly speaking, it is as you say. Then there is no task allotted to the administrators of a state that belongs to a woman because she is a woman or to a man because he is a man. But the natural capacities are distributed alike between both creatures, and women naturally share in all pursuits and men in all, [455e] except that for all the woman is weaker than the man."

"True."

"Shall we, then, assign all tasks to men and nothing to women?"

"How could we?"

"Rather, I suppose, it is the case that one woman is naturally suited to be a physician and another not, and one is naturally musical, and another unmusical?"

"Surely."

"And that one woman is naturally athletic (456a) and warlike and another unwarlike and dislikes gymnastics?"

"True."

"And what about this, that one is a lover, another a hater, of wisdom? And one high-spirited, and another lacks spirit?"

"That also is true."

"Then it is likewise true that one woman has the qualities of a guardian and another not. Did we not choose men as guardians on the basis of their natural qualities?"

"Yes."

"Women and men, then, have the same natural propensities for guardianship of the state, except that the one is weaker, the other stronger."

"That's apparent."

(456b) "Women of this sort, then, must be selected to live with men of this sort and to serve with them as guardians, since they are capable and kin to them by nature."

"True."

"And should not the same tasks be assigned to those with the same natures?"

"Yes."

"We return, then, to our previous formulation and agree that it is not unnatural to assign music and gymnastics to the wives of the guardians."

"A ridiculous question," he said. (456e)

"I know," I said; "and are these not the best of all the citizens?"

"By far."

"And will these women not be the best of all the women?"

"Yes, by far."

"Is there anything better for a state than that its women and men are the best that is possible?"

"There is not."

"And music and gymnastics (457a), as we outlined, if applied, will accomplish this?"

"Surely."

"Then, we have proposed what is not only possible but the best legal usage for the state."

"That is so."

"The wives of the guardians, then, must remove their clothing when they exercise, since they will be clothed with virtue as their garment, and must share with the men in war and the other duties related to guarding the city and have no other occupation. But in these same duties lighter tasks must be given to women than to men (457b), because their sex is naturally weaker. But the man who ridicules naked women exercising their bodies for the best reason 'plucks the fruit of unripe wisdom' and does not know, it appears, why he is laughing or what he is doing. For the fairest thing said or that will be said is this, that 'the beneficial is fair and the harmful shameful.'"

22h. *Laws* bk. 7, 795d–796b: Physical Education for Youth

Plato's Laws *is generally acknowledged to be the latest of his works. It provides a very detailed account of how an ideal state should function. The setting is Crete, where three men converse: an Athenian Stranger, a Spartan citizen named Megillus, and the Cretan Clinias, who has been given the responsibility of making laws* (nomoi) *for a Cretan colony called Magnetes. The dialogue primarily concerns what laws will be made for this colony, and some important information is provided on education and athletics. Although the conversation concerns idealized laws and customs, the discussion may not differ too greatly from traditional practices.*

(795d) It would be most useful to divide the education [of boys and girls in the city] into two parts—the one relates to physical training (*gymnastikē*) of the body, and the other is music for the sake of goodness of the soul. Physical training may be divided into two parts—dancing and wrestling. (795e) In dancing, there is one type for those who imitate the language of the Muses, which preserves magnificence and freedom, but the other is used for the sake of good condition, lightness, and beauty, and it is fitting for bending and extending the limbs and parts of the body. It also gives balanced movement (*eurythmou kinēseōs*), which accompanies the whole of dance and is part of it. (796a) And the aspects of wrestling which Antaeus or Ceryon introduced through their techniques for the sake of a useless ambition (*philonikia*), those are not worth praising.[24] But those aspects of the proper form of wrestling, with the releasing of neck, hands, and sides, when practiced with both ambition and poise for the sake of health together with well-maintained strength, those are entirely useful and must not be omitted. Instead, they should be set forth for students and teachers whenever we come to that part of our

---

[24] Antaeus and Cercyon belonged to the mythic traditions of wrestling. Antaeus was the son of Poseidon and Gaia. He was said to have challenged all passersby to a wrestling match and, ultimately, he killed them. As long as he was in touch with the earth, he was invincible. Heracles encountered Antaeus on the way to the garden of the Hesperides and defeated him by lifting him off the ground and squeezing him to death. Cercyon was a mythic king of Eleusis and challenged passersby to a wrestling match to the death. Just as Antaeus was killed by Heracles, so Cercyon was killed by Theseus, as part of his own labors in imitation of Heracles. Antaeus and Cercyon were known for brute strength in opposition to skill, on which, see **22c** and Pausanias 1.39.3, **37aa.**

laws. (796b) The teachers are to give all these things generously, and the students are to receive them gratefully.

22i. *Laws* bk. 7, 813d–814b: Athletic Training for Women

In this passage, the speaker, an anonymous Athenian, argues for an education of women that mirrors that of Sparta. It fleshes out much of what Socrates argued in the Republic *in imagining an ideal state (see* **22g***).*

(813d) ATHENIAN I am establishing gymnasia and all physical training related to military training: the bow and all types of missiles, light- and every type of heavy-armed fighting, (813e) military evolution, all military marching, bivouacking, and as much as extends to cavalry training. In all these subjects there should be instructors paid at public expense; and their pupils should be not only the boys and men in the city, but also the girls and women should be knowledgeable in these matters. As girls they should be practiced in every maneuver in armed fighting; when grown to womanhood, they should take part in evolutions and formations and the taking up (814a) and shouldering of arms, if for no other reason than this: If ever the guardians of the children and of the rest of the city should be obliged to leave the city and march out, these women should be competent to this extent; if, on the other hand—and this is not impossible—an enemy should invade with great strength and force, whether Greek or barbarian, and should force a battle around the city itself, (814b) then it would be a great dishonor to the state if its women were reared so shamefully that they were not willing to do as mother birds do in fighting for their young against the strongest beasts and be willing to die, but, rather than risking even death itself, they take themselves to the temples and throng the shrines and holy places, and heap disgrace upon mankind by being the most cowardly of all creatures.

22j. *Laws* bk. 7, 814d–816a: Athletics and Military Training

(814d) ATHENIAN We will decide this then when word matches deed and clearly establishes what we are speaking about, namely that wrestling is closest to warlike fighting in all its motions, and that it is not necessary to practice fighting for the sake of wrestling, but wrestling must be learned for the sake of fighting.

CLINIAS Well spoken.

ATHENIAN And now, concerning the functions of the wrestling school, let what has been said suffice for now. (814e) Concerning forms of motion (*kinēsis*) of the whole body, besides wrestling, someone might say the other major aspect is dancing and he would be right. Dancing has two parts: One is related to the august imitation of beautiful bodies, and the other is related to frivolous movement of ugly bodies. Again, there are two parts to the frivolous movement and to the earnest movement. Concerning the earnest type, there is the movement related to war for beautiful bodies engaged in violent toil—this is the movement of the brave soul. Then, there is the movement of the moderate soul engaged in good work and in sweet measures. (815a) Someone might call this dancing "peaceful" by nature. The warlike form, different from the peaceful, is rightly called "pyrrhic dancing" (*pyrrhikē*). It involves the eluding of all strikes and thrusts with nodding and ducking, and high leaps out of the way and also with forms of crouching—and also moves opposite to these—which are for active postures; it attempts to imitate the shooting of arrows and striking with all types of spears. In these movements, the tension is correct when there is an imitation of noble bodies and souls, (815b) and there is a straightening of the limbs of the body—such a one we call correct (*orthon*),[25] and the other one we call incorrect. But we must consider the peaceful type of dancing and whether someone does it correctly or not according to the nature of beautiful dancing in a way that is fitting for law-abiding men. And so first it is necessary to separate dancing that can be questioned from that which is beyond questioning. We must consider what the dancing is and how it is necessary to separate each. (815c) Bacchic dancing is one form, cultivated by those who, being intoxicated, imitate Nymphs, Pans, Silenuses, and Satyrs (as they call them), performing purifications, and other rites. This type of dance is not easily defined as either peaceful or warlike. And so, it seems best for me to define this type of dancing in the following way. (815d) First one must separate it from peaceful and warlike dancing and assert that this type of dancing is not civic. In that we have established and dismissed this type, now it remains for us to return to the peaceful and warlike dancing that are ours beyond question.

The type related to the unwarlike Muse, when people honor the gods and children of gods through dances, that will be all one type related to the performance of prosperity. And we might divide this type of dancing into two types also. (815e) One is fitting for those who have escaped from certain labors and dangers into a good state, and it presents greater pleasures. The other relates to the preservation and increase of pre-existing goods, though the pleasures received are gentler. In these types of dances, all men move with greater movement of the body when the pleasures are greater, and less with lesser pleasures. (816a) But the man who has been trained for courage (*andreia*) is more orderly. But when a man is cowardly and untrained for temperance, he has greater and more excessive changes of movement. Besides, when someone vocalizes in song or speech, he is unable to keep his body entirely still. Hence, when the imitation of what was spoken through gesture came about, it produced the entire technique (*technē*) of dance. One man among us moves in tune in all matters, another out of tune.

---

[25] The term *orthon* has both physical and ethical dimensions, meaning both "straight" or "upright" and "correct."

22k. *Laws* bk. 12, 950e–951a: Delegations to Panhellenic Festivals

Here Plato describes the necessity of sending delegations to the major Panhellenic sanctuaries, a prac-
tice that was common for most major city states, and further provides some reason for doing so.

(950e) It is right to send delegates to Pythian Apollo and to Zeus at Olympia, as well as
to Nemea and Isthmia, in order to take part in the sacrifices and contests for the gods.
And one should send as many as one is able who are the most beautiful and the best—
whoever will make the city seem most glorious in festivals and in peaceful gatherings,
and who will provide a reputation that rivals (951a) that of those engaged in war. And
when they come home, they will teach the youth that the customs of their city are second
to none.

23. Aristotle

Aristotle was a major philosopher of the fourth century, living from roughly 384 to 322 BCE. He was a
student of Plato and teacher of Alexander the Great. Aristotle wrote on a wide variety of topics rang-
ing from anatomy and physics to ethics and metaphysics. He discusses the topic of athletics mostly in
the context of social values and public education, with a predominant focus on the topic of excellence
(aretē). Like Plato, Aristotle also established his own school of philosophy at another of the well-
known gymnasia of Athens, the Lyceum.

23a. *Rhetoric* bk. 1, 1361b: Bodily Excellence

The Rhetoric, dated to the fourth century BCE, is a work that focuses on the practice and principles of
persuasion. As the work explains, all humans, both individually and in common, have a primary
goal, which is "happiness" or "blessedness" (eudaimonia) and its respective parts. According to the
Rhetoric, happiness consists of noble birth, numerous friends, good friends, wealth, good children,
numerous children, a good old age, as well as forms of bodily excellence (aretē), such as health, beau-
ty, strength, stature, agonistic ability, in addition to a good reputation, honor, good luck, and vir-
tue. In the section provided, Aristotle defines these bodily excellences in greater detail with a privileged
position for the pentathlete.

Excellence of the body consists of health so that one makes use of the body free from
disease. For many are "healthy," in the manner of Herodicus [see **22f, 39a, 39b**], but no
one would call them happy in their health, since they are compelled to abstain from all
human activities.

Beauty (*kallos*) is different for each age. Beauty of youth is most useful for the body to
possess for labor, running, and acts of violence, and it is most sweet to look upon for

pleasure. For this reason, pentathletes are the most beautiful, because they are by nature best suited to force and speed. For a man in his prime, beauty is related to acts of war, and he is both beautiful and fearsome. For an old man, beauty means being sufficient for the labors of necessity and to be free from pain by not having the typical ailments of old age.

Strength (*ischus*) consists in the ability to move another's body as one wishes. It is necessary to move another either by pulling or pushing, lifting or pressing down, or crushing, so that a strong man is strong in all these activities or in some of them.

Excellence of stature is being superior in height, depth, and width than many men in a way that does not render one's movements slower on account of excess.

Agonistic excellence of the body consists of size, strength, and speed—for speed is strong. One who is able to move his legs in a certain way, to move quickly forward is a runner; one who is able to squeeze and hold is a wrestler; one who is able to use his fists is a boxer. And one who is able to do two of them [i.e., wrestling and boxing] is a pankratist, but one who does all is the pentathlete.

23b. *Nicomachean Ethics* bk. 1, 1098b–1099a: Happiness and Excellence

There are some who say that happiness (*eudaimonia*) is excellence (*aretē*) or some form of excellence. For excellence includes activity (*energeia*) that is in accordance with excellence. But there is not a small difference in supposing that the best (*to ariston*) is achieved by possession or by use, and whether it occurs in disposition (*hexis*) or activity. Indeed, a man may have the right disposition, but that disposition may not produce anything good, (1099a) as when he is asleep or has relaxed in some other way. This is not possible for activity, for it will act out of necessity and act well. Just as the most beautiful and strongest are not crowned at the Olympic Games, but only those who compete, and of those only the ones that win, so it is that those who act rightly become the ones who obtain the beautiful and good things in life.

23c. *Nicomachean Ethics* bk. 2, 1104a: Moral and Bodily Qualities Compared

First one must consider that such forms of excellence are naturally destroyed by deficiency and excess as we observe with strength and health, since it is necessary to use the visible as witnesses to the invisible. Excessive and deficient physical training (*gymnasia*) destroys strength, just as excessive or deficient food and drink will destroy health. But proper proportion (*symmetria*) will cause, add, and preserve both strength and health.

So it is the case with temperance (*sōphrosynē*), courage (*andreia*), and other forms of excellence (*aretē*). The man who flees in fear and remains for nothing becomes a coward, and the one who is afraid of nothing and runs headlong into all events is too bold. The one who delights in every form of pleasure and abstains from none is undisciplined, but those who shun all pleasure, as do those who live in the country, are anesthetized. Thus, temperance and courage are destroyed by excess and deficiency, but they are preserved by the means (*mesotēs*). Not only are these forms of excellence created, increased, and destroyed by these methods, but the same will be true for the related activities. For from other more visible examples this is the case, as with strength. For strength comes about when taking in much nourishment and enduring much labor, and a strong man is especially capable of these things. And such is the case with the forms of excellence. For we become temperate when we abstain from pleasures, and when we are temperate, we are able to abstain.

23d. *Politics* bk. 8, 1337a–1339a: Education and Athletics

Aristotle's Politics *is a work that discusses the various aspects of civic life and practice in the Greek polis. In this section, Aristotle discusses the education (*paideia*) of the children of citizens, both its nature and purpose. As part of the discussion, Aristotle spends significant time on physical training (*gymnastikē*), and also makes some interesting observations on what he views as inappropriate training of the youth, including the Spartan system of training as well as the possible "overtraining" of youth in competitive athletics.*

(1337a) No one would dispute that matters concerning education of the youth must be conducted by the lawgiver. When this is not the case in the cities, harm comes to the citizens. For it is necessary that there be education according to a city's constitution, for the character (*ēthos*) normally establishes and preserves what is specific to each constitution, just as a democratic character preserves democracy and an oligarchic character preserves oligarchy. In addition to the powers and skill, one must consider what it is necessary to teach and introduce for the sake of the activities of each city. It is clear that such matters are for the sake of the performance of excellence (*aretē*).

But since there is one purpose (*telos*) for all cities, it is clear that there must exist one form of education for all cities, and that this be a public concern and not a private one, in the manner as now, where each citizen is concerned with the private education of his own children, and teaching whatever private lessons he thinks best. For it is necessary that a common education and training (*askēsis*) be created for all citizens in common. At the same time, it is necessary that each citizen not think that he belongs to himself, but that all citizens belong to the city. For each citizen is part of a city. So concern over each part necessarily looks toward concern for the whole. One might praise the Spartans for this reason, since they pay the greatest attention to the children and their public education.

And so laws must be made and implemented about the children and their common education. These laws will address what type of education, how is it necessary to teach, and what not to forget. For now, there is debate about the work. For not all agree on what it is necessary to teach the young, neither for the sake of excellence (*aretē*) nor for the sake of the best possible life (*bios aristos*). Nor is it clear whether attention should be given to the intellect (*dianoia*) or to the character (*ēthos*) of the soul (*psychē*). A disturbing perspective arises out of present education: It is not clear whether it is necessary to practice matters useful for life or for the sake of excellence (*aretē*) or higher matters—for some judges have supported all these views.

(1337b) Regarding excellence (*aretē*), there is no agreement. For all men do not honor the same form of excellence. Thus, there is a difference of opinion as to the practice (*askēsis*) of it. It is clear that those things that are necessarily useful must be taught. But it is also clear that not all things should be taught, if one makes a distinction between those activities that are free versus those that are not free. And it is necessary that participation in whatever are useful practices does not make the one who participates a base tradesman (*banausos*). One ought to consider a base activity either a craft or a form of learning that renders the body of free citizens, whether in soul or intellect, useless for the enjoyment and practice of excellence. Thus, we call base crafts all those which make the condition of the body worse and those activities which are done for pay. For such tasks provide no leisure for the intellect and make it low. Such is the case even with free forms of knowledge, although it is not unfree to take part up to a certain point, but to sit and work at them excessively would produce a harsh condition rendered by the harms already mentioned. Also, why one does something or learns something makes a big difference. It is characteristic of the free to do something for its own sake or for friends or for the sake of excellence. But if one does the very same thing for the sake of other reasons, he would seem menial and slavish in his activity.

The established forms of learning, as was said earlier, are in both categories. There are four parts which it is customary to teach: letters, physical training (*gymnastikē*), music, and the fourth for some is drawing. Letters and drawing are the most useful and serviceable for life. Physical training is taught as training for courage (*andreia*). But one might question music. Now most take part in music for the sake of pleasure. But some established it in education from the beginning because, as is often said, nature seeks not only to be busy in the right way but also to be able to be at leisure well. For this is the one principle (*archē*) of all things, and let us discuss it again. For if both are necessary, it is better to choose leisure rather than business as an end, and so we must seek what it is necessary that one do when in leisure. For it is not play, since play would be our compulsory purpose. But if that is not possible, then one must instead make use of play in business. (For the one who is engaged in labor needs rest, and play is for the sake of rest. And being at work in business comes with labor and stress.) For this reason, it is necessary that play be introduced by those who look for the right time for its use, like those introducing medicine. For relaxation is movement of the soul, and rest is for the sake of pleasure.

(1338a) But leisure itself seems to provide pleasure and happiness and living in a blessed way. Such qualities do not exist for those who are engaged in business, but for those in leisure. For the one who is busy is busy for the sake of something whose end is not yet achieved, but happiness (*eudaimonia*) is the end, which all suppose is accompanied by pleasure and not by pain. But they do not all establish this pleasure as the same, but each defines it differently according to his disposition. The best man (*aristos*) has the best pleasure, which comes from the things which are most beautiful. Hence, it is clear that it is necessary to learn and be taught for the purpose of pursuing leisure, and that these forms of education and learning are for their own sake, but those aspects of education related to business are treated as necessary and for the sake of other things. This is why earlier men established music for the sake of play and not as a necessity (for it is not a necessity), nor as a form of utility (in the same way that letters are useful for money, for the household, for learning, and for many civic affairs, while it seems to me that drawing is useful for judging the work of artists better). Nor, again, is music useful in the same way as physical training is for the sake of health and strength (for we do not see either of these qualities born out of music). And so what remains is that music is useful for the purpose of passing the time in leisure, and this appears to be the reason people introduced it. For they think it is how the freeborn citizens pass the time and established it in this capacity. Thus, Homer said, "He alone is the sort to call to the bountiful feast," and speaking to his companions thus, "They call him a singer," he says, "who delights everyone." And in other verses Odysseus say this is the best pastime when there are men in good spirits: "Guests, sitting in a row, they listen to the singer." For this reason, it is apparent there are certain forms of education which must be taught to our sons, which are not useful or necessary, but are free and beautiful. Whether there is one or many types, and what they are and how they are to be taught—this must be discussed later.

But now the path is before us, since we have testimony of the established modes of education from the ancients—for music makes this clear. And with regard to useful matters, it is clear that it is necessary that children be taught something not only because it is useful, such as the lessons of letters, but also because it can lead to learning other things. Similarly, drawing should be implemented not in order that they not make a mistake in their private purchases and not be deceived in the purchase and sale of goods, but rather because it makes one observant of bodily beauty. But seeking what is useful everywhere is the least suited to great-souled and free men. But since there must be education by habits rather than by word, whether this applies to the body or the intellect, it is clear from this that children must be provided with physical training (*gymnastikē*) and physical education (*paidotribikē*). For the one provides bodily disposition (*hexis*), and the other provides bodily action (*erga*).

(1338a) Now of the states that seem to provide care for their children, some produce an athletic disposition in them. But these states harm their form and the growth of their bodies. The Spartans do not make this mistake, though they make their children wild through hardships, as though this were most conducive to courage (*andreia*). But, as has often been said, the care of children must not be made with a view to this single mode, and if it is made to this single mode, nor do they even discover it. For neither in other living creatures nor in other tribes do we see that courage follows the wildest, but rather courage is found in the gentler and lion-like natures. And there are many tribes which are tolerant of murder and cannibalism, as among the Achaeans and Heniochi around the Black Sea, and others on the continent, some more, some less. These tribes are piratical, but they have no share of courage. And still we know the Spartans themselves, as long as they persisted in their love of labor, they excelled all others. But now they are left behind in the naked contests and in matters of war. For they did not differ from others in the manner of training their youth, but they alone practiced against those who did not practice. Hence it is beauty (*to kalon*) and not animality which must take the lead. For neither the wolf nor any other animal would compete in any beautiful danger, but the noble man (*anēr agathos*) alone. Those who allow children to pursue these exercises in excess and make them uneducated in necessary matters, they render them truly base and useful for one purpose only for the city, and even for this one purpose worse than others. And so we must not judge from earlier deeds, but from those of today. For the Spartans now have rivals in their education; formerly they did not.

And so it is agreed that physical training must be employed and how it is to be used. Until the age of puberty light exercises must be used, and preventing hard diets and exertions by compulsion, in order that there be no block in a child's development.

(1339a) It is not an insignificant sign that severe training at an early age produces this effect in so far as one would only find two or three among the Olympic victors who won as men and as boys because training in youth robs one of ability because of the hard exercises. But when youth have been engaged in other studies for three years after puberty, then it is fitting at that age to take up labors and strict eating. For it is not appropriate to work the intellect together with the body, for each produces an opposite effect based on the types of labor. The labor of the body impedes the intellect, and the labor of the intellect impedes the body.

23e. *Constitution of Athens* 42: Ephebic Education

The Constitution of Athens *is not part of the traditional Aristotelian corpus but was discovered on two leaves of a papyrus codex from Oxyrhynchus Egypt at the end of the nineteenth century. Aristotle is believed to have recorded numerous constitutions as part of his research for the* Politics, *and that of Athens is particularly important, given the centrality of the city in Greek history. In this section*

Aristotle describes the registration and physical training of Athenian citizens when they have come of age as ephebes.

The current form of the constitution goes as follows. Those who are born from citizens on both sides of the family take part in the constitution, and they register in the demes when they become 18 years old. When they register, the members of the deme vote on them through declaration, first if they appear to be of age according to the law, and if they do not, they go back among the children. Second, they vote as to whether they are free and have become so according to the laws. Then, if they vote that the person is not free, he is sent to the jury courts, and the members of the deme choose five men from among them to speak against him. And if it seems that he is not legally registered with the deme, the state sells him. But if the youth wins, the members of the deme are compelled to register him. After this the council approves those registered, and if someone appears younger than 18, then it would fine the demesmen who registered him. When the ephebes have been validated, the fathers gather their tribes, take an oath, and choose three from the tribesmen who are more than 40 years old, whom they consider to be the best and most suited to care for the ephebes, and from these the people select from each tribe a disciplinary officer (*sōphronistēs*), and from the other Athenians they elect an organizer for all of them. And after they have collected the ephebes, they first go around to the temples, then they go to the Piraeus and some keep watch at Munichia and others at Akte. And the people elect two trainers (*paidotribai*) and teachers for them, who teach them how to fight in armor, shoot bows, throw spears, and use slingshots. It also gives one drachma each to the disciplinary officer for food, and four obols each to the ephebes. Each disciplinary officer takes the pay for his tribesmen and buys the provisions for all in common (for the tribesmen eat together), and he takes care of all other matters. They live in this way for the first year. The next year, there is an assembly in the theater, and they demonstrate to the people matters concerning battle arrangements, taking up shields and spears from the state, they patrol the countryside, and they spend time at the guard-posts. They serve as guards for two years wearing a mantle, and they pay no taxes, nor are they able to sue or be sued in court, in order that there is no excuse for not being present, except regarding an estate, an heiress, and if a priesthood is granted to them. After two years, they then join the rest of the citizens.

23f. *Constitution of Athens* 60: Panathenaic Games

This section from the Constitution of Athens *describes the organization of the Panathenaic Games with a focus on the prizes given. Although the four sacred games at Olympia, Delphi, Isthmia, and Nemea did not offer prizes beyond a crown, many other athletic contests did offer prizes with monetary value. Of those contests, the Panathenaic contest was one of the most popular and it was unique in so far as its prizes for athletic and horse racing events consisted of amphoras of olive oil. These*

*Panathenaic amphoras were decorated on one side with an image of the contest for which the prize was awarded and on the other with an image of Athena, often Athena in a warrior stance (known as Athena Promachos). There was also an inscription—tōn Athēnēthen athlōn ("of the prizes from Athens"). In later periods, the name of the archon for that festival year was also recorded. For further discussion of the Panathenaic Games and their prizes, see **I14f** and Appendix B I.*

These are the duties of archons. They select by lot ten men as organizers of the games (*athlothetai*), one from each tribe. After being examined, they are in charge for four years, and they organize the procession of the Panathenaic festival, the musical, athletic, and horse-racing contests. They have the robe (*peplos*) for Athena made. Together with the council they have the prize amphoras made, and they distribute the olive oil to the athletes. The oil is collected from the sacred trees. The archon takes it from the land where the sacred trees are located, three quarters of a pint from each. Before that, the state sold the olives, and if anyone uprooted or cut down a sacred olive tree, the Council of the Areopagus[26] indicted him. And if he was found guilty, he was sentenced to death. But from the time when the olive oil has been used as rent for the land, though the law still exists, the trial has ceased. And the oil for the city is based on the estate and not on the number of trees. The archon collects the olive oil for the year and then hands it over to the treasurers of the Acropolis, and he is not able to go to the Areopagus until he has given the full amount to the treasurers. The treasurers watch over the oil the rest of the time on the Acropolis, and they measure it out to the organizers of the games for the Panathenaic festival, and the organizers give it to the victors in the contest. The prizes (*athla*) to those victorious in the musical contest are silver and gold; shields are prizes for the *euandria*,[27] and olive oil is the prize for athletic contests and horse races.

---

[26] This council was normally reserved for cases of murder.

[27] *Euandria* literally means "good manliness" and the event may have been a type of male beauty contest; see **17a-b**, **42c**, **I4g** and the introduction to *Tragedy and Comedy*.

3 The Hellenistic Period

The Hellenistic Period is traditionally dated from the death of Alexander the Great (323 BCE) to the death of Cleopatra VII (30 BCE). These three hundred years saw the widespread expansion of Greek culture into newly established cities of Egypt and Asia Minor such as Alexandria in Egypt or Antioch in Syria, and within these environments the promotion of familiar athletic behaviors. The successors of Alexander, who became the monarchs of these new regions—the Ptolemies, the Antigonids, the Seleucids, and the Eumenids—used competitive athletics to enhance their status with mainland Greeks as well as to reinforce their identities as Greek.[1] They and their family members not only competed in the four Panhellenic crown games, but they also instituted local festivals, some of which were deliberately set up to be the equal to the Panhellenic four. Then, at the local level, these new Greek cities established gymnasia that became centers for the training of elite Greek youth and a place in which to maintain and reinforce cultural identity in areas where the immigrant Greek populations were a very small minority.[2]

*Alexandria presents the clearest picture of these cultural strategies. The city was originally founded by Alexander the Great in 332, but at his death it came into the possession of one of his Macedonian satraps, Ptolemy, the son of Lagus, who established a line that ruled for 300 years until the death of Cleopatra VII. The Ptolemies and their families followed the pattern of Philip II by participating frequently in the Panhellenic crown games. They would not have competed in person or in gymnic events but in horse and chariot racing, which had long been used as status markers by the Sicilian tyrants in the sixth and fifth centuries BCE (see **2a–b, 3a**) and in late fifth century most ostentatiously by the Athenian Alcibiades (**9g, 12c, 17a–b, 18a**). Literary evidence for this interest comes from a papyrus roll discovered in Egypt and dating to the late third century BCE and published in 2001. It contained a book of epigrams now attributed to Posidippus of Pella in Macedon, who wrote at the court of the Ptolemies; one section of this new book (**27a–p**) contains eighteen epigrams celebrating victors in horse racing and chariot racing, including several of the Ptolemaic royal women. In style they imitate the kinds of brief dedications actually found on statue groups for victorious athletes at Olympia and elsewhere. One of them (**27o**) not only commemorates the victory of a Ptolemaic queen, but claims that she surpassed the glory of Cynisca of Sparta (**10a, 35a, 37x**) whose earlier victory was commemorated with a dedication at Olympia itself. Callimachus wrote an elegiac epinician for Berenice II (**26a**) and another for Sosibius, a high-ranking member of court (**26b**). For both of these Pindar is a model.*

In addition to their active participation in crown games, the Ptolemies also established games in Alexandria that from their inception were intended to vie in stature with the more famous Panhellenic games. The most important of these was the Ptolemaea, a quadrennial festival established around 276 BCE by Ptolemy II Philadelphus in honor of his deceased father. In order to promote the

---

[1] See Herodotus, **8e**.
[2] For the growth and importance of the gymnasium in the Roman period, see **38a, 115g**.

Sourcebook of Ancient Greek Athletics. Charles H. Stocking and Susan A. Stephens, Oxford University Press (2021).
© Charles H. Stocking and Susan A. Stephens. DOI: 10.1093/oso/9780198839606.003.0004

importance of these new games, the crown sent ambassadors to the cities from which it hoped to attract athletes, asking the cities to honor victors in a way that was equal to the four Panhellenic crown games. (The crown games did not give money prizes, but only a crown to mark the prestige of the victor; therefore, cities subsequently rewarded their victorious citizen athletes with substantial emoluments.) It was this "Is-Olympic" reward for the athlete victorious at the Ptolemaea that the Ptolemies were requesting (see **I5e**).

Alexandria was not alone: Cos apparently asked for Is-Olympic status in 242/241 (IG XII 4 220–1, 223); Miletus in 218/217 (IG XII 4 153), and at least thirteen more such venues were established in this same region in the early second century BCE.[3] In addition to competitions that held out lucrative rewards because of their Is-Olympic or crown status, local competitions (agōnes) could be sponsored by smaller cities and towns as part of gymnasium culture. Especially common was wrestling, which came to function as a mechanism of social bonding; elite youths wrestled as part of their gymnasium training, and as adult males they continued to engage in recreational wrestling, as does Socrates with Alcibiades in Plato's Symposium or Galen with his friends. Boxing never had the recreational cachet of wrestling, no doubt because of its disfiguring brutality, but it achieved some prominence in the period. Cleoxenus of Alexandria won an Olympic victory as a boxer in 240 BCE and he was said to have been a periodonikēs. Ptolemy IV was said to have sponsored the boxer Aristonicus who was defeated at Olympia in 212 BCE (see **28a**). These successful athletes surely contributed to the interest that boxing held for Hellenistic artists (see **24**, **25a**, **29**).

24. Theocritus

According to his own testimony Theocritus was Syracusan by birth, though he must have spent several years in Ptolemy's new city of Alexandria, where he wrote poetry that featured the royal couple— Ptolemy II and Arsinoë II. He lived in the first half of the third century BCE and is regarded as the inventor of pastoral poetry. His works (called Idylls) included a number of short poems in epic meter (dactylic hexameter), including an encomium to Ptolemy II Philadelphus and epic topics including Heracles, Helen and Menelaus, and the Argonauts. In Idyll 22 Theocritus gives a long, detailed poetic account of a boxing match. The Greek Argonauts had just passed through the straits to enter the Black Sea on their way to Colchis to retrieve the Golden Fleece. They stop for provisions and encounter Amycus, a local king, whose unfriendly behavior marks him and his people as noticeably barbarian. Two members of the Argo crew, Polydeuces (or Pollux) and his brother Castor, were known as the Dioscuri ("children of Zeus"). These brothers were Spartan, one born mortal, the other immortal, and at the death of the mortal, the other wished to share his immortality, so they took turns living on earth and in the underworld. They exemplified excellence in two sports—Castor was a great horseman, Polydeuces a boxer (see Figure 2), a sport especially associated with Sparta (see **40a** 9–10). They had a cult in early Alexandria. In this excerpt, Amycus challenges Polydeuces to a boxing match.

---

[3] See Pleket (2014: 368).

The bout begins with Polydeuces getting the favorable position so that Amycus has the sun in his eyes. Polydeuces' strategy is to hit the face, which was standard Greek boxing practice, while Amycus goes for body blows.[4]

24a. *Idyll* 22.27–135: Boxing Match between Polydeuces and Amycus

Then having escaped the clashing rocks and the dire mouth of the snowy Pontus, the Argo, bearing the dear sons of the gods, arrived at the land of the Bebrycians. (30) There down one ladder on either side the many men disembarked from Jason's ship. When they stepped upon the wide shore and sheltered beach, they spread beds for themselves and turned fire sticks in their hands. Castor of the swift horses and dark-skinned (35) Polydeuces together went apart from the heroes and gazed at the wide woodland everywhere on the hill. They found a perennially flowing spring beneath a smooth rock, full of pure water. The pebbles shone like crystal or silver from the bottom. (40) Lofty pine trees grew nearby and white plane trees and tufted cypresses and sweet flowers (the work of furry bees), all the kinds that fill the meadow at the end of spring. There an enormous man was sitting taking the sun. (45) Terrible to look at, with his ears broken by the blows of fists. His monstrous chest and broad back were rounded with iron flesh like a metal colossus. The muscles in his brawny arms under the point of his shoulders stood out like boulders that (50) a river had rounded and polished by circling them with great eddies of winter rains. On his back and neck was a lion skin fastened by its paws. The prize-winning Polydeuces addressed him first in this way: "Greetings, friend, whoever you are. Who are the mortals whose land this is?"

(55) AMYCUS How shall I rejoice when I see men whom I have not seen before?
POLYDEUCES Take heart. You do not look upon unjust men or men descended from the unjust.
AMYCUS I don't need courage. I'm not likely to learn that lesson from you.
POLYDEUCES Are you fierce, perverse, and arrogant to all?
AMYCUS I am such as you see. But I am not entering your country.
(60) POLYDEUCES You should come and happen to return with gifts of friendship.
AMYCUS Don't give me gifts of friendship—I don't have any for you.
POLYDEUCES My good man, would you not give us some of this water to drink?
AMYCUS You will know if thirst parches your dried lips.
POLYDEUCES Silver or some fee—tell us what you want.
(65) AMYCUS Raise your fists and meet me man to man.

---

[4] For a discussion of boxing and its techniques, see Appendix CII; see also **1a** *Iliad* 23.658–99, **1e, 29, 34a-b, 41c**.

POLYDEUCES Boxing or kicking legs with our feet and straightforward gaze? [i.e., boxing or *pankration*].

AMYCUS Boxing, and don't spare your skill.

POLYDEUCES Now who is it with whom I shall contend with bound fists?

AMYCUS You see him next to you. He is no gull and is called the Boxer.

(70) POLYDEUCES And is there a suitable prize for which we will contend?

AMYCUS I shall be yours or you shall be called mine, if I beat you.

POLYDEUCES Red-combed roosters contend on terms like this.

AMYCUS Whether we are like roosters or lions, we shall fight on no other terms.

(75) Amycus spoke and taking up a hollow conch shell he blew it; and after he blew it, the Bebrycians with their uncut hair quickly assembled under the shady plane trees. And in the same way mighty Castor went and called all the heroes from the Argo. (80) After the two had reinforced their hands with oxhide strips and wrapped long thongs around their arms, they came together in the center of the men, breathing out death for each other. They each made a great effort to get the sun behind their backs, (85) but Polydeuces outwitted the large man with his skill, and Amycus' whole face was struck by the sun's rays. Now in his anger he attacked, pummeling with his fists, and as he attacked, Polydeuces struck him on the chin. He grew angrier than before, and fought wildly, and (90) with his head lowered to the ground he attacked with force. The Bebrycians cheered and the heroes on the other side shouted encouragement to mighty Polydeuces, fearing that by closing him in the narrow space the Giant-like man might defeat him. (95) But Polydeuces sidestepped again and again, striking repeatedly, he cut him with both fists, and checked the onslaught of the arrogant man. As if drunk from the blows, he stood still and spat out crimson blood, and all the heroes shouted out (100) when they saw the deep wounds around his mouth and jaws, and his eyes were narrowed to slits in his swollen face. Then Polydeuces confused him with feints on all sides; but when he saw him to be helpless, he drove his fist down between his brows onto the center of his nose (105) and cut his forehead open to the bone. Amycus lay flat on his back on the dead leaves. When he got up, the grim battle commenced again, and they traded deadly blows with their hard thongs. While the king of the Bebryces kept punching the chest and around the neck, (110) unconquerable Polydeuces kept pounding the other's face with numerous blows. Amycus' flesh shrank as he sweated, and he seemed to shrink from a large to a smaller man. As the struggle increased, Polydeuces' limbs became stronger and his skin took on a better color.

(115) How did the son of Zeus overcome that glutton?[5] In fact, when Amycus, in his eagerness for a knockout punch, grabbed Polydeuces' left fist with his own left hand, and (120) leaning sideways as he lunged forward, he stepped into him and he brought up his wide fist from his right side. If he had happened to connect, he would have done damage,

---

[5] Boxers and other athletes were notorious for their large meat consumption.

but Polydeuces ducked his head and at the same time struck his opponent on the left temple with his iron fist and led with his shoulder. (125) Black blood immediately flowed from the gaping head wound. And with his left, he hit him in the mouth, and rattled his teeth. With increasingly rapid blows he pummeled his face until his cheeks were crushed. Amycus lay full out on the ground and (130) held up both hands to stop the fight, since he was near death. Polydeuces, although he had won, did no further harm, and Amycus swore a great oath by his father Poseidon that he would never again willingly harm strangers.

Figure 2. Boxer at Rest, Hellenistic bronze of nude, seated boxer, Museo Nazionale Romano: Palazzo Massimo alle Terme, Rome, Italy

25. Apollonius of Rhodes

Apollonius (c.295–220 BCE) lived and wrote in Alexandria. In his epic poem, the Argonautica, *Apollonius recounts this same incident at the beginning of book 2.1–95. As in the earlier section, this vignette opens with a set of verbal challenges, then Polydeuces agreeing to fight Amycus. The two men find a place that can serve as a makeshift stadium, seat their respective comrades, and commence the fight. Apollonius spends much more time on scene-setting than on the actual bout and he uses similes rather than description to communicate the violence of the exchanges. We translate only the bout itself below. The description of Amycus rising up to deliver a blow from above is found elsewhere (see* **1a**, *Iliad 23.680–90), as is the ease with which the opponent dodges the blow. Note that Amycus is killed in Apollonius but survives in Theocritus' version.*

25a. *Argonautica* bk. 2.67–97: Boxing Match between Polydeuces and Amycus

Now when in opposite corners they had fitted themselves with thongs, they immediately raised their weighted fists before their faces and attacked, bearing down in strength against each other. (70) Then the lord of the Bebryces, like a rough sea wave that rises above a swift ship that barely escapes through the skill of the clever pilot, when the impetuous billow pours over its sides, like this did he pursue the son of Tyndareus in order to frighten him and allowed him no respite. But Polydeuces, (75) completely untouched, by his skill evaded him as he attacked. And as soon as he had taken the measure of his opponent's brutal boxing technique, namely, where his strength was invincible, where weaker, he held his position without wavering and traded blow for blow. (80) As when carpenters strike ship's timbers repeatedly with hammers driving in the sharp pegs, and blow after blow the sound echoes without end, in this way the cheeks and chins of both were pummeled and their teeth clashed. (85) They did not stop trading blows until a terrible breathlessness overcame them both. Standing back, the two wiped sweat from their foreheads, as they panted for breath in exhaustion. Then they rushed each other like enraged bulls fighting over a grazing cow. (90) Amycus, having risen up on his tiptoes, stretched out like a man about to slay an ox and swung his weighted hand down upon Polydeuces. But he fended him off as he attacked by tilting his head sideways and receiving only a glancing blow on his shoulder. But closing on him, Polydeuces slipped his knee past the other's knee and (95) struck him with a swift lunge above the ear and shattered the bones within. Amycus fell to his knee in pain. The Argonauts cheered and Amycus' life poured out of him altogether.

25b. *Argonautica* bk. 4.1765–72: Foundation of the Hydrophoria on Aegina

This passage from the end of the epic provides the mythological basis for a local contest on the island of Aegina, though it is not clear what the actual historical festival is. The contest is the hydrophoria; it required young men to run the course carrying full water jars. This same event is apparently the subject of an epinician in iambics by Callimachus (26e).

From there they quickly passed through a vast expanse of sea to land on the shores of Aegina. Immediately they engaged in a harmless competition of fetching water, that is, who, after drawing it up, might first return to the ship, since both necessity and a stiff breeze pressed upon them. Now to this day [the Aeginetans] placing full amphoras upon their shoulders compete for victory in a contest of swiftness of foot.

26. Callimachus

Callimachus (c.305–240 BCE) of Cyrene lived and wrote in the court of the Ptolemy II and III. He wrote two victory odes that we know of. One was for Berenice II, who won in the four-horse chariot race at Nemea in 245 or 241 BCE. She was the wife of Ptolemy III (he ruled from 246 to 222 BCE) and a Cyrenean by birth. The other was written for an Alexandrian, Sosibius, who was most likely a high-ranking official in the court of Ptolemy III. If so, it must date from around 240. Both are fragmentary, although a considerable number of lines from each remains. Callimachus also wrote in prose on Olympic victory lists (see 46, line 44) and on specific agōnes, *though nothing of these works has survived.*

26a. *Aetia* bk. 3, frr. 54, 54i Harder: *Epinician for Berenice II:* Chariot Victor at the Nemean Games

Fr. 54. To Zeus and Nemea I owe, as a gift of thanksgiving, bride [Berenice II], sacred blood of the sibling gods [Ptolemy II and Arsinoë II, his sister and wife],... our victory song for your horses; for there came recently (5) from the land of cow-born Danaus [Argos, the site of the Nemean games] to Helen's small island and to the Pallenean seer, the herder of seals [Proteus], a golden story that near the tomb of Opheltes, the son of Euphetes, your horses ran, without breathing upon any charioteers in front...(10) but running like the winds, no one saw their traces.

The remainder of this song tells the story of Heracles' defeat of the Nemean lion as a precursor to the establishment of the Nemean games and how Heracles was hosted by a poor man named Molorchus, as an example of model guest–host behavior. The only other detail about the games themselves is Callimachus' comment that the Isthmian Games replaced the pine crown used for victors in favor of the wild celery crown, in deliberate imitation of Nemean practice.

Fr. 54i…and the sons of Aletes, performing games far more ancient than this one at the Aegean god's place, will make it a sign of an Isthmian victory, in imitation of the victors from Nemea; they will slight the pine, which previously crowned the competitors at Ephyra.

26b. *Epinician for Sosibius,* fr. 384 Pfeiffer: Chariot Victor at Nemea and Isthmia

This victory ode celebrates Sosibius' recent victories at the Nemean and Isthmian Games but mentions his earlier victories as well: one apparently in Athens, where he wrestled in the men's class although probably still a youth (ageneios), and another as a boy in the diaulos at an Alexandrian festival [probably the Ptolemaea].[6]

…for [Sosibius] the celery-wreathed chariot (5) had returned from Corinth [site of the Isthmian games] and the Asbystian horse[7] still hears the sound of the axle in his ears. And just as today this word darts to my lips, pronouncement of sweet tidings. "[Poseidon], who sits on either side of the sea-girt narrows, (10) receiver of oaths of the ancient Corinthians, the sacred isthmus at the foot of Pelops' land, with Cromma on one side and Lechaeon on the other, there where contest of feet, and of hand, and of swift horse is adjudicated, and (15) fair judgment surpasses gold [i.e., no money prize is given]…"

(20) He hastened to Nemea and brought another celery crown from the Argolid [the region of Nemea] to those from Pirene [i.e., the Isthmian games], so that an Alexandrian and a dweller on the banks of the Cinyps[8] might know of Sosibius twice crowned (25) by the two sons—the brother of Learchus and the nursling of Myrina—and the Nile, bringing the most fertile of waters annually, might say this: "A fair recompense has my nursling paid me…for never has anyone before (30) brought a double prize to the city [Alexandria] from these funeral games. And as great as I am, whose source no mortal man knows, in one thing at least I am lesser than those streams [i.e., inferior rivers] whom pale-ankled women may cross without difficulty or a child on foot without wetted knees."

[The speaker is probably Sosibius.]

---

[6] For competitors successful in both hippic and gymnic events, see Golden (1998: 119–20) and Pindar, *Isthmian* 3–4 on Melissus of Thebes.

[7] The victorious horses were from the Asbystian region of Cyrene, famous for horse-breeding.

[8] Cinyps was the river at the western edge of Cyrenean territory that formed the border with Carthage.

(35) "—for among the Athenians also the jars are kept under a sacred roof,[9] not as a mark of ornamentation, but of wrestling skill—and without fear of men we provided the opportunity for a chorus to lead a sweet *kōmos* in the temple of Athena, crying out (40) the victory song of Archilochus.[10] Ptolemy, son of Lagus, by you I first chose to carry off the prize from the *diaulos*..."

[The speaker is probably the poet.]

"The stranger was victorious in both. (45) No longer will we set up the unclad daughters of Eurynome [i.e., statues of the Graces] in the temple of Hera." A man will sing a song in agreement with what was said. And this dedication I heard about from others, but I myself saw the one that was dedicated at the outermost branch of the Nile, (50) as a visitor to the Caspian sea... And we sing of him for his victories, with his regard for the people and not forgetting those who are poor, (55) a thing that one rarely sees among the rich, whose minds are not stronger than their good fortune. Neither shall I praise him as he deserves nor forget—for I am afraid of the complaint of the people on both counts."

26c. *Aetia* bk. 3, frr. 84–5 Harder: Euthycles the Locrian Pentathlete

Callimachus seems to have included other tales about famous athletes in books 3–4 of his Aetia, *probably to enhance the status of Berenice II's victory by association with these earlier victors. In addition to the two who are mentioned below, Callimachus may also have related tales about Milo of Croton and Theogenes, though these have not survived. Euthycles was a famous fifth-century Olympian victor in the pentathlon (see* **37q**, *Pausanias 6.6.4–10). Callimachus' story is now only a small fragment.*

...when you came from Pisa, Euthycles, having gotten the better of men...returning from there again, (5) you came leading wagon mules as a gift; and when the people—always choking with envy of the rich—said that you received them through cutting deals against your country, they all secretly cast an evil vote. And your bronze statue which the town of Locri itself set up [they pulled down and did?] many things hateful to the blessed ones; for that reason a harsh [penalty?] was sent to them by the one they call [Zeus] on High, (15) who is unable to view sinners with a cheerful eye...

---

[9] These are the amphoras used as prizes for the victors; see **23f**.

[10] That is, Sosibius won a victory in men's wrestling as a youth. The victory permitted him to have a celebratory chorus that sang the Archilochian *kōmos* (see **2d**, n. 28).

26d. *Aetia* bk. 4, fr. 98 Harder: Euthymus the Locrian Boxer

This is a story about the Olympic boxing champion Euthymus of Locri. Apparently in Temesa, a city of the Brutii in southern Italy, one of Odysseus' crew was abandoned on the shore during the return voyage from Troy. The crewman then raped a local woman and was stoned to death. In expiation for the stoning, the locals were required to appease his ghost by leaving him a bed and a virgin as an annual tribute. Euthymus put an end to the practice by wrestling with the ghost. The text itself is lost, but this partial ancient summary exists. The story is well attested: see the version in Pausanias (37q, 6.6.4–7.1) and in Pliny's Natural Histories *7.152.*

… in Temesa a hero abandoned by Odysseus' ship demanded tribute from the locals and their neighbors, namely, that they should (5) bring him a couch and a girl of marriageable age and leaving them, they should go away and not look back. The next morning her parents got the girl back as a woman in place of a virgin. The boxer Euthymus ended this tribute by boxing…

26e. *Iambus* 8, Synopsis: The Hydrophoria at Aegina

The text is lost but this ancient summary exists. See also **25b***.*

This is an epinician for Polycles the Aeginetan, who was victorious in the *diaulos* race of the amphora bearers in Aegina, his fatherland. This is the contest: At the end of the stadium there is an amphora full of water to which the contestant runs empty-handed, picks up the amphora, and returns. If he is first, he is the victor. It came about in this way: The Argonauts disembarked on Aegina and competed with one another to see who was faster in carrying water. This contest is called the Hydrophoria ("Water-Carrying").

27. Posidippus of Pella

Posidippus was a Macedonian writer of epigrams who lived in the early half of the third century BCE. *Among his recently discovered epigrams there is a section of eighteen poems dedicated to victories in horse racing and chariot racing, and at least five of these celebrate victories not just of the male Ptolemies but of their queens and daughters. The extent of Ptolemaic engagement in these exhibitions of wealth and power can be gauged by* **271***, spoken by Ptolemy III's sister, Berenice Syra, on the occasion of her victory at Olympia. It begins by reciting a long line of Ptolemaic victors who include her grandfather (Ptolemy I) and grandmother (Berenice I), her father (Ptolemy II), and Arsinoë II. About Arsinoë we learn that she won in a single year all three victories for harnessed races—tethrippon teleion, the four-horse race for adult horses, the* synōris, *the two-horse race for adult horses, and the* tethrippon pōlikon, *the four-horse chariot race for foals. This deceptively simple epigram inserts the whole family into that exclusive club of horse-racing monarchs like the Spartan Eurypontids in the fifth century, and more importantly Philip II of Macedon, who had a small temple erected at Olympia that housed statues of him with his parents, his wife Olympias, and Alexander.*

In another epigram Posidippus singles out Berenice I's chariot victory for foals (tethrippon pōlikon)*, claiming that she now bests the earlier Spartan queen, Cynisca. This very pointedly constructs dynastic rivalries: Cynisca was the daughter of the chariot-mad Spartan king Archidamus II and her brothers were the equally horsey Agis II and Agesilaus II. Even in this family she apparently stood out as a breeder of horses and entered her own teams to win chariot victories at Olympia in 396 and 392* BCE *(**10a, 35a, 37x**). Other high-placed women after Cynisca had won chariot races, but Berenice's distinction seems to be that she was the first woman to do it with foals. See Appendix AIV.*

*In this section, Posidippus mixes praise of individual victors with praise of horses or teams and praise of the Ptolemies. Each epigram can be understood as a dedication on a statue or statue group of the victors; hence statements like "as though running" (**27b**). Often the victor's homeland is celebrated (see **27a, 27e-h, 27k**). The Ptolemies are often called Macedonian, because they were originally from Macedon, and Macedon, rather than Egypt, was counted as Greek for the purpose of Panhellenic competition. Many of these poems are fragmentary.*

27a–h. Single-Horse Victories

27a (ep. 71 AB)

This my single horse (*mounokelēs*) Aethon[11] [won a victory],
      and I [won the *stadion*?] at the same Pythian Games.
I, Hippostratus, was twice a victor,
      my horse and I, oh venerable Thessaly.

27b (ep. 72 AB)

Behold the sleekness of the colt, how it draws in its breath
      with every hoof beat and gallops at full stretch
as though running the Nemean race; it brought Molycus the celery crown
      winning by its outstretched head.

---

[11] The horse's name, "Fiery," seems to have been common; a different horse is so named in **27h** and in **1a** (*Iliad* 23.299), Menelaus' horse (*Aithē*).

27c (ep. 73AB)

This epigram is as if spoken by the victorious horse.

> At once from the starting line at Olympia I ran like this,
> > [with no need of] whip…
> [carrying?] a sweet weight, they crowned
> > Trygaeus with an olive branch.

27d (ep. 76 AB)

> This Arabian horse, running extended at full gallop on the edges of his hooves,
> > thus brings a victory for Etearchus.
> Having won in the Ptolemaea, and Isthmia, and Nemea twice,
> > he does not wish to omit the Delphic crown.

27e (ep. 83 AB)

> This Thessalian was the fastest single horse (*mounokelēs*), winning three victories
> > at Olympia and was dedicated as a sacred monument to the Scopadae.
> The first and only horse, this one. Test me: three times I won
> > …at the Alpheus, the Iamids[12] are my witness.

27f (ep. 84 AB)

> …as an Olympic victor, you washed your swift horse
> > in the Alpheus river, Thessalian Phylopidas;
> …a great house [was] hereafter crowned with wreaths,
> > but the first delights [*charites*, i.e., victory] are the more divine.

27g (ep. 85 AB)

> Distinguished for his swiftness, I, Amyntas,
> > brought this horse from my own herd
> to you, Pisan Zeus, and I did not undo my Thessalian fatherland's
> > ancient reputation for horses.[13]

---

[12] The Iamidae of Elis were one of the two local clans administering the Olympic Games.
[13] Thessaly, like Cyrene, was well known for breeding excellent horses, and several of these epigrams commemorate Thessalian victors.

27h (ep. 86 AB)

...he ran boldly; and indeed, this horse
      won four times as a single horse at Nemea
and twice in the Pythian stadium, Messenian *Aethon*,
       and he brought me, Eubotas, the crown on both occasions.

27i–j. Non-Royal Chariot Victories

27i (ep. 75 AB)

We four mares with a chariot
       ...that was driven in the presence of Zeus the Charioteer,
Pisans, [won] another Olympic crown
      for...the Spartan.

27j (ep. 77 AB)

...with a chariot I won three times at Olympia
       ...at a not inconsiderable cost
...and if it suffices for glory,
      I have no other need.

27k (ep. 74 AB)

In Delphi this filly, when competing against a Thessalian chariot
      in the four-horse race, finished alongside but won by a nod.
There was great outcry among the charioteers
      in the presence of the Amphictyonic judges,[14] Phoebus [= Apollo].
The judges cast their staffs to the ground,
      thinking that the charioteers should cast lots for victory.
But then our horse on the right side nodded to the ground and,
      guileless, she dragged the staff away,
a clever female among males, whereupon the myriads
      roared in one commingled voice to proclaim
a great wreath for her; in the uproar,
      Callicrates, a man from Samos, won the laurel crown.

---

[14] *Agōnothetai*, the judges at the Pythian Games (see Appendix BI).

> And to the brother-loving gods [Ptolemy II and his wife Arsinoë II] he dedicated
> this lifelike image, namely, the chariot and the charioteer in bronze.

27l–p. Panhellenic Royal Chariot Victories

27l. (ep. 78 AB)

> Speak, all you poets, of my fame…
> to say what is known, because my reputation…
> For my grandfather Ptolemy I won with his chariot,
> driving his team on the racecourses at Pisa
> and my father's mother, Berenice I. Again, with his chariot
> my father [Ptolemy II] won a victory, a king from a king,
> with his father's name. Arsinoë won all three victories for harness events in one
> competition… Olympia saw from one house children's children
> as prize-winners with their chariot. Celebrate, Macedonians, the crown of
> Berenice for her four-horse team.

27m (ep. 79 AB)

> The maiden queen with her chariot, indeed, Berenice,
> has won all the crowns for chariot races in the games,
> near you, Zeus of Nemea. By the speed of her horses
> her chariot left behind the rest of the charioteers.
> And her horses flying with slack reins
> came first into the presence of the judges (*agōnothetai*) of the Argolid.

27n (ep. 82 AB)

> … Berenice [Syra]'s horse
> winning on the racecourse
> .. near to the Corinthian citadel,
> the holy water of Pirene marveled at the Macedonian girl
> with her father Ptolemy. You alone, princess, proclaimed at the Isthmus
> how many times your house was victorious.

27o (ep. 87 AB)

When we were still foals, people of Pisa,
  we won the Olympian crown for Macedonian Berenice,
a crown that brings much-vaunted glory, by which we took away
  the ancient glory of Cynisca of Sparta.[15]

27p (ep. 88 AB)

This is supposedly spoken by Ptolemy II; his parents were Ptolemy I and Berenice I.

We alone were the first three kings to win
  in chariot racing at Olympia, both my parents and I.
I am one of them, named after Ptolemy, the son of Berenice,
  of Eordean stock, as are my two parents.
To my father's great glory, I add my own, but that my mother, a woman, won a
  victory in chariot racing, this is a great thing.

28. Polybius

Polybius (200–c.118 BCE) was a Greek born to a prominent Arcadian family. He was the first Greek historian to take the rise of Rome seriously and is our best ancient source for the early Hellenistic period.

28a. *Histories* bk. 2.12.8: Romans Allowed to Participate in Isthmian Games

The first incursion of the Roman army into Illyria and these parts of Europe [in 228 BCE], and further connection via an embassy with places in Greece, happened for these reasons. And from that beginning the Romans immediately sent other ambassadors to the Corinthians and the Athenians; at that time the Corinthians first granted the Romans the right to participate in the Isthmian Games.

---

[15] See also **10a**, **35a**, **37q** (5.12.5, 6.1.6), **37x**, **I1i**.

28b. *Histories* bk. 27.9.3–13: Cleitomachus and Aristonicus, Olympic Boxers

In this passage he likens the reaction of the populace to a Macedonian cavalry victory to a famous boxing match between Cleitomachus and Aristonicus at Olympia at which the crowd's allegiance altered during the match and was said to have affected the outcome. Cleitomachus was a boxer, a pankratist, and perhaps a wrestler (see 29). The event took place in 216 BCE.

(3) Their disposition, I think, was like this. What happened was very like the situation in gymnastic contests; when an inferior and much weaker opponent is matched against an outstanding and seemingly undefeatable athlete, the sympathy of the crowd is immediately for the weaker man; they urge him on to be bold and support him with enthusiasm. (4) And if he should strike his opponent's face and mark him with a blow, it straightaway becomes (5) a small contest for all of them. Sometimes they try to mock the other man, not out of dislike or contempt, but they become oddly sympathetic to the weaker man and apportion to him (6) their own good will. If someone at a critical moment makes them aware, they quickly correct their error. This, they say, Cleitomachus did. For he seemed to be invincible in the contest, and as his fame had spread throughout the world, they say that Ptolemy, in his eagerness to undermine his reputation, trained the boxer Aristonicus with great care, seeing as (8) he had a natural aptitude for this event. When Aristonicus had arrived in Greece and was matched against Cleitomachus at Olympia, the majority, it seems, took the former's side and cheered for him, happy that someone for a moment dared to stand (9) against Cleitomachus. But when, as the bout progressed, he appeared matched in the contest and somehow even landed an opportunistic blow, there was clapping and the crowd grew excited, and urged Aristonicus on. At that point, they say that Cleitomachus stood back and recovered his breath for short time and then turned to the crowd and asked them what they were thinking (10) by rooting for Aristonicus and siding with him (11) as much as they could. Did they think he was not fighting fairly or were they unaware that Cleitomachus was now fighting for Greece, but Aristonicus (12) for King Ptolemy? Did they want an Egyptian[16] to wear the Olympic crown by conquering Greeks or to hear a Theban and a Boeotian proclaimed victor (13) in the men's boxing match? When he said these things, they say, there was such a great change in the crowd that from the reversal Aristonicus was beaten by the crowd rather than Cleitomachus.

---

[16] This Egyptian must have been a Greek citizen of Alexandria to compete, but such Greeks were often subject to mainland Greek prejudices against anyone from Egypt.

29. Alcaeus of Messene

29a. *Greek Anthology* 9. 588: Cleitomachus the Boxer

Alcaeus was a writer of epigrams, some of which were written against Philip V of Macedon, which means that he must have lived around the end of the second century BCE. Twenty-two of his epigrams are now collected in the Greek Anthology. *His epigram on Cleitomachus of Thebes commemorates his triple victory in boxing,* pankration, *and wrestling. See* **28b** *and* **37o** *(Pausanias 6.15.3)*

> O Stranger, you see the bronze courage in the image
>   of Cleitomachus, just as Greece looked upon his power.
> When he had just unwrapped the thongs, bloodied from the boxing match,
>   from his hands, he fought in the fierce *pankration*.
> In the third contest, he did not get dust on his shoulders, but wrestled
>   without a fall; he won three matches at the Isthmian games.
> He alone of the Greeks has this honor. Seven-gated
>   Thebes and his father Hermocrates received the crown.

30. *Maccabees*

30a. Bk. 2.4.9–15: Setting Up a Gymnasium

Second Maccabees is a non-canonical text that some religious authorities include in the Old Testament. It was written in Greek, probably in Alexandria in 124 BCE. It treats mainly the Maccabean revolt against Antiochus IV Epiphanes and events from 180 to 161 BCE. This passage shows the importance of the gymnasium structure in promoting Greek identity to the detriment of Jewish identity.

After Seleucus died and Antiochus, called Epiphanes, succeeded to the kingdom, Jason the brother of Onias was proclaimed the high priest through corruption, having promised the king in a meeting 360 talents of silver and 80 talents of other revenue. In addition, he promised to pay another 150 if he was given permission for a gymnasium under his own authority in which he might establish an ephebate and enroll citizens of Jerusalem as Antiochenes. The king consented, and as soon as he took office, he converted the local stock to Greek customs. Jason abrogated the royal philanthropy toward the Jews that had been established through John, the son of Eupolemus, when he conducted an embassy to the Romans for friendship and alliance, and he destroyed the polity's lawful ways of living with novel behaviors contrary to the law. For he happily built his gymnasium at the foot of the very acropolis and induced the best of the ephebes to put on the *petasos*.[17] There was such a peak of Hellenizing behavior and increase in foreign customs that resulted from the impiety and the overwhelming ungodliness of Jason, who was no high priest, that the priesthood no longer paid heed to the services at the altar, but spurning the sanctuary and neglecting the sacrifices, they hastened to take part in the unlawful activities of the *palaestrae* after the summons to practice the *diskos*. They disdained the values of their ancestors while considering the Greek honors to be of the greatest importance.

31. Diodorus Siculus

Diodorus, who lived between 90 and 30 BCE, was a Greek writer of a universal history that set out to synchronize events that happened in the ancient Near East with those of Greece and Rome. He used the list of Olympic victors to provide an accurate temporal framework for the history (see Appendix BII).

31a. *Library of History* bk. 13.82.7: Exaenetus of Acragas

Exaenetus of Acragas won [the *stadion*] in the ninety-second Olympiad [412 BCE]; they conducted him into the city upon a chariot. Apart from the other participants, three hundred two-horse chariots (*synōrides*) with white horses participated in his victory parade. All of them belonged to the citizens of Acragas.

31b. *Library of History* bk. 14.109: Multiple Entries in Chariot Races at Olympia

The events described here supposedly took place in 388 BCE. How much of the story is true and how much dependent on Lysias' now fragmentary Olympic speech (16b) is moot. It is evidence for multiple entries in chariot racing. The Sicilian tyrant is Dionysius I of Syracuse (432–367 BCE).

As the time for the Olympic Games drew near, [Dionysius I] dispatched a greater number of four-horse chariots than the other contenders, and his teams were much faster. He also sent pavilions for the festival ornamented with gold and very rich and variegated hangings. He sent the best rhapsodes,[18] so that by performing his poetic compositions

---

[17] The acropolis was the Temple Mount. The *petasos* was a broad-brimmed hat characteristically worn by ephebes.

[18] Public performers of all types of poetry. At Olympia they did so as entertainment, not part of poetic competition.

during the festival they would glorify him, since he remained dedicated to his poetry. He sent his brother Thearides to oversee these matters. When he arrived at the festival, Thearides was the focus of admiration for the beauty of the pavilions and the number of chariots. When the rhapsodes began to proclaim Dionysius' poems, at first, because of the fine voices of the actors, the crowd came together and all were lost in admiration. But after a while, recognizing the poor quality of the poetry, they began to mock Dionysius, and their contempt reached the point that some of the crowd rifled through the pavilions. Lysias, the orator, who was then present in Olympia, exhorted the crowd not to admit the delegation sent by an impious tyrant to the sacred contests, and that is when he read his Olympian oration. Now during the contests, by chance it happened that some of Dionysius' chariot teams deviated from the course and others collided with one another and were damaged. Likewise, the ship that was conveying the delegation home from the games to Sicily was wrecked near Tarentum in Italy by storm winds. Accordingly, they say that the sailors who made it safely back to Sicily spread the story throughout the city that because the poetry was so bad not only the rhapsodes, but with them the chariot teams and the ship were wrecked.

32. Dionysius of Halicarnassus

32a. *Roman Antiquities* bk. 7.72.3: Athletes Competing Naked

Dionysius (c.60 BCE–c.7CE) was a historian and teacher of rhetoric. Born in Greek Halicarnassus, he moved to Rome at the beginning of Augustus' rule (c.30 BCE). His Roman Antiquities *attempted to set out the history of Rome, their customs, and their monuments for Greeks, who were now subject to Roman domination. Through recourse to parallels between Greek and Roman myths and behaviors, he argued that Romans were originally Greek in descent. Compare his version of the origin of athletic nudity with Pausanias 37ab, who attributes the practice to Orsippus of Megara, and I5m.*

The first who endeavored to strip the clothing from his body and run naked was Acanthus the Spartan at the fifteenth Olympiad [720 BCE]. Before that time all Greeks felt shame to appear at the games with their bodies completely naked, as Homer, our most credible and earliest witness, bears witness when he has his heroes wrapping a cloth around their loins (see **1b**, *Iliad* 23.685, **37ab**, and Appendix AIV).

4 The Roman Period

From the middle of the second century BCE the Greek cities of the Mediterranean, including the regions of southern Italy, Sicily, and mainland Greece, had gradually come under Roman authority; and shortly after the civil war between Octavian and Antony (aided by Cleopatra, the queen of Egypt) came to a bloody conclusion at the Battle of Actium in 31 BCE, Egypt, the last remaining independent Greek kingdom, fell to Rome. That event marked the beginning of the Roman Empire, as the Roman Republic gave way to the rule of one man, Octavian (later Augustus). He was the first in a long line of Roman emperors who ruled over a territory that eventually included Britain and Spain in the west, North Africa and Egypt in the south, and Turkey, Syria, Iraq, Saudi Arabia, and Palestine in the east. Rome exerted military authority over this vast territory and built an infrastructure of forts and roads throughout it to facilitate its economic and political interests. However, it governed its conquered Greek cities by allowing them to maintain many of their cultural traditions, including the gymnasium and the civic festival structures that subtended athletic competitions. In these municipalities, now without real political or military power, the gymnasium came to function as the main instrument of education for Greek youth. Members of civic gymnasia were the privileged citizen class, but non-Greeks could at times acquire this status through education. The civic gymnasium was thus a way of becoming Hellenized. The gymnasium was maintained by citizens chosen for their wealth who for a stipulated period provided the necessary services (see 115g). As a central gathering place, gymnasia were places for literary and musical education, visiting orators and other types of public speakers, as well as sites for more general male social interaction—many contained ball courts and baths (see 38e). At the same time, athletic festivals also grew in number, offering lucrative prizes to attract the best athletes, a means of demonstrating both local civic pride and their Greek heritage.

In general, Romans viewed the practice of Greek athletics with disdain, especially the habit of competing naked and the fact that Greek athletes were often elite citizens. In Rome, competitive spectacles were gladiatorial shows featuring slaves or men of low social status who often fought to the death. This Roman practice seems to have evolved from staging battles to the death between groups of war captives at funerals as a tribute to the dead. However, it quickly grew in popularity. and the Roman emperors, in particular, used exhibitions of gladiatorial combat to advertise and strengthen their power, with the result that the games grew exponentially in size and magnificence over the course of the first three centuries of the empire.[1] The contrast between the two types of physical display further enhanced the

---

[1] See Futrell (2008) and the essays in Scanlon (2014, vol. 2: 151–311).

Sourcebook of Ancient Greek Athletics. Charles H. Stocking and Susan A. Stephens, Oxford University Press (2021).
© Charles H. Stocking and Susan A. Stephens. DOI: 10.1093/oso/9780198839606.003.0005

gymnasium as an emblem of Greek culture. However much these emperors staged gladiatorial shows, they simultaneously encouraged Greek-style athletics and even established new Greek games to be held in their honor (see Table 2, p. 371). The majority of these games gave money or other valuable prizes, while those declared Is-Olympic, or equal (isos) to the Olympic Games, expected the victorious athlete's city to provide guaranteed support during his lifetime. As a result of imperial fiat and civic pride, under Roman rule the number of Greek athletic competitions increased substantially, to the financial advantage of the individual athlete. More and more, they were able to support themselves and their families with victories on an ever-increasing games circuit established throughout the empire, as is the case with tennis or golf today.

This brought a greater level of professionalization and continued debates about the place of athletics within the civic structure as well as about its intrinsic value for the individual. Earlier, Plato and Aristotle used familiar athletic practices to frame discussions about training the soul, while doctors argued about the viability and limits of strenuous athletic exercise for health. These and other debates about athletics as a form of knowledge or skill (technē) are magnified in the writings from the Roman period, as is clear from the selections from Epictetus, Lucian, Galen, and Philostratus, as well as many of the briefer anecdotes. The sheer amount of material has compelled us to limit our selections to Greek intellectuals writing between the first to the fourth centuries CE.[2]

33. *The Greek Anthology*

The Greek Anthology, a collection of short poems (epigrams) in various meters, was compiled in the Byzantine period, though the majority of the poets collected there wrote much earlier. All but one of the epigrams below are attributed to Lucillius, a writer of satirical epigrams, over a hundred of which were collected in this anthology. All that is known about his life is that he wrote under the Emperor Nero, who ruled from 54 to 68 CE. These epigrams on boxers, runners, and pentathletes are typical of his satirical style. Boxers are so often punched in the face that they are unrecognizable; runners are so slow that they never seem to finish the course. The poems imitate in form the dedicatory epigram, which was used extensively to praise individuals for their accomplishments. Note how each epigram sets up a situation that culminates in a twisted or barbed conclusion.

33a. Bk. 11.75

Olympicus is probably not a proper name but a descriptor: an Olympic man. Augustus was a title used for all of the Roman emperors, here for Nero.

---

[2] For Roman writing on Greek athletics, see König (2005: 205–53 [ch. 5]).

This Olympicus, as he now is, Augustus, used to have a nose, chin, brow, ears, and eyelids. Then, signing up to be a boxer, he lost them all. So much so that he did not even get a portion of his paternal inheritance. When his brother showed the image that he had of him, he was declared a stranger, since he bore it no resemblance.

33b. Bk. 11.76

Narcissus was so beautiful that when he saw himself in clear water, he fell in love with his own image and wasted away from desire. If Olympicus sees himself, it will have the opposite effect.

With a mug like yours, Olympicus, do not approach a fountain or look into any clear water; if you saw your face clearly, as Narcissus did, you will hate yourself until you die.

33c. Bk. 11.77

After twenty years Odysseus returned safe to his country and his hound Argos recognized his form (*Odyssey* 17.290–327). But since you have been boxing for four hours, Stratophon, you are unrecognizable to your dog and your city. If you want to look at your face in a mirror, you will say on oath: "I am not Stratophon."

33d. Bk. 11.78

Your head, Apollophanes, has become like a sieve, or the bottom of a worm-eaten book, really like the holes bored by ants, both crooked and straight, or Lydian and Phrygian musical notes. But fearlessly box on. If you are struck on your head, you will have the same marks; you cannot have more.

33e. Bk. 11.79

Cleombrotus retired from boxing. Then he got married. Now at home he has a pugnacious old woman throwing him the punches of Isthmia and Nemea and Olympia; and he is more afraid to see his own home than the stadium. Whenever he catches his breath, he is beaten with the punches of every bout, so that he might yield; and if he yields, he is beaten.

33f. Bk. 11.80

His opponents erected a statue of Apis, the boxer. For he never wounded anyone.

33g. Bk. 11.81

As many boxing matches as the Greeks officially sponsored, I, Androcles, competed in them all. I saved one ear at Pisa, one eyelid at Plataea. At Delphi I was carried out unconscious. My father Damoteles along with my fellow citizens was summoned to carry me from the stadium, either a corpse or mutilated.

33h. Bk. 11.82

We include this epigram because it falls within the sequence on runners. It is attributed to Nicarchus, a writer of forty-two epigrams now collected in the Greek Anthology; he lived in the first-century CE.

Charmus, with five others, ran the *dolichos* in Arcadia. Amazingly, but it's a fact, he came in seventh. "There were six," you are quick to say. "How did he come in seventh?" A friend of his, in his cloak, said, "Take heart, Charmus," so he was seventh. If he had had five friends, Zoilus, he would have come in twelfth.

33i. Bk. 11.83

Lately, when everything was shaking, only the runner Erasistratus was unmoved by the great earth.

33j. Bk. 11.84

The speaker is a competitor in the pentathlon—wrestling, running, discus, long jump, and javelin. The epigram plays on the fact that the winner of the pentathlon need not actually win any event; he could come in second in all of them.

No one among the competitors was swifter than I in taking a fall; no one was slower in running the *stadion*; I never came near with the discus; I never had the strength to lift my feet for the jump, and a deformed man could throw the javelin better. Out of five events I am the first to be proclaimed beaten five times.

33k. Bk. 11.85

Running in armor, Marcus continued until the middle of the night, with the result that the stadium was everywhere closed. The public attendants thought that he was one of the honorary stone statues of hoplites erected there. What then? They opened the track in a year and then Marcus came in, behind the field by a *stadion*.

34. Dio Chrysostom

Dio Chrysostom ("Golden-tongued") was an orator writing in the first century CE. *A philosopher and adviseor to emperors, he wrote on a wide variety of subjects, including two discourses on the boxer Melancomas ("Black-haired") of Caria. The first, translated below, describes a brief interlude when the narrator and friends were in Naples for the games held in honor of the emperor.[3] They encounter an old man who tells them about the marvelous endurance and boxing strategy of the man who had just died. Melancomas trained for endurance by holding his arms and fists in the pugilist's stance and dancing around the ring, but never actually engaging in blows. In this way he tired out his opponents, whose energy faded before the bout timed out. Because Greeks boxed upright and mainly tried to punch the opponent's face and head, arms were elevated quite high, and thus the stance was even more exhausting to hold for a long time. What attracts the spectators to Melancomas is his beauty, which athletes often possessed, but which is highly unusual for boxers, whose faces and ears were scarred from repeated blows. It is not clear whether Melancomas was a real boxer or a fiction (for boxing, see Appendix CII).*

34a. *Discourse* 28: Melancomas 2

(1) We came up from the harbor and immediately went to see the athletes, almost as if we had made the whole trip in order to watch the spectacle of the contest. When we got near to the gymnasium, we saw some running on the track outside, and there was a shout from those encouraging them; and we saw others engaged in other activities. They did not seem worth our attention, so we went over to where we saw the largest crowd. (2) Now, we saw very many men standing around the arcade of Heracles and others continually arriving, and some even leaving because they were not able to see. At first, we tried to see by peering over others, and could barely see the head of a man working out with his hands raised up.[4] Little by little we edged closer. He was a young man, very tall

---

[3] The Sebasta, first organized in 2 CE in honor of Augustus. They were held in Naples and designated Is-Olympic.

[4] He is practicing by shadow boxing.

and good-looking, and besides, it seemed, his body appeared taller and more beautiful from his exercise. He was exercising quite brilliantly and with purpose, with the result that he looked more like a man actually competing. (3) Then, when he stopped exercising and the crowd was going away, we considered him more carefully. He resembled those well-crafted statues and besides had a skin color like melted bronze.

(4) After he left, we asked one of the bystanders, an old man, who he was. "That is Iatrocles, the opponent of Melancomas, and the only one who does not ask to yield, at least if he can help it. Still he could not best him, for he always lost, sometimes competing for a whole day. Then he had already stopped trying, with the result that in this last contest in Naples Melancomas defeated no one more quickly than Iatrocles. But now look at how he struts and what a large crowd he practices in front of. I myself think that he is taking pleasure at that one's misfortune. And this is natural. For he knows that not only this crown, but even all the others will be his." (5) "What," I said, "is Melancomas dead?" For we too knew his name, although we had never seen him.

"Recently," he said. "He was buried two days ago."

"How did he distinguish himself from this man, and others?" I said, "Was it size or courage?"

"That one," he said, "my good man, was more courageous and larger than all other men, not only his opponents, and he was the best-looking. And if he had stayed an amateur (*idiōtēs*) and had not done this at all [i.e., boxing], because of his beauty alone he would have been widely acclaimed, for he attracted everyone, whenever he went anywhere, even those who did not know who he was. (6) He did not deck himself out in finery or do anything to be recognized, but to escape notice. But when he had stripped down, no one would look at another, although there were many boys and many men exercising naked. Although beauty often leads to softness, even for those moderately endowed with it, as beautiful as he was, he possessed even more self-control. And despising his beauty, he nonetheless preserved it in his harsh line of work. (7) Although competing at boxing, he was as unmarked as any of the runners, and he trained so strenuously and exceeded in punishing exercises to such an extent that he was able to remain for two consecutive days with his hands raised up and no one would see him letting them down or resting, as is the normal practice. He compelled his opponents to yield, not only before he himself was hit, but even before he hit them. For he did not think it manly to strike and be wounded, but that this resulted from being incapable of hard work and wanting to put an end to the bout. (8) But to last out the time and not be bested by the weight of one's arms or a lack of breath, or distressed by the heat, this was a worthy accomplishment." Taking him up, I said, "That's true, for in war the weakest throw away their shields, even though they are aware that, being unprotected, they are more likely to be wounded. In this way they are defeated by their fatigue more than their wounds." (9) "Well then," he said, "from when he began to compete at the Pythian games, he was the first of whom we know to have remained undefeated (*aleiptos*), to have won the most and most important crowns, and against opponents who were neither weak nor few in number. And before he was yet competing as a man, he surpassed his father, that most distinguished and well-known Melancomas from Caria who was a victor at Olympia and in many other competitions. For his father was not undefeated. (10) But as great as [the younger Melancomas] was, he died unfortunately. Having endured to the utmost laborious athletic training, he experienced none of life's pleasures. He was so excessively competitive that even when he was dying, he asked about the pankratist Athenodorus, a friend from childhood, 'How many days are left of his competition?'" And saying this, the old man burst into tears.

(11) "Your excessive grief is pardonable," I said, "because of your close kinship with him."

"By the gods," he said, "He isn't kin to me. He was not a family member, nor did I train him; I trained one of the boy pankratists. But he was such a great man that everyone who knew him grieved at his death."

(12) "Then," I said, "you should not call him wretched. On the contrary, he would have been the luckiest and most blessed of men if he was such as you say. For he came from a distinguished family, had beauty, and in addition courage, strength, and self-control, which are the greatest of good things. But what is the most marvelous in the man is to have been undefeated not only in his matches, but undefeated by hard work and heat and gluttony and sexual desire. It is necessary to be undefeated first by these things for one who is not going to be bested by any opponent. (13) And who enjoyed greater pleasures? A man who is the most competitive always winning, being admired, and who knew that he was? I think the gods loved him very much and especially honored him in death so that he might not experience any of the terrible things in life. For he must have, if he had lived, become less attractive, lost his strength, and perhaps even been defeated. Whoever passes away amidst the greatest of goods, having achieved the best that is possible, this man dies in the most fortunate way of all. And you would find that in times past those whom the gods loved died young."[5]

"Whom do you mean?" he said.

(14) "Achilles," I said, "and Patroclus and Hector and Memnon and Sarpedon."

As I was naming still others, he said, "You have fairly spoken these things for the ease of men's pains, and I would have wished to hear more. But it is time to train the boy, and I am going."

34b. *Discourse* 29.15–16: Melancomas 1

*The following section comes from the funeral oration for Melancomas. For the most part it duplicates the information in the earlier discourse but includes this favorable comparison of athletics and war. See **35j** (Plutarch) and **38a** (Lucian,* Anacharsis*) for different views.*

---

[5] See **8a** for similar sentiments.

(15) In general I prefer this to the excellence (*aretē*) that accrues from war because, first, the best of men in athletics would surpass in war, for the man who is stronger in body and capable of enduring hardship for a longer period with or without armor, I think is better. Second, it is not the same thing to compete against the skilled and those who are inferior in every way as to have opponents who are the best from the whole world. In war the man who wins one time kills his opponent (*antagōnistēs*) with the result that he does not have the same opponent again. In athletics, victory is for that one day but then the victor has as opponents likewise those he defeated and anyone else who wishes. (16) Then in athletics the better man triumphs over the lesser, since he must win with nothing other than his courage and his strength. But against the enemy the power of iron, since it is much greater than that of human nature, does not allow the excellence of the body to be tested, but often takes the side of inferior men. As many things as I have said about athletics are also true of the athlete.

34c. *Discourse* 9.1–2, 10–13: On Diogenes the Cynic at the Isthmian Games

Diogenes (c.412–323 BCE) from Sinope on the Black Sea was a wandering philosopher, notorious for his rudeness in confronting what he perceived as corrupt and disingenuous social behavior. He lived a simple life that defied social conventions, sleeping and eating and eliminating wherever he pleased and often in public spaces. He regarded himself as a physician of the soul, ready to critique bad behaviors and offer models for remedy. In this fictional narrative, written centuries after Diogenes had died, his attendance at the Isthmian festival is used to contrast behavior truly worthy of a crown with that of the contending athletes. Elements of this anecdote also occur in Dio's Discourse *8.4–6, 9–12.*

(1) During the Isthmian Games, Diogenes went down to the Isthmus, it seems, while living in Corinth. He attended the festival, not, as was the case with many others, in a desire to see the athletes and to eat his fill, but, I think, to observe men and their foolishness, since he knew that human behavior was at its most transparent on festival occasions, while in war and in encampments it escaped notice because of danger and fear. (2) And, to be sure, he thought that these men were most treatable, since diseases of the body whenever they are visible, are more easily treated by physicians than while they remain hidden.

[The locals were familiar with his antisocial behaviors and usually ignored him, but those visitors from abroad (Ionia, Sicily, Italy, Libya, Massilia, and Borysthenes) came to watch him and hear him speak, more to take a story home about him than with the object of personal improvement.]

(10) Generally, the managers of the Isthmian games (*athlothetai*) and the other dignitaries and powerful men were quite at a loss and withdrew themselves whenever he happened by, and they all passed by in silence, scowling at him. But when he crowned himself with

pine, the Corinthians sent some of their attendants to order him to take off the crown and to do nothing that was against the law. (11) He asked them why it was against the law for him to crown himself with pine, but not for others. One of them responded to him, "You have not won a victory, Diogenes." He replied, "I have defeated many great opponents (*antagōnistai*), not like these slaves now wrestling and throwing the discus and running here, (12) but more difficult in every respect—poverty, exile, ill-repute, and anger, pain, desire, and fear, and the most irresistible beast of all, festering and without restraint—pleasure, which no one of the Greeks or of the barbarians has resolved to fight against and conquer by overpowering with his soul, but they are all bested and failed in this contest—Persians and Medes and Syrians and Macedonians and Athenians and Lacedaemonians—except for me. (13) Do I seem worthy to you of the pine crown or will you take it and give it to the one full of the most meat?[6] Now give this answer to those who sent you: It is they who break the law. For without having won any contest they go about wearing crowns. And say that I have made the Isthmian Games more distinguished by taking the crown myself and that this should not be fought over by men, but by goats."

35. Plutarch

Plutarch (c. 46–120 CE) lived and wrote in Chaeronea in Boeotia. A member of the Greek upper class under Roman imperial power, he is best known for his Parallel Lives of the Greeks and Romans, *a series of biographical essays that paired famous Greeks with similar types of Romans, e.g., founders (Theseus and Romulus), lawgivers (Lycurgus and Numa), generals (Alexander and Julius Caesar), orators (Demosthenes and Cicero), as well as the* Lives of the Roman Emperors, *of which only two,* Galba *and* Otho, *have survived. He served as a magistrate in his hometown and as a priest of the cult of Apollo at Delphi. He was widely known for his writings and lectures, many of which are now collected under the title of* Moralia, *seventy-eight short essays on a wide range of topics from the education of children to the decline of oracles, to a series of questions on Greek and Roman customs. His sources were eclectic; he had available earlier historians and cites many who have not survived. Throughout his vast corpus there are numerous anecdotes that shed light on Greek athletic practices.*

35a. *Life of Agesilaus* 20.1: Cynisca

See also **27o, 37x, 11i.**

When Agesilaus saw that some of the citizens took undue pride in their breeding of horses, he persuaded his sister Cynisca to furnish a chariot to compete in the Olympic

---

[6] Athletes were often fed meat diets, though the average person ate very little meat.

Games, because he wished to show the Greeks that the victory was not a matter of personal excellence (*aretē*) but of wealth and expenditure.

35b. *Life of Alexander* 4.9–11: Why Alexander Does Not Compete at Olympia

This was a very well-known anecdote; a version of it occurs in Plutarch's Fortunes of Alexander *(Moralia 331B) as well.*

[Alexander] did not desire any type of fame and from any source, as Philip did, who fancied himself clever at sophistic argument and had his chariot victories engraved on his coinage. But when those in Alexander's circle asked him if he might like to compete in the *stadion* at Olympia, since he was a swift runner, he replied: "If in fact I was going to have kings as my opponents." And he seems in general to have had an aversion to the race of athletes, seeing as he established a large number of competitions, not only for tragedians and *aulos* players and lyre players, and even rhapsodes, and for all types of hunting and competing with cudgels, but he did not establish a prize for boxing or *pankration*.

35c. *Life of Alexander* 15. 7–9: Alexander at Troy

Going to Troy, he sacrificed to Athena and poured out libations to the heroes. He anointed the gravestone of Achilles with oil and with his companions competed in a foot race, naked, as was the custom. Then he crowned the gravestone with garlands, proclaiming him blessed because, while alive, he happened upon a trustworthy friend [Patroclus] and, when he died, a great herald [Homer].

35d. *Life of Alexander* 34.3: Alexander Honors a Valiant Athlete

For Phayllus, see **46a** *(710).*

[Alexander] sent the citizens of Croton in Italy a portion of the spoils, honoring the zeal and valor of the athlete Phayllus, who, during the Persian Wars, when the rest of the Italiote Greeks refused help, took a ship at his own cost and sailed to Salamis to have a share in the danger. Alexander was thus well disposed to all valor and a guardian and friend of noble actions.

35e. *Life of Aratus* 28.4: Violation of Right to Participate in the Nemean Games

Normally, the four crown games began with a proclamation that was intended to insure safe passage to the competition through all Greek territories, even those at war. The events described took place in 100 BCE. On the various locations of the Nemean Games, see Appendix B1.

[Aratus, the tyrant of Sicyon] brought Cleonae into the Achaean League and the Nemean Games to the people in Cleonae on the grounds that by virtue of their homeland (*patria*) the games were more properly theirs. But the Argives also celebrated them, and then, for the first time, they abrogated the right of safety of person (*asylia*) and safe passage for all Argive competitors; and as many as they captured traveling through the land to compete in Argos, they sold [into slavery] on the grounds that they were enemies.

35f. *Life of Lycurgus* 1: Evidence from Olympia for Dating Lycurgus

The biography opens with a discussion of the various ancient attempts to date Lycurgus, the famed Spartan lawgiver, as well as the beginning of the Olympic Games.

Some say that he flourished with Iphitus and together they established the Olympic truce.[7] Among them is the philosopher Aristotle, using as his evidence the discus at Olympia on which Lycurgus' name has been inscribed and preserved. But others calculating the time by the successions of the kings of Sparta, as Eratosthenes and Apollodorus, show that he lived many years before the first Olympiad.

35g. *Life of Lycurgus* 14.2: Lycurgus' Policy on Educating Women

This material is undoubtedly dependent on Xenophon's earlier account (see 10c).

[Lycurgus] exercised the bodies of unmarried women in running, wrestling, throwing the discus, and javelin, so that the growth in their wombs, having a strong beginning in a strong body, would emerge in better condition, and that having come with strength to the fullness of their pregnancy, they would endure the pains of labor easily and well. Freeing them from a soft, sedentary, and delicate lifestyle, he accustomed the boys as well as the girls to parade naked and at some festivals to dance and sing with young men present and observing them.

---

[7] Athenaeus, bk. 14.635f states that "It is agreed by all that Lysander the lawgiver along with Iphitus of Elis organized the first numbered Olympic Games." See Appendix BII.

35h. *Life of Numa* 1.4: Hippias of Elis' List of Olympic Victors

Hippias of Elis (443–399 BCE) is credited with inventing or at least systematically organizing Olympic victory lists, but this passage of Plutarch is the only actual mention of Hippias' authorship. Despite Plutarch's skepticism, Hippias' Elean citizenship, his interest in systematic record-keeping, and the fact that such Olympionikai begin to appear shortly after his lifetime support the identification of him as the inventor of such lists. See Appendix BII.

It is difficult to determine chronologies accurately, and especially chronologies arranged on the basis of Olympic victors, the list of which, they say, Hippias of Elis published late, based on nothing that compels trust.

35i. *Life of Pericles* 36.4–5: Death of a Pentathlete Struck by an *Akontion*

This brief anecdote stigmatizes Pericles for treating an athlete's death as material for a rhetorical dispute. It mirrors the debate found in Antiphon (15) and indicates that these types of accidents were not unusual.

Now the elder of his legitimate sons, Xanthippus [annoyed at his scanty allowance], mocked his father by relating for a laugh the conversation at home and [Pericles'] time spent in conversations with sophists. For when a pentathlete in throwing an *akontion* accidently struck and killed Epitimus the Pharsalian, [Pericles] spent the whole day with Protagoras debating whether the *akontion* or the thrower or the umpire (*agōnothetēs*) was responsible in accordance with correct reasoning.

35j. *Life of Philopoemen* 3.3–4: The Difference between Athletes and Soldiers

Because [Philopoemen] seemed naturally suited for wrestling, when some of his friends and guardians urged him to the athletic life, he asked them whether he would be harmed for military training by athletic training. They said what was true, namely, that the athletic body and lifestyle differed from the military in every respect, especially in diet and exercise. For athletes a great deal of sleep, continual eating to fullness, regulated movements and rest augmented and protected their condition from every slip or deviation from their usual state as being a change for the worse. But experience of all change and irregularity was fitting [for the soldier's lifestyle], especially accustoming themselves to endure deprivation easily and lack of sleep. Upon hearing this, Philopoemen not only abandoned the matter [wrestling] and mocked it, but later, when he became a general, he cast dishonor and abuse upon athletes, as much as he could, because they turned those with the most useful bodies unfit for the contests that were necessary [i.e., war].

35k. *Life of Phocion* 20.1: The *Apobatēs* Race

For the apobatēs *race, see* **19e** *and Appendix C IV.*

When his son Phocus wanted to compete at the Panathenaea, he urged him to the *apobatēs* race, not expecting a victory, but on the grounds that the regimen and bodily exercise would improve him. For the young man loved to drink and led a disorderly life. When he did win and many invited him to join in a victory banquet, Phocion refused other invitations but accepted this sought-after honor of one man. When he went to the banquet and saw the imposing scale of the preparations, even the foot basins with aromatics brought to them as they entered, he urged his son: "Stop your companion from ruining your victory." Wishing to remove the youth entirely from that lifestyle, he sent him to Sparta and enrolled him among those engaged in the so-called *agōgē*.[8]

35l. *Life of Solon* 23: Compensation for Panhellenic Victories

This brief passage comes from a discussion of Solon's law on prices. Plutarch adds the following information on commodities by way of comparison. These amounts were said to be a reduction of earlier levels of support.

With respect to the pricing of sacrificial offerings, a sheep and a measure of wheat were both valued at one drachma. [Solon] ordered that the victor at Isthmia be given 100 drachmas, and an Olympic victor 500 drachmas.

35m. *Life of Theseus* 25.4–5: Theseus and the Isthmian Games

Theseus established the Isthmian Games in rivalry with Heracles; just as the Olympic Games had been established for Zeus by Heracles, the Isthmian Games were established by him for the Greeks to celebrate in honor of Poseidon. The games in honor of Melecertes had been established there, but they were celebrated at night and organized like a mystic rite rather than a spectacle and festival assembly for all Greeks. Some say

---

[8] This was the training that young Spartan men engaged in before coming of age. See **10d**.

that the Isthmian Games were established for Sciron, whose murder Theseus was expiating because they were kin. Sciron was the son of Canethus and Henioche, the daughter of Pittheus.[9] Others say that it was Sinon, not Sciron, and the games were established for the former by Theseus, not the latter. He stipulated that the Corinthians should provide a seating area for those Athenians who attended that was as large as the area covered by the sail of the ship that brought the delegation; this is according to the histories of Hellanicus and Andron of Halicarnassus.

35n. *Moralia 38B: On Listening to Lectures.* Ear Protectors

Plutarch is concerned with the young hearing inappropriate things before their characters are formed and they can make sensible judgments. This seems to have been a familiar anecdote; it occurs also in Table Talk (Moralia 706C).

[In order to keep the ears of the young unsullied] Xenocrates urged that ear protectors (*amphōtides*) be placed on children even more than on athletes; the ears of the latter are disfigured by blows, but the character of the former by words.

35o. *Moralia 224F: Sayings of the Spartans.* Fairness in Competition

A comment attributed to Leon, an early seventh-century Spartan king.

When he saw the runners at Olympia at the starting line jockeying for position, he remarked: "The runners are much more interested in a quick start than fairness."

35p. *Moralia 347C: Fame of the Athenians.* Marathon

On Marathon, see also **8g** *and* **38c.**

Now Heraclides Ponticus records in his histories that Thersippus of Eroeadae announced the [victory of] the battle of Marathon, but most say it was Eucles, who ran in his armor, while heated from the battle, and after he had burst into the doors of the first men of the state, said only this: "Rejoice; we are victorious." Then he immediately expired.[10]

---

[9] Pittheus was Theseus' grandfather. For Sciron, see **22c.**

[10] A similar anecdote is told about a torch racer in Plutarch's *Life of Aristides* 20.5.

36. Epictetus

Epictetus, born in Phrygia c.50 CE, was a Stoic philosopher. He began life as a slave, migrated to Rome, and was later freed, but exiled from Rome along with other philosophers by the Emperor Domitian. He then established a school on the Adriatic coast in Epirus (modern Albania). His moral and ethical teachings were successful because of their clarity of vision and application. In these brief selections from his Discourses, *he uses examples from athletics to illustrate his views on the importance of management of the self.*

36a. Bk. 1.2.25–37: "How One May Preserve Character on Every Occasion"

Epictetus concludes this discourse with examples of the way in which athletes by virtue of training and habits of mind will persist with what they deem proper.

(25) An athlete once acted in a way that put him in danger of dying unless he had his genitals removed. His brother, who happened to be a philosopher, came to him and said, "Come brother, what are you going to do? Shall we have that part of you cut off and then go back to the gymnasium?"[11] He did not tolerate that option, and he persisted until he died. (26) Someone might then ask: "How did he do this? As an athlete or a philosopher?" But Epictetus said, "As a man—a man who was announced and competed at Olympia—a man experienced with such a place and not merely one oiled up at the gymnasium of Baton.[12] (27) Someone else might allow his head to be cut off, if he could live without it. (28) But such is the nature of character. It is so strong among those accustomed to it that they include it in their deliberations. (29) And someone might say, 'Epictetus, shave your beard.'[13] And 'Philosopher,' I say, 'I will not shave.' And he might say, 'But if you don't, I will cut your throat.' And I say, 'If that seems better to you, cut it.'

(30) And someone asked, 'How are we supposed to perceive the character proper to each?' How, when a lion approaches, does a solitary bull perceive its preparation and endanger itself on behalf of the entire herd? Or is it clear that perception of character happens at the same time as preparation in all matters? (31) And whoever among us has such preparation, he will not be ignorant of it. (32) A bull does not become a bull or a man a man all of a sudden, but it is necessary to train in winter, to prepare oneself and not jump at that which is not appropriate to us.

(33) Consider only, at what price you sell your ability to choose. If nothing else, do not sell it for a small sum. But that which is great and remarkable belongs to others, to

---

[11] Since men exercised naked, the loss of genitals would also be a visual deformity.
[12] Baton was a gymnasiarch in the time of Marcus Aurelius.
[13] The beard was a mark of the philosopher, and so the request is to reject one's identity.

Socrates and others like him. (34) Why then, if we have been born in a similar way, are not all men or at least many like such great people? Do all horses become swift and dogs good at tracking? (35) What then? If I am without natural talent, do I disavow all self-care for this reason? May it not be so. (36) Epictetus will not be better than Socrates. But if not better, at least not worse, this is enough for me. (37) For I will not be a strongman like Milo, and nevertheless I do not neglect my body. Nor will I be rich like Croesus, but I do not neglect my possessions. We do not neglect any act of care simply because we are denied reaching the highest point."

36b. Bk. 1.6.23–9: "On Providence." Hardships at Olympia

Epictetus compares the hardships that spectators endure at Olympia to what one must endure in daily life. The passage also provides insights into Olympia as a tourist attraction.

(23) You travel to Olympia in order to view the work of Pheidias,[14] and each of you considers it a misfortune to have died without seeing it. (24) But where there is no need to travel, and you are there and already present before other works, do you not desire to view and understand these? (25) Do you not perceive either who you are or for what you have been born or why you have received the ability of perception? (26) Some things are unseemly and difficult in life. Are there not difficulties at Olympia? Do you not suffer from the heat? Are you not closed in by the crowd? Do you not bathe badly? Are you not soaked when it rains? Do you not take delight in the noise and shouts and other difficulties? (27) But I suppose these things are compensated for by the worthiness of the spectacle and you bear and endure it. (28) But come, have you not received the abilities by which you may endure all that happens to you? Do you not have a greatness of spirit (*megalopsychia*)? Have you not received courage (*andreia*)? (29) Do you not have endurance (*karteria*)? And why do I care about what can happen to me when I have greatness of spirit? What shall disrupt me or disturb me or appear painful? Will I not make use of that power for the very purpose I received it? And will I be in pain and lament at that which happens to me?

36c. Bk. 1.18. 21–3: "One Ought Not to Be Disturbed by the Mistakes of Others." Thinking like an Athlete

(21) "Who then is unconquered? He whom nothing disturbs which is beyond his choice. Then when I approach the remainder of a set of circumstances, I think in the manner of an athlete. "That man won the first lot. What then about the second? And what if there is heat? (22) What about at Olympia?" And so on and so forth. And if you try to bribe him,

---

[14] Pheidias created the cult statue of Zeus at Olympia, which was considered one of the seven wonders of the ancient world.

he will show contempt at such an act. And what if you put a young woman in front of him? And what if the contest takes place in the dark? And what if reputation is at stake? And what if blame is involved? Or praise? Or even death? (23) He is able to conquer all these things. So what if there is heat or rain or if there is some sadness? Or if he is tired? This man is my unconquerable athlete (*anikētos athlētēs*).

36d. Bk. 1.29.33–40: "On Stability (*Eustatheia*)." Athletics as a Metaphor for Training in Life

(33) When one is called into any particular situation, that is the proper time (*kairos*) to demonstrate whether one has been taught well. (34) For the one coming into danger is like a young boy having come from school who has practiced solving syllogisms. And if someone provides him with an easily solvable syllogism, he says, "Give me a refined and complicated one, in order that I might train myself (*gymnazein*) with it." Even athletes are dissatisfied with slight young men. (35) One says, "He cannot lift me up." A young man who reacts in this way has a fine disposition. But not always. When the occasion presents itself, it is necessary that one weeps and says, "I wish I had learned." (36) What then? If you did not learn it in order to demonstrate it in action, why then did you learn it at all? I think there is someone of you sitting there who are in labor pains with yourself, saying, "May difficulties not come to me which have come to this man. Why do I waste my time sitting in a corner when I am able to be crowned at Olympia? When will someone announce such a contest for me?" All of you need to have such a disposition. (37) But even among the gladiators of Caesar, there are those who are upset because no one has brought them forth for competition and paired them with another fighter, and they pray to god and approach their overseers requesting to fight. Among you, will no one appear as such? (38) I would like to sail to Rome and see what my athlete is doing, how he takes care in his subject matter. (39) "But I do not want such a subject," he says. But is it in your power to choose what subject you wish? You have been given a body as such, and parents as such, and such brothers, and a fatherland as such, and a station in that fatherland. Then you come and say, "Change my subject matter." Do you not have the means for using what has been given to you? (40) You ought to say, "It is your lot to give to me, mine to care for it well." But you do not say this and say instead, "Do not offer this to me, but such as I choose."

36e. Bk. 3.15.1–4: "On Circumspection in All Matters." Enduring Hardships like Olympic Athletes

(1) In all activities, consider what precedes and what follows, and approach it thus.

If not, first you will have enthusiasm, since you have not considered what comes next. Later, when some lamentable events have appeared, you will stop. And you say, (2) "But I wish to be an Olympic victor." But consider all the things that precede and follow this. And if it is fitting for you, seize upon the work. (3) It is necessary that you conduct yourself in an orderly fashion, eat according to necessity, abstain from desserts, be trained by compulsion, directed at fixed times, in heat and in cold. You will not drink cold water or wine. In short, you must surrender yourself to a trainer as you do to a doctor. (4) And then in the contest, you will be covered in dirt; there will be times when you break a hand, and your ankle will be dislocated, when you eat much dust and are physically whipped. And after all this there comes a time when you will lose.

36f. Bk. 3.22.51–2: "On Cynicism." The Risks in Olympic Competition

In this excerpt, we see the use of athletic metaphor extended. Indeed, Diogenes the Cynic is also reported to have relied extensively on athletics as a metaphor for the philosophical life (see Dio Chrysostom Discourse 8 and **34c***).*

(51) Do you see what a great affair you are about to undertake? First, take a mirror; look at your shoulders; know your loins, your thighs. For you are going to be enrolled in the Olympic Games, a contest that is not cold or miserable. (52) In the Olympics it is not possible simply to be conquered and excused, but first it is necessary to be shamed with the entire habitable world looking on, not just among the Athenians or Spartans or Nicopolitans. And then one must be whipped if one steps out from what is proper, and before being beaten, one must suffer thirst and heat, and eat much dust. Reflect more carefully, know yourself, consult the divinity, and attempt nothing separate from god. For if he advises you, know that he wishes you to be great or he wishes you to suffer many blows.

37. **Pausanias**

Very little is known about Pausanias beyond what he reveals in his writings. He was probably from Lydia (see **37f***) and lived and wrote in the middle of the second century* CE, *under the Roman emperors from Hadrian to Marcus Aurelius. He was dead by 180* CE. *His surviving writing is an immensely valuable travelogue, the* Description of Greece, *in ten books. It provides detailed descriptions of the main areas of mainland Greece from his own experience as a visitor. In his extensive treatment of Olympia, he includes descriptions of the buildings, dedications by individuals and states, background on the history of the site and the games held there (the quadrennial Olympic Games and the Heraea), as well as numerous anecdotes about successful athletes. He spends far less time in describing the other* *three Panhellenic sites, which doubtless reflects their relative importance during the Roman period.* **37q**, *the longest section we print, provides a good example of his technique: He describes the monuments as if he is moving past them. Each individual statue is positioned relative to others around it, with biographical, historical, and mythological information occasionally inserted. Pausanias occasionally makes critical judgments about his material, though for the most part he simply presents it. Much of the information he provides can be found in earlier material, particularly Pindar's Olympian Odes and inscriptions found at Olympia. Pausanias' own descriptions were also a source for subsequent writers who mention Olympia and its victorious athletes.*

37a. Bk. 5.7.6–8.4: Mythic History of the Olympic Games

These various mythic accounts link the origin of the Olympic Games with the beginning of the rule of Zeus as king of the gods. Note how many of the gods are said to have engaged in athletic contests.

As far as the Olympic contest is concerned, those men of Elis who remember most ancient matters say that Cronus held the first kingship [of the gods] in the sky, and that a temple was built for Cronus in Olympia by those men called the Golden Race.[15] When Zeus was born,[16] Rhea entrusted the protection of her son to the Dactyls of Ida, who are the same as those called Curetes. They came from the Cretan Mount Ida: Heracles, Paeonaeus, Epimedes, Iasius, and Idas.

(5.7.7) Heracles, who was the oldest, played a game where he matched his brothers in a running race, and crowned the winner with a branch of wild olive. They had so much wild olive that they slept on heaps of its leaves while they were still green. They say that the wild olive tree was introduced to Greece by Heracles from the land of the Hyperboreans, who were men living beyond the home of the North Wind, Boreas.[17]

(5.7.8) In his hymn to Achaea, Olen the Lycian was the first to say that from these Hyperboreans Achaea came to Delos. And then Melanopus of Cyme composed an ode for Rhea and Apollo, declaring that these gods came to Delos from the Hyperboreans, even before Achaea.

(5.7.9) And Aristeas of Proconnesus—for he too made mention of the Hyperboreans—may perhaps have learned even more about them from the Issedones, whom he mentions visiting in his poem. And so Heracles of Ida is generally thought to be the first to set up a contest (*agōn*) there, and first to have called it Olympic. So he established

---

[15] In Greek myth the Golden Age of men was a time of peace and prosperity, the first of five ages, each of which declined from the previous state. See Hesiod, *Works and Days*, 109–201.

[16] Zeus was Cronus' son. Cronus had swallowed his previous children in fear that they would overthrow him. Therefore, his wife, Rhea, hid the newborn Zeus to prevent this from happening. When Zeus came to adulthood, he did overthrow his father to become the ruler of the Olympian gods.

[17] This Heracles (from Mt. Ida) is one of the Curetes, not the son of Zeus and Alcmene. For a version of this story, see Pindar **2b**.16–18.

the custom of holding them every fifth year because he and his brothers were five in number.[18]

(5.7.10) Now some say that Zeus wrestled here with Cronus himself for rule, while others say that he was administrator of the contest (*agōnothetēs*) in honor of his victory over Cronus. But there were other contests, and Apollo is said to have outrun Hermes and beat Ares at boxing. And they say this is why the Pythian flute song is played while the pentathletes are jumping—because the flute song is sacred to Apollo and Apollo won Olympic victories.

(5.8.1) After these games, they say Clymenus, the son of Cardys, came from Crete, about fifty years after the flood came upon the Greeks in the time of Deucalion.[19] He was descended from Heracles of Ida, and he re-established the contest at Olympia. There he set up an altar in honor of Heracles, his ancestor, and the other Curetes, and gave the epithet of *Parastates* ["Assistant"] to Heracles. Endymion, the son of Aethlius, brought an end to Clymenus' rule, and then he established a race for his sons at Olympia, with the kingship as the prize (*athla*).

(5.8.2) And about a generation after Endymion, Pelops held a contest in honor of Olympian Zeus that was most remarkable compared to any of his predecessors.[20] When the sons of Pelops were scattered from Elis over all the rest of the Peloponnese, Amythaon, the son of Cretheus, and cousin of Endymion on his father's side, also set up Olympic contests. For they say that Aethlius was also a son of Aeolus [the god of the winds], though he was called a son of Zeus. And after him Pelias and Neleus set up contests in common.

(5.8.3) Augeas too held them, and likewise Heracles, the son of Amphitryon,[21] after his conquest of Elis. The victors crowned by Heracles include Iolaus, who won with the mares of Heracles. And so even in ancient times it was customary to compete with another's horses. In the funeral games of Patroclus, Homer made it so that Menelaus drove a pair of horses, where one was *Aethē*, a mare of Agamemnon, while the other was his own horse.[22]

(5.8.4) In addition, Iolaus was charioteer to Heracles. So Iolaus won the chariot race, and Iasius, an Arcadian, won the horse race; while one of the sons of Tyndareus, Castor, won the foot race and the other, Polydeuces, won the boxing match. And it is said that Heracles himself won victories at wrestling and the *pankration*.

---

[18] The event is every four years, but Pausanias is counting first and last Olympic year, plus three intervening years.

[19] After Zeus destroyed men by flood for their baseness, he ordered Deucalion and his wife Pyrrha to repopulate the earth by sowing rocks ("the bones of their mother"). This was the Greek version of a widely known flood myth.

[20] See **2a** (Pindar *Olympian* 1).

[21] This is the later and more famous Heracles of the twelve labors.

[22] See **1b** (*Iliad* 23.290).

37b. Bk. 5.8.5–9.6: When Olympic Contests Were Introduced

(5.8.5) After the reign of Oxylus, who also established a contest, the Olympic festival was discontinued until the reign of Iphitus. When Iphitus renewed the games, as I have already mentioned [Pausanias 5.4.5], men had by this time forgotten the ancient contests. The memory (*hypomnēsis*) of the ancient contests was recovered little by little. And whenever they remembered something, they reintroduced it into the program of the contests.

(5.8.6) This much is clear. For when there was a continuous observance of the Olympic festival, the first prize established was for the foot race, and **Coroebus** the Elean was victor [in 776 BCE]. There is no statue (*eikōn*) of Coroebus at Olympia, but his grave is on the borders of Elis. Afterward, at the fourteenth Olympiad [724 BCE], the *diaulos* was added. **Hypenus** of Pisa captured the crown of wild olive in that contest. At the next Olympiad, **Acanthus** of Sparta won in the *dolichos* [distance race].[23]

(5.8.7) At the eighteenth Olympiad [708 BCE], they remembered the pentathlon and wrestling. **Lampis** won in the pentathlon and **Eurybatus** won in wrestling. Both were Spartans. At the twenty-third Olympiad [688], prizes for boxing were given out, and the victor was **Onomastus** of Smyrna, which at that time was already part of Ionia. At the twenty-fifth Olympiad [680 BCE], they brought back the race of full-grown horses, and **Pagondas** of Thebes was recognized as best in the chariot race.

(5.8.8) At the eighth Olympiad [648 BCE] after this they admitted the *pankration* for men and the *kelēs* [race on horseback]. The horse of **Crauxidas** of Crannon won, and **Lygdamis** of Syracuse overcame all who entered for the *pankration*. Lygdamis has his tomb near the quarries at Syracuse, and according to the Syracusans he was equal in size to Theban Heracles, though I am not so sure.

(5.8.9) There is no recollection (*mnēmē*) of contests for boys in the ancient Olympic contests, but the Eleans enjoyed them and so they introduced them. The prizes for boys' running and wrestling were set up at the thirty-seventh Olympiad [632 BCE]. **Hipposthenes** of Sparta won the prize for wrestling, and **Polyneices** the Elean won the foot race.[24] At the forty-first Olympiad [616 BCE] they announced boys' boxing, and of those who entered this contest, **Philytas** of Sybaris was preeminent.

(5.8.10) The men's race with armor was sanctioned at the sixty-fifth Olympiad [520 BCE], for the sake of attention to military matters, or so it seems to me. **Damaretus** of Heraea was the first to beat those running with shields. They established the harness race for two full-grown horses, called the *synōris*, at the ninety-third Olympiad [408 BCE], and **Euagoras** of Elis was victorious. At the ninety-ninth Olympiad [384 BCE], they decided to have contests for chariots drawn by [four] foals, and **Sybariades** of Sparta won the crown with his chariot.

---

[23] See Appendix CI-IV for further discussion of events.
[24] On Hipposthenes' illustrious career, see also **40a**.

(5.8.11) Afterward they added races for chariots and pairs of foals [264 BCE], and for single foals with a rider [256 BCE]. For the chariot and pair of foals, it is said that **Belistiche**, a woman from the Macedonian seaboard, was victorious.[25] For the horse race with foal, **Tlepolemus** of Lycia was the winner. They say that Tlepolemus won at the hundred-and-thirty-first Olympiad [256 BCE], and Belistiche at the third before this. At the hundred-and-forty-fifth Olympiad [200 BCE], prizes were established for the boys' *pankration*, and **Phaedimus**, an Aeolian from the city Troas, won.

(5.9.1) Some contests at Olympia were dropped, because the Eleans decided to discontinue them. The pentathlon for boys was established at the thirty-eighth Olympiad [628 BCE], but after **Eutelides** of Sparta took home the wild olive, it was no longer acceptable to the Eleans to have boys enter the contest. The races for mule carts, and the *kalpē* were introduced at the seventieth Olympiad [500 BCE] and the seventy-first [496 BCE] respectively, but announcements were made at the eighty-fourth [444 BCE] that both would be stopped. When they were first instituted, **Thersius** of Thessaly won the race for mule carts, while **Pataecus**, an Achaean from Dyme, won the *kalpē*.

(5.9.2) The *kalpē* was for mares, where the riders jumped off and ran beside the mares, holding on to the bridle in the last part of the race, just like those today who are called "mounters" (*anabatai*). The mounters, however, differ from the riders in the *kalpē* because they have different marks of identification (*sēmeia*), and they ride stallions instead of mares. The cart race was neither an ancient invention nor beautiful in itself. Moreover, each cart was drawn by a pair of mules, not horses, and there is an ancient curse on the Eleans if this animal is ever born in Elis.

(5.9.3) The arrangement of the festival in our time was established at the seventy-seventh Olympiad [472 BCE]. In this arrangement, sacrifices to the god are made, and afterward, contests for the pentathlon and chariot races, which occur before the other contests. Earlier, the contests for men and for horses were held on the same day. But at the Olympiad I just mentioned, the pankratists prolonged their contests until night-time, because they were not called forth in a timely manner (*kata kairon*). The cause of the delay was partly the horses, but still more the contest for the pentathlon. Callias of Athens defeated the pankratists on this occasion, but never afterward was the *pankration* to be impeded by the *pentathlon* or the chariots.

(5.9.4) The rules concerning the contest organizers (*agōnothetai*) are not the same now as they were at the first contests. Iphitus acted as sole presider, as likewise did the descendants of Oxylus after Iphitus. But at the fiftieth Olympiad, [580 BCE] two men, appointed by lot from all the Eleans, were entrusted to put on the Olympic contests, and for a majority of time after this the number of organizers remained two.

(5.9.5) But at the ninety-fifth Olympiad [400 BCE] nine *Hellanodikai* ("Judges of Greece") were appointed. The chariot races were turned over to three of them, another

---

[25] For further discussion of women competing in the Olympic Games, see Appendix AIV.

three oversaw the pentathlon, and the rest looked after the remaining contests. At the second Olympiad after this, a tenth judge was added. At the hundred-and-third Olympiad [368 BCE], because the Eleans had twelve tribes, one judge was selected from each.

(5.9.6) But the Eleans were weighed down by a war with the Arcadians and gave up a portion of their territory, along with the people included in the surrendered land. As a result, the number of tribes was reduced to eight in the hundred-and-fourth Olympiad [364 BCE]. Then *Hellanodikai* equal in number to the tribes were selected thereafter. At the hundred-and-eighth Olympiad [348 BCE], they returned to ten judges, which has remained unchanged to this day.

37c. Bk.5.10.1–10: The Temple of Olympian Zeus

(5.10.1) One might see and hear many things worthy of amazement (*thauma*) among the Greeks, but the greatest share of divine thought goes to those who participate in the divine rites of Eleusis and to those competing in the contest at Olympia. From ancient times, the grove sacred to Zeus has been called by a derivative term, Altis. Pindar also calls the place Altis in an ode made for an Olympic victor.[26]

(5.10.2) The temple and the image for Zeus were made from spoils of war, when the Eleans seized Pisa and as much of the surrounding area as was given up by the Pisans in war.[27] The image itself was made by Pheidias, and an inscription written under the feet of Zeus attests to this: "Pheidias, son of Charmides, an Athenian, made me" (see Figure 3).

(5.10.3) The height from the pediment is 68 feet, its width is 95, its length 230 feet. The architect of the temple was a local named Libon. The tiles are not made from baked earth, but from Pentelic marble cut into the shape of tiles. This invention is attributed to Byzes of Naxos, who reportedly made the images in Naxos on which is the inscription: "Euergus the Naxian fashioned me for the offspring of Leto, a son of Byzes, who first fashioned tiles from stone." This Byzes lived around the time of Alyattes the Lydian, when Astyages, the son of Cyaxares, ruled over the Persians [*c.* early sixth century BCE].

(5.10.4) In Olympia, a gold-plated cauldron stands on each end of the roof of the temple of Zeus, and an image of Victory, also gold plated, is set in the middle of the pediment. Under the image of Victory has been dedicated a golden shield, with Medusa the Gorgon in relief. The inscription on the shield states who dedicated it and why. It says: "The temple has a golden shield; from Tanagra the Spartans and their allies dedicated it, a gift taken from the Argives, Athenians and Ionians, a tithe offered for victory in war."

---

[26] See **2c**, Pindar *Olympian* 10.55.

[27] Pisa and Elis struggled intermittently for centuries. Pisa probably controlled Olympia in the late seventh and early sixth centuries BCE, but lost out to Elis around 570, the time Pausanias is referring to. For fourth-century BCE conflicts, see **10j** (Xenophon) and **37k**.

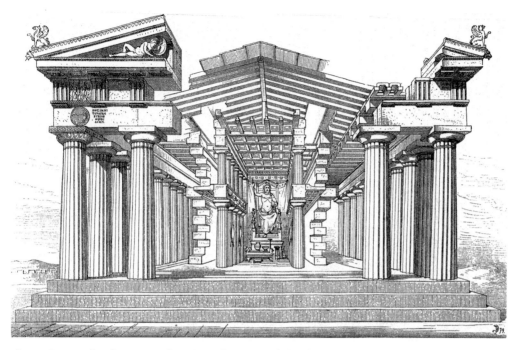

Figure 3. Temple of Zeus at Olympia with statue of Pheidias. Reconstruction by Chipiez, xylography, nineteenth century, Europe

I also mention this battle in my history of Attica, when I described the tombs that are at Athens.[28]

(5.10.5) On the outside of the frieze on the outside of the temple at Olympia, above the columns, are twenty-one gold plated shields, an offering made by the Roman general Mummius after he defeated the Achaeans, captured Corinth, and drove out its Dorian inhabitants.

(5.10.6) Now on to the images in the pediments: In the front pediment one finds the contest between Pelops and Oenomaus about to take place, and both are making preparations for the race. An image of Zeus is carved in the middle of the pediment; on the right of Zeus is Oenomaus with a helmet on his head, and next to him Sterope, his wife, one of the daughters of Atlas. Myrtilus too, the charioteer of Oenomaus, sits in front of the four horses. After him are two men. They have no names, but Oenomaus must have ordered them to attend to the horses as well.

(5.10.7) On the side at the edge one finds the Cladeus, the river which the Eleans honor most of all, second to the Alpheus. On the left of Zeus are Pelops, Hippodamia, the charioteer of Pelops, horses, and two men, who are the horse attendants of Pelops. Then the pediment narrows again, and in this part, the Alpheus is represented. According to

[28] Pausanias mentions this work several times in his *Description of Greece*, but it no longer exists.

Figure 4. East Pediment of Temple of Zeus, c.460 BCE, Archaeological Museum, Olympia

Figure 5. West Pediment of Temple of Zeus, c.460 BCE, Archaeological Museum, Olympia

the Troezenians, the name of the charioteer of Pelops is Sphaerus, but my guide (*exēgētēs*) at Olympia called him Cillas.[29]

(5.10.8) The sculptures in the front pediment are by Paeonius, who came from Mende in Thrace. Those in the back pediment are by Alcamenes, a contemporary of Pheidias, ranking next after him for skill as a sculptor. What he carved on the pediment is the battle between the Lapiths and the Centaurs at the marriage of Pirithous. Toward the center of the pediment is Pirithous.[30] On one side of him is Eurytion, who has seized the wife of Pirithous, with Caeneus bringing help to Pirithous, and on the other side is Theseus defending himself against the Centaurs with an axe. One Centaur has seized a maid, another a boy in the prime of youth. Alcamenes, I think, carved this scene, because he had learned from Homer that Pirithous was a son of Zeus, and because he knew that Theseus was a great-grandson of Pelops [cf. Homer *Iliad* 14.318].

(5.10.9) Most of the deeds of Heracles are represented at Olympia. Above the doors of the temple are carved the hunting of the Arcadian boar, his work against Diomedes the Thracian, and that against Geryon at Erytheia; he is also about to receive the load [of the earth] from Atlas, and he cleans dung from the land for the Eleans. Above the doors of the rear chamber he takes the Amazon's girdle; and there are the events pertaining to the deer, the bull at Cnossus, the Stymphalian birds, the Hydra, and the Argive lion.[31]

(5.10.10) As you enter the bronze doors you see on the right, before the pillar, Iphitus being crowned by a woman; the elegiac couplet on the statue says she is Truce (*Ekecheiria*). Within the temple are pillars, and inside are porticoes above, with an entrance through them to the image (*agalma*). A curving ascent to the roof has also been constructed.

37d. Bk. 5.11.1–11: The Statue of Olympian Zeus

(5.11.1). The god, made of gold and ivory, sits on a throne (see Figure 6). On his head lies a crown made in imitation of olive branch. In his right hand he carries Victory, which is also made of ivory and gold; she wears a ribbon and a crown on her head. In the left hand of the god is a scepter ornamented with every kind of metal, and the bird sitting on the scepter is the eagle. The sandals of the god are also made of gold, as is his robe. On the robe there are figures of animals and lily flowers.

(5.11.2) The throne is adorned with gold, jewels, ebony, and ivory. Upon it are painted figures and wrought images. There are four Victories, in the arrangement of dancing women, one at each foot of the throne, and two others at the base of each foot. On each

---

[29] On the story of Pelops, see **2a**, (Pindar *Olympian* 1).
[30] At the very center of the pediment is Apollo, but Pausanias makes no mention of him.
[31] Heracles' killing of this lion ravaging Nemea was his first labor. See **26a**.

Figure 6. Historical Reconstruction of Pheidias' Olympian Zeus by Quatremère de Quincey, 1814

of the two front feet are fixed Theban children snatched by sphinxes, while under the sphinxes Apollo and Artemis are shooting down the children of Niobe.[32]

(5.11.3) Between the feet of the throne are four rods, each one stretching from foot to foot. The rod straight opposite the entrance has on it seven images, and no one knows how the eighth disappeared. These must be representations of ancient contests, since contests for boys had not yet been introduced in the time of Pheidias.[33] The figure of one binding his head with a ribbon resembles Pantarces, a native of Elis, who was reportedly the beloved of Pheidias. Pantarces also earned a victory for boys wrestling at the eighty-sixth Olympiad [436].

(5.11.4) On the other posts is the group that fights against the Amazons with Heracles. The number of figures in the two parties is twenty-nine, and Theseus too is stationed

[32] See Apollodorus, *Library* 3.5.6 for the myth of Niobe.
[33] This is not true, even according to Pausanias. Here the text is most likely corrupt.

with the allies of Heracles.[34] The throne is supported not only by the feet, but also by an equal number of pillars standing between the feet. It is impossible to go under the throne in the way that we enter the inner part of the throne at Amyclae. At Olympia there are fences constructed like walls which keep people out.

(5.11.5) Of these fences, the part opposite the doors is only covered with dark blue paint; the other parts show images by Panaenus. Among them one finds Atlas supporting heaven and earth, by whose side stands Heracles ready to receive the burden of Atlas, along with Theseus; Pirithous, Hellas, and Salamis carrying in her hand the ornament made for the top of a ship's bow; then there is Heracles' exploit against the Nemean lion, the outrage (*paranomēma*) committed by Ajax against Cassandra,

(5.11.6) Hippodamia, the daughter of Oenomaus, with her mother, and Prometheus still held by his chains, and Heracles is lifted up to him. For this is also said about Heracles, namely that he killed the eagle which tortured Prometheus in the Caucasus, and Heracles set free Prometheus from his chains. Last in the picture come Penthesilea releasing her soul while Achilles holds her; two Hesperides carry the apples, which they were entrusted with to protect. This Panaenus was a brother of Pheidias; he also painted the battle of Marathon in the Painted Stoa at Athens.

(5.11.7) On the uppermost parts of the throne above the head of the image, Pheidias has made three Graces on one side and three Seasons on the other. In epic they are said to be daughters of Zeus. In the *Iliad* Homer says that the Seasons have been entrusted with the sky, like guards at the court of the king [*Iliad* 5.470]. The footrest of Zeus, called by the Athenians *thranion*, has golden lions on it and the fight of Theseus against the Amazons in relief, which is the first manly deed (*andragathēma*) of the Athenians against foreigners.

(5.11.8) On the pedestal supporting the throne and Zeus with all his adornments are works in gold: Helios mounted on a chariot, Zeus and Hera, Hephaestus, and by his side Charis. Close to her comes Hermes, and close to Hermes, Hestia. After Hestia is Eros receiving Aphrodite as she rises from the sea, and Aphrodite is being crowned by Persuasion (*Peithō*). There are also reliefs of Apollo with Artemis, Athena, and Heracles; and near the end of the pedestal Amphitrite and Poseidon, while the Moon is driving what I think is a horse. But others have said that the horse of the goddess is a mule and not a horse, and they tell a simple-minded story about the mule.

(5.11.9) I know that the height and width of the Olympic Zeus have been measured and recorded; but I will not praise those who made the measurements, because their measurements fall far short of the impression made by a sight of the image. No, they say the god himself was witness to the artistic skill of Pheidias. For when the image was finished, Pheidias prayed for the god to give a sign if the work was pleasing to him. They say

---

[34] On the genealogical and thematic connections between Theseus and Heracles, see, among other sources. Plutarch, *Life of Theseus*.

a thunderbolt immediately struck that part of the floor where today a bronze jar stands to cover the place.

(5.11.10) All the floor in front of the image is paved, not with white, but with black tiles. In a circle round the black stone runs a raised rim of Parian marble, to keep in the olive oil that is poured out. For olive oil is beneficial to the image at Olympia, and it is olive oil that keeps the ivory from being harmed by the marshy conditions of the Altis. On the Athenian Acropolis the ivory of the image they call Parthenos is supported, not by olive oil, but by water. For the Acropolis, owing to its great height, is very dry, so that the image, being made of ivory, needs water or dampness.

(5.11.11) And at Epidaurus, when I asked why they pour neither water nor olive oil on the image of Asclepius, the attendants at the sanctuary informed me that both the image of the god and the throne were built over a cistern.

37e. Bk. 5.12.4–8: Votive Offerings in the Temple of Zeus

[5.12.4] In Olympia there is a wool curtain adorned with Assyrian weaving and Phoenician purple which was dedicated by Antiochus,[35] who also gave as offerings the golden aegis with the Gorgon on it above the theater at Athens. This curtain is not drawn upward to the roof like the one in the temple of Artemis at Ephesus, but it is let down to the ground by cords.

[5.12.5] The offerings inside and in the *pronaos* include a throne of Arimnestus, king of Etruria, who was the first foreigner to present an offering to Olympic Zeus, and the bronze horses of Cynisca, tokens (*sēmeia*) of her Olympic victory.[36] These are not as large as real horses, and stand in the *pronaos* on the right as you enter. There is also a bronze tripod on which the crowns for the victors were displayed before the table was made.[37]

[5.12.6] There are also statues of emperors: a statue of Hadrian made of Parian marble dedicated by the cities of the Achaean confederacy, and a statue of Trajan dedicated by all the Greeks. This emperor subdued the Getae beyond Thrace and made war on Osroes, the descendant of Arsaces, and on the Parthians. The most remarkable of his architectural achievements is the baths named after him, a large circular theater, a building for horse races which is actually two stades long, and the Forum at Rome, which is worth seeing not only for its general beauty but especially for its roof made of bronze.

(5.12.7) Of the statues set up in the round buildings, the amber one represents Augustus the Roman emperor, and the ivory one they told me was a portrait of Nicomedes, king of Bithynia. After him the greatest city in Bithynia was renamed Nicomedia; before him it

---

[35] Most likely Antiochus Epiphanes, who was king of Syria from 175 to 164 BCE.
[36] For Cynisca, see **10a, 35a, 37x**. [37] This is the table in the temple of Hera, on which, see **37j**.

was called Astacus, and its first founder was Zypoetes, a Thracian by birth, it seems, given his name. The amber from which the statue of Augustus is made is very rare and precious to men for many reasons when found native in the sand of the Eridanus. The other "amber" is an alloy of gold and silver.

(5.12.8) In the temple at Olympia are four dedications by Nero—three crowns representing wild olive leaves, and one representing oak leaves.[38] Here too are located twenty-five bronze shields, which the armed men carry in the race. Stelai are also set up, including one on which is written the oath sworn by the Eleans to the Athenians, the Argives, and the Mantineans that they would be their allies for one hundred years.

37f. Bk. 5.13.1–4, 7: The Temple of Pelops

(5.13.1). Within the Altis there is also a walled-off sacred area (*temenos*) dedicated to Pelops, whom the Eleans honor above the other heroes of Olympia in the same way that they honor Zeus above the other gods. To the right of the entrance to the temple of Zeus, on the north side, lies the Pelopion. It is far enough from the temple that statues and other offerings stand in the intervening space, and it begins at about the middle of the temple and extends as far as the rear chamber. It is surrounded by a stone wall within which trees grow and male statues (*andriantes*) have been set up.

(5.13.2) The entrance is on the west. It is said that Heracles, the son of Amphitryon, set up the sanctuary for Pelops. Heracles too was a great-grandson of Pelops, and he is also said to have sacrificed to him into the pit. Right down to the present day the magistrates of the year sacrifice to Pelops, and the victim is a black ram. No portion of this sacrifice goes to the seer, but it has been established to give only the neck of the ram to the so-called "woodman."

(5.13.3) The woodman is one of the servants of Zeus, and the work given to him is to provide cities and private citizens with wood for sacrifices at a fixed rate. Wood of the white poplar, but no other tree, is allowed.

(5.13.7) Down to the present day, signs have remained that Pelops and Tantalus used to live in my country [i.e., Lydia]. There is a lake named after Tantalus and a famous grave, and on a peak of Mount Sipylus there is a throne of Pelops beyond the sanctuary of Plastene the Mother. If you cross the river Hermus, you see an image of Aphrodite in Temnus made of a living myrtle tree. There is a tradition that it was dedicated by Pelops while propitiating the goddess and asking for Hippodamia to be his bride.

---

[38] Nero participated in Olympic Games in his tour of Greece in 66–7 CE and apparently "won" new contests at Olympia made strictly for his participation, including a ten-horse chariot race and musical contests. See Suetonius, *Nero* 23–5, 53; Cassius Dio 62.9.3–21.1.

37g. Bk. 5.13.8–10: The Altar of Zeus

(5.13.8) The altar of Olympic Zeus is equally distant from the Pelopion and the sanctuary of Hera, but in front of both. Some say it was built by Idaean Heracles; others say it was built by the local heroes two generations after Heracles. It is made from the ashes of the thighs of the victims sacrificed to Zeus, like the altar at Pergamus. There is also an ash altar of Samian Hera, but it is not much larger than what the Athenians call "improvised hearths" in Attica.

(5.13.9) The first stage of the altar at Olympia, called the *prothysis*, has a circumference of 125 feet. The circumference of the stage on the *prothysis* is 32 feet. The total height of the altar reaches to 22 feet. It has been established that the victims themselves are sacrificed on the lower stage, the *prothysis*. But they carry up the thighs to the highest part of the altar and dedicate them there.

(5.13.10) The steps that lead up to the *prothysis* from either side are made of stone, but those leading from the *prothysis* to the upper part of the altar are made of ashes like the altar itself. It is possible for unmarried women (*parthenoi*) and married women to ascend to the *prothysis*, when they are not shut out from Olympia. But men alone are allowed to ascend from the *prothysis* to the highest part of the altar. Even when the festival is not being held, sacrifice is offered to Zeus by private individuals, and daily sacrifices are made by the Eleans.

37h. Bk. 5.16.1–17.1: The Temple of Hera and the Heraea

(5.16.1) It remains for me to describe the temple of Hera (see Figure 7) and the outstanding objects contained in it. The Eleans say that it was the people of Scillus, one of the cities in Triphylia, who built the temple about eight years after Oxylus came to the throne of Elis. The style of the temple is Doric, and pillars stand all round it. In the rear chamber one of the two pillars is made of oak. The length of the temple is 169 feet, the width 63 feet, and the height is roughly 50 feet. They do not remember who the architect is.

(5.16.2) Every four years, the Sixteen women weave a *peplos* for Hera, and these same women also hold a contest (*agōn*) called the Heraea. The contest consists of foot races for unmarried women (*parthenoi*). These women are not all of the same age. The first to run are the youngest. After them, the next in age, and the last to run are the oldest of the girls. They run in the following way:

(5.16.3) Their hair hangs down. They wear a small tunic, which reaches to a little above the knee, and they bare the right shoulder as far as the breast. This contest is also put on by them in the Olympic stadium, but the race in the stadium is shorter in distance by one-sixth. The victors are given crowns of olive and a portion of a bull sacrificed to Hera. And it is possible for them to dedicate statues with inscriptions on them. Those who administer to the Sixteen, who preside over the games, are married women like them.

Figure 7. Remains of temple of Hera at Olympia

(5.16.4) They conducted the contests for the unmarried women in ancient times as well. They say that Hippodamia [the wife of Pelops] assembled the Sixteen Women, and with them inaugurated the Heraea as an act of gratitude (*charis*) for her marriage to Pelops. And they recollect that **Chloris** won, who was the only surviving daughter of the house of Amphion. But they say one of her brothers also survived with her. As far as the children of Niobe are concerned, what I myself chanced to learn about them I have made clear in my account of Argos [2.21.9].

(5.16.5) They also give the following story about the Sixteen Women. They say that when Damophon was tyrant of Pisa, he did much harm to the Eleans. But when Damophon died, the people of Pisa refused to have a share in the wrongs of his tyranny, and the Eleans were also willing to give up their grievances. And so they chose women from each of the cities in Elis to settle their differences. The woman chosen from each city was to be the oldest of the women and the most preeminent in public esteem and reputation. [*The text breaks off here.*]

(5.16.6) The women from these cities brought about a reconciliation between Pisa and Elis. Later on these women were entrusted with the management of the Heraea, and they were responsible for weaving the *peplos* for Hera. The Sixteen Women also arrange two choral dances, one named after Physcoa and the other for Hippodamia. This

Physcoa they say came from Elis in the Hollow, and the name of the deme where she lived was Orthia.

(5.16.7) They say Physcoa mated with Dionysus and bore him a son called Narcaeus. When he grew up, he made war against the neighboring areas, and rose to great power, and he established a sanctuary of Athena Narcaea. They say too that Narcaeus and Physcoa were the first to worship Dionysus. So various honors are paid to Physcoa, especially the choral dance named after her and managed by the Sixteen Women. The Eleans still protect the ancient customs, even though some of the cities have been destroyed. Now the Eleans are divided into eight tribes, and they choose two women from each.

(5.16.8) Whatever ritual has been established for either the Sixteen Women or the *Hellanodikai* to perform, they do not perform them before they have purified themselves with a pig suitable for purification and with water. The purification takes place at the spring Piera. It is possible to reach this spring by going along the flat road from Olympia to Elis. (5.17.1) These things are as I have described them.

37i. Bk. 5.17.9–11: Funeral Games of Pelias Depicted on the Chest of Cypselus

*This chest was a votive offering by the Cypselids, the ruling family of Corinth, in gratitude for the saving of their ancestor Cypselis, the seventh-century tyrant. As a child his life was endangered by a rival faction (the Bacchiadae), so his mother hid him in this chest. Pausanias describes the rich decorative art on the chest, including the funeral games for Pelias, the son of Poseidon, who ruled Iolcus in Thessaly. Most of the competitors were members of crew of the Argo; see **40a** (3).*

(5.17.9) [Next comes] the contest (*agōn*) at the funeral of Pelias, with the spectators looking at the competitors. Heracles is seated on a throne, and behind him is a woman. There is no inscription saying who the woman is, but she is playing on a Phrygian flute rather than a Greek one. Driving chariots drawn by pairs of horses are Pisus, son of Perieres, and Asterion, son of Cometas [Asterion is said to have been one of the Argonauts], Polydeuces, Admetus, and Euphemus. The poets declare that Euphemus was a son of Poseidon and a companion of Jason on his voyage to Colchis. He is the one winning the chariot race.

(5.17.10) The ones who dare to box are Admetus and Mopsus, the son of Ampyx. Between them stands a man playing the flute. As in our time, they are accustomed to play the flute while competitors in the pentathlon are jumping. The wrestling match between Jason and Peleus is an equal one. Eurybotas is shown throwing the discus. Indeed, Eurybotas had a reputation as a discus thrower. Those engaged in a running race are Melanion, Neotheus, and Phalareus. The fourth runner is Argeius, and the fifth is Iphiclus. Iphiclus is the victor, and Acastus is holding out the crown to him. He is probably the father of the Protesilaus who joined in the war against Troy.

(5.17.11) Tripods are set up as prizes for the victors. The daughters of Pelias are also present, though the only one with her name inscribed is Alcestis. Iolaus, who willingly helped Heracles in his labors, is shown as a victor in the chariot race. At this point the funeral games of Pelias come to an end.

37j. Bk. 5.20.1: Votive Offerings in the Temple of Hera

(5.20.1) There are also other dedications in the temple: a couch of no great size and adorned mostly with ivory, the discus of Iphitus, and the table upon which are set the crowns for the victors. The couch is said to have been a personal item of Hippodamia. The discus of Iphitus has inscribed upon it the truce (*ekecheiria*), which the Eleans proclaim at the Olympic festivals. The inscription is not written in a straight line, but the letters run in a circle round the discus.

37k. Bk. 5.20.4–5: Elean and Spartan Battle around the Altis

(5.20.4) I must also be sure not to skip over the story told by Aristarchus, who is the guide at Olympia. He said that in his day the roof of the temple of Hera was damaged. When the Eleans repaired it, they found the corpse of a soldier with wounds between the roof supporting the tiles and the ornamented ceiling. This soldier fought in the battle in the Altis between the Eleans and the Spartans. (5.20.5) The Eleans defended themselves in that battle by climbing onto the sanctuaries of the gods as well as other high places. Apparently, this soldier crept under there after becoming weak from his wounds and then died. Because he was in a completely sheltered spot, the corpse was not going to suffer harm from the stifling heat or the cold in winter. Aristarchus also said that they carried the corpse outside the Altis and buried him with his armor.[39]

37l. Bk. 5.20.9–10: The Metroon and Prytaneion

(5.20.9) As it was being excavated, I myself saw a temple of no great size in the Doric style, which they have called the Metroon, "Temple of the Mother," up to the present, keeping its ancient name. There is no image of the mother of the gods inside, but there are statues of Roman emperors. The Metroon is within the Altis, and there is also a round building called the Philippeion. On the roof of the Philippeion is a bronze poppy which binds the beams together.

---

[39] See **9f, 10h** and Hornblower (2000: 219–20).

(5.20.10) This building is on the left of the exit near the Prytaneion. It is made of burnt brick and is surrounded by columns. It was built by Philip after the fall of Greece at Chaeronea. Here are set statues of Philip and Alexander, and with them is Amyntas, Philip's father. These works too are by Leochares. Like the statues of Olympias and Eurydice, they are made of ivory and gold.

37m. Bk. 5.21.1–22.1: The Zanes

(5.21.1). My account will now move to an explanation of the statues and dedications, but it would not be fitting to mix the two categories in my description. On the Athenian Acropolis, for instance, statues are dedications like everything else. But in the Altis some things are dedicated only in honor of the gods, whereas statues are also given as part of the prizes awarded to the victors. I will make mention of the statues later. But first, I will turn to the dedications and will go over the most noteworthy of them.

(5.21.2) As you go to the stadium along the path from the Metroon, there is a platform of stone, with steps through it, on the left at the bottom of the hill of Cronus. By the platform have been set up bronze images of Zeus. These have been made from the fines inflicted on athletes who have committed acts of hubris in the contests. The natives call the images Zanes (see Figure 8).[40]

(5.21.3) The first six were set up in the ninety-eighth Olympiad [388 BCE], since Eupolus of Thessaly bribed the boxers who entered the competition, including Agenor the Arcadian and Prytanis of Cyzicus, as well as Phormio of Halicarnassus, who had won at the preceding Olympics. They say this was the first time that an injustice (*adikēma*) was committed by athletes in the Olympic contest. The first to be fined by the Eleans were Eupolus and those who accepted bribes from Eupolus. Two of these images are the work of Cleon of Sicyon. I do not know who made the other four.

(5.21.4) Except for the third and the fourth, the other images have elegiac inscriptions on them. The first of the inscriptions is intended to make it clear that an Olympic victory is to be achieved, not by money, but by swiftness of foot and strength of body. The inscription on the second image declares that the image stands in honor of the deity, thanks to the piety (*eusebeia*) of the Eleans, and it is also intended to be a source of fear for athletes who break the rules. The basic idea of the inscription on the fifth image is praise for the Eleans, especially for fining boxers. The purpose of the sixth dedicated image is as a lesson (*didaskalia*) to all the Greeks not to give bribes to obtain an Olympic victory.

(5.21.5) They say that next after Eupolus, Callippus of Athens, a competitor in the pentathlon, bought off his fellow competitors with money, and that this offense occurred

---

[40] Zanes means "Zeuses." See **11m** for the inscriptions of the Zanes statue bases still *in situ*.

Figure 8. Statue bases of Zanes at Olympia, funded by fines of athletes found cheating

at the hundred and twelfth festival [332 BCE]. When the fine had been imposed by the Eleans on Callippus and his fellow competitors, the Athenians commissioned Hyperides to persuade the Eleans to give up the fine, but the Eleans refused this favor (*charis*). The Athenians were so disdainful of them that did not pay the fine, and they boycotted the Olympic Games. Finally, the god at Delphi declared that he would deliver no oracle on any matter to the Athenians until they had paid the fine to the Eleans.

(5.21.6) So when it was paid, another six images were made in honor of Zeus. On them are inscribed elegiac verses equal in elegance to those related to the fine of Eupolus. The gist of the first inscription is that the images were dedicated because the god expressed his approval of the Elean decision against the pentathletes through an oracle. On the second image and likewise on the third are praises of the Eleans for the fines against the competitors in the pentathlon.

(5.21.7) The fourth purports to say that the contest at Olympia is based on excellence (*aretē*) and not money. The inscription on the fifth declares the reason for dedicating the images, while the inscription on the sixth commemorates the oracle from Delphi given to the Athenians.

(5.21.8) There are two images next to those I have just described, and they were dedicated from a fine imposed on wrestlers. As to their names, neither I nor the Elean guides knew them. There are also inscriptions on these images. One says that the Rhodians paid money to Olympian Zeus for the injustice (*adikia*) committed by a wrestler. The other says that certain men wrestled for bribes and that the image was made from the fines imposed upon them.

(5.21.9) The rest of the information about these athletes comes from the Elean guides, who say that it was at the hundred and seventy-eighth Olympiad [69 BCE] that Eudelus accepted a bribe from Philostratus, and that this Philostratus was a Rhodian. This account I found was different from that of the Elean record of Olympic victories. In this record it is stated that Strato of Alexandria won the victory in the *pankration* and wrestling on the same day at the hundred and seventy-eighth Olympiad. (Alexandria on the Canopic mouth of the Nile was founded by Alexander, the son of Philip, but it is said that previously there was on the site a small Egyptian town called Racotis.)

(5.21.10) Three competitors before Strato, and three others after him, are known to have received the wild olive for winning the *pankration* and wrestling: Caprus from Elis, and the Greeks from the other side of the Aegean: Aristomenes of Rhodes and Protophanes of Magnesia on the Lethaeus, were earlier than Strato. After Strato, there was Marion, his compatriot, Aristeas of Stratonicea (in ancient times, both land and city were called Chrysaoris), and the seventh was Nicostratus, from Cilicia on the coast, though he was in no way a Cilician except in name.

(5.21.11) While still a baby, this Nicostratus was stolen from Prymnessus in Phrygia by robbers, because he was a child of a noble family. He was conveyed to Aegeae and bought by someone or other, who later had a dream. He thought that a lion's cub lay beneath the pallet bed on which Nicostratus was sleeping. And so when Nicostratus grew up, he won other victories elsewhere, in addition to *pankration* and wrestling at Olympia.

(5.21.12) Afterward, others were fined by the Eleans, including an Alexandrian boxer at the two hundred and eighteenth Olympiad [93 CE]. The name of the man fined was Apollonius, and his surname was Rhantes—it is a general characteristic for Alexandrians to have a surname. This man was the first Egyptian to be charged by the Eleans with a wrongdoing.

(5.21.13) He was not charged for giving or taking a bribe. Rather, he was charged for the following hubristic behavior at the Olympic contest. He did not arrive at the prescribed time (*kairos*), and in accordance with their own rules, the Eleans had no option but to exclude him from the competition. As an excuse, he said that he had been kept back in the Cyclades islands because of contrary winds. Heraclides, himself an Alexandrian by birth, proved this was entirely untrue. He showed that Apollonius was late because he collected some money at the Ionian Games.

(5.21.14) Given these circumstances, the Eleans excluded Apollonius along with any other boxer who came after the prescribed time, and they gave the crown to Heraclides without a contest. At that point, Apollonius put on his boxing straps (*himantes*) for a fight, rushed at Heraclides and jumped on him, although Heraclides had already put the wild olive on his head and fled to the *Hellanodikai*. Apollonius was to pay dearly for this great and thoughtless offense.

(5.21.15) There are also two other images of modern craftsmanship. For at the two hundred and twenty-sixth Olympiad [125 CE] they detected that two boxers, while fighting for victory, came to an agreement on a sum of money. For this misconduct a fine was inflicted. One of the images of Zeus that was made stands on the left of the entrance to the stadium and the other on the right. The bribed boxer was called Didas, and the briber was Sarapammon. They were from the same district, the newest in Egypt, called Arsinoites.

(5.21.16) It is a wonder that a man would have so little respect for the god of Olympia that he would take or give a bribe in the contests. It is an even greater wonder that one of the Eleans dared such a deed. But it is said that the Elean Damonicus was indeed that daring at the hundred and ninety-second Olympiad [12 BCE]. They say that collusion occurred between Polyctor the son of Damonicus and Sosander of Smyrna, who has the same name as his father. These were competitors for the wrestling prize of wild olive. They say that Damonicus was exceedingly ambitious for his son to win, and he bribed the father of Sosander.

(5.21.17) When the transaction became known, the *Hellanodikai* imposed a fine, but instead of imposing it on the sons, they directed their anger against the fathers. It was they who committed the injustice. From this fine, images were made. One is set up in the Elean gymnasium; the other is in the Altis in front of what is called the Painted Stoa, because there were pictures on the walls in ancient times. Some call this Stoa the Echo Stoa, because when a man has shouted, his voice is repeated by the echo seven or even more times.

(5.21.18) They say that a pankratist of Alexandria named Sarapion, at the two hundred and first Olympiad [25 CE], was so afraid of his fellow competitors (*antagōnistai*) that on the day before the *pankration* was about to be announced he ran away. This is the only occasion on record when any man, not to say a man of Egypt, was fined for cowardice.

(5.22.1) I found these to be the reasons the images were made. There are also images of Zeus dedicated by city states and by individuals. There is in the Altis an altar near the entrance leading to the stadium. On it the Eleans do not sacrifice to any of the gods, but it is customary for the trumpeters and heralds to stand upon it when they compete.

37n. Bk.5.23.4: Treaty for the Thirty Years' Peace

In front of this Zeus there is a bronze stele, on which are the terms of the Thirty Years Peace between the Spartans and the Athenians. The Athenians made this peace after they had reduced Euboea for the second time, in the third year of the eighty-third Olympiad [446 BCE], when Crison of Himera won the foot race. One of the articles of the treaty is to the effect that although Argos has no part in the treaty between Athens and Sparta, yet the Athenians and the Argives may privately, if they wish, be at peace with each other. Such are the terms of this treaty.

37o. Bk.5.24.4: Roman Dedications at Olympia

We know of no Roman, either private citizen or senator, who gave a dedication to a Greek sanctuary before Mummius. At Olympia, he dedicated a bronze Zeus from the spoils of Achaea [c.146 BCE]. It stands on the left of the offering of the Spartans, next to the first pillar on this side of the temple. The largest of the bronze images of Zeus in the Altis is 27 feet high. It was dedicated by the Eleans themselves from the plunder of the war with the Arcadians.

37p. Bk.5.24.9–11, 26.3: Swearing Oaths Not to Violate the Rules of the Contest

(5.24.9) But of all the images of Zeus, it is the Zeus in the Bouleuterion, which is the one most likely to strike terror into the hearts of wrongdoers. He is called Zeus Horkios, oath-god, and in each hand, he holds a thunderbolt. Beside this image it is the custom for athletes, their fathers, their brothers, and their trainers to swear an oath upon slices of boar's flesh. They swear that they will commit no evil deeds in the Olympic contest. The athletes take an additional oath also, that they have strictly followed the regulations for training for ten successive months.

(5.24.10) An oath is also taken by those who examine the boys and the foals entering for races. They swear that they will decide fairly and without taking bribes, and that they will keep secret what they learn about a candidate, whether the candidate is accepted or not. I forgot to inquire what it is customary to do with the boar after the oath of the athletes, although the ancient custom is that no human being might eat the meat from a victim on which an oath had been sworn.

(5.24.11) Homer makes this point clearly. For when Agamemnon swore that Briseis had not slept with him, Homer says the boar was thrown by the herald into the sea:

> He spoke, and cut the boar's throat with ruthless bronze;
> And Talthybius swung the boar and threw it into the great depths
> of the grey sea, food for the fishes (*Iliad* 19.266–8).

Such was the ancient custom. Before the feet of Zeus Horkios is a bronze plate, with elegiac verses inscribed upon it. The purpose is to strike fear into those who go against their oaths.

From 5.25.1–5.27.11 Pausanias describes the many different types of dedications that could be found on the site. The one dedication relevant to athletic competition is:

(5.26.3) Among the offerings made by Micythus is Agon carrying jumping weights (*haltēres*), the shape of which is as follows: They are half of a circle, not an exact circle, but elliptical, and made so that the fingers pass through as they do through the handle of a shield.

37q. Bk. 6.1.1–18.7 (with omissions): Statues, Shrines, and Stories about Victors

(6.1.1) After my description of the dedications I must now go on to mention the memorials (*mnēmē*) of competition horses, athletic men, and private individuals. Not all the Olympic victors have had statues erected. Some, in fact, who demonstrated shining deeds, either at the games or by other exploits, have had no statue.

(6.1.2) My work forces me to omit these, since this is not a list of all athletes who have won Olympic victories, but an account of statues and of dedications. I shall not even record all those whose statues have been set up, since I know how many have before now won the crown of wild olive not by strength but by the chance of the lot. Those only will I mention who themselves gained some reputation (*doxa*), or whose statues happened to be better made than others.

(6.1.3) On the right of the temple of Hera is the statue of a wrestler, **Symmachus** the son of Aeschylus. He was an Elean by birth. Beside him is **Neolaidas,** son of Proxenus, from Pheneus in Arcadia, who won a victory in the boys' boxing match. Next comes **Archedamus,** son of Xenius, another Elean by birth, who like Symmachus overthrew wrestlers in the contest for boys. The statues of the athletes mentioned above were made by Alypus of Sicyon, pupil of Naucydes of Argos.

(6.1.4) The inscription on **Cleogenes** the son of Silenus declares that he was a native, and that he won in the single horse race (*kelēs*) with a horse from his own private stable. Next to Cleogenes are set up Deinolochus, son of Pyrrhus, and Troilus, son of Alcinous. These also were both Eleans by birth, though their victories were not the same. **Troilus,** when he was one of the *Hellanodikai*, succeeded in winning victories in the chariot races, one for a chariot drawn by a full-grown pair and another for a chariot drawn by foals. The date of his victories was the hundred and second festival [372 BCE].

(6.1.5) After him, the Eleans passed a law that in future no judge was to compete in the chariot races. The statue of Troilus was made by Lysippus. The mother of **Deinolochus** had a dream, in which she thought that the son she clasped to her bosom had a crown on his head. For this reason Deinolochus was trained to compete in the games and outran the boys. The artist was Cleon of Sicyon.

(6.1.6) As for **Cynisca,** daughter of Archidamus, her ancestry and Olympic victories, I have given an account thereof in my history of the Lacedaemonian kings.[41] By the side of the statue of Troilus at Olympia has been made a basement of stone, whereon are a

---

[41] See **37x** and compare Plutarch, **35a**.

chariot and horses, a charioteer, and a statue of Cynisca herself, made by Apelles; there are also inscriptions relating to Cynisca.[42]

(6.1.7) Next to her also have been erected statues of Spartans. They gained victories in chariot races. **Anaxander** was the first of his family to be proclaimed victor with a chariot, but the inscription for him declares that his paternal grandfather previously received the crown for the pentathlon. Anaxander is represented in an attitude of prayer to the god, while **Polycles**, who gained the nickname of Polychalcus, likewise won a victory with a four-horse chariot, and his statue holds a ribbon in the right hand. Beside him are two children; one holds a wheel and the other is asking for the ribbon. Polycles, as the inscription says, also won the chariot race at Delphi, the Isthmus and Nemea.

(6.2.1) The statue of a pankratist was made by Lysippus. This man was the first to win the *pankration* not only from Stratus itself but from the whole of Acarnania, and his name was **Xenarces** the son of Philandrides. Now after the Persian invasion the Spartans became keener for horse breeding. than any other Greeks. Beside those I have already mentioned, the following horse-breeders from Sparta have their statues set up after that of the Acarnanian athlete Xenarces, Lycinus, Arcesilaus, and Lichas his son.

(6.2.2) **Xenarces** succeeded in winning other victories, at Delphi, at Argos and at Corinth. Lycinus brought foals to Olympia, and when one of them was disqualified, entered his foals for the race for full-grown horses, winning with them. He also dedicated two statues at Olympia, works of Myron the Athenian. As for **Arcesilaus** and his son **Lichas**, the father won two Olympic victories; his son, because in his time the Spartans were excluded from the games, entered his chariot in the name of the Theban people, and with his own hands bound the victorious charioteer with a ribbon. For this offense the *Hellanodikai* beat him.[43]

(6.2.3) And on account of this Lichas the Spartan invaded Elis in the reign of King Agis, when a battle took place within the Altis. When the war was over Lichas set up the statue in this place, but the Elean records of Olympic victors give as the name of the victor, not Lichas, but the Theban people.

(6.2.6) By the statue of Thrasybulus stands **Timosthenes of Elis**, winner of the foot race for boys, and **Antipater of Miletus**, son of Cleinopater, conqueror of the boy boxers. Men of Syracuse, who were bringing a sacrifice from Dionysius to Olympia, tried to bribe the father of Antipater to have his son proclaimed as a Syracusan. But Antipater, thinking nothing of the tyrant's gifts, proclaimed himself a Milesian and wrote upon his statue that he was of Milesian descent and the first Ionian to dedicate his statue at Olympia.

(6.2.7) The artist who made this statue was Polycleitus, while that of Timosthenes was made by Eutychides of Sicyon, a pupil of Lysippus. This Eutychides made for the Syrians on the Orontes an image of Fortune, which is highly valued by the locals.

---

[42] For the inscription see Inscriptions **I1i**.   [43] See **9f**.

(6.2.8) In the Altis by the side of Timosthenes are statues of **Timon** and of his son **Aesypus**, who is represented as a child seated on a horse. In fact, the boy won the horserace, while Timon was proclaimed victor in the chariot race. The statues of Timon and of his son were made by Daedalus of Sicyon, who also made for the Eleans the trophy in the Altis commemorating the victory over the Spartans.

(6.2.9) The inscription on the Samian boxer says that his trainer Mycon dedicated the statue and that the Samians are best among the Ionians for athletes and at naval warfare; this is what the inscription says, but it tells us nothing at all about the boxer himself.

(6.2.10) Beside this is the Messenian **Damiscus**, who won an Olympic victory at the age of twelve. I was exceedingly surprised to learn that while the Messenians were in exile from the Peloponnesus, their luck at the Olympic games failed. For with the exception of Leontiscus and Symmachus, who came from Messene on the Strait, we know of no Messenian, either from Sicily or from Naupactus, who won a victory at Olympia. Even these two are said by the Sicilians to have been not Messenians but Zancleans.

(6.2.11) However, when the Messenians came back to the Peloponnesus their luck in the Olympic games came with them. For at the festival celebrated by the Eleans in the year after the settlement of Messene, the foot race for boys was won by this Damiscus, who afterward won in the pentathlon both at Nemea and at the Isthmian Games.

(6.3.1) Nearest to Damiscus stands a statue of someone, whose name they do not give, but it was Ptolemy son of Lagus who set up the offering. In the inscription Ptolemy calls himself a Macedonian, though he was king of Egypt. On the statue of **Chaereas of Sicyon**, a boy boxer, is an inscription that he won a victory when a young man, and that his father was Chaeremon. The name of the artist who made the statue is also written, Asterion son of Aeschylus.

(6.3.2) After Chaereas are statues of a Messenian boy Sophius and of Stomius, a man of Elis. **Sophius** outran his boy competitors, and **Stomius** won a victory in the pentathlon at Olympia and three at the Nemean games. The inscription on his statue adds that, when commander of the Elean cavalry, he set up trophies and killed in single combat the general of the enemy, who had challenged him.

(6.3.3) The Eleans say that the dead general was a native of Sicyon in command of Sicyonian troops, and that they themselves with the force from Boeotia attacked Sicyon out of friendship to the Thebans. So the attack of the Eleans and Thebans against Sicyon apparently took place after the Spartan disaster at Leuctra.

(6.3.4) Next stands the statue of a boxer from Lepreus in Elis, whose name was **Labax** son of Euphron, and also that of **Aristodemus**, son of Thrasis, a boxer from Elis itself, who also won two victories at Delphi. The statue of Aristodemus is the work of Daedalus of Sicyon, the pupil and son of Patrocles.

(6.3.5) The statue of **Hippus of Elis**, who won the boys' boxing match, was made by Damocritus of Sicyon, of the school of Attic Critias, being removed from him by four generations of teachers. For Critias himself taught Ptolichus of Corcyra, Amphion was the pupil of Ptolichus, and taught Pison of Calaureia, who was the teacher of Damocritus.

(6.3.6) **Cratinus of Aegeira** in Achaia was the most handsome man of his time and wrestled with skill (*technē*); when he won the wrestling match for boys the Eleans allowed him to set up a statue of his trainer as well. The statue was made by Cantharus of Sicyon, whose father was Alexis, while his teacher was Eutychides.

(6.3.7) The statue of **Eupolemus of Elis** was made by Daedalus of Sicyon. The inscription on it informs us that Eupolemus won the foot race for men at Olympia, and that he also received two Pythian crowns for the pentathlon and another at the Nemean games. It is also said of Eupolemus that three judges stood on the course, of whom two gave their verdict in favor of Eupolemus and one declared the winner to be **Leon the Ambraciot**. Leon, they say, got the Olympic Council to fine each of the judges who had decided in favor of Eupolemus.

(6.3.8) The statue of Oebotas was set up by the Achaeans by the command of the Delphic Apollo in the eightieth Olympiad [460 BCE], but **Oebotas** won his victory in the foot race at the sixth festival [756 BCE]. How, therefore, could Oebotas have taken part in the Greek victory at Plataea? For it was in the seventy-fifth Olympiad [c. 479 BCE] that the Persians under Mardonius suffered their disaster at Plataea. Now I am obliged to report the statements made by the Greeks, though I am not obliged to believe them all. The other incidents in the life of Oebotas I will add to my history of Achaea.[44]

(6.3.9) The statue of Antiochus was made by Nicodamus. A native of Lepreus, **Antiochus** won the *pankration* once at Olympia, and the pentathlon twice at the Isthmian games and twice at the Nemean. For the Lepreans are not afraid of the Isthmian games as the Eleans themselves are. For example, **Hysmon of Elis**, whose statue stands near that of Antiochus, competed successfully in the pentathlon both at Olympia and at Nemea, but clearly kept away, just like other Eleans, from the Isthmian games.

(6.3.10) It is said that when Hysmon was still a boy he was attacked by a flux in his nerves, and he practiced the pentathlon so that he become a man healthy and free from disease as a result of his effort (*ponos*). His training was also to enable him to win famous victories in the games. His statue is the work of Cleon, and he holds old fashioned jumping weights (*haltēres*).

(6.3.11) After Hysmon comes the statue of a boy wrestler from Heraea in Arcadia, **Nicostratus** the son of Xenocleides. Pantias was the artist, and if you count the teachers you will find five between him and Aristocles of Sicyon. **Dicon**, the son of Callibrotus, won five foot races at Pytho, three at the Isthmian games, four at Nemea, one at Olympia in the race for boys besides two in the men's race. Statues of him have been set up at Olympia equal in number to the races he won. When he was a boy, he was proclaimed a

---

[44] See Pausanias 7.17.6

native of Caulonia, as in fact he was. But afterward he was bribed to proclaim himself a Syracusan.

(6.3.13) Close to Dicon is a statue of **Xenophon**, the son of Menephylus, a pankratist of Aegium in Achaia, and likewise one of **Pyrilampes** of Ephesus after winning the distance race (*dolichos*). Olympus made the statue of Xenophon; that of Pyrilampes was made by a sculptor of the same name, a native, not of Sicyon, but of Messene beneath Ithome.

(6.3.14) A statue of Lysander, son of Aristocritus, a Spartan, was dedicated in Olympia by the Samians, and the first of their inscriptions runs:

> In the much-seen precinct of Zeus, ruler on high, I stand, dedicated at public expense by the Samians.

So this inscription informs us who dedicated the statue; the next is in praise of Lysander himself:

> Deathless glory (*athanaton kleos*) by thy achievements, for fatherland and for Aristocritus, have you won, Lysander, and you have the reputation (*doxa*) of excellence (*aretē*).

(6.4.1) Next to the statue of Lysander is an Ephesian boxer named **Athenaeus** who beat the other boys, his competitors, and also a man of Sicyon who was a pankratist, **Sostratus** nicknamed Acrochersites. For he used to grip his opponent by the fingers and break them, and would not let go until he saw that his opponent had given in.

(6.4.2) He won at the Nemean and Isthmian games combined twelve victories, three victories at Olympia and two at Pytho. The hundred and fourth festival [364], when Sostratus won his first victory, is not reckoned by the Eleans, because the games were held by the Pisans and Arcadians and not by themselves.

(6.4.3) Beside Sostratus is a statue of **Leontiscus**, a mens' wrestler, a native of Sicily from Messene on the Strait. He was crowned, they say, by the Amphictyons and twice by the Eleans, and his mode of wrestling was similar to the *pankration* of Sostratus the Sicyonian. For they say that Leontiscus did not know how to throw his opponents but won by breaking their fingers.

(6.4.4) The statue was made by Pythagoras of Rhegium, an excellent sculptor if ever there was one. They say that he studied under Clearchus, who was likewise a native of Rhegium, and a pupil of Eucheirus. Eucheirus, it is said, was a Corinthian, and attended the school of Syadras and Chartas, men of Sparta.

(6.4.5) The boy who is binding his head with a fillet must be mentioned in my account because of Pheidias and his great skill as a sculptor, but we do not know whose portrait the statue is that Pheidias made. **Satyrus** of Elis, son of Lysianax, of the clan of the Iamidae, won five victories at Nemea for boxing, two at Pytho, and two at Olympia. The artist who made the statue was Silanion, an Athenian. Polycles, another sculptor of the Attic school, a pupil of Stadieus the Athenian, has made the statue of an Ephesian boy pankratist, **Amyntas** the son of Hellanicus.

(6.4.6) **Chilon**, an Achaean of Patrae, won two prizes for men wrestlers at Olympia, one at Delphi, four at the Isthmus and three at the Nemean games. He was buried at the public expense by the Achaeans, and his fate it was to lose his life on the field of battle. My statement is borne out by the inscription at Olympia:

> In wrestling I alone conquered twice the men at Olympia and at Pytho [=Delphi], Thrice at Nemea, and four times at the Isthmus near the sea; Chilon of Patrae, son of Chilon, whom the Achaean folk buried when I died in battle, because of my excellence (*aretē*).

[6.4.7 omitted.]

(6.4.8) Next to Chilon two statues have been set up. One is that of a man named Molpion, who, says the inscription, was crowned by the Eleans. The other statue bears no inscription, but tradition says that it represents Aristotle from Stageira in Thrace, and that it was set up either by a pupil or else by some soldier aware of Aristotle's influence with Antipater and at an earlier date with Alexander. **Sodamas** from Assos in the Troad,

(6.4.9) a city at the foot of Ida, was the first of the Aeolians in this district to win at Olympia the foot-race for boys. By the side of Sodamas stands Archidamus, son of Agesilaus, king of the Spartans. Before this Archidamus no king, so far as I could learn, had his statue set up by the Spartans, at least outside the boundaries of the country. They sent the statue of Archidamus to Olympia chiefly, in my opinion, on account of his death, because he met his end in a foreign land, and is the only king in Sparta who is known to have missed burial.

(6.4.10) I have spoken at greater length on this matter in my account of Sparta. **Euanthes** of Cyzicus won prizes for boxing, one among the men at Olympia, and also among the boys at the Nemean and at the Isthmian games. By the side of Euanthes is the statue of a horse-breeder and his chariot; mounted on the chariot is a young maid. The man's name is Lampus, and his native city was the last to be founded in Macedonia, named after its founder Philip, son of Amyntas.

(6.4.11) The statue of **Cyniscus**, the boy boxer from Mantinea, was made by Polycleitus. **Ergoteles**, the son of Philanor, won two victories in the *dolichos* at Olympia, and two at Pytho, the Isthmus and Nemea. The inscription on the statue states that he came originally from Himera; but it is said that this is incorrect, and that he was a Cretan from Cnossus. Expelled from Cnossus by a political party he came to Himera, was given citizenship and won many honors besides. It was accordingly natural for him to be proclaimed at the games as a native of Himera.[45]

---

[45] On Egoteles, see **2e** and **I1g**.

(6.5.3) [The massacre by Alexander of Pherae] befell Scotoussa when Phrasicleides was archon at Athens, in the hundred and second Olympiad [372 BCE], when **Damon of Thurii** was victor for the second time, and in the second year of this Olympiad. The people that escaped remained but for a while, for later they too were forced by their destitution to leave the city, when the divine power brought a second calamity in the war with Macedonia.

(6.5.4) Others have won glorious victories in the *pankration*, but **Poulydamas**, besides his prizes for the *pankration*, has to his credit the following exploits of a different kind. The mountainous part of Thrace, on this side the river Nestus, which runs through the land of Abdera, breeds among other wild beasts, lions, which once attacked the army of Xerxes, and mauled the camels carrying his supplies.

(6.5.5) These lions often roam right into the land around Mount Olympus, one side of which is turned toward Macedonia, and the other toward Thessaly and the river Peneius. Here on Mount Olympus Poulydamas slew a lion, a huge and powerful beast, without the help of any weapon. He was driven to this exploit by an ambition to rival the labors of Heracles, because Heracles also, legend says, overthrew the lion at Nemea.

(6.5.6) In addition to this, Poulydamas is remembered for another wonderful performance. He went among a herd of cattle and seized the biggest and fiercest bull by one of its hind feet, holding fast the hoof in spite of the bull's leaps and struggles, until finally it put forth all its strength and escaped, leaving its hoof in Poulydamas' grasp. It is also said of him that he stopped a charioteer who was driving his chariot onward at a great speed. Seizing with one hand the back of the chariot he kept a tight hold on both horses and driver.

(6.5.7) Dareius, the bastard son of Artaxerxes, who with the support of the Persian common people put down Sogdius, the legitimate son of Artaxerxes, ascended the throne in his stead. When he was king, he learned of the exploits of Poulydamas and sent messengers with the promise of gifts and persuaded him to come before his presence at Susa. There Poulydamas challenged three of the Persians called Immortals to fight him—one against three—and killed them. Of his exploits, some are represented on the pedestal of the statue at Olympia, and others are set forth in the inscription.

(6.5.8) But after all, the prophecy of Homer respecting those who glory in their strength[46] was to be fulfilled also in the case of Poulydamas; he too was fated to perish through his own strength (*rhōmē*). For he entered a cave with the rest of his drinking companions. It was summer-time, and, as ill-luck would have it, the roof of the cave began to crack. It was obvious that it would quickly fall in and could not hold out much longer.

(6.5.9) Realizing the disaster that was coming, the others turned and ran away; but Poulydamas resolved to remain, holding up his hands in the belief that he could prevent the falling in of the cave and would not be crushed by the mountain. Here Poulydamas met his end.[47]

---

[46] *Iliad* 6.407: "this strength of yours will be your doom."
[47] A similar story is told about Milo of Croton, see below 6.14.8.

(6.6.1) Beside the statue of Poulydamas at Olympia stand two Arcadians and one Attic athlete. The statue of the Mantinean, **Protolaus** the son of Dialces, who won the boys' boxing match, was made by Pythagoras of Rhegium; that of **Narycidas**, son of Damaretus, a wrestler from Phigalia, was made by Daedalus of Sicyon; that of the Athenian **Callias**, a pankratist, is by the Athenian painter Micon. Nicodamus the Maenalian made the statue of the Maenalian pankratist **Androsthenes**, the son of Lochaeus, who won two victories among the men.

(6.6.2) By these is set up a statue of **Eucles**, son of Callianax, a native of Rhodes and of the family of the Diagoridae.[48] For he was the son of the daughter of Diagoras and won an Olympic victory in the boxing match for men. His statue is by Naucydes. Polycleitus of Argos, not the artist who made the image of Hera, but a pupil of Naucydes, made the statue of a boy wrestler, **Agenor of Thebes**. The statue was dedicated by the Phocian Commonwealth, for Theopompus, the father of Agenor, was a state friend (*proxenos*) of their people.

(6.6.3) Nicodamus, the sculptor from Maenalus, made the statue of the boxer **Damoxenidas** of Maenalus. There stands also the statue of the Elean boy **Lastratidas**, who won the crown for wrestling. He won a victory at Nemea also among the boys, and another among the beardless youths (*ageneioi*). **Paraballon**, the father of Lastratidas, was first in the *diaulos*, and he left to those coming after an object of ambition (*philotimia*), by writing up in the gymnasium at Olympia the names of those who won Olympic victories.

(6.6.4) So much for these. But it would not be right for me to pass over the boxer **Euthymus**, his victories and his other glories.[49] Euthymus was by birth one of the Italian Locrians, who dwell in the region near the headland called the West Point, and he was called son of Astycles. Local legend, however, makes him the son, not of this man, but of the river Caecinus, which divides Locri from the land of Rhegium and produces the marvel of the grasshoppers. For the grasshoppers within Locri as far as the Caecinus sing just like others, but across the Caecinus in the territory of Rhegium they do not utter a sound.

(6.6.5) This river then, according to tradition, was the father of Euthymus, who, though he won the prize for boxing at the seventy-fourth Olympic festival [484], was not to be so successful at the next. For Theagenes of Thasos, wishing to win the prizes for boxing and for the *pankration* at the same festival, overcame Euthymus at boxing, though he had not the strength to gain the wild olive in the *pankration*, because he was already exhausted from his fight with Euthymus.[50]

(6.6.6) Thereupon the umpires fined Theagenes a talent, to be sacred to the god, and a talent for the harm done to Euthymus, holding that it was merely to spite him that he entered the boxing competition. For this reason, they condemned him to pay an extra fine privately to Euthymus. At the seventy-sixth festival [476] Theagenes paid in full the

---

[48] For the family see **2f**.   [49] On Euthymus see also **26d, 46, I1f** and Appendix AI.
[50] On Theagenes see also **42a, I12b** and Appendix AI.

money owed to the god,…and as compensation to Euthymus did not enter the boxing match. At this festival, and also at the next following, Euthymus won the crown for boxing. His statue is the handiwork of Pythagoras and is very well worth seeing.

(6.6.7) On his return to Italy Euthymus fought against the Hero, the story about whom is as follows. Odysseus, so they say, in his wanderings after the capture of Troy was carried down by winds to various cities of Italy and Sicily, and among them he came with his ships to Temesa. Here one of his sailors got drunk and violated a maiden, for which offense he was stoned to death by the natives.

(6.6.8) Now Odysseus, it is said, cared nothing about his loss and sailed away. But the ghost of the stoned man never ceased killing without distinction the people of Temesa, attacking both old and young, until, when the inhabitants had resolved to flee from Italy for good, the Pythian priestess forbade them to leave Temesa, and ordered them to propitiate the Hero, establishing for him a sanctuary apart and building a temple, and to give him every year as wife the fairest maiden in Temesa.

(6.6.9) So they executed the commands of the god and suffered no more terrors from the spirit. But Euthymus happened to come to Temesa just at the time when the spirit was being propitiated in the usual way; learning what was going on he had a strong desire to enter the temple, and not only to enter it but also to look at the maiden. When he saw her, he first felt pity and afterward love for her. The girl swore to marry him if he saved her, and so Euthymus waited with his armor for the attack of the spirit.

(6.6.10) He won the fight, and the Hero was driven out of the land and disappeared, sinking into the depth of the sea. Euthymus had a distinguished wedding, and the inhabitants were freed from the spirit forever. I heard another story also about Euthymus, how that he reached extreme old age, and escaping again from death departed from among men in another way. Temesa is still inhabited, as I heard from a man who sailed there as a merchant.

(6.6.11) This I heard, and I also saw by chance a picture dealing with the subject. It was a copy of an ancient picture. There was a stripling, Sybaris, a river, Calabrus, and a spring, Lyca. Besides, there were a hero-shrine and the city of Temesa, and in the midst was the spirit that Euthymus cast out. Horribly black in color, and exceedingly dreadful in all his appearance, he had a wolf's skin thrown round him as a garment. The letters on the picture gave his name as Lycas.

(6.7.1) So much for the story of Euthymus. After his statue stands a runner in the foot race, **Pytharchus** of Mantinea, and a boxer, **Charmides** of Elis, both of whom won prizes in the contests for boys. When you have looked at these also you will reach the statues of the Rhodian athletes, Diagoras and his family.[51] These were dedicated one after the other in the following order. **Acusilaus**, who received a crown for boxing in the men's class; **Dorieus**, the youngest, who won the *pankration* at Olympia on three

---

[51] On Diagoras, see **2f**.

successive occasions. Even before Dorieus, **Damagetus** beat all those who had entered for the *pankration*.

(6.7.2) These were brothers, being sons of Diagoras, and by them is set up also a statue of **Diagoras** himself, who won a victory for boxing in the men's class. The statue of Diagoras was made by the Megarian Callicles, the son of the Theocosmus who made the image of Zeus at Megara. The sons of the daughters of Diagoras also practiced boxing and won Olympic victories: in the men's class **Eucles**, son of Callianax and Callipateira, daughter of Diagoras; in the boys' class **Peisirodus**, whose mother dressed herself as a man and a trainer and took her son herself to the Olympic games.

(6.7.3) This Peisirodus is one of the statues in the Altis and stands by the father of his mother. The story goes that Diagoras came to Olympia in the company of his sons Acusilaus and Damagetus. The youths, on defeating their father, proceeded to carry him through the crowd, while the Greeks pelted him with flowers and congratulated him on his sons. The family of Diagoras was originally, through the female line, Messenian, as he was descended from the daughter of Aristomenes.

(6.7.4) **Dorieus**, the son of Diagoras, besides his Olympian victories, won eight at the Isthmian and seven at the Nemean games. He is also said to have won a Pythian victory without a contest. He and Peisirodus were proclaimed by the herald as [being citizens] of Thurii, for they had been pursued by their political enemies from Rhodes to Thurii in Italy. Dorieus subsequently returned to Rhodes. Of all men he most obviously showed his friendship with Sparta, for he actually fought against the Athenians with his own ships, until he was taken prisoner by Attic men-of-war and brought alive to Athens.

[6.7.5] Before he was brought to them the Athenians were angry with Dorieus and threatened him; but when they met in the assembly and beheld a man so great and famous in the guise of a prisoner, their feeling toward him changed, and they let him go without doing him any harm, even though they might, with justice, have punished him severely.

[6.7.6] The death of Dorieus is told by Androtion in his Attic history. He says that the fleet of the great King [of Persia] was then at Caunus, with Conon in command, who persuaded the Rhodian people to leave the Spartan alliance and to join the great King and the Athenians. Dorieus, he goes on to say, was at the time away from home in the interior of the Peloponnese and having been caught by some Spartans he was brought to Sparta, convicted of treachery by the Spartans and sentenced to death.

[6.7.7] If Androtion tells the truth, he appears to me to wish to put the Spartans on a level with the Athenians, because they too are open to the charge of precipitous action in their treatment of Thrasyllus and his fellow admirals at the battle of Arginusae. Such was the fame (*doxa*) won by Diagoras and his family.

[6.7.8] Alcaenetus too, son of Theantus, a Leprean, himself and his sons won Olympian victories. **Alcaenetus** was successful in the boxing contest for men, as at an earlier date he had been in the contest for boys. His sons, **Hellanicus** and **Theantus**, were proclaimed winners of the boys' boxing match, Hellanicus at the eighty-ninth festival [424] and Theantus at the next. All have their statues set up at Olympia.

(6.7.9) Next to the sons of Alcaenetus stand **Gnathon**, a Maenalian of Dipaea, and **Lucinus of Elis.** These too succeeded in beating the boys at boxing at Olympia. The inscription on his statue says that Gnathon was very young indeed when he won his victory. The artist who made the statue was Callicles of Megara.

(6.7.10) A man from Stymphalus, by name **Dromeus** ["Runner"], proved true to it in the *dolichos*, for he won two victories at Olympia, two at Delphi, three at the Isthmus and five at Nemea. He is said to have also conceived the idea of a meat diet; up to this time athletes had fed on cheese from the basket.[52] The statue of this athlete is by Pythagoras; the one next to it, representing Pythocles, a pentathlete of Elis, was made by Polycleitus.

(6.8.1) **Socrates of Pellene** won the boys' race, and **Amertes of Elis** the boys' wrestling at Olympia, besides beating all competitors in the men's wrestling match at Delphi. It is not said who made the statue of Socrates, but that of Amertes is from the hand of Phradmon of Argos. **Euanoridas of Elis** won the boys' wrestling match both at Olympia and at Nemea. When he was made an umpire (*Hellanodikēs*), he himself recorded the names of the victors in Olympia.

(6.8.2) As to the boxer, by name **Damarchus**, an Arcadian of Parrhasia, I cannot believe (except, of course, his Olympic victory) what romancers say about him, how he changed his shape into that of a wolf at the sacrifice of Lycaean [= "Wolf-like"] Zeus, and how nine years after he became a man again. Nor do I think that the Arcadians record this of him, otherwise it would have been recorded as well in the inscription at Olympia, which runs:

> This statue was dedicated by Damarchus, son of Dinytas, Parrhasian by birth from Arcadia.

(6.8.3) Here the inscription ends. **Eubotas of Cyrene**, when the Libyan oracle foretold to him his coming Olympic victory for running, had his portrait statue made beforehand, and so was proclaimed victor and dedicated the statue on the same day. He is also said to have won the chariot race at that festival which, according to the account of the Eleans, was not genuine because the Arcadians presided at it.

(6.8.4) The statue of **Timanthes of Cleonae**, who won the crown in the *pankration* for men, was made by Myron of Athens, but Naucydes made that of **Baucis of Troezen**, who defeated the male wrestlers. Timanthes, they say, met his end through the following cause. On retiring from athletics, he continued to test his strength by drawing a great bow every day. His practice with the bow was interrupted during a period when he was away from home. On his return, finding that he was no longer able to bend the bow, he lit a fire and threw himself alive on to it. In my view all such deeds, whether they have

---

[52] For diet see **14b, 14f, 14i, 42a, 44b.**

already occurred among men or will take place hereafter, ought to be regarded as acts of madness (*mania*) rather than manliness (*andreia*).

(6.8.5) After Baucis are statues of Arcadian athletes: **Euthymenes from Maenalus** itself, who won the men's and previously the boys' wrestling match; **Philip**, an Azanian **from Pellana**, who beat the boys at boxing, and **Critodamus from Cleitor**, who like Philip was proclaimed victor in the boys' boxing match. The statue of Euthymenes for his victory over the boys was made by Alypus; the statue of Damocritus was made by Cleon, and that of Philip the Azanian by Myron. The story of Promachus, son of Dryon, a pankratist of Pellene, will be included in my account of the Achaeans.

(6.8.6) Not far from Promachus is set up the statue of **Timasitheus**, a Delphian by birth, the work of Ageladas of Argos. This athlete won in *pankration* twice at Olympia and three times at Pytho. His achievements in war too are distinguished by their daring and by the good luck which attended all but the last, which caused his death. For when Isagoras the Athenian captured the Acropolis of the Athenians with a view to setting up a tyranny, Timasitheus took part in the affair, and, on being taken prisoner on the Acropolis, was put to death by the Athenians for his crime against them.

(6.9.1) **Theognetus of Aegina** succeeded in winning the crown for the boys' wrestling match, and Ptolichus of Aegina made his statue. Ptolichus was a pupil of his father Synnoön, who in turn was a pupil of Aristocles the Sicyonian, a brother of Canachus and almost as famous an artist. Why Theognetus carries a cone of the cultivated pine and a pomegranate I could not conjecture. Perhaps some of the Aeginetans may have a local story about it.

(6.9.2) After the statue of the man who the Eleans say did not have his name recorded with the others because he was proclaimed winner of the *kalpē* stands **Xenocles of Maenalus**, who defeated the boys at wrestling, and **Alcetus**, son of Alcinous, victor in the boys' boxing match, who also was an Arcadian from Cleitor. Cleon made the statue of Alcetus; that of Xenocles is by Polycleitus.

(6.9.3) **Aristeus of Argos** himself won a victory in the *dolichos*, while his father **Cheimon** won the wrestling match. They stand near to each other, the statue of Aristeus being by Pantias of Chios, the pupil of his father Sostratus. Besides the statue of Cheimon at Olympia there is another in the temple of Peace at Rome, brought there from Argos. Both are in my opinion among the most glorious works of Naucydes. It is also told how Cheimon overthrew Taurosthenes of Aegina in wrestling, how **Taurosthenes** at the next Festival overthrew all who entered for the wrestling match, and how an apparition similar to Taurosthenes appeared on that day in Aegina and announced the victory.

(6.9.4) The statue of **Philles of Elis**, who won the boys' wrestling match, was made by the Spartan Cratinus.

As regards the chariot of Gelon, I did not come to the same opinion about it as my predecessors, who hold that the chariot is an offering of the Gelon who became tyrant in Sicily. Now there is an inscription on the chariot that it was dedicated by Gelon of Gela, son of Deinomenes, and the date of the victory of this Gelon is the seventy-third festival [488 BCE].

(6.9.5) But the Gelon who was tyrant of Sicily took possession of Syracuse when Hybrilides was archon at Athens, in the second year of the seventy-second Olympiad [492 BCE], when **Tisicrates of Croton** won the foot race. Plainly, therefore, he would have announced himself as of Syracuse, not Gela. The fact is that this Gelon must be a private person, of the same name as the tyrant, whose father had the same name as the tyrant's father. It was Glaucias of Aegina who made both the chariot and the portrait-statue of Gelon.

(6.9.6) At the Festival previous to this it is said that **Cleomedes of Astypalaea** killed Iccus of Epidaurus during a boxing match. On being convicted by the judges for foul play and being deprived of the prize he became mad through grief and returned to Astypalaea. He attacked a school of about sixty children there when he pulled down the pillar which held up the roof.

(6.9.7) The roof fell upon the children, and Cleomedes, pelted with stones by the citizens, took refuge in the sanctuary of Athena. He entered a chest standing in the sanctuary and drew down the lid. The Astypalaeans toiled in vain in their attempts to open the chest. At last, however, they broke open the boards of the chest, but found no Cleomedes, either alive or dead. So they sent envoys to Delphi to ask what had happened to Cleomedes.

(6.9.8) The response given by the Pythian priestess was, they say, as follows:

> Last of heroes is Cleomedes of Astypalaea, Honor him with sacrifices since he is no longer a mortal.

So from this time have the Astypalaeans paid honors to Cleomedes as to a hero.[53]

(6.9.9) By the side of the chariot of Gelon is dedicated a statue of **Philon**, the work of the Aeginetan Glaucias. About this Philon Simonides the son of Leoprepes composed a very neat elegiac couplet:

> My fatherland is Corcyra, and my name is Philon; I am The son of Glaucus, and I won two Olympic victories for boxing.

There is also a statue of **Agametor of Mantineia**, who beat the boys at boxing.

(6.10.1) Next to those that I have enumerated stands **Glaucus of Carystus**.[54] Legend has it that he was by birth from Anthedon in Boeotia, descended from Glaucus the sea-deity. This Carystian was a son of Demylus, and they say that he first worked as a farmer. The ploughshare one day fell out of the plough, and he fitted it into its place, using his hand as a hammer.

---

[53] See Appendix AI.   [54] See also **40a** (§20) and **46**.

(6.10.2) Demylus happened to be a spectator of his son's performance, and thereupon brought him to Olympia to box. There Glaucus, inexperienced in boxing, was wounded by his opponents, and when he was boxing with the last of them, he was thought to be fainting from the number of his wounds. Then they say that his father called out to him, "Son, the plough strike." So he dealt his opponent a more violent blow which forthwith brought him the victory.

(6.10.3) He is said to have won other crowns besides, two at Delphi, eight at the Nemean and eight at the Isthmian games. The statue of Glaucus was set up by his son, while Glaucias of Aegina made it. The statue represents a figure sparring, as Glaucus was the best exponent of the skill of all his contemporaries. When he died the Carystians, they say, buried him in the island still called the island of Glaucus.

(6.10.4) **Damaretus of Heraea**, his son and his grandson, each won two victories at Olympia. Those of Damaretus were gained at the sixty-fifth festival [520] (at which the race in full armor was instituted) and also at the one succeeding. His statue shows him, not only carrying the shield that modern competitors have, but also wearing a helmet on his head and greaves on his legs. In course of time the helmet and greaves were removed from the armor of competitors by both the Eleans and the Greeks generally. **Theopompus**, son of Damaretus, won his victories in the pentathlon, and his son Theopompus the second, named after his father, won his in the wrestling match.

(6.10.5) Who made the statue of Theopompus the wrestler we do not know, but those of his father and grandfather are said by the inscription to be by Eutelidas and Chrysothemis, who were Argives. It does not, however, declare the name of their teacher, but runs as follows:

> Eutelidas and Chrysothemis made these works, Argives, who learnt their skill (*technē*) from those who lived before.

Iccus the son of Nicolaidas of Tarentum won the Olympic crown in the pentathlon, and afterward is said to have become the best trainer of his day.

(6.10.6) After Iccus stands **Pantarces the Elean**, beloved of Pheidias, who beat the boys at wrestling. Next to Pantarces is the chariot of **Cleosthenes**, a man of Epidamnus. This is the work of Ageladas, and it stands behind the Zeus dedicated by the Greeks from the spoils of the battle of Plataea. Cleosthenes' victory occurred at the sixty-sixth festival [516], and together with the statues of his horses he dedicated a statue of himself and another of his charioteer.

(6.10.7) There are inscribed the names of the horses, Phoenix and Corax, and on either side are the horses by the yoke, on the right Cnacias, on the left Samus. This inscription in elegiac verse is on the chariot:

> Cleosthenes, son of Pontis, a native of Epidamnus, dedicated me After winning a victory in the glorious games of Zeus with his horses.

(6.10.8) This Cleosthenes was the first of those who bred horses in Greece to dedicate his statue at Olympia. For the offering of **Evagoras the Laconian** consists of the chariot without a figure of Evagoras himself; the offerings of Miltiades the Athenian, which he dedicated at Olympia, I will describe in another part of my story. The Epidamnians occupy the same territory to-day as they did at first, but the modern city is not the ancient one, being at a short distance from it. The modern city is called Dyrrhachium from its founder.

(6.10.9) **Lycinus of Heraea, Epicradius of Mantineia, Tellon of Oresthas,** and **Agiadas of Elis** won victories in boys' matches; Lycinus for running, the rest of them for boxing. The artist who made the statue of Epicradius was Ptolichus of Aegina; that of Agiadas was made by Serambus, also a native of Aegina. The statue of Lycinus is the work of Cleon. Who made the statue of Tellon is not related.

(6.11.1) Next to these are offerings of Eleans, representing Philip the son of Amyntas, Alexander the son of Philip, Seleucus and Antigonus. Antigonus is on foot; the rest are on horseback.

(6.11.2) Not far from the kings mentioned stands a Thasian, **Theagenes** the son of Timosthenes. The Thasians say that Timosthenes was not the father of Theagenes, but a priest of the Thasian Heracles, a phantom of whom in the likeness of Timosthenes had intercourse with the mother of Theagenes. In his ninth year, they say, as he was going home from school, he was attracted by a bronze image of some god or other in the marketplace; so he caught up the image, placed it on one of his shoulders and carried it home.

(6.11.3) The citizens were enraged at what he had done, but one of them, a respected man of advanced years, bade them not to kill the lad, and ordered him to carry the image from his home back again to the marketplace. This he did, and at once became famous for his strength, and his feat was broadcast throughout Greece.

(6.11.4) The achievements of **Theagenes**[55] at the Olympian games have already—the most famous of them—been described in my story, how he beat Euthymus the boxer, and how he was fined by the Eleans. On this occasion the *pankration*, it is said, was for the first time on record won without a contest, the victor being Dromeus of Mantineia. At the festival following this, Theagenes was the winner in the *pankration*.

(6.11.5) He also won three victories at Delphi. These were for boxing, while nine prizes at Nemea and ten at the Isthmus were won in some cases for the *pankration* and in others for boxing. At Phthia in Thessaly he gave up training for boxing and the *pankration*. He devoted himself to winning fame among the Greeks for his running also and beat those who entered for the *dolichos*. His ambition was, I think, to rival Achilles by winning a prize for running in the fatherland of the swiftest of those who are called heroes. The total number of crowns that he won was one thousand four hundred.

---

[55] See above 6.6.10 and also **42a, I12b** and Appendix AI.

(6.11.6) When he departed this life, one of those who were his enemies while he lived came every night to the statue of Theagenes and flogged the bronze as though he were ill-treating Theagenes himself. The statue put an end to the outrage by falling on him, but the sons of the dead man prosecuted the statue for murder. As a result, the Thasians dropped the statue to the bottom of the sea, adopting the principle of Draco, who, when he framed for the Athenians laws to deal with homicide, inflicted banishment even on lifeless things, should one of them fall and kill a man.

(6.11.7) But in course of time, when the earth yielded no crop to the Thasians, they sent envoys to Delphi, and the god instructed them to receive back the exiles. At this command they received them back, but their restoration brought no remedy of the famine. For the second time they went to the Pythian priestess, saying that although they had obeyed her instructions the wrath of the gods still abode with them.

(6.11.8) Whereupon the Pythian priestess replied to them:

But you have forgotten your great Theagenes.

And when they could not think of a contrivance to recover the statue of Theagenes, fishermen, they say, after putting out to sea for a catch of fish caught the statue in their net and brought it back to land. The Thasians set it up in its original position and are accustomed to sacrifice to him as to a god.

(6.11.9) There are many other places that I know of, both among Greeks and among barbarians, where images of Theagenes have been set up, who cures diseases and receives honors from the natives. The statue of Theagenes is in the Altis, being the work of Glaucias of Aegina.

(6.12.1) Hard by is a bronze chariot with a man mounted upon it; racehorses, one on each side, stand beside the chariot, and on the horses are seated boys. They are memorials of Olympic victories won by Hieron the son of Deinomenes,[56] who was tyrant of Syracuse after his brother Gelon. But the offerings were not sent by Hieron; it was Hieron's son Deinomenes who gave them to the god, Onatas the Aeginetan who made the chariot, and Calamis who made the horses on either side and the boys on them.

(6.12.2) By the chariot of Hieron is a man of the same name as the son of Deinomenes. He too was tyrant of Syracuse and was called Hieron the son of Hieroncles. After the death of Agathocles, a former tyrant, tyranny again sprung up at Syracuse in the person of this Hieron, who came to power in the second year of the hundred and twenty-sixth Olympiad [276], at which **Idaeus of Cyrene** won the *stadion*.

(6.12.3) This Hieron made an alliance with Pyrrhus the son of Aeacides, sealing it by the marriage of Gelon his son and Nereis the daughter of Pyrrhus. When the Romans went to war with Carthage for the possession of Sicily, the Carthaginians held more than half the island, and Hieron sided with them at the beginning of the war. Shortly after,

---

[56] See also the victory poems for Hieron, **2a** and **3a**.

however, he changed over to the Romans, thinking that they were stronger, and firmer and more reliable friends.

(6.12.4) He met his end at the hands of Deinomenes, a Syracusan by birth and an inveterate enemy of tyranny, who afterward, when Hippocrates the brother of Epicydes had just come from Erbessus to Syracuse and was beginning to harangue the multitude, rushed at him with intent to kill him. But Hippocrates withstood him, and certain of the bodyguard over-powered and slew Deinomenes. The statues of Hieron at Olympia, one on horseback and the other on foot, were dedicated by the sons of Hieron, the artist being Micon, a Syracusan, the son of Niceratus.

(6.12.5) After the likenesses of Hieron stand Areus the Spartan king, the son of Acrotatus, and Aratus the son of Cleinias, with another statue of Areus on horseback. The statue of Aratus was dedicated by the Corinthians, that of Areus by the people of Elis.

(6.12.6) I have already given some account of both Aratus and Areus, and **Aratus** was also proclaimed at Olympia as victor in the chariot race. **Timon**, an Elean, the son of Aesypus, entered a four-horse chariot for the Olympic races…this is of bronze, and on it is mounted a maiden, who, in my opinion, is Victory. **Callon** the son of Harmodius and **Hippomachus** the son of Moschion, Elean by race, were victors in the boys' boxing match. The statue of Callon was made by Daippus; who made that of Hippomachus I do not know, but it is said that he overcame three opponents without receiving a blow or any physical injury.

(6.12.7) **Theochrestus of Cyrene** bred horses after the traditional Libyan manner; he himself and before him his paternal grandfather of the same name won victories at Olympia with the four-horse chariot, while the father of Theochrestus won a victory at the Isthmus. So declares the inscription on the chariot.

(6.12.8) The elegiac verses bear witness that **A gesarchus of Triteia**, the son of Haemostratus, won the boxing match for men at Olympia, Nemea, Pytho and the Isthmus; they also declare that the Tritaeans are Arcadians, but I found this statement to be untrue. For the founders of the Arcadian cities that attained to fame have well-known histories; while those that had all along been obscure because of their weakness were surely absorbed for this very reason into Megalopolis, being included in the decree then made by the Arcadian confederacy.

(6.12.9) There is no other city [named] Triteia in Greece, except the one in Achaia. However, one may assume that at the time of the inscription the Tritaeans were reckoned as Arcadians, just as nowadays too certain of the Arcadians themselves are reckoned as Argives. The statue of Agesarchus is the work of the sons of Polycles, of whom we shall give some account later on.

(6.13.1) The statue of **Astylus of Croton**[57] is the work of Pythagoras; this athlete won three successive victories at Olympia, in the *stadion* and the *diaulos*. But because on the

---

[57] Plato, *Laws* bk. 8.840a1–7 lists Astylus as one of several athletes who abstained completely from sex during their training.

two latter occasions he proclaimed himself to be a Syracusan in order to please Hieron the son of Deinomenes, the people of Croton condemned his house to be a prison and pulled down his statue.

(6.13.2) There is also set up in Olympia a slab recording the victories of **Chionis the Spartan**. They who have supposed that Chionis himself dedicated the slab and not the Spartan people are foolish. Let us assume that, as the slab says, the race in armor had not yet been introduced; how could Chionis know whether the Eleans would at some future time add it to the list of events? But those who say that the statue standing by the slab is a portrait of Chionis, it being the work of the Athenian Myron, are even more so.

(6.13.3) Similar in renown to Chionis was **Hermogenes of Xanthus**, a Lydian, who won the wild olive eight times at three Olympic festivals and was surnamed "Horse" by the Greeks. **Polites** also you would consider a great marvel. This Polites was from Ceramus in Caria and showed at Olympia every excellence in running. For from the *dolichos*, demanding the greatest stamina, he changed, after the shortest interval, to the *stadion*, and after winning a victory in the distance race and immediately afterward in the *stadion*, he added on the same day a third victory in the *diaulos*.

(6.13.4) Polites then in the second...,[58] as they are grouped together by lot, and they do not start them all together for the race. The victors in each heat run again for the prize. So, he who is crowned in the *stadion* will be victorious twice. However, the most famous runner was **Leonidas of Rhodes**. He maintained his speed at its prime for four Olympiads and won twelve victories for running.

(6.13.5) Not far from the slab of Chionis at Olympia stands **Scaeus**, the son of Duris, a Samian, victor in the boys' boxing match. The statue is the work of Hippias, the son of... and the inscription on it states that Scaeus won his victory at the time when the people of Samos were in exile from the island.

(6.13.6) By the side of the tyrant is a statue of **Diallus**, the son of Pollis, a Smyrnean by descent, and this Diallus declares that he was the first Ionian to receive at Olympia a crown for the boys' *pankration*. There are statues of Thersilochus of Corcyra and of Aristion of Epidaurus, the son of Theophiles, made by Polycleitus the Argive; **Aristion** won a crown for the men's boxing, **Thersilochus** for the boys' boxing.

(6.13.7) **Bycelus**, the first Sicyonian to win the boys' boxing match, had his statue made by Canachus of Sicyon, a pupil of the Argive Polycleitus. By the side of Bycelus stands the statue of a man-at-arms, Mnaseas of Cyrene, surnamed the Libyan; Pythagoras of Rhegium made the statue. To Agemachus of Cyzicus from the mainland of Asia...the inscription on it shows that he was born at Argos.

(6.13.8) Naxos was founded in Sicily by the Chalcidians on the Euripus. Of the city not even ruins are now to be seen, and the fact that the name of Naxos has survived to later ages must be attributed to **Tisander**, the son of Cleocritus. He won the men's boxing

---

[58] The text is missing.

match at Olympia four times; he had the same number of victories at Delphi, but at this time neither the Corinthians nor the Argives kept complete records of the victors at Nemea and the Isthmus.

(6.13.9) The **mare of the Corinthian Pheidolas** was named (as the Corinthians say) Aura ["Wind"], and at the beginning of the race she chanced to throw her rider. But, nevertheless, she went on running properly, turned around the post, and, when she heard the trumpet, quickened her pace, reached the judges first, realized that she had won and stopped running. The Eleans proclaimed Pheidolas the winner and allowed him to dedicate a statue of this mare.

(6.13.10) The sons of Pheidolas were also winners in the horse-race, and the horse is represented on a slab with this inscription:

The swift Lycus by one victory at the Isthmus and two here
Crowned the house of the sons of Pheidolas.

But the inscription is at variance with the Elean records of Olympic victors. These records give a victory to the sons of Pheidolas at the sixty-eighth Olympiad [508] but at no other. You may take my statements as accurate.

(6.13.11) There are statues to Agathinus, son of Thrasybulus, and to Telemachus, both men of Elis. **Telemachus** won the race for four-horse chariots; the statue of Agathinus was dedicated by the Achaeans of Pellene. The Athenian people dedicated a statue of **Aristophon**, the son of Lysinus, who won the men's *pankration* at Olympia.

(6.14.1) **Pherias of Aegina**, whose statue stands by the side of Aristophon the Athenian, at the seventy-eighth Olympiad [468] was considered very young, and, being judged to be as yet unfit to wrestle, was prevented from participating in the contest. But at the next festival he was admitted to the boys' wrestling match and won it. What happened to this Pherias was different, in fact the exact opposite of what happened at Olympia to **Nicasylus of Rhodes**.

(6.14.2) Being eighteen years of age he was not allowed by the Eleans to compete in the boys' wrestling match but won the men's match and was proclaimed victor. He was afterward proclaimed victor at Nemea also and at the Isthmus. But when he was twenty years old, he met his death before he returned home to Rhodes. The feat of the Rhodian wrestler at Olympia was in my opinion surpassed by **Artemidorus of Tralles**. He failed in the boys' *pankration* at Olympia because of his extreme youth.

(6.14.3) When, however, the time arrived for the contest held by the Ionians of Smyrna, his strength had so increased that he beat those who had competed with him at Olympia, after the boys, the beardless youths (*ageneioi*) as they are called, and thirdly the pick of the men, all on the same day. His match with the *ageneioi* was the outcome, they say, of a trainer's encouragement; he fought the men because of the insult of an older pankratist. Artemidorus won an Olympic victory among the men at the two hundred and twelfth festival [69 CE].

(6.14.4) Next to the statue of Nicasylus is a small bronze horse, which **Crocon of Eretria** dedicated when he won a crown with a racehorse. Near the horse is **Telestas of Messene**, who won the boys' boxing match. The artist who represented Telestas was Silanion.

(6.14.5) The statue of **Milo**[59] the son of Diotimus was made by Dameas, also a native of Croton. Milo won six victories for wrestling at Olympia, one of them among the boys; at Pytho he won six among the men and one among the boys. He came to Olympia to wrestle for the seventh time, but did not succeed in mastering **Timasitheus**, a fellow citizen who was also a young man, and who refused, moreover, to engage in close quarters with him.

(6.14.6) It is further stated that Milo carried his own statue into the Altis. His feats with the pomegranate and the discus are also remembered by tradition. He would grasp a pomegranate so firmly that nobody could wrest it from him by force, and yet he did not damage it by pressure. He would stand upon a greased discus and make fools of those who charged him and tried to push him from it. He used to perform also the following exhibitions of strength.

(6.14.7) He would tie a cord round his forehead as though it were a ribbon or a crown. Holding his breath and filling with blood the veins on his head, he would break the cord by the strength of these veins. It is said that he would let down by his side his right arm from the shoulder to the elbow, and stretch out straight the arm below the elbow, turning the thumb upward, while the other fingers lay in a row. In this position, then, the little finger was lowest, but nobody could bend it back by pressure.

(6.14.8) They say that he was killed by wild beasts. The story has it that in Croton, he came across a tree-trunk that was drying up; wedges were inserted to keep the trunk apart. Milo in his pride thrust his hands into the trunk, the wedges slipped, and Milo was held fast by the trunk until the wolves—a beast that roves in vast packs in the land of Croton– made him their prey.

(6.14.9) Such was the fate that overtook Milo. Pyrrhus, the son of Aeacides, who was king on the Thesprotian mainland and performed many remarkable deeds, as I have related in my account of the Athenians, had his statue dedicated by Thrasybulus of Elis. Beside Pyrrhus is a little man holding flutes, carved in relief upon a slab. This man won Pythian victories next after **Sacadas of Argos.**

(6.14.10) For Sacadas won in the games introduced by the Amphictyons [i.e., the Pythian games] before a crown was awarded for success, and after this victory two others for which crowns were given; but at the next six Pythian festivals **Pythocritus of Sicyon** was victor, being the only flute-player so to distinguish himself. It is also clear that at the Olympic festival he fluted six times for the pentathlon. For these reasons the slab at Olympia was erected in honor of Pythocritus, with the inscription on it:

This is the monument of the flute-player Pythocritus, the son of Callinicus.

---

[59] See also **36a, 39a** (13), and **42a**.

(6.14.11) The Aetolian League dedicated a statue of Cylon, who delivered the Eleans from the tyranny of Aristotimus. The statue of **Gorgus**, the son of Eucletus, a Messenian who won a victory in the pentathlon, was made by the Boeotian Theron; that of **Damaretus**, another Messenian, who won the boys' boxing match, was made by the Athenian Silanion. **Anauchidas**, the son of Philys, an Elean, won a crown in the boys' wrestling match and afterward in the match for men. Who made his statue is not known, but Ageladas of Argos made the statue of **Anochus of Tarentum**, the son of Adamatas, who won victories in the *stadion* and *diaulos*.

(6.14.12) A boy seated on a horse and a man standing by the horse the inscription declares to be **Xenombrotus of Meropian Cos**, who was proclaimed victor in the horse-race, and **Xenodicus**, who was announced a winner in the boys' boxing match. The statue of the latter is by Pantias, that of the former is by Philotimus the Aeginetan. The two statues of Pythes, the son of Andromachus, a native of Abdera, were made by Lysippus, and were dedicated by his soldiers. Pythes seems to have been a captain of mercenaries or some sort of distinguished soldier.

(6.14.13) There are statues of winners of the boys' race, namely, **Meneptolemus of Apollonia** on the Ionian Gulf and **Philo of Corcyra**; also **Hieronymus of Andros**, who defeated **Tisamenus of Elis** in the pentathlon at Olympia, and who afterward served as soothsayer in the Greek army that fought against Mardonius and the Persians at Plataea [see **8j**]. By the side of this Hieronymus is a statue of a boy wrestler, also of Andros, **Procles**, the son of Lycastidas. The sculptor who made the statue of Lycastidas was named Stomius, while Somis made the statue of Procles. **Aeschines of Elis** won two victories in the pentathlon, and his statues are also two in number.

(6.15.1) **Archippus of Mitylene** overcame his competitors in the men's boxing match, and his fellow townsmen hold that he added to his fame by winning the crown, when he was not more than twenty years old, at Olympia, at Delphi, at Nemea and at the Isthmus. The statue of the boy runner **Xenon**, son of Calliteles from Lepreus in Triphylia, was made by Pyrilampes the Messenian. Who made the statue of Cleinomachus of Elis I do not know, but **Cleinomachus** was proclaimed victor in the pentathlon.

(6.15.2) The inscription on the statue of Pantarces of Elis states that it was dedicated by Achaeans, because he made peace between them and the Eleans, and procured the release of those who had been made prisoners by both sides during the war. This **Pantarces** also won a victory with a racehorse, and there is a memorial of his victory also at Olympia. The statue of **Olidas of Elis** was dedicated by the Aetolian nation, and **Charinus of Elis** is represented in a statue dedicated for a victory in the *diaulos* and in the race in armor. By his side is **Ageles of Chios**, victorious in the boys' boxing match, the artist being Theomnestus of Sardes.

(6.15.3) The statue of **Cleitomachus of Thebes** was dedicated by his father Hermocrates, and his famous deeds are these. At the isthmus he won the men's wrestling match, and on the same day he overcame all competitors in the boxing match and in the *pankration*. His victories at Delphi were all in the *pankration*, three in number. At Olympia this Cleitomachus was the first after Theagenes of Thasos to be proclaimed victor in both boxing and the *pankration* [see **28b**].

(6.15.4) He won his victory in the *pankration* at the hundred and forty-first Olympiad [216 BCE]. The next Olympiad saw this Cleitomachus a competitor in the *pankration* and in boxing, while **Caprus of Elis** was minded both to wrestle and to compete in the *pankration* on the same day.

(6.15.5) After Caprus had won in the wrestling match, Cleitomachus put it to the judges that it would be fair if they were to bring in the *pankration* before he received wounds in the boxing. His request seemed reasonable, and so the *pankration* was brought in. Although Cleitomachus was defeated by Caprus he tackled the boxers with sturdy spirit and unwearied in his body.

(6.15.6) The Ionians of Erythrae dedicated a statue of **Epitherses**, son of Metrodorus, who won two boxing prizes at Olympia, two at Delphi, and also victories at Nemea and the Isthmus; the Syracusans dedicated two statues of Hieron at the public charge, while a third is the gift of Hierpon's sons. I pointed out in a recent chapter that this Hieron had the same name as the son of Deinomenes, and, like him, was a tyrant of Syracuse.[60]

(6.15.8) At the thirty-eighth festival [628] **Eutelidas the Spartan** won two victories among the boys, one for wrestling and one for the pentathlon, this being the first and last occasion when boys were allowed to enter for the pentathlon. The statue of Eutelidas is old, and the letters on the pedestal are worn dim with age.

(6.15.9) After Eutelidas is another statue of Areus the Spartan king, and beside it is a statue of **Gorgus the Elean**. Gorgus is the only man down to my time who has won four victories at Olympia for the pentathlon, beside a victory in the *diaulos* and a victory in the race in armor.

(6.15.10) The man with the boys standing beside him they say is Ptolemy, son of Lagus [reigned 323–285 BCE]. Beside him are two statues of the Elean **Caprus**, the son of Pythagoras, who received on the same day a crown for wrestling and a crown for the *pankration*. This Caprus was the first man to win the two victories. His opponent was overcome in the *pankration*, as I have already mentioned; in wrestling the man he overcame was the Elean **Paeanius**, who at the previous festival had won a victory for wrestling, while at the Pythian games he won a crown in the boys' boxing match, and again in the men's wrestling match and in the men's boxing match on one and the same day.

(6.16.1) The victories of Caprus were not achieved without great toils and strong effort. There are also at Olympia statues to **Anauchidas** and **Pherenicus**, Eleans by race who won crowns for wrestling among the boys. Pleistaenus, the son of the Eurydamus who commanded the Aetolians against the Gauls, had his statue dedicated by the Thespians.

---

[60] See Pausanias 6.12.2 above.

(6.16.4) **Aristeides of Elis** won at Olympia (so the inscription on his statue declares) a victory in the race in armor, at Delphi a victory in the *diaulos*, and at Nemea in the "horsey" race (*hippios*) for boys. The length of the horse-race is twice that of the double course (*diaulos*); the event had been omitted from the Nemean and Isthmian games but was restored to the Argives for their winter Nemean Games by the Emperor Hadrian.

(6.16.5) Quite close to the statue of Aristeides stands **Menalces of Elis**, proclaimed victor at Olympia in the pentathlon, along with Philonides son of Zotes, who was a native of Chersonesus in Crete, and a courier of Alexander, the son of Philip. After him comes **Brimias of Elis**, victor in the men's boxing match, Leonidas from Naxos in the Aegean, a statue dedicated by the Arcadians of Psophis, a statue of **Asamon**, victor in the men's boxing match, and a statue of **Nicander**, who won two victories at Olympia in the *diaulos* and six victories in foot-races of various kinds at the Nemean games. Asamon and Nicander were Eleans and the statue of the latter was made by Daippus, that of Asamon by the Messenian Pyrilampes.

(6.16.6) **Eualcidas of Elis** won victories in the boys' boxing match, **Seleadas the Spartan** in the men's wrestling match. Here too is dedicated a small chariot of the Laconian Polypeithes, and on the same slab Calliteles, the father of Polypeithes, a wrestler. **Polypeithes** was victorious with his four-horse chariot, **Calliteles** in wrestling.

(6.16.7) There are private Eleans, Lampus the son of Arniscus and... of Aristarchus; these the Psophidians dedicated, either because they were their public friends or because they had shown them some good will. Between them stands **Lysippus of Elis**, who beat his competitors in the boys' wrestling match; his statue was made by Andreas of Argos.

(6.16.8) **Demosthenes the Spartan** won an Olympic victory in the men's *stadion*, and he dedicated a slab in the Altis by the side of his statue. The inscription declares that the distance from Olympia to another slab at Sparta is six hundred and sixty stadia. **Theodorus** gained a victory in the pentathlon, **Pyttalus** the son of Lampis won the boys' boxing match, and **Neolaidas** received a crown for the *stadion* and the race in armor; all were Eleans. About Pyttalus it is further related that, when a dispute about boundaries occurred between the Arcadians and the Eleans, he delivered judgment on the matter. His statue is the work of Sthennis the Olynthian.

(6.16.9) Next is Ptolemy, mounted on a horse, and by his side is an Elean athlete, **Paeanius** the son of Damatrius, who won at Olympia a victory in wrestling besides two Pythian victories. There is also **Clearetus of Elis**, who received a crown in the pentathlon, and a chariot of an Athenian, Glaucon the son of Eteocles. This **Glaucon** was proclaimed victor in a chariot race for full-grown horses.

(6.17.1) These are the most remarkable sights that meet a man who goes over the Altis according to the instructions I have given. But if you will go to the right from the Leonidaeum to the great altar, you will come across the following notable objects. There is **Democrates of Tenedos**, who won the men's wrestling match, and **Criannius of Elis**, who won a victory in the race in armor. The statue of Democrates was made by Dionysicles of Miletus, that of Criannius by Lysus of Macedonia.

(6.17.2) The statues of Herodotus of Clazomenae and of Philinus, son of Hegepolis, of Cos, were dedicated by their respective cities. The Clazomenians dedicated a statue of **Herodotus** because he was the first Clazomenian to be proclaimed victor at Olympia, his victory being in the boys' *stadion*. The Coans dedicated a statue of **Philinus** because of his great renown, for he won at Olympia five victories in running, at Delphi four victories, at Nemea four, and at the Isthmus eleven.

(6.17.3) The statue of Ptolemy, the son of Ptolemy Lagus, was dedicated by Aristolaus, a Macedonian. There is also dedicated a statue of a victorious boy boxer, **Butas of Miletus**, son of Polyneices; a statue too of **Callicrates of Magnesia** on the Lethaeus, who received two crowns for victories in the race in armor. The statue of Callicrates is the work of Lysippus.

(6.17.4) **Enation** won a victory in the boys' *stadion*, and **Alexibius** in the pentathlon. The native land of Alexibius was Heraea in Arcadia, and Acestor made his statue. The inscription on the statue of Enation does not state his native land, though it does state that he was of Arcadian descent. Two Colophonians, **Hermesianax** son of Agoneus and **Eicasius** son of Lycinus and the daughter of Hermesianax, both won the boys' wrestling match. The statue of Hermesianax was dedicated by the commonwealth of Colophon.

(6.17.5) Near these are Eleans who won in boys' boxing, **Choerilus** the work of Sthennis of Olynthus, and **Theotimus** the work of Daitondas of Sicyon. Theotimus was a son of Moschion, who took part in the expedition of Alexander the son of Philip against Dareius and the Persians. There are two more from Elis, **Archidamus** who was victorious with a four-horse chariot and **Eperastus** the son of Theogonus, victor in the race in armor.

(6.17.6) That he was the soothsayer of the clan of the Clytidae, Eperastus declares at the end of the inscription:

> Of the stock of the sacred-tongued Clytidae I boast to be,
> Their soothsayer, the scion of the god-like Melampodidae.

For Mantius was a son of Melampus, the son of Amythaon, and he had a son Oecles, while Clytius was a son of Alcmaeon, the son of Amphiaraus, the son of Oecles. Clytius was the son of Alcmaeon by the daughter of Phegeus, and he migrated to Elis because he shrank from living with his mother's brothers, knowing that they had been involved in the murder of Alcmaeon.

(6.17.7) Mingled with the less illustrious offerings we may see the statues of **Alexinicus of Elis**, the work of Cantharus of Sicyon, who won a victory in the boys' wrestling match, and of Gorgias of Leontini. This statue was dedicated at Olympia by Eumolpus, who, as he himself says, was the grandson of Deicrates who married the sister of Gorgias.

(6.17.8) This Gorgias was a son of Charmantides and is said to have been the first to revive the study of rhetoric, which had been altogether neglected, in fact almost forgotten by mankind. They say that Gorgias won great acclaim for his eloquence at the Olympic assembly, and also when he accompanied Tisias on an embassy to Athens. Yet Tisias improved the expertise of rhetoric. In particular he wrote the most persuasive speech of his time to support a Syracusan woman's claim to a property.

(6.17.9) However, Gorgias surpassed his fame at Athens; indeed Jason, the tyrant of Thessaly, placed him before Polycrates, who was a shining light of the Athenian school. Gorgias, they say, lived to be one hundred and five years old. Leontini was once laid waste by the Syracusans, but in my time was again inhabited.

(6.18.1) There is also a bronze statue of **Cratisthenes of Cyrene**, and on the chariot stand Victory and Cratisthenes himself. It is thus plain that his victory was in the chariot race. The story goes that Cratisthenes was the son of **Mnaseas** the runner, surnamed the Libyan by the Greeks. His offerings at Olympia are the work of Pythagoras of Rhegium.

(6.18.6) **Sotades** at the ninety-ninth festival [384 BCE] was victorious in the *dolichos* and proclaimed a Cretan, as in fact he was. But at the next Festival he made himself an Ephesian, being bribed to do so by the Ephesian people. For this act he was banished by the Cretans.

(6.18.7) The first athletes to have their statues dedicated at Olympia were **Praxidamas of Aegina,** victorious at boxing at the fifty-ninth Olympiad [544 BCE], and **Rexibius the Opuntian**, a successful pankratist at the sixty-first Olympiad [536 BCE]. These statues stand near the pillar of Oenomaus, and are made of wood, Rexibius of figwood and the Aeginetan of cypress, and his statue is less decayed than the other.

37r. Bk. 6.19.1–6 (with omissions): The Treasuries

In this next section Pausanias discusses some of the treasuries built by city states, most notably the Sicyonian. We print only the part of this discussion directly relevant to athletic competition.

(6.19.1) There is in the Altis to the north of the Heraeum a terrace of conglomerate, and behind it stretches Mount Cronius. On this terrace are the treasuries, just as at Delphi certain of the Greeks have made treasuries for Apollo. There is at Olympia a treasury called the treasury of the Sicyonians, dedicated by Myron, who was tyrant of Sicyon.

[6.19.2–19.3 omitted.]

(6.19.4) On the smaller of the chambers at Olympia are inscriptions, which inform us that the weight of the bronze is five hundred talents, and that the dedicators were Myron and the Sicyonian people. In this chamber are kept three *diskoi*, being used for the contest of the pentathlon. There is also a bronze-plated shield, adorned with paintings on the inner side, and along with the shield are a helmet and greaves. An inscription on the armor says that they were dedicated by the Myanians as first-fruit offerings to Zeus. Various conjectures have been made as to who these Myanians were.

[6.19.5 omitted.]

(6.19.6) There are placed here other offerings worthy to be recorded, the sword of Pelops with its hilt of gold, and the ivory horn of Amaltheia, an offering of Miltiades the son of Cimon, who was the first of his house to rule in the Thracian Chersonesus.

37s. Bk. 6.20.7–21.3: The Stadiums and Gymnasia

This is Pausanias' description of the layout of the athletic facilities at Olympia in his day. See Plan 2, p. 374.

(6.20.7) There is within the Altis by the processional entrance the Hippodamium, as it is called, about a quarter of an acre of ground surrounded by a wall. Into it once every year the women may enter, who sacrifice to Hippodamia, and do her honor in other ways. The story is that Hippodamia withdrew to Midea in Argolis, because Pelops was very angry with her over the death of Chrysippus. The Eleans declare that subsequently, because of an oracle, they brought the bones of Hippodamia to Olympia.

(6.20.8) At the end of the statues which they made from the fines levied on athletes, there is the entrance called the Hidden Entrance. Through it judges and competitors enter the stadium. Now the stadium is an embankment of earth, and on it is a seat for those presiding over the games. Opposite the judges (*Hellanodikai*) is an altar of white marble.

(6.20.9) Seated on this altar a married woman looks on at the Olympic games, the priestess of Demeter Chamyne, which office the Eleans bestow from time to time on different women. Maidens (*parthenoi*) are not debarred from looking on at the games. At the end of the stadium, where is the starting place for the runners, there is, the Eleans say, the tomb of Endymion.

The Hippodrome at Olympia

(6.20.10) When you have passed beyond the stadium, at the point where the judges sit, is a place set apart for the horse-races, and also the starting place (*aphesis*) for the horses. The starting place is in the shape of the prow of a ship, and its prow is turned toward the course. At the point where the prow adjoins the porch of Agnaptus it broadens and a bronze dolphin on a rod has been made at the very point of the ram.

(6.20.11) Each side of the starting place is more than 400 feet in length, and in the sides are built stalls. These stalls are assigned by lot to those who enter for the races. Before the chariots or racehorses is stretched a cord as a barrier. An altar of unburnt brick, plastered on the outside, is made at every festival as near as possible to the center of the prow.

(6.20.12) And a bronze eagle stands on the altar with his wings stretched out to the fullest extent. The man appointed to start the racing sets in motion the mechanism in the altar, and then the eagle has been made to jump upward, so as to become visible to the spectators, while the dolphin falls to the ground.

(6.20.13) First on either side the barriers are withdrawn by the porch of Agnaptus, and the horses standing thereby run off first. As they run, they reach those to whom the second station has been allotted, and then are withdrawn the barriers at the second station. The same thing happens to all the horses in turn, until at the ram of the prow they are all abreast. After this it is left to the charioteers to display their skill and the horses their speed.

(6.20.14) It was Cleoetas who originally devised the method of starting, and he appears to have been proud of the discovery, as on the statue at Athens he wrote the inscription:

Who first invented the method of starting the horses at Olympia,
He made me, Cleoetas the son of Aristocles.

It is said that after Cleoetas some further device was added to the mechanism by Aristeides.

(6.20.15) The racecourse has one side longer than the other, and on the longer side, which is a bank, there stands, at the passage through the bank, Taraxippus, the terror of the horses. It has the shape of a round altar, and as they run along the horses are seized, as soon as they reach this point, by a great fear without any apparent reason. The fear leads to disorder; the chariots generally crash, and the charioteers are injured. Consequently, the charioteers offer sacrifice, and pray that Taraxippus may show himself propitious to them.

(6.20.16) The Greeks differ in their view of Taraxippus. Some hold that it is the tomb of an original inhabitant who was skilled in horsemanship; they call him Olenius and say that after him was named the Olenian rock in the land of Elis. Others say that Dameon, son of Phlius, who took part in the expedition of Heracles against Augeas and the Eleans, was killed along with his charger by Cteatus the son of Actor, and that man and horse were buried in the same tomb.

(6.20.17) There is also a story that Pelops made here an empty mound in honor of Myrtilus and sacrificed to him in an effort to calm the anger of the murdered man, naming the mound Taraxippus ("Frightener of horses") because the mares of Oenomaus were frightened by the trick of Myrtilus. Some say that it is Oenomaus himself who harms the racers in the course. I have also heard some attach the blame to Alcathus, the son of Porthaon. Killed by Oenomaus because he wooed Hippodamia, Alcathus, they say, here got his portion of earth; having been unsuccessful on the course, he is a spiteful and hostile deity to chariot-drivers.

(6.20.18) A man of Egypt said that Pelops received something from Amphion the Theban and buried it where is what they call Taraxippus, adding that it was the buried thing which frightened the mares of Oenomaus, as well as those of every charioteer since. This Egyptian man thought that Amphion and the Thracian Orpheus were clever magicians, and that it was through their enchantments that the beasts came to Orpheus, and the stones came to Amphion for the building of the wall. The most probable of the stories in my opinion makes Taraxippus an epithet of Poseidon Hippios.

(6.20.19) There is another Taraxippus at the Isthmus, namely Glaucus, the son of Sisyphus. They say that he was killed by his horses, when Acastus held his contests in honor of his father. At Nemea of the Argives there was no hero who harmed the horses, but above the turning-point of the chariots rose a rock, red in color, and the flash from it terrified the horses, just as though it had been fire. But the Taraxippus at Olympia is much worse for terrifying the horses. On one turning post is a bronze statue of Hippodamia carrying a ribbon, and about to crown Pelops with it for his victory.

(6.21.1) The other side of the course is not a bank of earth but a low hill. At the foot of the hill has been built a sanctuary to Demeter surnamed Chamyne. Some are of opinion that the name is old, signifying that here the earth gaped for the chariot of Hades and then closed up once more. Others say that Chamynus was a man of Pisa who opposed Pantaleon, the son of Omphalion and despot at Pisa, when he plotted to revolt from Elis; Pantaleon, they say, put him to death, and from his property was built the sanctuary to Demeter.

(6.21.2) In place of the old images of the Maid and of Demeter new ones of Pentelic marble were dedicated by Herodes the Athenian.

The Gymnasium at Olympia

In the gymnasium at Olympia it is customary for pentathletes and runners to practice, and in the open has been made a foundation of stone. Originally there stood on the foundation a trophy to commemorate a victory over the Arcadians. There is also another smaller enclosure to the left of the entrance to the gymnasium, and the athletes have their wrestling-schools here. Adjoining the wall of the eastern porch of the gymnasium are the dwellings of the athletes, turned toward the southwest.

(6.21.3) On the other side of the Cladeus is the grave of Oenomaus, a mound of earth with a stone wall built round it, and above the tomb are ruins of buildings in which Oenomaus is said to have stabled his mares.

37t. Bk.10.7.2–8: Delphi and the Pythian Games

The Pythian Games originally held only musical contests, but they were reorganized in 582 BCE on a quadrennial schedule and athletic events added in imitation of the Olympic Games (see Appendix BI). The first two sections give the names of mythological victors in musical contests.

(10.7.2) The oldest contest at Delphi and the one for which they first offered prizes was, according to tradition, the singing of a hymn to the god. The man who sang and won the prize was **Chrysothemis of Crete**, whose father Carmanor is said to have cleansed Apollo.[61] After Chrysothemis, says tradition, **Philammon** won with a song, and after him his son **Thamyris**. But they say that Orpheus, a proud man and conceited about his mysteries, and **Musaeus**, who copied Orpheus in everything, refused to submit to the competition in musical skill.

(10.7.3) They say too that **Eleuther** won a Pythian victory for his loud and sweet voice, for the song that he sang was not of his own composition. The story is that **Hesiod** too was debarred from competing because he had not learned to accompany his own singing on the harp. **Homer** too came to Delphi to inquire about his needs, but even though he had learned to play the harp, he would have found the skill useless owing to the loss of his eyesight.

(10.7.4) In the third year of the forty-eighth Olympiad [586 BCE] at which **Glaucias of Croton** was victorious, the Amphictyons [the Delphic judges] held contests for harp playing as from the beginning but added competitions for flute-playing and for singing to the flute. The conquerors proclaimed were **Melampus**, a Cephallenian, for harping, and **Echembrotus**, an Arcadian, for singing to the flute, with **Sacadas of Argos** for flute-playing. This same Sacadas won victories at the next two Pythian festivals.

(10.7.5) On that occasion they also offered for the first-time prizes for athletes, the competitions being the same as those at Olympia, except the four-horse chariot. And the Delphians themselves added to the contests *stadion* for boys, the *dolichos* and the *diaulos*. At the second Pythian festival [582] they no longer offered prizes for events, and hereafter gave a crown for victory. On this occasion they no longer included singing to the flute, thinking that the music was ill-omened to listen to. For the tunes of the flute were most dismal, and the words sung to the tunes were lamentations.

(10.7.6) What I say is confirmed by the votive offering of Echembrotus, a bronze tripod dedicated to the Heracles at Thebes. The tripod has as its inscription:

> Echembrotus of Arcadia dedicated this pleasant gift to Heracles when he won a victory
> at the games of the Amphictyons, singing for the Greeks tunes and lamentations.

In this way the competition in singing to the flute was dropped. But they added a chariot race, and **Cleisthenes, the tyrant of Sicyon**, was proclaimed victor in the chariot race.

(10.7.7) At the eighth Pythian festival [558] they added a contest for harpists playing without singing; **Agelaus of Tegea** was crowned. At the twenty-third Pythian Festival they added a race in armor [498]. For this **Timaenetus of Phlius** won the laurel, five Olympiads after **Damaretus of Heraea** was victorious. At the forty-eighth Pythian festival [398] they established a race for two-horse chariots, and the winning chariot

---

[61] Carmanor was a Cretan priest who freed Apollo from the pollution he incurred from killing the giant serpent who resided in Delphi.

belonged to Execestides the Phocian. At the fifth festival after this [378] they yoked foals to a chariot, and the chariot of **Orphondas of Thebes** came in first.

(10.7.8) The *pankration* for boys, a race for a chariot drawn by two foals, and a race for ridden foals, were many years afterward introduced from Elis. The first was brought in at the sixty-first Pythian festival [346], and Iolaidas of Thebes was victorious. At the next festival but one [338 BCE] they held a race for a ridden foal, and at the sixty-ninth festival a race for a chariot drawn by two foals [314]; the victor proclaimed for the former was Lycormas of Larisa, for the latter **Ptolemy the Macedonian**. For the kings of Egypt liked to be called Macedonians, as in fact they were.

The reason why a crown of laurel is the prize for a Pythian victory is in my opinion simply and solely because the prevailing tradition has it that Apollo fell in love with the daughter of Ladon.[62]

37u. Bk. 2.1.5–2.2.2: The Isthmus

See Appendix BI.

(2.1.5) The Corinthian Isthmus stretches on the one hand to the sea at Cenchreae, and on the other to the sea at Lechaeum. For this is what makes the region to the south mainland. He who tried to make the Peloponnesus an island gave up before digging through the Isthmus. Where they began to dig is still to be seen, but into the rock they did not advance at all. So it still is mainland as its nature is to be. Alexander the son of Philip wished to dig through Mimas, and his attempt to do this was his only unsuccessful project. The Cnidians began to dig through their Isthmus, but the Pythian priestess stopped them. So difficult it is for man to alter by violence what is divine.

(2.1.6) A legend of the Corinthians about their land is not peculiar to them, for I believe that the Athenians were the first to relate a similar story to glorify Attica. The Corinthians say that Poseidon had a dispute with Helius [a Sun god] about the land, and that Briareos arbitrated between them, assigning to Poseidon the Isthmus and the parts adjoining, and giving to Helius the height above the city. Ever since, they say, the Isthmus has belonged to Poseidon.

(2.1.7) Worth seeing here are a theater and a white-marble race-course. Within the sanctuary of the god stand on the one side portrait statues of athletes who have won victories at the Isthmian games, on the other side pine trees growing in a row, the greater number of them rising up straight. On the temple, which is not very large, stand bronze Tritons. In the fore-temple are images, two of Poseidon, a third of Amphitrite [his wife],

---

[62] In some versions of her story, Daphne was the daughter of the river god, Ladon, with whom Apollo fell in love. She rejected him, running from his embraces. When pleaded with her father for help, she was turned into the laurel tree. Laurel trees grew on the site of Delphi and their leaves came to be used for victory crowns.

and a Sea, which also is of bronze. The offerings inside were dedicated in our time by Herodes the Athenian, four horses, gilded except for the hoofs, which are of ivory,

(2.1.8) and two gold Tritons beside the horses, with the parts below the waist of ivory. On the car stand Amphitrite and Poseidon, and there is the boy Palaemon upright upon a dolphin. These too are made of ivory and gold. On the middle of the base on which the car is located has been wrought a Sea holding up the young Aphrodite, and on either side are the nymphs called Nereids. I know that there are altars to these in other parts of Greece, and that some Greeks have even dedicated to them precincts by shores, where honors are also paid to Achilles.

(2.1.9) Among the reliefs on the base of the statue of Poseidon are the sons of Tyndareus [Castor and Polydeuces], because these too are saviors of ships and of sea-faring men. The other offerings are images of Calm and of Sea, a horse like a whale from the breast downward, Ino and Bellerophontes, and the horse Pegasus.

(2.2.1) Within the enclosure on the left is a temple of Palaemon, with images in it of Poseidon, Leucothea, and Palaemon himself. There is also what is called his Holy of Holies, and an underground descent to it, where they say that Palaemon is concealed. Whoever, whether Corinthian or stranger, swears falsely here, can by no means escape from his oath. There is also an ancient sanctuary called the altar of the Cyclopes, and they sacrifice to the Cyclopes upon it.

(2.2.2) With respect to the graves of Sisyphus and of Neleus—for they say that Neleus came to Corinth, died of disease, and was buried near the Isthmus—I do not think that anyone would look for them after reading Eumelus. For he says that not even to Nestor did Sisyphus show the tomb of Neleus, because it must be kept unknown to everybody alike, and that Sisyphus is indeed buried on the Isthmus, but that few Corinthians, even those of his own day, knew where the grave was. The Isthmian games were not interrupted even when Corinth had been laid waste by Mummius, but so long as it lay deserted the celebration of the games was entrusted to the Sicyonians, and when it was rebuilt the honor was restored to the present inhabitants.

37v. Bk. 2.15.3–4: Nemea

See Appendix BI.

(2.15.2) From Cleonae to Argos are two roads; one is direct and only for active men, the other going along the pass called Tretus ("Pierced"), is narrow like the other, being surrounded by mountains, but is nevertheless more suitable for carriages. In these mountains is still shown the cave of the famous lion,[63] and the place Nemea is distant some

---

[63] Heracles' first labor was to kill the lion sent by Hera to devastate Nemea.

fifteen stadia. In Nemea is a noteworthy temple of Nemean Zeus, but I found that the roof had fallen in and that there was no longer any image remaining. Around the temple is a grove of cypress trees, and it is here, they say, that Opheltes was placed by his nurse in the grass and killed by the serpent.

(2.15.3) The Argives offer burnt sacrifices to Zeus in Nemea also, and elect a priest of Nemean Zeus; moreover they offer a prize for a race in armor at the winter celebration of the Nemean games. In this place is the grave of Opheltes; around it is a fence of stones, and within the enclosure are altars. There is also a mound of earth which is the tomb of Lycurgus, the father of Opheltes. The spring they call Adrastea for some reason or other, perhaps because Adrastus found it. The land was named, they say, after Nemea, who was another daughter of Asopus. Above Nemea is Mount Apesas, where they say that Perseus first sacrificed to Zeus of Apesas.

37w. Bk. 1.30.1–2: The Academy in Athens

(1.30.1) Before the entrance to the Academy is an altar to Eros, with an inscription that Charmus was the first Athenian to dedicate an altar to that god. The altar within the city called the altar of Anteros ["Love Avenged"] they say was dedicated by resident foreigners, because the Athenian Meles, spurning the love of Timagoras, a foreign resident, bade him ascend to the highest point of the rock and cast himself down. Now Timagoras took no account of his life and was ready to gratify the youth in any of his requests, so he went and cast himself down. When Meles saw that Timagoras was dead, he suffered such pangs of remorse that he threw himself from the same rock and so died. From this time the foreign residents worshipped the avenging spirit of Timagoras as Anteros.

(1.30.2) In the Academy is an altar to Prometheus, and from it they run to the city carrying burning torches. The contest is while running to keep the torch still alight; if the torch of the first runner goes out, he has no longer any claim to victory, but the second runner has. If his torch also goes out, then the third man is the victor. If all the torches go out, no one is left to be winner. There is an altar to the Muses, and another to Hermes, and one within to Athena, and they have built one to Heracles. There is also an olive tree, accounted to be the second that appeared.

37x. Bk. 3.8.1–5: Agis and Cynisca of Sparta

See also Thucydides **9f** *and Xenophon* **10h**.

(3.8.1) Archidamus left sons when he died, of whom, Agis, was the elder and inherited the throne instead of Agesilaus. Archidamus also had a daughter, whose name was

Cynisca; she was exceedingly ambitious to succeed at the Olympic games and was the first woman to breed horses and the first to win an Olympic victory. After Cynisca other women, especially women of Sparta, have won Olympic victories, but none of them was more distinguished for their victories than she.

(3.8.2) The Spartans seem to me to be of all men the least moved by poetry and the praise of poets. For with the exception of the epigram upon Cynisca, of uncertain authorship, and the still earlier one upon Pausanias that Simonides wrote on the tripod dedicated at Delphi, there is no poetic composition to commemorate the doings of the royal houses of the Spartans.

(3.8.3) In the reign of Agis the son of Archidamus the Spartans had several grievances against the people of Elis, being especially exasperated because they were debarred from the Olympic games and the sanctuary at Olympia. So they dispatched a herald commanding the people of Elis to grant home-rule to Lepreum and to any other of their neighbors that were subject to them. The people of Elis replied that, when they saw the cities free that were neighbors of Sparta, they would without delay set free their own subjects; whereupon the Spartans under king Agis invaded the territory of Elis.

(3.8.4) On this occasion there occurred an earthquake, and the army retired home after advancing as far as Olympia and the Alpheus but in the next year Agis devastated the country and carried off most of the booty. Xenias, a man of Elis who was a personal friend of Agis and the state-friend of the Spartans, rose up with the rich citizens against the people but before Agis and his army could come to their aid, Thrasydaeus, who at this time championed the interests of the popular party at Elis, overthrew in battle Xenias and his followers and cast them out of the city.

(3.8.5) When Agis led back his army, he left behind Lysistratus, a Spartan, with a portion of his forces, along with the Elean refugees, that they might help the Lepreans to ravage the land. In the third year of the war the Spartans under Agis again prepared to invade the territory of Elis. So Thrasydaeus and the Eleans, reduced to dire extremities, agreed to forgo their supremacy over their neighbors, to dismantle the fortifications of their city, and to allow the Spartans to sacrifice to the god and to compete in the games at Olympia.

37y. Bk. 8.38.2–7: Mount Lycaeus

(8.38.2) On the left of the sanctuary of the Mistress is Mount Lycaeus. Some Arcadians call it Olympus, and others Sacred Peak. On it, they say, Zeus was reared. There is a place on Mount Lycaeus called Cretea, on the left of the grove of Apollo surnamed Parrhasian. The Arcadians claim that the Crete, where the Cretan story has it that Zeus was reared, was this place and not the island.

(8.38.3) The nymphs, by whom they say that Zeus was reared, they call Theisoa, Neda, and Hagno. After Theisoa was named a city in Parrhasia; Theisoa to-day is a village in the district of Megalopolis. From Neda the river Neda takes its name; from Hagno a spring on Mount Lycaeus, which like the Danube flows with an equal volume of water in winter just as in the season of summer.

(8.38.4) Should a drought persist for a long time, and the seeds in the earth and the trees wither, then the priest of Lycaean Zeus, after praying toward the water and making the usual sacrifices, lowers an oak branch to the surface of the spring, not letting it sink deep. When the water has been stirred up there rises a vapor, like mist; after a time the mist becomes cloud, gathers to itself other clouds, and makes rain fall on the land of the Arcadians.

(8.38.5) There is on Mount Lycaeus a sanctuary of Pan, and a grove of trees around it, with a race-course in front of which is a running-track. Of old they used to hold here the Lycaean games. Here there are also bases of statues, with now no statues on them. On one of the bases an elegiac inscription declares that the statue was a portrait of Astyanax, and that Astyanax was of the race of Arceas.

(8.38.6) Among the marvels of Mount Lycaeus the most wonderful is this. On it is a precinct of Lycaean Zeus, into which people are not allowed to enter. If anyone takes no notice of the rule and enters, he must inevitably live no longer than a year. A legend, moreover, was current that everything alike within the precinct, whether beast or man, cast no shadow. For this reason when a beast takes refuge in the precinct, the hunter will not rush in after it, but remains outside, and though he sees the beast cannot see a shadow. In Syene also just on this side of Ethiopia neither tree nor creature casts a shadow so long as the sun is in the constellation of the Crab, but the precinct on Mount Lycaeus affects shadows in the same way always and at every season.

(8.38.7) On the highest point of the mountain is a mound of earth, forming an altar of Zeus Lycaeus, and from it most of the Peloponnesus can be seen. Before the altar on the east stand two pillars, on which there were of old gilded eagles. On this altar they sacrifice in secret to Lycaean Zeus. I was reluctant to pry into the details of the sacrifice; let them be as they are and were from the beginning.

37z. Bk. 8.40.1–5: Deaths of Arrhachion [Arrhichion] and Creugas

*See also Philostratus, **40d**, for a description of Arrhichion.*

(8.40.1). The Phigalians have on their marketplace a statue of the pankratist Arrhachion; it is archaic, especially in its posture. The feet are close together, and the arms hang down by the side as far as the hips. The statue is made of stone, and it is said that an inscription was written upon it. This has disappeared with time. But Arrhachion won two Olympic victories at festivals before the fifty-fourth, while at this festival [564 BCE] he won one due partly to the fairness of the judges and partly to his own manliness.

(8.40.2) For when he was contending for the wild olive with the last remaining competitor, whoever he was, the latter got a grip first and held Arrhachion, hugging him with his legs, and at the same time he squeezed his neck with his hands. Arrhachion dislocated his opponent's toe, but expired owing to suffocation. Yet he who suffocated Arrhachion was forced to give in at the same time because of the pain in his toe. The Eleans crowned and proclaimed the corpse of Arrhachion victor.

(8.40.3) I know that the Argives acted similarly in the case of Creugas, a boxer of Epidamnus. For the Argives too gave to Creugas after his death the crown in the Nemean Games, because his opponent Damoxenus of Syracuse broke their mutual agreement. For evening drew near as they were boxing, and they agreed within the hearing of witnesses that each should in turn allow the other to deal him a blow. At that time boxers did not yet wear a sharp thong on the wrist of each hand, but still boxed with the soft gloves, binding them in the hollow of the hand, so that their fingers might be left bare. These soft gloves were thin thongs of raw oxhide plaited together after an ancient manner.

(8.40.4) On the occasion to which I refer Creugas aimed his blow at the head of Damoxenus, and the latter bade Creugas lift up his arm. On his doing so, Damoxenus with straight fingers struck his opponent under the ribs; and because of the sharpness of his nails and the force of the blow he drove his hand into the other's inside, caught his bowels, and tore them as he pulled them out.

(8.40.5) Creugas expired on the spot, and the Argives expelled Damoxenus for breaking his agreement by dealing his opponent many blows instead of one. They gave the victory to the dead Creugas and had a statue of him made in Argos. It still stood in my time in the sanctuary of Lycian Apollo.

37aa. Bk. 1.39.3: Theseus Discovers the Skill of Wrestling

In this passage, Pausanias attributes the expertise of wrestling as a skill (techne) to Theseus.

After the graves of the Argives is the tomb of Alope, who, legend says, being mother of Hippothoon by Poseidon, was on this spot put to death by her father Cercyon. Cercyon is said to have mistreated strangers by wrestling with them against their will. As a result, even to my day this place is called the Wrestling Ground of Cercyon and is a small distance from the grave of Alope. Cercyon is said to have killed all those who went against him except Theseus, who outmatched him mainly by his skill (*sophia*). For Theseus was the first to discover the craft (*techne*) of wrestling, and through him afterward was established the teaching of the craft. Before him men used only size and strength of body in wrestling.

37ab. Bk. 1.44.1: Orsippus and the Origin of Nude Athletics

See the discussion in Appendix AIII.

Near to Coroebus is buried Orsippus, who won the *stadion* by running naked while the athletes at Olympia wrapped clothes around themselves in the competitions, as was the ancient custom…I think that at Olympia he deliberately let the loincloth (*perizōma*) fall away, recognizing that a naked man ran more easily than a man wearing a loincloth.

38. Lucian

Lucian of Samosata (c.125–80 CE) was a Syrian by birth but Hellenized by education. He became a professor of Greek rhetoric under the Romans, teaching at some point in Gaul (southern France). He wrote about eighty dialogues on a wide variety of subjects, most of which were in a dialect (Attic) derived from the writings of fifth-century Athens. His status as an outsider provided him with a perspective on Greek social behaviors like athletics as they were practiced in the Greek cities of the eastern Roman Empire, but also on the pretensions of those who wished to pass as Greek or as educated. Much of his writing, therefore, satirized what he saw. In the following selections that discuss athletics, it is not always clear how much is based on actual contemporary behaviors, how much is exaggeration, and how much is fantasy.

38a. *Anacharsis* (with omissions)

*This is a satirical dialogue set in the sixth century BCE. The two speakers are **Anacharsis**, a philosopher from the area of the Black Sea who was numbered among the Seven Wise Men of Greek antiquity. In this fiction, he travels to Athens to learn about the Athenian ways of government. He and the Athenian statesman **Solon**, another of the Seven, are watching young men exercising in the gymnasium. Anacharsis finds what they are doing both strange and silly. Solon defends the practice as cultivating virtuous citizens, thus expressing an opinion found often in Classical writers about the link between athletic training and military preparedness. By Lucian's time Greek cities no longer depended on citizen soldiers; rather, the gymnasium functioned as a status marker and a place to inculcate and solidify Greek identity under foreign (Roman) rule. The practices described here are an amalgam of the views of earlier writers, particularly Plato, and the gymnasium of Lucian's day.*

(1) ANACHARSIS Why are your young men doing these things, Solon? Some of them grip and trip each other; some throttle and twist away and wallow together in the mud like so many pigs. Yet, initially, when they have removed their clothes—for I saw this—they take

turns as they anoint and rub each other down with oil quite peacefully; but then I have no idea what happens to them: They push one another and lowering their heads, they butt their foreheads together like rams. There, look! That one has lifted the other up off his legs and dropped him on the ground; now he has fallen on top and will not let him get up, but presses him down into the mud; and finally he wraps his legs tight round his belly, putting his elbow against his throat; he throttles the wretch, who meanwhile is slapping him on his shoulder, imploring him, I suppose, not to choke him to death.[64] Despite their application of oil, they do not hesitate to get dirty; rubbing off the oil, they cover themselves in mud and sweat and provide a good laugh for me at least, just like eels slipping through one's hands. (2) Others in the open part of the court are doing the same thing, not in mud at least, but they have a deep layer of sand placed under them in a pit, and they sprinkle one another and willingly pour dust over themselves like roosters. They want to be less able to escape in the clinches, I suppose, and the sand neutralizes the slipperiness of the oil, and in its dryness provide a firmer grip. (3) Others are upright after dusting themselves and are attacking each other with blows and kicks. This poor fellow is likely to spit out his teeth; his mouth is full of blood and sand; he has taken a fist to the jaw, as you see. But not even this official here separates them and puts an end to the fight—I infer from his purple cloak that he is an official. But he encourages them and praises the one who struck that blow. (4) All the others in various places are exerting themselves. They bob up and down as if they were running but stay in the same place, and they leap up and kick the air.

(5) Now I want to know what is the good of doing such things? To me it's more like madness. It will not be very easy to convince me the ones who are acting like this are not out of their minds.

(6) SOLON Naturally, these practices strike you that way, since they are so strange and so completely unlike Scythian behaviors. Just as there are many aspects of your education and customs that would seem very strange to us Greeks, if we should become acquainted with them, as you now are of ours. But take heart, my good man; these activities are not madness; it is not from violence that they hit each other, wallow in the mud, and sprinkle dust. This behavior has its use, is not without pleasure, and culminates in an admirable physical condition. If you stay for some time in Greece, as I think you will do, you yourself will be a mudder or a duster in no time; the pleasure and profit of the pursuit will become apparent to you.

ANACHARSIS Back off. I wish you all joy of your pleasures and your profits; but if any of you treats me like that, he will learn that we do not wear our swords to no purpose. (7) But tell me, what do you call what is happening? What do we say they are doing?

---

[64] See description of death of Arrhichion, **37z**.

The Gymnasium and Prizes for Winners

SOLON This place, Anacharsis, we call a gymnasium, and it is dedicated to Apollo. You see his statue there; he is the one leaning on the pillar, with a bow in his left hand. The right arm bent over the head indicates that the God is resting after some great exertion.

As for these exercises here, the one in the mud is called wrestling; those in the dust are also wrestling, and those who strike each other while standing upright are engaged in what we call the *pankration*. We have other gymnasia for boxing, discus throwing, and high jumping; and in all these we hold contests; the winner is considered to be the best of those with whom he has competed, and he takes the prize.

(9) ANACHARSIS And the prizes, what are they?

SOLON At Olympia a wreath of wild olive, at the Isthmus one of pine, in Nemea one of celery, at Delphi some of the God's sacred laurel berries, and for us at the Panathenaea, oil from the sacred olives. Why are you laughing, Anacharsis? Do you think the prizes too small?

ANACHARSIS Oh no; you list prizes that are most imposing and worthwhile so that those who have given them may bask in their munificence and the competitors be especially keen to take up the such prizes as these. For laurel berries and celery, who would not take on such preparation as this, then risk being choked, or a limb dislocated? As if it was impossible to procure fruit without effort, or a wreath of celery or pine without mud smeared on his face or being kicked in the stomach by his opponent.

(10) SOLON My dear sir, it is the face value of the gifts that we regard. They are the signs of victory, tokens by which winners are recognized. The attending fame is worth everything to these victors; to be kicked in pursuit of this is acceptable for those who are trying to capture great repute from such pains. Fame does not accrue to a man without effort; the man who covets fame must put up with hardship at first; afterward he may look for the pleasure and profit from his exertions.

ANACHARSIS This pleasure and profit, you say, Solon, result from being seen in their wreaths by everyone and congratulated on their victory by those who before commiserated with them on the blows they received; and they become happy exchanging laurel berries and celery for their labors.

SOLON You are still unacquainted with our ways. After a short time, you will revise your opinions about these things, when you go to the festival games and see such a great number of men gathering for the spectacle, the stands that hold thousands filling up, the competitors being cheered, and the victor being thought equal to the gods.

Anacharsis Objects to the Sufferings Involved in Competition to No Purpose

(11) ANACHARSIS This very thing, Solon, is most pitiable; they suffer these pains not in front of a few, but in front of so many spectators, witnesses to the insult, who, to be sure,

count them happy when they see them dripping with blood or being throttled by their opponents. For these are the most blessed accompaniments of victory. Among us, the Scythians, Solon, if someone were to strike one of the citizens, overturn and throw him down, or tear his clothing, our elders would mete out a severe punishment, even though he should endure this with few witnesses, not like your vast throngs at Olympia or Isthmia. However, though I cannot help pitying the competitors who are suffering, I am still more astonished at the spectators, who you say are the most prominent people from all over, if they leave their serious concerns and idle away their time on such things. I cannot comprehend how it gives them pleasure to see men being struck, pummeled, thrown to the ground, and pounded down by one another.

(12) SOLON If it were the time of the Olympian, Isthmian, or Panathenaic Games, what happens there would have taught you that we have not pursued these activities vainly. For no one by speaking would convince you of the pleasure of what they are doing as by sitting in the middle of the spectators, looking at the men's courage and physical beauty, their marvelous condition, amazing skill and unconquerable strength, their boldness, rivalry, unbeatable mindset, and their inexpressible pursuit of victory. I know well, you would never have stopped praising and cheering and clapping.

(13) ANACHARSIS By god, Solon, and laughing and mocking as well. All the things that you have listed, courage and conditioning, beauty and daring, I see that you are wasting them to no great purpose; your country is not in danger; your lands are not being ravaged; your friends or relations not being carried off in insolence. It would be that much more ridiculous if, being the best of men, as you claim, they endured such great indignities and made themselves wretched, spoiling their good looks and their fine figures with sand and black eyes, so that by their victories they might become possessors of fruit or the wild olive. It does give me pleasure to recall those prizes! But do all the competitors get them?

The Reason for Only One Winner at Olympia

SOLON By no means; there is only one winner.

ANACHARSIS Then, Solon, why do so many endure hardships with an uncertain and precarious chance of victory, knowing that there will be only one victor and many losers, wretches who have taken blows and wounds in vain?

Solon now embarks on a long explanation of how this kind of athletic training makes for the best citizens of the state. Anacharsis says that that is why he came to Athens—to learn about the Athenian laws and customs.

(14) SOLON You seem to have never yet considered at all what a good political constitution is, or you would never disparage the best of our customs. If you ever take the trouble to learn how a state may be organized in the best way and its citizens become the best they can be, at that point you will commend these practices and the spirit of rivalry by

means of which we cultivate them; then you will recognize that they gain much that is useful, but inseparable from hardships, even if they now seem to spend their energy in vain.

ANACHARSIS Well, Solon, I came from Scythia to this land of yours, traveling through the vast and storm-laden Euxine, for no other purpose than to learn the laws of Greece, observe your customs, and learn the best constitution. That was why I chose you of all Athenians for my friend and host on the basis of your reputation. I was accustomed to hear that you were a writer of laws, an inventor of the best institutions, an introducer of helpful practices, and the fashioner of a constitution. Before all things, then, teach me. Make me your pupil. I would gladly sit beside you without food or drink, as long as you keep on speaking, and with mouth agape I would listen to you explaining about the constitution and the laws.

(15) SOLON It is not easy, friend, to explain everything briefly. But by going through different areas, one by one, you will learn our views about the gods, then about parents, about marriage, and everything else. What we think about the young and how we treat them from the time when they begin to understand higher things and their bodies approach manhood and they are capable of endurance, these things I shall now tell you. Then you will grasp why we propose these exercises for them and compel them to train their bodies. Not simply for the sake of the contests, so that they may carry off prizes— very few of the whole number ever reach that point, but seeking a more important good for their city and themselves. There is another contest in which all good citizens get prizes, and crowns not of pine or wild olive or celery, and whoever takes part in it obtains human happiness, including individual freedom and political independence, wealth and fame, enjoyment of our traditional festivals, safety for our families, and all together, the best of all that a man might ask of gods. The crown of which I speak is woven from all of these things, and they are acquired in that contest to which this training and these toils lead.

(16) ANACHARSIS You amazing man! You had prizes like all of these to talk about and you regaled me with laurel berries and celery and sprigs of wild olive and pine.

SOLON But those prizes will no longer seem trivial to you when you have grasped what I am saying. They stem from the same concept, all small parts of that greater contest, and of the wreath of complete happiness that I spoke of. But our discussion somehow deviated from its proper order, as there was mention of the Isthmus and Olympia and Nemea. However, now, since we are at leisure and you say that you are eager to hear, it is easy for us to go back to the beginning and the common competition that is, I say, the basis for all of these customary behaviors.

[We omit 16–19, where Solon explains a number of civic institutions to Anacharsis as they walk along the road.]

(20) SOLON Well, you must first hear a preliminary statement of our views upon city and citizens. We do not consider a city to be its buildings like walls, temples, or docks. These are no more than a fixed and immovable frame that provides the members of the

community with shelter and safety. We place our whole authority in the citizens; they replenish and organize it and carry out and guard each element; they are like the soul that is in each of us. Thinking of it in this way, we take care, as you see, of our city's body; ornamenting it to be as beautiful as we can make it, providing it internally with buildings and encircling it as securely as possible with external walls. But above all, we especially think how to make our citizens noble in soul and strong in body; for such men will in peacetime make the most of themselves and their political unity, while in war they will keep the city safe and guard its freedom and prosperity. Their early nurture we entrust to their mothers, nurses, and tutors, who raise and provide them with a liberal education. But as soon as they understand what is good, and when modesty, shame, fear, and ambition begin to grow in them, when their bodies appear ready for toil and they become firmer and stronger, at that point we take and teach them, prescribing studies and exercises (*gymnasia*) for the soul, but we also accustom their bodies to endure hardship. We do not think the natural development of either body or soul is sufficient, but we also want systematic teaching and learning for them, which will improve their good qualities and reform their baser ones. Our model is that of the farmer who shelters and fences his plants while they are small and tender so that they are not buffeted by the winds, but, as soon as the shoot thickens, he prunes the excessive growth and allows it to be shaken by the winds to make them bear more fruit.

Education of the Minds of the Young

(21) SOLON At first, we use music and arithmetic to stimulate their minds; we teach them to write and to read aloud clearly. Then, as they get on, we set out for them the sayings of wise men, the deeds of olden times, and valuable tales performed in meter, on the grounds that it is easier to remember. And as they hear of certain feats of valor or famous deeds, they yearn little by little, and are fired up to emulate, so that they too may be sung of and marveled at by posterity. (Hesiod and Homer have composed much of this sort of poetry for us.) When they attain full citizenship, and it is necessary for them to take their part in governing—but all this, perhaps, is irrelevant. The subject proposed for discussion was not how we train their souls, but why we think fit to train their bodies with such strenuous exercise.

[*We omit 22–3, Solon's digression on tragedy and comedy. He continues with a discussion of the training of the athlete's body and how it fits a man for warfare.*]

(24) SOLON Then their bodies, which you especially wanted to hear about, we train as follows. We strip them naked, as I said, when they are no longer soft and uncoordinated. We think it best to accustom them to the open air, habituating them to each of the seasons, so that neither heat nor frost distresses them. Then we anoint them with oil and make them supple. Since we believe that leather when softened with olive oil is more

supple and harder to break, and much more durable (and it is already dead), it would be illogical if we thought that the living body would not be improved by the application of olive oil. After that, we have thought up a variety of gymnastic exercises and appointed instructors for each type. Then we teach one boxing, another the *pankration*, so that they grow accustomed to hard work. They become habituated to endurance, to meet blows, and never to shrink for fear of injury. This has worked for us to produce two most valuable traits in them: It makes them courageous in the face of danger, heedless of their bodies, and at the same time strong and enduring.

Wrestling

SOLON Those whom you saw lowering their heads and wrestling learn to fall safely and get up easily, to be able to push, grapple, and twist, to endure throttling, and lift their opponent up high in the air. They are not acquiring useless skills, but one thing beyond dispute; their bodies are hardened and more capable of enduring pain because of this harsh exercise. There is another and not insignificant advantage: They acquire experience from this, in case they come to need in war what they have learned. Obviously, such a man, when he closes with a real enemy, throws him more quickly, or if he falls, will know better how to get up again. We provide all these preparations for that real test in arms and we expect much better soldiers so furnished with this training, when beforehand we have made their naked bodies supple and hardened and made them stronger and healthier, light and fit (though heavy for their opponents to endure).

(25) You see, I suppose, the results, what they are likely to be when they are armed, when even naked, they implant fear in their enemies. They show no white, pasty fleshiness, no cadaverous thinness, like the bodies of women washed out from the shade, trembling and with rivulets of sweat pouring down and panting under their helmets especially if the sun, as now, burns down at midday. Who would need men who are thirsty and averse to dust, who, if they see blood, break ranks and die before they come within range of the enemy's spear and come to grips with the enemy? But our young men are ruddy, darkened by the sun, with virile faces, displaying great spirit, fire, and courage. They glow with good health, neither lean and emaciated nor carrying weight, but sculpted and symmetrical. They have sweated out any useless excess of flesh, but strength and suppleness, purged of any worthless admixture, are left in them, and they preserve this healthy condition vigorously. The gymnastic exercises have the same effect on our bodies as the winnowing fan which blows away chaff and husks from the wheat and sifts and heaps up the clean grain.

(26) Training like this necessarily produces sound health and the capacity to endure fatigue. A man like this does not sweat quickly and seldom appears to be sick. It is as if someone with a torch would thrust it into the pile of wheat and at the same time into the straw and chaff—I am returning to my winnower simile—the straw, I think,

would catch fire more quickly, but the wheat would burn gradually, without a great blaze and not all at once; it would smolder slowly and be consumed over a longer period of time.

Neither sickness nor fatigue will easily attack this sort of body or readily overwhelm it. Internally, it is well fortified and externally strongly resistant to such assaults, so that it neither admits nor receives sun or frost to the detriment of the body. As a defense against yielding to hardships, abundant internal heat, long beforehand readied and stored up, fills them at once, restores the vital force, and lengthens endurance to the utmost. Previous exertion and hardship do not dissipate their strength but increase it, and it grows stronger the more it is fanned.

Running, Long Jump, Javelin, Discus

(27) SOLON Further, we train them to run, habituating them to endure long distances and to be as quick and light-footed as possible in the sprint. The running is not on hard, resistant ground, but in deep sand, on which you can neither plant your foot firmly nor get a good push off, since the foot slips against the yielding sand. Then, we train them to leap a trench, if necessary, or other obstacle, and in addition we train them to practice with weights as large as they can grasp in their hands. And again, they compete for distance in throwing the javelin. You also saw a round bronze in the gymnasium, like a small shield, but without handle or straps. You tested it as it lay there and found it heavy and hard to handle from its smooth surface. Well, they hurl that up and forward into the air and for distance, competing to see who can throw the greatest distance and out-throw his competitors—an exercise that strengthens the shoulders and tones extremities.

The Value of Mud and Dust for Training

(28) SOLON The mud and dust that you found quite laughable, this is why it is put down. In the first place, so that they may fall not on a hard surface, but without harm on a soft surface. Secondly, slipperiness is necessarily better when they are sweating in the mud. Behavior you compared to eels is neither useless nor absurd, but contributes appreciably to strength and flexibility when, in grappling with each other, they are compelled to grip an adversary tightly who is trying to slip from their grasp. Do not think that to lift up a man who is muddy, sweating, and covered with oil and trying to break out of your grasp and slip away is no small thing. All these things, as I said before, are useful against an enemy: If you need to take up a wounded friend and carry him out of danger easily or seize an enemy and carry him back in your arms. For these reasons we train them beyond what is necessary, having set them to harder tasks, so that they may carry out the smaller with much greater ease.

(29) We think that the usefulness of dust is just the reverse, to prevent one who is gripped from slipping away. After practicing in the mud to hold onto something that is escaping because of its oiliness, they are accustomed in turn to escape themselves even from a firm grasp. Also, the dust sprinkled on a profuse sweat seems to check it and makes their strength last longer, and prevents the ill effects of the wind blowing upon their bodies when the pores are open. In addition, it wipes away dirt and makes the skin glisten. I would enjoy placing side by side one of the white-skinned people who live in the shade and any of those exercising in the Lyceum that you choose (after he had washed off the mud and dust), and then ask you which you would rather resemble. I know you would choose at first glance, even without testing their skills, to be solid and well built rather than to be delicate and soft and white, because the blood is thin and hides itself away inside the body.

(30) Such are the exercises we prescribe to our young men, Anacharsis, thinking that they will become good guardians of their country and that we will live our lives in freedom because of them, defeating our enemies, if they invade us, and amaze those living around us to the extent that most of them yield to us and pay us tribute. In peace also we find them much better, since their ambitions extend to nothing shameful and they are not inclined toward arrogance when they are idle. They have athletic exercise to occupy their leisure. When I spoke of the common good and peak of happiness for the city, this is what I meant. These are attained in peace or in war, when our youth, having prepared themselves in the best possible way, strive for all that is noblest.

Anacharsis Ridicules the Usefulness of These Exercises for Warfare

(31) ANACHARSIS Then, Solon, if ever an enemy attacks you, anointing yourselves with oil and dusting yourselves over, you attack brandishing your fists at them; they, it is clear, cower before you and flee, afraid that you will throw a handful of sand in their mouths (open in amazement), or that by leaping around to get behind them, you would wind your legs round their bellies and throttle them by ramming your arm under their chin-pieces. And, of course, they will shoot their arrows and throw their javelins, but these will not hurt you any more than they would statues, seeing as you are so sunburned and supplied with much blood. You are not straw and chaff to yield as quickly as possible to the blows you receive; but after long and difficult fighting, cut to pieces with deep wounds, you would shed a few drops of blood. You did say this sort of thing, unless I completely misunderstood your example.

(32) Do you not see that these refinements of yours are all silly—childish games and occupations for young men who are idle and want an easy life? If you really want to be free and happy, you will need other exercises and true training in arms. The competition will not be against each other with playfulness, but against the enemy, practicing valor in real danger. Having them give up the dust and oil, teach them to use bow and javelin, not

by giving them the light javelin that can be diverted by the wind, but let it be a heavy spear that whistles as it flies and a stone that fills the hand, a double ax, a wicker shield in their left hand, a breastplate, and a helmet.

(33) As you are now, you appear to me to be saved by the grace of one of the gods, since you have not been destroyed under the attack of a few light-armed troops. See, if I draw this little dagger at my belt and alone fall upon all of your young men, I could capture the gymnasium without a blow; they would all run away and no one would dare face the cold steel, but they would stand around the statues, hide behind pillars; they would make me laugh when most of them wept and trembled. Then you would see that they no longer have the ruddy bodies that they now do; they would all immediately grow white in fear. Profound peace has placed you in the position that you could not easily endure the sight of a single plume on an enemy's helmet.

Solon Counters by Pointing to Examples of Athens' Success in War

(34) SOLON Anacharsis, the Thracians who invaded us with Eumolpus did not say this. Nor did your women who attacked Athens with Hippolyta,[65] nor anyone else who has tested us in warfare. My dear man, it does not follow that because our youths work out naked that we expose them without armor to real dangers. When they have become self-sufficient in bodily development, they are trained in weapons, and would make much better use of them because they are so well disposed by their training.

Weapons Training

ANACHARSIS Where is your gymnasium for arms training? I have seen no such thing in the city, although I have walked around all of it.

SOLON You would see, if you visit longer, that each man has many weapons which he uses whenever it is necessary. You will see our crests and bosses and our horses and horsemen amounting to almost a quarter of our citizens. But we think it excessive to bear arms and carry short swords on our belts in peacetime; indeed, there is a penalty for anyone who brings weapons into town unnecessarily or produces weapons in public. You, of course, may be pardoned for living in arms. Living without fortification makes conspiracy easy. You have many enemies; you do not know when somebody may come upon you in your sleep, pull you out of your cart, and dispatch you. Then, your mutual distrust and civic interactions that are governed by no law but by free choice mean that steel must be always at hand, in case another uses force against you.

---

[65] These are the mythical Amazons, female warriors who were thought to live in the region of the Black Sea from which Anacharsis comes.

(35) ANACHARSIS Then, you think the wearing of arms without real necessity is excessive; you take care of your weapons, so that they may not be ruined by handling, and put them away so that you might use them when the need arises; but the bodies of your youth you wear out even when no danger presses, knocking them about and wasting them in sweat; instead of husbanding their strength for the day of need, you expend it vainly in mud and dust.

SOLON You seem to conceive of force like wine or water or liquid of some sort. You are afraid that it may flow away unnoticed in exercise as from an earthenware jar and be lost, leaving the body empty and dry, since it is not filled up again from internal reserves. That is not the case; the more someone draws upon it in the course of exercise, the more it flows in, like the story about the Hydra—have you heard it? If one of its heads was cut off, two immediately sprang up in its place. But if someone does not exercise from the beginning and lacks muscle tone, without any reserves, then he might be made weaker by the exertions. This is the case with a fire and a lamp: With the same breath you may kindle the fire in a short time and increase it with your breath; you can quench the light of the lamp, which does not have an adequate supply of fuel to resist the blast. The root from which it sprang is not strong.

Why Do the Panhellenic Games Not Have Contests with Weapons?

(36) ANACHARSIS I don't understand that, Solon; what you said is too subtle for me;, it requires exact thought and keen intelligence. But do tell me why at the Olympic, Isthmian, Pythian, and other games, where many, so you say, attend to see your young men competing, you never have matches that involve weapons? Instead, you bring them out naked into the middle of the assembly and exhibit them being kicked and taking punches, and when they win, give them laurel berries or wild olive. It would be good to know why you do this.

SOLON Well, we think it will increase their eagerness for exercise if they see those who excel in these contests honored and proclaimed by name among the assembled Greeks. Having to strip off their clothes before such a crowd that makes them take pains with their condition; they do not want to be ashamed when naked, so each does his best to be worthy of victory. And the prizes, as I said before, are not small things: the praise of the spectators, to be the mark of all eyes, and to be pointed at by a finger as the best of one's contemporaries. Accordingly, many of the spectators who are at an age for training depart with a passion for hard work and excellence. Anacharsis, if the love of fair fame were to be banished from our lives, what good would remain? Who would care to do something splendid? But from these contests they provide you with a reasonable opportunity to infer what sort of fighters they would be like against the enemy on behalf of their country and children and wives and sacred places when they have weapons who now naked are so keen for victory in competing for a sprig of wild olive or laurel berries?

(37) I wonder how you would feel if you were a spectator at our quail- and cockfights and the excitement they raise? You would laugh, no doubt, especially when you learn that we do it in accordance with the law, and that all of military age are ordered to attend and see how the birds spar till they are utterly exhausted. And yet it is not laughable either; an urge for danger is thus instilled gently into men's souls so that they may not be less ignoble or courageous than fighting cocks? Or give in too soon from wounds or fatigue or any other hardship? But as for testing our men in armed combat and watching them be wounded, no! That is brutal and quite perverse and besides being unprofitable to slaughter our best men, whom we could better use against our enemies.

Spartan Training of Young Men

(38) SOLON Since you say you are going to visit the rest of Greece also, if you ever go to Sparta, remember not to laugh at them either or think that they are laboring vainly when they collide with and pummel one another over a ball in the theater; or when they go into a place surrounded by water, divide into troops, and treat one another as enemies (and they are naked as we are), until one company drives the other out of the perimeter—the side of Lycurgus beating the side of Heracles or vice versa—and into the water. Afterward, there is peace going forward and no one would any longer strike a blow. Above all, you may see them being scourged at the altar, streaming with blood, while their fathers and mothers standing by, far from being distressed by what is taking place, even threaten them if they do not hold up under the blows, imploring them to endure pain as long as possible and endure the terrible treatment. Many youths may even die in these trials, thinking that it is unworthy to yield in the sight of their kinsmen, while they are alive, or even to flinch. You will see statues of them being honored which have been dedicated at public expense by the Spartans. Whenever you see these things, do not suppose that they are madmen or say that they are suffering to no necessary purpose, neither compelled by a tyrant nor so treated by an enemy. Lycurgus, their lawgiver, would give you many reasonable arguments for thus punishing them. He did not do this from enmity or hatred, nor was he wasting the state's young blood for nothing; he deemed it proper that those who were going to defend their country should be extremely tough and be entirely superior to fear. However, even if Lycurgus does not say this, you can see for yourself, I think, that such a man, if captured in war, would never betray Sparta's secrets if he was tortured by the enemy. But mocking them, he would be whipped, competing with the flogger to see which of the two would yield.

(39) ANACHARSIS Was Lycurgus himself whipped as a young man, Solon, or did he introduce such innovations when safely past the age of the contest?

SOLON He was an old man when he drafted these laws for the Spartans, after returning from Crete. He visited the Cretans when he heard that they had the best possible laws, since Minos, son of Zeus, had devised them.

ANACHARSIS Why then, Solon, do you not emulate Lycurgus and whip your young men? It is a fine practice and quite worthy of you Athenians.

SOLON We are content with our own exercises; we do not think it a good idea to imitate other nations.

ANACHARSIS No, you realize, I think, what it is like to be stripped and scourged with your arms raised up, with no benefit either to yourself or for the common good of the country. If I do happen go to Sparta when they are doing this, I imagine that very soon I will be stoned to death publicly at their hands for laughing at them, whenever I see them being whipped like thieves or evildoers or other such miscreants. Really, the state looks to be in need of hellebore, behaving so ludicrously.

(40) SOLON My good man, I do not think that you are winning an undefended case, speaking alone in the absence of opponents. In Sparta there will be someone who can make a reasonable case in favor of their customs. But since you do not seem to be very pleased with those of our customs that I have described to you, it is not unfair of me to ask you to describe in turn how you train your youth in Scythia. How do you Scythians train your youth? With what sort of exercises do you raise them? How do you make them good men?

ANACHARSIS That is a very fair request, Solon. I will explain Scythian customs to you, not imposing, perhaps, or on the same level as yours, for we would never dare to receive a single blow to the head—we are such cowards—but such as they are, they will be stated. It seems that we must delay our talk until tomorrow, so that I might reflect quietly over what you have said and gather my thoughts for what I should say. But for now, let's go away on these conditions. It's already evening.

38b. *Herodotus* 1–3: Public Speaking at the Games

This dialogue sets out the benefits of the games circuit for writers (historians, orators, and philosophers) to promote their works to a wide audience. See **34c** *on Diogenes the Cynic taking advantage of this ready audience at the Isthmian games.*

(1) [We cannot successfully imitate Herodotus' style, but we can imitate] what he did to promote his writing and how quickly he established himself as an important man for all of the Greeks. As he sailed from his home in Caria for Greece, he thought to himself how he and his writings might become distinguished and well known as quickly and effortlessly as possible. The lecture circuit—now in Athens, now Corinth, now Argos or Sparta in turn—he thought laborious and time-consuming and no small effort would be required for such a thing… He planned, if he were able, to capture all the Greeks together somehow. The great Olympic Games were approaching, and Herodotus, thinking that this was the ideal time for which he was hoping, waited for the moment when the festival

was filled with people and crowded with the most important men from everywhere. Having entered the rear court of the temple of Zeus, not as a spectator, but as a competitor in the Olympic Games, he recited his own *Histories* and so charmed those present that his books were named after the Muses, since they were also nine in number.

(2) Therefore, he became better known than the Olympic victors themselves; there was no one who did not know the name of Herodotus—some who had heard him at Olympia for themselves, others learning from those who attended the festival. Wherever he would appear, someone would point to him: "This is the Herodotus who told the story of the Persian Wars in the Ionic dialect, who celebrated our victories." These are the benefits he enjoyed from his *Histories*. From that one assembly he got acclaim throughout all Greece and was proclaimed not by one herald, but in every city from which there had been spectators.

(3) It was later recognized that this was a short path to fame; Hippias the sophist and native of Elis, Anaximenes of Ceos, Polus from Acragas, and many others gave recitations, always in person and before the festivalgoers, from which they became well known in a short time.

38c. *A Slip of the Tongue in Greeting* 3: Marathon

This anecdote about the runner who announced the victory at Marathon puns on the various meanings of the Greek word chairete: *"hail," "farewell," "rejoice." In* **35p** *Plutarch identifies the runner as Eucles, but the runner's statement is the same (*chairete nikōmen*).*

The first [to use it in this sense] is said to have been Philippides the runner from Marathon who announced the victory. To the archons who had assembled and were worrying about the outcome of the battle he said: "Rejoice (*chairete*)! We are victorious." When he had spoken, he died at the same time as the announcement, breathing his last on *chairete* ("farewell").

38d. *Portraiture Defended* 11: Victor Statues at Olympia

This is addressed to Panthea, a favorite of the Emperor Verus (130–69 CE). She objects to extravagant praise by citing the practice of erecting victory statues in Olympia that could not exceed life size.

Now she herself praised your model and the inventiveness of the portraits but did not acknowledge the similarity. [She said] she was not nearly worthy of such a flattering image and neither was any other mortal woman … Further, she ordered me to say to you, "I hear—many say this—whether it is true, you men know, that Olympic victors are not permitted to erect statues greater in size than their own bodies, that the judges

(*Hellanodikai*) make sure that none of them exceeds the truth, and the scrutiny of the statues is more exacting than the scrutiny of the athletes. So, see to it that we do not incur a charge of exaggerating the height and then the judges might overturn our statue."

38e. *Lexiphanes* 5: Attending the Gymnasium

This dialogue takes on the widespread practice among the educated Greek elite of insisting on a Classical Attic vocabulary and dialect, even though by Lucian's time Attic was as far removed from contemporary speech as we are from Shakespeare's, and most Greeks spoke a koine that incorporated pronunciation, spelling, and vocabulary from the Ionic dialect. Within Greek rhetorical schools the fierce debate about what constituted proper Attic usage led some to be hypercorrect in their choice of words. The title character, Lexiphanes ["Vocabulary Flaunter"], consistently parades his Attic vocabulary, even if the word is rare and not in common use. Here we learn about the various activities in the gymnasium beyond the contested events. Upright wrestling and swinging the arms are mentioned as exercises in **14e** *(Regimen bk. 2.64).*

After he had narrated such things as these, all of us who were present departed. When we came to the gymnasium, we exhausted ourselves: one with the hand wrestling (*akrocheiriasmos*), another with neck holds, still another with upright wrestling. Another who had anointed himself was eluding holds, another exercised with the punching bag (*kōrykos*), another swung his arms with lead balls (*molybdainai chermadioi*) grasped in his hands. Then after pounding each other, turning our backs, after enjoying our sport in the gymnasium, Philinus and I steeped ourselves in a hot bathing tub and then left, but the others after ducking their heads in a cold bath swam marvelously underwater.

38f. *Hermotimus* 40: Selecting Pairs for Competition at Olympia

The speakers (Lycinus and Hermotimus) are discussing how the opponents are paired for Olympic events in wrestling and pankration.

A silver urn is set out sacred to the god [Zeus Olympios]. Into it are cast small lots, the size of a bean, inscribed with letters. Two are marked with alpha, two with beta, another two with gamma, and so on in the same way, if there are more athletes—two lots always have the same letter. Each of the athletes comes forward, prays to Zeus, puts his hand in the urn, and takes one of the lots. They do this one after another. A whip-bearer (*mastigophoros*) who stands by each of them holds his hand, preventing him from reading what the letter is that he has drawn. When they have all drawn a lot, the *alytarch*, I think, or one of the *Hellanodikai* (I can't remember which) going around examines the lots of the athletes standing in a circle; in this way he matches the one having an alpha to the one who has drawn the other alpha to wrestle or compete in the *pankration*. Likewise, he matches the one with beta to the other beta and the others with the same letters in the same way, if the number of competitors is even (such as eight or four or twelve); if the number is odd (five, seven, nine), he throws an odd letter written on one lot among the others, one that does not have a duplicate. Whoever draws this lot, he has a bye, waiting until the others have competed their rounds, since he has no matching letter. This is no small piece of luck for the athlete, to be able, while at his peak, to compete against tired opponents.

38g. *On Slander* 12: Why Athletes Cheat

The example given is from running. The hysplēx *is the starting mechanism, the* terma, *the end point of the race. For cheating in athletic events, see Plutarch* **35o** *and Appendix BIII.*

The man who is slandered is also a man who is especially honored and for this reason is envied by those inferior to him. It is the same in gymnic competitions of running. There, when the *hysplēx* is released, the good runner focuses only on what is in front of him, turning his mind to the *terma*, with the hope of victory in his feet; he does not trouble himself with those running against him or do them harm. But the bad runner and unskilled athlete turns his expectation of victory from swiftness to unsportsmanlike behavior. He thinks how he might check or trip the runner because, if he does not do this, he could not win.

38h. Pseudo-Lucian, *The Ass Tale* 8–9: An Erotic Episode Modeled on a Wrestling Match

This is a famous story of an overcurious young man named Lucius who seeks out magic practices. When he does find a witch to instruct him, he finds himself turned into an ass. Before that happens he meets a young woman, appropriately named Palaestra, who engages him in a "wrestling match" with Lucius. Her instructions mimic standard wrestling protocols; see **P6** *and Appendix CII. See further the* Palatine Anthology *12.206 (attributed to Strato), for a similar use of wrestling terms in an erotic context.*

(8) PALAESTRA Now undress and let's wrestle. Provide me with a demonstration as I please. I shall, in the manner of a trainer or overseer, discover and call out the names of the holds that I want you to use, and you should be ready to obey and to do all that is ordered.
LUCIUS Order away and note how adaptable and pliant and vigorous are my holds."
(9) She took off her clothing and, standing completely naked, she began her instruction.

PALAESTRA Now young man, strip down and oil up with that fragrant ointment over there and grip (*symplekou*) your adversary (*antagonistēs*). Grab both my thighs and put me on my back. Then, from on top insert yourself between my thighs, pushing them apart and lift and stretch my legs up. Then, relaxing and staying fixed on it, coming closer, hit the mark and push in everywhere until you are worn out and let your loins show their strength. Then, withdrawing on a level, stab through the groin, and again push forward to the wall and then pummel it. When you see some relaxation, then is the time, coming in for the clinch (*hamma*), lock around the waist with a tight hold. Try not to rush, but with a bit of self-control, match your speed to mine. Now you can leave the ring.

39. Galen

Galen is one of the best-known medical figures in the ancient world, second only to Hippocrates (see **14***). He was born in Pergamum in Asia Minor in 129* CE. *After completing his studies, he began his medical career as a physician for gladiators in Pergamum in 157* CE. *From 162 until 166, he worked in Rome, where he experienced a meteoric rise to fame and treated the highest levels of Roman society. Although he traveled extensively, he spent most of the remainder of his life and career in Rome. He died either in 199 or sometime between 204 and 207* CE. *His writings provide some of our most important evidence for the role of athletics as a specialized form of knowledge in the ancient world. Athletics and medicine were considered to be two separate but interrelated areas of knowledge and practice in antiquity, both focused on the physical body. Just as there were professional doctors (*iatroi*) in the ancient world, so there were also professional coaches and trainers (*gymnastai, paidotribai*) who specialized in physical exercise, not just for competition, but also for military training and leisure. During the Roman Imperial period, various forms of exercise related to Greek athletic competitions, such as wrestling, were considered an essential part of an elite education, coupled with a focus on the Greek intellectual tradition of rhetoric and philosophy. Galen himself was well trained in philosophy, and he often aligned himself, not just with the medical figure of Hippocrates, but also with the philosophers Plato and Aristotle. Although Galen promotes many aspects of earlier ancient Greek culture, he is at times ambivalent and at other times outwardly hostile to Greek athletics as a legitimate form of knowledge and practice. In the texts that follow, it becomes apparent that the physical training and treatment of the body are deeply implicated in much larger philosophical issues. At the same time, Galen's texts also reveal how competitive athletics and physical exercise are both related to and separate from medicine.*

39a. *Protrepticus* or *Exhortation to Acquire Expertise* 9–14

This essay is a programmatic criticism of athletic training in antiquity. Its primary aim is to encourage young elite males to take up the study of what the ancients termed a technē. *The concept of* technē *has a long and complex history in Greek intellectual tradition. In our earliest sources, it seems to refer to* *skill or craft and can apply to a range of practices from carpentry to prophecy. By the Classical period the term extends to more abstract forms of knowledge, and the concept becomes a major topic of philosophical discourse as well as rhetorical theory (see Plato **22b, 22d**). A critical aspect of the philosophical discourse relates not just to the objects of study and practice regarding different types of* technē, *but also to the social roles and authority attributed to those who are defined in society by their knowledge and practice. Hence, there is an equally important social aspect of authority implicit in the concept. Galen's use of the term seems to incorporate these various usages. As a result, we translate the term* technē *as "expertise" in order to capture the threefold implications of physical ability, knowledge, and authority.*

In exhorting his young readers to take up a form of expertise, Galen distinguishes the different types of expertise. But the majority of the text argues against the knowledge and practice of athletics as a legitimate and valuable form of expertise, even though his impassioned arguments signal the opposite. Galen's primary basis for his extreme distaste of athletics is the issue of "health" (hygieia) (on which, see **39b** *introduction). However, Galen also makes arguments regarding other aspects of elite social standing including beauty, wealth, and birth. One should also take special note of Galen's use of earlier texts and authorities. In evaluating his various arguments, one must consider whether Galen is relying on a history of anti-athletic sentiment or whether he is manipulating his ancient sources in order to strengthen his own perspective. The extant text of the* Protrepticus *ends with Galen's discussion of athletics, but some sources suggest that there was a second part specifically advocating the pursuit of medicine.*

The Problem with Athletics and Athletes

(9) Come then my children, those of you who have heard my words, you are urged to acquire an expertise. And do not let some charlatan of a man deceive or mislead you by teaching you a bad or useless skill. And recognize that of all the practices, those are not forms of expertise that do not have as an end (*telos*) what is beneficial to life. And concerning the different activities, I am sure you recognize that none of the following is a form of expertise: activities such as acrobatics, tightrope walking, and spinning in a circle without vertigo, or some other practice of small-scale art, like those practiced by Myrmecides of Athens or Callicrates of Sparta.[66]

The only practice I am suspicious of is that of the athletes. For this practice proclaims strength of body and brings fame (*doxa*) among the many. It is honored by the elders at public expense (*dēmosia*) and daily gifts of silver, and one practicing it is respected in a way equal to our best leaders. And it may deceive some of the youth that it should be considered a form of expertise. Thus, it is a good idea to analyze athletics. For anything that has not been examined can easily deceive.

The race of humans has commonalities with the gods and with the irrational animals. It has in common with the gods the capacity for reason (*logikon*), and it has commonality with animals in so far as the race of humans is mortal. It is better, therefore, in realizing

---

[66] These two were engravers of miniatures (see Plutarch, *Moralia*, On Common Conceptions 1083e).

our commonality with our superiors, to give attention to education (*paideia*), by which we may obtain the greatest of goods if we are successful, and, even if we are not successful, we at least do not suffer the shame of being less than irrational animals. Now athletic training (*askēsis*) of the body is the most shameful when it fails, but even successful training of the body makes us no better than irrational animals. For who is stronger than a lion or an elephant? Who is faster than a hare? And who does not know that we praise the gods for no other reason than for the many forms of expertise, and that we consider the best of men worthy of divine honor (*timē*) not because they ran well in the contests or threw the discus or wrestled, but because of the good work (*euergesia*) in their expertise. Asclepius and Dionysus, whether they were formerly mortals or were gods from the beginning, are considered worthy of the highest honors, the one because of medicine, and the other because he taught us the art of the grapevine. If you do not wish to be persuaded, at least have respect for Pythian Apollo. It is that god who said that Socrates was the wisest of them all and who said the following when he spoke to Lycurgus:

> You have come, Lycurgus, to my rich temple,
> Dear to Zeus and all the Gods who have Olympus as their home.
> I am at a loss whether to prophecy to you as man or god,
> But, I expect, rather as a god, oh Lycurgus. [Herodotus 1.65.3]

The same god also appeared and honored Archilochus in an extraordinary way when he died. Apollo stopped the murderer of Archilochus, who wished to enter his temple, and said, "You killed the servant of the Muses, depart from the temple!"

What Wise Men Say against Athletes and Athletics

*Much of this argument is modelled on Plato (see, e.g., **22b**).*

(10) Come then, what honors do you confer on athletes? But do not say that you are not able to say, unless you condemn something from this witness as insufficient. For you seem to show precisely that when you make appeal to the many as a witness and you choose praise from them. But I know that when you are sick, you would not turn to the many but to the few who are most skilled in medicine, nor when sailing would you turn to fellow sailors but to the steersman, and when building to the carpenter, and when in need of sandals to the shoemaker. How then, when this is a contest of utmost importance, could you give to yourself the power of judgment, considering the opinion of very wise men to be less than your own? And I leave aside mention of the gods. Listen to how Euripides[67] speaks concerning athletes:

---

[67] From Euripides' *Autolycus* (see **12a**). The play is now lost, but these lines were cited by others in antiquity (see, e.g., Athenaeus 10.413c; Diogenes Laertius 1.56; Plutarch, *Moralia* 581f).

Of the countless evils that exist throughout Greece
none is worse than the race of athletes.
First, they neither learn to manage a household well,
nor would they be able to. How could any man
who is a slave to eating and dominated by his belly
garner wealth that exceeds his father's?
Then, they are unable to cope with poverty or misfortunes;
without the acquisition of good habits,
a change toward the worse leaves them without resources.

Also, each of their practices is also useless. Listen again, if you wish, to what he has to say:

For the man who wrestles well, who is swift of foot,
who throws a discus, or boxed well,
has he defended his fatherland by winning a crown?

Or if you wish to hear something even more subtle, listen again to what he says:

Are they going to fight the enemy
with a discus in their hands or cast the enemy from their fatherland
by penetrating a shield with their fists?
No one is this foolish when he is near a sword.[68]

Should we look down on Euripides and these sayings of his? Let us turn then to the philosophers for judgment. But even for them, as though from one mouth, they all agree that it is a trifling practice. Nor have any of the doctors ever praised it. First, consider what Hippocrates says, "the athletic disposition (*diathesis*) is not natural; better the healthy condition (*hexis*)" [see **14i**]. Then there are also the sayings of all of the best doctors of his era. But I do not think it best that these matters be judged entirely by authorities. Such is the practice of a rhetorician rather than of a man who honors the truth. Nevertheless, since some take refuge in the praise of the many and in their empty opinion, and they shirk from looking at the practice naked (*gymnos*) from the outside in and of itself, I am compelled to make use of such authorities in order that they recognize that they do not have an advantage even there.

At this point it is not ill-timed for me to tell a story about Phryne. She was once at a symposium, and there was one of those games where each in turn gives orders to the symposiasts to do what one wishes. Phryne saw the women beautified with rouge, white paint, and seaweed, and she order that water be brought and that they take it up with their hands and bring it to their face once, and after this wipe it away immediately with a napkin. Phryne was the first to do this. The faces of the other women were filled with slime, and they were like monsters in their appearance. Phryne alone was unadorned,

---

[68] See **38a** (*Anacharsis* 31).

and she was naturally beautiful. She had no need whatsoever of cosmetic adulteration. Just as true beauty is accurately examined in and of itself, stripped of all external additions, so it is fitting to analyze athletic practice in isolation. And one should consider whether it seems to have some advantage either for the cities in common or for those practicing it individually.

Body and Soul, Health and Moderation

(11) Of those things which qualify as good by nature, there are some related to the soul, some to the body, and some external. There are no other thinkable goods beyond these types.

Now it is clear to everyone that athletes have never taken part in the goods of the soul, not even in a dream. In the first place, they do not know whether they even have a soul, so much are they lacking in knowledge of its rational quality. Always engaged in increasing the amount of flesh and blood, they have a soul that has been extinguished entirely as though by much filth. Such a soul is unable to think clearly but is mindless in a way similar to the irrational animals. Perhaps they might respond that they are in possession of goods concerning the body. But will they lay claim to health, that most valuable good? You would find no others in a more dangerous disposition, if one trusts Hippocrates when he says that the good condition (*euexia*) at its peak (*akron*), which they pursue, is dangerous [see **14a**]. He also says, "The practice (*askēsis*) of health (*hygieia*) comes from moderation in food and not shirking from labor" [*Epidemics* 6.4.18]. This fine statement of Hippocrates is praised by all. But athletes practice the opposite. They overwork and overfill themselves, and they completely ignore the advice of that ancient man, just like Coroebus. In establishing a healthy regimen, Hippocrates also said "Labor, food, drink, sleep, sex: moderation in all" [*Epidemics* 6.6.2]. These men train at exercises beyond what is fitting every day, and they force themselves to eat; and often they lengthen out their eating well into the middle of the night. Thus one might say about them:

> The gods and mortal charioteers were sleeping
> All night, bound by soft sleep;
> But sleep did not come upon the wretched athletes.[69]

Indeed, the amount they sleep is also beyond reason. At the time when men who live by nature have rest from their labor and need food, those men are just waking up from sleep, so that their life seems similar to that of pigs—except pigs do not overwork or eat by compulsion. Athletes suffer these things and sometimes rub their backs with rhododendrons.

---

[69] Galen has altered lines from Homer's *Iliad* 24.677–9 by replacing "luck-bringing Hermes" found in Homer with "wretched athletes."

In addition to the things said before, the ancient Hippocrates also says, "Activities done in excess and suddenly, filling and emptying, heating or cooling, or moving the body in certain ways are dangerous." And he says: "For all forms of excess are hostile to nature (*physis*)" [Hippocrates, *Aphorisms* 2.51]. But they do not pay attention to these things or to others, and they pass over whatever else has been well said by Hippocrates. And they practice all things contrary to the advice given for health.

And I would assert that athletic activity is not a practice (*askēsis*) in health, but in disease. I agree with Hippocrates, since he says, "The athletic disposition is not natural; the healthy condition is better" (see **14g**). First, he says that the practice of athletics is contrary to nature, by which he means that athletics destroys it. In addition, he specifies their "disposition" (*diathesis*) and not "condition" (*hexis*), and he denies applying the term "condition" to athletes, since all the ancients use the term "condition" in referring to the truly healthy. For condition is a lasting disposition and hard to change, but the good condition (*euexia*) of athletes at its peak is dangerous and unstable. Nor is it able to improve because it is a peak, and it eventually gives way. As such, it is not able to remain in the same place and stay constant but leads down a path of deterioration. Such is the state of the body for athletes, and when the athlete stops training, it is much worse. Some die after a short time, and some reach a later stage of life, but none reach old age. And if they do, at the end of life they differ little from Homer's prayers: "Lame, shriveled, and deprived of their eyes" [Homer *Iliad* 9.503].

Just as walls that have been shaken by engines of war are ready to dissolve under any accidental harm and are able to endure neither an earthquake nor any heavier attack, so the bodies of athletes, cracked and weakened by the blows that occur in practice, are ready to suffer as the result of unintended events. Their eyes are hollowed out often and when their strength is gone, the space fills with fluid. And when their strength fails in time, their teeth readily fall out, since they have been shaken so often. The joints which have been twisted become weak for the rest of the athlete's life, and all breaks and sprains easily come back. In terms of bodily health, therefore, it is clear that no race is more miserable than athletes. Thus, someone might appropriately call athletes miserable (*athlios*)—either the term "athletes" comes from the term *athlios*, "miserable," or the term *athlios* comes from the condition of athletes—or perhaps both have a common source in the term "misery," (*athliotēs*).[70]

Beauty and Athletics

(12) Now that we have examined health as the greatest of bodily goods, let us turn to the remaining forms of goodness. Concerning beauty, it has very little to do with the nature

---

[70] The term "athlete" is actually derived from the Greek term *athlon*, meaning "prize," and later refers to a contest or struggle for a prize. The term *athlios,* meaning "miserable," is a result of the secondary meaning of *athlon* as contest/struggle.

of athletics. Often, trainers (*gymnastai*] have taken aside those who are proportional in their limbs, fattened them up, stuffed them with blood and flesh, and eventually brought them into the opposite of their original state. And the faces of others have often become misshapen and disfigured in every way, especially for those training in *pankration* and boxing. When they twist or completely break each other's limbs or gouge out each other's eyes, then the so-called "beauty" of this practice is seen clearly. These are the tasks supposedly performed "for beauty," so long as they are healthy, but they lose and destroy the rest of their bodily abilities. And as I just said, the limbs are twisted in every which way and cause disfigurement.

The Failures of Strength

(13) If none of the things said is true, perhaps the athletes will lay claim to strength. For I know well that they will say they are the strongest of all men. But what sort of strength, by the gods, and what is its use? Is it the type of strength good for agriculture? Certainly, it would be great for them to be able to dig or harvest or sow or any other thing on a farm. Or is it strength for war? Recall again Euripides, who would praise them by saying "Will they fight the enemy with discus in hand?" (see **12a**). Are they strong in the cold and the heat? But, like imitators of Heracles, do they cover their skin with the same cloak in winter and summer, do they persevere without sandals, lie on the ground, and sleep in the open? In all these matters, they are weaker than newborn children. On what occasion, then, will they show their strength? For what reason are they so proud? Surely it is not, I suppose, because they are able to beat shoemakers, carpenters, and masons in the wrestling school and stadium. Perhaps they demand that we admire their ability to roll in the dirt all day long. But this is also the case for quails and partridges, and if that is the case, then it is also necessary to pride oneself on washing in the mud all day (see **38a** for similar arguments).

But what about Milo of Croton, who lifted one of the sacrificial bulls onto his shoulders and did a lap of the stadium? What excessive ignorance! He did not even recognize that, just a short time before, the soul of the animal carried that most heavy body of the bull. And it did it with far less strain than Milo when it lifted it up and enabled it to run. But nevertheless, the soul of the animal was worth nothing compared with Milo. And the death of Milo was the stupidest thing of all! Once Milo saw a youth chopping wood lengthwise with the use of wedges. Then Milo laughed and pushed the youth aside, and he dared to split the wood with his own hands. He expended however much strength he had on the first attempt and managed to move apart both parts of the tree, and then the wedges fell out from their place. Milo tried but was unable to split the remainder of the tree. In the end he was conquered and did not recover his hands quickly enough. When the two parts shut back together, the edges of his hands were caught and crushed. This would later be the cause of Milo's pitiful death. (See **37q**, Pausanias 6.15.8). The dead bull being lifted did nothing at all for his suffering. Or do you think Milo's efforts with the bull saved all of Greece when they warred with the barbarians? Was it not the wisdom of Themistocles which saved Greece, first in interpreting the oracle correctly, then in his capacity as general: "For one wise plan conquers many hands, and ignorance is a worse evil when accompanied with weapons?"[71]

By now I am certain that it has been shown clearly that the practice of athletics is of no use in the affairs of life. And you would learn that athletes are worthless even in their own endeavors if I should narrate to you that story which a certain inspired man compiled and stretched out into an epic. Here it is:

If, by Zeus' will, there should be peace and harmony in life for all the animals, so that the herald at Olympia could call all the athletes and also lead into the stadium all the animals, I do not think any of the humans would be crowned in the contests:

In the *dolichos* the horse will be best;
the hare will carry away the crown in the *stadion*;
in the *diaulos* the gazelle will be best.
No man would be accounted for in the foot races,
Wretched (*athlios*) men, training for nothing.

Not even those descended from Heracles would be stronger than an elephant or lion, and I suspect that a bull would be crowned in boxing.

With the foot the ass will carry away the crown,
If someone wishes to contend with him.
But it will be written down in the records of the much-tested contest,
that Brayer once beat a man in the *pankration*.
It was in the twenty-first Olympiad that he won.[72]

This entirely pleasing story shows that there is no athletic strength in human modes of training. But if men do not beat animals in strength, in what type of good do they participate?

Pleasure and Wealth

(14) Some might say that bodily pleasure is a good. Yet they do not enjoy this either, not while training and not when they have stopped. They are in pain and hardship during the time of training, not only from exercising but also from forced eating, and when they happen to stop, most parts of their body are mutilated. Perhaps you think they are respected for their ability to collect the most money. But you will be able to see that they are all in debt, not only during their athletic career, but also when they have stopped. Nor

---

[71] Euripides *Antiope* fragment 200, v. 3–4.   [72] The poet is unknown.

would you find one athlete who is wealthier than any man whose wealth is from a normal household business. But wealth obtained from one's own activity is of no value, but only wealth obtained from expertise. This is wealth, which will "float in a shipwreck," so to speak. This does not apply to wealth managers, tax collectors, or merchants. They themselves also gain wealth from their own activity. But if they lose their wealth, they also lose their practices, since they need a certain amount of money as capital for their endeavors. But in the absence of that capital, they are unable to start up their former practices, and no one lends to them without pledge or security. But there is a basic divide in the types of expertise (*technai*). Some of them are both rational and respected, while others are looked down upon because they involve labor of the body. This second group are called "banausic" and "manual." It would be better for one to partake of the former types of expertise. For the second type is often given up when one reaches old age. In the first group are included medicine, rhetoric, music, geometry, mathematics, logic, astronomy, grammar, and law. If you wish, you may add to these sculpture and drawing. For even if they use their hands, the work does not require youthful strength. A youth, therefore, ought to take up and practice one of these forms of expertise, provided his soul is not that of a beast. In my opinion, the best of these is medicine.

39b. *Thrasybulus, or Whether Health is Part of Athletics or Medicine 30–47*

The Thrasybulus *(named after the addressee of the text) is concerned predominantly with establishing the category of "health" (*hygieia/to hygieinon*) and its relationship to both athletics (*gymnastikē*) and medicine (*iatrikē*). "Health" was viewed as a deity, the daughter of Asclepius, the god of medicine, from at least the mid-fifth century* BCE*. Although Galen relies on earlier works such as Hippocratic writings for his arguments, he himself seems largely responsible for introducing the discourse of "health" in antiquity as a unique and separate form of expertise (*technē*). As in the* Protrepticus, *in the* Thrasybulus, *Galen criticizes the excesses of athletic practice as well as its purpose, i.e., for physical conquest. But despite his criticism of athletics, he does not dismiss exercise in general. In this text he gives far greater attention to defining health as a matter of moderation and balance regarding the timing, amount, and quality of exercise. If the* Protrepticus *gave greater attention to athletes, the* Thrasybulus *focuses more on the experts themselves, both doctors and trainers. Because expertise in medicine and athletics was not regulated by any form of administrative or governing body, it was determined partly by practical results and partly through agonistic rhetoric and self-promotion, which is well documented in the* Thrasybulus. *This text demonstrates the extent to which Galen and medical practitioners in general were engaged in much broader social contests regarding who had the greatest knowledge and authority over the body.*

Sections 1–29 of the Thrasybulus *involve a long, complicated argument on the division of knowledge in order to categorize "health." Because the results of that argument are summarized in the remainder of the work, those sections are omitted from this translation.*

Expertise Concerning the Good of the Body

(30) I think I have demonstrated sufficiently that there is only one expertise (*technē*) concerning the good of the body, and this will be demonstrated no less adequately in what follows. We have not yet come to the point of naming this form of expertise. It could very well be neither medicine (*iatrikē*) nor athletics (*gymnastikē*), but something else. Or it may be that this expertise is entirely without a name, just as many others are without a name. But we will consider that point shortly. There is indeed one good for our bodies, whatever it may be, as is the case for many other things, and also one form of expertise for our bodies, as there is for others. This I am certain is true, and I am also certain there is one mode of inquiry for both.

Now let us analyze all the parts of the one expertise concerning the good of the body. In doing so we should be able to identify the power of the part called "health." In order that we make this division according to proper method, let us also analyze under what type (*genos*) we might classify expertise concerning the body. It is obvious that its objective (*telos*) is not contemplation for its own sake, as with mathematics, astronomy, and physics. But it is entirely clear that it accomplishes something in relation to the body. It is also clear that the activity is not the end in itself, as with dancing, which has nothing to show for it once the activity ceases.[73] It is obvious then that it is part of either the productive or acquisitive modes of expertise, since it is not part of either the theoretical or practical modes. But it is not one of the acquisitive forms like angling, fishing, or hunting in general, since those practices involve conquering and taking possession of something that exists but does not produce something that did not already exist. It follows that the expertise related to the human body is productive.

Productive Expertise

The work of the productive expertise is twofold. Productive expertise will make something entirely new which did not previously exist, or it will fix a part of something that has already been made. Now the expertise in question is not able to produce an entire human body, but it is able to fix parts of it, like mending shirts, although not entirely in the same manner. For it is nature (*physis*) which makes the body and also repairs it when it is distressed, just like the expertise related to clothes. The expertise we are inquiring into is a kind of servant of nature. In order for the argument to move forward, let us agree to call this mode "restorative." Now this mode makes either big or small repairs. That part which makes big repairs is called both medical and therapeutic. Small repairs are called protective.

---

[73] See **10n** and **22j** for an opposite opinion of the health value of dancing.

Protective Expertise

To be sure, there are all sorts of divisions regarding the first type involving large repairs. For any amount is able to be divided into so many more numbers. But since it is not fitting to speak about those things now, let us pass over them and let us divide up the expertise concerning small repairs. There seem to be three significant divisions. One may take aside a person who is completely healthy and protect him in that condition, and this category is called the expertise of good condition (*euektikon*). The other form of restoration is for someone who has been sick, which some young doctors call "recuperative" (*analēptikon*). In between these two is what is properly called "health" (*to hygieinon*). Health is commonly referred to both as health and as "protection" (*phylaktikon*). Now the three parts of protective expertise—recuperative, health, and good condition—are parts of the expertise dealing with small repairs, but they also differ to a greater or lesser extent. Good condition involves the most minor rehabilitations, health smaller, and the recuperative involves larger rehabilitations. And some might add a fourth division for the protective mode, which is called "prophylactic." It has a power equivalent to the one that rehabilitates those who have just recovered from sickness. But it is clear that both of these divisions partake in the two opposing portions of the whole mode of expertise, namely between large and small restorations. Indeed, it is clear to everyone that therapeutic expertise involves large repairs. And it should be equally clear that the expertise pertaining to the good condition and health deals with small repairs. In between these two are the recuperative and prophylactic, whose forms of rehabilitation are not small compared with the expertise of health, but not large compared with the therapeutic mode. And it seems to me that those who call both groups "neither" are not too far off, although that is part of a different argument.

With regard to the present problem regarding the expertise of the body, we should divide the parts of the protective aspect into three: one for those with health as a state (*schesis*), one with health as a condition (*hexis*), and one for those in good condition (*euektikon*). Let us not bicker over nomenclature. Let us call the first "recuperative" (*analēptikon*), the second "health" (*to hygieinon*), and the third "good condition" (*euektikon*). The first two bring about bodily improvement, while good condition protects it.

Is Health Part of Medicine or Athletics?

(31) Since that is now settled, let us recall the current problem, namely, "Is what one calls 'health' a part of medicine or athletics?" In a well-reasoned manner, we said at the outset that the entire investigation is a matter of definition. It would not be difficult to discover to which category health belongs if we knew what medicine is and what athletics is. As far as "health" is concerned, it seems to me to have been shown quite clearly: Either it is

the protective expertise entirely or it is the middle part of the three parts of the protective mode, namely the one dealing with health according to condition. The investigation beyond what is named seems to me to be unnecessary, since the facts are no longer in dispute, given that what has been established is agreed upon and remains. After going through the major points of the demonstrations, I will turn to an explanation of the names.

I claim, just as with good clothes, houses, and shoes, that there is one expertise concerning the body. There are two parts to this one expertise. One part is productive; the other is restorative, and both of these parts belong to nature. The restorative part also consists in a human expertise which helps in the work of nature. This human restorative expertise, in turn, has two parts—the one is called the "therapeutic" or "medical," and the other is called "protective." The protective mode is also called "health" (*hygieinon*) and has three parts: the recuperative, the good condition, and the one known by the same term as the larger category, namely, health. If someone investigates the protective mode, either in part or as a whole, and whether it is part of medicine or athletics, then it is necessary to go through the whole matter, just as I have now done. And it follows that one must assert that there is only one expertise concerning the body. One may call this expertise "medicine," or if one does not want to call it that, then one may even call it "athletics." Or one might assert that the single expertise is nameless but consists of two parts, one known as medicine, the other athletics. And if one does not want to make this claim either, then one might assert that there is an expertise of health that is in opposition to the therapeutic expertise. And if you wish, you may assert that it has two parts—one dietetic (*diaitētikē*) and another athletic. For if you give an explanation of the terms of each, then the rest will follow.

[(32) We omit this section, which presents an argument about the meaning of words in other languages.]

The Term "Athletics" Not Found before Plato

(33) Now I do not dare conjecture whether the third type of medicine known as dietetic existed in the time of Homer. But one older than me and more trusted to know the affairs of the Greeks, the philosopher Plato, says that the ancient disciples of Asclepius did not use that part of the expertise of medicine at all. But it cannot be denied that there is an expertise involving these three parts naturally which is called "medicine" for all the Greeks. In Homer's time there was no term for "athletics," nor was anyone called a "trainer" (*gymnastēs*), as one calls a "doctor," and the term "athletics" is not found much before the time of Plato, who prefers to call the practitioner of such an expertise a *paidotribēs*, rather than a *gymnastēs*. For the formalized expertise of the trainer began a little before Plato, at the same time as the formal training of athletes began. For a long time ago, a man who worked according to nature was truly well conditioned in labor.

Such a man entered contests not just in wrestling but also in running, and one man often won both, as well as the javelin, archery, discus, and chariot racing. Only later were they separated and made into figures like Homer's Epeius, who was worst of all men in all the natural works, but good at boxing, the only use of which is competition [see **1b**, Homer *Iliad* 23.664–76]. Just like him, they were not able to sow, dig, travel, or perform peacetime labors, let alone the works of war.

(34) We have already criticized the "good condition" of such men before, as well as athletics, which brought about such a state. In its place, we have praised another form of good condition which is safe and entirely useful for activity based in nature. Regarding this other good condition, there are two materials which are productive and protective of it: regimen (*diaita*) and exercise (*gymnasia*). There are four type of material which cause the body to change: surgery, drugs, diet, and exercise. One is of no use to the sick, and two are of no use to one in a natural state. The sick have much need of drugs, surgery, and diet, but no need of exercise, while the one who is completely healthy will make use of diet and exercise but will have no need of drugs or surgery.

(35) Thus, athletics is part of the expertise of health, and Hippocrates has taught us sufficiently about both. He has explained what it is necessary to know about air, place, water, wind, and seasons, and he has written most accurately on food, drink, and activity. And these are the things of which regimen consists. Similarly, he had explained the proper time, amount, and nature of both exercise and massage.

It seems that Plato referred to the entire expertise of the body not as "health" but as "athletics" (*gymnastikē*). He did this because it is specifically suited to the healthy, but not at all used by the sick, and he thought that this activity alone required a supervisor. For a body that is completely healthy and makes use of natural desires will make no mistake in the type of food or timing of its use. You will learn from our discussion that what Plato knew as "athletics," that is, as part of the expertise concerning the body, is something different from what is called "athletics" today. I will now cite for you some passages of Plato, first from the *Gorgias*.

> I say there are two forms of expertise (*technai*) with two forms of practice (*pragmata*). I call the one pertinent to the soul politics, but the one pertinent to the body I am not able to name so easily, since there is not one treatment (*therapeia*) of the body, but I say there are two parts—one is called physical training (*gymnastikē*) and the other is medicine (*iatrikē*) [see **22d**, 464b].

Here Plato makes it quite clear that there is one therapy with two parts. He also makes it clear that the two parts have names, but the whole does not, and that the whole looks to what is best as the "good condition." And the following is also clear, from what he wrote in that same book:

> You say there is something called "body" and something called "soul"?
> How could I not?

And you think there is a good condition for each?

I do.

Are there apparent good conditions, but not actual ones? What I mean is that there are many who seem to have a good condition with respect to their bodies, and it would not be easy to detect if they did not, unless one were a doctor or a trainer [463e-464a].

In what follows Plato goes on to explain that those people look to what is best, while cooks and beauticians look to what causes the most pleasure.

Athletic Trainers Use a Base Form of Expertise

(36) The type of athletics practiced by those who train athletes is truly a base mode of expertise (*kakotechnia*), but it puts on airs with an august name. With Plato, it was not yet in such a state contrary to nature, but it was already beginning to be aimed not at the best possible ends, since it was viewed simply as the strong skill in conquering one's opponents. Plato finds fault with it in the third book of the *Republic*.

The excessive care of the body which goes beyond basic physical training is the greatest hindrance of all. For it is a problem in household affairs, the military, and in civic positions in the city. And most of all, it is a hindrance to learning of any sort, and thoughtfulness and makes care of oneself difficult, causing one to always anticipate headaches and blaming philosophy for their cause. So that whenever this "excellence" is pondered and practiced, in every way it is a hindrance. For it makes you think you are suffering and never stop from suffering with respect to your body [see **22f**, Plato *Republic* 407b].

And it is even clearer in the next passage that he does not think the objective of athletics is the strong skill in conquering, but it is for the use of one's efforts according to nature. He demonstrated this by saying the following:

He will work at exercises (*gymnasia*) and labor (*ponos*) for the purpose of invigorating his nature and awakening those qualities rather for the sake of strength. This is unlike the other athletes who partake of bread and labor for the sake of strength [Plato *Republic* 410b5–8].

So it is clear from what has been said that Plato is fiercely protecting the opinion of Hippocrates concerning this form of athletics, whose purpose is the good condition of the athletes. For he condemns that type as useless for all political matters, just as Hippocrates had said, in the speech quoted before: "The athletic disposition is not natural, better the healthy condition (*hexis*)" (see **14g** and Galen, **39a** 10). For the physical disposition of the athlete, which is taken to the extreme, is not safe for health; and both Hippocrates and Plato recognized this, as has been said elsewhere.

Health Is Balance; Athletics Creates Imbalance

(37) But since I am now set up to say something about the bad type of good condition and athletics, I will make mention of these issues too, although in the briefest time possible. Health consists in a type of balance (*symmetria*); but the kind of athletics under discussion creates a type of imbalance (*ametria*), since it produces much thick flesh and a great amount of blood, making it especially "sticky." For its purpose is not only to increase the strength, but also the bulk and thickness of the body, so as to conquer an opponent with it. It is not difficult to discover that on account of this it is not useful in the activities based on nature and is dangerous in other ways as well. In every form of expertise that exists, the greatest object to strive for is to arrive at the peak of one's purpose. But with regard to this form of athletics, that purpose is the worst, because it is not a natural disposition, but, as Hippocrates says, unnatural.

That which is naturally good becomes better through progress, increase, and augmentation. But that which is unnatural becomes worse, the bigger it becomes. Thus, all of a sudden, some have lost their voice, others have lost their sight, or have become paralyzed and completely crippled from their unnatural size and mass, which block the naturally hot air and exhalation of air. The softest harm some of them suffer is breaking a blood vessel and then vomiting or spitting blood. And so I will completely put aside from my writing the producers of such a "good condition," who have the most incredible writings which are carried about by those with damaged ears. In any case, my dear Thrasybulus, you will recognize that they are not worth a reply from me. What more could there be for those people who just yesterday or the day before had stopped from filling themselves and sleeping more than is natural. Indeed, they have come to such a state of daring that they talk about things of which even those sufficiently practiced are not able to give an analysis because they are difficult and contested. What would they learn even if they heard deep, intelligent, and penetrating theories? If there is not always good judgment in such a type of theory even for those who have been trained since childhood in the best lessons, it would be amazing that those men alone would have an excessive presence of mind in such matters, when such men were trained so as to win in contests, but were unfit and did not even win crowns.

But indeed, wakefulness and a not unlearned mind awaken a sharp mind more than sleep does, and it is observed in song amongst almost all people, because it is entirely true, that a fat stomach does not give birth to a nimble mind. Perhaps the dust alone endowed them with wisdom. But can someone suppose that the mud in which they roll is the creator of wisdom when they see swine spending time in the same manner? Nor is it likely for there to be wisdom in the latrines in which they spend most of their time. Yet they spend their time doing nothing other than these things; for we have observed their lives in the periodic cycle of eating, drinking, sleeping, defecating, and rolling in the dust and mud.

True Expertise of the Body—Health and Medicine

(38) And so after sending those people away, because we will be analyzing modes of expertise and not bad expertise (*kakotechnia*), let us call forth those who are knowledgeable of true athletics: Hippocrates, Diocles, Praxagoras, Philotimus, Erasistratus, Herophilus, and the rest who have learned the complete expertise of the body.[74]

We have just learned that Plato said there was no single name for this form of expertise. Do not then go looking for a single name for this entire expertise on the body. For you will not find one. If you happen to speak on this form of expertise, let it be enough for you to recall what Plato explained, namely, that there is one therapy for the body with two parts—athletics for the healthy, medicine for the sick.

But this is especially worthy of consideration, namely, that Plato did not differentiate between the expertise pertaining to health and that regarding medicine, as did all those men mentioned just now. Let me make mention of one of them, if you will, since his writings are available to everyone. In the first part of his work "On Matters of Health," Erasistratus says the following: "It is not possible to find a doctor who has dedicated himself to the business of health." And later: "Indigestion that occurs from some disease and the treatment of these matters falls to the business of medicine and not to the business of health." And if he continues further still: "If there is some poor condition of the body which causes everything taken in to be corrupted, so that the body will come to the state of bad humors the same as those before, this is a condition for the doctor and not the health practitioner to cure." And again later, "It is for doctors and not practitioners of health to talk about such matters and to cure them."

Thus, he makes clear there is not only "health," which he names as a form of expertise similar to all others. And he also names a "practitioner of health" just as a doctor is a practitioner of medicine. And so the therapeutic expertise of the body, for which there is no single name in Greek, is divided into two parts. And just as the two parts are called "medicine" and "health," so the practitioners are called doctors and health practitioners. Many other doctors have used these terms in the same manner.

(39) It seems, however, that in Plato's time it was not a common term for the expertise of health or for the practitioner of health. For Hippocrates' notion of health is not called health, but it is described in his work "Regimen" and in "Airs, Waters, Places." Nor, as I said, did Plato think there was a use of regimen for the healthy, but athletics alone was sufficient. And maybe he did not think that the recuperative and protective parts of this form of expertise belonged to athletics. As I said earlier, these were positioned in the middle and are able to be categorized wherever one wishes. But if one categorizes these with medicine, then health is little more than air, water, places, exercises, and food, and not all foods, but only those that are fitting for the healthy.[75] Perhaps, because the matters

---

[74] These are all famous doctors in antiquity.

[75] These topics were already treated by the Hippocratics. One of the most famous treatises was *Airs, Waters, and Places*, or the effect of the environment on health and disease.

of airs, waters, and places were already known to doctors, since they comprise the first part of the therapeutic portion of expertise on the body, there remains nothing to learn specifically for practitioners of health that is also for doctors, except the expertise of exercises (*gymnasia*). It is not unlikely, therefore, that the whole was named on the basis of the one discussed before, that is, athletics. But this is a consideration of the name rather than the facts.

(40) And if someone thought that this account was about terminology and not facts and ordered me to make statements about it, I would say that it is better to name the two primary divisions of the whole as health and therapeutics. For we have learned in our logical methods that it is better to divide groups that are similar in type to each other. For, if one were to make a division between air animals and water animals, it would be entirely strange to add a category of "rational animals." Instead, the distinction requires fire and earth animals, while the "rational animals" category would require a distinction with "irrational" animals, just as "immortal" is in opposition to "mortal," "tame" in opposition to "wild," "flying" and "swimming" in opposition to "on foot." It would be completely illogical to say that some animals are immortal, others go by foot, and some have two feet.

Expertise of the Doctor and the Expertise of Health

Similarly, regarding the expertise of the body, if someone wishes to discover its parts through division, it will be said that taking care of the sick belongs to the expertise of the doctor, while attention to the healthy pertains to the expertise of health. And better than this, as I said earlier, is to assert that there is a restorative expertise of the body, which makes large-scale healing restorations, called "medicine," and there is one that makes unnoticed small scale repairs, even if restored at the beginning, which is a protective expertise. It is even better still to name them from their subject matter—one pertaining to sickness, the other to health. And if you should wish to divide the healthy or preservative form of expertise (for it has already been said that either term can be used), with that subject matter, there will be three divisions, as stated above: recuperative, health proper, and, in addition to these, the expertise of good condition (*euektikon*). There is a subject that is proper to each. For the first, it is the body that is healthy as a state, one that is healthy "in condition," and the third is called "well conditioned." The different bodies are named according to the relevant parts of the expertise.

If there is a division of remedies based on subject matter, a division into fours will be made for the protective and healthy expertise. For the expertise is comprised of the following: substances taken, produced, emptied, and external. It is on account of these things that health is protected. The part of the expertise of health pertaining to substances taken involves a knowledge of food and drinks aimed at the protection of health. The part dealing with substances emptied is knowledge of sweat, feces, urine, and everything that needs to be emptied from the body. The "external" category involves knowledge of air and water, sea salt, olive oil, and all other matters of that sort. The fourth area, things produced, relates to exercises and related practices. Wakefulness, sleeplessness, sleep, sex, desire, thought, and bathing also are part of this group. The healthy person is to be recognized by how the nature, the amount, and the timing of the activities are described.

Expertise of Athletics

(41) Knowledge of exercises is, therefore, a small part of the expertise concerning health. I think it is more appropriate to associate the expertise of athletics with knowledge of the function of all types of exercise, especially since knowledge of those exercises in the *palaestra* comprises only a small part and is the least useful for everyone. Rowing, digging, reaping, spear-throwing, running, jumping, riding, hunting, and fighting with armor, chopping and carrying wood, and farming and other natural activities are better than exercising in the *palaestra*. And it is possible for you to see not only that athletics is a small part of the expertise concerning health, but again that the part of athletics practiced in the *palaestra* is the least useful because it is practiced by athletes, and it produces an unnatural condition, and it has a bad form of expertise as its foundation. It pretends to produce good condition for a useful objective, but it accomplishes something other than good condition. Those who train badly suddenly appear as authorities in this bad form of expertise. But Hippocrates and the ones mentioned with him are the true experts in athletics. To be sure, just as all things said by all of them are not correct with regard to medicine, so the same is true concerning exercises. But now is not the time to cross-examine them on their mistakes. Instead, my purpose is to explain the term "athletics," what type of knowledge (*epistēmē*) it is and what is the power (*dynamis*) of its exercises, just like pharmacology's relationship to drugs (*pharmaka*). Both take their names from their objects, in the same way as other aspects just discussed.

(42) And so it is clear that anyone who distinguishes athletics from medicine is misinformed. For the one gets its name from its subject matter, the other from the entire general activity. The first level involves activities according to its parts: purgation by hellebore or scammony;[76] as well as cutting veins, cutting out a bone, and denying and giving nourishment. After this is a more general and complete level involving pharmacology, surgery, dietetics. For all these, what is common is the act of healing, just as for all those who are healthy there is a common practice of protection. And whoever differentiates the expertise concerning protection from medicine makes an antithesis from a common category. Both are named from their activities, just as disease and health are named after their subject matter. Pharmacology and athletics are both named from the material of

---

[76] A plant from the bindweed and morning glory family.

their remedies. For the one is related to expertise concerning disease and medicine, and the other to health and protection.

(43) But we must consider whether we have unknowingly demonstrated that there is one person who is knowledgeable of exercises in the *palaestra*, whether we have made the expertise of the *palaestra* a part of the expertise of athletics. For one knowing all the exercises in the *palaestra* and all types of massage is similar to a baker, cook, or house-builder—they know how to make bread, and cooked food, and houses, but they do not perceive nor do they know at all what is useful or not useful and what among them has powers for health. As has been said before, there is one perceivable expertise of the body, and others provide matter for this one expertise. It is not very good to ask a shoemaker whether one should wear shoes or go shoeless, or whether to wear this or that type of shoe.

(44) As a type of master-science, the therapeutic expertise of the body stands over these other forms, demanding from the housebuilder a certain type of house, from the shoemaker a type of shoe, from the baker a loaf, from the cook a certain dish, and others from others, according to their nature. But health is one part of this therapeutic expertise of the body, and it has four parts, and athletics is one part. Athletics, therefore, is the master-science for the following forms of expertise: for horsemanship, while teaching measure, time, and type, for hunting with hounds and other types of hunting, when they are called upon. And it directs, begins, and arranges digging, reaping, woodcutting, rowing, dancing, and whatever other physical activities.

Exercises in the *Palaestra*

(45) And among these subforms of expertise, we may include exercises in the *palaestra*. Let us call it, if you wish, "child-training" (*paidotribikē*). But this form of expertise has no knowledge of either help or harm of the body. Rather, it invents holds and moves, like dance, which are aesthetic and complex and designed to overtake an opponent and to relieve pain. But dance makes no claims as a therapeutic form of expertise of the body. Indeed, "child training" is entirely ignorant of athletics, like some impulsive servant who rises against his good master out of extreme misperception. It is as if a soldier, cavalryman, archer, slingsman, or spearsman were to go against his general when he is stationing them, arming them, leading them into battle, or calling for silence. A soldier would be mad if he were to call upon his general to act on some single action, and then finding himself either to be better or just as good, would consider himself worthy of command or proclaim himself to have a part of the expertise of generalship. No less mad would be the child trainer who thinks he partakes in athletics or that he possesses a part of it. Just as the soldier is a servant to generalship, so the child trainer is only a servant to that part of athletics in which he trains, that is, in the expertise pertaining to the *palaestra*. But I call this second form of expertise concerning the *palaestra* the skill in takedowns

[*katablētikē*, i.e. in wrestling]. But those training athletes do not call themselves according to this name. Rather, they call themselves trainers (*gymnastai*).

But in truth, child training is only one aspect, like archery, and then there is the skill in conquering, which is like generalship, and lastly athletics, which is like medicine. Each of the subsidiary forms of expertise serves two modes of expertise above them. Thus, a shoemaker may be instructed by a general on how to make a shoe useful for a soldier, or he may be instructed by one with expertise concerning the body to produce a shoe useful for health. Similarly, one with expertise in cooking will provide a healthy dish thanks to a doctor or health practitioner. But if he makes a dish for pleasure, he is instructed by no mode of expertise, only by a form of flattery, whose purpose is not health. And even exercises in the *palaestra* have some value for health for the trainers and health practitioners, but it is of value for the "athletic disposition" (*diathesis*), which we have already said is based on a bad form of expertise. It calls itself "athletics," but it is more appropriately called the "art of takedowns" (*katablētikē*). The Spartans do, in fact, call it "superiority in throwing" [i.e., an opponent] and those trained in this skill are called "more capable of throwing [an opponent]" rather than "stronger."

Competition between Athletic Trainers and Doctors

This section provides an excellent example of the competitive social practices that those with competing forms of expertise engaged in. Compare the strictures leveled against athletic trainers with the material in the Gymnasticus *(40a).*

(46) The healthy polity, therefore, hates and loathes this practice, because it is destructive to the strength for daily life and creates a disposition of the body that is not good. Even I have proven myself to be stronger than those who seem to be the best athletes and who have carried off many victor's crowns in competitions. For they were completely useless in any kind of walking, in the actions of war, in activities of the citizen, and in farming. And if they need to stay by the bed of a sick friend, they are completely useless at giving advice, examination, and action. They are about as useful as swine. Still, the worst ones, who have never won, suddenly call themselves trainers. And then they clamor in some barbarous voice like pigs. Some of them even try to write about massage, good condition, health, and exercises, and they engage in and argue about matters in which they have no learning. For example, there was a man who was finding fault with Hippocrates' views on massage. And when I arrived, some of the doctors and philosophers asked me to give them an account, and it became clear that Hippocrates' account was the first and best on this subject. And then a self-taught trainer came into the middle, stripped a boy down, and ordered us to massage and train him, or otherwise to keep silent on massage and training. And then he shouted, "What jumping pit did Hippocrates frequent? Where was his *palaestra*? He probably didn't even know how to anoint himself with oil!" That man

went along screaming and was not even silent enough to hear and learn what was being said, but I gave an explanation to those present in a leisurely manner. I explained that this fool was behaving in a way similar to a cook or a baker who dared to talk about the properties of barley or bread and then remarks, "In what mill or kitchen did Hippocrates spend his time? Let him first prepare some cake, bread, sauce, or other dish, and then let him talk about these matters."

(47) Why, then, you ask, do we call Hippocrates and the group after him "doctors," if we do not apply that term to the entire expertise of the body, but only to that part which applies to healing the sick? But they do make use of the whole area of expertise pertaining to the body, and they do not even leave out the part related to exercises. The therapeutic was the first part of the expertise of the body to be established, because it was the most pressing, and later the other aspects concerning prevention and health were introduced at leisure, but the entire mode of expertise took its name from one part, although it consisted of many other parts. We apply the term "geometer" not just to those working in flat figures, but also to those dealing with solid objects. We do not say one person is a geometer and the other a "stereometer"—we simply leave out the other term.

The same is true for the term "health," not in relation to bodies or regimens, but in relation to those who know such matters, and whom Erasistratus differentiated from doctors. The same is true when the ancients applied the term "trierach" to the captain of a trireme, but now it applies to any commander of a ship. A similar thing happened with medicine and doctors. It happened that the whole expertise of the body was named from the first established part, namely, as "medicine" and one who is knowledgeable of medicine as "doctor." And so it is not inappropriate, when someone asks what is health a part of, to reply "medicine." With the term medicine being applied no longer to part but to the whole expertise of the body, Hippocrates and all the others today are rightly called "doctors." For they know the two largest aspects of this expertise, namely, therapy and health. And they know athletics, which is part of the second group, as has already been shown.

And so just as Hippocrates and Diocles and Praxagoras, and Philotimus and Herophilus were knowledgeable of the whole expertise concerning the body, as indicated in their writings, so then again the followers of Theon and Tryphon also addressed the bad form of expertise for athletes, as the writings of those men also indicate, calling one preparatory exercise, and another middle exercise, and another complete, and another restorative, and they considered whether one must practice and train an athlete according to this cycle or some other way. And I am amazed at these trainers of athletes when I hear them assert that health is a part of their expertise.

Indeed, health is not actually a part of athletics, but athletics is a part of health. What is it possible to say about this base form of expertise, which is not even part of the expertise of the body and was deemed to have no value, not just by Plato and Hippocrates, but by all other doctors and philosophers?

39c. *Exercise with a Small Ball*

Although Galen appears quite hostile to athletics as a socially and philosophically valuable form of expertise, he was not opposed to exercise per se. In this text, he promotes exercise with a small ball as the best means for achieving the ultimate aim of health. If Galen had a specific exercise in mind in this discussion, which one is not entirely clear. But it does involve catching, throwing, and blocking, as well as considerable physical contact. He could be referring to a Roman game known as harpastum, *which may have resembled something like rugby (see* **43a***). Or he may be referring to another popular Roman game known as* trigon, *which involved three players who passed a ball with their right hand to the player on the right and caught it in their left hand as it came from the player on their left. It was probably played with more than one ball, rather like juggling. A third option may be that he is referring not to a single game but to several different types of ball play.*

This text is a distillation of many of Galen's key arguments regarding athletics and physical health. He highlights the accessibility of this mode of exercise as opposed to other more elaborate and expensive endeavors such as hunting. This basic form of exercise seems also to have had an egalitarian appeal. According to Galen, exercise with a small ball may also be calibrated for varying levels of intensity and relaxation and offer balanced training of the entire body. These qualities align it with Galen's more general conceptions of health as moderation (to meson) and balance. Lastly, as described in the other works of Galen in this volume, one of Galen's primary criticisms of athletics is the excessive levels of violence and danger which it enacts on the body.

(1) Epigenes, men of old, including the best doctors and philosophers, have sufficiently proven that exercise (*gymnasia*) is good for health (*hygieia*), and that it is better than food for its health benefits. But no one has demonstrated how much better exercise with a small ball is than all other forms of exercise. It is right then for me to say what I know on the subject. May what I say be judged by you, who have been trained better than anyone in the expertise (*technē*) of exercises. And if what I say seems sufficient, may it be of use to others, with whom you may share my account.

I claim that the best of all exercises are those which not only work the body (*sōma*), but which are also able to please the soul (*psychē*). Whoever discovered hunting with dogs and other types of hunting mixed labor with pleasure, delight, and ambition. Those men were wise and had an accurate understanding of human nature. The movement of the soul is so strong in this form of exercise that many have altered the state of their illness because of the pleasure alone. And many who have been distressed recovered entirely. No suffering of the body is so great that it can have power over the experiences of the soul. It is necessary not only to pay attention to the nature of the movements of the soul, but also to care for them much more than those of the body. This is common to all exercises performed with pleasure. But I will now explain the more outstanding benefits of exercise with a small ball.

Accessibility

(2) The first outstanding feature is its accessibility. If you considered how much preparation and leisure are required for the practice of different types of hunting, you would

clearly understand that no one involved in politics or practicing other forms of expertise would be able to participate in those forms of exercise. For it requires that a man have a lot of wealth and leisure. But this form of exercise alone (i.e., exercise with a small ball) is so good for mankind (*philanthrōpos*) that not even the poorest are without the means to practice it, since it requires no nets, weapons, horses, or hunting dogs. It only requires a small ball.

It is also beneficial for other forms of activity. Thus, nothing is neglected because of it. What could be more convenient than this exercise, which also provides for every human occasion and activity? There is no easy access to the benefits of exercise in hunting. For it requires wealth, preparation of the equipment, and the leisure for watching for the right time for the hunt. But the preparation of equipment for exercise with a small ball is accessible even to the poorest, and the time it takes is available even for those with the least amount of leisure. This is how good the exercise with a ball is for accessibility.

A Complete Exercise

But it is also the most sufficient of all exercises. You would especially understand this if you considered other forms of exercise, what they are capable of and their nature. You will find that other exercises are either too excessive or too soft, that they move the lower parts of the body more than the upper, or they affect some part of the body more than others such as the groin, head, hands, or chest. But there is no other exercise in which all the parts of the body are moved equally and are able to be trained either in the most excessive or softest manner, except in the exercise with a small ball. It can be performed at the swiftest or slowest pace, most excessively or most softly, as one wishes and as the body seems to require. And one can move parts of the body or the whole body, or some parts rather than others, however one thinks best.

For when people are standing in front of each other and working hard to block the space between them, this exercise is considered the greatest and most violent, since many neck grabs and wrestling holds are part of the mix. Thus, there is much exertion on the head and neck with the neck grabs. The lungs, chest, and stomach are trained with the holds, pushes, levers, and other wrestling maneuvers. The groin and legs are also strained excessively, and steadiness on one's feet is strengthened in this labor. Moving forward, moving under, and jumping from one side to the other are also not a small exercise for the legs. But, if one must speak the truth, these aspects alone are the best ways to move the whole body. For certain nerves and muscles are used in the movements forward, and others are exercised more by going under, and others still for those moving from one side to the other. But the person who practices only one type of movement for the legs, such as running, trains the parts of the body in an unbalanced and uneven manner.

(3) Just as those types of movement are best for the legs, so, seizing the ball in every position is best for the hands, at least for those who are accustomed to the exercise. In the

many different positions, it is necessary to exert some muscles sometimes and others at other times, so that all the parts are able to work equally, and there is rest for those taking it easy during the period of the activity. Thus, they exercise all parts of the body, and when they rest, they do not remain entirely idle, nor when they are exerting themselves are they simply seized with fatigue. The eyes are also trained. This is possible to comprehend when one observes that, if someone does not accurately observe the trajectory along which the ball travels, he necessarily misses the catch. In addition, it sharpens the mind, in thinking about not dropping the ball, blocking the middle, or taking away the ball. Thought alone is thinning, but when mixed with exercise and ambition, while also aimed at pleasure, then such combinations provide the greatest benefit to the body for health and to the soul for intelligence.

Indeed, this is no small good, when an exercise is able to bring benefit to the body and soul in their respective points of excellence (*aretē*). And it is able to exercise both in the best forms of training, which generals take part in according to the ruling laws of a city. This is not difficult to see. The activities of a general include attacking at the right time, escaping from attack, seizing an opportunity in battle, taking possession of the enemies' property either by force or unexpectedly when being attacked, and also protecting those goods which have been obtained. To speak plainly, it is necessary that a general be good as both guard and thief. This is the most important part of his expertise. Is there any other exercise that accustoms one sufficiently to guard what one has obtained, to recover what one has previously given up, or to anticipate the thoughts of the enemy? I would be surprised if one could name another such exercise. The majority of exercises have the opposite effect, making people slow, sleepy, and heavy in their thoughts. For all the exercises performed by those laboring for crown competitions [i.e., the Olympic, Pythian, Isthmian, and Nemean Games] promote more flesh rather than the training of excellence. Many have been so beefed up that they cannot breathe without difficulty. Such men could hardly become good generals in war or administrators in royal and political affairs. One would sooner look to pigs than such men.

Perhaps you think that I praise running and other such exercises which thin the body. But this is not so. In every case I find a lack of proportion (*ametria*) contemptible. And I assert that practice in every form of expertise (*technē*) makes use of proportion (*to symmetron*). And if there is some lack of measure, then it cannot be good. And so I praise running neither for its ability to slim the bodily disposition nor for its ability to provide any training in courage. For victory does not come from running away swiftly, but from the ability to overpower the opponent in close quarters. For this reason, the Spartans did not take much pleasure in running quickly, but in standing bravely. But if you inspected running in terms of health, it trains the parts of the body so unequally that it cannot be healthy. For in this exercise, some overwork, while others are entirely idle. Neither of these is good and both cultivate the seeds of disease and cause weakened powers.

(4) Therefore, I most especially praise that form of exercise which provides sufficient health for the body, as well harmony in its parts and excellence of soul. All of these exist in the exercise with a small ball. For it is able to benefit the soul in every way and trains all parts of the body equally. And it is especially beneficial for health and provides proportion in bodily disposition. Nor does it produce a disproportionate amount of flesh or excessive thinness, but it is sufficient for the practices that require strength as well as those which make use of speed. And with regard to the violence in this sport, there is no more than in any other. But let us again consider its gentleness. For there are times when it is needed, such as because of age or because participants are not yet or no longer able to endure strong labors, and they wish to lessen the exertion, or they are recovering from illness. And it seems to me to have more gentleness than any other form of exercise. For there is no other gentler exercise, provided one takes part in it gently. Thus, it is necessary to make use of moderation and not revolt against proportion. Thus, one may make slow advances at one point or remain in the same place at another. And then, after not too much competing, one should make use of gentle massage with oil and hot baths. This is the gentlest form of all exercises. It is the most beneficial for those in need of rest and it is the most capable of restoring strength for the weak, both for the elderly and children.

But so many other exercises are also practiced with the small ball, which are either stronger or gentler. Anyone who wishes to learn all the forms of the practice should also know these exercises. If there is some necessary work, as often happens, and you work the parts of the body disproportionately, either the upper parts or all the lower parts, or just the feet or hands, you will be able to rest some parts which were previously exhausted and put other parts through equal motion which were entirely idle before. For throwing the ball vigorously from a sufficient distance makes use of the legs either not at all or just a little, and it provides rest for the lower parts of the body, while it provides motion for the upper parts. But if one runs swiftly and makes use of throws from a distance less often, one works the lower parts of the body instead. And that movement exercises the lungs and is hurried and quick in this exercise but without strained effort. But that movement which is not quick but involves effort in holds, throws, and catches strains and strengthens the body. But if the practice is both straining and quick, then it works the body and breath greatly and is definitely the most vigorous of all exercises.

It is not possible to commit to writing the extent to which one needs both intensity and relaxation in each different case, since the number of variables for each circumstance cannot be expressed. Rather, it is necessary to discover and teach those uses through action. And this is especially important. For the nature of an exercise is of no use if the quantity of the exercise is not determined. But let this be a concern for the *paidotribēs*, whose concern is instruction in exercise.[77]

---

[77] On the *paidotribēs,* see also Galen **39b**, 45, Philostratus **40a**, 14.

Conclusion

(5) Let me now finish what remains of the argument. For I wish to add to the list of benefits from exercise with a small ball that there is no outside danger in the nature and amount of this form of training. But there is danger in other types of exercise. For swift running has already ruined many men when it breaks vital vessels. Just as great noises which are violent and happen all together at one time have been established as the cause of the greatest problems for more than a few people. Vigorous horse riding has ruptured regions of the kidneys and harmed areas around the chest, and also in the spermatic channels. And I do not even mention the mistakes of the horses, on account of which riders are thrown from their seats and die immediately. In addition, jumping, the discus throw, and the other exercises in the pit [i.e., the place in stadium dug out for boxing, wrestling, and *pankration*] have twisted the limbs of many trained athletes. Is it even necessary to mention those injured in the *palaestra* who have been mutilated no less than Homer's "prayers"? For the poet says this about them: "Lame, shriveled, with squinting eyes."[78] You would see the same types coming from the *palaestra*—lame, twisted, crushed, or entirely maimed in some part of the body. But when I add to the list of benefits from exercise with a small ball that there is no chance of danger, then exercise with a small ball is surely the best of all in its benefits.

40. Philostratus

"Philostratus" was a name of at least three men from the same Athenian family who lived and wrote in the late second and third centuries CE. Consensus now assigns the Gymnasticus, *the* Life of Apollonius of Tyana, *the* Heroicus, *and the first book of the* Imagines *to Flavius Philostratus, born c.170. He was a prominent speaker (a sophist) and civil magistrate, and the Athenians erected a statue in his honor at Olympia (see Bowie 2009: 19–32).*

40a. *Gymnasticus*

This treatise, written sometime in the third century CE, remains our closest approximation to an ancient manual on athletic training. Although we know that training manuals were a genre of ancient literature, the Gymnasticus *is not a training manual per se, but serves instead as a defense of athletic training (gymnastikē). Its purpose is to present athletic training as a socially and culturally legitimate form of bodily knowledge, an aim which may be viewed in part as a reaction to the attacks on athletics by medical writers such as Galen. In order to achieve this objective, Philostratus argues for the*

---

[78] Personified in *Iliad* 9.503; cf. Galen **39a**, 11.

reclassification of athletics as a form of knowledge that is comparable to sophistic rhetorical practice such that the body itself becomes a vehicle for elite Greek identity within the Roman Imperial period. In many ways it responds to the critiques of athletic trainers found in Galen.

Athletics as a *Sophia*

(1) Let us consider wisdom (*sophia*) to include the following, namely, philosophy and rhetoric, as well as the understanding of poetics, music, geometry, and even astronomy, within reason. But such knowledge is also the organization of an army, and still also the following: all forms of medicine and painting and sculpture, including the forms of statues as well as stonecutting and engraving in iron. But concerning physical (*banausoi*) crafts, let the term "expertise" (*technē*) be given to them, when some instrument or object fulfills its purpose correctly. But let the term "wisdom" (*sophia*) be reserved for those practices alone, which I have named. I do not include the navigator in the class of craftsmen, because he understands the stars and the winds and grasps that which is not visible.

Why I have said these things will be made clear shortly. But concerning athletic training (*gymnastikē*), let us consider it a form of wisdom (*sophia)* inferior to no other expertise (*technē*), so that it can be summarized in manuals for those wishing to practice athletics (*gymnazein*). For the old form of athletics used to make Milos and Hipposatheneses, and Poulydamases, and Promachuses and Glaucus son of Demylus, and also athletes before them, Peleus, and Theseus, and Heracles himself. But athletic training in the time of our fathers knew lesser men, but still amazing and worthy of recollection. However, the training that has been established now has harmed the affairs of athletes so much that many have contempt for exercise enthusiasts.

Nature (*Physis*)

(2) It seems best to me, therefore, to teach the reasons why athletics has declined and to collect all that I know for both athletes and coaches [the trained and the trainers], and to provide a defense of nature, which has been slandered, because athletes today are far worse than athletes of old. For nature nurtures lions that are no less today, and it is the same for dogs, horses, and bulls. And the matter of nature applies also to trees. Vines are the same and the gifts of the fig tree, and nothing has changed of gold, silver, and stone, but just as nature deemed it best, all things grow the same as before. Regarding athletes, however many of the forms of excellence (*aretai*) that they had before, nature did not abandon them. For she still produces brave, beautiful, and intelligent men—for such characteristics belong to nature. But exercising in an unsound manner and pursuing matters in an unhealthy fashion deprives nature of her power. How this happened, I will demonstrate later. But let us first consider the origins of running, boxing, wrestling, and other such events, when and where each began. The records of the Eleans will be

provided throughout, for it is necessary to provide such materials from the most accurate accounts.

Origins of the Events:

(3) In every athletic contest, there are, on the one hand, the light events: the *stadion*, the *dolichos*, the *hoplitai* (race in armor), and the *diaulos*. Then there are the heavier events: the *pankration*, wrestling, and boxing. The pentathlon is a combination of both. For wrestling and throwing the discus are heavy, but throwing the javelin, jumping, and running are light. Before the time of Jason and Peleus, the long jump was crowned individually, as was the discus, and the javelin could win a victory at the time when the Argo used to sail. Telamon was strongest in the discus, Lynceus was strongest in the javelin, but those born from Boreas [Calais and Zetes] were the best at running and jumping. Peleus was second in these matters, but he was strongest of all in wrestling. And so, when they competed in Lemnos, they say that Jason, pleasing Peleus, put together the five events, and Peleus thus collected the victory, being considered the most warlike of them in his time on account of his excellence, which he used in battles, and, on account of his practice in the five events, which were especially warlike, since javelin throwing was included in the contests. (4) This was the origin of the **dolichos**: Running heralds used to come often from Arcadia to Greece as messengers of matters in war, and they were prevented from using horses, but instead had to run. And so running in a single day the total number of *stadia*, of which the distance race comprises, made them heralds and trained them for war.

Stadion. (5) The *stadion* was discovered as follows: When the Eleans sacrificed in the customary fashion, they placed the offerings on the altar, but they did not bring fire. Instead, runners were put a *stadion*'s distance from the altar, and a priest stood before the altar with a torch, acting as judge. The one who won lit the offerings and went away as Olympic victor.

Diaulos. (6) But when the Eleans sacrificed, it was necessary that the envoys (*theōroi*) of all the Greeks perform sacrifices. And in order that their arrival not be in vain, the runners ran from the altar, as though calling Greece, and then they ran back to the same place as though making an announcement that Greece would come happily. These, then, are the affairs concerning the origin of the *diaulos*.

Race in Armor. (7) The old hoplite races and especially those in Nemea, which they call the armed race and horse race, are dedicated to Tydeus and the Seven [against Thebes]. But the Olympic hoplite race, as the Eleans say, was established for this reason: The Eleans were engaged in a war with the people of Dyme that was without the possibility of truce, and not even the Olympic Games brought a break from the fighting. When the Eleans themselves were victorious on the same day as the contests, a hoplite is said to have run from the battle to the *stadion* track bringing an announcement of victory. This story is persuasive, but I heard the same thing from the Delphians when they waged war against some of the Phocian cities, and I heard the same from the Argives, when they spent time in constant war against the Spartans, and from the Corinthians when they fought both in the Peloponnese and beyond the boundaries of the Isthmus. But there seems to me to be a different origin for the hoplite race. For I agree that the practice has origins in war, but that it came into contests to signal the beginning of war, with the shield demonstrating that the truce has ceased, and that there is need for arms. And if you listen carefully to the herald, you see that he announces to everyone that the prize-distributing competition is ending, and the war trumpet signals the work of Ares calling the youth to arms. This announcement commands that those taking olive oil carry it away, not so as to be anointed, but because they have stopped anointing themselves. (8) The hoplite race in Plataea in Boeotia was considered the best because of the length of the race and also because of the armor which reaches the feet, covering the athlete as if he were to fight. It is also considered the best because it was established as a brilliant deed against the Persians, and, more generally, because the Greeks established this event against the barbarians. In addition, it was the best because of the law established for competitors, which Plataea established long ago: If an athlete should compete again, after winning previously, it was necessary to establish trustees for his body, since death was decreed for the man if he was defeated.

Boxing. (9) Boxing is a Spartan discovery and it came to the Bebrycian barbarians. Polydeuces used it best, and therefore the poets sang of him because of this fact [see **24** and **25a**]. The Spartans used to box for the following reason: The Spartans had no helmets, and they did not consider it appropriate for their country to wage war under helmets. But a shield was enough instead of a helmet for the one who carried it with skill. And so in order that they might guard against blows to the face, and in order that they might also endure being beaten, they practiced boxing and exercised covering the face. Those from an earlier generation abandoned boxing and the *pankration* also, because they considered it shameful to contend in those events in which it is possible, when one single person declares defeat, that Sparta as a whole be reproached as though lacking bravery. (10) The ancient form of boxing was fought in the following manner: Four of the fingers were set into leather straps, and they wrapped so much of the strap that if one brought the fingers together, a fist was possible, and it was held together by a strap, which accordingly was tied to the forearm as a support. But now the equipment has changed, and they make boxing straps by softening hides of the fattest oxen and adding sharp knuckles, but the thumb is not wrapped with the fingers for striking in order that the entire hand not be used for fighting. This is for moderation in striking. Hence, they have banned the boxing straps made from pig from the stadium, considering the blows from them painful and hard to heal.

Wrestling and Pankration. (11) Wrestling and *pankration* were discovered for their usefulness in war. First, the battle fought at Marathon by the Athenians makes this evident, since it appeared closer to wrestling. In addition to this event, second is the battle at Thermopylae, when the Spartans fought with their bare hands when their swords and spears had been broken. However many events there are in a contest, the *pankration* is valued above all else, although it is a mixture of imperfect wrestling and imperfect boxing. Although it is valued by others, the Eleans have considered wrestling stronger and "painful," as the poets say, not only for the intermixture of wrestling moves, for which one needs a body that is fluid and flexible, but also because there are three contests in the competition, since it requires that many falls. Although they consider it terrible to give a dustless victory in the *pankration* and boxing, they do not deny the wrestler, since the law says to grant such a victory only in the crooked and painful wrestling match. The reason for this is clear to me, since the law is established thus: For a skilled athlete, the training is more difficult than the competition at Olympia. Concerning the light events, the *dolichos* is trained with eight or ten *stadia*, and the pentathlon, with something like three, and the runners specializing in the three events execute the *diaulos*, the *stadion*, or both. But there is nothing difficult in such matters. For this is the manner of light training, whether Eleans train the athletes or whether others do. But the athlete in the heavy events is trained by the Eleans in the season of the year when the sun burns the mud most in the Arcadian valley, and he endures dirt hotter than the sand of Ethiopia, and he holds out, starting in the afternoon.

Given these hardships, the wrestlers are the most hard-working. For when the time of competition comes, the boxer will be injured and inflict injury and get kicked in the shins. But when being trained, he will perform a shadow of the competition. The pankratist competes in all ways, however many there are in the *pankration*. But he is trained at one time in one way and at another time in another. Wrestling, however, is the same in pre-competition and competition. For it is possible to test each aspect, how much he knows and how much he is capable of, and wrestling has rightly been called "rounded," for the standing posture of wrestling is "rounded." For this reason, the Eleans crown the most well trained, and indeed he may be crowned for training alone.

Chronology of Events (compare **37b** for similar information)

(12) They say that all these events did not enter into the competitions at the same time, but one and then another was discovered and perfected by the practice of athletics. For the old Olympic Games up to the thirteenth Olympiad [728 BCE] consisted of the *stadion*

alone, and in these the Eleans won three, the Messenians won seven, and one each for a Corinthian, Dymaean, and Cleonaean, each in a different Olympiad, but no one won two Olympiads. In the fourteenth Olympiad [724 BCE], the *diaulos* began, and the victory for it went to the Elean **Hypenus**. And in the next Olympiad [720 BCE], the Spartan **Acanthus** won the contest of the *dolichos*.

The eighteenth Olympiad [708 BCE] gave shape to the pentathlon and wrestling for men, and **Eurybatus** the Lusian won in wrestling, and **Lampis** the Spartan won the pentathlon. But there are those who write that Eurybatus was a Spartan.

The twenty-third Olympiad [688 BCE] called forth the boxer, and the Smyrnaean **Onomastus**, having boxed in the strongest fashion, won and inscribed Smyrna with a beautiful deed: For however many Ionians and Phrygian cities there are throughout the Hellespont and Phrygia, and however many tribes of men there are in Asia, the city of Smyrna exceeded all of these at the same time and first obtained the Olympic crown. And this athlete wrote the rules of boxing, and the Eleans used them, on account of the wisdom of this boxer, and the Arcadians were not at all upset if he wrote contest rules for them, having come from luxuriant Ionia.

And in the thirty-third Olympiad [648 BCE] the *pankration* was established, which until then had not been established, and **Lygdamis** the Syracusan won. This Sicilian was so big that his foot was a cubit in length. And a *stadion* is measured by so many of his feet.

(13) They say that the boys' pentathlon entered the Olympic games in the thirty-eighth Olympiad [628 BCE], when **Eutelidas** the Spartan won, but that a boy never again competed in such a competition at Olympia.

The child who won the boys' *stadion* in the forty-sixth Olympiad [596 BCE]—for it was first established then—was the young goatherd **Polymestor** the Milesian, who overtook a hare by the strength of his feet.

Some say that boys' boxing began in the forty-first Olympiad [616 BCE], and **Philytas** the Sybarite won. But others say it was in the sixtieth Olympiad [540 BCE], and that **Leocreon** from the island of Ceos won.

Damaretus is said to be the first to have a victory in the hoplite race in the sixty-fifth Olympiad [520 BCE], I believe, being from Heraea.

In the one hundred and forty-fifth Olympiad [200 BCE] they introduced the boys' *pankration*. The reason for the slowness in acknowledging it I do not know, since it was already well known among others. It began late among the Olympiads, when Egypt was already being crowned, and indeed that victory was for an Egyptian, and Naucratis was declared victorious when **Phaedimus** the Egyptian won.

It seems to me that these events would not have entered into the competitions one after the other, nor would the Eleans and all the Greeks be so passionate about them, unless *gymnastikē* had advanced and shaped their practice. For the victories of the athletes may be attributed no less to the coaches (*gymnastai*) than to the athletes.

Characterizing Athletics (*Gymnastikē*)

(14) What then is it necessary to know about athletics? What else other than that it be considered a form of wisdom (*sophia*) composed from the crafts of medicine and *paidotribikē*, being more complete than the latter and a portion of the former. How much it partakes of both, I will demonstrate.

However many wrestling moves there are, the *paidotribēs* will demonstrate, establishing the right moments and the attacks and the distances and how one should guard oneself or overcome one who is guarding himself, but the athletics coach (*gymnastēs*) will also teach the athlete that which the athlete does not yet know.

There are occasions when it is necessary in wrestling and the *pankration* either to engage or to escape an existing advantage of one's opponents or to counterattack, about which the coach (*gymnastēs*) would have no clue unless he knew the skills of the *paidotribēs*. On this basis, they are equal disciplines (*technai*) (see **P6–7**).

But to cleanse the bodily humors and to take away the excess and to soften the rigid and to fatten or change or soften them by heat, this constitutes wisdom of the coaches (*gymnastai*). For either the *paidotribēs* does not know these things or, if he does know them at all, he uses them badly on the children, testing the nobility of pure blood. In this respect, athletics is more complete than the aforementioned profession, and it is related to medicine in the following manner:

Diseases, however many we name catarrh and dropsy and consumption, and however many sacred diseases there are, doctors treat with injections, washings, or plasters, but athletics will restrain such diseases through regimen and massage.

Having broken something or having been wounded or having the sight in one's eyes confounded or having one of the limbs dislocated, one must be taken to the doctors, since athletics has nothing to do with such matters.

(15) From these matters, I wish to demonstrate the extent to which athletics is related to each form of knowledge. But I think it best also to see these forms of knowledge in athletics. No one would be able to know all of medicine, but one person would be able to know fractures, and another would be able to know fevers, and another illnesses of the eyes, and another would know well all the consumptive diseases. And because it is a great task to master even a small portion of medicine, doctors rightly say that they know all. And no one could claim that he knew all of athletics at the same time. For if one coach knows the running events, he will not know wrestling and *pankration*. And the one training an athlete in the heavy events will understand another form of knowledge in an inexpert way.

(16) This is the symmetry of the expertise (*technē*), but the origin of athletics is the natural ability of man to wrestle and box sufficiently and to run upright. For there would not be any one of these sorts of events if it were not there beforehand, and on account of which it exists. And just as the origin of metalworking is iron and bronze, and the earth and things from the earth are the origin of agriculture, and the sea is the cause of the art

of navigation, thus let us consider athletics as innate and natural to the human race. And a certain story is told that once there was no form of athletics, and Prometheus was the first to train himself, but Hermes trained others also, and he admired Prometheus for his discovery, and the *palaestra* of Hermes was the first. And those formed by Prometheus were those who trained in the mud. They believed they were formed by Prometheus, since athletics made their bodies fit and well formed.

(17) And so, at the Pythian and Isthmian Games, and wherever on earth games have been established, the coach, while wearing a robe, anoints the athlete and no one will disrobe him who is unwilling. But in Olympia he attends the athlete naked. According to the opinion of some, this is because the Eleans are testing the trainer in the summer season, to see whether he knows how to endure also being hot in that season of the year. The Eleans, however, say this. The Rhodian Pherenice was the daughter of Diagoras and in manner was so strong that, at first, she seemed to be a man to the Eleans. And so she covered herself with a robe at Olympia and trained her son Pisidorus. And that boy was a boxer, and he was well skilled in his craft and not at all inferior to his grandfather. But when they learned of her deception, they hesitated to kill her out of respect for Diagoras and the children of Diagoras, since all the relations of Pherenice were Olympic victors. As a result, a law was written that the coach had to undress, and he was not to remain unexamined by the Eleans.[79]

(18) The coach carries a strigil at Olympia, perhaps for this reason: It is necessary that the athlete at Olympia apply dust and be covered in mud. And in order that he not ruin his bodily condition, the strigil reminds the athlete of the oil and to apply it so abundantly that it is necessary to scrape it off with a strigil after applying it. And some say that a coach at Olympia once killed his athlete with a sharp strigil because he did not strive for victory. And I support this story. For it is better [for it] to be believed than disbelieved. So then, let the strigil serve as a sword against bad athletes, and let the coach take precedence over the *Hellanodikai.*

(19) The Spartans wanted their coaches to know all war tactics also, since they considered athletic contests as preparation for war. And one should not be surprised at this, since Spartans related dancing, the lightest of activities in peacetime, to war. They dance as though they were guarding or throwing a spear or jumping off the ground and handling a shield skillfully.

Anecdotes of Coaches and Athletes

(20) How coaches were beneficial to athletes either through exhortations, rebukes, promises, or wise sayings, many more than a single account can enumerate. But let the best of those be reported here. The coach Tisias led to victory in the Olympic contest **Glaucus**

---

[79] This story is told in Pindar, **2f** and in Pausanias, **37q** (6.7.2).

of Carystus. When Glaucus was giving way to his opponent in boxing at Olympia, Tisias shouted "use the plow strike." This was a right-handed punch against his opponent. For Glaucus was so strong in that hand that he once straightened a bent plowshare by striking it with his right hand as though with a hammer.[80]

(21) And then there is **Arrhichion**, the pankratist, who had already won two Olympic victories. When he was contending for the crown as a third Olympic victory to add to these and was growing weary, Eryxias, the coach, inspired in him a desire for death, shouting from outside the ring how beautiful it would be that his epitaph say that he did not give up at Olympia.[81]

(22) The coach of **Promachus** of Pellene recognized that Promachus was in love at a time when the Olympic Games were approaching, and he said to Promachus, "You seem to be in love." And when he saw him turn red, he said "I did not ask you in order to test you, but in order to help you in your desire. For I could speak on your behalf to the woman." And although he did not speak to the woman at all, he returned, bringing a story to the athlete that was false, but worth much for the one that was in love: "She would not consider you unworthy of her affections, if you win at Olympia." And Promachus, encouraged when he heard these words, not only won, but defeated **Poulydamas** of Scotousa after the event with the lions, which he wrestled in front of the Persian king Ochus.[82]

(23) I myself have heard **Mandrogenes** of Magnes attributing to his coach his powers of toughness, which he used in his youth in the *pankration*. For he said that his father died, and his house came under the control of his mother, who was masculine and noble, and his coach wrote this sort of letter to her: "If you should hear that your son has died, believe it, but if you should hear that your son lost, do not believe it." He said that he displayed complete courage out of respect for this letter, in order that his coach might not be proven a liar or that his mother be deceived.

(24) **Optatus**, the Egyptian, won the race in Plataea. And there was a law established in Plataea, as I mentioned before, that someone who lost, but won before, would be publicly executed, and that one cannot participate in training until one establish guarantors for the body. But when none of his relatives offered for something so major, the coach offered himself up for the law and strengthened his athlete for a second victory. For those intending to seize upon a great deed, to not distrust is the best source of hope.

Analysis of the Coach and His Knowledge

(25) Since a crowd of such examples is pouring forth, new mixed with the old, let us inspect the coach himself who presides over the athlete—what he knows and what sort of person he is. Let the coach be neither too talkative nor untrained in his tongue, so that

---

[80] Pausanias **37q** (6.10.1–3).　　[81] See **40d**.　　[82] See **37q** (5.6.4–9).

the work of his craft not be dismissed due to talkativeness nor that it seem simple and executed without reason, and let him examine every aspect of physiognomics. I urge this for the following reason: A judge at Olympia (*Hellanodikēs*) or Delphi (*Amphiktyōn*) judges the child athlete on certain criteria: whether he has a tribe and fatherland, whether he has a father and a family, whether he is born from free parents and not a bastard, and above all whether he is young and not beyond the age of a *pais*. But even if they should know whether he is strong or weak, a drunkard or a glutton, brave or cowardly, they do not have any rules that pertain to such matters; but it is necessary that the coach know such things thoroughly, since he is a type of judge of nature. Let him recognize every sign of character in the eyes by which lazy men are revealed, the tightly wound, the sluggish, those lacking in endurance, and the powerless. For the character of black eyes is one thing and the character of blue, gray, and bloodshot eyes is another, and another still is the character of yellow or spotted and bulging or hollow eyes. For nature signifies the seasons in the stars and character in the eyes. But the character of the parts of the body must be subject to inspection in the following manner, as in sculpture: The ankle should correspond with the wrist, the forearm with the shin, the arm match with the thigh and the buttocks with the shoulder; the back should be seen in relation to the stomach, the chest should project similarly to the area below the hips, and the head, being the scale of the whole, have symmetry with all of these.

The Analysis of Athletes

(26) With that being said, let us not consider that the subject of training is to follow, but rather stripping the one to be trained and establishing an inspection of the athlete's nature, in what way he is put together and for what purpose. For it is not fitting that there is so much discussion of dogs and horses by hunters and horsemen, with the result that they do not use one dog for all types of hunting or for all prey hunted by them, but one type of dog for one and another for another, and they make some horses companions in the hunt and others battle horses and others still they use for contests and not simply as chariot horses, but each horse is assigned suitably to the shaft or the rope of the chariot. Yet those humans go unjudged (*akritos*) who are brought to the Olympic or Pythian Games for the sake of the victory proclamations, which even Heracles desired. Therefore, I encourage the coach to consider proportionality (*analogia*), which I mentioned, but before proportion, to consider the character of the humors.

(27) And yet there is an even more ancient matter than this, which seemed best to the Spartan Lycurgus. For in providing Sparta with warrior athletes, he said, "Let the young women be trained and let them be allowed to run in public." I suppose this was for the sake of good children and bearing better offspring because of their bodily strength. For when she comes to the house of her husband, she will not be reluctant to carry water or to grind grain, since she was trained from youth. And if she should marry a young man

who is also a training partner (*syngymnazomenos*), she will produce even better children, for they will be big and strong and free from disease. Indeed, Sparta became great as it was in war because their marriages were carried out in that way.[83]

(28) But since it is fitting to begin from one's birth, let the coach go to the child athlete and first look at him in terms of parentage, if they were married young and were noble and free from diseases which attack the nerves and often occur in the eyes and ears or organs. For these diseases by nature go away at some point and lurk unseen in children, but when they reach the age of ephebes and transition into men, going into their prime, the diseases become clear and manifest, since the blood undergoes a change with the changing of age. The youthfulness of the parents, if both parents are well born (*gennaioi*) when they come together, also adds strength to the athlete, and the blood is pure, and there is strength of bone, and unmixed humors and equal size, and I would say that they also add beauty. But suppose the parentage is unknown because they are not present at the time of judgment. How shall we test the seed? For the whole account will turn into stupidity if we should delay the athlete already standing in the stadium with olive and laurel while we inquire into the father and mother who could have died in his youth. For a method of viewing (*theōria*) is necessary by which we may seem not to be ignorant of the parents and the athlete's own disposition when we look at the naked athlete. The reasoning is difficult and not at all easy, but it is not beyond the limits of the discipline (*technē*). And so I shall provide this for the inquiry.

(29) I have demonstrated what kinds of athlete noble seed and youth will produce, but the seed of those advanced in years remains to be examined. Their skin is soft, their clavicle is hollow, their veins protrude like someone having labored, their hips are disjointed, and their muscles weak. There are more tests for them when being trained. They are heavy and raw in their blood because of their coldness, and their sweat comes to the surface rather than remaining in the curved and hollow parts of the body, nor do they bloom in labors unless we bring forth the sweat, nor is lifting suitable for them, but they require rest. And they are exhausted by their work beyond the measure of the work they have done. I consider them unworthy of all events in the contest, especially the *pankration* and boxing, for they are not firm in the contest against man. And with their skin not being strong, they are easily harmed by blows and wounds. Nevertheless, they ought to be trained, but they should be flattered by the one training them, since they need this while working and training. If the seed appears to be elderly in just one of the parents, the shortcomings will be similar, but less manifest.

(30) Blood will reveal the sickly in terms of bodily condition (*hexis*), for it will necessarily appear muddy and flooded with bile. And even if at some point the blood is awakened by the trainer, it reverts and becomes heavy again. For that which is not naturally good results in difficulties. A prominent throat would indicate as much, the shoul-

---

[83] See also **10c** and **35g**.

derblades, and a neck that is protruding and sunken where the clavicles come together. Those with narrow sides and those with sides broad beyond measure demonstrate many signs of illness. For with the first group, by necessity their organs are compressed, and they breathe in a poor manner; they cannot endure labors, and they digest food poorly. And with the other group, their organs are heavy and hanging, with the result that their breathing is slow and they are slow in the attack, and food will be less well digested, going to the belly [i.e., running to fat] rather than used for the nourishment of the body. This is what I say about the parents of those intending to compete. But now it is necessary to examine what is suitable for each event in the contests.

The Pentathlete

(31) Let the one going to compete in the pentathlon be heavier than the light athletes, but lighter than the heavier athletes, and he should also be tall, well put together, upright, not excessive or reduced in his muscularity And let him have legs that are large rather than proportional and hips that are fluid and flexible on account of the twisting motion of the javelin and the discus and the jump. Indeed, he will jump with less pain and will break nothing in his body if he is firm in his landing after lowering his hips. And it is necessary that he have large hands and long fingers. For he will throw the discus that much better if, on account of the size of his fingers, the edge of the discus is sent up from the hollow of his hand. And he will throw the javelin easily if the fingers, though they are small, do not touch at a high point of the sling of the javelin.

The Distance Runner

(32) Let the best of the distance runners be strong in the shoulders and neck like the pentathletes, but let him have light and nimble legs, just as the runners of the *stadion*. For the *stadion* runners move their legs for the quick course, as though winged by their hands, but the distance runners do this toward the end and at other times go almost at a walk, holding their hands up in front of them, for which reason they need strong shoulders.

(33) Ever since the time when **Leonidas** of Rhodes won the "triple" in four Olympic Games, no one distinguishes between competitors in the race in armor, the *stadion*, and the *diaulos*. Nevertheless, one should distinguish between the athletes competing in one event and those competing in all three. Let the one racing in armor be equipped with a long torso and well- developed shoulders and tapered knee muscles in order that the shield be carried well by those taking it up. As for the *stadion* runners, since this is the lightest of the events in the competition, the strongest are well proportioned, but the athletes that are not excessively tall, though taller than the well-proportioned by a small amount, are better still. For excessive height lacks stability, just like those plants that have

become too tall. Let them also be put together well, for the principle of good running is standing well. The balance of their body parts (*harmonia*) should be as follows: The legs should balance the shoulders, the chest should be less than that of the well-proportioned athlete and have good organs, the knees should be light, the shins straight, and hands bigger than normal. Their muscularity should be proportionate. Excessive muscles are the bonds against speed. As for competitors in the *diaulos*, they should be stronger than those who run the *stadion*, but lighter than those who run in armor. And let those competing in all three be arranged according to merit, combined from all those advantages, of which they make use for each one of the events. Let no one think this is impossible, for there have been such runners also in our time.

The Boxer

(34) Let the boxer have large hands, good forearms, strong upper arms, sturdy shoulders, and a high neck. Thick wrists are heavier for hitting, but smaller wrists are fluid and strike with ease. And let strong hips support him, for the forward attack of the hands renders the body unsteady unless he is carried upon strong hips. And I consider those with large calves unfit for any of the events in the contest, but least of all for boxing. For those athletes are slow in kicking the shins of their opponents and slow to defend against kicks. And let him have shins that are straight and well proportioned, with thighs that are separated and stand apart from each other. For the frame of the boxer is more suited for attacking if his thighs do not come together. The best stomach is one that is drawn in. For such boxers are lighter and breathe easily. But nevertheless, there is some need of a stomach for a boxer, for a stomach protects against blows to the face, projecting forward against the strike of the opponent.

The Wrestler

(35) Let us move on to the wrestlers. The wrestler should be tall, in principle, rather than proportional, but let him be put together like the well-proportioned, with neither a tall neck, not a neck yoked to the shoulders. For the latter [i.e., with neck yoked to shoulders] is naturally suitable, but, for those familiar with the statues of Heracles, it appears more similar to one punished than trained. How much more pleasing and godlike are the noble statues that do not have short necks. But let the neck be upright as one sees in a horse that is beautiful and aware of itself, with the base of the neck going down to each clavicle. Shoulders brought together and prominent heads of the shoulder add size to the wrestler, as well as nobility of form and strength, which are better for wrestling. For such shoulders, which provide support for the head from the arms, are good protection for a neck being bent and wrenched from wrestling. And arms that are well marked are good for wrestling. And I define a well-marked arm as follows. Broad veins run from the

neck and throat, one on each side, and they make a descent from the shoulder to the hands and are prominent in the arms and elbows. Those in whom the veins are on the surface and highly visible do not gain strength from them, and they are not sweet to look at, much like varicose veins. But those for whom the veins that swell and happen to be deep present a light and unique "breath" [*pneuma*, i.e., force] for the hands. And such veins make young the arms of the elderly, and for the young, they indicate readiness and appearance in the call for wrestling. And the chest is better that is forward and projecting. For the organs inside such a frame are situated as though in a solid and well-formed chamber and are noble, strong, free from disease, and passionate at the right time. And the chest is pleasing that is moderately projecting, lean with striations. For these types of chests are strong and vigorous but less suited to wrestling, but more wrestling-like than others. But those with hollow caved chests I consider not worthy to strip down or to train. For they often suffer stomach pains and are not well organed and have no wind (*pneuma*) And let the stomach be drawn in at the abdomen—for a heavy stomach is not useful for the wrestler—and let it be supported by a groin that is not slight, but let it be well developed. For such groins are capable of grabbing hold in every way that wrestling provides, and they cause pain rather than experience pain when brought together [around an opponent]. And a straight back is pleasing, but one that is rounded is better suited to wrestling, since it is more natural for the wrestling posture, which is rounded and bending forward. And be sure that a hollow spine does not divide the back. For it will lack marrow, and the vertebrae there could be twisted and compressed by the wrestling moves and could slip forward at some point. But this is more an assumption than how it is. The hip, like an axle fixed between the limbs above and below, should be fluid, flexible, and mobile. And the size and fleshiness of this region beyond reason achieves this effect, by Zeus. But let the area below the hip be neither slight nor excessive, for the one is weak, and the other is untrainable. But let it project strongly and in a way suitable for wrestling. And the flank that is curved and can bend the chest forward makes men capable of wrestling and being wrestled [i.e., on the attack or on the defense]. For when athletes of this type are underneath, they are difficult for their opponents to beat, and they are not easy to bear when the opponent is underneath them. And small glutes are weak, but overly broad glutes are slow. But well-formed glutes are good in all situations. A thigh that is firm and turned outward combines strength with beauty and supports everything well, and especially if the shin is not tilted outward, and the thigh is supported by a straight knee. Ankles that are not straight but slanting and falling inward cause the body to falter just as crooked pedestals make column drums unsteady. Such a sort is the wrestler and he will take part in the *pankration* in that part of the contest on the ground but will be less successful in the hand-to-hand combat. But the perfect pankratists are those who have a build that is more wrestling-like than the boxers, but more boxing-like than the wrestlers.

Athletes' Body Types

(36) There are also noble athletes who are "big" in their small stature. But let us consider them somewhat lacking in size compared with the "squared" and symmetrical types. They are built in body like the large and seem larger than their actual size, but they are also shown to be well fleshed, that is, unless they seem to be emaciated. Wrestling rather announces their skill. For they are flexible, versatile (*polytropoi*), strong, light, quick, and have good balance. They escape from many impossible and difficult wrestling holds, resting on the head as though on their feet. But they are not in the front ranks of boxing and *pankration*, since they stand below an opponent when he strikes, and it is quite laughable that they jump from the ground whenever they should strike. Let us establish as a standard for the "big in small" athlete the images of the wrestler **Maron** from Cilicia. But we must reject those athletes with long torsos. For they are good at eluding the hard-to-guard maneuvers of wrestling, but they are useless for wrestling throws because of the burden on their legs.

(37) "Lions," "eagles," "splinters," and those whom they call "bears"—such are the types of athletes. For the lions are broad-chested with big hands, but lacking in the hind parts, and the eagles are similar in build to the lion-like, but hollow in the legs, just like the build of eagles. But both types reveal daring, violent, and impetuous people. But they lose courage in the face of failure, which is no surprise if one considers the character of lions and eagles.

(38) The splinter-like and the strap-like (*himantōdeis*) are both tall with long legs and big hands, but they are different from each other in both small and larger matters. For the splinter-like are stiff and appear well defined, for which reason, I think, the name fits them. But the others are limber and rather loose, and they are fluid in their turns according to the properties of leather. The splinter-like are more vigorous in their maneuvers and the strap-like ones grip firmly and hold fast.

(39) The types of athletes capable of endurance are hard, muscular, hollow in the stomach, and quick in their vision. Often, they seem unconquerable. The phlegmatic are the most dependable. For those who are choleric are the type that can switch over into madness on account of their zealous nature.

(40) But athletes similar to bears are round, fluid, and well-fleshed. They are less defined and hunched over rather than upright. But they are difficult to wrestle and can slip through holds, and they grab hold firmly. And they rattle in breathing, just like bears when they run.

(41) And the ones who are equal in both hands, whom they call the ones with two right hands, they are a rare discovery of nature. They are invulnerable in their strength, hard to guard against, and indefatigable. For this equality of the body gives more strength to the limbs. How this is, I will tell you. For the Egyptian **Mys** [i.e., "Muscle"], as I heard from those older than me, was a young man, but not large, and he wrestled beyond the

limits of the discipline. And when he became ill, his left side got bigger. A dream came to him after he had decided to stop competing that encouraged him [to train] against the disease and to gain strength on the mutilated side more than on the unharmed and unmutilated side. And the vision was true. For by twisting with the damaged parts of his limbs, he produced holds that were difficult for his opponents, and he benefited from his disease by strengthening the damaged limbs. This itself is a source of wonder. Indeed, this is not something that happens regularly. Rather let it be considered the work of a god demonstrating something great for mankind.

(42) Concerning the proportions of the body, whether this one or that one is better, there are small disputes among those men who have not examined these matters in a rational manner. But concerning the humors, however many there are, there is no argument, nor could anyone deny that the hot and moist type is the best. For, like expensive statues, it consists of unmixed and pure matter. Free of clay, mud, and excessive fluids, those with a lack of flowing of bile and phlegm easily endure toiling at what is necessary. Because they are well nourished, seldom sick, and recover quickly from illness, they are easily trained and coachable in various forms of training on account of the good fortune of the mixture of their humors. But easily angered athletes are both hot and dry in their mixture of humors and useless for those coaching, just as hot sand is for one sowing seeds. But they are strong in their quickness of mind, for this is a strong characteristic for them. But the phlegmatic athletes are slow, and their bodily condition (*hexis*) is one of coldness. Such athletes must be trained with vigorous movement, but the ones easily angered should be trained step by step, with each breath. The former require the goad, the latter the reins; the former need to be covered in dust, and the latter need to be anointed with oil.

(43) Let these things be said about the humors for modern athletics, since the old form of athletics did not recognize the humors, but trained strength alone. And with respect to athletics, those men of old only knew physical training in and of itself. Some men of old trained by carrying loads not easy to carry, and some by competing in swiftness with horses and hares, some by bending and straightening iron that had been forged for thickness, and some were yoked with strong bulls and draft oxen. Some tamed bulls, and others, lions. Such was the training for athletes like **Polymestor, Glaucus, Alesias,** and **Poulydamas** of Scotousa. And the hands of **Tisander**, the boxer from Naxos, sent him swimming around the promontory of the island over much of the sea. This was training for his hands and the rest of his body. For them food consisted of barley cakes and unsifted and unleavened bread, as well as cow, bull, and goat flesh, and deer also nourished them; wild olive trees anointed them with oil, for which reason they trained without sickness, and grew old only after a long time. And they used to compete over eight Olympiads, and some nine, and they were good soldiers and fought "beyond the wall." Nor did they fall there but were worthy of rewards and war trophies (*tropaia*), and they made war a practice for athletics, and athletics a practice for war.

The Problems with Athletic Training

Diet. (44) But then things changed, and some athletes did not serve in war, and others were lazy from a lack of labor, and others became relaxed from weakness. The Sicilian diet took hold, and the stadiums were weakened considerably, since flattery was added to athletics. But medicine first introduced flattery, offering, as an adviser, a good craft to be sure, but too soft to be grasped in athletic events, since it taught leisure and recommended that one sit before exercising, filled like a Libyan or Egyptian food sack. And it introduced cooks and chefs for pleasure, who made athletes gluttonous and hollow in their stomachs, feeding them with bread flavored with poppy, made from husked wheat. They filled them with fish, an unnatural meat, making arguments about fish from the areas of the sea, how those from the mud are fatty, and those from the rocks are tender, those from the open sea are meaty, and that algae nourish slender ones, and seaweed produces weak ones. And medicine has also discussed pork meat with marvelous tales. Medicine commands that those herds of swine at the seashore be considered of poor quality on account of the sea garlic, of which the seashore is full, and the beach too. Medicine also warns to guard against those swine near the rivers on account of their feeding on crab and to only eat those that feed on cornelian cherries and acorns.[84]

Money. (45) Such soft living is also keen for the sex impulse. It also set athletes onto a path of lawlessness in money matters and in selling and buying victories.[85] For some give away their own fame (*eukleia*) on account of needing much, I think, and others buy victories without labor on account of soft living. The laws against temple robbers show great anger for one stripping a silver or gold dedication or defiling it, but the crown of Apollo or Poseidon, for which the gods themselves struggled greatly, that crown is sold without fear and bought without fear, and only the wild olive remains inviolate for the Eleans according to the ancient custom. But as for the rest of the contests, let me deliver this one story, from many, which tells all. A boy won in the wrestling match at Isthmia, after agreeing to pay 3,000 drachmas to one of his opponents for the victory. When both boys were present at the gymnasium the next day, the one asked for the money, and the other said he did not owe it, since he won while the other was unwilling to lose. Since that argument accomplished nothing, they turned to oaths. and the one who sold the victory came to the temple of Isthmia and swore before the people and before the eyes of Greece that in truth he sold the contest of the god and that 3,000 drachmas was promised to him. He admitted all of this, speaking with a clear and articulate voice. By however much this story is true, even if it is not without witnesses, by that much is it both unholy and unspeakable. Indeed, he swore at the Isthmus and before the eyes of Greece. What then would happen in Ionia and in Asia to the disgrace of the contest? Nor do I discount trainers and athletes in this corruption. For there are some with money for training, and they lend it to the athletes at rates greater than

---

[84] See Plato **22d**.　　[85] See Pausanias **37m**.

for those experienced in sea trade. They care nothing about the reputation (*doxa*) of the athletes, but they become financial advisers in buying and selling, thinking only of their own gain. So much can be said for the "traders." For they trade in the excellence (*aretai*) of the athlete by setting up a good deal for themselves.

(46) But they make this mistake also. They strip down a child athlete and train him as though already a man. They order him to preload his stomach and have him walk in the middle of training and belch. In this way, like bad educators, they deprive the children of their youthful step, and they train them to be sluggish, heavy, and timid in the prime of their life. But they ought to have trained movement as at the *palaestra*: I mean the movement of the limbs, however much is achieved from massage and from rubbing down with the hands. And the child should also practice clapping, since it makes their exercises more high-spirited The Phoenician **Helix** trained with this sort of exercise, not only as a child, but also when he came into adulthood.[86] He was amazing beyond description, more so than all those who I know cared for such recreation.

The Tetrad. (47) One should not pay attention to the tetrads of the coaches, because of which all aspects in athletics have been destroyed. We consider the tetrad a cycle of four days, doing one thing on one day, and another on another. The first day prepares the athlete, the next increases intensity, the day after that relaxes, and the last day mediates. The preparatory day involves short, intense exercise and quick movement rousing the athlete and making him sharp for the coming hardship. The [day of] intense exercise is an inexorable test of the stored strength of the athlete in his bodily condition (*hexis*). The day of ease is a time for regaining movement in a rational manner and the mediating day [teaches] how to escape one's opponent and how not to let go when an opponent is escaping. And by training athletes in this way with complete regularity and in repeating the tetrad, they take away the knowledge of truly understanding the naked athlete. For certain foods make the athlete sick, as does wine, and thefts of food, and contests and tiredness and other things still, some voluntary and some not. How then will we treat an athlete if we train with tetrads and the drawing of lots?[87]

Overeating, Drinking, and Sex

(48) A heavy brow will reveal those who overeat, as will shallow breathing, filled out hollows around the collarbone, and excessive flesh around the flanks. An excessively large stomach, quick-pulsing blood, and wetness in the flanks and behind the knee all indicate one who drinks too much. And there are more telltale signs of those athletes who train,

---

[86] Helix was victorious in the *pankration* at Olympia in 213 and 217 CE. This mention of Helix is the only indication of the treatise's date.

[87] Here Philostratus suggests that the regularity of the tetrad does not coincide with other aspects of irregularity such as the drawing of lots in the combat sports. See **39b** (47).

having come to the gymnasium right after sex. For they have less strength, they have shallow breathing, they are not daring in the attack, and they lack color from their labors, and other such symptoms conquer them. When stripped, they reveal themselves by hollow collarbones, loose hips, ribs in relief, and coldness of blood. And if we should seize upon them, there would be no contest for the crown. They have hollowness under their eyes, a faint beating of the heart, and a light steam from their sweat. Their sleep which regulates digestion is also light. The glances of their eyes are wandering and indicate that they are thinking of love.

(49) But those with wet dreams are cleansed of overflowing good health (*euexia*); yet they nevertheless seem pale and covered with sweat, and they lack strength. At the same time they are well nourished because of sleep, they are straight in their hips, and they have sufficient breath. Athletes with wet dreams are in the same general category as those who have sex. But the one group cleanses their bodily condition, and the others waste away. A good sign of exertion is when the external covering of the body seems rather delicate, the veins are swollen, the arms hang down, and the muscles are withered.

(50) And those who have overeaten, if they happened to be competitors in the light or heavy events, they are to be treated with downward massage, in order that the excess might be led away from the stronger parts of the body. The pentathletes are to be trained in one of the light exercises, runners trained by not straining, but going leisurely and still with a somewhat vigorous pace, and let the boxers work at arm's length lightly and striking the air. But wrestling and *pankration* are upright contests, though it is also necessary to roll on the ground. And so let them roll but lying on top rather than underneath and never tumbling headlong, in order not to maim the body with an incurable wound. But let the athletic coach soften the light and the heavy athletes through massage with a moderate amount of oil, especially on the upper parts. And he should also wipe this oil off.

(52) When wine abounds in the bodies of athletes, moderate training brings an outpouring of sweat. For it is necessary that such athletes do not train excessively or that they relax. For it is better to drain off the corrupted liquid so that the blood is not harmed by it. But let the coach wipe it away and use the strigil, with moderate amounts of oil, in order that the outpouring of sweat is not blocked.

(53) But if an athlete has come from the works of Aphrodite [i.e., sex], it is better not to train him. What sort of men would exchange crowns and heralds for base pleasure? But if they should be trained, let it be for the sake of admonishment, by testing their strength and their breath, since the pleasures of Aphrodite cut these short especially. But the bodily condition of those with wet dreams is also related to the work of Aphrodite, although involuntary, as I said. And so let those athletes be trained with care, and they should be nourished in their strength, since it is clearly lacking. And cleanse them of sweat, since it is excessive for them. Let their exercise be a warm-up, being conducted over time in order that they are trained aerobically. And they require sufficient oil thickened with dust, for this *pharmakon* supports the body and relieves it sufficiently.

(53) Let anxious athletes be soothed with words of wisdom that encourage them and stand them up but let them also be trained in the same way as those who are sleepless and have poor digestion. Their training should be continuous. For those timid in thought are more eager to learn what it is best to guard against. Exhaustion without cause is the beginning of disease. And so it is necessary that those struggling in the mud and *palaestra*, on the one hand, take moderate rest, as I said before, but those having worked in the dust should train in the mud next with a small amount of intensity. For immediate rest after training in the dust is a bad remedy for exhaustion, since it does not nurse strength but weakens the athlete. Such would be the wiser form of training and fitting for the athlete.

Criticism of the Tetrad

(54) But the argument against the tetrads (which I have rejected) is the error in judgement concerning **Gerenos** the wrestler, whose statue is in Athens on the right of the road to Eleusis. He happened to have just won at Olympia, and he had been drinking on the third day after his victory. He was being entertained at the homes of some of his friends, and because he indulged in unaccustomed extravagance, he was unable to sleep. When he came into the gymnasium on the next day, he conceded to his coach that he was raw and doing badly. But the coach was furious, listened angrily and was harsh with him for relaxing and interrupting the tetrads, until he killed him through ignorance of training, by not prescribing how it was necessary to train [in these circumstances], even when the athlete was silent. It is no small tragedy when tetrads are as they are, and the coach is himself untrained and uneducated. For how is it not a heavy matter for the stadiums to harm such an athlete? And how do those who welcome the tetrads make use of them when coming to Olympia? For them there is dust, as I have said, and the training has been predetermined, and the *Hellanodikai* do not train by prescription but all activities are improvised as appropriate, and even the coach is threatened with the rod if he should do something which is beyond what they order.[88] Indeed, what they command is beyond reproach, since those who refuse what they order are readily banned from the games. So much for the tetrads. And if we follow the advice I have given, we will demonstrate that athletics is a form of wisdom, and we will strengthen athletes and the stadiums will grow young from training well.

Athletic Training

Jumping Weights. (55) The *haltēr* [jumping weight] is an invention of the pentathletes, and it was discovered for the long jump, from which it derives its name.[89] Because they

---

[88] On the *Hellanodikai* carrying whips, see **36e, 36f, 38b**.
[89] On the long jump, see Appendix CIII.

considered the jump more difficult than other events in competition, the rules urged on the jumper with flutes and lightened him with the jumping weights. For the weights are the steadfast guide for the hands and bring a solid landing that is well marked in the earth. The law makes clear that this is the value of the jumping weights. For they do not agree to measure a jump if it does not make a suitable imprint. The large jumping weights train the shoulders and hands of jumpers, and the circular ones train the fingers. The jumping weights should be taken up by those who are light and heavy, in all forms of training, except in training used for relaxation.

Dust and Clay. (56) Regarding types of dust, the clay-like is sufficient for cleansing and to provide moderation for those who have been excessive. But the dust from ostraca is fit for opening closed pores and causing sweat, and the dust from asphalt is good for warming the parts of the body that have become cold. The black dust and the yellow dust are both earthy and good for softening and for nourishing the skin. But the yellow dust makes the limbs glisten and pleasing to look at, especially when it is on a noble and well-formed body. It is necessary to sprinkle the dust with a fluid wrist so and through separated fingers, sprinkling rather than spreading it out, in order that the fine dust falls on the athlete.

The Heavy Bag. (57) A heavy bag should be hung for the boxers, but also for those who participate in the *pankration*. Let the punching bag for boxers be light, since the hands of boxers train for timing alone, but the bag for pankratists should be heavier and bigger, in order that they may secure their footing against the attack of the bag, and train their shoulders, and fingers while striking against an opponent. And he should hit his head against it, and he should assume all the upright positions of the *pankration*.

Sunbathing. (58) All those who sun themselves unintelligently (*amathōs*) do it in all types of sun, but those who do it with knowledge and reason do not always sunbathe and only in so far as it is a benefit. For the sun's rays that go with the north wind are both calm and pure and warm, since they come from the clear air. But the south winds are cloudy and wet and excessively hot, which weaken rather than warm those that are training. Thus, I have described the days suitable of sunning. But the phlegmatic should take the sun more so, in order that they sweat out the excess [phlegm]. But those who are prone to anger should keep from this practice, in order that fire not be poured upon fire. And let those past their prime sun themselves lying in leisure in a manner fitting for those being roasted. But those in full strength should be active and trained in every way [in the sun], just as the Eleans see fit. But as for the saunas and dry anointing, since they are considered part of a more rustic type of training, let us leave those to the Spartans, whose training is similar neither to the *pankration* nor to boxing. Indeed, the Spartans say that they train in this very way, not for the sake of competition, but for the sake of toughness alone. One such example is being whipped, since their law prescribes being flogged at the altar.[90]

40b. *Life of Apollonius of Tyana* bk. 5.43: Training at Elis

This purports to be the biography of a traveling wise man, teacher of philosophy (he was a neo-Pythagorean), and miracle worker who lived between 15 and 100 CE. In this anecdote he uses the arduous training of the Olympic athletes as a model for his own followers, addressing them by claiming this is like "an Olympic exordium."

Whenever the Olympic Games are approaching, the Eleans train the athletes for thirty days in Elis itself, and Delphi, when the Pythian Games approach, gathers the athletes together, and the Corinthians, when the Isthmia approaches, say "Go into the stadium and become the sorts of men who win." The Eleans, whenever they process to Olympia, speak in this way to the athletes: "If your effort has made you worthy of coming to Olympia, and no slacking off or cowardice has been permitted, go forward with boldness; for those who have not practiced in this way, go away wherever you wish."

40c. *Imagines* bk. 1.24: Hyacinth

This is the description of a painting of the boy Hyacinth, whom Apollo loved but accidently struck with a discus and killed. The flower so named was said to have sprung from his blood.

A small *balbis*[91] was set apart, sufficient for one standing on it if it does not support the back parts and the right leg, the front parts lean forward, and the other leg is relieved of weight, since it must be straightened and brought forward with the right arm. The posture of the man holding the discus: Turning his head to the right, he must bend over far enough to look down at his side and throw by rising up and casting this discus with the entire right side of his body. Now, I suppose Apollo threw his discus in this manner, since he would not have thrown it in any other way, and struck the young man who now lies there upon the very discus. He was a Laconian youth with a straight leg not untrained in running, his arm muscles already delineated and the contour of the bones apparent from under his flesh. But Apollo has turned away, still standing on the *balbis*, and gazes at the ground.

---

[90] On the Spartan habit of flogging boys see **10d, 38a** (40).
[91] The word is used for the starting line in a foot race, but here for the area marked off for the discus throwers.

40d. *Imagines* 2.6: Arrhichion

The second book of the Imagines *is generally thought to have been composed by a later Philostratus.*[92]
The painting describes Arrhichion's victory and simultaneous death in the pankration *at the Olympic*
Games. The style of the description is vivid, detailed, and full of action, much of which could not be
simultaneously shown in static art. The story was well known. See Pausanias **37z,** *and Appendix CII.*

You have come to the Olympic Games [of 564 BCE] themselves and the fairest of the
events there. This is the men's *pankration*. Arrhichion is being crowned for it, but he died
after the victory and that Olympic judge (*Hellanodikēs*) there crowned him. He should be
called strict because he is careful of the truth and because he is painted as those [Olympic
judges]. The land provides the stadium in a single depression with sufficient extent, and
the stream of the Alpheus that comes out of it is shallow…Wild olive trees flourish
around it, gray in color, fair and curly like celery. (2) After the stadium we now turn our
attention to many other things, and let us consider the accomplishment of Arrhichion
before it has finished. For he seems to have conquered not only his adversary but all the
Greeks. At least they have leaped up from their seats and shouted, and some are waving
their hands, others their garments, others jump up from the ground, and other are wrestling their neighbors in delight, for this really astonishing accomplishment does not allow
the spectators to keep to their seats. Is there anyone so unfeeling that he does not applaud
the athlete? After he had already won twice at Olympia, this now is a greater deed, when,
after he had won this prize at the cost of his life, he is dispatched to the land of the blessed
in his very dust. Do not think this was chance, for he had cleverly planned this victory
beforehand. (3) And the wrestling? Pankratists, my boy, engage in a dangerous type of
wrestling. The must accept facial blows, which are not safe for the wrestler, and grappling
in which they must win as if they were falling. They need the skill to choke from time to
time in different ways, and they grasp an ankle and twist an arm, in addition to punching
and jumping on their opponent. These are the techniques of the pankratist, except for
biting and gouging the eye. The Spartans permit even these things, I suppose because
they are training themselves for battle. The Elean contests prohibit these things, but they
do approve of choking. (4) When his opponent had grabbed Arrhichion around his waist,
he thought to kill him and rammed his forearm against his throat and choked off his breath;
inserting his legs between his thighs, he pressed his feet against the back of his knees, and
he got ahead of Arrhichion, since at that point the sleep of death was stealing over his
senses. But when he relaxed the grip of his legs, he did not anticipate Arrhichion's strata-
gem. Arrhichion kicked back with the sole of his foot, as a result of which his opponent's
right side was exposed, since his knee was dangling. He pulled this opponent, now not
much of an opponent, to his groin, leaned to his left and caught the top of his opponent's
foot in the bend of his knee; he wrenched his ankle from its socket by the violence of his

---

[92] See Bowie and Elsner (2009: 6–7).

thrust in the opposite direction. Arrhichion's soul, although feeble as it departed from his body, did this. It gave him the strength for what he had striven for. (5) The man who is throttling him is depicted like a corpse, signaling with his right hand that he yields, but Arrhichion is depicted as all victors are, for his blood is still fresh and the sweat still glistens, and he smiles, as do the living whenever they perceive that they have won the victory.

40e. *Heroicus* 14.4–15.10: An Oracle Advises Athletes about Victory

This is a dialogue between the keeper of a vineyard on the site of a ruined shrine of a Homeric hero (Protesilaus) and a Phoenician sailor. The keeper recounts the many predictions of the oracle, including these, which feature athletes. The interest of the passage is the story about the invention of a wrestling technique and of the jealousy of the Elean overseers.

THE VINEDRESSER You have heard, I think, of the Sicilian pankratist whom our fathers used to call the Jumper, because he was short, much more so that his opponents.

(15.1) THE PHOENICIAN I do know from the testimony of his statues, for his bronze statues are found in many places.

THE VINEDRESSER He exceeded in skill and in heart, stranger, and his well-proportioned body was very strong. (15.2) He came to this shrine as a boy (and he was sailing immediately to Delphi to compete in the contest) and asked Protesilaus what he should do to defeat his opponent. (15.3) Protesilaus replied, "Be stepped on." At first, he was disheartened, thinking that the he had been rejected by the oracle, but being the first to discover stepping on the opponent's heel, he realized later that the oracle told him not to release his opponent's foot. For the one wrestling against the heel must continually be stepped on by his opponent, and in doing this, this athlete gained a glorious reputation and was never defeated. (15.4) I suppose you have heard of the clever Plutarch?…(15.5) When he was going to his second Olympic Games for the men's competition, he asked the hero to prophesy how he might win. He replied, "Pray to Archelous, god of the contest."

(15.6) THE PHOENICIAN "What did that mean?"

THE VINEDRESSER He was competing at Olympia with **Hermias the Egyptian** for the victory crown. When one man was weakened by his wounds and the other by thirst—the sun was at its peak during the boxing—a cloudburst broke over the stadium and Plutarch, in his thirst, drank the water that had collected on the sheepskin wrapped around his arms. Later he said that, recollecting the oracle, he took heart and got the victory. (15.7) Perhaps you wonder at the hardness of **Eudaemon the Egyptian**, if you have happened upon him boxing. When he asked how he might not be defeated, the oracle responded, "Spurn death."

THE PHOENICIAN And he obeyed the oracle, vinedresser. Having prepared himself in this way, the crowd finds him adamantine and godlike.

(15.8) THE VINEDRESSER The athlete **Helix** has never himself sailed to this shrine but sent one of his companions, who asked how many times he would win at Olympia. "Twice," the oracle said, "unless you do not wish to win three times."

(15.9) THE PHOENICIAN Marvelous, vinedresser. You will say, I suppose, how this happened at Olympia. Having gained one victory when he won in the men's wrestling, although, technically, he belonged in the boys' class. When he had stripped for both the wrestling and the *pankration* in the next Olympiad, the Eleans in their anger had in mind to bar him from both contests, charging him with breaking the Olympic rules. (15.10) They barely crowned him for the *pankration* [*They apparently cancelled the wrestling to deny him another victory.*]. Protesilaus predicted that he should guard against this envy, which is the opponent of those who are accomplished.

41. Aelian

Although Aelian (c.170–235) was born in Praeneste in Italy and lived in Rome, he wrote in Greek. His **Historical Miscellany** *is a collection of stories that reflect Greek cultural values of the past, particularly the period of the Athenian empire.*

41a. *Historical Miscellany* bk. 2.6: Hippomachus the Trainer

They say that Hippomachus the athletic trainer, when an athlete whom he was coaching caused his opponent to fall and the whole crowd of bystanders cheered, Hippomachus beat him with his staff and said, "You did badly and not what you should have to improve. These people would not have praised you if you had used proper technique." He was making the point that those who do each thing properly and well must please not the many but those with theoretical knowledge of what is being done.

41b. *Historical Miscellany* bk. 4.15: Straton the Pankratist and Democrates the Wrestler

These two anecdotes belong to a series, the theme of which is that illness can be the catalyst for significant change. Strato was a victor in 68 BCE (see Pausanias **37q**, *5.21.9–10 and for Democrates,* **37q**, *6.17.1).*

Strato, the son of Corrhagus, it seems, was sick for a reason. Although he came from a noble and wealthy family, he did not exercise in the gymnasium. Suffering with his spleen, needing the therapy of gymnastic exercise, at first he exercised as much as was necessary for health, but as he progressed in skill, he exercised with his whole focus. At Olympia on the same day he won the wrestling and the *pankration* and won in the following Olympiad and at Nemea and Isthmia and Pythia.

Democrates, the wrestler, also had problems with his feet. Going to competitions, he stood in the stadium, drew a circle around himself, and ordered his opponents to drag him outside of the circle. Unable to do so, they were defeated. Because he had held his stance unmoving, he departed as a crowned victor.

41c. *Historical Miscellany* 10.19: Eurydamus of Cyrene, a Boxer

Eurydamus the Cyrenean won at boxing, but his teeth were knocked out by his opponent. He swallowed them so that his opponent did not know.

41d. *Historical Miscellany* bk. 14.7: Spartan Scrutiny of Boys' Bodies

This is a Spartan law. It states that no Spartan is to be seen with a less than manly skin [i.e., tanned by healthy outdoor activities] or a have a bodily weight beyond what is acquired in exercise. It seemed to them that the latter was from idleness, and the former was not manly. It was also mandated that every ten days all the ephebes should present themselves naked to the ephors in public. If they were well muscled and strong from their exercises, as if they were sculpted and chiseled, they were praised. But if there was something soft or flaccid about their limbs and they were puffy and bloated with fat from idleness, they were immediately beaten in punishment. Daily, the ephors paid attention to the details of their dress so that no aspect of the necessary decorum was neglected. Spartan cooks need know only about meat. With skills beyond this, a cook was driven from Sparta, as if they were purging sickness from the state.

42. Athenaeus

Athenaeus from Naucratis in Egypt lived and wrote in the late second century CE. *A polymath, his work, the* Deipnosophists *("Philosophers at the Dinner Table") is a massive compendium of miscellaneous information, ranging from food and dining habits to music and poetry. Gluttony was a frequent topic.*

42a. *Deipnosophists* bk. 10, 412f–413b: The Gluttonous Habits of Athletes

Pausanias **37q** *profiles Theagenes (6.6.4–8) and Milo (6.14.5–9).*

Theagenes of Thasos consumed a bull all by himself, as Posidippus says in his epigram:

> For a bet I once ate a Maeonian ox,
>   since my country, Thasos, would not have furnished a meal
> for Theagenes. As much as I ate, I desired still more. For this reason
>   I am erected here in bronze with an outstretched hand.

Milo of Croton, according to Theodorus in his *On Athletic Contests*, was accustomed to eat twenty *minas* of meat, as much bread, and to drink three jars of wine [daily]. At Olympia he lifted a four-year-old bull upon his shoulders and carried him around the stadium. After this he butchered and ate it alone on the same day. Tithormus the Aetolian ate an ox in competition with Milo, as Alexander the Aetolian records. Phylarchus in the third book of his histories says that Milo ate the bull while reclining before the altar of Zeus [Olympios], and therefore the poet Dorieus wrote the following:

> Such was Milo, when he lifted a weight from the ground,
>   A four-year-old calf (at the feast of Zeus),
> The monstrous beast on his shoulders as if a newborn lamb
>   He carried lightly throughout the whole festival.
> That was a marvel, but he accomplished a greater spectacle than this,
>   Stranger, before the Pisan altar.
> For he carried the ox that had not borne a yoke in the procession; then
>   Cutting up its flesh, he ate the whole thing by himself.

Astyanax the Milesian, three times victor in the *pankration* in successive Olympiads, was invited to dinner by the Persian Ariobarzanes, and when he arrived, he promised to eat everything that had been prepared for all the others, and he did so. According to Theodorus, when the Persian asked him to do something worthy of his strength, he broke off a bronze bean-shaped knob from the couch and after softening it [in his hands] he straightened it. At his death, when he was burned on the pyre, one urn was insufficient for his bones, and two were scarcely enough. What had been prepared for the nine men invited to the feast at Ariobarzanes, Astyanax ate it all.

42b. *Deipnosophists* bk. 12, 539c: Craterus on Campaign

Perdiccas and Craterus were devoted to athletic activities. Goatskins sufficient to fill up a stadium accompanied them on expeditions, and when they had established a place in the encampment, they exercised under them.[93] Many teams of oxen followed as well, bringing the dust for use in the wrestling pit (*palaestra*).

42c. *Deipnosophists* bk. 13, 565f–566a: Beauty Contests for Men: The *Euandria*

In the *euandria* they choose the best-looking men and entrust them with leading the procession [bearing sacred objects]. In Elis there is actually a beauty contest. And to the first-prize winner they give the utensils of the goddess to carry, to the second-prize winner to lead the ox [for sacrifice], and the third-prize winner places the offerings [on the fire]. Heraclides of Lembos records that in Sparta the most beautiful man and the most beautiful woman are admired more than anything, since the most beautiful women are born in Sparta.[94]

42d. *Deipnosophists* bk. 13, 609e–610a: Beauty Contests for Women

I am aware of a contest of female beauty that was once established. Nicias in his History of Arcadia says that Cypselus instituted it when he founded the city [Elis] on the plain of the Alpheus. On the plain he settled some Parrhasians and dedicated an altar and sanctuary to Eleusinian Demeter. In her festival the beauty contest was celebrated. The first to win was his wife Herodice. The contest is held even up to the present, and the contestants are called "Wearers of Gold." Theophrastus says that there is a beauty contest [for men] at Elis, and the judgment is a serious occasion; the winners receive armor as prizes, which Dionysius of Leuctra says they dedicate to Athena. A ribbon is tied around the victor[95] by his friends and he leads the procession to the temple. Myrsilus in his *Historical Paradoxes* records that a crown of myrtle was given to the victors. The same Theophrastus says that in some places there are contests of prudence and household skills for women, just as there are among the barbarians. Elsewhere there are contests of beauty, as this too should be honored, as with those citizens of Tenedos and Lesbos. But he says that beauty is a matter of luck or nature, and an award for prudence (*sophrosyne*) ought to be given. For only with prudence should beauty be valued. If not, it runs the risk of undisciplined behavior.

---

[93] That is, the skins formed a roof that would cover a stadium. This is probably an exaggeration.

[94] Compare Xenophon, *Memorabilia* bk. 3.3.12.

[95] Victors are often portrayed with ribbons (called *tainia*) tied around their heads or upper arms.

43. Pollux

43a. *Onomasticon* bk. 9, 103–7, 119: On Varieties of Ball Games

Julius Pollux, like Athenaeus, from second-century Naucratis in Egypt, was a professor of rhetoric in Athens. He is responsible for a treatise on names and technical terms that now exists in a later abridgement. Book 9 includes these descriptions of various types of ball games. Ball-playing was ubiquitous, though not part of the usual athletic programs. See Galen **39c**.

(103) *Episkyros, phaininda, aporrhaxis*, and *ourania* are names of children's ball games.

(104) *Episkyros* has the variant names of *ephēbikē* ("for the young") and *epikoinos* ("for everyone"). It was mostly played with opposing teams of equal numbers who, with a stone chip (called a *skyron*), draw a line between themselves on which they place the ball. They draw two other lines, one behind each of the others' lines. Whichever team gets the ball first throws it beyond their opponents, whose task it is to intercept the oncoming ball and throw it back, until such time as one team pushed the other beyond the back line.

(105) *Phaininda* is named either from Phainindos, who first invented it, or from *phenakizein* ("to deceive"), because a player fakes a throw to one person, while throwing to another, deceiving the one who expected the ball. This very likely resembles the game with a small ball called *harpaston*, from the verb *harpazein* ("to snatch away"). Perhaps one could call it "the game with the soft ball."[96]

Aporrhaxis. One should bounce the ball forcibly on the ground, dribbling continuously with one's hand; the number of bounces is counted.

(106) *Ourania*. The player bends himself back and throws the ball in the air. The goal for each of the other players is to catch it before it hits the ground, as Homer made clear in Phaeacia.[97] Whenever they bounced the ball against a wall, they counted the number of bounces. The loser was called "the donkey" and had to do anything that was commanded; the winner was "the king" and did the commanding.

(119) *Ephedrismos*. Setting up a stone at a distance, the players aim at it with balls or stones. The one who does not knock the stone over has to carry the one who does; the latter covers the eyes of the former, until he comes unerringly upon the stone [called a *dioros*].

---

[96] Athenaeus bk. 1, 15a–c quotes a passage from the fourth-century comic poet Antiphanes about the grace of a young man playing *phaininda* in the gymnasium.
[97] *Odyssey* 9.373. Homer portrays Nausicaa, the daughter of the king of Phaeacia, playing this type of game with her attendants (see **1c**).

44. Diogenes Laertius

The author of the Lives and Opinions of the Ancient Philosophers, *Diogenes Laertius is otherwise unknown. His work is usually placed in the third century* CE, *because he does not treat philosophers later than this. The material he presents will have been culled from earlier sources, but it will not necessarily be accurate.*

44a. *Lives and Opinions of the Ancient Philosophers* bk. 1.55: Solon on Athletic Emoluments

Solon was a late seventh–early sixth-century BCE *Athenian who instituted a series of legal reforms to address various issues of civic inequity. He was also a poet. Here Diogenes claims that Solon actually reduced the allowances paid to athletes for victories in crown games. If accurate, then it means that such emoluments were a very early feature of Athenian life, and already in tension with other necessary pensions, such as for those whose fathers had died in war. See also* **35l**. *Solon is a main character in* **38a**.

[Solon] also limited the honors paid to athletes in competitions, ordering for the Olympic victor five hundred drachmas, for the Isthmian victor one hundred drachmas, and scaled for the others. For it was inappropriate to increase the honor of these men, but only of those who had died in war, and the support and education of their sons at state expense.

44b. *Lives and Opinions the Ancient Philosophers* bk. 8.12: Meat Diets for Athletes

This is only a small note in his much larger treatment of Pythagoras, but it has been widely quoted in discussions of athletic diets. Given the fact that this information came from collections of random anecdotes, it is not likely to be accurate. On diet, see Philostratus, Gymnasticus **40a** *(44).*

[Pythagoras] is said to have been the first to prescribe a diet of meat for athletes, for Eurumenes, as Favorinus tells us in the third book of his *Memorabilia*. Before that athletes were trained on a diet of dried figs and soft cheese, and also on wheat-meal, as again we learn from Favorinus in the eighth book of his *Historical Miscellany*. Some say that Pythagoras was a trainer (*aleiptēs*) who fed them this diet, not the philosopher.

45. Heliodorus

Heliodorus of Emesa was the last of the five surviving novelists of Greek antiquity. Apart from the information he appends at the end of his novel, An Ethiopian Story *(Ethiopika) he is otherwise unknown. The novel is usually dated to the end of the third century CE. This complex romance of Charicleia and Theagenes ends with the couple, who have traveled from Delphi in Greece, captive of the king of the Ethiopians. Theagenes is destined for sacrifice to their gods, but before then is forced to engage in several contests of strength, culminating in a wrestling match. Theagenes, of course, wins, Charicleia is discovered to be the white daughter of the black Ethiopian king, and together Theagenes and Charicleia go on as the heirs apparent to the throne. The novel was extremely popular in later ages, influencing Cervantes as well as French painting. Apart from this passage, athletic contests are rare in the novelists; what follows resembles the boxing in Theocritus (**24**) and Apollonius (**25a**), where a monstrous barbarian is pitted against a noble Greek youth, who wins. It may be significant that Theagenes of Thasos (see **37q**, Pausanias 6.15.3, and **42a**) was the name of a famous boxer and pankratist.*

45a. *An Ethiopian Story* bk. 10.31.1, 3–32.2: Theagenes Wrestles with a Giant Ethiopian

(1) When [Theagenes] drew near to their meeting place, looking at him, Hydaspes [the Ethiopian king] said to him, speaking Greek: "Stranger, you must compete with this man; the people order it." "Let it happen," answered Theagenes, "but what kind of contest is it?" "Wrestling," said Hydaspes.

(3) Then taking up the dust, he poured it over shoulders and arms that were dripping with sweat from the bullfight. Then he shook off what did not stick to him, raised his outstretched arms, planted his feet firmly, flexed his knees, and hunched his shoulders and back; bending his neck a little and tensing his whole body, he took his stance for the holds of the pain-filled wrestling match. (4) The Ethiopian looked at him with a mocking smile, and with a sarcastic shake of his head he indicated his contempt for his opponent. Suddenly darting forward, he slammed his forearm into Theagenes' neck like a hammer; the sound of the blow echoed, and he moved back nonchalantly with a smirk. (5) But Theagenes was a man who from childhood had exercised and oiled up in the gymnasium, perfecting the art (*technē*) of combat presided over by Hermes. At first, since he had received proof of his opponent's power, he decided to retreat and swore to himself not to come to grips with such a monstrous bulk of a man in his fury, but by skill outmaneuver his untrained strength. (6) To be sure, although he was troubled only a little from the blow, he pretended that he was in great pain, and gave up the other side of his neck to be struck. When the Ethiopian immediately struck a blow, Theagenes gave way to the punch and pretended nearly to fall on his face.

(32.1) When he observed this, the Ethiopian in his confidence let his guard down as he closed for the third time; having raised his arm, he was about to bring it down when suddenly Theagenes bent down and came in unnoticed and avoided the rush. With his right hand he grabbed other's left arm and threw his opponent, who by the impetus of his own arm, as it descended into empty space [since Theagenes had moved], was forced to the ground. Theagenes came up under his armpit and straddled his back. (2) Grappling his opponent around his broad belly with difficulty, he then with his heel kicked at the opponent's ankles in turn until he had forced him to his knees. Then he straddled the Ethiopian, inserted his legs between his thighs; then his wrists, which were taking all his weight, he yanked out from under him. Holding his body clear of the ground, he wrapped his arms around his temples and pulled back his head and shoulders, and then slammed him to the ground on his belly.

46. Eusebius

46. *Chronica*, 1–47, 482–535: Famous Athletes

The early fourth-century CE bishop, Eusebius of Caesarea, has preserved our only complete Olympic victor list in his Chronica. *The actual list is discussed in Appendix BII; here we translate the opening on Olympic chronology, and the final section on famous athletes that was appended by Panodorus, an Alexandrian monk who revised Eusebius a generation later. The* Chronica *was translated into Armenian and Latin, but a Greek copy of the victor list survives in a medieval manuscript (Parisinus 2600). For the historical section, compare Pausanias* **37a**.

Now I think it makes sense to append to my account the Olympiads as recorded by the Greeks, since what happened in Greece seems to have been organized on the basis of these chronological writings. Events prior [to these lists] appear to have been recorded as each writer thought fit.

About the Foundation of the Olympic Games

(10) It is necessary to say a few things about the games, since those who push their foundation back to the earliest times say that they were founded before Heracles by one of the Idaean Dactyls. Then they were held by Aethlius as a trial for his sons. From him the contestants were called "athletes." (15) After him, his son Epeius held the games. Then Endymion, next Alexinus, and then Oenomaus celebrated the festival. After him Pelops celebrated the games in honor of his father Zeus. (20) Then came Heracles, the son of Alcmene and Zeus. There were ten generations from the time of Heracles, but some say three complete game cycles up to Iphitus' restoration of the games. For he was an Elean, and with foresight for Greece and wanting the cities to cease from wars, he sent ambassadors

from the whole Peloponnese for the purpose of learning about the cessation of persistent warfare.

[Lines 25–32 omitted.]

[On the basis of the god's prophecy] Iphitus announced a truce...(35) and Iphitus established the contests along with Lycurgus the Spartan, who happened to be his relative, for they were both descended from Heracles. At that time there was only the contest of the *stadion* [sprint], but later the other contests were added piecemeal. According to Aristodemus of Elis, the contestants began to be recorded after the twenty-seventh Olympiad [from the time of Iphitus], that is, whichever athletes were victors. (40) Before that time no one was recorded, since earlier generations neglected this. In the twenty-eighth Olympiad, Coroebus of Elis won the *stadion* and was the first to be recorded, and this Olympiad was established as the first.[98] The Greeks number dates from it. Polybius' history relates the same things that Aristodemus does. Callimachus says that there were thirteen unrecorded Olympiads from the time of Iphitus, (45) with the Olympiad in which Coroebus was victor the fourteenth. Many say that from the foundation of the contest by Heracles to the first numbered Olympiad was 459 years. The Eleans conduct the penteteric contest, there being four years between.

[Lines 49–677 contain Eusebius' list of stadion victors.]

(678) Up to this point we found the record of Olympic victors. Eusebius devised them, but other writers of chronologies and Dexippus the Athenian recorded the Olympiads in order and those victorious in them. Accordingly, Dexippus, in writing his chronological history up until the two hundred and sixty-second Olympiad [269 CE], says that Dionysius of Alexandria was victorious in that year. Since the list of Olympic victors above (685) has omitted many of the distinguished athletes, we shall mention a few out of the many.

Tithormus, who lived at the time of the athlete Milo, was not an athlete, but a cowherd. When Milo tested his strength and marveled at his superiority, he cried out, "This man is another Heracles." The saying comes from this. (See also **42a**.)

(690) **Glaucus the Carystian** was a boxer; his strength was irresistible. (See also **37q**, Pausanias 6.10.1–3 and **40a**, *Gymnasticus* 20.)

Cleomedes the Astypalaian, about whom there was a prophecy, "Cleomedes the Astypalaian is the last of the heroes," was an undefeated boxer, as was **Areius the Egyptian** (see **37q**, Pausanias 6.9.6–8).

Strato, the son of Corrhagus, won in wrestling at Olympia and also in *pankration*, and again in the next Olympiad. (695) He also won in Nemea, Delphi, and Isthmia (see **37q**, Pausanias 5.21.9–10 and **41b**).

---

[98] Established by Hippias of Elis as 776 BCE.

Euthymus the Locrian was a boxer; because of his bodily strength he was marveled at exceedingly (see **26d**, **37q**, Pausanias 6.6.4–10).

Eurydamas the Cyrenean, was a boxer. When an opponent knocked out his teeth, he won his match by swallowing them, so that his opponent would not realize it (see **41c**).

(700) **Dioxippus the Athenian** athlete made a demonstration to King Alexander of his unique strength; shedding his clothes, he took up a club; one of the nobles attacked him in full armor, threatening him with a spear. The naked man conquered him, answering the challenge.

(705) **Cleitomachus the Theban** was a marvelous boxer, unvanquished because of his strength; equally marvelous was the discipline of his training regimen. For he did not endure even the bare mention of sex; when talk of sex took place in a symposium or any other place, he got up and left. He did this so that by never being defeated by sexual urges, the peak of his strength would not waste away (see **28b** and **37q**, Pausanias 6.15.3–5).

(710) The long jump of **Phayllus the athlete from Croton** is said to have been 52 feet. He alone came from Italy to aid the Greeks against the Persians, having equipped a trireme at his own expense (see **35d**).

Melacomas the boxer was both the greatest and the most handsome, with whom even the Emperor (715) Titus, they say, was in love. He never harmed or struck anyone, but merely stood there; with his arms in the raised position he destroyed all of his opponents (see **34a–b**).

Aurelius Helix, an athlete who lived in the time of the Emperor Severus, so surpassed his opponents that he competed in wrestling as well as (720) *pankration* in Rome; for the Eleans, jealous of him, did not summon any wrestler to the stadium; and he won each, which no one else had done, in the Roman contests (see **40e**, 15.8).

As I pass over many athletes, I content myself with one, **Nicophon the Milesian**:

(725) The deep tendon of a bull, iron shoulders
of Atlas, and the holy hair and beard of Heracles,
and leonine glance of the Milesian giant
not even Olympian Zeus saw without a shiver,
when Nicophon was
(730) victorious in men's boxing at Olympia.

In the time of Theodosius the Great [379–95 CE] there was a wrestler from Philadelphia in Lydia whose name was **Philumenus**. He is said to have struck a bronze statue and to have forced the bronze to settle deep inside itself. Now on the statue there happened to be this epigram, the final line of which is:

(735) "Bronze is much weaker than my hand."

Metagenes of Thasos captured innumerable victories in boxing, for in strength he was irresistible.

Part II
Inscriptions

Inscriptions present a unique form of evidence for athletic activity in Ancient Greek culture: they allow insight into the material reality of athletic competition and how it converges and diverges from other written forms of evidence. Most inscriptional evidence for athletics pertains to some particular athletic achievement or victory, and the inscription was often written on or accompanied a dedicatory object, whether that object was a statue or another type of athletic instrument such as a strigil or jumping weights, but sometimes the inscription on a plaque or stela was the object of dedication itself. On the one hand, victory inscriptions commemorate the athlete, along with his or her family and city. At the same time, these commemorations also functioned in a manner similar to other objects of religious dedication meant to praise a particular deity or show thanks for benefits received. Another important type of inscription erected by communities provides information on rules, regulations, and prizes for athletic activity. The number of inscriptions pertaining to athletics is vast, and those presented here are meant simply to be a representative sample. The inscriptions are organized chronologically by place, with a focus on Olympia and Delphi, where the number of inscriptions is greatest, and we have also included the two most well-documented cities of Greece, Athens and Sparta, along with select inscriptions from around the Mediterranean.

Sourcebook of Ancient Greek Athletics. Charles H. Stocking and Susan A. Stephens, Oxford University Press (2021).
© Charles H. Stocking and Susan A. Stephens. DOI: 10.1093/oso/9780198839606.011.0002

5   Inscriptions

1. Olympia

Olympia presents one of the earliest locations in Greece for formal athletic competition and also for inscriptional evidence about these competitions. As the venue of Olympia increased in popularity and expanded in physical size from the eighth to the fourth centuries BCE, so did the number of inscriptions and dedicatory objects (see Pausanias 37). Beyond victory dedications, Olympia also provides occasion for some of the earliest inscribed rules and regulations pertaining to athletic activity. While the inscriptional evidence from Olympia is vast, the following items offer a select sample with unique historical and cultural significance.

I1a. Rock of Bybon, mid-sixth century (*IvO* 717)

A large rock weighing 315.7 lbs. was discovered southeast of the Pelopion. On it is an inscription written in boustrophedon style (where lines are written in opposite directions) stating that it was lifted with one hand by a man named Bybon (see Figure 9). On the bottom of the rock are well worn grooves, most likely caused by handling the rock. Although "weightlifting" was not an Olympic contest, this artifact provides some of our best evidence that feats of strength were performed at the site.

Bybon, son of Phorys, lifted me over his head with one hand.

I1b. Wrestling Regulation, 525–500 BCE (*SEG* 48.541)

This fragmentary bronze tablet provides some of our earliest evidence for regulations in athletic competition at Olympia, with explicit instructions against finger breaking, as well as regulations on the extent of punishment. Despite this rule, Pausanias tells us of an Olympic victor (c.456 and 452 BCE), Leontiscus of Messene, who seems to have used finger breaking as a means to secure victory nevertheless; see 37q (6.4.3).

> The wrestler should not break a finger [
> the referee (*diaitētēr*) should strike, except at the head [
> wrongdoers shall be brought in and promise [
> [in] the Olympic Games and as one who is worthy of victory both in this [
> (5)   neither an ally nor a woman; if he knowingly goes [
> an Elean man and the allies, neither a deceitful man (?) [

Sourcebook of Ancient Greek Athletics. Charles H. Stocking and Susan A. Stephens, Oxford University Press (2021).
© Charles H. Stocking and Susan A. Stephens. DOI: 10.1093/oso/9780198839606.003.0006

Figure 9. Rock of Bybon, Archaic period, weight 143.5 kg (315 lbs.). Museum of the History of the Olympic Games, no. Λ 191. Photo courtesy of Charles Stocking

Figure 10. Hieron's dedication of a helmet, *c.*474 BCE, British Museum no. 1823, 0610.1

he would pay (?) drachmas as a fine, whether he does harm or [
but with foreign money an envoy should not [

I1c. Dedicated Strigil with Inscription, *c.*500 BCE (*CEG* 387)

A large strigil (an instrument used for scraping sweat) was discovered at Olympia with an inscription explaining that this was given as a gift to Zeus, presumably as a victory dedication (although it need not be). The dedicator explains that he himself made the strigil, and he proclaims his own technical skill or knowledge (sophia). This inscription presents one of the earlier uses of the term, specifically in relationship to physical craft; only later, in the Classical period and beyond, does it take on the more abstract sense predominantly associated with philosophy. See 22 (Plato), 39 (Galen), and 40a (Philostratus) for further correlations between sophia, sport, and technical craft.

Dikon dedicated this as a gift to Zeus from his work, having made it himself. He has skill (*sophia*).

I1d. Tellon Inscription, *c.*472 BCE (*CEG* 381)

This inscription comes from a marble statue base for a victory dedication by Tellon. The statue and base were also described by Pausanias, 37q (6.10.9). The inscription is unique for its inclusion of both regional and civic identity (Arcadian from Oresthasion) and the fact that the dedicator felt the need to mark out both.

Tellon, son of Daemon, dedicated this [statue], a boxer, an Arcadian from Oresthasion,
As a boy…

I1e. Deinomenid Inscription, Helmet, Olympia, *c.*474 BCE (*SEG* 23.253)

This inscribed helmet was dedicated as war spoils by the Syracusan tyrant, Hieron after the battle of Cumae, waged between the combined navies of Syracuse and Cumae against the Etruscans (see Figure 10). The inscription is nearly identical to those of two other helmets dedicated at Olympia. As a Sicilian, Hieron was especially concerned with demonstrating his participation in and identity with Greek culture. He did this not only through athletic participation and dedication at Olympia (see 2a and 3a), but he also sought to portray his activities in war as a distinctly Greek achievement through this type of dedication at Olympia.

Hieron, son of Deinomenes, and the Syracusans, [dedicated] to Zeus Etruscan [spoils] from Cumae.

11f. Euthymus of Locri, c.472 BCE (*CEG 399*)

This dedication by the boxer Euthymus of Locri was found on a marble statue base at Olympia. He was a well-known and very successful athlete in antiquity who received cult worship as a hero (see **26d, 37q** *(6.6.4-7.1) and Appendix AI).*

Euthymus of Locri, son of Astycles, won three times at Olympia.
He dedicated this image for mortals to look upon.
Euthymus from Epizephyrian Locri dedicated it.
Pythagoras from Samos made it.

11g. Ergoteles Inscription, 466 BCE (*CEG 393*).

This inscription was found on a bronze plaque excavated at Olympia. The dedication was made by Ergoteles, a distance runner with a complicated political biography. The inscription lists his various victories in the Panhellenic contests and states that his dedication is meant to memorialize the city of Himera, an important ancient Greek city in Sicily. His victory in the distance race at Olympia was also commemorated by a victory poem from Pindar (see **2e**)*, who explains that Ergoteles is, in fact, an exile from his native city of Cnossus on Crete, as a result of civil strife (stasis). Pausanias,* **37q** *(6.4.11), later described Ergoteles' victory dedication and further commented on the justified absence of Cnossus from his dedication.*

Ergoteles dedicated me…
Having won against the Greeks in the Pythian Games…
and twice at the Olympic Games, and…
an immortal monument for Himera.

11h. Cyniscus of Mantinea, c.460 BCE (*CEG 383*)

This inscription runs counterclockwise around the feet of a statue on a marble base. The dedicator Cyniscus is mentioned by Pausanias **37q** *(6.4.11) as a boxer in the boys' age division, and he further notes that the statue is made by Polyclitus, one of the most famous sculptors in Greek history, known for his ability to emphasize proportion and symmetry in the representation of the body.*

Cyniscus the boxer from famous Mantinea dedicated this [statue]
after his victory, he who has the name of his father.

11i. Cynisca of Sparta, *c.*390–380 BCE (*CEG* 820)

*Cynisca is famous for having been the first woman to have won a victory in the ancient Olympics, even though women seem to have been barred from attending the Olympic festival in antiquity. She won in the chariot race in c.396 and probably again in 392 BCE. She was able to win because it was the owner of the chariot team who was declared victor. The story of Cynisca is told by Xenophon **10a**, Plutarch **35a**, and Pausanias **37x** (3.8.1–5). According to the last, the bronze dedication for Cynica's first Olympic victory depicted her standing with her winning chariot team (see Figure 11). Cynisca's victory in turn paved the way for subsequent female victors in the hippic events. For the political ramifications of the inscription, see Dillery (2019).*

Kings of Sparta are my fathers and brothers.
Cynisca, victorious with my chariot of swift-footed horses and
having erected this image, I declare that I alone of women
throughout all of Greece took the crown.
Apelleas son of Callicles made it.

11j. Statue Base of an Unknown Olympic Victor in the Race in Armor, *c.*350–300 BCE (*NIvO* 25)

Stand and glory in the excellence (*aretē*) of his feet
for twice he took away the prize (*aethlon*) in the grove of Olympian Zeus
while holding up his thick bronze shield.
First…among all…
And he was crowned at the festival of Pallas Athena.
Twice he has obtained glory (*kleos*) at the foot of Parnassus [Delphi]
and in the *diaulos* and the armor carry he obtained the goal of first prize.
Not in vain…did he wash his light feet with divine water of Castalia [at Delphi].

11k. Deinosthenes of Sparta, *Stadion* Victor, *c.*316 BCE (*IvO 171*)

This unique victory dedication for Deinosthenes, a stadion *victor, marks the total distance from Sparta to Olympia. The dedication may imply, therefore, that Deinosthenes was a messenger or "day-runner" (hēmerodromos). See further Pausanias **37q** (6.16.8).*

Deinosthenes, the Spartan, son of Deinosthenes,
dedicated this to Olympian Zeus,
after winning the *stadion*.
From this stele to Sparta is six hundred and sixty (*stadia*)
from there to the first stele is thirty *stadia*.

Figure 11. Statue base of Cynisca of Sparta with inscription, *c.*390–380 BCE, Museum of the History of the Olympic Games, no. Λ 529

Figure 12. Daochus dedication, *c.*337 BCE, Delphi Archaeological Museum

11l. Philippus of Arcadia, *c.* 300 BCE (*CEG* 827)

Note in this inscription the connection between one of the mythical originators of boxing and Philippus' victory.

Standing on the Alpheus, Pelasgus once revealed
the custom of boxing with hands to Polydeuces,
where he was announced as victor.
And once again glory (*kleos*) came back to beautiful Arcadia,
honoring Philippus, who laid low with straight fighting
four boys from the islands.

11m. Zanes Inscription, early fourth century BCE (*IvO* 637)

*The Zanes were statues dedicated to Zeus from the fines levied against those found cheating (see Pausanias **37m** and Appendix BIII). The statue bases remain where Pausanias described them. Although we no longer have the didactic inscriptions, Pausanias' observation that "Two of these images are the work of Cleon of Sicyon" (5.21.3) is confirmed by this material record from one of the inscriptions.*

Cleon of Sicyon made it.

11n. Arsinoë II, mid-third century BCE (*IvO* 307)

*Arsinoë II, daughter of Ptolemy I and Berenice I, was the first to win all three chariot victories in the same Olympics: the two- and four-horse chariot races as well as the four-horse race for colts. Her victory is mentioned in conjunction with the long line of victories for the Ptolemies in Posidippus' epigrams for hippic victories (see **27l**). Callicrates of Samos, who made this dedication, was the commander of the Ptolemaic navy and also a victor in the Pythian chariot race for colts sometime after 270 BCE. The dedication made by Callicrates involved two columns with statues of Ptolemy II and Arsinoë II (see **27k**).*

Callicrates the Samian, son of Boescus,
dedicated this to Olympian Zeus
for queen Arsinoë,
daughter of King Ptolemy and Queen Berenice.

11o. Diogenes of Ephesus, *c.*69 BCE (*IvO* 232)

This inscription is part of a dedication for a series of victories in trumpet contests at Olympia and elsewhere under an expanded program of games that were first initiated by the Ptolemies and continued into the Roman era. The contests for both trumpeters and heralds were introduced perhaps around 396 BCE.

Diogenes of Ephesus, son of Dionysius,
who won the trumpeting contest at Olympia five times,
twice at the Pythian Games, three times at Isthmia,
three times at Nemea, twice at the Asian Common Games,
twice at Neapolis, at the Heraean Games at Argos,
and at eighty other sacred and crown contests,
he [dedicates this] to Olympian Zeus.

11p. Olympic Officials, *c.*28 BCE (*IvO* 64)

This inscription is one of many that list the officials for the sanctuary at Olympia, and it gives a good indication of the various activities and agents involved in the sanctuary, not just during the athletic festival, but throughout the year.

Sacred to Zeus
The administrators for the 189th Olympiad
Priests:
      Eudamus, son of Euthymenes,
      Sophon, son of Lycus,
      Aphrodisius, son of Euporus.
Libation bearers/heralds (*spondophoroi*):
      Antiachus, son of Antiachus,
      Heraclides, son of Heraclides,
      Lycidas, son of Lycidas.
Prophets:
      Callitus Clytiad, son of Antias,
      Pausanias Iamid, son of Diogenes,
Keyholders:
      Arcesus, son of Harmodius,
      Callias, son of Pausanias
      Hippias, son of Carops
      Moschion, son of Dameas
      Pausanias, son of Diogenes
Flute player:
      Aristarchus, son of Aristocles

Guide:

> Polychares, son of Aristcrates

Daily sacrificer:

> Zopyrus, son of Olympiachus

Registrar:

> Heraclides, son of Heraclides

Wine pourer:

> Alexas, son of Sophron

Libation dancer:

> Epictetus, son of Heraclides
>
> Hilarus, son of Antiochus
>
> Epictetus, son of Aphrodisius

Woodman:

> Euthymus. son of Sotion

Master of the house and butcher:

> Alexas, son of Lycus

I1q. Is-Olympic Games, 2 BCE (*IvO* 56.11–28)

In the Hellenistic period new games were instituted throughout the Mediterranean that were intended to have a cultural symbolic value equivalent to the original crown games and were therefore referred to as "Is-Olympic" Games and "Iso-Pythian Games." This strategy was continued in the Roman period. The Is-Olympic Games discussed here were those instated in Naples by the Roman emperor Augustus. Rules for the Is-Olympic Games in Italy were set up in Olympia as a symbolic gesture of the connection between the two regions.

No one younger than 17 years is permitted to take part in the Italian Is-Olympic Games. Those aged 17 to 20 years are to compete in the boys' category, and those who are older in the men's category. Concerning prizes: they are to be given to victors…An *opsōnion* is to be distributed to the athletes thirty days before the festival so that all who are competing should each be given a drachma each day, beginning thirty days before the festival. From the fifteenth day on, two and half drachmas should be given to the boys, and three drachmas to the men. In accordance with the decree of Caesar, honors are to be to everyone…a crown, but to the men one of wheat. There will be a proclamation of the crown…The crowns for any contests which either have no competitors or which result in a tie are to be dedicated by the organizer of the games in the gymnasium in Naples, and may they be inscribed with the contest for which each had been the prize. Whichever athletes wish to sign up for the Italian Games in Naples, let them appear in Naples no less than thirty days before the festival. And they should register before the organizers of the games with their patronym and their fatherland and what competition they choose. Let the athletes go to the gymnasium … It is necessary that each athlete be registered by the name he uses, whether by reference to his father or however it is established by law. If not, let him be fined by the organizer of the games, and if he does not pay the fine, let him be whipped. If anyone is later than the established time, let him announce the reason for his lateness to the organizers of the games—let the reasons be illness or pirates or shipwreck. If anyone wishes to make an accusation … if he is guilty, let him be barred from the games by the organizers.

11r. P. Cornelius Ariston, c. 49 CE (*IvO* 225)

This lengthy and elaborate epigram was a dedication for a boy victor in the pankration.

P. Cornelius Ariston son of Irenaeus, Ephesian,
(5)   a boy pankratist, having won in the 207th Olympiad,
      this boy, at the height of his youth, has the strength of a man,
      this boy, in whom beauty and strength are seen.
      Where are you from, and from whom [were you born]? Tell me.
      Against what enemies did you increase your victories,
      when you stood before the proponents of Zeus?
(10)   Irenaeus is my father, stranger; my name is Ariston;
      My fatherland, Ionic on both sides, is Ephesus.
      I was crowned at Olympia without drawing a bye in the boys' *pankration*
      after struggling in the dust for three contests against opponents.
      I will be announced throughout all of Asia. I am Ariston,
(15)   the one crowned with wild olive in the *pankration*,
      whom Greece spoke of fully, when she saw me at the height of my youth,
      having demonstrated the excellence of men with my hands.
      For my crown was not by a lucky lot, but without a bye
      I was received warmly by Zeus and the Alpheus.
(20)   And I did not rest in seven bouts of wrestling in the boys' group,
      but ever engaged, I was crowned in all.
      For I bring glory with immortal ribbons
      to my father Irenaeus and to my fatherland Ephesus.

11s. Nero, c. 68 CE (*IvO* 287)

The Roman emperor Nero notoriously postponed the Olympic Games in order that he might also participate, and he created both a music contest and unprecedented new horse races, in which he crowned himself victor, although he fell from his chariot (on which, see Suetonius Nero 23–4). Despite

Nero's own efforts, his self-imposed popularity seems short lived, as indicated by this inscription in which Nero's name is carefully erased.

> …] from the…of Caesar [[Nero]]
> …Dio]nysios to Olympian Zeus…

I1t. Tiberius Claudius Rufus, during the reign of Trajan (*IvO 54*)

This inscription is a rare dedicatory offering that was not made for a victorious athlete. Rufus was honored for his endurance when a match came to a draw after he competed with an opponent until nightfall. The inscription provides an account of how and why such a dedication for a non-victor existed at all.

> The decree of the Eleans.
> Marcus Betilenus Laetus revealed to me
> that Tiberius Claudius Rufus, a pankratist,
> (5)   having come to the Olympic contest, resided with all decorum in the city,
> with the result that he was judged fitting for every commendation among all in
> his temperance both by common consent and individually.

(10) Rufus gave care to his exercises in sight of the *Hellanodikai* according to the inherited custom of the contests, and since it was clear there was hope of obtaining a sacred crown for himself, and because he entered into the stadium worthy of Olympian Zeus, and when the combat was established and his undertaking against all, (15) he competed greatly and in a way to be marveled at, since he was worthy. For he thought that the Olympic crown would be placed upon him, and he conquered all without a bye, having obtained lots against the most respectable men. (20) He entered into such a state of excellence and positive spirit that when he was competing for the crown and he obtained a lot against a better man, he was thought to be competing for his soul rather than for hope of the crown. And he fought until nightfall, until the stars came out, (25) and he endured until the end. And because of the hope of victory, he was urged to fight to the utmost, so that he was marveled at in the most sacred contest of Olympia by our citizens and by those of the administration gathered to watch. (30) For these reasons, Laetus said that Rufus requires honor and that a vote should be made for him who has increased and decorated the contest at Olympia so much. And he proposed giving him a statue at Olympia with (35) an inscription with an account of the other contests and a demonstration of the offering which he alone among his age-mates made. And this seemed best to those in charge and all the people, to praise Laetus (40) for his proposal, and that Rufus be honored by the citizen body, and to set up a statue with an inscription set forth.

I1u. Death of an Athlete, second century CE (*BCH* 88: 186–7)

*Death was a known and perhaps not too uncommon danger for those competing in Greek athletics, especially the combat sports. This inscription commemorates Agathus Daemon, who died at Olympia in the boxing match. We are not told whether he won or lost. Such tales of death in athletic achievement can be found throughout the history of ancient Greek athletics, but especially in the Roman Imperial period, with accounts of Melancomas in Dio Chrysostom (see **34a** and **34b**) and the story of Arrhichion (see **37z, 40a** (21), **40d**).*

Agathus Daemon, named "the Camel" from Alexandria, a victor at Nemea. He died here, boxing in the stadium, having prayed to Zeus for victory or death. Age 35. Farewell.

2. Delphi

According to tradition, the Pythian Games at Delphi began sometime at the end of the sixth century (c.586 BCE). Unlike the sanctuary at Olympia, which was involved with athletic competition from an early date, Delphi was already a well-known Panhellenic sanctuary because of its oracle, well before the athletic competitions were instituted. As a result, athletic dedications and inscriptions at Delphi can be seen as an extension of the dedicatory activities already practiced at Delphi designed to showcase the status, wealth, and successes of individuals and cities to the larger Greek and Roman worlds.

I2a. Polyzalos Inscription, c.478 BCE (*CEG* 397)

This statue base belongs to the famous bronze charioteer discovered at Delphi (see Figure 26, p. 402). The inscription is written in hexameter verse. The underwritten text, which was erased has posed problems of interpretation for the dedication and its historical context. It is generally assumed that the dedication is meant to commemorate an unattested chariot victory in either 478 or 474 BCE for Polyzalos, who was a son of Deinomenes, and brother to the famous Sicilian tyrant Hieron, who also won a chariot victory at the Pythian Games in 470 BCE. In order to explain the erasure, it is believed that Polyzalos originally made the dedication while including the title "lord of Gela," but that this title was erased (perhaps by Hieron) because Polyzalos never held an official ruling title over Gela. For Hieron was ruler over Gela, while their brother Gelon was tyrant of Syracuse (485/484–478 BCE), but when Gelon died, Hieron became tyrant of Syracuse, and presumably retained power over Gela, while Polyzalos may have had an unofficial position of authority in Gela. Hence, the erasure seems to speak to interfamilial politics among the sons of Deinomenes. Thus, much like Hieron's patronage of Pindar and his victory dedications, the dedication and inscription for the bronze charioteer demonstrate the intimate ways in which athletics and politics are entangled and represented at Panhellenic sanctuaries.

Polyzalos dedicated me,
the son of Deinomenes; exalt him, famous Apollo.

Under the first line of text is the line that has been erased:

…dedicated me as lord of Gela.

12b. Theogenes (or Theagenes) of Thasos, 370–365 BCE (*SIG³* 36A)

One of the most famous and successful of all ancient athletes, he won not only in boxing and pankration, *but also in the* dolichos. *Because of the powers associated with one of his statues, Theogenes received cult worship as a hero after his death. See further Pausanias* **37q** *(6.6.5–6, 6.11.2–9, 6.15.3),* **42a**, *as well as Appendix AI.*

…son of Timoxenus, you have the greatest praise for toughness (*karteria*) from the Greeks. For no man was crowned so often winning in boxing and the *pankration*. And in the Pythian Games you received three crowns, one without competition (*akoniti*). No other mortal accomplished this…nine victories in the Isthmian Games, and twice the herald shouted for you alone in the circle of men as victor in boxing and the *pankration*. And nine times [did you win] at Nemea, Theogenes. And you won 1,300 private victories, and I declare that you were not defeated in boxing in twenty-two years. Theogenes, son of Timaxenos, from Thasos, won the following:

Olympia—boxing
Olympia—*pankration*
Pythia—boxing
Pythia—boxing
Pythia—boxing without competition (*akoniti*)
Isthmia—boxing
Isthmia—boxing
Isthmia—boxing
Isthmia—boxing
Isthmia—boxing
Isthmia—boxing
Isthmia—boxing
Isthmia—boxing
Isthmia—boxing and *pankration* in the same contest
Nemea—boxing
Nemea—boxing
Nemea—boxing

Nemea—boxing
Nemea—boxing
Nemea—boxing
Nemea—boxing
Nemea—boxing
Nemea—boxing
Hekatombaia[1]
dolichos
in Argos

12c. Daochus Dedication, *c.*337–332 BCE (*Delph.* III 4.460)

Daochos was a member of the Amphictyonic League who dedicated a group of statues of his ancestors who had previously won victories in the four sacred crown games. The statues held an important position overlooking the temple of Apollo. The statues of these victors were not erected in their lifetimes, but about 150 years after their victories, Daochus honored their memory with this dedication (see Figure 12). They also served to increase his own prestige.

Pharsalius, first you won the *pankration* at Olympia.
Agias, son of Acnonius, from the Thessalian land,
five times [you won] in Nemea, three times at the Pythian Games,
five times at Isthmia—no one ever erected a victory trophy
for your hands.
And I was this man's brother (*homadelphos*),
and I carried away the same number of crowns
on the same day, victorious in wrestling…
I killed the strongest man, though I did not wish to,
my name is Telemachus.
Those men had equal prize-winning strength. And I
Agelaus, was a relative of both of them.
And I won in the *stadion* in the boys' age group in Pythia.
We alone of mortals have these crowns.
I am Daochus Agias, my fatherland is Pharsalus,
ruling all of Thessaly not by force but by law
for twenty-seven years,
and Thessaly was filled with glorious peace and wealth
and Pallas did not lie to you in sleep, Sisyphus son of Daochus.

---

[1] The Hekatombaia was a New Year's festival in honor of Hera. The term *hecatomb* refers to a sacrifice of one hundred oxen, which also took place at this festival.

What she said clearly was a promise she made.
From the first time you put the armor around your skin,
you neither ran from your enemies nor suffered any wound.
After augmenting the excellence of his household ancestors,
he [Daochus] set up these gifts to Phoebus, honoring family and fatherland.
Daochus made use of the honored gift,
Tetrarch of Thessaly, representative of the Amphictyonic League.
Sisyphus, son of Daochus.

12d. Archon, Chariot Victory, c.321 BCE (*SEG* 18.222)

Archon was an officer of Alexander the Great and a governor of Babylonia after Alexander the Great's death. This inscription commemorates his victories at the Isthmian and Pythian Games.

Blessed Archon, twice you have received the wreath of fair glory,
when you won in horsemanship at the Isthmian and Pythian Games.
Cleinus is envied because of his famous son
and Pella, the fatherland will receive a glory that is forever remembered.

12e. Organization of Pythian Games, c.246 BCE (*CID* 2.139)

This inscription provides a list of payments to individual contractors for various tasks needed to prepare the site for the Pythian Games. The heading gives the date by naming the ruling official and the members of the Amphictyony who were responsible for hiring contractors.

In the archonship of Dio in Delphi and the Amphictyonic representatives: Aeacidas, Nicanor, Nicias, Agemachus, Lycopus?, Alcidamus, Pantaenetus, Dio, Polyclitus from the Aetolians; Gannon from the Chians; Echecratidas and Nicaidas from Delphi; Euptolemus and Lanicus from the Boeotians; Archidamus from the Phocians.

(5) These men have been awarded the work for the Pythia.

Agazalus: for hoeing and leveling the covered practice track (*xystos*) and the peristyle: 18 staters, 1 drachma; for hoeing and leveling the open-air practice track (*paradromis*): 16 staters, 1 drachma; for 270 measures of white earth for the *xystos*, at 1¾ obol per measure, total 43 staters, ½ obol.

Critolaus: for fencing [...]: 37 staters.

(10) Olympichus: for maintenance of the *xystos* and the *paradromis* and the ballcourt (*sphairistērion*) and the gymnasium: 36 staters.

[Cr]itolaus: for [repairs] to the drain alongside of the Demeter shrine: 20 staters, 1 drachma, 2 obols.

Soch[ares]: for the furnishing of six hoes: [?].

Eucharus: for roping off the peristyle: 1 stater, 1 drachma.

(15) Cleon: for repairs to the wall of the ballcourt: 30 staters.

Asandros: for sifting the arena: 5 staters.

Euthydamus: for the hoeing and the leveling of the ballcourt and to make [?]; for 201 measures of black earth on the ballcourt, at 1 obol per measure: total 16 staters, 1 drachma, 3 obols

Cleon: for repairs to the wall by the shrine of Demeter: 29 staters, ? drachmas.

(20) Pasion: for plastering the disrobing room (*apodytērion*) and the wall by the shrine of Demeter: 8 staters.

Lyson: 15 measures of white earth for plastering the *apodyterion* and the wall at ¾ obol per measure: 2 staters, 2¼ obols.

Smyrnaeus: for cleaning out the Pythian stadium and repairing the surroundings: 10 staters, 1 drachma; for hoeing the Pythian stadium and hoeing and leveling the jumping pits: 110 staters.

(25) Nikon: for construction of the Odeum: 44 staters, 1 drachma, 3 obols.

Xenon: for 600 measures of white earth for the Pythian stadium at 1⅔ obols per measure: total: 33 staters, 4 obols.

Melission: for a pedestal in the Pythian theater: 28 staters.

Euthydamus: for fencing the Pythian stadium: 10 staters.

Nikon: for setting up the proscenium in the Pythian stadium: 10 staters; for the platform in the Pythian stadium, at [?] per foot for [?] feet: [?] 6 staters.

(30) Euthydamus: for construction of the vaulted entrance in the Pythian stadium: 20 staters.

Smyrnaeus: for cleaning out the [?]: 8 staters.

Anaxagoras: for construction of the 36 turning posts (*kamptēres*): 12 staters.

Agazalos: for the ? by the pentathletes: 9 staters:...

Damastratus: [?] for the boxers: 77 staters, 1 drachma.

(35) Melission: for repair to the [?] in the vaulted entrance: 1 stater, 1 drachma.

[?]: for cleaning out the hippodrome: [?].

Dionysius: for hoeing around the turning posts (*kamptēres*) in the hippodrome: [?].

Euthydamus: for [hoeing?] around the turning posts (*kamptēres*) in the hippodrome: [?]

Callōn: for furnishing [?] in the hippodrome: 89 staters.

Diōn: the [?] in the hippodrome: 38 staters; for the [?] of the houses: 24 staters.

(40) Pleistus: for the prizes (*brabeia*): an Aeginetan mina [= 100 drachmas].

Euthydamus: for plating the [?] with bronze: 9 staters, 3 obols.

Cleon: for cleaning out and fencing the Castalian [spring] with the Gorgon's head spout: 9 staters.

Agazalos:...for cleaning out the forge [?]...

12f. Honorary Inscriptions for Athletic Trainers, Imperial period (*Delph.* III 1.200)

Athletic training was a vital aspect of preparation for sport. In the Roman Imperial period, the importance and social standing of the athletic trainer was such that he could receive public honors in much the same way as athletes. In the examples provided, two athletic trainers are made citizens and council members for Delphi.

Good Fortune
P. Fla. Claudianus...Ephesian and Elean...
citizen and council member...
the Delphians made the *paidotribēs*
a Delphic citizen and council member,
by the vote of the council.
Good Fortune
The Delphians [decree that] the *gymnastēs* Lucius Itollenus Apolaustus, a Zmyrnean,
on account of his beauty and nobility (*kalokagathia*), and his habit of life, [and
consider] that he is fit for citizenship and council among them.

12g. Female Victors in Pythian Games, *c.*47 CE (*SIG³* 802)

This dedication was made by Hermesianax, son of Dionysus, from Tralles on behalf of his daughters, who won multiple athletic victories in the sacred crown games. The inscription provides important evidence that women's categories of competition were included in these games, perhaps beginning in the Hellenistic period.

Hermesianax, son of Dionysius, of Caeserea in Tralles, he, [as both Athenian and Delphian honors] his daughters, who themselves have the same [citizenship].

Tryphosa won at the Pythian Games organized by Antigonus and Cleomachis, at the Isthmian Games organized by Juventius Proclus, each time in the *stadion*, first in the maiden division.

Hedea won at the Isthmian Games organized by Cornelius Pulcher the chariot race in armor and she won the *stadion* at the Nemean Games organized by Antigonus, and also at the games in Sicyon organized by Menoites. She also won the *kithara* singing in the boys' category at the Sebasteia in Athens organized by Nuvius, son of Philinus; she was first in her age group...as a maiden.

Dionysia won the *stadion* at [the Isthmian Games] organized by Antigonus, and in the Asclepian Games at the sanctuary of Epidaurus organized by Nicoteles.

To Pythian Apollo

The city of the Delphians [honors] Hermesianax, son of Dionysius, of Caesarea in Tralles, and his daughters, on account of their excellence and their piety toward the god.

3. Sparta

*Despite objections to athletic competition voiced by the Spartan poet Tyrtaeus (see **4**), athletics was a major focus of Archaic and Classical Spartan society. The level and involvement of Spartan participation in both local and Panhellenic contests is well attested by the epigraphic and archaeological evidence. There is some debate as to whether Spartan involvement in competition declined sometime around the mid-sixth century, on the basis of a decline in the recorded numbers from Olympic victor lists. Such declines, however, could be explained by the expanded number of participants from beyond the Peloponnese as well as the expanded circuit of Panhellenic competitions.*

During the late Classical period, Sparta seems to have undergone a dramatic crisis and significant reduction in manpower and territory. This loss in political and military power gave way to a type of renaissance for Spartan culture in the Hellenistic period and culminated in the Roman Imperial period. This resurgence in Spartan cultural activity has been dubbed the "Spartan Mirage", indicating efforts on behalf of the Spartans to revitalize their earlier institutions and solidify their former reputation for war and training. Two indications of this cultural resurgence were the development of new international athletic contests, including the Ourania and Eurycleia festivals (as indicated in the inscriptions below) as well as a significant increase in evidence for the Spartan educational program known as the agōgē, *which included the rites of Artemis Orthia, discussed in two inscriptions below. The following are some of the main examples of inscriptions pertaining to Spartan athletics.*

13a. Aeglatas Stele, Found near the Leonidaeum, *c.* 500 BCE (*CEG 374*)

This inscription on a marble slab records two victories of Aeglatas: the makros *may have been a distance race that involved a torch relay while the* dolichos *was presumably the same as that practiced at Olympia. The victory stele is dedicated to Apollo Carneius, for whom the athletic festival of the Carneia was held in Sparta.*

Aeglatas dedicated this object to Carneius, after winning five times in the *makros*, and added..., and having won three times in the *dolichos* at the Athenaea...

13b. Damonon Stele. *c.* 400 BCE (Christesen 2018)

This dedicatory marble slab records the victories of two Spartans, Damonon and Enymacratidas, who won hippic contests and foot races at nine different local festivals. This dedication records a particularly unique hippic event using mares only, the kalpē, *in which the rider dismounted from the mare and finished the race by running beside the mare. For further discussion of the* kalpē, *see Appendix CIV.*

> Damonon dedicated [this] to Athena Poliachos, after he won victories,
> in a way that no one of the present era has ever accomplished.

He won the following contests with his own four-horse chariot,
and he himself held the reins:

(5)   He won four times in the contest for the Earth Holder [= Poseidon]
and four times in the Athenaea,
and four times in the Eleusinian Games,
and he won in the single-horse race in the Poseidonia Games at Helos,
holding the reins himself,

(10)   and he won in the *kalpē* from horses
[bred] from his own mares and stallion.
and he won the Poseidonia Games at Thouria eight times
in the *kalpē*, holding the reins himself,
from horses [bred] from his own mares and stallion,

(15)   and he won in the single-horse race then as well.
And Damonon won at the Eleusinian Games
in the *kalpē* four times, holding the reins himself.
Enymacratidas won the following victories,
first in the boys' *dolichos* at the Lithesia Games,

(20)   and he won on that same day with his racehorse.
And in the youth age group, Enymacratidas won the *dolichos* in the Ariontia Games
and he won with his racehorse on the same day.
At the Parparonia Games, Enymacratidas won the boys' *stadion*, *diaulos*, and
    dolichos,
and he won with his racehorse on the same day.

(25)   And as a boy, Damonon won the *stadion* and the *diaulos*,
entering the games of the Earth Holder.
And as a boy, Damonon won the *stadion* and the *diaulos*,
entering the Lithesia Games.
And as a boy, Damonon won the *stadion* and the *diaulos*,

(30)   entering the Malateia Games.
And as a boy, Damonon won the *stadion* and the *diaulos*,
entering the Lithesia Games.
And as a boy, Damonon won the *stadion* and *diaulos*,
entering the Parparonia Games.
(35) And at the Athenaea, [he won] the *stadion*.
In the ephorate of Echemenes,
Damonon won the following:
the *kalpē* at the Athenaea, while he held the reins,
and he won with his racehorse on the same day.

(40)   And his son won the *stadion* on the same occasions.
In the ephorate of Euippus,

Damonon won the following:
the *kalpē* at the Athenaea, while he held the reins,
and he won with his racehorse on the same day.

(45)   And his son won the *stadion* on the same occasion.
In the ephorate of Aristeus,
Damonon won the following:
the *kalpē* in the games of the Earth Holder,
while he held the reins,

(50)   and he won with his racehorse on the same day.
And his son won the *stadion*, the *diaulos*, and *dolichos*
on the same occasion in a single day.
In the ephorate of Echemenes,
Damonon won the following:

(55)   the *kalpē* in the games of the Earth Holder,
while he held the reins,
and his son won the *stadion* and…

[the text breaks off]

13c. Ourania Festival, *c.*97 CE (*IG* V, 1 667)

This inscription on the refounding of the Ourania festival c.97 CE offers an example of how early Spartan practices pertaining to religion and sport were revived and/or reinvented in the Roman Imperial period. The Ourania festival was held in honor of Zeus Ouranios, and the priesthoods for the festival were originally reserved for former Spartan kings by hereditary right. After the end of dual kingship in Sparta, the festival was revived under Nerva and was intended to honor the Roman emperor.

In the greatest Augustan Nervan Games of Ourania,
in which Gaius Julius Agesilaus was the overseer of the competition (*athlothetēs*,
   "prize giver"),
as well as Titus Flavius Charixenus along with his children,
the first contest was carried out by Menecles,

(5)   while Gaius Julius Menecles and Tiberius Claudius Agemon were organizers
   (*agōnothetai*),
Titus Flavius Attinas, a Phocaean, son of Mnason Pasicles won the boys' wrestling,
and he set up this statue according to the sacred customs and public vote.

I3d. Eurycleia Festival, Roman period (*IG* V, 1 666)

The Eurycleia was another new athletic contest in Sparta established c.136/137 CE *and named after the Hadrianic senator Eurycles Herculanus. The Eurycleia Games offered cash prizes to attract foreign (i.e., non-Spartan) athletes. The victory inscription provided here for the Alexandrian wrestler Marcus Aurelius Asclepiades, a circuit victor in the crown games, provides a good indication of the ways in which Spartan athletic contests started to take on an international reputation.*

Marcus Aurelius Asclepiades, an Alexandrian and Athenian,
two-time victor in the circuit of crown games (*periodonikēs*),
a trainer in the gymnasium (*aleiptēs*),
won the men's wrestling contest at the Eurycleia festival
twice in succession while Marcus Aurelius Areto and Gaius Julius Autocrates
were organizers of the games.

I3e. Artemis Orthia Inscriptions, second century CE (*IG* V, 1 290, 306)

These two inscriptions are examples of victory dedications for what is known as a contest of endurance and toughness (karteria). Held in honor of Artemis Orthia, the contest was part of Spartan education of the youth known as the agōgē. *The Spartan* agōgē *seems to have been reformed in the Hellenistic period, and the violence and intensity of its training and system of education may have been dramatically increased, especially in the Roman Imperial period, from which most of the inscriptions relevant to the rites of Artemis Orthia come. The contest seems to have involved being whipped at the altar of Artemis Orthia, and the youth who demonstrated the greatest endurance for pain was proclaimed victorious. For further discussion of the Spartan* agōgē *and the rites of Artemis Orthia, see Xenophon's* Constitution of the Lacedaemonians *(10c–g) as well as Plutarch,* Life of Lycurgus *(35f–g). In addition, Philostratus, in the* Gymnasticus, *40a (58) also points to the rites of Artemis Orthia as a form of training for karteria in opposition to traditional competitions (agōnia). On the basis of the language of the dedications and their form, however, it is clear that the Spartans viewed these practices as a form of competition equal to other sporting competitions.*

I3e.1. *c.*138–61 CE (*IG* V, 1 290)

The…brother (*kasen*) to Alcastus
when Deximachus was *patronomos* [a Spartan official probably in charge of the
    agōgē],
he won the contest in toughness (*karteria*)
for Orthia.

I3e.2. *c.* late second century CE (*IG* V, 1 306)

> Cleandrus,
> also known as Menis,
> son of Callistratus,
> leader (*boagos*) while Gorgippus, son of Gorgippus
> having won the contest,
> dedicated [this] to Artemis Orthia

4. Athens

*Although the city of Athens was a major venue for athletic competition, from at least the Archaic period with the advent of the Panathenaic Games sometime in the mid-sixth century, nevertheless, the number of dedications for athletic victories is relatively rare. Even in antiquity, Athens seems to have been understood as an exception to the practice of athletic dedication. A passage from a speech of Lycurgus against Leocrates (**21a**) explains that Athenians preferred to honor those who benefited the state, not athletes. Although we need not take this account literally, it nevertheless does correlate with the relative paucity of athletic dedications in Athens, despite the popularity of athletic competition. The following are some select dedications and other types of inscriptional evidence for athletics in Athens.*

I4a. Early Inscriptional Evidence for the Panathenaea, mid-sixth century BCE (Raubitschek)

I4a.1. 326

> The race [they made…]
> …Crates Thrasycles Aristodicus
> Bruson Antenor [...
> The [priests] first set up the contest (*agōn*) for the gray-eyed maiden [= Athena].

I4a.2. 327

> The race [they made…]
> …
> The priests established the contest for the gray-eyed maiden. [= Athena]

14b. Inscribed Jumping Weight, Eleusis, 575–550 BCE (*CEG* 299)

This inscribed jumping weight (haltēr) *was discovered at Eleusis. Jumping weights were typically the property of an athlete and were common dedications for victorious athletes in competition. They were also the main object of dedication for the pentathlon event. The athlete named may have been an Eleusinian and/or the contest may have taken place at Eleusis, since we know that games were held there, although the testimony on such games is sparse (e.g. Pindar Olympian 9.99). See Appendix CIII and Figure 25 (p. 397).*

> In jumping Epaenetus won on account of these
> ha[*ltēres*]

14c. Callias Dedication, mid-fifth century BCE (*IG* I², 606)

This base was found near the Propylaea on the Acropolis. Callias was a victor in all four sacred crown games (periodonikēs) *and his career is briefly discussed in Pausanias* **37q** *(6.6.1), since he also had a dedication at Olympia.*

> Callias, son of Didymias, dedicated this
> for victory
> at Olympia
> Pythia: twice
> Isthmia: five times
> Nemea: four times
> Great Panathenaea.

14d. Pronapes Dedication, mid-fifth century BCE (*IG* II², 3123)

This Athenian chariot victor may have also been a prosecutor of Themistocles, the Athenian general who orchestrated the battle of Salamis during the Persian Wars.

> Pronapes, son of Pronapes, dedicated this to the gods
> Nemea, Isthmia, Panathenaea…

14e. *Sitēsis* for Athenian Victors, c.430 BCE (*IG* I³, 131)

The institution of sitēsis, *free meals for life, at the Prytaneion was granted to Athenian citizens who were victors in one of the four sacred crown games, and also given to other notable people (see* **35l**). *It was precisely this reward that Socrates proposed as his punishment in the* Apology (**22a**).

[…] was secretary.

[The Council and the people decided] when Erechtheus was…

[…] thippus was chairman; […] icles

[proposed *sitēsis*] in the Prytaneion first for

(5)   according to ancestral tradition; then for descendants of

Harmodius and Aristogeiton, then whoever is closest in ancestry;

[…] and may there be *sitēsis* for them, if

[…] from the Athenians, in accordance with [tradition?];

[…] whom Apollo chose, when expounding

(10)   […] *sitēsis*, and in the future those whom he may

choose for them,

on the same… basis, and those who [have won at the Olympic Games] or at the

Pythian Games [or Isthmian or] N[emean Games]

[or will win in the future, also for them let there be] *sitēsis* based on [what is written on

(15)   the stele…]

The inscription goes on to stipulate the same privilege for those victorious in horse and chariot competitions at the four crown games.

I4f. List of Prizes Given at the Panathenaea, *c.*350 BCE (*IG* II², 2311)

This Athenian festival was held annually for Athenian citizens, but every four years, beginning in 566/565, the city sponsored a nine-day version with athletic contests open to non-citizens. The competitions included musical, gymnic, and hippic events, as well as events restricted to citizens, who were probably organized by tribe. In the latter the prize is an ox, meant to be sacrificed and shared by the whole group. Competition takes place in three age categories: men, boys, and ageneioi *(literally, those who have yet to grow a beard). Unlike the crown games, the Panathenaea gave substantial prizes in the form of money, golden crowns, and jars of olive oil, which had a commercial as well as a practical value, and more than one prize was given in each category. Thanks to a large, though now broken inscription that recorded the prizes offered in each category, we are able to get a sense of the scale of the awards. No date remains on the inscription, but it was probably made between 400 and 350 BCE.*

The first part is now missing.

For the *kithara* singers:

(5)   First place, a crown of olive in gold

1,000 drachmas in weight and

500 drachmas in silver.

Second prize: 1,200 drachmas

Third prize: 600 drachmas

(10)   Fourth prize: 400 drachmas

Fifth prize: 300 drachmas

For the men's *aulos* singers:

First prize: this crown weighing 300 drachmas

Second prize: 100 drachmas

(15) For the men's kithara players:

First prize: this crown weighing 300 drachmas

Second prize: *[the number is lost]*

Third prize: 100 drachmas

For the *aulos* players:

First prize: this crown

[The text is broken, and a number of the figures are missing, even when the categories are visible.]

For the boy victor in the *stadion*:

50 amphoras of olive oil

(25) Second prize: 10 amphoras

For the boy victor in the pentathlon:

30 amphoras of olive oil

Second prize: 6 amphoras of olive oil

For the boy victor in wrestling:

(30) 30 amphoras of olive oil

Second prize: 6 amphoras of olive oil

For the boy victor in boxing:

30 amphoras of olive oil

Second prize: 6 amphoras of olive oil

(35) For the boy victor in the *pankration*:

40 amphoras of olive oil

Second prize: 8 amphoras of olive oil

For the *ageneios* victor in the *stadion*:

60 amphoras of olive oil

(40) Second prize: 12 amphoras of olive oil

For the *ageneios* victor in the pentathlon:

40 amphoras of olive oil

Second prize: 8 amphoras of olive oil

For the *ageneios* victor in the wrestling:

(45) 40 amphoras of olive oil

Second prize: 8 amphoras of olive oil

For the *ageneios* victor in the boxing:

40 amphoras of olive oil

Second prize: 8 amphoras of olive oil

For the *ageneios* victor in the *pankration*:

[The prizes for the men's gymnic contests are now missing from the stone.]

For the two-horse chariot race with colts:
    40 amphoras of olive oil
    Second prize: 8 amphoras of olive oil
For the two-horse chariot race with adult horses:
    140 amphoras of olive oil
    Second prize: 40 amphoras of olive oil

Prizes for warriors [i.e., contests restricted to Athenian citizens]

For the victor in the horse race:
    16 amphoras of olive oil
    Second prize: 4 amphoras of olive oil
For the victor in the two-horse chariot race:
    30 amphoras of olive oil
    Second prize: 6 amphoras of olive oil
For the victor in the processional two-horse chariot race:
    4 amphoras of olive oil
    Second prize: 1 amphora of olive oil
For the victor in the javelin throw from horseback:
    5 amphoras of olive oil
    Second prize: 1 amphora of olive oil

Victors' *nikētēria* [*This category lists a single prize for each event.*]

For the pyrrhic dancers in the boys' category: a bull and 100 drachmas
For the pyrrhic dancers in the *ageneioi* category: a bull and 100 drachmas
For the pyrrhic dancers in the men's category: a bull and 100 drachmas
For the winning tribe in *euandria*: a bull and 100 drachmas
For the winning tribe in the torch race: a bull and 100 drachmas
For the individual victor in the torch race: a water jar and 30 drachmas

Prizes for the contest of boats:

For the winning tribe: 3 bulls, 300 drachmas, and 200 meals at the city's expense.
Second prize: 2 bulls and 200 drachmas

14g. *Sōtēria* Festival, *c.*246 BCE (*IG* II³, 1005)

This stele, located in the Agora of Athens, pertains to the reorganization of the Sōtēria festival at Delphi as a festival equivalent to the Pythian Games (Iso-Pythian). The festival was held to honor victory over the Celtic invader Brennus (c.279 BCE).

When Polyeuctus was archon, in the ninth prytany of Aigeis, where Chaerephon, son of Archestratus of Cephale, was secretary. On the twenty-second of Elaphebolion, the thirtieth of the prytany, the people decreed. Cybernis, son of Cydias of Halimous, proclaimed:

> The federation of the Aetolians, in demonstrating their piety to the gods, voted that the *Sōtēria* contest take place for Zeus the Savior and Pythian Apollo, as a memorial of the battle against the barbarians when they attacked the Greeks and the sanctuary of Apollo, common to the Greeks, against whom the people sent out select troops and cavalry to fight on behalf of common safety (*sōtēria*). Concerning this, the federation of the Aetolians and the general Charixenus have sent to the people an embassy for discussion, in order that the people might accept the competition in music as equal to the Pythian and in athletics and equestrian events as equal to the Nemean...

14h. Inscription Honoring the Ephebes, *c.*122 BCE (*IG* II², 1039, 45–68)

*In Athens, young men of 18 and 19 spent two years in training and military service under the watch of a magistrate charged with oversight, a **kosmētēs**, and trainers (**paidotribai** or **gymnastai**). They were honored with this public tribute after having completed their service successfully. The Athenian* ephēbeia *may, therefore, be viewed as a counterpart to the rites of passage for young men that were practiced throughout Greece, as in the Spartan **agōgē** (see further Appendix AII).*

(45) The ephebes during the archonship of Apollodorus acted well and with decorum during the whole year of training. They were obedient to the *kosmētēs* [magistrate in charge of ephebes] and trainers (*paideutai*) and attended lessons of the philosophers and behaved appropriately at the gymnasium, and they showed care for the exercises and training of the body, and in their weapons training, and they were not lacking in eagerness and love of honor. (50) They provided guardianship for the city and the Piraeus according to the orders of their director and the generals. They made expeditions into the county as best as they could, doing all tasks together, and they carried out the orders of their superiors with eagerness. They maintained piety to the gods and participated in civic processions and also performed acts of public good. They sacrificed at the Proeresia (55) and Mysteria, and Piraea and Dionysia, and they provided the most beautiful sacrifices possible. They sacrificed at the Diogeneia within the precinct and performed other appropriate exercises with favorable omens for all of them. They also sacrificed at the Sylleia[2] with good omens, and likewise performed sacrifices on the day of departure on the Acropolis for Athena Polias, Kourotrophos, and Pandrosus, also with favorable omens. In order that the council be

---

[2] The Sylleia was a festival in Athens held in honor of the Roman general Sulla after the conquest of Athens, although the precise chronology of the festival is uncertain.

seen to approve the excellence of the ephebes and their love of honor in their good deeds, with good fortune, (60) the council decided to praise the ephebes under the archonship of Apollodorus and to crown them with a golden crown for their good order and because they maintained their zeal for the most beautiful matter [and] to announce the crown at the competition for new tragedies of the Great Dionysia, and also at the Panathenaea and Eleusinia in athletic competitions. The generals and herald of the Council of the Areopagus shall attend to the proclamation of the crown. And it is permitted for them to dedicate (65) the image in the place that seems best and to inscribe the decree with the others on the same stele. This is so that when these matters are brought to pass, the council may be shown to honor those who devote themselves from the first stage of youth to the most beautiful things, and others may become envious for similar matters.

14i. Theseia Games, second century BCE (*IG* II², 956)

The games in honor of Theseus were first instituted in Athens to mark the seizure of the island of Scyros and the returning of the bones of Theseus to Athens around 476/5 BCE. The Theseia was reinstituted by the Romans to mark the return of the island Scyros as well as Delos, Imbros, and Lemnos to Athenian control. The gaps in this inscription can be filled in from a series of others on this same topic (see IG II² 956–65, 1014 and Bugh 1990: 20–37).

Antidemus, the son of Cleip[pides, spoke:

> Nicogenes, son of Nicon, of the deme of the Philiadae [elected
> by the people as [*agōnothetēs* of the Theseian Games
> for one year in the year that Aristolas [was archon, he sent a well-formed procession
> (5)　and carried out a sacrifice according to ancestral custom,
> for the Theseia] and took care of a torch race and athletic contest
> with foresight so that none of the contestants fell to foul play.
> (10)　And he set up prizes for the contests with great eagerness,
> leaving out nothing in accordance with the vote of the people.
> and he prepared for the victorious tribes the best horses as prizes,
> and also for those of rank from the foreigners,
> and he established these prizes.
> (15)　And he gave to the Council as a fee for attendance 1,200 drachmas
> and to members of the prytany he gave 200 drachmas for sacrifice.
> And he set up a stele in the precinct of Theseus on which he wrote down the
> 　　victors' names.
> In addition to this, he provided an account of all, having spent from his private
> 　　accounts
> over two thousand six hundred and ninety drachmas.

(20)   And about all these things which he managed, he brought accounts
to the Metroon and also provided corrections to the auditors.
In order that the council and the people manifestly remember
those who provided honor for themselves and readily gave to their causes,

(25)   with good fortune, the Council decided that those who have been selected as
officers for the approaching assembly issue orders for payment about these matters and communicate the opinion of the Council to the people, namely, that the
Council decided to praise Nicogenes, son of Nicon, of the deme of the Philiadae

(30)   and to crown him with a gold crown according to custom for his goodwill and
the ambition with which he executed the affairs of the Council and the people
of Athens, and to proclaim the crown at the new tragedies at the city Dionysia
and at the

(35)   gymnic contests of the Panathenaea, Eleusinia, and Ptolemaea. The recorder for
the Prytany should record this decision on the stele upon which are the victors.

[What follows after this is a victor list from this Theseia festival.]

5. Other Significant Inscriptions from the Ancient Mediterranean

The following are a selection of other exemplary inscriptions that provide important information about ancient athletics in the Greco-Roman World.

15a. Cleombrotus Inscription, sixth century (*CEG* 394).

*This inscription, dated to between 600 and 550 BCE, is on a bronze plaque found in the ancient territory of Sybaris. It seems to have been part of a larger dedication of an athletic victor statue. The dedication was made by a figure named Cleombrotus, whose name means "glory" (kleos) of "man" (brotos), and the inscription is one of the oldest we have pertaining to Olympic victors. Unique to this inscription is the insistence that the dedication is "equal in width and height." This may be related to issues of likeness between victor and the dedicated statue or it may also relate to regulations at Olympia requiring that statues not be larger than life size (see **38d,** Lucian, Portraiture Defended 11)*

Cleombrotus,
the son of Dexilaus,
after winning at Olympia

dedicated [this statue],
which is equal to him in height and thickness,
after he promised a tenth of his prize to Athena.

15b. Aristis of Cleonae, Nemea, c.565 BCE (*IG* IV, 290)

This statue base found at Nemea is in honor of a victor in the pankration. *In this inscription, we see the dedication itself speaking. This was a known practice in early Greek dedicatory epigrams.*

Aristis dedicated me to lord Zeus Kronios,
having won four times in the *pankration* at Nemea.
He is the son of Pheidon from Cleonae.

15c. Drymus Inscription, Run from Olympia to Epidaurus, c.320 BCE (*IG* IV, 2 1.618)

This is from the statue base of a victor erected in his home city of Epidaurus. Its interest is his claim to have run from Olympia back to his home city, a distance of about 140 miles, on the same day as his victory. This is just barely possible.

I, Drymus, the child of Theodorus, announced my Olympic victory here in Epidaurus, on the same day, running into the renowned precinct of the god, an example of manly courage. My country is horsey Argos.

15d. Subsidizing Athletes, Ephesus, c.300 BCE (*I. Eph.* 1415–16)

These two inscriptions on the same stone statue base provide the earliest evidence for subsidizing promising athletes who would bring glory to a city. They also show that athletes could change their citizenship to their advantage. Athenodorus, after winning in local festivals and at Nemea, has himself declared an Ephesian and is eligible for subsidy. Another more fragmentary inscription (I. Eph. 2005) claims that Athenodorus lacks the means to train and asks for a subsidy for training and travel. In I. Eph.1416, the father proposes that the city subsidize Timonax, who was a boy victor at Isthmia and Nemea, for his promise for future competitions.

(1415) Resolved by the council and the people [of Ephesus]. Neumus, the son of Andronicus, proposed: Since Athenodorus, the son of Semon, who is entitled to pay of taxes equal to that of a citizen and is resident in Ephesus, has won at Nemea in the boys' boxing and, having been proclaimed as an Ephesian, has won a crown for the city, [it was resolved] by the council and the people that Athenodorus, the son of [Semon], be an Ephesian, as he was proclaimed in the competition, and he shall accrue the honors that are assigned by law to whoever wins a contest for boys at Nemea, and his victory shall be proclaimed in the agora, just as other victors are proclaimed. The steward (*oikonomos*) shall give the money stipulated by law for the crown and enroll him in the tribe and "the thousand." He is assigned to the Carenaeus tribe and "the thousand" of Cheloneus.[3]

(1416) Resolved by the council and the people [of Ephesus]. Herogiton proposed: seeing as Timonax, the son of Dardanus, was victorious earlier at Isthmia and Nemea in the boys' [...] and the city crowned him, having promised that he will win other contests and that the city will again crown him, Timonax's father has brought forward a petition to request the senate to provide...

15e. Decree of the League of the Islanders (Nesiotic League) to Designate the Ptolemaea as "Is-Olympic," *c.*280 BCE (*Syll.*[3] 390)

The league (koinon) was a federation of city states of the Cyclades in the Aegean Sea. It was originally organized under the Antigonids of Macedon around 314 BCE, but around 287 fell under the sway of the empire of the Ptolemies of Egypt. The league was headed by a nēsiarch *and a council. In this decree the league agrees to accord victors at the Ptolemaea the same honors that they would accord to Olympic victors—this is the meaning of "Is-Olympic" (see lines 40–5).*

Resolved by the delegates of the Islanders: with respect to what [Philocles] the king of the Sidonians and Bacchon the *nē[siarch]* wrote to the cities, namely, that they should send delegates to Samos (5) to deliberate about the sacrifices, the sacred embassy, and the contest that Ptolemy is establishing in honor of his father in Alexandria, which is to be Is-Olympic, and that Philocles and Bacchus have discussed with the delegates [now] arriving from their cities, (10) it has been resolved by the League of the Islanders: since King Ptolemy the Savior was responsible for many great and good things for the islanders and the other Greeks, having freed the cities, restored their laws, (15) returned all to their ancestral constitutions, and rescinded their taxes, the current King Ptolemy, who has inherited the kingdom from his father, continuing to demonstrate the same goodwill and concern towards the islanders and (20) the other Greeks, is offering sacrifice to his father and establishing a contest (*agōn*) for gymnic, musical, and hippic events to be Is-Olympic, preserving his piety toward the gods and maintaining his goodwill toward his forefathers, he urges for these reasons (25) that the islanders and the other Greeks vote that the contest may be Is-Olympic; it is fitting that all the islanders, who were the first to honor Ptolemy the Savior with godlike honors both for his communal benefactions and for (30)

---

[3] That is, he is now included in these two citizen groups. See Brunet (2003: 219–35, esp. 227–2).

[his assistance to private parties] ... vote ... (35) in their own goodwill to accept the sacrifice and send the sacred embassy at the designated times for all time to come, as the king has urged, and for the contest to be Is-Olympic, (40) and for the victors of the islanders to have the same honors as each of the islanders has prescribed in law for those who are victorious at the Olympic Games, and to crown King Ptolemy, the son of Ptolemy the Savior, with a golden crown (45) worth one thousand *staters* because of his excellence (*aretē*) and goodwill towards the islanders, and the delegates should inscribe (50) the vote on a stone slab (*stēlē*) to stand in Delos alongside of the altar of Ptolemy the Savior. Accordingly, (50) the cities that participate in the council should pass this decree, inscribe it on stone slabs, and dedicate it in the sanctuaries in which other honors are inscribed in each of the cities. The delegates should appoint three sacred embassies, which on arrival (55) in Alexandria should offer sacrifice on behalf of the League of the Islanders to Ptolemy the Savior and give over the crown to the king [Ptolemy II]. The money for the crown, the travel, and income for the sacred delegation the cities shall bear, each according to its share, and they shall give it to whomever Bacchon designates. Glaucon of Cythnos, ... of Naxos, and Cleocritus of Andros were appointed.

15f. Prize List, Ephebic Training, Coresia on Ceos, third century BCE (*IG* XII, 5 647)

This inscription provides details of catering for a local festival, the exact identity of which is unknown. In addition to instructions for food and animals for sacrifice, the inscription provides a list of victors and their prizes. Finally, it notes that the victors' names should be inscribed on the temporary surface of a white board (leukōma), and only with the approval of the council should they be carved in stone. The opening is broken.[4]

... On the 22nd day of the month of Maimakterion[5] the *probouloi* shall pay the provider 150 drachmas (5) for sacrificial animals. The provider shall give a surety that is acceptable to the *probouloi* that he will cater the feast in accordance with the law, namely, sacrifice an adult ox and an adult sheep; if he sacrifices a pig, it should not be more than one and a half years old. He shall cater a feast for the citizens and whomever the city invites and (10) the resident foreigners and as many freedmen as pay taxes in Coresia. He shall provide food, wine, fruits and nuts, and everything else suitably, and meat per man of not less than two minas in raw weight and of the entrails as much as the sacrificial animals have. The *probouloi*, the (15) treasurer (*tamias*), and the herald shall scrutinize the sacrificial animals, weigh the meat, and preside over the sacrifices. He shall provide the meal ... and suitable wine until sunset. If the feast meets with approval, the treasurer shall pay the

---

[4] For the date, see Van Minnen (2010).   [5] November/December in the Attic calendar.

remainder of the money on the next day. If it does not meet with approval, he shall deduct a fifth part [20%] from what is left.

(20) The *probouloi* shall establish a contest at the festival at the cost of 65 drachmas, and a gymnasiarch shall be chosen at the same time as the other officials, not under 30 years of age. This gymnasiarch shall conduct a torch race of the young men at the festival and shall take care of all other matters of gymnastic training and shall lead them out three times per month for practice in javelin, archery, and (25) catapult discharging (*katapaltaphesia*). Whoever of the young men is able but does not present himself, the gymnasiarch shall have authority to fine him up to a drachma. The *probouloi* shall award prizes to the winners as follows in the men's class:

> Winning archer: a bow and quiver of arrows, 15 drachmas[6]
>> Second prize: a bow, 7 drachmas
> Javelin thrower: three spear tips and helmet, 8 drachmas
>> Second prize: three spear tips, 1 drachma, 4 obols

(30) Catapulter: helmet and pole, 8 drachmas
>> Second prize: pole, 2 drachmas
> Victor in the torch race: shield (20 drachmas)

The [*probouloi*] shall establish a contest for boys and award prizes of a portion of meat for the winning boy archer and boy javelin thrower. The outgoing *probouloi* shall prepare the weapons and give them to the incoming *probouloi*; (35) the treasurer shall provide the cost and give a portion of meat to the rhapsode, and the *probouloi* currently in office shall hold the catapult and thirty missiles as long as it seems fit to the council. It is not possible for someone who has received a prize to give it away. The military commanders (*stratēgoi*) shall revue the troops in armor. (40) The scribe shall record in order those eternal victors on a white board (*leukōma*), and if the law is approved, record them on a stone slab placed in the precinct.

15g. Gymnasium Inscription, Beroia in Macedonia, *c.* 180 BCE (*SEG* 27.261)

This inscription provides considerable detail about the workings of the Hellenistic gymnasium. The law is prefaced with an instruction to deposit a copy in the public archives as well as to inscribe a copy on a stone slab (stēlē) and erect it in the gymnasium. The purpose of this is to encourage those who are appointed as overseers (gymnasiarchs) to discharge their office appropriately and to spend their allocated sums prudently. The young men who exercise will also profit from the public placement of the law, in that it will compel them to be more obedient and have a greater sense of shame.

(Side A) The city shall appoint a gymnasiarch whenever the other officials are appointed, not younger than 30 or older than 60. (25) The man appointed gymnasiarch should begin

---

⁶ The amount given for each prize is the amount that the officials pay for the item.

by swearing the oath appended below: "I swear by Zeus, Earth, Sun, Apollo, Heracles, and Hermes that I will act as gymnasiarch in accordance with the law of the gymnasiarchy, and for as much as is not stipulated in the law, using my own judgment, as piously and justly as I am able. Neither favoring a friend (30) nor harming an enemy unjustly, I shall not myself deprive the young men of the existing revenue or knowingly permit anyone in any way on any pretext to do so. May all be well with me if I abide by my oath; if I contravene it, may the opposite happen."

(Side B) Let no one of those under 30 years of age undress, when the sign down, unless the leader consents. When the sign is raised, no one else may do so, unless the leader consents. Nor may anyone anoint himself in any other *palaestra* in the same city. (5) If he does, the gymnasiarch will prevent him and fine him fifty drachmas. Whoever the gymnasiarch appoints to be in charge, all who frequent the gymnasium should obey this man, in accordance with what is mandated for the gymnasiarch. Whoever does not obey, the gymnasiarch should beat with a staff; (10) he should fine the others. The ephebes and those under 22 should practice with javelin and bow daily, when the boys have anointed themselves, and likewise if some other time seems necessary to their instructors.

With respect to the boys: none of the young men (*neaniskoi*) may enter the gymnasium with the boys or have conversation with the boys. If someone does, (15) the gymnasiarch should fine him and prohibit him from doing any of these things. The physical trainers (*paidotribai*) should present themselves twice daily at the hour that the gymnasiarch appoints, unless someone is ill or there is some other necessary engagement. If not, he should report to the gymnasiarch. If one of the trainers is negligent and does not appear (20) at the appointed hour for the boys, he should be fined five drachmas a day. The gymnasiarch shall have the power to beat the boys and the trainers who are undisciplined if they are not free and to fine them if they are free. He should compel the trainers to hold a review of the boys (25) three times a year, every four months, and he should appoint judges for them; he should crown the victor with a branch of olive.

Those who should not share in the gymnasium: No slave should undress in the gymnasium or a freedman or those who are the sons of these if he has not been to the wrestling school (*palaestra*), if he is a lover of boys, if he is employed at a trade in the marketplace, if he is drunk, or if he is insane. (30) If the gymnasiarch should knowingly allow anyone showing these characteristics to anoint himself or after someone points this out or reports to him, he should be fined 1,000 drachmas. In order to extract the fine, the one reporting should give a written report to the city auditors, and they should submit a written complaint to the city debt collector. If they do not submit a written report or the collector does not act, they should pay an equal (35) fine and one-third should be given to the one who has brought the suit. If the gymnasiarch thinks he has been accused unjustly, it should be possible for him, after filing a counter-plea within ten days, to obtain judgment in the established court. Future gymnasiarchs should prevent those appearing to act contrary to the law from anointing themselves. If they do not, they should be liable for the same fines.

No one should (40) insult the gymnasiarch in the gymnasium. If he does, he should be fined fifty drachmas. If someone strikes the gymnasiarch in the gymnasium, those present should prevent this and not allow it, and in the same way he should fine the person who struck the blow one hundred drachmas, and apart from this he should be liable to the gymnasiarch in accord with the public laws [i.e., the gymnasiarch could bring a case against the man in court]. And whoever of those present who is able but does not come to the aid of the gymnasiarch, should be fined fifty drachmas.

(45) With respect to the Festival of Hermes (*Hermaea*): The gymnasiarch should conduct the Festival of Hermes in the month of Hyperberetaios[7] and sacrifice to Hermes and offer as a prize a weapon and three others for fitness (*euexia*), good discipline (*eutaxia*), and hard training (*philoponia*) for those up to 30 years of age. The gymnasiarch should select seven men from the place as judges for fitness; they should draw lots, and the three who are selected should swear an oath (50) to Hermes to judge fairly whoever seems to have developed the best body, without favor or prejudice. If those who are selected do not act as judges or swear an oath that they are unable to do so, the gymnasiarch shall have the authority to fine those who refuse to obey ten drachmas and shall draw lots from the remainder in place of the defaulter. With respect to the contests of good discipline and hard training, the gymnasiarch, after swearing an oath (55) to Hermes, shall judge the contest of good discipline, whoever seems to be the most disciplined of those up to 30 years of age, and of hard training, whoever seems to him to have trained the hardest in the current year of those up to 30 years of age. Those who win shall, on that day, wear crowns and whoever wishes to do so may tie on a headband. At the Festival of Hermes, the gymnasiarch should produce a torch race for boys and young men. (60) The money for the weapons [the prizes] should come from existing revenues. The overseers of the temple (*hieropoioi*) should conduct the festival, receiving no more than two drachmas from each of those who use the gymnasium, and holding a feast in the gymnasium, they should choose others who will serve as overseers for Hermes in their place for the future. The physical trainers should participate in the sacrifice to Hermes whenever the overseers celebrate it, (65) receiving from the boys no more than one drachma from each, and they should divide up proportionally the raw meat from the sacrifices. The overseers and the gymnasiarch should not allow any performance during the drinking.

With respect to the prizes: the prizes that the victors win they should dedicate within eight months of the beginning of the term of the incoming gymnasiarch; if they do not, the gymnasiarch should fine them each one hundred drachmas. Those who cheat and (70) who do not compete fairly the gymnasiarch has the power to beat and fine, and likewise if someone sells his victory to another.

Selection of lampadarchs ("officers in charge of the torch race"): the gymnasiarch should choose three lampadarchs from the place in the month of Gorpiaeus.[8] Those

---

[7] September in the Macedonian calendar.   [8] August in the Macedonian Calendar.

chosen should provide the young men (*neaniskoi*) with oil, each for a ten-day period. He should choose three lampadarchs for the boys, and those chosen (75) should provide oil for an equal number of days. If any of those chosen objects, either his father or his brother or the guardian of orphans, on the grounds that he is unable to serve as lampadarch, let him swear under oath within five days the grounds on which he should not be chosen. If he does not fulfill the duties of the lampadarch or does not swear under oath, the one chosen must pay a fine of fifty drachmas and must provide the oil and serve as lampadarch. Likewise, if the man who has sworn under oath should be found not to have sworn suitably, if convicted (80) by the gymnasiarch and the young men (*neoi*), he should be fined fifty drachmas and likewise be compelled to provide the oil and to serve as lampadarch. In the place of one who has justly sworn an oath that he cannot serve, the gymnasiarch should appoint another. He should conduct the torch race for boys from the participants in the gymnasium, those who seem to him to be suitable, and likewise with the young men.

With respect to judges, the gymnasiarch should appoint judges whom (85) he thinks to be qualified, for the torch race (*lampadēdromia*) at the Festival of Hermes and for the long race and for the other contests. If anyone complains about one of the judges, saying that he has been treated unfairly by someone, he shall examine his conduct in accordance with the laws.

The gymnasiarch has authority over existing funds for the young men, and he should spend from them. Whenever he leaves his office, the amount of the funds and if any monies have been (90) acquired from fines or convictions, and the amount spent from these, recording the total sum on a tablet, he should display it in the gymnasium in the month of Dios[9] of the following year. He shall hand these accounts over to the city auditors within four months, and it shall be possible, if anyone wishes, to examine the accounts with them. The balance of the funds he should hand over to his successor within thirty days of the day on which he has left office. If he does not hand over the accounts and (95) the balance in accordance with what has been written, he shall pay a fine of 1,000 drachmas to the young men. The city debt collector will exact the fine from him when the auditors have submitted his name. Likewise, he shall hand over his account and the balance.

The sweat collector. Whoever has purchased the revenue from the *gloios* shall provide the service of guardian of the wrestling school (*palaistrophylax*), doing what the gymnasiarch orders, as is appropriate in the gymnasium. If he does not obey or is in any way unruly, he should be beaten by the gymnasiarch.

If (100) someone steals something from the gymnasium, he shall be liable to prosecution for sacrilege, if convicted in the established court. For all the fines, the gymnasiarch shall inscribe the reason for the fine and announce it in the gymnasium and display the

---

[9] October in the Macedonian calendar.

names of those fined on a white board (*leukōma*) and report them to the city tax collector, who, when he has collected the fines, give them to the gymnasiarch in office. If someone should protest that he was fined unfairly, it shall be possible for him, (105) upon filing a complaint, to be judged by the appropriate magistrates. If the man fined wins his suit, the gymnasiarch shall pay him one and a half times the fine, and in addition he shall be fined another 15 percent. Whoever wishes shall indict the gymnasiarch within twenty-four months after he has left office and the complaints shall be decided by the appropriate courts.

The law was passed by the city magistrates.

15h. Polycreon, Olympic Victor, Rhodes, *c.*172 BCE (*I. Lind.* 699)

These are two different commemorative inscriptions, one for a Nemean victory, the other for an Olympic victory; the latter is in verse.

a. Polycreon, the son of Agesistratus, the grandson of Polycreon, victorious at Nemea in the class of *ageneioi*, wrestling.
b. O Zeus Olympios, I announce that a Rhodian boy, Polycreon, the son of Agesistratus, prevailed in heavy-handed wrestling at your contest without taking a fall, who first gave this happy reward to sacred Lindos, extending to the broad land of the Halys, three times. Divine report came to Rhodes, his fatherland, bringing everlasting delight for his labors, for which his victory-ennobling fame is eternal.

15i. List of Victors at the Eleutheria at Larissa, *c.* first century BCE/first century CE (*IG* IX, 2 531)

This local festival at Larissa in Thessaly provides information about a number of contests not found at the Panhellenic Games. These include a bull-hunting contest unique to this region in which a rider pursues a bull to tire it, then dismounts, and wrestles it to the ground. There are several different types of target shooting and horsemanship that are derived from military training, and several different poetry contests typical of those found in the Roman period.

The victors:

> Bull-hunting (*taurothēria*): Marcus Arrontius
> Old-style recitation: Philon the younger, the son of Philon
> Cavalry charge: Dionysius, the son of Dionysius
(15) Foot race: Demetrius, the son of Xenon

Two-horse chariot charge: Timostheus, the son of Gorgopas
Torch race on horseback: Marcus Arrontius
Trumpeter: Lysicles, the son of Leptines

(20) Herald: Petalon, the son of Dionysius
Boys' *stadion*: Gaius Claudius, the son of Claudius
Men's *stadion*: Demetrius, the son of Demetrius
Boys' *diaulos*: Neomenes, the son of Ariston

(25) Men's *diaulos*: Aristonicus, the son of Hermias
Boys' torch race: Empedion, the son of Homerus
Boys' boxing: Demonicus, the son of Eudemus
Men's boxing: Demetrius, the son of Demetrius

(30) Boys' *pankration*: Philo the younger, the son of Philo
Second trial (*krisis*), boys' *pankration*: Eupalides, the son of Themistogenes

(35) Men's *pankration*: Asclepiades, the son of Asclepiades
Race in armor: Cteson, the son of Pausanias
Horse race with dismount (*aphippodroma*): Aristomenes, the son of Asandrides
Chariot race with dismount (*apobatikos*): Ladus, the son of Argeius

(40) Infantry marksmanship: Alexander, the son of Cleon
Archery: Onomarchus, the son of Heraclides
Cavalry marksmanship: Aristomedes, the son of Asandrides
Prose encomium: Quintus Ochrius, the son of Quintus

(45) Epic encomium: Ameometus, the son of Philoxenides
New recitation: Philo the younger, the son of Philo
Epigram: Ameometus, the son of Philoxenides

15j. Epidaurus, c. first century CE (*IG* IV², 1 652)

The sanctuary of Asclepius in Epidaurus was the major healing sanctuary of the ancient Greek world, and an athletic festival was held there from c.520 BCE onward. This inscription provides a good demonstration of the expanded circuit of games in the Roman period, including the Sebasta Games held in honor of Augustus.

The city of the Epidaurians [honors]
Cornelius Nicates, son of Sodamus,
twice victor in the Caesarian Sebasta Games,
organizer at the Apollonian and Asclepian Games,
and founder of the festival and games for Caesar,
and first organizer of those games,
[the city honors him]

because of his excellence and goodwill
to the city.

15k. Titus Flavius Victory Monument, Iaso, c. 86 BCE (*CIG* 2682)

*This victory dedication demonstrates the expanded circuit of contests in Asia Minor, as well as the
expanded circuit of "Sacred Games," including the newly established Capitoline Games in Rome, the
first Greek-style competitions held in Rome, begun by Domitian in 86 CE.*

Titus Flavius Metrobius, son of Demetrius,
won the "shield at Argus" [Argive Heraea] and the Olympic Games in Ephesus
and the Asian Common Games in Ephesus twice,
and the Asian Common Games in Pergamum three times,
the games in Smyrna twice, the Asian Common Games in Sardis twice,
twice in Miletus, the Elusinian Games, and Panathenaic Games in Athens,
the games for Caesar in Sparta, twice in Rhodes,
and he won 120 other quinquennial and triennial games
with the help of Heracles.
Titus Flavius Metrobius son of Demetrius
won the *periodos* in the men's *dolichos* first in the games of Iasos,
first in the men's category in the Capitoline Games in Rome in honor of Olympian
    Zeus.

15l. Shrine for Theogenes (or Theagenes) of Thasos, c. 100 BCE
(Martin 1940:175)

*This inscription was found on Thasos outside the shrine of Theogenes, who received hero worship at
this time. It is written on a circular marble block which has a large space in its center with a slot on
the top of the block that allowed visitors to deposit money into it. For Theogenes' victory inscription
at Olympia, see* **I2b**, *and for Theogenes' athletic life and career, see further Pausanias* **37q***) 6.6.5–6,
6.11.2–9, 6.15.3).*

Those who sacrifice to Theogenes must give no less than one obol to the treasury. For
anyone who does not abide by what is written will be remembered. The deposited money
for each year will be given to the main priest. He will protect it until 1,000 drachmas are
collected. When this amount is collected, the council and the people will decide whether
it is to be used for some dedication or for repairs for Theogenes…

15m. Orsippus of Megara, after first century CE (*IG* VII, 52)

Orsippus of Megara is thought to have been an Olympic victor in the stadion *around c.720 BCE and the first man to run naked in the* stadion, *thereby introducing nudity into Greek athletics (see Appendix AIII). Here an honorary dedication dated to after the first century CE is made by the Megarians in honor of Orsippus. See also* **37ab**.

> The Megarians set up this distinct memorial for wise Orsippus of Megara here,
> because they were persuaded by the reports from Delphi.
> [Orsippus] who released the greatest boundary stones for his fatherland,
> while enemies were cut off from much land.
> He was first of the Greeks in Olympia to be crowned nude (*gymnos*),
> where earlier men wore loincloths in the foot race.

15n. Honorary Inscription for Marcus Aurelius Demetrius, c.200 CE (*IG* XIV, 1102)

This honorary inscription for an athlete shows both his victories on an expanded competition circuit in the Roman era as well as his post-athletic career, which follows in the footsteps of his father. It also presents a significant degree of boasting and explanation in order to prove that his victories were genuine and worthy of praise, a style that become common in the later Roman Empire (see also **P10**).

I am the son of Marcus Aurelius Demetrius. He was priest and xystarch for life of the Sympas Xystos (entire *xystos*), director of the Imperial Baths, citizen of Alexandria and Hermopolis, *periodonikēs*, an incredible pankratist and wrestler. I am Marcus Aurelius Asclepiades, also named Hermodromus, the oldest of the trustees of great Sarapis, main priest of the Sympas Xystos, xystarch for life, director of the Imperial Baths, citizen of Alexandira, Hermopolis, and Puteoli, council member of Naples, Elis, and Athens, and a citizen and council member of many other cities. I am a pankratist, unconquered, unchallenged, not to be dislodged *periodonikēs*. I won every contest in which I enrolled. I was never called out nor did any other dare to be called out against me, nor was I in a tie, nor did I debate, nor did I withdraw, nor did I miss a contest, nor by royal favor did I take part or win in the common games. But I was crowned in every contest I entered in the *skamma* [i.e., the dug-up area where events take place], and I was tested in every qualifying round.

I was a competitor in the three groups of peoples in Italy, Greece, and Asia, and I won the following competitions in the *pankration*: the Pisa Olympics in the 240th Olympiad, the Pythian Games in Delphi, twice in the Isthmian Games, twice in the Nemean Games—the second time when my opponent withdrew, the shield games in Argos for Hera, twice in the Capitoline Games (in the second my opponent withdrew after the first lot), twice in the Eusebeia Games at Puteoli (the second when my opponent withdrew after the second round of lots), twice in the Actian Games at Nikapolis (the second when my opponent withdrew), five contests in Athens (the Panathenaic Games, the Olympics at Athens, the Panhellenics, and the Hadrianic Games twice), five contests at Smyrna: Asian Common Games twice (the second when my opponent withdrew), and also the Olympics in Smyrna and Hadrianic Olympics, three times in the games of Augustus at Pergamum (the second when my opponents withdrew in the beginning, the third when they withdrew after the first lot), three times at Ephesus (the Hadrianic, the Olympic, and the Barbilleia Games, where opponents withdrew after the first lot), the Games for Asclepius at Epidaurus, the Games of Haleia at Rhodes, the Chrysanthic Games at Sardis, and many money games, including the Eurycleia Games at Sparta, the Mantineia, and others. In total, I participated in competitions for six years. But I ceased competing at the age of 25 because of the dangers and jealousies against me. After I had stopped for several years, I was compelled to compete in my fatherland Alexandria and won the *pankration* in its sixth Olympiad.

l5o. Aurelius Achilles, Aphrodisias, third century CE (Roueché 1993)

*This honorary inscription is notable, first because Ephesus, the city responsible for the decree, explicitly rejects an intercity rivalry that was otherwise typical. Second, even though the decree does contain typical boasting similar to that in the **l5m**, it also contains a certain degree of moralizing praise, such as a focus on nobility and the excellence of both body and soul.*

…since the most marvelous city of the Ephesians always welcomes those who have shown enthusiasm with testimonies that are fitting and just for their worth, and because she takes pleasure in the advantages of all as if they were her own, and whatever outstanding benefits accumulate for the good reputation of other cities from distinguished men, these present good fortune; (10) and since she assigns a special portion of her goodwill to the most splendid city of the Aphrodisians, for whom she has many clear justifications for the exchange of affection. For these reasons, the city has welcomed Aurelius Achilles; he has undertaken the training of the body and is most noble in training, and he is the most impressive of men in his life and character, so that in him all excellence (*aretē*) of body (*sōma*) and soul (*psychē*) is combined… [The city has honored him] often, both in earlier contests, which he adorned by fighting remarkably and with great courage, and especially in the Olympic contest. When the city encouraged him—as if it were his own fatherland—to proceed to the finals, and to the category of men (30), he listened and obeyed the exhortation, and he defeated his opponents. He was crowned with the olive with such glory that his courage and enthusiasm are to be considered among the most distinguished of contests. For these reasons it was decided that the testimony about these events should not only go as far as the knowledge of those who were present in the stadium at the time, but by means of this decree he should be praised even more to his fatherland.

Epigram located on the side of the stone:

…but if you proclaim…of Varianus in verse, I hold the olive after I defeated him; or if you praise the youth Arion, better than men, against him Zeus also granted me the olive. In all the *stadia* of the peoples…My skill (*mētis*) is so great that none of my fellow-citizens surpasses…The many other crowns proclaim to you my fame (*kleos*)…in a stone image and my likeness. Often…in Pythia, and divine Olympia, having defeated rivals with glorious fame, while none of the men who have fought against me for victory was called to confront a second contest…

Part III
Papyri

Sourcebook of Ancient Greek Athletics. Charles H. Stocking and Susan A. Stephens, Oxford University Press (2021).
© Charles H. Stocking and Susan A. Stephens. DOI: 10.1093/oso/9780198839606.011.0003

6   **Papyri**

Texts written in Greek on papyrus or parchment that had been preserved in the sands of Egypt started coming to light in the nineteenth century. They record the activities of immigrants to Egypt, initially under the Ptolemies, then later under the Romans. Some of the earliest documents testify to the importance of athletic culture and competitions (agōnes) for these immigrants. Since the majority are private letters or petitions, they provide a different and personal perspective on the gymnasium, ephebic and other athletic training, and the tax status of those training athletes and those posting victories in crown or Is-Olympic games.

P1–4 are from the Hellenistic Period. They are letters that mention athletes or athletic equipment. They come from an extensive archive of Zenon, who was the estate manager for Apollonius, the chief financial minister for Ptolemy II Philadelphus. P1 is from Hierocles to Zenon about a promising young athlete, who may well bring Zenon (or his employer Apollonius) a victory crown; P2 provides evidence for the favored tax status of athletes and athletic trainers; P3 announces a victory in the newly established festival of the Ptolemaea near Alexandria; and P4 is a routine instruction to purchase scrapers, apparently in two sizes, since they are specified for men and for boys. A century later we learn from P5 that oversight of and payment for athletic events associated with ephebes were subject to liturgy, that is, those whose names were listed as having sufficient means could be chosen to pay for certain events. The remainder of the text is missing its ending, but the gist is clear. The petitioner has been asked to pay for the torch race for forthcoming games. He claims insufficient means and asks to be relieved of the burden. The man himself is characterized as "an 80-aroura man," which indicates that he is at the high end of the economic scale. He is also a cavalryman, undoubtedly one of the many settled in the area of the Fayum opened up under Ptolemy II.

Papyri from the Roman period are much more plentiful than from the Hellenistic, with a commensurate increase in texts that mention athletes and athletics. By the end of the Hellenistic period athletes were organized into professional societies and competed on an international games circuit. After the Romans conquered the Greek east, the growth in Greek athletic competitions continued, although the Romans imposed stricter rules for the scheduling of games and rewards for victors. Two types of games evolved: "sacred" and "eiselastic."[1] The former title seems to have designated those who won in games established by or in honor of Roman emperors. The latter entitled a victor to a procession into his home city when he returned, as well as a pension (usually paid monthly) called an opsōnion. *Of the large number of existing Roman papyri, we present only the few that provide unique insights about athletic behaviors.*

P6 and P7 are fragments from ancient training manuals. P8 is an athlete's will. From it we learn that his son was fostered, probably because the games circuits required constant travel, and that the emoluments that the man had received for his victories were heritable. This sheds light on the

---

[1] "Eiselastic" is derived from the Greek *eiselaunein*, "to drive in a victory procession."

Sourcebook of Ancient Greek Athletics. Charles H. Stocking and Susan A. Stephens, Oxford University Press (2021).
© Charles H. Stocking and Susan A. Stephens. DOI: 10.1093/oso/9780198839606.003.0007

motivations behind **P9**, *where one father signs an agreement with another to have the latter's son throw a wrestling match at an eiselastic games to the former's son. The benefits accruing from the win would have been substantial.* **P10** *is a familiar type of petition for release from the imposed burden (called a "liturgy") of paying for some public expense. The extremely flattering style of referring to the reigning emperors is typical of these late Roman documents and revelatory of the continued support that athletes received even under the Roman Empire.*[2]

P1. Letter about a Promising Athlete, 257 BCE (P. Cairo Zenon 59060)

Hierocles to Zenon, greetings. It would be good if you are in good health. I too am in good health. You wrote me about Pyrrhus: If I thought he was apt enough, to train (*aleiptein*) him, but if not, that I should not incur useless expenses and detract him from his education. As to what I think, the gods would know best, but it seems to Ptolemaeus, who should know as much as is humanly possible of those now training, though they began long before him [i.e., Pyrrhus], that he is much better, and within a very brief time he will far surpass them. And in addition, he is continuing with his other studies. To speak with the will of the gods, I hope you will be crowned. Now send him a bathing apron as soon as possible, and if possible, let it be goatskin, and if not, soft calfskin and a chiton and cloak and the mattress and coverlet and pillows, and the honey. You wrote that you were amazed that I did not know that these things were subject to taxation. I do know, but you are able to manage that it be sent as safely as possible.

P2. Tax Status of Athletes and Trainers, *c.*256 BCE (P. Hal 1.160–5)

Apollonius to Zoilos, greetings. We hold exempt from the tax on salt, as the king has decreed, the following individuals and their households: teachers of grammar, athletic trainers (*paidotribai*), the [practitioners] of Dionysus, and those victorious in the games at Alexandria, both the Basileia and the Ptolemaea.[3]

P3. Victory at the Ptolemaea, 251 BCE (PSI IV 364)

Zenodorus to Zenon, greetings. It would be good if you are in good health. I too am in good health. Know that my brother Dionysius has won a victory in the games of the

---

[2] See further Mann, Remijsen, and Scharff (2016); Remijsen (2014) and (2015).
[3] See Bagnall and Derow (2004: no. 124).

Ptolemaea held on the Sacred Island.[4] I have received the cloak that you sent; at this point, please send me another also. It should be thicker and of soft wool, so that my brother Dionysius might have it for the Festival of Arsinoë.

P4. Instruction to Purchase Scrapers, c.250 BCE (P. Cairo Zenon 59488)

Paramonos to Zenon, greetings. I forgot to give you instructions about the scrapers (*xystrai*) when you were visiting. Since they are cheap in Memphis, buy me six for men and six for boys of Sicyonian manufacture, of the best quality possible, and one and one half artabas of dried capers, not old, but as fresh as possible.

P5. Petition for Release from the Lampadarchy, c.147–136 BCE (BGU 6.1256)

Claims of unfair treatment and of penury were standard in these petitions; they were not necessarily accurate.

To Peteharpocrates, the village scribe of Philadelphia, from Hermon the son of Theocritus, a Macedonian, from the troop of Protogenes and his son Protogenes, of the sixth hipparchy [cavalry troop], an 80-aroura man. On Thoth 16 of the current 35th year, some have been drawn up to serve as lampadarchs (*lampadarchai* "overseers of the torch race") for the proposed games. On the 19th of the same month, I have been tasked with the liturgy of the lampadarchy (*lampadarchia*) for the men's foot race. This is not proper, because I have neither the capital nor the circumstances to defray the cost of the lampadarchy, living as I am on a small income that is hardly sufficient for me and my wife and children. Further, those whom they drew up before me as lampadarchs for the same contest (*agōn*) have been released, since [the officials] conspired to favor them. I request that you do not overlook me being subject to unfair treatment but refer my petition to the gymnasiarch and the young men (*neaniskoi*) of the gymnasium in Philadelphia,[5] so that I may be released from the lampadarchy. If not, at least append my petition to whom fitting, so that...

---

[4] For the Sacred Island, see Remijsen (2014: 354).

[5] *Neaniskoi* seem to have been members of a committee that dealt with the organization and supervision of the gymnasium. The title occurs in this role throughout Hellenistic Egypt. See Legras (1999: 209–12) and Habermann (2004: 342–3).

P6. Fragment of a Wrestling Manual, first–second century CE (P. Oxy 3.466)

This is a page from a carefully written instruction manual on how to train wrestlers (the rest of the text has been lost). It describes a series of holds for a drill involving a pair of wrestlers; the format is to instruct each wrestler in turn addressed as "you," and then conclude with "engage" or "grapple" (plexon or sumplexon*). Poliakoff (1987: 52) observes that "such manuals must have served to create a standardized and widely known* palaestra *vocabulary," including a complicated wrestling terminology. These exercises were sufficiently familiar that they could be parodied in an erotic context, most notably in* Ps-Lucian, The Ass Tale (**38h**). *We have preserved the layout of the original in our translation. For wrestlers, see Figure 24 (p. 396).*

You stand up to his side, attack with your foot, engage.
You throw him, stand up and turn around, engage.
You throw him, sweep and knock his foot out from under him.
You stand to the side of the opponent, lock his head with your right arm, engage.
You grasp him around the waist. Get under his hold. Step through it and engage.
You underhook with your right arm. Where he has taken the underhook, wrap
    your arm around his arm and attack his side with your foot.
You push away with your left hand. Force the hold and engage. Turn around. Fight
    by gripping both sides.
You throw your foot forward. You grab him around his body. Step forward and force
    back his head. Face him and bend back and throw yourself at him, bracing your
    foot.

P7. Instructions for *Pankration*?, second century CE (P. Oxy. 79.5204.7–13)

This fragment is written in a much less formal hand than **P6**, *though it is a similar instruction manual. Since it mentions striking the opponent, which was prohibited in wrestling, the instructions are probably for the* pankration. *It is set up in the same way as* **P6**, *with each athlete addressed in turn, though the instructions in the original were set out, as here, as continuous text. We translate the most legible portion, though there are still many gaps. For an image of the text, see 5204 at* http://www.papyrology.ox.ac.uk/POxy/. *For the* pankration, *see Figure 21 (p. 394).*

You stretch out your hands and grasp him…shake. You…place your foot opposite his knee and engage. You force him round by an underhook with your left arm. You thrusting… you sit up. You strike him and drag him along. You…elbow…with your knee below his side (*lagōna*) turn him over. You strike him and drag him along. You grab a finger.[6]

---

[6] Finger grabbing was apparently permitted; finger breaking was not; see **I1b**.

You…his wrist. You extend…You strike and pull back your hand. Put him on his back…elbow…disengage, pull back, sit up…

P8. Athlete's Will, second century CE (P. Ryl. 2.153.15–33)

I designate as heir to all that I now possess or may acquire or that may accrue to me in any way and in any form and to all the furnishings that I leave and my supplies and other property and to the sums which are or shall be due to my son Hellenicus by my wife Claudia Leontis. He is a minor, and I have left him in Smyrna in Asia, since he is still a foster child. I appoint as his guardians until he reaches the legal age or until he decides to come to Hermopolis after he reaches legal age the aforesaid persons, whom I know to suitable and worthy of the position, my friend Maximus, son of Hermaeus, and my cousin, Achilles, son of Sabourion, on the condition that they provide my aforesaid son and heir with food and clothing as they think fit…until my son reaches legal age or comes to Hermopolis. When he reaches legal age or after reaching it comes to Hermopolis, he himself shall supply to the said persons the said provisions as long as each of them survives as aforesaid. The allowances (*opsōnia*) due to me from the property of Hermopolis on account of my athletic crown, in accordance with the ordinances of our lord Antoninus and his deified father Hadrian, shall be claimed by my aforesaid guardians and heirs and delivered to my son.

P9. Contract to Lose a Wrestling Match, 267 CE (P.Oxy 79.5209)

This extraordinary document is framed as a legal contract between two fathers for the son of one to lose a wrestling match to the son of the other in exchange for a cash payment. The fathers are Aurelius Aquila, his son Nicantinous, a wrestler in the boy's class, and Marcus Aurelius Lucammon and Gaius Julius [Theon] (the name is restored), who are guarantors, most probably the trainers of another boy wrestler, Demetrius. The date of the papyrus indicates that the match in question was the final of the boys' wrestling competition at the 138th Great Antinoeia in the city of Antinoopolis in Egypt, which seems to have been an annual event. The festival was instituted by Hadrian in honor of his favorite Antinous, who had drowned in the Nile on a visit to the country. Demetrius has agreed to throw the match in return for 3,800 drachmas. The contract stipulates that if Demetrius does not lose, then his guarantors will pay an indemnity. The incentive for the father and son to cheat was that, as the winner in this festival, the son would have been awarded a pension by his native city. The pension at that time would have been about 200 drachmas a month for life. So, the bribe would have paid for itself within about a year and a half. But why would another agree to lose? Most likely, and this seems to be confirmed by an earlier example on the Zanes, where an adult wrestler bought off his rival who had won a previous Olympic crown, the boy who agreed to throw the match had already won a crown, and this was merely an opportunity to make more money; see **37m** *(5.21.3) and* **40a** *(44). For an image of the text, see 5209 at* http://www.papyrology.ox.ac.uk/POxy/.

Aurelius Aquila also called Sara[p…high] priest of the illustrious city of the Antinoites… to Marcus Aurelius Lucam[mon…of the Hadr]ianic tribe of the Olympian deme, and to Gaius J[ulius Theon? through the agency of Marcus] Aurelius Serenus…, both guarantors for A[urelius] Demetrius, a wrestler, greetings.

Seeing as he has entered into an agreement with [my son, Aure]lius Nicantinous, he being [Aurelius] Demetrius, who has been guaranteed by you, in the competition for the boy [wrestlers] to fall three times and yield, [in compensation for this] receiving through you [Lucammon and Theon] 3,800 drachmas of silver…without risk, on the condition that—may it not happen!—if yielding and not falling short [on his part], the crown is reserved as sacred [i.e., it is not awarded], we do not take action against him in these matters. But if Demetrius contravenes the terms written and agreed upon with my own son, likewise you are to pay to my son necessarily for the insult three talents of silver without delay or excuse, in accordance with the law of guarantee, because we have contracted on these terms. The contract is binding and written in two duplicate copies, one of which I hold, the other you hold. When formally asked, I stated my agreement.

14th year of Emperor Gallienus, Mecheir 29 [=February 23, 267 CE].

P10. Petition of a Sacred Victor, 298/9 CE (P.Oxy. 79.5210)

For an image of the text, see no. 5210 at http://www.papyrology.ox.ac.uk/POxy/

To Aelius Publicus, *vir perfectissimus*, prefect of Egypt, from Gaius Julius Theon?, son of Serenus, a sacred victor (*hieronikos*) and multiple victor, *paradoxos*,[7] citizen of Oxyrhynchus, Antinous and many other cities. I make my request on the basis of the general laws and your experience in all matters. I am confident that I shall obtain from your generosity (*philanthrōpia*) what I request. That sacred victors should not be subject to burdens or certain levies, as you know, has been decreed by the laws, as well as by our masters Diocletian and Maximian, the Augusti, and Constantius and Maximian, the most noble Caesars. It has been decreed that those who are 60 years or older be released from all types of levies and burdens. Thus, nothing is lacking from both parts of the existing pleading other than your magnificent consent. Now, I happen to be a sacred victor; I bound my head in victory gloriously and majestically at the sacred games in everlasting perpetuity of our masters Diocletian and Maximian, the Augusti, and Constantius and Maximian, the most noble Caesars. Having come to old age after my prime and my training during that time, and after a lifetime of 64 years, so that in accordance with this right,

---

[7] *Paradoxos* was a title given to distinguished athletes and artists, "the Admirable."

I am the beneficiary of the divine declaration of our greatest kings and most noble Caesars. I request, since I am of modest means, if it pleases your genius, that you consent on both of these grounds, and order through your sacred signature below that I may be released in some fashion, in order that too, having experienced your benefaction, may acknowledge the greatest thanks to your unsurpassed genius.

Farewell.

APPENDIX A THE ATHLETE IN GREEK CULTURE

I. Heroes and Athletes

Today, a "hero" is generally defined as someone distinguished by noble actions and admired for qualities of character. The notion of the hero in antiquity (Greek *hērōs*), however, had much more precise mythic and religious connotations. The ancient hero was understood to be a human, male or female, with superhuman abilities who underwent the ordeal of death and then received cult worship from a given community, usually in the form of sacrifice. Although mythic persons were the main heroes of ancient Greece and Rome, athletes also received similar cult worship.

Throughout antiquity, the mythical figure of Heracles served as the prototypical hero athlete. As the son of Zeus and the mortal woman Alcmene, he had physical strength that exceeded all mortals. But because of the anger of Hera, the wife of Zeus, he was forced to undertake twelve labors. Heracles' labors are often described in Greek as *athla* (see, e.g., **3b**: Bacchylides 9). The Greek word means "struggles" or "toil" and is etymologically related to the Greek term for "prize in a contest," *athlon*, as well as the term "athlete," Greek *athlētēs*. Hence, the Greek "athlete" is one who undergoes labors (*athla*) for a prize (*athlon*). According to various traditions, in the course of Heracles' labors, he established the contests at Olympia in honor of his father Zeus (**2b**: Pindar *Olympian* 3; **37a**: Pausanias 5.8.3) and his twelve labors are depicted on the metopes of the temple of Zeus at Olympia (**37c**: Pausanias 5.10.9). Like many Greek heroes, Heracles suffered a tragic death but underwent an apotheosis in which he was reconciled with the goddess Hera, immortalized, and married to Hebe (= "Youth"), the daughter of Hera and Zeus. Heracles' own immortalization after suffering from his labors may have served as a paradigm for victorious athletes who might expect a proxy form of immortality through reputation and glory (Greek *doxa* and *kleos*) as compensation for their own physical ordeals (see Nagy 2013). Heracles received cult worship throughout the Greek and Roman worlds, and there were several athletic festivals, especially in the Roman period, in honor of Heracles (on which, see Stafford 2012).

Heracles' exploits also served as a paradigm for the mythic hero Theseus, who was believed to be responsible for the unification of Athens. According to tradition, Theseus was a distant cousin of Heracles and desired to imitate his exploits. When the time came for Theseus to travel to Athens to claim his heritage, he decided to travel by land and undertook six of his own labors similar to those of Heracles. The labors of Theseus are depicted on the Athenian treasury at Delphi and also on the Temple of Hephaestus in Athens. In one foundation myth, Theseus established the Isthmian Games for Poseidon in imitation of Heracles' foundation of the Olympic Games (**35m**: Plutarch *Life of Theseus* 25.4–5). In Athens and elsewhere, Theseus received hero cult worship, and an athletic festival known as the Theseia was established in his honor in the fifth century BCE and continued through the Hellenistic and Roman periods (see **I4i**: Theseia Inscription *IG* II² 956).

Another equally significant mythic hero athlete was Pelops, who is also thought to be a founder of the Olympic Games (**2a**: Pindar *Olympian 1*). It is not uncommon to have several foundation myths for the same cultural institution, and Pausanias attempts to justify the double foundation of Olympic Games in terms of chronological sequence (**37a**: Pausanias 5.7.6–5.8.4). At Olympia there was a sanctuary dedicated to Pelops known as the Pelopion, where Pelops received the blood sacrifices of a black ram (**2a**: Pindar *Olympian* 1; **37f**: Pausanias 5.13.1–2) Similarly, there were blood sacrifices performed for Pelops' wife Hippodamia (**37s**: Pausanias 6.20.7) and even for the chariot driver Myrtilus, who had cursed Pelops (**37s**: Pausanias 6.20.17). In these cases, as with most instances of hero cult worship, the blood offerings were intended to appease the deceased and avoid any potential harm that the deceased might bring about as a result of their supernatural powers.

Hero cult worship also took place at the Panhellenic sanctuaries of Nemea and Isthmia. Like Olympia, both the Nemean and Isthmian Games had double foundation myths. On the one hand, the Nemean Games were held in honor of Zeus and related to Heracles' labor against the Nemean lion (**3b**: Bacchylides 9), but they were also held in honor of the mortal infant Opheltes. Opheltes was tragically killed by a serpent, and the games are said to have been first established in his honor as Archemorus ("Beginning of doom") by the famous Seven against Thebes (Pausanias 2.15.2, 8.48.2–3). Similarly, the Isthmian Games, which were in honor of Poseidon, also have a foundation myth related to hero cult. They were believed to have begun as funeral games in honor of the infant Melicertes. Melicertes was a son of woman named Ino, and a grandson of Cadmus, whose family line was cursed by the goddess Hera. Ino and Melicertes were said to have been chased off a cliff by Ino's husband. The mythic figure Sisyphus then found the child's body and held the first Isthmian Games in his honor. Ino is said to have been transformed into the goddess Leucothea and Melicertes into a divine being known as Palaemon (**37u**: Pausanias 2.2.1). Although neither Opheltes nor Palaemon accomplished physical exploits as Heracles, Theseus, or Pelops did, they nevertheless received worship as "heroes" in order to avert the harm that might come from their ill-omened deaths.

In addition to these mythic figures associated with ancient athletic sanctuaries, many historical athletes also received hero-cult worship. Euthymus of Locri was a three-time Olympic victor in boxing (*c.*484, 476, 472 BCE) and is reported to have defeated an evil spirit that was tormenting the city of Temesa (**37q**: Pausanias 6.6.7–10; **26c**: Callimachus). He was unique for having received hero worship while still living. Although Euthymus was a successful athlete, he was defeated by one of the most successful athletes in ancient history, Theogenes (or Theagenes) of Thasos, who also received hero worship. Theogenes is reported to have won between 1,200 to 1,400 competitions, primarily in boxing, but also in the distance race. He was reported to have had superhuman strength, even as a child. But he did not receive hero worship because of his victories or his physical power. When his statue fell and killed his enemy, who had been vandalizing it, the statue was first thrown into the sea, but the community of Thasos suffered from a plague until the Delphic oracle instructed them to worship Theogenes as a hero (**37q**: Pausanias 6.11.2–9). A marble block at his shrine on Thasos shows that worship could take the form not only of blood sacrifice but also of monetary deposits (**15l**).

Another athlete worth mentioning who received hero cult worship was Poulydamas of Scotousa, an Olympic victor in the *pankration* in 408 BCE, famous for various exploits of strength, which are depicted on his statue base. Like the statues of Euthymus and Theogenes, Poulydamas' statue was believed to be endowed with special power and healing properties. Those exploits and Poulydamas' tragic death, which came from overconfidence in his strength, are recorded by Pausanias (**37q**: 6.5.4–9).

It is important to note that not all athlete heroes were actual victors. Such is the case with Cleomedes of Astypalaea. Cleomedes is said to have killed his opponent in a boxing match at Olympia (*c*.492 BCE), but was not given the victory. In a fit of rage at the loss, he is said to have torn down a school and killed the children inside. When the townspeople sought revenge, Cleomedes sought sanctuary at a temple of Athena and mysteriously disappeared. The Delphic oracle then instructed the people to worship him as a hero (**37q**: Pausanias 6.9.6–8). This fits the pattern of hero worship as a way to avert harm.

Our historical evidence on ancient hero cult, like so much of ancient athletics, is made up of a bricolage of ancient sources, and it is not always clear why some athletes received cult while others did not. One such example is Milo of Croton, perhaps the most famous athlete from Greek and Roman antiquity. Milo won six Olympic victories in wrestling, starting in 540 BCE, as well as seven Pythian, ten Isthmian, and nine Nemean victories. Like Euthymus of Locri, he is famed for amazing feats of strength (**37q**: Pausanias 6.14.5–8). He is reported to have dressed as Heracles and worn his six Olympic crowns in a war between Croton and Sybaris, and this may have indicated Milo's own desire for heroization. Like other mythic and historical hero athletes, Milo is reported to have died tragically as a result of overconfidence in his strength: When his hand got stuck in a tree, he was eaten by wolves (**37q**: Pausanias 6.14.8; **39a**: Galen *Protrepticus* 13). Despite his tremendous accomplishments and the fantastic stories that surround Milo, there is no evidence that he received cult worship.

There are many other athletes in the ancient world who are reported to have received hero worship (see Polignac 2014). From the brief list presented here, it is clear that historical hero athletes did not receive cult worship simply as a way to glorify their individual accomplishments. Instead, the reason for worship is historically contingent on issues surrounding the communities from which the athletes came. As François de Polignac explains, "The cult of the athlete eclipses weaknesses, divisions, and past crises by placing them in the sphere of the sacred, where each takes on a new meaning, affirms and strengthens the unity of the group, and maintains a hero at a reasonable distance from the city" (Polignac 2014: 111).[1]

II. Athletics and Education

Organized, civic education in Ancient Greece was intimately associated with athletic training from sometime in the sixth century BCE. Throughout the Archaic and Classical periods, *gymnasia* became an increasingly central aspect of every Greek city. The formal building for athletic training was referred to either as a *palaestra* ("wrestling place") or, more generally, as a *gymnasion* ("nude place"). On athletic nudity, see Appendix AIII. *Gymnasia* generally involved a dirt area for physical training surrounded by a colonnade, along with additional classrooms and storage spaces on the periphery (see Plan 1). Running tracks were often located nearby.

In Archaic and Classical Greece, boys between the ages of 7 and 14 underwent physical training at *gymnasia* under the guidance of an instructor known as a *paidotribēs*, who trained the youth in the competitive events as well as other forms of physical training. In addition, the youth were taught reading, writing, mathematics, and music. In contrast to the *paidotribēs*, a coach who

---

[1] See further Azouley (2016); Currie (2005); Nagy (2013); Pache (2004); Polignac (2014); and Stafford (2012).

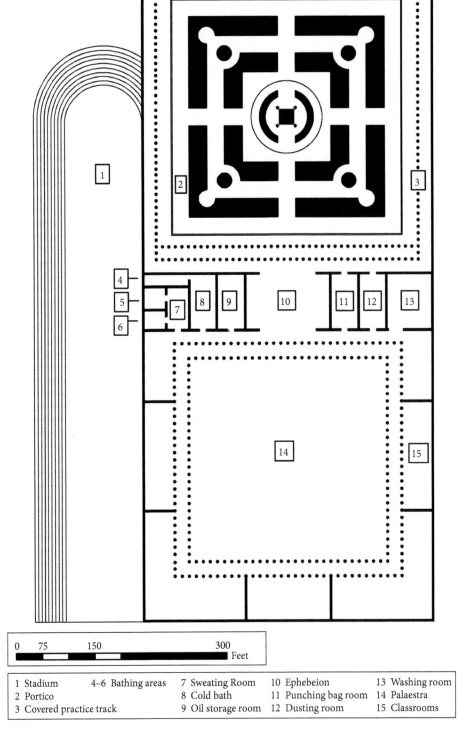

0	75	150	300

Feet

1 Stadium	4–6 Bathing areas	7 Sweating Room	10 Ephebeion	13 Washing room
2 Portico		8 Cold bath	11 Punching bag room	14 Palaestra
3 Covered practice track		9 Oil storage room	12 Dusting room	15 Classrooms

Plan 1. Schematic of the gymnasium based on Vitruvius

specialized in training athletes for competition was known generally as a *gymnastēs*. (On the activities of the *paidotribēs* and *gymnastēs*, see **22f**: Plato *Republic* 406a–409a; **23d**: Aristotle *Politics* 1337a–1339a; **39b**: Galen *Thrasybulus*; **40a**: Philostratus *Gymnasticus* 14–19). The official in charge of rules, regulations, and daily operations of the *gymnasion* was known as a *gymnasiarch*. Although *gymnasia* were public places of education, there were often a number of rules implemented by the gymnasiarch to exclude certain groups and populations of the city, such as women, slaves, and "madmen" (**I5g**: Inscription at Beroia). Beyond the public gymnasia, private places of training and education also existed in many city states. And in addition to general education for young men, cities such as Athens had compulsory physical and military training for potential citizens known as the *ephēbeia* (*ephēbos* = "young man"), which also took place at *gymnasia* (see **23e**: Aristotle *Constitution of Athens*; **I4h**: Ephebic Inscription, Athens). Similarly, Sparta had its own elaborate rites of passage and education for all citizen soldiers known as the *agōgē* (see **10d**: Xenophon *Constitution of the Lacedaemonians*). From our sources pertaining to Athens, Sparta, and elsewhere, it is clear that one of the main purposes of athletic training was to cultivate what the ancient Greeks referred to as *aretē*, a value traditionally defined as "virtue" but perhaps better translated as "excellence." The concept of *aretē* included a broad number of values and modes of behavior but was never narrowly defined. As Aristotle states in the *Politics*, "Regarding *aretē*, there is no agreement" (**23d**: Aristotle *Politics* 1337a–1339a).

Indeed, the values of education were often debated throughout antiquity, and this is perhaps why *gymnasia* were not only places of physical training and basic education, but they also became major venues for the development of philosophy, especially in Athens. In the Classical period, philosophers and other intellectual figures known as "sophists" first frequented *gymnasia* on an informal basis (see **13b**: Aristophanes *Clouds*; **22d**: Plato *Gorgias*). The three best-known *gymnasia* in Athens were the Academy, the Lyceum, and the Cynosarges, and each eventually became the site for a major philosophical school. The philosopher Antisthenes, a student of Socrates and Gorgias, is said to have set up his own school of thought, which developed into Cynicism, first in the Cynosarges gymnasium. And Plato established his school of philosophy in the Academy, while Aristotle established his at the Lyceum. Even later philosophic movements which were distinctly anti-athletic, such as Stoicism, nevertheless retained a significant number of athletic metaphors that may result from the historical connections between athletics and education beginning in the Classical period (on which, see **36a–f**: Epictetus).

In the Hellenistic and Roman periods, the gymnasium became a distinctive locale for establishing and confirming elite Hellenic identity, which was determined in part through education, in part through citizenship. In Egypt, for instance, there was a class of elites referred to as *hoi apo tou gymnasiou* "those from the gymnasium" (see Remijsen 2014). In the period of Rome's expansion and empire, even though bath complexes became the major venue for leisure and athletic activity, *gymnasia* remained associated with a distinctly Greek-style education and hybrid bath-gymnasium complexes developed in the Eastern provinces. Such complexes were indicative of the persistent value of Hellenism even in a Roman context. This persistence is signaled by the fact that the majority of our sources on ancient Greek athletics come from the Roman Imperial period.[2]

---

[2] See further Decker (2012); Murray (2015); Newby (2005); Papakonstantinou (2019); Pleket (2012); Remijsen (2014); and Scott (2014).

III. Nudity and the Athletic Body

A unique and defining characteristic of ancient Greek athletics is that it was performed in the nude (see Figure 13). The Greek word "naked" (*gymnos*) is the basis for several key terms related to athletics: *gymnazein* (to exercise in the nude); *gymnastikē* (the art of athletic training/exercise in the nude); *gymnastēs* (the trainer of the nude athlete); *gymnasion* (the building for athletic training in the nude and the word for exercise). In the ancient Olympics and other athletic festivals, the *gymnikos agōn*, "nude competition" referred to all athletic events performed by individual athletes, and this category was opposed to the horse events or *hippikos agōn*. How and why it became customary for ancient Greek athletics to be practiced in the nude was a source of debate in antiquity and remains so today.

First and foremost, it is generally agreed that exercise in the nude became a cultural norm sometime in the early Archaic period, between the eighth and sixth centuries BCE. In the Homeric epics, we see that athlete warriors did not participate in sport entirely nude but girded themselves with belts or loincloths before performing activities such as wrestling (**1b:** Homer *Iliad* 23). And one of our first attestations of exercise in the nude appears in an erotic fragment of the Archaic Greek poet Theognis (see **6a**). In the Classical period, the philosopher Plato discusses how practices and values may be historically and culturally relative and refers to the practice of athletic nudity as a relatively late Greek cultural practice. Plato further asserts that nudity in athletics

Figure 13. Attic red-figure vase of nude athlete cleansing by scraping off dirt with strigil, National Archaeological Museum of Madrid

Figure 14. Panathenaic prize amphora, Cleophrades Painter, c.525–500 BCE, Metropolitan Museum, New York, no. 07.286.79

began with the Cretans and then the Spartans (see **22g**: 452c). Similarly, the historian Thucydides also asserts that the practice of nude athletics began with Sparta, as part of a general effort to reduce the opportunities for social distinction through luxury and modes of dress (**9a**). Later authors offer more historically contingent reasons for nudity in ancient Greek sport: the Roman travel writer Pausanias tells the story of Orsippus of Megara, who is believed to have competed and won in the *stadion* foot race at the Olympics around 724 BCE. It appears Orsippus lost his loincloth (*perizōma*) either accidentally or on purpose. Pausanias suggests that Orsippus' reason was to enhance his athletic performance (**37a–b**). Pausanias' account is also corroborated by a Roman period inscription (first century CE), where the Megarans commemorated Orsippus for the first nude victory in Greek history (see **I5m**). Whatever the historical origins of nudity in Greek sport, it is clear that the practice was the norm by the Classical period, especially with the development and increasing importance of the gymnasium as a fixture in every Greek city.

The only major equipment for the nude athlete also served to emphasize the fact of nudity. For every athlete carried with them a small bottle of oil known as an *aryballos* or *lēkythos*, as well as an oil and sweat scraper (*stlengis* or, later, *xystra*) or strigil (from the Latin *strigilis*). Olive oil was a universal commodity in the ancient Mediterranean with myriad uses, but one of the most popular was its application to the exercising body. There may have been multiple reasons for the application of olive oil: for health and function by warming up the body and making it supple and also for aesthetic and potentially ritual purposes by making the body glisten and shine. After exercise, the oil, sweat, and dirt were scraped off the body. This mixture was called *gloios* and was often collected and sold as a medical remedy (see **I5g**: Inscription at Beroia). Both the oil flask and scraper came to be signifiers of an individual's status as an athlete, as indicated by numerous epitaphs depicting nude individuals with oil bottle and strigil in hand. Strigils were also used in athletic dedications and took on a symbolic significance of their own (see **I1c**; **40a**:18).

Overall, the nude body on display in Greek athletics had significant social implications. First, the practice of nudity may have had an exclusionary effect by presenting the body as visual evidence for differentiating those who had the means and leisure to train regularly from those who did not. And yet the practice of training nude may have also had an inclusive component, as indicated by the passage in Thucydides, since those of different social groups would literally be stripped bare of any external signifiers of wealth and status and would train together in the gymnasia. In addition, because of the pederastic practices of ancient Greek culture, the nudity of athletes further promoted the male body as an object of sexual desire. Female athletes, by contrast, did not regularly perform athletics in the nude, except in the case of Sparta and in Plato's ideal city in the *Republic* (see further discussion at Appendix AIV). Finally, athletic nudity was clearly a marker of Greek versus non-Greek identity, and even in the Hellenistic and Roman periods such athletic nudity continued to signal the Hellenic heritage of athletic competition and training.[3]

IV. Women and Greek Athletics

For men, most Greek city states provided athletic training either as part of military preparedness or in a civic or private gymnasium. At the same time the majority of these city states restricted the role of women to the private sphere of the household and to religious festivals. Athletic competitions for men were part of the public religious festival structure, but during the Archaic and Classical periods women's athletic competitions were found only in festivals restricted to women, which were usually conducted without male spectators. A few such established festivals were known to include running contests for girls and unmarried women, and there is a little more evidence for women's competitions in male venues by the Roman period.

Since men provide all of the information we have about ancient Greek athletics, we have almost no information about the extent and types of these female athletic activities. The information we do have comes from a few literary sources, archaeological remains, artifacts, inscriptions, and epigrams about female victors in the Roman period. The myth of Atalanta, as seen in visual arts as well as texts, provides an image of a female athlete (wrestler and runner) who competes with and often defeats men.

The Heraea at Olympia

Married women were not allowed to be spectators at the Olympic Games; sources claim that women discovered there would be punished by death (see, e.g. **40a**: Philostratus *Gymnasticus* 17). But according to Pausanias (**37h**: 5.16.2–7), writing in the second century CE, the Eleans held a festival to Hera in the sanctuary at Olympia on a four-year cycle exclusively for women. It was said

---

[3] See further Bonfante (1989); Christesen (2012); and Miller (2004).

Figure 15. Bronze statuette of female runner, found at Prizien, Serbia, c.520–500 BCE. British Museum 1976.5–10.1 Bronze 208

to have been established by Hippodamia, in gratitude for her marriage to Pelops.[4] As part of the festival, there were foot races for women in three age classes, girls, young unmarried women, and those who aged in between (probably 16- to 18-year olds, a clear parallel to young men competing as *ageneioi*). Greek women normally wore garments that fell from shoulder to ankle, but Heraea runners wore a short tunic ending mid-thigh, with the right shoulder bared to the breast.

A series of small statuettes of female runners with a costume that resembles Pausanias' description are thought to represent the event (see Figure 15). They date from the sixth century (the Heraea probably began sometime in the sixth century BCE or even earlier). The victors received olive crowns, as did the male athletes, and were also able to dedicate statues with inscriptions on them. The victor also received a cow for sacrifice to Hera, which suggests that the victory had a communal component.

Arcteia

Running events for very young girls (7–14) from elite Athenian families were also staged at the Arcteia in Brauron (outside of Athens), a festival in honor of Artemis. Most of the evidence comes

---

[4] This is an obvious symmetry with the myth told by Pindar in Olympian 1 (**2a**) that Pelops initiated the Olympic Games in gratitude to Zeus for his victory over Oenomaus.

from excavation of the site itself, where small jugs (*kratēriskoi*) were found depicting little girls running. Similar jugs were found at an Artemis shrine in Munichia.

Spartan Women

The education of Spartan women was the exception to normal Greek practice. According to Xenophon and Plutarch, the Spartan lawgiver Lycurgus mandated that young women train and even compete with men, though the purpose of the training was to make women healthier and stronger for childbearing, not to provide them with rudimentary military training in order to defend their city if necessary (see **10c**, **35g**). Athenian sources were ambivalent about Spartan women: In Plato's *Republic*, Socrates, in creating his ideal, if imaginary state, does seem to reflect Spartan practices in arguing for the need for athletic training for women as well as men (**22g**), and in the *Laws* (**22i**) Plato specifically names Sparta as a model. A Spartan festival to Dionysus included running events for unmarried women, but since Pausanias claims it came to Sparta from Delphi, it may date to the Roman period (Pausanias 3.13.7).

Equestrian Events

Despite the fact that women did not attend the Olympic Games, from the fourth century BCE onward women did compete and post victories in equestrian events at both Panhellenic and local games. This was possible because the owner of the horse or team received the crown, not the jockey or charioteer. The earliest such victor was Cynisca, the sister of Agesilaus II, a Spartan king; she won with a four-horse chariot at Olympia in 396 and probably again in 392 (see **10a**, **35a**, **37x**, **I1i**). According to Pausanias (3.17.3), her victory statue was erected in Sparta. In the Hellenistic period, the royal women of the house of Ptolemy posted multiple victories in equestrian events, as Posidippus and Callimachus record (**26a**, **27l-o**). Subsequently, inscriptions include the victories of at least fifteen women who competed in Panhellenic as well as local competitions.[5]

Roman Period

The Roman period saw the introduction of events for women in many local and some Panhellenic contests. The proximate cause for this seems to have been to honor Livia, the wife of the Emperor Augustus. Livian Games were introduced in Sparta, with races for young women, and into the Isthmia around 2 BCE. Evidence is meager, but there is one inscription from Delphi (*c.*45 CE) erected by a father to commemorate the multiple victories of his three daughters in the *stadion* at Delphi, Isthmia, and Nemea; one daughter also won in lyre playing at Athens; a third in a race in armor (**I2g**). The multiple victories suggest that these girls competed regularly, though probably not after they reached the age of marriage. How frequently other women competed in similar events is not known.

The indirect role of women in athletics is well attested. They served as overseers in the actual running of a civic gymnasium (*gymnasiarchoi*) and in sponsoring games (*agōnothetai*). They may have taken on these roles as a duty assigned by lot to the wealthy citizens of a city (called a liturgy) or as part of a priestly office, but inscriptions do record many women who held such positions.[6]

---

[5] See Mantas (1995: 128–9).   [6] See the list in Mantas (1995: 137–9).

The increasing participation of women in affairs of the gymnasium makes sense, because in the Roman period the gymnasium became a marker of Greek social status and women as well as men were eager to distinguish themselves as "of the gymnasium class."

The Myth of Atalanta

According to Apollodorus (*he Library*, 3.9.2, *c*. first century BCE), Atalanta was the daughter of Iasus and Clymene of Arcadia but was exposed by her father because she was a girl. She was suckled by a bear until hunters found and reared her. As an adult she refused to marry and continued to hunt in the forests. She was part of the expedition to hunt the Calydonian boar, and at the funeral games in honor of Pelias she wrestled with Peleus (the father of Achilles) and won. (This event was occasionally portrayed on Greek vases and friezes: see Figure 16.) Later discovering her parents, she again refused to marry unless the suitor could beat her in a foot race. She raced in armor, and the man, if defeated, was killed. After many had raced against her and died, a contender named Melanion used the strategy of bringing golden apples from Aphrodite. He threw the apples into Atalanta's path as he ran; because she stopped to pick them up, she was beaten in the race. Fifth-century BCE images of Atalanta and a few other women in gymnasium settings[7] present them in a bikini-like costume that persists into later Roman images of female athletes.[8] Whether this represents actual dress for women

Figure 16. Atalanta wrestling Peleus, black-figure hydria, c.550 BCE, Staatliche Antikensammlungen, Munich, no. 596

[7] See Arrigoni (1985: plates 16–20).
[8] The Villa Romana del Casale in Piazza Armerina has a fourth-century CE mosaic of young women apparently competing in gymnic events; they wear a costume similar to that found in much earlier representations.

in gymnasia or male imaginings is not at all clear. Atalanta's importance as a female athlete led Plato in *Republic*, bk.10 (620b5–8) to place her among the souls of other well-known Greek mythic figures who were choosing which type of creature they wished to be in returning to life on earth. He wrote that "in the middle was Atalanta selecting her lot; having seen the great honor of an athletic man, she could not pass over it, but chose [to be a male athlete]."[9]

---

[9] See further Arrigoni (1985) with illustrations; Golden (1998); Mantas (1995); Scanlon (2014).

APPENDIX B SITES AND CONDUCT OF FESTIVAL GAMES

I. Major Festivals

Athletic competitions were a pervasive feature of Greek civic life; they appear as soon as we have written records, and the major games sites were established by the sixth century BCE. The most important of these games (Olympic, Pythian, Isthmian, and Nemean) were open to all Greek male citizens and, because they gave only crowns and only for a first-place victory, they were collectively known as *stephanitic* or "crown" games. Each game had its own individual plant from which the crowns were formed (see Table 2); images of these crowns served as shorthand to mark the game on coins or on victory monuments. By the fifth century their sequencing into a circuit over four years was referred to as the *periodos* (see Table 3) and an athlete who won a victory in all four in succession was a *periodonikēs* (circuit victor).[1]

Apart from these crown games, competitions took place in small local venues, in *polis*-sponsored festivals either limited to citizens or open to both citizens and non-citizens and at sanctuaries dedicated to a deity. Competitions took place in the context of a religious festival dedicated either to a city's divine patron (e.g., the Panathenaea at Athens dedicated to Athena) or to the deity to whom a specific site was dedicated (e.g., the Asclepieia at Epidaurus dedicated to the healing god Asclepius). Most festivals were held on a regular schedule annually, biennially, or quadrennially. Athletic contests might take up the major portion of the festival or, as with the Panathenaea, be only

Table 2 When important Greek athletic contests were established

Games	Location	Established	Dedicated to	Cycle	Prize
Lycaea	Arcadia	Bronze Age?	Zeus	5-year?	
Olympic	Olympia	776 BCE	Zeus	4-year	olive crown
Heraea	Olympia	sixth century	Hera	4-year	
Pythian	Delphi	586 or 582	Apollo	4-year	laurel crown
Isthmian	Isthmia	582 BCE	Poseidon	2-year	pine crown
Nemean	Nemea, Argos	573 BCE	Zeus	2-year	celery crown
Heraea	Argos	Archaic?	Hera	3-, then 5-year	myrtle crown, bronze objects
Panathenaea	Athens	566 BCE	Athena	4-year	money
Eleutheria	Plataea	479 BCE	Zeus	4-year	trophy
Soteria	Delphi	279/278 BCE	Zeus	4-year	crown, Is-Olympic
Ptolemaea	Alexandria	278 BCE	Ptolemy I	4-year	Is-Olympic
Sebasta	Naples	2 CE	Augustus	4-year	Is-Olympic
Neronia	Rome	60 CE	Nero	4-year	eiselastic
Capitolia	Rome	85 CE	Jupiter	4-year	crown, is-olympic

---

[1] A modern parallel would be the winner of a grand slam in tennis.

Table 3 Circuit (*periodos*) of the four crown games

Olympiad	Festival	Month	Year
75.1	Olympia	July/August	480
75.2	Nemea	August/September	479
	Isthmia	April/May or June/July	478
75.3	Delphi	July/August	478
75.4	Nemea	August/September	477
	Isthmia	April/May or June/July	476
76.1	Olympia	July/August	476

part of a much broader celebration. The organization of some festivals is known in detail either from textual sources or from local inscriptions (see, e.g., **23f, I2e, I3c, I3d, I4g, I4i,** and below).

Not all Greek religious festivals had athletic contests[2] and why athletics became attached to certain festivals is disputed, though prestige and economic benefits must have been significant factors, especially in the Hellenistic and Roman periods. The earliest games for which we have written testimony occur in Homer, and they are of two types: the funeral games organized by Achilles for Patroclus (see **1b**), and what appears to be civic games held by the Phaeacians (**1d**). Each of the crown games had at least one origin myth claiming the event was established to honor a dead hero (as in **1a**) or an important local figure, but other myths of origin are told as well: Pindar, for example, provides two different stories for the foundation of the Olympic Games (see **2a, 2b**) and Eusebius (**46**) provides several others. (On hero cult attached to the game sites, see Appendix AI). Civic festivals were established to honor local divinities, and most seem to have added athletic events in imitation of the crown games. In contrast to crown games, civic festivals normally offered prizes of monetary value—gold crowns, vessels filled with olive oil, and weapons or objects of metal as well as sacrificial animals which would be slaughtered and consumed as part of the victory banquets. Hence, they were called *agōnes chrēmatitai* (from *chrēma* = money).

The Hellenistic and Roman periods saw the establishment of a number of new Greek-style games, but now often dedicated to a monarch, as with the Ptolemaea in Alexandria in Egypt around 278 BCE (dedicated to Ptolemy I) or the Neronia in 60 CE (dedicated to the Roman emperor Nero). The most important of these were the Capitoline Games (Capitolia) celebrated in Rome first in 85 CE, and immediately included as the fifth member of the old Greek *periodos*. In addition, cities increasingly added athletic competitions to existing or newly organized festivals, which expanded an athlete's opportunities for financial rewards. Festivals that attained the desirable designation of "Is-Olympic" guaranteed that the victorious athlete would, when returning to his home city, be accorded benefits equal (*isos*) to those that winners at Olympia would have received. These could be considerable, including a victory parade into the city (*eiselasis*), support for life at the city's expense (*opsōnion*), and publicly placed statues and/or inscriptions to celebrate the victory. By the fourth century CE there were hundreds of known venues for Greek-style competitive athletics within the Roman Empire (Table 2 lists a few of the most important). This growth in games meant that athletes could earn a living by competing throughout the year in

---

[2] For example, there were no games attached to the Attic Anthesteria or Plynteria.

various games and led to professionalization in training (see **40a**; *Gymnasticus* 45–6) and to formal guilds of athletes (Young 2012).

   Olympia is by far the most famous and the oldest of the crown game sites. It is situated in the northwestern Peloponnese in a flat plain where two rivers (the Cladeus and the Alpheus) join. Olympia itself has extensive ruins (visible today) that, in conjunction with Pausanias' detailed discussion (**37a–s**), provide a very full idea of the site and how competitions were conducted. Religious activity seems to have taken place there as early as 1000 BCE, well before games were formally organized—according to ancient sources in 776.[3] By the mid-sixth century BCE, the sanctuary had come under the control of the nearby city of Elis, which took responsibility for all aspects of the festival and imposed an organization that persisted for centuries. Officials (*Hellanodikai* = "judges of the Greeks") were chosen by lot from the Elean elite to act as overseers for the festival as a whole and as judges for the games. (Their number varied over the centuries from an initial two to as many as ten; see Pausanias **37b**, 5.9.4–6). They were responsible for readying the site when games were held, certifying and guaranteeing the preparedness of the athletes and horses, and overseeing the competitions and sacrifices. Every fourth year at the first full moon after the summer solstice (between July and August), the *Hellanodikai* proclaimed the beginning of the sacred month during which cities were supposed to observe the Olympic truce (see **37j**). The truce allowed athletes and trainers to pass safely through territories that might be warring with each other, and during this month athletes were required to train in Elis under the supervision of the *Hellanodikai*, a requirement that seems to have been unique to the Olympic Games. At the end of the sacred month organizers, athletes, horses, and chariots walked in procession for two days from Elis to the games site, a distance of about 55 km (35 miles). Spectators, as many as 40,000, would have made their way separately. Initially, the only competition was said to have been the foot race the length of the stadium (called the *stadion*), and later the Olympiad was named for the victor in the event. Other events were quickly added (see Table 7, p. 391, and Table 8, p. 399) and the festival grew in length to five days during the fifth through the first centuries BCE. The program is shown in Table 4.

Table 4   Schedule of events for Olympic festival c.350 BCE

Day 1	Oaths of athletes and trainers
	Examination of athletes and horses to ensure they compete in the proper categories
	Contests for trumpeters and heralds
Day 2	Equestrian events
	Pentathlon
Day 3	Sacred procession and sacrifices to Zeus
Day 4	Boys' contests
Day 5	Men's foot races
	Men's combat events
	Race in armor
	Crowning of victors in temple of Zeus
	Banquet of victors in Prytaneion

---

[3] This date was questioned even in antiquity; see Appendix BII

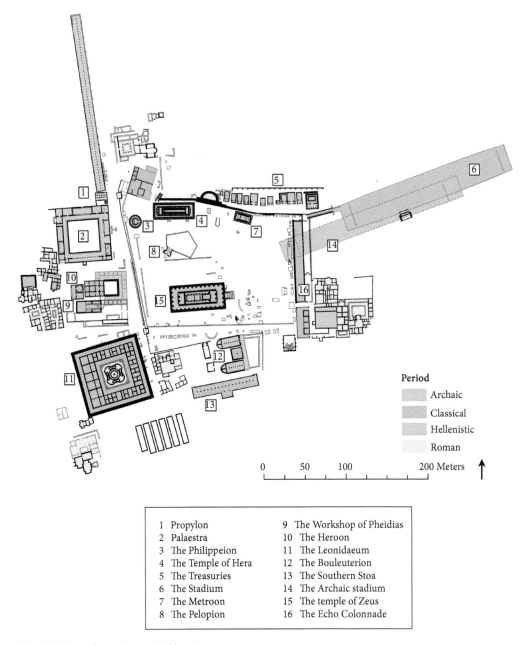

Period

Archaic

Classical

Hellenistic

Roman

1	Propylon	9 The Workshop of Pheidias
2	Palaestra	10 The Heroon
3	The Philippeion	11 The Leonidaeum
4	The Temple of Hera	12 The Bouleuterion
5	The Treasuries	13 The Southern Stoa
6	The Stadium	14 The Archaic stadium
7	The Metroon	15 The temple of Zeus
8	The Pelopion	16 The Echo Colonnade

Plan 2. Plan of sanctuary at Olympia

The original site held a sacred enclosure with an altar to Zeus (the *Altis*) and a tomb identified as that of Pelops (see Pindar **2a,** Pausanias **37f**). The oldest temple, erected in the sixth century BCE, was to Hera, the wife of Zeus, and a festival in her honor (the Heraea) was held every four years, in a staggered sequence with the Olympic Games, and included a foot race for girls and women (see Appendix AIV). The central temple to Zeus Olympios was built in 471 BCE, and its

statue was one of the seven wonders of the ancient world.[4] As the number of games and participants grew over time, temples and other facilities were added (see Plan 2). Facilities were only
provided for the athletes and their trainers, and it was usual for the wealthy to have elaborate tents,
but the majority of the attendees will have slept outdoors. (For the discomforts, see **36b**: Epictetus
1.6.23–9). The gymnic events took place in the stadium, which was entered by an arched passage;
it had a few seats for the judges, but only sloping earthen banks for the majority of the spectators.
Equestrian events were held in the hippodrome, the exact location of which is no longer evident
(see Pausanias **37s**). By the Hellenistic period, facilities included an athletic complex (*palaestra*,
baths, gymnasium), a hotel for distinguished visitors (*Leonidaeum*), a meeting chamber
(*bouleutērion*), and treasuries built by various cities in which to house their valuable dedications.
Statues and inscriptions to commemorate victors were erected throughout the area (see Pausanias
37q). A remarkable feature of the Olympian landscape was the line of Zanes erected between 388 BCE
and 127 CE and placed for athletes to see as they entered the stadium to compete (see Pausanias **37m**
and Figure 8). These sixteen statues were paid for by fines from athletes and trainers found guilty
of cheating or bribery (see **37m** and Appendix B3). In 393/394 CE, the Roman emperor Theodosius
closed all pagan temples, and the Olympic Games may have ceased at that time, as did other
athletic contests, but another edict was issued forty years later, which suggests that they continued
for a bit longer. They were revived in 1896 in direct imitation of what was known about the
ancient contests.

   In contrast to Olympia, the site of the **Pythian Games** was located in the mountainous terrain
of central Greece, which imposed physical constraints on the placement of its two central athletic
venues: the stadium and the hippodrome. Second in prestige after Olympia, Delphi was a very old
sanctuary, holding the most important oracle of the ancient Greek world. The site was sacred to
Pythian Apollo, who supposedly killed a monstrous snake (the Python) that guarded the place.
Originally, the site held only musical contests, since Apollo was also the patron god of music and
musicians, and musical competitions always remained central. But after local city states banded
together to form a loose council (the Amphictyonic League) and won control of the area, in
582 BCE, the contests were reorganized on a quadrennial schedule and athletic events added that
resembled the Olympic Games (see Pausanias **37t**). Six months before the games officially began,
it was the responsibility of the Amphictyony to choose nine citizens (called *theōroi*) to travel
around to Greek cities and announce the date of the games. They also proclaimed the sacred
month (*hieromēnia*) during which the sacred truce was supposedly held. The Amphictyony was
also responsible for preparing the athletic venues, which were not, unlike the temple complex, in
constant use. An inscription from 247/246 BCE allows insight into the work. Forty independent
individuals were contracted to clear growth from the stadium and gymnasia, level them, and
spread a layer of fine earth for practice and competition (see **I2e**).[5] See further Appendix BII1.

   Control of Delphi was contested often in the course of Greek history, more for its prestigious
oracle than its athletics: It was invaded by a nomadic people, the Gauls, in 279 BCE and Thracians
tribes in 83 BCE, who burned the temple. Roman conquerors looted the site, removing its valuable

---

   [4] It was destroyed by fire in the fifth century CE.
   [5] Comparable information about site maintenance does not exist for the other three crown games, but it
is reasonable to infer that similar processes were necessary.

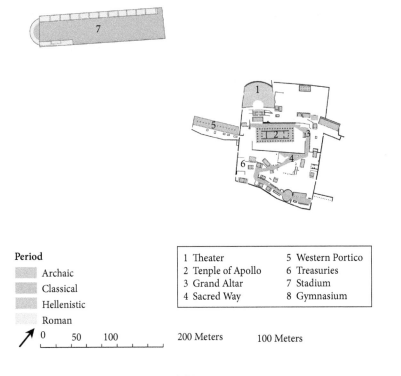

Period		1 Theater	5 Western Portico
	Archaic	2 Temple of Apollo	6 Treasuries
	Classical	3 Grand Altar	7 Stadium
	Hellenistic	4 Sacred Way	8 Gymnasium
	Roman		

0   50   100   200 Meters   100 Meters

Plan 3. Plan of sanctuary at Delphi

dedications. Earthquakes destroyed many of the buildings over time, until the games presumably ended sometime in the fifth century CE.

The original site was rectangular and filled with a central temple to Apollo, a theater for musical and later dramatic contests, and a way lined with treasuries housing the dedications of individual cities. Equestrian events took place in a hippodrome situated below the sanctuary in the plain of Crisa, with the gymnic events in a stadium located above the sanctuary (see Plan 3). The current stadium was built in the Hellenistic period and renovated in the second century CE, when stone seating was added sufficient for around 6,500 spectators. The stadium is U-shaped and measures 600 feet in length with a set of stone starting blocks and lanes for twenty contestants. The remains of the fourth-century BCE gymnasium complex were built on a lower terrace and contained a 180-meter track for running practice as well as a covered colonnade (*stoa*) for use in inclement weather. Below it were the *palaestra* and baths.

In addition to the standard athletic contests known from Olympia, the Pythian program included contests in singing to the *kithara* (a small harp-like instrument) and to the *aulos* (a double-barreled oboe-like instrument), *kithara* and *aulos* playing, and later competitions for acting, recitations, and a foot race for girls (see **I2g** and Appendix BII2).

Games at Isthmia and Nemea were established later than the Olympian and Pythian and were held biennially. Both sites are located in the northeastern corner of the Peloponnese. **Isthmia** sits on the narrow neck (isthmus) on the Gulf of Corinth, a central artery that connected the Peloponnese with Attica and northern Greece. It was controlled by Corinth, an important and prosperous mercantile city roughly 10 km (6 miles) to the west. The sanctuary shows evidence of cultic activity in the Bronze Age, and the first temple was built in the seventh century to Poseidon, the god of the sea. Athletic events were said to have been added by the rulers of Corinth (the Cypselids) in 582 on the model of the Olympic Games and held every other year in the spring. In addition to the usual competitions, events included a boat race (*hamilla neōn*), the *hippios*, which was not a horse race, but, a foot race for men and boys that was longer (four stades) than the *stadion* or *diaulos* (see Pausanias **37q** (6.16.4) and **37u**, and Euripides, *Electra* 825), and music and poetry contests. The site included a theater built around 400 BCE (see Plan 4). Originally, the

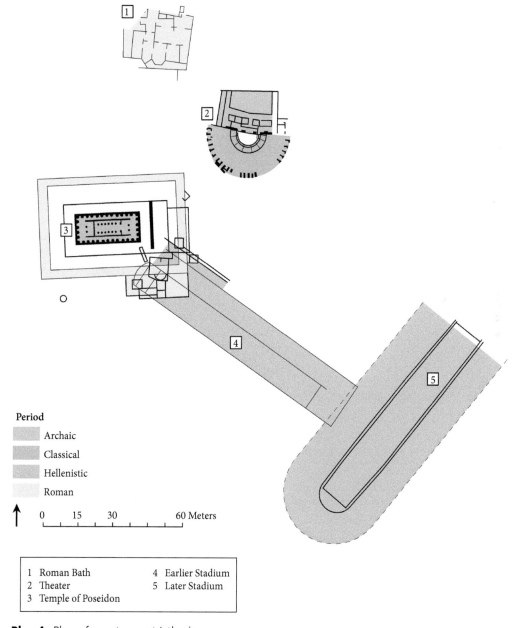

Period

Archaic

Classical

Hellenistic

Roman

0   15   30   60 Meters

1	Roman Bath	4	Earlier Stadium
2	Theater	5	Later Stadium
3	Temple of Poseidon		

Plan 4. Plan of sanctuary at Isthmia

games awarded a crown of pine but changed in the fifth century to one of wild celery in imitation of Nemea, and the reasons for the change are a topic of discussion in antiquity. Both types were used in the Roman period. The Isthmian Games, like the Nemean, sometimes experienced interruptions due to local conflicts (see Xenophon **10i**). In the third century BCE, the Isthmia was the first of the crown games to permit Romans to compete (see Polybius **28a**). According to Dio Chrysostom (**34c**) the games were organized by *athlothetai*. (The term is known also from Athens, where it is a rough equivalent of *Hellanodikai*.)

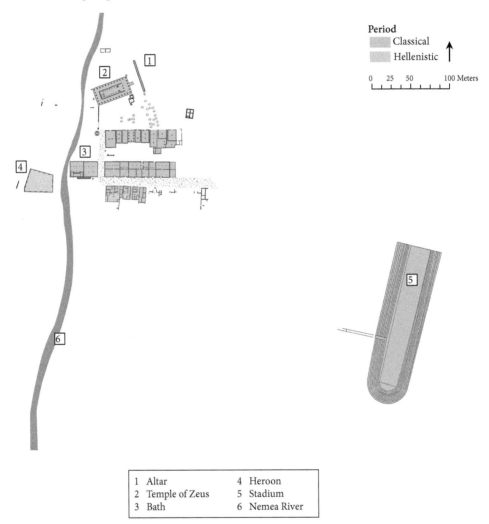

1 Altar	4 Heroon
2 Temple of Zeus	5 Stadium
3 Bath	6 Nemea River

Plan 5. Plan of sanctuary at Nemea

The **Nemean Games** were the last established of the four crown games and the first to end, sometime in the third century CE. The site was a fertile plateau far from urban centers where four regions converge (Corinthia, Achaea, the Argolid, and Arcadia). The powerful city of Argos founded the games there near Cleonae, a small city that originally oversaw their organization, but by the end of the fifth century they were moved to Argos. The games were a political pawn in dynastic struggles, as they were moved back to Nemea for about eighty years after 330 BCE, and in 235 competing games were held at both Nemea and Argos (see Plutarch **35e**). The site itself was dedicated to Zeus and had the standard accommodations for athletes as well as a well-excavated stadium that held remains of a starting mechanism (a *hysplēx*) (see Plan 5). It was entered by a vaulted tunnel, as at Olympia. Spectators sat along the banked sides of the stadium and coin finds suggest they sat by civic group (i.e., Argive, Corinthian). But by Pausanias' time much of the site was in ruins. As with Olympia, the judges were *Hellanodikai* appointed by the controlling city (usually Argos). Competition was in three age classes (as in the Panathenaea)—boys, beardless youths (*ageneioi*), and men. The program included the *hippios* (see above) and in the Roman period a *stadion* for girls (see **I2g**).

The **Greater Panathenaea** was the most important of the city-sponsored games, a celebration of Athens' power, wealth, and cultural importance. Originally it was an annual festival dedicated to the city's patron goddess Athena, whose temple, the Parthenon, was situated on the Acropolis. In 566/565 BCE the tyrant Peisistratus reorganized the Panathenaea on a quadrennial basis and added athletic events to the musical and dramatic competitions. Victorious contestants were awarded money prizes, including gold crowns and specially produced amphoras (see Figure 14, p. 365) filled with olive oil[6] and decorated with an image of the event (see **I4f**: *IG* II[2] 2311). The events were divided into three ages classes (as at Nemea), but also included separate events for Athenian citizens only, organized by civic units known as tribes. These events included a beauty contest for men (*euandria*), a boat race, *anthippasia*, and the *apobatēs* race. The prizes for winners in these contests often included an ox, meant for a sacrificial feast for the entire tribe (see **4f**). See Table 5 for a comparison of events at these games.

In imitation of crown games, the city sent ambassadors throughout Greater Greece to announce the date of the games and invite participants. According to Aristotle (see **23f**) officials (*athlothetai*), one for each of Athens' ten tribal units, were appointed to organize the procession, oversee the musical, gymnic, and hippic events, the making of the *peplos*[7] and the amphoras, and the making of the prize oil from olive trees sacred to Athena. The eight-day festival began with a procession that included officials, the bearer of the *peplos*, and young men and women. The procession is memorialized on the Parthenon frieze. The events took place in the city itself. A night-time torch race came from the Academy to the Acropolis to light the sacred fire, an event that became a model for the bringing of the Olympic torch when the Olympic Games were reintroduced in 1896. The dedicated stadium was built in 330 BCE and refurbished for the 1896 games. The Panathenaea survived until about 410 CE (see also Appendix BII4).[8]

---

[6] The oil was used by athletes both before and after exercise, but also it was important for lighting and cooking.

[7] As part of the festival a garment (called a *peplos*) was woven by selected women to be presented to the goddess at the start of the festival.

[8] See further Nijf (2000); Romano (2014); Valavanis (2004); Young (2012); and Remijsen and Clarysse, KU Leuven website.

Table 5 Events at the four Panhellenic sites and the Panathenaea compared

Games	Gymnic contests	Equestrian contests	Musical contests	Other
Olympic	*stadion, dolichos, diaulos,* wrestling, *pankration,* boxing, pentathlon, race in armor	two- and four-horse chariot race (for adult horses and foals) single-horse race (adult and foal)	trumpeter	
Pythian	same	only four-horse chariot race	*aulos, kithara* playing, and singing	dithyramb, tragic, comic acting, *stadion* for girls
Isthmian	same			*hippios*
Nemean	same, but three age classes			boat race *hippios* *stadion* for girls
Panathenaea	same, but three age classes	same	same as Pythian	tribal contests: *euandria,* pyrrhic dancing, torch race, *apobatēs,* boat race

II. Record-Keeping

Modern athletic competitions have records of every sort, most notably the Olympic records of height, speed, and distance that the Olympic motto itself encourages an athlete to break (*Altius, Citius, Longius* = Higher, Faster, Farther). Without the technological advances that the modern world enjoys ancient Greeks kept fewer records, but they shared the same desire to record athletic achievements. Their records were of two kinds: locally inscribed stone and those written in book form (usually on papyrus).

Inscriptions on stone walls, statue bases, or on a free-standing slab (called a stele) were commonly used to record an individual victor in one or more contests (see, e.g., **I1d, I2a, I2b,** etc.) or several victors within a city (see **I5i**). These could be erected by the victor's family or the city honored by his victory (see **I5j**). These monuments are now extremely useful in constructing a picture of the range of cities that sponsored games or honored victorious athletes (both in local and Panhellenic venues). They also provide a snapshot of games in which an individual might compete (see **I3b**) and the type of benefits that an individual victor might accrue. However, they are widely dispersed in time and place, so cannot provide a systematic or complete picture.

An additional tool for reconstructing the history of ancient Greek athletics is the various types of **victors' lists compiled for individual games**. The bulk of these are for Olympia, but examples survive for other crown games (Delphi, Isthmia, Nemea), as well as for many local contests.[9] Some lists were recorded on stone and found on or near the game sites, but others were written in book form. These were portable, and thus available to be consulted by writers of other types of

---

[9] For a list of Olympic victors, see Moretti (1953). Christesen (2007: 130–2) lists inscriptions of victors for local games. For a list of Isthmian victors, see Christesen (2007: 129 n. 191 and 134–6).

texts (i.e., historians, geographers; see Pausanias **37q**, 6.13.8). As they were transmitted over the centuries, information could be added or subtracted as a need arose (see below for examples).

1. Lists of Olympic victors (*Olympionikai*)

The most significant (and numerous) are the Olympic victory lists. Unlike records of individual games, their form was chronological, listing victors in order beginning with the first Olympiad. The earliest and most significant event was the *stadion* (foot race), and its victor gave his name to the whole Olympiad (see Eusebius below). After the *stadion*, victors would usually be recorded in the order in which their event was added to the Olympic program, clustered first by gymnic events (running, pentathlon, wrestling, boxing, *pankration*), then hippic events (single-horse race, two-horse chariot, four horse-chariot, etc.). For gymnic events, the boys' victories were recorded immediately after the men's victories. (Hippic events had no age categories.) The format was simple, as P. Oxy 2.222 illustrates: Lines 7–19 record the victors of 476 BCE, among whom are Euthymus of Locri (see **I1f**); Theogenes of Thasos (see **I2b**); Theron of Acragas (see **2b**); and Hieron of Syracuse (see **2a**, **3a**):

96th [Olympiad] Scamander the Mytilenean [won] the *stadion*.
Dandis the Argive, *diaulos*.
[…] *dolichos*.
[…] the Tarantine, pentath(lon).
[…] the Maronite, wrestling.
[Euthymos the] Locrian from Italy, boxing.
[Theogenes] of Thasos, *pankration*.
[…], boys' *stadion*.
[Theognetos the Aegi]netan, boys' wrestling.
[Hag]esi[da]mos the Locrian from Italy, boys' boxing.
[Ast]yros the Syracusan, race in armor, the greatest.[10]
The four-horse chariot of [Ther]on of Acragas [won].
The horse of [Hier]on of Syracuse [won].

This list circulated as a standalone work, and its basic framework could be adapted easily for chronographic studies. Many such studies integrated unique local information about athletes as well as political events (for example, magistracies of various cities) that fell within the Olympiad. In these cases, only the year of the Olympiad and the *stadion* victor were necessary to provide the frame. Sections of Eusebius' *Chronographia* use this format:

54th. Hippostratus of Croton, *stadion*.

Arechion of Phigaleia was being strangled and died, even as he was winning the *pankration* for the third time. His body was crowned victor, since his opponent yielded in defeat, when his leg was broken by Arechion.[11]

55th. Hippostratus, the same man, *stadion* for a second time.

This happened when Cyrus became king of the Persians.

---

[10] "The greatest" appears to be a personal comment of the compiler; it refers to the victor, not the event.
[11] For Arechion (also spelled Arrhichion/Arrhachion) see **37z**, **40d**.

56th. Phaedrus of Pharsalus, *stadion*.

57th. Laodromus of Laconia, *stadion*.

A somewhat more elaborate example is provided by POxy 1.12, which records events of 348–345 BCE:

> In the one hundred and eighth Olympiad Polycles the Cyrenean won the stadion; in Athens, Aristodemus [348 BCE], Thessalus [347], Apollodorus [346], and Callimachus [345] were the archons. In the first year of this [Olympiad] the philosopher Plato died and Speusippus succeeded him as head of his school [i.e., Plato's Academy].

Work on Olympic victor lists seems to have begun systematically in the late fifth century BCE with Hippias of Elis, who is credited with establishing the date of 776 BCE for the first Olympiad.[12] Others who compiled or depended upon such lists included Aristotle, Philochorus (a writer of local Athenian history), Timaeus of Tauromenium (the historian of Sicily), Eratosthenes of Cyrene, Diodorus Siculus, Dionysius of Halicarnassus, and Eusebius.[13] Today, fragments of several lists copied in the Roman period occur on papyrus (POxy. 1.12, 2.222, and 17.2082) and partial lists are used or embedded in historical or other types of writing. The only complete list is that of Eusebius in his *Chronologia* (see **46**), though historians like Diodorus Siculus[14] depended on the framework of the *Olympionikai* to write annalistic histories that attempt to synthesize historical events from all parts of the world known to Greeks, as this brief excerpt makes clear:

> As for the dates included in this work, we cannot securely establish the events before the Trojan War because no trustworthy annals have been passed down, but after the Trojan War, following Apollodorus the Athenian, we [i.e., Diodorus] have established 80 years from the return of the Heraclidae, and from that event to the first Olympiad 320 years, reckoning the dates from the kings in Sparta and from the first Olympiad to the beginning of the Celtic War [the end of his history]. (1.5.1)

The value of these lists for the ancients resided in their strict chronological organization from the fixed date of 776. Because Greek city states did not have synchronized calendars or systematic record-keeping of historical events, Greek writers were particularly concerned to find ways of aligning events. This need grew more urgent in the Hellenistic and Roman periods, when Greeks encountered other cultures with their own systems of record-keeping. Many turned to the *Olympionikai* as a reliable structure against which to locate specific regional, national, or international events. This is borne out by the more elaborate versions of *Olympionikai*, which included important historical or cultural events or information about athletes for each of the four years within the Olympiad (see examples above). From these many lists and inscriptions it is possible to gain insight into the range and growth of Olympic victors over time (see Table 6).

---

[12] Christesen (2007: 146–57) discusses how the date was arrived at and the likelihood of its accuracy.

[13] Only the works of the last three survive.

[14] As did Dionysius of Halicarnassus in his *Roman Antiquities*. See Christesen (2007: 296–347) for what he calls these "Olympiad Chronicles."

2. Lists of Pythian victors (*Pythionikai*)

The sanctuary of Apollo at Delphi was famous for its oracle; it was also the site where the Pythian Games were held, after being reorganized in 586 BCE on a four-year cycle to include gymnic and hippic events (see Appendix BI). Lists of Pythian victors were first compiled in the late fourth century BCE; these were likely to have been circulating texts, as were the Olympic lists, but partial lists were also inscribed on stone slabs (stelai) and erected in the precinct at Delphi. Primary evidence for this comes from a fragmentary inscription (*SEG*³ 275 = *Fouilles de Delphes* 3.1.400) at Delphi commending Aristotle and Callisthenes for compiling it:

> Since Aristotle, the son of Nicomachus the Stagirite, and Callisthenes, the son of Damotimus, composed the list (*pinax*) of those who were victorious at the Pythian Games and of those who organized the contest from the beginning, praise Aristotle and Callisthenes and crown them; the stewards will set up the list (*pinax*) in the sanctuary...

References by later sources, particularly those who commented on Pindar's victory poems, make it clear that the victor list was organized by Pythiad, for which Aristotle and Callisthenes had introduced the idea of numbering.[15] In addition to the list of athletic victors, Aristotle is credited with an account of the musical victors at Delphi.[16]

3. Local festival records

The Panathenaea was held annually for Athenian citizens, but every four years, from 566/565 BCE, the city sponsored a nine-day festival with athletic contests open to noncitizens. Unlike the crown games, the Panathenaea gave substantial prizes in the form of money, golden crowns, and jars of olive oil. Thanks to a large inscription (see **I4f:** *IG* II2 2311) that recorded not individual victors, but the prizes awarded in each event, we are able to get a sense of the relative value placed on events. For example, the largest prizes are not for athletes but for musicians, and competitions are in two categories, namely, those contests standard at Panhellenic games and a second group restricted to citizens, some of which were organized on the basis of civic units called "tribes." The latter group includes the male beauty contest (*euandria*), the torch race (*lampadēdromia*), and the boat race, prizes for which include oxen, which would be sacrificed to provide a feast for the winning tribe.

In contrast to the prizes at the Panathenaea, the third-century BCE list from Coresia on Ceos, (see **I5f:** *IG* XII,5 647) records much smaller prizes, which suggests that there were many local competitions that did give prizes but were unlikely to be held for more than local citizens or ephebes.

---

[15] Aristotle is likely to have been instrumental in numbering the *Olympionikai* as well.
[16] See Christesen (2007: 179–202) for a discussion of the evidence for the dating and construction of *Pythionikai*.

Table 6 Where Olympic victors are from over time

Archaic
776 BCE – 481 BCE

Classical
480 BCE – 323 BCE

Hellenistic
322 BCE – 31 BCE

Roman
31 BCE – 393 BCE

Kilometers

0   275   550   1,100

4. Other works on athletic contests

The late Classical and early Hellenistic period saw a growing interest in the history of the Panhellenic games, their sites, types of event, and famous athletes. In addition to the cumulative lists of victors by site, there were numerous annalist-style essays detailing significant events that happened within each game cycle, collections of historical and anecdotal information about victors, and treatises on specific sites (though none has survived intact). The Hellenistic poet Callimachus, for example, wrote a treatise *On Contests* (*peri agōnōn*, fr. 403 Pf.), and Eusebius cites him as a source for the chronology of Olympic victor lists (see **46**). Another Hellenistic poet, Euphorion of Chalcis wrote *On the Isthmian Games*, while a poetic fragment mentions the origin of the wild celery crown.[17]

These and similar writings on athletic events and practices belong to a serious tradition of systematizing knowledge about Greek institutions, in part to affirm the continuity of Greek cultural forms over time, especially as Greeks moved to lands distant from Greece proper.[18]

III. Breaking the Rules

Because the stakes were so high and the rewards to victors in status and money so great, the temptation to cheat in Greek athletic competitions must have been enormous. All competitions had rules that disqualified or fined an athlete or trainer found guilty of cheating, but there is ample testimony that it occurred throughout the history of Greek athletic games. Also, there were always a number of possibilities to game the system that fell short of cheating, such as trying to enter a competition in a younger age category, where the competitors would be less skilled, using prohibited holds or punches, biting, gouging, or tripping opponents, starting a race too soon, or cutting out a competitor in chariot racing. As early as Homer's description of the funeral games for Patroclus, Antilochus defeated Menelaus by running a better chariot race strategically, though his horses were not as good. Menelaus was furious at the defeat and insisted that the younger man won by trickery (see **1b**: Homer, *Iliad* bk. 23.566–95).

At Olympia the official judges, the *Hellanodikai*, were in charge of certifying that the competitors were adequately trained and in the proper age class to prohibit unequal matches; they monitored the matches and could disqualify or even beat an offender for infractions like biting and gouging, and all athletes swore a solemn oath to abide by the rules. A small fragment from the late sixth century BCE has been found that lists a few of these rules:

> *The wrestler should not break a finger[*
> *the referee should strike, except at the head[*
> *wrongdoers should be brought in and promise[(see* **I1b**)

But apparently the constant breaking of rules required more stringent measures. At Olympia, as the athletes entered the stadium along the road from the Metroon, bronze images of Zeus (called Zanes) were erected. These were made from the fines levied on athletes who wantonly

---

[17] Quoted in Plutarch, *Table Talk*, *Moralia* 667A.   [18] See further Christesen (2007).

broke the rules of the contests. Pausanias describes a few examples ranging in date from 338 BCE to 125 CE, the first with the explicit statement that "an Olympic victory is to be achieved, not by money but by swiftness of foot and strength of body" (**37m**: 5.21.4 and Figure 8).

The majority of these fines were for bribing the opponent to throw the match, a practice that is attested in other places (see **40a**: Philostratus, *Gymnasticus* 45). In wrestling, especially, the practice was sufficiently common that the Greeks had a word for it: *hypopalaiein*, "to go down voluntarily in wrestling." There are a number of anecdotal mentions of cheating in Greek writing (see **13a**: 25, **14c**, **38g**), but the most egregious example is what appears to have been a contract between two fathers in which one pays the other for his son to throw a wrestling match (**P9**).

The extreme pressure under which the athletes competed and which led to cheating is illustrated by an account in Pausanias (**37q**: 6.9.6–7). He tells the tragic and frightening story of Cleomedes of Astypalaea, who was competing in boxing (*pyx*). He killed his opponent, which in itself was not disqualifying, but the *Hellanodikai* determined that he had cheated in doing so and stripped him of the victory crown. He subsequently went mad, and when he returned to his hometown, he killed a schoolroom full of children (see Appendix A1).[19]

---

[19] See further Golden (1998: 15–16, 38, 42, 109); Miller (2004: 211–12); Potter (2012: 60–1, 286–7).

APPENDIX C THE EVENTS (*AGŌNES*)

I. Running Events

1. The *stadion*

Our earliest accounts of running competitions in Greek culture occur in the *Iliad*, where they are associated both with warfare (see **1a**: *Iliad* 22.159–66) and with more general conceptions of human-divine interaction (see **1b**: *Iliad* 23.740–92). The earliest and most prominent of the running events was the *stadion*—a foot race on a straight track, which measured 600 ancient feet, although the actual distance of the track varied from place to place (from 165 m at Corinth to 192.28 m at Olympia) (see Figure 17). According to Philostratus, the *stadion* race had its origin in Olympia as a race to the altar (see **40a**: *Gymnasticus* 5). According to several ancient sources, the *stadion* was the only event at the Olympics for the first thirteen Olympic Games, which were presumably held every four years (**37b**: Pausanias 5.8.6; **40a**: Philostratus *Gymnasticus* 12). The first Olympic victor in the *stadion* was Coroebus of Elis, and the race was so important in the ancient world that the four-year period after the Olympic Games was named after the *stadion* victor and was used as a standard for measuring historical time throughout antiquity. These historical periods were recorded in documents known as Olympic victor lists (see Appendix BII). For examples of praise poems (*epinikia*) written for *stadion* victors in the Archaic and early Classical periods, see Pindar *Olympian* 13 (**2g**) as well as Bacchylides 10 (**3c**). For criticism that running presents neither civic nor martial virtue, see Tyrtaeus 12 (**4**) and Lucian's *Anacharsis* (**38a**).

2. The *diaulos*

After the *stadion* other events were apparently added slowly over time. The second such event to be added to the Olympic program was the double *stadion* race or *diaulos* (literally "double flute").[1] This race involved running the length of a *stadion*, turning around a single post, and running back (see Figure 18). According to Philostratus, this event symbolized the gesture of inviting Greece to the games (**40a**: *Gymnasticus* 6) According to several sources, the *diaulos* race was added at the fourteenth Olympic Games, and Hypenus of Pisa was the victor (**37b**: Pausanias 5.8.6; **40a**: *Gymnasticus* 12; **46**: Eusebius).

3. The *dolichos*

The third running event added to the Olympic program was the distance race, known as the *dolichos* (see Figure 19).[2] The actual distance of this race varied from 7 to 24 *stadia*. The race was

---

[1] It would be difficult to visually distinguish a *diaulos* runner from a *stadion* runner, but this particular fragment presents the inscription "*Diaulodromō eimi*": "I am for the runner of the *diaulos*"

[2] The distance runner not only presents less arm action, but also decreased leg drive compared with the *stadion* runner.

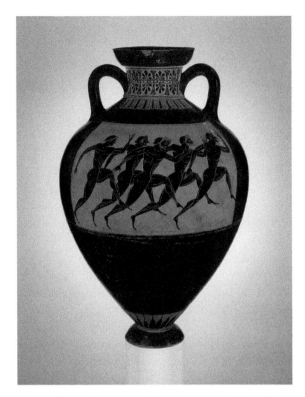

Figure 17. Panathenaic amphora showing *stadion* runners, attributed to Euphiletus Painter, c.530 BCE, Metropolitan Museum, New York, no. 14.130.12

Figure 18. Fragment of Athenian amphora showing *diaulos* runner, c.560–550 BCE, National Museum, Athens, no. 2468. Photo courtesy of Charles Stocking

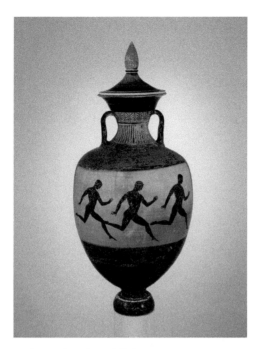

Figure 19. Panathenaic amphora showing *dolichos* runners, c.333 BCE, British Museum, no. 1856,1001,1

run on a *stadion* track and involved all competitors turning around a single turning post. According to Philostratus, the *dolichos* came about from the practice of messengers who had to run in times of war (**40a**: *Gymnasticus* 6). Several sources say that the *dolichos* was introduced in the fifteenth Olympiad (720 BCE); it was won by Acanthus of Sparta (**37b**: Pausanias 5.8.6; **40a**: Philostratus *Gymnasticus* 12; **46**: Eusebius). Indeed, we have evidence that the *dolichos* was a competitive event in early Spartan history (on which, see **I3a**). Also of significance is the *dolichos* victory of Ergoteles of Himera, a political exile from Crete, for which we have the praise poem of Pindar, *Olympian* 12 (**2e**) as well as a dedicatory inscription from Olympia (**I1g**; and **37q**: Pausanias 6.4.11)—a rare case of coincidence between literary and material evidence in ancient athletic history.

4. Running in armor

The race in armor was the last running event thought to have been added to the Olympic program. It was also known as the *hoplitēs* or *hoplitodromos* (see Figure 20). According to Philostratus, there was debate in antiquity as to its significance, although it clearly had its origins in war (**40a**: *Gymnasticus* 7). The amount of armor and length of the race differed for each festival, but the race in armor at Plataea was said to have been the longest and the most heavily armed (**40a**: *Gymnasticus* 8). According to several sources, the race in armor was thought to have begun in the sixty-fifth Olympiad (520 BCE) and the victor was Damaretus of Heraea (**37b**: Pausanias 5.8.10; **40a**: Philostratus *Gymnasticus* 12; **I1J**).

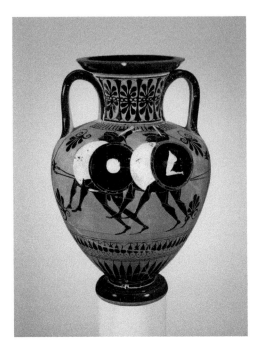

Figure 20. Terracotta neck-amphora (jar), showing hoplite runners, c.510 BCE. Edward C. Moore Collection, Bequest of Edward C. Moore, 1891

Each of the running events required different physiological demands and different techniques (**40a**: Philostratus *Gymnasticus* 32, 33). Such differences can be seen in the way they are represented on Panathenaic amphoras (see Figures 17–20; for the prize awarded at the Panathenaea, see **I4f**).

5. Torch relay and marathon

The *stadion*, *diaulos*, *dolichos*, and *hoplitēs* were standard forms of competition at Panhellenic festivals. But two of the running events associated with the modern Olympic Games, the torch relay and the marathon were not part of the Panhellenic festival program.

The torch relay of the modern Olympics was introduced in the highly controversial Berlin Olympics in 1936. In antiquity, torch races were practiced at many festivals, although the most well known are those of Athens (**37w**: Pausanias 1.30.1–2; **I4f**). As in Philostratus' account of the origin of the *stadion* (**40a**: 5), the goal of the torch relay was to light an altar for sacrifice.

In contrast to the torch relay, the marathon is an entirely modern construct, although inspired by ancient accounts. There are, in fact, two ancient stories concerning distance running and the famous battle of Marathon of 490 BCE. First, according to Herodotus, an Athenian "day runner" (*hēmerodromēs*) named Pheidippides (Philippides in some manuscripts) ran from Athens to Sparta (a distance of roughly 250 km) in order to request aid from the Spartans against the Persian invasion at Marathon, although the request was ultimately denied (Herodotus **8g**). A second story from Plutarch tells of a man named either Thersippus or Eucles, who ran from Marathon to

Athens after the battle, and when arriving, famously announced "Rejoice! We are victorious" (*Chairete nikōmen*) and then died (**35p**: Plutarch *Moralia* 347c). And in reference to the form of greeting, "Rejoice!" "*chairete*," Lucian discusses the same story of the announcement and death of the herald, but refers to him as Philippides, thus conflating the two stories from Herodotus and Plutarch (**38c**). In modern times, these stories were further conflated by Robert Browning in his 1879 poem, "Pheidippides." Both the ancient accounts and Browning's poem inspired organizers of the first Olympic Games to introduce the "marathon" race at the 1896 Olympics in Athens. To the joy of modern Greeks, a Greek water carrier Spyridon Louis won this first, highly symbolic race. He subsequently became a national hero.[3]

6. Running events for women

See Appendix AIV. For a list of when gymnic events were added to the Olympic program, see Table 7.

Table 7 When gymnic events were added to Olympic program

Event	Year Added
stadion, 200 meter race	776 BCE
diaulos, 400 meter race	724 BCE
dolichos, 5000 meter race	720 BCE
pentathlon	708 BCE
palē (wrestling)	708 BCE
pyx (boxing)	688 BCE
pankration	648 BCE
stadion for boys	632 BCE
palē for boys	632 BCE
pentathlon for boys (dropped immediately)	628 BCE
pyx for boys	626 BCE
hoplitēs (= race in armor)	520 BCE
pankration for boys	200 BCE

II. Combat Events

The ancient heavy events or combat sports consisted primarily of **wrestling, boxing, *pankration***, and the late addition of an event known as the ***pammachon***. In antiquity, these combat sports were called the "heavy events," because there were no weight classes, and there was a significant competitive advantage for weighing more than your opponent (see **40a**: Philostratus *Gymnasticus* 3). In training, the combat sports were practiced in the dirt area known as the *skamma* in facilities called *palaestrae* and *gymnasia* (see Appendix AII and Plan 1, p. 362). In competition, a *skamma*

---

[3] See further Christesen (2007: 202–15): Miller (2004: 31–6); Young (2004: 165–70).

was typically made in the area of the *stadion* track, since the *palaestrae* and *gymnasia* at sites such as Olympia could not accommodate the crowds of spectators. Not only did the heavy athletes need to be very large and strong, but they also had to have extreme endurance, since they competed in tournaments which often consisted in many elimination rounds. Pairings for each round were determined by lot, so an element of chance was also at play. If there was an odd number of competitors, one athlete was able to secure a bye, which meant he could move on to the next round without having to compete (see Lucian **38f** and **I1r**). Overall, there were very few regulations in place to ensure the health and safety of competitors. But judges for these events did carry sticks and were allowed to physically beat competitors who were found to be in violation of the few rules that were in place (see Lucian **38f** and **I1b**). Indeed, the heavy events were marked by extreme violence and brutality, and death was not entirely uncommon in these competitions. The majority of ancient athletes who received hero cult worship were heavy athletes, and this may be due to the extreme danger to which these athletes subjected themselves (see Appendix AI). Because of the violence in these sports, Philostratus suggests that the heavy events originated in training for war (**40a**: Philostratus *Gymnasticus* 9–11).

1. Wrestling

The quintessential heavy event was wrestling, known in Greek as *palē*. Wrestling in ancient Greece and Rome was performed standing, and victory was achieved when an athlete was able to throw his opponent to the ground three times (see Figure 24, p. 396). There were certain regulations in place for wrestling, but it seems that athletes would try to bend the rules as much as possible in efforts to inflict pain upon their opponents (**I1b**; **37q**: Pausanias 6.4.3) There is no question, however, that wrestling in antiquity was extremely technical and required significant skill. This is indicated both by textual descriptions as well as visual evidence on vases and mosaics, where very complex wrestling moves are depicted. This is borne out by fragments from wrestling manuals as well (see **P6**). Although Heracles is understood to be the paradigmatic heavy athlete, the invention of wrestling as a distinct and teachable skill is attributed variously to Hermes (**40a**: Philostratus *Gymnasticus* 16) and to Theseus (**37aa**: Pausanias 1.39.3). Unlike other forms of competition, training for wrestling seems to have been the same as, and therefore as difficult as, the actual competition. For this reason, the wrestler is known to be the "hardest-working" (*epiponōtatos*) athlete (**40a**: Philostratus *Gymnasticus* 11)

2. Boxing

The ancient boxing competition, known in Greek as *pyx* "fist" (related to English "pugilist") may be considered even more violent than wrestling. In Greece, from earliest times until the fourth century BCE, boxers wrapped their fists and wrists with leather straps called *himantes*. These lightweight straps seem to have served as protection for the one wearing them. Unlike modern boxing gloves, these leather straps did not lessen the severity of the blows and may have even increased it. Indeed, from in the fourth century, heavier, "sharp" leather straps were used, whose purpose seems to have been to inflict more damage on an opponent, since the sharp, thick leather could more easily lacerate the skin. Not only was the equipment designed for pain, but the rules for the contest also made boxing an extremely difficult event. For there were no rounds in boxing, but only one continuous match. Hence, endurance was a critical component of success. This is why the boxer Melancomas was praised so greatly, in that he seems to have won by avoiding blows and outlasting his opponents (**34a–b**: Dio Chrysostom 28, 29). Victory in boxing was established in only one of two ways: either by knockout or when someone quit, which was signaled by the raising of one's index finger. As a result, boxers typically experienced disfiguring injuries that are well reflected in sculpture such as the Terme boxer (see Figure 2, p. 141).

3. *Pankration*

A third form of competition in the heavy events, which combined wrestling and boxing, was known as the *pankration*, which translates as "all-force" or "total victory." The *pankration* is not represented in the poetry of Homer, and it seems to have been introduced later than boxing and wrestling, perhaps around 648 BCE (**37b**: Pausanias 5.8.8). There are infamously few rules in the *pankration*—no biting, no eye gouging—and victory was declared when an opponent quit or simply could not continue. One might conclude that the *pankration* was as much a test of will as it was of skill and endurance of pain (see Figure 21). The implications of this are famously portrayed in the story of the pankratist Arrhichion, who was said to have forced his opponent to quit and thereby won the match, even though Arrhichion himself died in the process of securing his victory (**40a**: Philostratus *Gymnasticus* 21; **40d**: *Imagines* 2.6; **37z**: Pausanias 8.40.1–5).

4. *Pammachon*

Lastly, from about 300 CE, a new event known as *pammachon* or "all-fighting" was included in the circuit of Greek competitions in the Roman Empire. The term *pammachon* was used throughout Classical and Hellenistic Greek history as a synonym for the *pankration* event, but in the Roman period it seems to indicate a competitive event entirely separate from the *pankration* (see Remijsen 2010). We are not entirely clear on the rules of the *pammachon,* but it seems to have been less technical than the *pankration*. Greek-style competitions underwent significant changes in the Roman Imperial period, and the addition of a new heavy event is one such change. This may have resulted from the increased popularity of the heavy events in the Roman period, since the heavy events are the best attested in Roman honorary inscriptions and art.[4]

III. Pentathlon

The pentathlon for men was introduced into the Olympic program in 708 BCE, the pentathlon for boys was introduced in 628 BCE, but immediately dropped (**37b**: Pausanias 5.9.1). This competition was unique in that it involved five events; hence its name (*pent-* = "five"; *athlon* = "contest"). It was held on a single day, with the individual events following each other without a break, and took place in the stadium. The events were running (the exact length is not known, but probably the *stadion*), wrestling, javelin, discus, and long jump. Philostratus **40a** (4) provides the mythological background for this event, claiming that Jason invented it for the Argonauts. While running and wrestling were also separate competitions, at the Panhellenic Games, javelin, discus, and

---

[4] See further Poliakoff (1987) and Remijsen (2010).

Figure 21. *Pankration*, Panathenaic prize amphora, attributed to the Cleophrades Painter, c.500 BCE. Metropolitan Museum, New York, Rogers Fund, 1916

Figure 22. Events of the pentathlon, Panathenaic prize amphora, attributed to the Euphiletus Painter, *c.*530–520 BCE, British Museum 1842.0314.1

Figure 23. The discus thrower, Roman copy of Greek original, first century CE. British Museum 1814.7-4.43/Sculpture 250

long jump only took place as part of the pentathlon, and many visual images represent these three together as on the Panathenaic amphora shown in Figure 22. The man on the left holds up jumping weights (*haltēres*) for the long jump; the man in the middle holds a javelin; next to him is a man with a discus, followed by another javelin thrower.

Evidence for the order of events comes from a passage in Pindar, *Nemean* 7.70–3 that implies that the winner of the javelin throw did not need to wrestle. This would mean that javelin preceded wrestling and that these two were the final events. Bacchylides *Ode* 9. 26–34 (see **3c**), also for a Nemean victory, lists discus, javelin, wrestling, but not the other two, while an epigram of Simonides (**7b**) on an Isthmian and Pythian pentathlete gives the order as jumping, running, discus, javelin, and wrestling, which aligns with the other two statements. Whether the order changed in later periods or differed at regional venues is not known. There is no consensus on how the event was judged, but it does seem that if the competitor won three of the five events, he was declared a winner and, if no one did so, the winner would be the one who came in second in all five events. This led to ambivalent attitudes toward victors in this event; for example, Longinus in *On the Sublime* (34.2), in comparing the orators Hyperides and Demosthenes, claims that Hyperides "is nearly as good a second as the pentathlete with the result that he loses to all of the first-place winners [i.e., Demosthenes], but beats the amateurs." A dialogue attributed to Plato (*Amatorius* 135e–136a) describes the pentathlete as someone who in competing with runners or wrestlers is inferior, but superior to ordinary athletes. More positively, the philosopher is compared to a pentathlete, because he was not a slave to any one area of expertise which would weaken his interests in other things.

Figure 24. Detail of wrestlers, statue base, late sixth century BCE. National Museum, Athens, no. 3476

Figure 25. The long jump, red-figure kylix, attributed to the Onesimus Painter, c.500–490 BCE, Museum of Fine Arts, Boston, no. 01.8020

Of the five events comprising the pentathlon, running is discussed in Appendix AI1, wrestling in Appendix AII1.

1. The Long Jump (*halma*)

Unlike the modern event, jumpers held weights in their hands (called *haltēres*) of around 2 kg (4 lbs.) and shaped like dumbbells (see Figure 25). As the jumper ran toward the landing pit and jumped, he used the momentum of his weighted arms to propel him forward, and at the top of his leap, he may have dropped the weights; see Pausanias **37o**; Lucian **38a** (27); Philostratus **40a** (55). In addition, images show an *aulos* player, who would give the competitor a rhythm for his jump or for his run-up to the jump (see Pausanias, **37q** [6.14.10] on Pythocritus of Sicyon, who played for the pentathlon). The jump began at a starting stone (called a *batēr*) and ended in a dugout area of earth or sand (called a *skamma*). Much is made of late statements about the Crotoniate pentathlete Phayllus' jump of 55 feet, and beyond the *skamma* (Zenobius 6.23, Scholium on Aristophanes' *Acharnians* 2.14; **46**: Eusebius), but whether this was a humorous exaggeration or a mistake in copying a number (e.g., 55 for 22), it cannot be an accurate statement unless contestants took several steps that counted as part of the distance, as in the modern triple jump.

2. The Discus Throw (*diskos*)

Like the javelin throw, the discus thrower threw out from a starting line and was judged for distance. The discus itself was a round disc made of stone or metal (iron or bronze), tapered at the edges. In contrast to the modern discus, with an established weight of 2 kg and a diameter of 22 cm for men, 1kg in weight and 18 cm in diameter for women, there was considerable variety in size (diameter varied from 17 to 35 cm) and weight (from 1.3 to 6.6 kg) in ancient competitions, because individual festivals set their own standards, and there were different weights for men and for boys (as today with men and women). Pausanias **37r** (6.19.4) states that three discuses used for the pentathlon were kept in the Sicyonian Treasury at Olympia. In Philostratus (**40c**) the thrower seems to stand on a block or pedestal, perhaps like the starting stone in the long jump. Like the javelin throw, it could be dangerous. An iconic statue of a discus thrower (*diskobolos*) has come to represent the modern Olympic Games (see Figure 23, p. 395).

3. The Javelin Throw

The javelin (*akōn* or *akontion*) was a weapon of war, and throwing it was commonly practiced in gymnasia even by young boys, sometimes with fatal consequences (**15a**: Antiphon *Second Tetralogy*; **35i**: Plutarch). The shafts were of wood, 5 or 6 feet long, and metal-tipped for sticking in the ground. The throw was aided by a leather thong (*ankylē* or *mesankylon*) wrapped around the shaft at its balance point and controlled by two fingers. It acted as a catapult. In crown competitions the event was judged for distance from the starting line, and the contestant could not overstep the line. At the Panathenaea and some other festivals the javelin was cast at a target (see Figure 22).[5]

IV. Equestrian Events

Hippic events came to the Olympic program a century after running, wrestling, and the pentathlon, according to ancient sources.[6] They differ from gymnic events in that they depended on horse breeding and the training of skilled teams. Unlike gymnasium training, hippic events were not supported by civic structures, though cities did occasionally pool resources to sponsor teams. Some owners did drive their own chariot teams, particularly in the early Classical period (**2k**: Pindar *Isthmian* 2), but the more usual circumstance was for owners to employ professional jockeys and charioteers. However, it was the owner of the horse or the team who received the crown, a circumstance that enabled those winning in these events to manipulate a victory for political gain (see **8f**: Herodotus; **18a**: Isocrates *On the Chariot Team*). It also allowed women to compete in these normally all-male venues, and to post victories (see **10a**: Xenophon *Agesilaus* 9.1; **35a**: Plutarch

---

[5] See further Golden (1998: 60–2 [on the jump], 69–73 [on determining victors]); Kyle (2014); Lee (1976); Langdon (1990); Valavanis (2004: 414–23 with illustrations).

[6] Modern scholars have questioned the accuracy of the ancient accounts, believing that chariot racing must have begun much earlier, especially given its prominence on the temple of Olympian Zeus. Bell (1989, esp. 171–3) discusses the arguments for and against an earlier date.

Life of Agesilaus 20.1; **I1i**: Inscription *CEG* 820; **26a**: Callimachus, *Epinician for Berenice* II; **27l-o**: Posidippus, Royal Chariot Victories).

The importance of chariot racing for Olympia can be seen from the temple of Olympian Zeus, completed in 457 BCE; the temple's east pediment featured a chariot race between king Oenomaus of Pisa and Pelops, who wished to marry his daughter (see **37c** and Figure 4). Pelops is victorious and, according to one version of this myth, founded the Olympic Games in gratitude. Pindar features this origin myth at length in *Olympian* 1 (**2a**).

The first hippic event introduced at Olympia was the four-horse chariot race (*tethrippon teleion*) in 680 BCE. Other equestrian events were later added to the Olympic program: the horse race (*kelēs*) in 648, the two-horse chariot team (*synōris*) in 408, the four-horse team for colts (*tethrippon pōlikon*) in 384; the two-horse team for colts (*synōris pōlikē*) in 268, and the horse race for colts (*kelēs pōlikon*) in 256. The mule car race (*apēnē*) was introduced in 500 BCE but dropped by 444; the *kalpē* (in which runners dismounted and ran alongside their horses) was introduced at Olympia in 496 but also dropped by 444 (see Table 8). According to Pausanias (**37b**: Pausanias 5.8.11) the hippic events took place last in the Olympic program.

Table 8 When equestrian events were added to Olympic program

Event	Year Added
tethrippon (=four-horse chariot race)	680 BCE
kelēs (=horse race)	648 BCE
apēnē (=mule car race)	500 BCE (dropped in 444 BCE)
kalpē (=mares' race)	496 BCE (dropped in 444 BCE)
synōris (=two-horse chariot race)	408 BCE
tethrippon for foals	384 BCE
synōris for foals	264 BCE
kelēs for foals	256 BCE

1. Horses

Greeks distinguished cavalry and racing horses, not by specific breeds, but by training and preferred characteristics. Cavalry horses tended to be large; they were trained for obedience, not speed. They needed to perform in battle conditions, where they would carry adult males in full armor who might need to mount and dismount. Training that mimicked battle conditions is the source of several hippic events mentioned below (*kalpē, anthippasia, apobatēs*, javelin throw from horseback). The Athenian inscription (**I4f**: *IG* II² 2311) that lists prizes for events marks off several as "for warriors" (*polemistēriois*), including horse and chariot races. Inscriptions from Larisa in the second century CE list contests for dismounting from a chariot, a torch race on horseback, and cavalry charges (**I51**: IG 9.2.526–34). Cavalry horses were expensive to acquire and maintain, but they served a central purpose in Greek warfare, and many states had citizen classes of *hippeis* or cavalrymen, who possessed the means to own and train a warhorse. Racing horses, in contrast, were purely luxury items and always associated with the rich. Horses trained for racing were lighter and required speed, stamina, and a competitive drive. They were accustomed to the bridle, but not a saddle, and carried only the very light weight of a boy jockey. Chariot horses also needed speed and stamina but were trained to bear a yoke as they ran. Greeks raced both mares and stallions (they did not geld), but for chariot racing mares were preferred. Certain regions of Greece and the wider Mediterranean were notable for their horses. In part this depended on the physical contours of the region; the relatively flat plains of Thessaly, for example, afforded space for breeding and training, as did parts of the Peloponnese, Sicily, southern Italy, and the area around Cyrene in North Africa. The region in which the horse was bred is often part of the description of a successful horse or team.

2. Chariots

Racing chariots were light in weight, made of wood, with a curved front and an open back. The driver stood balancing on a platform mounted on an axle that connected the two wheels. Horses were yoked to a central pole that extended from the chariot. The two center horses were attached abreast to the yoke; the charioteer controlled them with two pairs of reins, one pair in the left hand, the other in the right. The reason for this was the need to curb the left horse while slackening the reins on the right horse in making turns and other maneuvers. This was the set-up for the two-horse chariot, which alone was used in warfare. For four-horse competition, two additional horses were added to the yoked pair to increase pulling strength; these outside or trace horses were loosely attached to the yoke and were not reined. Charioteers are normally represented as wearing a belted tunic that fell almost to the feet and sometimes a cap; they carried a whip (see Figure 26, p.402).

3. Racecourses

Chariot racing took place in a hippodrome; this was a large elliptical field with posts (*kamptēres*) at either end, but without a central divider. However, the length of the tracks was not standardized; known lengths include three stades from the starting post to the turning post at Olympia and eight stades at Athens. The standard race at Olympia was twelve laps, but there is little evidence for racetracks elsewhere. Lots were drawn for a starting position, which was staggered to insure fairness at the start. This might be done by simple positioning, but some elaborate starting mechanisms are known (see Pausanias **37s**, 6.20.10–14). The field of racers could often be quite large: Pindar records that over forty chariots participated in the race at Delphi in 462 (*Pythian* 5.49–51). Hippodromes that survive from the Roman period (e.g., the Circus Maximus in Rome, the Hippodrome in Constantinople) all have a substantial low wall as a central divider (*spina*); they were used for Roman chariot racing, which was essentially a team sport.

Horse racing also took place in the hippodrome, but it was much shorter than the chariot race, akin to the sprint in running. At Olympia it was either one length of the hippodrome (three stades) or one full lap, a distance of six stades.

4. Chariot racing

Ancient chariot racing was thrilling, violent, and frequently lethal. For Greek spectators the drama of the race enmeshed them in a cycle of hope, anxiety, terror, then elation or despair as a favored team might win, place, or crash (see **11a**: Sophocles *Electra* 698–763). So popular was chariot racing in the Roman Empire that it came to enjoy imperial sponsorship and eventually to become a team sport essential for the entertainment of the masses (the circus part of "bread and circuses"). But the trajectory of such racing was different in the Greek city states. Chariots were introduced to Greece during the Bronze Age and used in warfare—a practice clearly reflected in the Homeric poems—but they had disappeared as early as the eighth century, as the advent of the hoplite phalanx and the social revolution that accompanied it made the chariot marginal or even obsolete for later Greek conflicts. Thus, chariot racing cannot be understood as a seamless byproduct of military preparedness. In Greek contests, the two-horse team that was used in warfare was replaced by the four-horse team. Given the enormous costs associated with the breeding and training of suitable horses, chariot racing was de facto a rivalry of wealth. For kings and tyrants especially, the venues of the Panhellenic Games became *the* place to exhibit their wealth and mark their presence as power players on an international stage. Pindar, Bacchylides, and Simonides provide ample evidence of this in their victory odes for Sicilian tyrants and Cyrenean kings (see, e.g., **2a**; **2b**; **2k**; **3a**). Victory monuments were erected at games sites by victors like Philip of Macedon (the Philippeum). Athenian victors (Cimon, Alcibiades) were often important political figures (see **8f**: Herodotus 6.103; **9g**: Thucydides 6.16.1–3) while the kings of Sparta, and later the Ptolemies, used racing to further their political and dynastic goals (see **10a**: Xenophon *Agesilaus* 9.1; **35a**: Plutarch, *Life of Agesilaus* 20.1; **27l–p**: Posidippus, Royal Chariot Victories).

In addition to literary evidence for chariot racing, there are numerous inscriptions commemorating chariot victors at Panhellenic sites; and images on vases that range in date from the Mycenean to the Roman period provide some insight into the mechanics of yoking and driving. Unfortunately, larger commemorative bronze statues have almost all been lost. The exception is the charioteer at Delphi (478 or 474 BCE; see Figure 26), but even he now holds reins from a chariot and team that have disappeared (for the dedication, see **I2a**).

Greek chariot racing continued as long as Greek civic and athletic festivals themselves survived, well into the Roman Empire, where it became a status marker for Roman emperors (or potential emperors). Germanicus, Tiberius, and most notoriously Nero all won victories at Olympia. (Nero insisted in driving his own team, and apparently fell off, though he was declared victor, nonetheless.[7]) For those who could not compete or attend such races, the Greek literary chariot race modeled on Homer remained popular. As the Emperor Julian's tutor is said to have admonished him, "Do you have a passion for horse racing? The one in Homer is most cleverly described. Take that book and study it!"[8] In fact, the late Greek epics of Quintus of Smyrna and Nonnus entertained their audiences with increasingly more elaborate renditions of chariot competitions.[9] They did so without betraying any obvious influence of contemporary Roman racing practices, a testament to the persistence of Greek ways of athletic life.

5. Mule Cart Race (*Apēnē*)

This event was short-lived. Introduced at Olympia in 500, it was dropped from the program in 444 (**37b**: Pausanias 5.9.1–2), and the victors are not included in stone or papyrus victory lists for

---

[7] Suetonius, *Nero* 24.   [8] Julian, *The Beard-Hater* 21.14–15.
[9] Quintus, *Posthomerica* 4.180–595, Nonnus, *Dionysiaca* 37.103–484.

Figure 26. The Charioteer at Delphi, life-size bronze statue, dedicated by Polyzalos, 478 or 474 BCE, Delphi Museum, nos. 3484, 3520, 3540

Olympia. The *apēnē* was a cart pulled by mules with a seated driver, rather like the sulky used in modern harness racing. Images of the race appear on Panathenaic amphoras[10] as well as on some coins.[11] Three of the four known victors in this race were from Western Greece (Sicily, southern Italy), which suggests that the event had its origins there. Powerful local dynasts may have wanted more options to compete for the status of an Olympic victor. For example, Anaxilas of Rhegium, who won this event in 480 or 484 BCE, commemorated it in his coins, and the coin type persisted in nearby Messene for a generation.

6. Horse racing (*kelēs*)

The single-horse race was introduced into the Olympic program in 648 BCE and was held at the Pythian Games from 586.[12] This was for adult horses, which ran a single length of the hippodrome or the whole lap, that is, either to the turning post (*kamptēr*) at the end of the course or around it and back to the starting position, a length somewhere between 800m and 1.2 km. The boy jockeys rode without saddle or stirrups; they are shown wearing a loose tunic or sometimes naked. They controlled their mounts with whip and reins threaded through a bit in the horse's mouth. There were no weight categories for horses or handicapping, though the preference for small boys as jockeys indicates awareness of the importance of carrying the least weight possible. The courses could be dangerous, since the single-horse events followed the chariot races. Pausanias even records one incident of a horse which threw its jockey, but finished the course ahead of the rest, and thus was awarded the victory (**37q**: Pausanias 6.13.9–10). A few famous horses were commemorated along with their owners: Pherenicus ("Victory-bearer") the prize-winning horse of Hieron was commemorated by Pindar and Bacchylides (see **2a**, **3a**). Horse racing continued to be popular well into the Roman period.

The horserace for foals (*kelēs pōlikōn*) was introduced in 256 BCE in the Hellenistic period, no doubt to give wider scope for prizes to competing elites but also to introduce young horses to competition earlier.

7. *Apobatēs*

This event seems to have been developed first in Athens (and held at the Panathenaea), before it was later adopted by other cities.[13] It is possible that the event was instituted by Peisistratus, as part of his broadening of the Panathenaic program. Called the *apobatēs* or "dismounter," it is the name for the contestant as well as for the event, and it seems to have had a uniformly positive press. As the speaker in the pseudo-Demosthenic *Erotic Essay* (**19e**) explains, "the *apobates* is open only to citizens and the best men aspire to it . . . [it is] the noblest and best of the competitions." The contestants were required to dismount from a moving four-horse chariot while holding their shields, and then to run alongside the chariot, probably for the length of the stadium. The runners may have been required to remount as well, but on this point the sources and the images are ambiguous. One Panathenaic amphora depicts the event with the charioteer wearing

---

[10] BM inv. no. B 121 (1837.6–9.75).
[11] HFMA nr. 2006.010.016. Ref.: SNG ANS 317; Caltabiano Series IV; cf. obverse of Nr. 145 (D 89).
[12] Bell (1989: 167–90).   [13] Oropus (*IG* VII, 4254), Aphrodisias (*CIG* 2758).

the usual long garment and the *apobatēs* wearing a helmet and carrying a shield but otherwise naked. However, other vases show the *apobatēs* wearing a tunic, so the exact status of his attire remains moot. It is featured on the Parthenon frieze, which dates to 440 BCE, on both the north (XIII–XXII) and the south panels (XXIV–XXXI). Although most of these panels are badly broken or known now only from earlier drawings, one panel allows us to see the event. The only other surviving textual (as opposed to visual) reference to this event comes from Plutarch in his life of the fourth- century BCE Athenian statesman Phocion (see **35k**). Phocion, in his desire to strengthen his son's character, encouraged him to compete in the *apobatēs* at the Panathenaea on the grounds that the training for and discipline of the event would have the desired effect. As in the *Erotic Essay*, this anecdote privileges character as the mark of the *apobatēs*, and the extensive coverage that the event receives on the Parthenon frieze necessarily elevates this race in Athens over other hippic events.

8. *Kalpē*

This event is known only from Olympia, where it was introduced in 496 BCE but discontinued in 444. It consisted of an armed rider racing his horse, dismounting, and then running beside his horse to finish the course. The length of the race is not known.[14]

9. *Anthippasia*

For this event two groups, each composed of cavalry from five tribes and led by a hipparch, rode directly at each other as if attacking, and then interpenetrated the other group's line. This was done three times as a demonstration of equestrian skill. It is known only from Athens, where in the third century BCE it was part of the Panathenaea and also the Athenian festival of the Olympieia in honor of Zeus Olympios (see *IG* II² 3079.5–13). Xenophon's *Hipparchus* (**10l**: 3.10–13) is the only detailed description of the event.[15]

10. Javelin throw from horseback

The only evidence for this event comes from Athens, where it was introduced at the Panathenaea at the end of the fifth century BCE. Riders mounted on horses threw at a stationary target. Like the *anthippasia*, it was an event designed to display the military skills of ephebes. The event occurs on the Athenian list stipulating a prize of five amphoras of olive oil (see **I4f**). A similar event occurs on the prize list from Coresia (see **I5f**).[16]

---

[14] See Christesen 2018 for a thorough discussion of the *kalpē*.
[15] See Kyle (1987: 189–90) for the inscriptional evidence.
[16] For hippic events, see further Bell (1989); Christesen (2018); Kyle (1987): Neils and Schultz (2012); Papakonstantinou (2003); Willis (2014).

GLOSSARY OF GREEK TERMS

The glossary contains all Greek terms found in the readings that are relevant to athletics. In the readings these words are transliterated from Greek and italicized within the texts, usually with an accompanying translation. they may appear in passages as *agōn* ("competition") or competition (*agōn*). We have provided page numbers for the relevant passages.

adikēma act of wrongdoing, injustice, 190

adikia injustice, 192

aethlon (aethlion/athlos/aethlos) see *athlon*

agalma object of wonder, often in the form of a statue dedicated to the gods, 181

ageneios boy in his late teens (literally, "beardless"), 144, 331

agōgē Spartan rites of passage, 86, 168, 324, 327, 333, 363

agōn, plural **agōnes** competition (the singular is often used for an entire event; see, e.g., **gymnikos agōn**), 5, 65, 69, 72, 78, 81, 138, 143, 174, 186, 188, 327, 328, 337, 351, 353, 364, 372

agōnothetēs, plural **agōnothetai** sponsor or supervisor of an athletic event, 149–50, 167, 175, 177, 326, 334, 369

agora place of assembly; marketplace, 17, 332, 337

akōn javelin, 31, 66, 398

akoniti literally, "dustless" (used to describe a victor who won without a competition), 319

akontion javelin; see also *akōn*, 167, 398

akritos unjudged, 280

akron peak (of physical condition), 250

aleiptein anoint with oil, and therefore to train, 352

aleiptēs trainer who specializes in massage (literally, "one who anoints"), 300, 327

aleiptos not left behind, therefore "undefeated", 161

altis sacred precinct of Zeus at Olympia, 31, 90, 178, 184, 185, 189–90, 193–4, 196–7, 204, 210, 214, 217, 219–20, 373

alytarch official at the Olympic Games with duties including crowd control and selecting and disciplining athletes, 244

ametria imbalance, 260, 269

amphōtis, plural **amphôtides** ear protector (for a boxer), 169

anabatēs, plural **anabatai** rider (literally, "one who mounts"), 177

analēptikon restorative, 256

analogia proportion (in respect to the body), 280

andragathēma manly deed, 183

andragathia character of a virtuous man, 76

andreia manliness, courage, 128, 131–2, 134, 171, 206

andrias, plural **andriantes** statue, 185

anēr agathos noble man; see also *kalos kagathos*, 134

anikētos unconquerable, 172

ankylē six-foot rawhide thong used to throw the javelin (*akōn*), 398

antagonistēs opponent, 163–4, 193, 246

anthippasia horse event in the Panathenaea involving two squads of cavalry in a mock battle, 91, 378, 399, 404

apēnē wagon drawn by mules, 399, 403

aphesis starting line for foot races and horse races, 220

aphippodroma horse race in which riders dismount during the race, 344

apobatēs competitor in a chariot race where the driver occasionally jumps out and runs alongside the chariot, 95, 105, 114, 168, 378, 399, 403–4

apobatikos relating to the *apobatēs*, e.g., *apobatikos agōn*, 344

apodytērion place where athletes disrobed before practice, 322

aporrhaxis game in which the ball was dribbled or bounced, 299

apotheōsis elevation to divine status, 359

aretē, plural **aretai** excellence, goodness, valor, 5, 7, 11–12, 62–65, 77, 122, 129–132, 163, 165, 191, 199–200, 269, 272, 288, 311, 338, 347, 363

aristos best (referring to a singular male), 10, 12, 14, 16–17, 63, 76, 132–3

aryballos small flask with a narrow neck used to hold oil, 365

askēsis exercise, practice, training., 131–2, 248, 250–1

asylia safety of person, of competitors at games, 166

Athēnēthen athlōn "of the prizes from Athens" (inscribed on Panathenaic amphoras)

athlētēs athlete, 172, 251

athlios miserable, 251, 253

athliotēs misery, 251

athlon (or **aethlon/aethlion/athlos/aethlos**), plural **athla** (or **aethla/aethlia/athloi/aethloi**) prize, labor (for the relationship of these words to one another, see Appendix AI), 64, 136, 251, 311, 359, 393

athlothetēs organizer of games, one who offers a prize, 326

aulos wind instrument formed with two pipes joined by a mouth strap, 28, 43–4, 76, 93, 165, 331, 376, 380, 397

balbis starting block for *stadion* race, 292

banausos artisan, one who works with his hands, 132

batēr starting place for the long jump, 397

bia (or **biē**) violent force (often opposed to *mētis*, craft/intelligence), 11–12

boagos overseer of Spartan *agōgē*, 328

boulē plan; Council at Athens, 68, 91

bouleutērion meeting place for local officials. The *bouleutērion* at Olympia was where athletes were registered for competition and where they swore an oath to Zeus, 90, 194, 374, 375, 377

brabeia prizes, 322

caestus Latin term for strip of leather, sometimes weighted with lead or iron, that boxers wrapped around the hands and wrists, 407

chairete nikōmen "Rejoice! We are victorious," (famous phrase associated with the victory of the Greeks at the battle of Marathon), 243, 391

charis gratitude, grace, joy, delight, especially in conditions of reciprocity, 12, 18, 24, 187, 191

chermadioi, molybdainoi leaden balls used for arm exercises, 244

chorēgia role of chorus leader, 116

daimōn divine spirit, god, 60

dēmos people, 82, 95

diaita regimen, diet, 258

diaitatēr judge, umpire, 307

diaitētikē dietetics, in reference to expertise, 257

dianoia thought, intention, 132

diathesis physical disposition, 249, 251, 265

diaulos foot race that is the length of a *stadion* and back, 39, 41, 56–7, 102, 144–5, 146, 176, 202, 211–12, 215–17, 223, 253, 273, 275–6, 282–3, 311, 325–6, 344, 377, 380, 381, 387–91

didaskaleion school, 407

didaskalos teacher, 190

dikaiosynē justice, 118

dioros stone used in the game *ephedrismos*, 299

diskos discus, 17–18, 398

dolichos long-distance race, 35, 57, 85, 159, 176, 199–200, 205–6, 209, 212, 219, 223, 253, 273, 275–6, 319–20, 324–6, 380, 387, 389–91

doxa reputation, thought, opinion, 59, 62, 64, 195, 199, 204, 247, 288, 359

drachma silver coin worth six obols[1], 108, 135, 168, 287, 300, 309, 315, 321–2, 330–2, 334, 338–42, 345, 355–6

dynamis power, potential, 16, 263

eikōn statue, likeness, 176

eiselasis parade for victorious athlete sponsored by home city, 372

ekecheiria declaration of cessation of hostilities in month preceding games, 181, 189

empeiria experience, 120

energeia activity, 130

ephēbeia compulsory physical and military training for a city's youth (ephebes), 333, 363

ephēbikē another name for *episkyros*, 299

ephēbos an 18- or 19-year-old youth who spent two years in military training; youth age category, 363

---

[1] It is impossible to give accurate modern equivalences for the money amounts given in these texts, so we have provided ancient equivalences where possible. See Loomis (1998: 261–340) for the collected evidence for Athenian labor costs from the fifth century BCE to the third century CE.

ephedrismos game that required throwing a ball or stone at a target, 299

epikoinos another name for *episkyros*, 299

epiponōtatos most hard-working, 392

episkyros team ball game in which one side tried to force the other to retreat beyond a set line (played in Sparta as part of youth training), 299

epistēmē knowledge, 263

erastēs older adult male lover in a pederastic relationship, 66

eris strife, 16

erōmenos youth in a pederastic relationship with an older adult male lover, 66, 114

ēthos custom, habit, 70, 131–2

euandria male beauty contest for "good manliness," probably physical fitness, 95, 109, 136, 298, 332, 380, 383

eudaimōn blessed, happy, 118

eudaimonia state of blessedness, happiness, 129, 130, 133

euergesia good work, 248

euexia good bodily condition, 250–1, 289, 341

eukleia good repute, glory, 287

eunomia good order, 33, 65

eustatheia good disposition, stability, 172

exedra arcade furnished with recesses and seats in a *gymnasion*, 262

exēgētēs interpreter, guide, 181

gennaios noble, well-born, 281

gloios mixture of sweat, olive oil and dirt collected from athletes after training and sold as a medical remedy, 342, 365

gymnasiarchos director of a *gymnasion*, 369

gymnasion, *plural* **gymnasia** 1 building for physical training and education; 2 exercise, 78, 93, 106, 115, 117, 119, 123, 127, 129–30, 137, 156, 232, 235, 258–9, 262, 267, 361, 363, 364, 366, 369, 375, 376, 398

gymnastēs coach for athletes, 257, 277, 323, 363, 364

gymnazein/gymnazesthai 1 to train in the nude; 2 to exercise, 66, 118, 172, 272, 364

gymnikos agōn "naked competition", i.e., a non-hippic competition, 69, 72, 364

gymnos nude, 66, 249, 346, 364

halma long jump, 17, 66, 397

haltēr, plural **haltēres** weight held in the hands during the long jump, 194, 198, 290, 329, 396–7

hamma clinch, in wrestling, 246

harmonia balance, 283

harpaston ball game, perhaps similar to rugby, 299

harpazein to seize, 299

Hellanodikēs, plural **Hellanodikai** umpire at the Olympic Games (literally "judge of Greece"), 28, 74, 177–8, 188, 192–3, 195–6, 205, 220, 244, 278, 280, 290, 293, 317, 373, 378, 385, 386

hēmerodromos messenger (literally "day runner"), 75, 311

hērōs hero, 359

hexis bodily disposition, 130, 133, 249, 251, 256, 259, 281, 286, 288

hieromēnia month declared "sacred" during which the truce (*ekecheiria*) was in place for the Olympic Games, 113, 374

hieropoioi overseers of the temple, 341

himas, plural **himantes** leather strap wrapped around the fist for boxing, 192, 285, 392

hippikos agōn contests involving horses, 364

hippios foot race for men and boys that was twice the length of the stadium, 217, 376, 378, 380

hoplitēs armored soldier, 3, 82, 160, 389–90

hoplitodromos race in armor, 41, 44, 389

hubris insolence, 38, 40, 190

hydrophoria relay race in which participants carry amphoras filled with water, 143, 146

hygieia/to hygieinon health, 247, 250, 254, 256–7, 267

hypomnēsis memory, 176

hysplēx starting mechanism for running events, 245, 377

iatrikē medicine, 120, 254–5, 258

iatros, *plural* **iatroi** doctor, physician, 246

idiotēs private citizen, amateur athlete, 161

kairos right time; also an anthropomorphized deity with wings on back and feet., 41, 172, 192

kakotechnia incorrect form of expertise, 259, 261

kalokagathia condition of possessing "beauty and goodness" (usually applied to elite individuals), 88, 323

kalpē horse event for mares in which the rider jumped from his horse and ran alongside the horse for the final distance of the event, 177, 206, 324–6, 399, 404

kampē/kamptēr turning post in a race, 322, 400, 403

karteria toughness, endurance, 171, 319, 327

kasen Spartan term for the relationship of a boy to the leader (*boagos*) of his group (*agelē*)., 327

katablētikē skill of conquering/wrestling, 265

kelēs race on horseback, 23, 176, 195, 399, 403

kinēsis movement, 127

kithara lyre or harp, 323, 330–1, 376, 380

kleos glory, fame, 5, 17, 22, 60, 64, 199, 311, 313, 335, 348, 359

klēros lot used in draws for the combat events, 7. see *lot* in General Index

koinon league or federation (literally, "common thing"), 337

kōmos band of revellers; song sung in honor of victor, 145

korykos punching bag, 244

kosmētēs magistrate in charge of ephebes at Athens, 333

krisis trial, 344

kudos glory, reputation, 7, 31, 34, 62

lampadarchēs official in charge of the torch race, 353

palaistrophylax guardian of the wrestling school, 342

palē wrestling, 31, 144, 289, 391–2

pammachia/pammachos synonym for *pankration*, but also a separate fighting event introduced in 300 CE., 391, 393

pankration combat sport meaning "all power" or "all victory" with only two rules no eye gouging and no biting; techniques included boxing, wrestling, kick boxing, 53, 56, 65, 81, 85, 91–4, 140, 153, 165, 175–7, 192–3, 196, 198–9, 201–6, 209, 212–13, 215–16, 224, 232, 236, 244–5, 252–3, 271, 273–7, 279, 281, 284–5, 288–9, 291, 293, 295, 296, 297, 303–4, 316, 319–20, 331, 336, 344, 346–7, 354, 360, 380–1, 391, 393–4

paradromis practice track in the *gymnasion*, 321

paranomēma transgression, 183

parthenos, *plural* **parthenoi** virgin, unmarried woman, 184, 186, 220

patria fatherland, 177

patronomos guardian of ancestral tradition, holder of a Spartan office instituted in 227 BCE, probably to oversee the revived *agōgē*, 327

peithō persuasion, anthropomorphic goddess of persuasion, 183

pentathlon contest consisting of five events jumping, running, discus, javelin, and wrestling, 37–9, 51, 56–7, 59–60, 65, 78, 90, 145, 159, 176–8, 188, 190–1, 196–8, 208, 214–19, 273. 275–6, 282, 329, 331, 374, 380–1, 391, 393, 395–8

peplos embroidered garment, given as a sacred offering to Athena in the Panathenaea, 136, 186–7, 380

periodonikēs victor in the four sacred crown competitions at Olympia, Delphi, Isthmia, and Nemea, but later including the expanded circuit of sacred crown games, 32, 35, 36, 138, 327, 329, 346, 371

periodos circuit of sacred crown games, 345, 371–2

perizōma loincloth or belt worn by athletes, 230, 365

petasos characteristic hat worn by ephebes, 154

phaininda ball game that involves deception in throwing, 299

pharmakon, plural **pharmaka** drug(s), 263, 289

phēmē rumor, report, 62

phenakizein to deceive, 299

philonikia love of victory; competitiveness, 126

philoponia love of labor; used in the sense of hard training, 341

philotimia love of honor, ambition, 202

phylaktikos protective, in reference to expertise, 256

physis nature, 251, 255, 272

pneuma breath, wind, 284

polymētis crafty, 13

ponos labor, 198, 259

pragmata deeds, affairs, 120, 258

probouloi standing members of committee to examine measures before they were proposed to the full group, 338–9

proedria seats in front row at events set aside for officials

pronaos forecourt of temple, 184

prothysis first stage of ash altar of Zeus at Olympia, 186

proxenos consul, citizen of one state and representative to another, 202

prytaneion public building, hearth of the city, where honorary meals for citizens were given, 74, 117–18, 189–90, 329–30, 373

prytanis chief magistrate, 190

psychē spirit, soul, 4, 110, 116, 119, 121, 132, 267, 347

pygmē boxing, 31

pyx boxing, 12, 17, 188, 386, 391–2

rhabdouchoi umpires (literally, "those who carry a rod (*rhabdos*)"), 82

rhōmē strength, 65, 70, 201

schēsis state, disposition, 256

sēma marker, sign, usually a grave marker, 6

sitēsis feeding, in reference to free meals in the *prytaneion* for victorious athletes, 117–18, 329–30

skamma dug-up area for jumping and fighting events, 346, 391, 397

skyron stone chip used in *episkyra*, 299

sōma body, 116, 267, 347

sophia wisdom, knowledge, 65, 121, 229, 272, 277, 309

sōphronistēs person in charge of training ephebes in Athens (literally, one who "makes temperate"), 135

sōphrosunē temperance, 131, 298

sphairē (*or* episphaira) ball for playing; padded boxing glove used in practice, 17

sphairistērion, plural sphairisteria room for ball play in the *palaestra/gymnasion* complex, 321

spondophoros libation bearer, who announced the truce in preparation for the Olympic Games, 314

stadion foot race competition, measuring 600 ancient feet (with variations), 31, 37–9, 44, 57, 74, 84, 114, 147, 154, 159–60, 165, 210–12, 215, 217–18, 223, 230, 253, 273–6, 282–3, 303, 311, 320, 323, 325–6, 331, 344, 346, 365, 369, 373, 377, 378, 380–2, 387–393

statēr coin weight used by various Greek cities; equivalent to four drachmas (see n. 1), 321–2, 338

stēlē block of stone with various functions, including victory monuments, 193, 311, 324, 330, 332, 334–5, 338–9, 381

stlengis scraper used to remove sweat and oil, the equivalent of the Latin *strigilis* (strigil), 365

symmetria/to symmetron proper proportion, balance, 130, 260, 269

syngymnazomenos training partner, 281

synōris, plural **synōrides** chariot team of two horses, 146, 154, 176, 399

tainia ribbon used to mark a victorious athlete, worn around forehead or arm, 298

tamias treasurer, 338

taurothēria bull hunting, 343

technē expertise, craft, art, 43, 119–20, 124, 128, 157, 198, 208, 229, 246–7, 254–5, 267, 269, 272, 277, 281, 301

temenos sacred area, precinct at a sanctuary, 185

terma endpoint, turning point and/or finish in racecourse, 245

tethrippon chariot team of four horses, 146–7, 399

tropaia trophies, 286

thauma/thaumasia amazement, 178

theōria embassy, sending of state ambassadors to the games; spectacle, viewing, 281

theōros, *plural* **theōroi** envoys, 273, 375

therapeia service, attention, care, 120, 258

timē honor, respect, 248

xenos (*or* **xeinos)** guest-friend, host, honorary guest at major competitions, 58

xyēlē curved knife used to shape javelin, 84

xystos covered practice track at a *gymnasion*, 321, 346, 362

xystra scraper used to remove sweat and oil; a later term for *stlengis* that became common in the Roman period, 253, 265

SELECT BIBLIOGRAPHY

Arrigoni, G. "Donne e sport nel mondo Greco, religione e società," in B. Gentili et al. (eds.), *Le Donne in Grecia* (Rome and Bari, 1985), 129–201.

Azoulay, V. "Les Statues de Théogénès de Thasos: Entre vénération et outrage," in C. M. Annoville and Y. Riviere (eds.), *Faire parler et faire taire les statues: De l'Invention de l'écriture à l'usage de la poudre,* (Rome, 2016) 149–96.

Bagnall, R. S. and P. Derow (eds.). *The Hellenistic Period: Historical Sources in Translation* (Oxford, 2004).

Bell, D. "The Horse Race (*keles*) in Ancient Greece from the Pre-Classical Period to the First Century BC," *Stadion* 15 (1989): 167–90.

Bonfante, L. "Nudity as a Costume in Classical Greece," *American Journal of Archaeology* 93/4 (1989): 543–70.

Bowie, E. and J. Elsner (eds.). *Philostratus* (Cambridge, 2009)

Brunet, S. "Olympic Hopefuls from Ephesos," *Journal of Sport History* 30/2 (2003): 219–35.

Bugh, G. "The Theseia in Late Hellenistic Athens," *Zeitschrift für Papyrologie und Epigraphik* 83 (1990): 20–37.

Cairns, D. L. *Bacchylides: Five Epinician Odes* (Cambridge, 2010).

Christesen, P. *Olympic Victor Lists and Ancient Greek History* (Cambridge, 2007).

Christesen, P. *Sport and Democracy in the Ancient and Modern Worlds.* (Cambridge, 2012).

Christesen, P. *A New Reading of the Damonon Stele. Histos* Supplement 10 (Newcastle upon Tyne, 2019).

Christesen, P. and D. G. Kyle (eds.). *A Companion to Sport and Spectacle in Greek and Roman Antiquity* (Chichester, 2014).

Christesen, P. and C. Stocking (eds.) *A Cultural History of Sport in Antiquity* (London, 2021).

Crowther, N. B. *Athletika: Studies on the Olympic Games and Greek Athletics. Nikephoros* Beihefte 11 (Hildesheim, 2004).

Crowther, N. B. *Sport in Ancient Times* (Westport, CT, 2007).

Currie, B. *Pindar and the Cult of Heroes* (Oxford, 2005).

Decker, W. *Sports and Games of Ancient Egypt*, trans. A. Guttmann (New Haven, CT, 1992).

Decker, W. "Gymnasion," in T. Scanlon (ed.), *Sport in the Greek and Roman Worlds*, vol. 2 (Oxford, 2014), 95–107.

Dillery, J. "Cynisca's Swift-Footed Horses: *CEG* 820 (*IG* V.1 1564a) and the Lame Kingship of Agesilaus," *Zeitschrift für Papyrologie und Epigraphik* 210 (2019): 17–19.

Dova, S. *The Poetics of Failure in Ancient Greece* (New York, 2020).

Ebert, J. *Griechische Epigramme auf Sieger an gymnischen und hippischen Agonen.* Abhandlungen der sächsischen Akademie der Wissenschaften zu Leipzig, Philologisch-historische Klasse 63.2 (Berlin, 1972).

Fisher, N. and H. van Wees (eds.). *Competition in the Ancient World* (Swansea, 2011).

Futrell, A. *The Roman Games* (Malden, MA, and Oxford, 2008).

Gardiner, E. N. *Greek Athletic Sports and Festivals* (London, 1910).

Gardiner, E. N. *Athletics in the Ancient World* (Oxford, 1930).

Gerber, D. *Greek Elegiac Poetry*. Loeb Classical Library 258 (Cambridge, MA, 1999).

Goff, B. E. and Simpson, M. (eds.). *Thinking the Olympics: The Classical Tradition and the Modern Games* (London, 2011).

Golden, M. *Sport and Society in Ancient Greece* (Cambridge, 1998).

Golden, M. *Sport in the Ancient World from A to Z* (London and New York, 2004)

Golden, M. *Sport and Social Status in Ancient Greece* (Austin, TX, 2008).

Habermann, W. "Gymnasien im ptolemäischen Ägypten—eine Skizze" in D. Kah and P. Scolz (eds.), *Das hellenistische Gymnasion*. Wissenskultur und gesellschaftlicher Wandel 8 (Berlin, 2004) 335–48.

Harder, A. *Callimachus,* Aetia: *Introduction, Text, Translation, and Commentary*. 2 vols. (Oxford, 2012).

Harris, H. A. *Greek Athletes and Athletics* (London, 1964).

Harris, H. A. *Sport in Greece and Rome* (London and Ithaca, NY 1972).

Hornblower, S. "Thucydides, Xenophon, and Lichas: Were the Spartans Excluded from the Olympic Games from 420 to 400 B.C.?" *Phoenix* 54/3–4 (2000): 212–25.

Hornblower, S. and C. Morgan (eds.). *Pindar's Poetry, Patrons, and Festivals* (Oxford, 2007).

Jackson, D. F. "Philostratos and the Pentathlon," *Journal of Hellenic Studies* 111 (1991): 178–81.

Jones, W. H. S. *Pausanias: Description of Greece* (London, 1918).

König, J. *Athletics and Literature in the Roman Empire* (Cambridge, 2005).

König, J. (ed.). *Greek Athletics* (Edinburgh, 2010).

Kurke, L. "The Economy of *Kudos*." in Leslie Kurke and Carol Dougherty (eds.), *Cultural Poetics in Archaic Greece: Cult, Performance, Politics* (Oxford, 1993), 131–63.

Kyle, D. G. "Non-Competition in Homeric Sport: Spectatorship and Status," *Stadion* 10 (1984): 1–20.

Kyle, D. G. *Athletics in Ancient Athens*. Mnemosyne Supplement (Leiden, 1987).

Kyle, D. G. "Winning and Watching the Greek Pentathlon Again," *Journal of Sport History* 17 (1990): 291–305.

Kyle, D. G. "Philostratus: 'Repêchage,' Running and Wrestling: The Greek Pentathlon Again." *Journal of Sport History* 22 (1995) 60–5.

Kyle, D. G. *Sport and Spectacle in the Ancient World*. 2nd edn. (Malden, MA, 2015).

Langdon, M. K. "Scoring the Ancient Pentathlon: Final Solution?" *Zeitschrift für Papyrologie und Epigraphik* 78 (1989): 117–18.

Langdon, M. K. "Throwing the Discus in Antiquity: The Literary Evidence," *Nikephoros* 3 (1990): 177–82.

Larmour, D. H. J. *Stage and Stadium: Drama and Athletics in Ancient Greece*. *Nikephoros* Beihefte 4 (Hildesheim, 1999).

Lee, H. M. "The *terma* and the Javelin in Pindar, *Nemean* vii 70–3 and Greek Athletics," *Journal of Hellenic Studies* 96 (1976): 70–9.

Lee, H. M. "The Late Greek Boxing Glove and the Roman 'Caestus'," *Nikephoros* 10 (1997): 161–78.

Lee, H. M. "The Ancient Olympic Games: Origin, Evolution, Revolution," *Classical Bulletin* 74 (1998): 129–41.

Legras, B. *Néotés: Recherches sur les jeunes grecs dans l'Égypte ptolémaïque et romaine*. Hautes études du monde gréco-romain 26 (Geneva, 1999).

Loomis, W. *Wages, Welfare Costs and Inflation in Classical Athens* (Ann Arbor, MI, 1998).

Mann, C., S. Remijsen and S. Scharff (eds.). *Athletics in the Hellenistic World* (Stuttgart, 2016).

Mantas, K. "Women and Athletics in the Roman East," *Nikephoros* 8 (1995): 125–44.

Martin, R. "Un Nouveau Règlement de culte thasien," *Bulletin de Correspondance Hellénique* 64 (1940): 163–200.

McDonnell, M. "The Introduction of Athletic Nudity: Thucydides, Plato, and the Vases," *Journal of Hellenic Studies* 111 (1991) 182–93.

McDonnell, M. "Athletic Nudity among the Greeks and Etruscans: The Evidence of the 'Perizoma Vases'" in *Spectacles sportifs et scéniques dans le monde étrusco-italique*. Collection de l'École française de Rome (Rome 1993), 395–407.

Measham, T., E. Spathari, and P. Donnelly. *1,000 Years of the Olympic Games* (Sydney, 2000).

Miller, S. "Turns and Lanes in the Ancient Stadium," *American Journal of Archaeology* 84 (1980): 159–66.

Miller, S. *Ancient Greek Athletics*. (New Haven, CT, and London, 2004).

Miller, S. *Arete: Greek Sports from Ancient Sources*. 3rd edn. (Berkeley and Los Angeles 2004).

Minnen, P. van. "Contracting the Caterers on Keos," in J. Dijkstra, J. Kroesen and Y. Kuiper (eds.), *Myths, Martyrs, and Modernity: Studies in the History of Religions in Honour of Jan N. Bremmer* (Leiden, 2010), 209–17.

Moretti, J.-C. and P. Valavanis. *Les hippodromes et les concours hippiques dans la Grèce antique. Bulletin de Correspondance Hellénique*, Supplement 62 (Athens, 2019).

Moretti, L. *Inscrizioni agonistiche greche* (Rome, 1953).

Moretti, L. *Olympionikai: I vincitori negli antichi agoni olimpici*. Accademia Nazionale dei Lincei (Rome, 1957).

Moretti, L. "Nuovo supplemento al catalogo degli Olympionikai," *Miscellanea greca e romana* 12 (1987) 67–91.

Morgan, C. *Athletes and Oracles: The Transformation of Delphi and Olympia in the Eighth Century B.C.* (Cambridge 1990)

Morgan, K. *Pindar and the Construction of Syracusan Monarchy in the Fifth Century B.C.* (Oxford, 2015).

Mouratidis, J. "Anachronism in the Homeric Games and Sports," *Nikephoros* 3 (1990): 11–22.

Murray, S. "The Role of Religion in Greek Sport," in P. Christesen and D. G. Kyle (eds.), *A Companion to Sport and Spectacle in Greek and Roman Antiquity* (Chichester, 2014), 309–19.

Murray, S. "Sport and Education in Ancient Greece and Rome," in W. M. Bloomer and P. Bannard (eds.), *A Companion to Ancient Education* (Chichester, 2015), 430–43.

Nagy, G. *Pindar's Homer: The Lyric Possession of an Epic Past* (Baltimore, MD, 1990).

Nagy, G. *The Ancient Greek Hero in 24 Hours* (Cambridge, MA, 2013).

Neils, J. and P. Schultz, "Erechtheus and the Apobates Race on the Parthenon Frieze (North XI–XII)," *American Journal of Archaeology* 116/2 (2012): 195–207.

Newby, Z. *Greek Athletics in the Roman World* (Oxford, 2005).

Newby, Z. *Athletics in the Roman World* (Bristol, 2006).

Nicholson, N. *Aristocracy and Athletics in Archaic and Classical Greece* (Cambridge, 2005).

Nicholson, N. *The Poetics of Victory in the Greek West* (New York, 2016).

Nijf, O. van. "Athletics, Festivals and Greek Identity in the Roman East," *Proceedings of the Cambridge Philological Society* 45 (2000): 176–200.

Pache, C. *Baby and Child Heroes in Ancient Greece* (Urbana, IL, 2004).

Papakonstantinou, Z. "Prizes in Early Archaic Greek Sport," *Nikephoros* 15 (2002): 51–67.

Papakonstantinou, Z. "Alcibiades in Olympia: Olympic Ideology, Sport and Social Conflict in Classical Athens," *Journal of Sport History* 30/2 (2003): 173–82.

Papakonstantinou, Z. "Agariste's Suitors: Sport, Feasting, and Elite Politics in Sixth-Century Greece," *Nikephoros* 23 (2010): 71–93.

Papakonstantinou, Z. (ed.). *Sport and the Cultures of the Ancient World: New Perspectives* (New York, 2010).

Papakonstantinou, Z. "The Athletic Body in Classical Athens: Literary and Historical Perspectives," *International Journal of the History of Sport* 29/12 (2012): 1657–68.

Papakonstantinou, Z. *Sport and Identity in Ancient Greece.* (New York, 2019).

Papalas, A. J. "Boy Athletes in Ancient Greece", *Stadion* 17 (1991) 165–72.

Pfeiffer, I. L. "Athletic Age Categories in Victory Odes," *Nikephoros* 11 (1988): 21–38.

Pfeiffer, R. *Callimachus*, vol. 1 (Oxford, 1965).

Phillips, D. and D. Pritchard (eds.). *Sport and Festival in the Ancient World* (Swansea, 2003).

Pleket, H. W. "On the Sociology of Ancient Sport," in T. Scanlon (ed.), *Sport in the Greek and Roman Worlds*, vol. 1 (Oxford, 2014), 29–81.

Pleket, H. W. "Sport in Hellenistic and Roman Asia Minor" in P. Christesen and D. G. Kyle (eds.), *A Companion to Sport and Spectacle in Greek and Roman Antiquity* (Chichester, 2014), 364–76.

Poliakoff, M. *Studies in the Terminology of the Greek Combat Sports* (Königstein, 1986).

Poliakoff, M. *Combat Sports in the Ancient World: Competition, Violence, and Culture.* (New Haven, CT, 1987).

Poliakoff, M. "Melankomas, ἐκ κλίμακος, and Greek Boxing", *American Journal of Philology* 108 (1987): 511–18.

Polignac, F. de, "Athletic Cults in Ancient Greece," in T. Scanlon (ed.), *Sport in the Greek and Roman Worlds*, vol. 1 (Oxford, 2014), 91–116.

Potter, D. *The Victor's Crown* (Oxford, 2012).

Pritchard, D. *Sport, War, and Democracy in Classical Athens* (Cambridge, 2013).

Raschke, W. J. "Aulos and Athlete: The Function of the Fluteplayer in Greek Athletics," *Arete* 2 (1985): 177–200.

Raschke, W. J. (ed.). *The Archaeology of the Olympics* (Madison, WI, 1988).

Raubitschek, A. *Dedications from the Athenian Acropolis: A Catalogue of the Inscriptions of the Sixth and Fifth Centuries B.C.* Edited in Collaboration with L. H. Jeffrey (Cambridge, MA, 1949).

Reed, N. B. "The *Euandria* Competition Reconsidered," *Ancient World* 15 (1987): 59–64.

Reid, H. *Athletics and Philosophy in the Ancient World: Contests of Virtue* (New York, 2011).

Remijsen, S. "Pammachon: A New Sport." *Bulletin of the American Society of Papyrologists* 47 (2010): 185–204.

Remijsen, S. "Greek Sport in Egypt: Status Symbol and Lifestyle" in P. Christesen and D. G. Kyle (eds.), *A Companion to Sport and Spectacle in Greek and Roman Antiquity* (Chichester, 2014), 349–63.

Remijsen, S. *The End of Athletics in Late Antiquity* (Cambridge, 2015).

Remijsen, S. and W. Clarysse. *Ancient Olympics*, http://ancientolympics.arts.kuleuven.be/, accessed May 29, 2021.

Renfrew, C. "The Minoan-Mycenean Origins of the Panhellenic Games," in W. J. Raschke (ed.), *The Archaeology of the Olympics* (Madison, WI, 1988), 26–34.

Riele, G. J. (ed.). "Inscriptions conservées au Musée d'Olympie," *Bulletin de Correspondance Hellénique* 88 (1964): 186–7.

Robinson, R. S. *Sources for the History of Greek Athletics* (Chicago, 1981).

Romano, D. "Athletic Festivals in the Northern Peloponnese and Central Greece" in P. Christesen and D. G. Kyle (eds.), *A Companion to Sport and Spectacle in Greek and Roman Antiquity* (Chichester, 2014), 176–91.

Roueché, C. *Performers and Partisans at Aphrodisias in the Roman and Late Roman Periods* (London, 1993).

Rusten, J. and J. König, *Philostratus: Heroicus, Gymnasticus, Discourses 1 and 2.* Loeb Classical Library 521 (Cambridge, MA, 2014).

Scanlon, T. "The Vocabulary of Competition: Agôn and Aethlos, Greek Terms for Contest," *Arete* 1/1 (1983): 147–62.

Scanlon, T. *Eros and Greek Athletics* (New York, 2002).

Scanlon, T. (ed). *Sport in the Greek and Roman Worlds*, 2 vols. (Oxford, 2014).

Schaus, G. P. and S. R. Wenn (eds.), *Onward to the Olympics: Historical Perspectives on the Olympic Games* (Waterloo, ON, 2007).

Scott, M. *Delphi and Olympia : The Spatial Politics of Panhellenism in the Archaic and Classical Periods* (New York, 2010).

Scott, M. "The Social Life of Greek Athletic Facilities," in P. Christesen and D. G. Kyle (eds.), *A Companion to Sport and Spectacle in Greek and Roman Antiquity* (Chichester, 2014), 352–67.

Sinn, U. *Olympia: Cult, Sport and Ancient Festival.* Trans. T. Thornton (Princeton, NJ, [1996] 2000).

Sinn, U. (ed.). *Sport in der Antike: Wettkampf, Spiel und Erziehung im Altertum* (Würzburg 1996).

Spivey, N. The Olympics: A History. (Oxford, [2004] 2012).

Stafford, E. *Heracles.* (New York, 2012).

Stocking, C. "The Use and Abuse of Training 'Science' in Philostratus' *Gymnasticus*," *Classical Antiquity* 35/1 (2016): 86–165.

Stocking, C. "Athletic Competition" in C. Pache, S. Lupack, R. Lamberton, and C. Dué (eds.), *The Cambridge Guide to Homer* (Cambridge 2020), 296–9.

Swaddling, J. *The Ancient Olympic Games* (Austin, TX, 2008)

Sweet, W. E. "Protection of the Genitals in Greek Athletics," *Ancient World* 11 (1985): 43–52.

Sweet, W. E. *Sport and Recreation in Ancient Greece: A Sourcebook with Translations* (Oxford, 1987).

Tzachou-Alexandri, O. (ed.). *Mind and Body: Athletic Contests in Ancient Greece* (Athens, 1989).

Valavanis, P. *Hysplex: The Starting Mechanism in Ancient Stadia* (Berkeley, CA, 1999).

Valavanis, P. *Games and Sanctuaries in Ancient Greece: Olympia, Delphi, Isthmia, Nemea, Panathenaia* (Los Angeles, 2014).

Weiler, I. *Der Agon im Mythos: Zur Einstellung der Griechen zum Wettkampf* (Darmstadt, 1974).

Williamson, C. and O. van Nijf. *Connected Contests*, http://connectedcontests.org, accessed May 29, 2021.

Willis, W. "Athletic Contests in Epic," in T. Scanlon (ed.), *Sport in the Greek and Roman Worlds*, vol. 1 (Oxford, 2014), 60–90.

Young, D. *The Olympic Myth of Greek Amateur Athletics* (Chicago, 1984).

Young, D. *A Brief History of the Olympic Games* (Malden, MA, 2004).

Young, D. "Professionalism in Archaic and Classical Greek Athletics," in T. Scanlon (ed.), *Sport in the Greek and Roman Worlds*, vol. 2 (Oxford, 2014), 82–94.

INDEX OF NAMES

GENERAL INDEX

Words in **bold** print appear in the Glossary.